THE WHEELS OF THE WORLD

THE WHEELS OF THE WORLD
300 YEARS OF IRISH UILLEANN PIPERS

COLIN HARPER WITH
JOHN McSHERRY

*For Tíona McSherry, lady of encouragement,
and Cormac O'Kane, wizard of sound* — C.H.

*For Áille, Denis & Olive McSherry and all
the McSherry clan, Trisha & Úna Brady* — J.McS.

A Jawbone book
First edition 2015
Published in the UK and the USA by
Jawbone Press
2a Union Court,
20–22 Union Road,
London SW4 6JP,
England
www.jawbonepress.com

ISBN 978-1-908279-93-4

Volume copyright © 2015 Outline Press Ltd. Text copyright © Colin Harper and John McSherry. All rights reserved. No part of this book covered by the copyrights hereon may be reproduced or copied in any manner whatsoever without written permission, except in the case of brief quotations embodied in articles or reviews where the source should be made clear. For more information contact the publishers.

DESIGN Mark Case
EDITOR Sarah McQuaid

Printed in the Czech Republic by PB Print UK

1 2 3 4 5 19 18 17 16 15

CONTENTS

Introduction		6
Chapter 1	John McSherry	18
Chapter 2	Introducing Finbar Furey, Paddy Keenan and Liam O'Flynn	56
Chapter 3	Finbar & Eddie Furey: A Dream In Their Hands	64
Chapter 4	Liam O'Flynn: The Quiet Man	107
Chapter 5	Paddy Keenan: Rakish Paddy Blues	123
Chapter 6	Three Kings: Leo Rowsome, Séamus Ennis, Willie Clancy	160
Chapter 7	Leo Rowsome: Keeper Of The Flame	170
Chapter 8	Leo Rowsome At The BBC	186
Chapter 9	Séamus Ennis: The Master Outside	217
Chapter 10	Séamus Ennis At The BBC	267
Chapter 11	Willie Clancy: The Minstrel From Clare	345
Chapter 12	Johnny Doran: Along The Road Forever	372
Chapter 13	The Only Patsy Touhey	405
Chapter 14	Uilleann Piping Before 1900	409
Chapter 15	Piping In Ulster	445
Chapter 16	Brian Vallely & Armagh Pipers' Club	496
Appendix 1	*Melody Maker* Interviews, 1976 & 1978	510
Appendix 2	Discographies & Sessionographies	520
Appendix 3	John McSherry Tune Transcriptions	565
Endnotes		599
Acknowledgements		611
Index		614

Introduction

This book may appear, at first, to the casual observer, somewhat sprawling and eccentric – a bit like the uilleann (pronounced 'ill-in') pipes themselves. Hopefully, it will also, like the pipes, be entertaining, full of intrigue and allow a little glimpse into a world that seems magical … for the pipes are at the mystical heart of Irish music. *The Wheels Of The World* may reflect, as a title, something of the otherworldly with which the pipes have long been associated, but it is written as much for the curious outsider, the interested listener or the general reader of music histories and biographies, as for the devotee.

Finbar Furey, a master and ambassador of the instrument during the 1960s and 70s, describes his fingers and his mind locking into a 'wheel' when a performance clicks into place – like a man climbing the stairs and never getting to the top. For the non-playing outsider, it conjures an image of a lone figure far from help wrestling a wild beast, or a surfer clinging onto the crest of a colossal wave (which, as it happens, is not dissimilar to the experience of interviewing Finbar Furey). For the general reader, I hope this book will be a map to a hitherto unknown region. There may be dragons. There are certainly fairies. And there are three hundred years of heroes.

What are the uilleann pipes, and why should we care? They are the most complex of all the world's bagpipes: seven pipes in total – one chanter, three drones, three regulators – linked to a cloth or leather bag which holds a constantly renewed supply of air. Two full octaves can be attained. Sympathetic chords can be played, simultaneous to the melody, with the wrist via 13 keys on the three regulators. Air is pumped continuously via under-arm bellows; the pipes are elbow-driven, unlike the simpler mouth-blown varieties of Scotland, Galicia and elsewhere. Controlling the pressure of the air flow, along with fingering techniques and physical manipulation of the chanter, allows for an infinite variety of nuance and the execution of dazzling artistry. In the hands of a master, the machine is capable of extraordinary emotional impact and unique 'voice'. It is the only instrument truly indigenous to Ireland.

Closest in tone to the oboe (among the instruments of the Western orchestra), the uilleann pipes have a stylistic range that's chameleonic. Listen to Leo Rowsome, recorded in the first half of the 20th century, and you hear an artist for whom Vivaldi would have written concerti; listen to Johnny Doran, from the same period, and you hear a man with whom Jimi Hendrix would have jammed in a heartbeat. The pipes are both a chamber instrument, capable of integrating within an orchestral setting, and a self-contained equivalent to the electric guitar. Those who have mastered them – those few in any generation stretching back to the beginning of the 18th century – have displayed as much individual character and singularity of expression as any of the great chamber soloists and guitar heroes of the 20th and 21st.

First recorded on wax cylinder in 1897, the instrument is essentially a separate tradition within the Irish music tradition, and has not always been welcome within it. The numbers of instruments that have existed and of individuals who could play them, at any point in history before the most recent times, have never been great. The number of people who could make the things at any point in history, even unto the present day (if quality is taken into consideration), has never required more than the fingers of two hands to count. The instrument, its players and its makers have, for most of the past three centuries, been the virtual panda of musical culture: a creature hovering at the brink of extinction, loved by the cognoscenti yet barely within the realistic possibility of salvation, frequently propped up by the intervention of a faithful few.

That the instrument and its music *have* survived, and are now in relative terms flourishing, is a remarkable story. It's a story that relies on the extraordinary careers and artistry of a handful of individuals, most of whom are chronicled in detail herein. It could be described as a microcosmic version of the story of the blues – and the music of the pipes, in great part, *is* the blues – save that here, instead of Blind Lemon Jefferson, Charley Patton, Robert Johnson, Muddy Waters and Howlin' Wolf, we have Blind Garrett Barry, John Cash, Johnny Doran, Séamus Ennis and Willie Clancy. And in the 'rock era', where the blues birthed Buddy Guy, Jimi Hendrix and Peter Green, the uilleann pipes found new life through Finbar Furey, Paddy Keenan and Liam O'Flynn – lightning speed, smouldering fire and deep soul. For the first time in history the instrument had 'volume', in the sense not only of amplification on a concert stage but of the ability to connect to a mass popular audience through modern communication systems and the infrastructure of the post-Beatles international music industry.

While the blues cannot document its origins back beyond 1900, the history of uilleann piping and its practitioners can be glimpsed in primary sources almost as far back as the origins of the instrument. A remarkable number of named players emerge from the mists and spring to life on the pages of antiquarians' books and travellers' journals. In the age of recorded sound the sources become greater still. For the second half of the 20th century, the print sources are joined by living recollection. It is a wide, deep and intricate portrait that one can paint of this most curious instrument's story and its oft curiouser practitioners.

Being a creator of polyphonic sound in a pre-electronic age, the uilleann pipes were once known as 'the Irish organ'. It was only, perhaps, a quirk in history that during the 1970s, in the hands of a small number of now legendary figures, they became a feature in bands. It was also, perhaps, a quirk in history that those same bands, with repertoires of harmonically- and decibel-enhanced traditional music, occupied a space within the popular music world – operating within the machinery of its touring, recording and marketing infrastructure. The 'ballad boom' that had gripped Irish popular culture, alongside the singular phenomenon of Irish showbands during the 1960s, was duly superseded in the following decade by this series of bands (some with pipes, some without) who either fused or shoehorned Ireland's twin traditions of vocal and instrumental music together into one marketable package.

As one commentary has noted:

> Some have claimed that the prime cause for the rise of interest in traditional music in Ireland [in the 1960s and 70s] was the US folk boom of the late 40s and 50s. However, probably the most potent catalyst for change was the British 'folk music revival' of the early 60s, which had taken traditional song as its focus and, along the way, drawn in many young Irish immigrants.[1]

The examination of the fortunes of Irish traditional musicians within the context of the British 'folk revival' has been a somewhat neglected field. One types a sentence like that and imagines drawbridges going up and sabres being rattled in the castles of the Irish trad faithful. But there is nothing to be feared. Irish music is what it is, but it is not a culture that has lived within a vacuum. During the Early Modern era, interactions between the war-piping traditions of Ireland and Scotland appear to have been regular and mutually beneficial, to the extent that the two traditions are essentially the same; during the 20th century, the cultural melting pot (and manual labour market) of London loomed large in the lives of many significant Irish musicians.

Leo Rowsome, a man who almost single-handedly kept uilleann piping visible during the first half of that century, made records, gave concerts and sought broadcasts in London from the 1920s to the 1950s. Séamus Ennis, a piper of similar stature and importance, lived there through most of the 50s, broadcasting extensively on the folk music of the British Isles and performing in the earliest British folk clubs and in concert events with Ewan MacColl, architect of the British folk revival. The BBC work of both Leo and Séamus is documented fully in this book for the first time, revealing very clearly the extent to which the general public in the Britain of those times, when radio was king, was aware of the uilleann pipes. Willie Clancy, the third great piper of that era, worked as a labourer in London during the mid-50s, performing in the vibrant

Irish pub scene and being commercially recorded for the first time whilst there. Finbar Furey and Paddy Keenan, pipers from the next generation, each found their way to London during the following decade: the former securing record deals and national publicity, the latter finding his way back to piping through a bit of cultural tourism.

While Irish traditional music lingered on in various states of health in pockets around Ireland in the 20th century, it was only in Britain that the oxygen of revitalisation through engagement with a mass public – if that was what was wanted – could be accessed. In the entertainment industry, then as now, Ireland was a satellite of Britain. Radio Éireann's belated commitment to Ireland's traditional music only came about, as Séamus Ennis was to note with a frisson of *schadenfreude*, through the overwhelming success of his own BBC vehicle *As I Roved Out*. Finbar Furey only became appreciated as 'the Jimi Hendrix of the pipes' because he was touring up and down the very same country as Jimi Hendrix himself, and at the very same time causing a sensation of his own. Through virtuoso players with a youthful appeal like Finbar and, in his wake, Liam O'Flynn with Planxty and Paddy Keenan with The Bothy Band, people saw the instrument and felt its music afresh, without the cultural baggage that an Irish listener might have had, and responded to it instinctively.

Uilleann piping is, in some ways, an outlier even within Irish traditional music. It is a revered but difficult instrument, and until recently its proponents – let alone its masters – have been few. A specialist activity will always lie a little to one side, even within its own broad community. That position was helped along by the persistent impression of pipers being a breed apart, their community down the ages attracting what would appear to be more than its fair share of eccentrics and awkward characters. Added to that, and perpetuated with relish by the deft storytelling of Séamus Ennis, is an extensive fund of lore linking the uilleann pipes and much of its repertoire to mystical little beings who live in hedges, dance at midnight and grant wishes. It's not a million miles from Robert Johnson and his crossroads.

The instrument itself was at its own crossroads in the 1960s. Disillusioned with the apparent lack of interest in their art from Comhaltas Ceoltóirí Éireann ('The Music Association of Ireland', founded in 1951 to promote Irish traditional music), as many pipers as could be found came together in a kind of critical mass, in both senses, in May 1968, and within six months had founded Na Píobairí Uilleann ('The Uilleann Pipers'). It was perhaps the most significant turning point in the instrument's history. To this day, the NPU is the only support, resource and representation organisation for any of the instruments associated with Irish music; and, even with the usual blips of defections and controversies typical of any such interest group, it has seen its membership grow from the founding few of 1968 to the 3,000-plus of 2014. And that's not counting John McSherry, who is something of a lone wolf with his own circle of protégés, nor Brian Vallely, a remarkable man who has been independently running the Armagh Pipers' Club, a prolific bulwark against any future threat of extinction, in a small town in Northern Ireland since 1966. But then all great pipers are, as I have said, a breed apart. Trying to organise them into one happy band is a proposition with built-in layers of oxymoron.

Leaving aside the unique figures of Leo Rowsome, Séamus Ennis and Johnny Doran (who all lived by their piping in different ways), the global popular music explosion of the 1960s and beyond allowed uilleann pipers, for the first time in the 20th century, an opportunity to be professional musicians. To a great extent, through the visibility they achieved and through the popularity of their recordings, the handful of pipers who scaled the walls of the popular music castle in this golden age have had an overwhelming influence on what the general listening public knows – insofar as it knows anything – of uilleann piping. They have influenced the sound and style of piping within their own generation and the next.

These key individuals, with the bands within which they made their mark, are: Finbar Furey (Finbar & Eddie Furey, 1967–76; The Fureys, 1976–97); Paddy Moloney (The Chieftains, 1968 onward); Liam O'Flynn (Planxty, 1972–75; 1978–83; 2003–05); Paddy Keenan (The Bothy Band, 1975–79); and Davy Spillane (Moving Hearts, 1981–86; Davy Spillane Band, 1987–91).

While inquisitive newcomers, either learning the instrument or simply appreciating it as listeners, will almost inevitably discover the great names of the past, who played almost exclusively solo, the band players of the 1960s to the 1980s, and the apparent exoticism of the lifestyle they represented, still hold a certain aspirational sway over young players to this day. Even piping has its rock stars.

*

The impetus to create what has become *The Wheels Of The World* came from John McSherry. Few pipers have ever become genuine household names, even in Ireland – arguably, only Leo Rowsome and Séamus Ennis in their own times, through their extensive broadcasting in an era when radio pervaded society. There is a tendency to this day for even the best uilleann pipers to be 'musicians' musicians' rather than 'personalities' easily accessible to the general public (although both Paddy Moloney and Finbar Furey can hold their own on TV light entertainment shows and have often done so, at least in Ireland). Partly, this is down to the nature of the instrument: head-down, seated concentration does not lend itself to showmanship, and the solitary dedication required to master the instrument plays to the strengths of those whose personalities do not crave public affirmation.

John is no extrovert on a stage, but he somehow exudes a kind of rock-star cool, rather like Paddy Keenan. Possibly it's the shared haircut. The best comparison might be to snooker's Ronnie O'Sullivan: a soft-spoken, slightly awkward character whose abilities in his field are instinctive, brilliant and inspirational and whose image is consequently more exotic than his offstage personality might suggest.

While the numbers of those involved in uilleann piping today (perhaps 6,000 worldwide) is greater than at any time in history, there remain only a handful of full-time professional pipers. No one interviewed for this book could think off the cuff, when asked, of more than seven or eight. There are perhaps a dozen in the world today, with apologies to anyone not on the list below.

Finbar Furey, by his own admission, no longer plays the pipes for a living; Davy Spillane has essentially retired from touring and recording. Paddy Moloney, Liam O'Flynn and Paddy Keenan are still granted a hero's welcome wherever they perform. In America, Jerry O'Sullivan and Eric Rigler are the leading practitioners, each with extensive recording and performing credentials including orchestral and film soundtrack specialisms respectively. In Brittany, Ronan Le Bars and Patrick Molard have been great ambassadors for the instrument. In Great Britain, Michael McGoldrick is a professional musician with flute and uilleann pipes in his weaponry in equal measure. In Ireland, John McSherry, Cillian Vallely, who replaced John in Lúnasa and has remained there ever since, and Ronan Browne all live by their instrument.

John McSherry is an exceptional, instinctive, naturally gifted musician. He is also naturally shy, which is why he's most comfortable in ensemble settings, with someone else doing the talking. He is, nonetheless, a prime living example of the continuum of uilleann piping. He is admired and held in some awe for his musical mind, technical innovations and improvisational flair, not only within his own peer group in the Irish music world but by the generation before him (those, in fact, who first influenced *him*), the generation after him (numerous students and up-and-coming players) and artists from other musical disciplines.

To give one example, while working on this book I was also assisting veteran English rock guitarist Andy Powell, of Wishbone Ash, with an autobiography. I didn't need to explain John's music to Andy; he already knew and loved it. In a different corner of the music world, inspirational Irish jazz trumpeter Linley Hamilton exudes admiration for John's improvisational ability to anyone who'll listen, describing him as 'a monster', in the jazz lingo, daddy-o. Country artist Nanci Griffith, for whom John recorded in 1999, has said that 'his playing brought me to tears'. In a good way, one hopes.

Young pipers like Sheila Friel in Scotland, Calum Stewart in Brittany, Tyler Duncan in America, 2014 'Northern Ireland Musician of the Year' Conor Mallon, acclaimed singer/songwriter Barry Kerr and numerous other protégés in Belfast and around the world cite John's influence, while 70s icons Dónal Lunny and Paddy Keenan will happily go on record to declare him, respectively, 'a musical giant' and 'the only piper I'd give my pipes to in a concert'.

Nine years older than John, and a key early mentor, flautist Marcas Ó Murchú (now a major figure in the Comhaltas Ceoltóirí Éireann world) saw the potential from day one: 'It seemed clear to me that John Mc Sherry was a genius in his own right, from the first time we met when he was barely a teenager.'

From John's own generation, Kevin Rowsome, grandson of Leo Rowsome and a formidable piper himself, says: 'I really like the innovative nature of John's playing. It's really refreshing to hear a highly competent piper who isn't intimidated by trying out new things with the instrument … being able to carry them off with ease.'

Michael McGoldrick, an alumnus of Capercaillie, Afro Celt Sound System and many other Irish, Scottish and world music entities, goes further still:

> John McSherry would be a huge influence on my own playing. As soon as you hear John playing, it's recognisable – and it wouldn't be just me saying that. I think John has taken the bits that he's been inspired by from Paddy Keenan's playing and Johnny Doran's playing, and yet John's chanter playing doesn't sound like them. In the sense that his timing is better than theirs and his groove is different. There's a bit of rock'n'roll in John's playing as well.

I first encountered John during the mid-90s, when his international career as a piper and recording artist was beginning to take off. I saw him performing several times with Tamalin, his family band, and once in Dublin with Dónal Lunny's Coolfin. Time passed; John went around the world a few times and occasionally did something in Belfast. One concert at the Whitla Hall with free jazz pioneer Ornette Coleman in 2000 was particularly memorable: a grand folly of public-subsidy con-fusion. A performance at the King's Head launching his band At First Light a few years later was less challenging but much easier on the ear.

In 2012, early in the process of writing *Bathed In Lightning: John McLaughlin, the 60s and the Emerald Beyond* (Jawbone Press, 2014), I was asked by John's sister Tíona – a great friend who has often helped me out on musical projects of my own without ever asking for anything in return – if I might be interested in helping John with a book. The timing was no good, but the thought was filed away. If Tíona was finally asking me for something, I should try and deliver it if at all possible. A year later the McLaughlin book was complete, and I called with John to see what he had in mind.

After 20 years on the road, he felt it was time to take stock, and was also foreseeing a gradual shift in his career: fewer bands, more solo/duo work. His initial thoughts revolved around transcriptions of tunes associated with him, accompanied by biographical text and perhaps a brief history of the instrument. His inspiration arose from having a piping student with notational skills who had offered to pay for lessons by creating detailed transcriptions from John's playing.

During our discussion it became clear that John had been inspired, as a kid learning the pipes in Belfast, by recordings of three of the 'band players' mentioned above: Finbar Furey, Paddy Keenan and Liam O'Flynn. I felt we might expand the book to include chapters on these three directly inspirational figures from the generation before John. From there, it was only a short leap of imagination to stretch the structural concept further by including the heroic figures of the generation before: Séamus Ennis, Leo Rowsome, Willie Clancy and Johnny Doran. Beyond that, we might look at Patsy Touhey at the very dawn of the recording era – selling uilleann piping to the masses in America years before the first jazz or blues record was ever made – and thence backward, as far as was possible, to the very beginnings of the instrument.

In short, I might approach the book as a history of uilleann piping through the prism of John McSherry. That concept felt just about achievable, assuming the co-operation of certain people and the existence of primary print and other documentary sources. Finding and accessing such sources would prove challenging but not impossible. In a way, it was all 'there'. There just wasn't a big arrow pointing at it.

Being an historian rather than a musicologist, I was drawn to exploring the theme of how the uilleann pipes found a wider audience, initially in Britain. That theme begins with the BBC broadcasting groundwork of Leo Rowsome and Séamus Ennis, and moves thereafter to the British performing and recording careers of The McPeake Family and Finbar & Eddie Furey in the 1960s, then on to the opening up of mainland Europe as a market for Irish music in the 1970s – a situation that would sustain the band-based model of Irish traditional music in the commercial arena for many years.

With that approach in mind, the book's parameters are necessarily selective. That there are no chapters on, for example, Paddy Moloney or Davy Spillane has no pejorative implication. Similarly, there are no specific chapters on other important figures in the current piping world such as Gabriel McKeon, Mick O'Brien and others in the Dublin piping fraternity.

The Chieftains occupy a singular place in the international music world as a kind of Irish trad chamber group. They've managed to accrue an ambassadorial function *vis-à-vis* Irish music over their near 50-year history, being remarkably adept at collaborative projects involving the music of other cultures and remarkably adept at sustained success.

Davy Spillane, alone of the significant band pipers, brought uilleann piping into the world of electric guitar-based rock and ambient music, and did so successfully, in both a musical and a commercial sense. I can recall buying his 1988 album *Out Of The Air* at Dougie Knight's record store – the place where Van Morrison's Them had rehearsed barely 25 years earlier – when I was at university. It is a moot point that while the music industry has more or less collapsed in the 27 years since then, uilleann piping has forged steadily, stealthily onward.

My own tastes in piping are now firmly for it as a solo instrument or in a duo with guitar (if the guitarist is a master like Steve Cooney or Tony Byrne), but I would still have great affection for the sound of that Spillane record – the first artefact of uilleann piping I owned. While Davy has now stepped back from the commercial touring and recording world, he was the most prominent piper of the 1980s and early 90s, and remains a significant part of the story of uilleann piping. It may be argued that Davy's collaborative album with Andy Irvine, *East Wind* (1992), was an influence on the globally successful *Riverdance*. And if history is part truth, part perception, it must be accepted that for a lot of people, *Riverdance* represents what they understand of traditional Irish music.

Within the parameters described, I have sought to make the history of uilleann piping accessible to the general reader, to bring to life some of its greatest exponents and characters, to synthesize or distil existing knowledge and to bring into print new testimony and new knowledge, where possible, with the hope that such knowledge may enhance appreciation of the piping art and the recorded works of the artists featured. A lot of commentary around Irish traditional music focuses on 'the music'; this book focuses on 'the people'.

However much those within Irish traditional music may feel 'the music' is a quasi-spiritual entity which performers should only approach as custodians or as vehicles, there are two reasons, in the context of this book, to look primarily at the individuals who have performed it. Firstly, while other instruments associated with Irish traditional music have regional styles and aspects, piping as we currently know it is defined by individual players rather than by regions, schools or repertoires. To put it bluntly, fiddlers may play in a Donegal, Sligo or East Clare style; pipers, on the other hand, may play in a Séamus Ennis, Johnny Doran or Leo Rowsome style. Or, just possibly, they may sound like no one but themselves. Secondly, from Patsy Touhey in the 1890s up to John McSherry in the present, the pipers profiled in this book have operated within the commercial music world. Personality, in that arena, is an integral part of the package and a factor that contributes toward an individual's success or failure, however spiritual his or her repertoire may be.

While the core of the book is, then, a 'patchwork narrative' of interlinked but loosely sequential biographies, exploring the continuum of piping influence backward to the 18th century from the starting point of John McSherry, a couple of tangential chapters suggested themselves along the way.

One of these chapters looks at the history of uilleann piping in Ulster (Northern Ireland plus Donegal, Cavan and Monaghan). Having encountered dusty old print references to Ulster being the runt of Ireland's four ancient provinces where piping is concerned, it seemed time to interrogate that view. Aside from John, there are several notable pipers from the North; and its history, while periodically lean (as is the case with every province), includes names of significant importance: 18th century pipe maker William Kennedy; the almost mythical composer 'Piper' Jackson; the prominent, if eccentric, pipe maker and broadcaster R.L. O'Mealy; Comhaltas Ceoltóirí Éireann and NPU co-founder Seán Reid; 1960s touring group the McPeakes; Presbyterian polymath Wilbert Garvin; and the indefatigable Brian Vallely, driving force behind the 50-year success of the Armagh Pipers' Club and its associated William Kennedy Piping Festival. Brian's singular achievement deserves a chapter to itself.

Finally, a substantial 'Discographies & Sessionographies' appendix brings together new, hitherto scattered and sometimes hard-to-find information on the recorded works and BBC broadcasts of many of the artists profiled in the main text.

As the content of the book has evolved in parallel with detailed transcriptions of John's music being made, it was felt that we should focus here on prose content. Twenty-five piping transcriptions are nonetheless included. It is assumed that those interested in learning them will scan and enlarge, while the aspiration remains for a future publication focused fully on transcriptions and aimed squarely at practising pipers – in both senses.

A few words need to be said about the 'voice' of the prose. John's chapter was written by himself, with a little help from his friend, and is (naturally) in the first person. The rest of the book was written by me and is largely presented with third-person narration. When John's voice is heard in chapters other than his own, it appears as quotation. Only very occasionally beyond this Introduction, if the context demands it, will I be heard in first person.

*

That brings me to the second part of this Introduction. Revisiting an interview I conducted with Liam O'Flynn in 1996, it struck me that Liam had said a great deal that could easily stand alone as a snapshot introduction to the instrument. He makes it all sound so easy. Given the depths of arcane delving to come in this volume, expanding in great detail on many of the people and themes to which he refers, we might as well paddle in now via the shallow end with Liam – a direct link between the masters of the past and the John McSherry of the present:

Liam O'Flynn: The uilleann pipes developed out of the Irish equivalent of the Scottish war pipes. Dates aren't really known, except that around 1700 a bellows was added and the Irish pipes began to take on their own identity. I've seen kind of hybrid pipes, which look like a cross between Highland and uilleann pipes. But during the 18th century the instrument evolved. The biggest breakthrough was the reed which is in the chanter, because you get a second octave with it by overblowing, so that was a really huge technical breakthrough because all pipes before that had only the one octave. There are three parts to what's described as the full set of pipes: the chanter, which produces the tune; the drones, which are sounding all the time; and the regulators. You've seven reeds altogether. Sometimes in, say, a slow air, you might decide to use only one drone, but almost always it's all three. The regulators are the keys you operate with your wrist for harmonies and chords – they're like closed-off chanters.

They've developed a very complex system of keys on the Northumbrian pipes to get the second octave. I think the uilleann pipes are the only pipes to have that sort of reed where you can shoot from the first to the second octave by overblowing. Keys have been added so that you can get a chromatic scale, although it isn't that easily accessible.

By its very nature, the instrument demands from the player a commitment, a real involvement, because it's complex not only to play but in its maintenance as well. It's affected by things like the temperature, and extremes of that cause all sorts of problems.

The whole business of the mystique of the instrument – I can only imagine that during the 18th century, when this instrument was evolving, it must have been absolutely amazing to appear with, when it was still largely unknown to people: some fellow arriving along with this extraordinary instrument with its own built-in accompaniment. It's bound to have created some impression.

And because pipers superseded harpers in the big houses, I'm sure they took advantage of those positions and added to their own mystique. Around the same time, you'd have pipers who travelled a lot, so that their arrival in an area was a big deal – not just because they were entertainers, but because they were news-gatherers as well.

In the earlier part of the century there were a huge amount of uilleann pipers in America, probably the best known being Patsy Touhey, a Galway man originally, who made 78rpm recordings that would be as influential today as Michael Coleman's fiddle recordings from the same era.

There's certainly shared material [among players of all traditional instruments], but there are particular tunes which we all regard as piping tunes or fiddle tunes – some of them just don't translate from one instrument to the other, particularly Donegal fiddle tunes. It's difficult to put into words, but there are musical intervals which are comfortable on the fiddle which wouldn't be on the pipes, like the difference between tunes composed on keyboard and on guitar.

In most sessions these days there's almost always a piper, but in former times it was very much a solo instrument, and partly the reason was that the instruments were in these odd keys. It was really down to what materials were available to the pipe maker – if he had a piece of ebony a particular length, it didn't matter to him what key it was in, so you'd often find pipes that are in between notes. The only instrument these pipes could comfortably play with was the fiddle, because the fiddle could tune itself to the pipes, so pipes and fiddle are traditionally a popular duet.

The pipes I mostly play are concert pitch pipes. The keys you can play in there are D, G, A minor, E minor, but the bottom note is D above middle C. There are other sorts of pipes that come under the heading 'flat pipes': they're flat, or below concert pitch, and they can be in almost any key. In fact, in the 19th century people were almost exclusively making low-pitch pipes and they have a different sound – mellow, quiet, sweet-toned instruments. Séamus Ennis recorded with those sort of pipes. Whereas the concert pitch pipes are more strident and were developed in America by the Taylor brothers, who came from Drogheda originally. There was a need in America for a louder instrument because of the size of the concert halls.

I've been fortunate enough in having known probably the three most important names in piping this [20th] century – Leo Rowsome, Willie Clancy and Séamus Ennis – and having known them very well. They had a very direct contact with the tradition that was untainted, if you like, and what I am is a synthesis of those people's styles, I suppose … I still play a set of Leo Rowsome pipes.

What's really fantastic is when people come up to you and say, 'You were the first person who introduced me to the sound of the pipes.' That's a wonderful compliment, and I have to say it happens quite a lot. There are pipe makers now in France, Germany, Australia and so on. And they reckon there are more young people playing pipes now than ever, really. There's been a huge growth in interest in the instrument, especially considering that 40 or 50 years ago [in the 1940s] it nearly died out. A handful of musicians, like the three fellows I mentioned, kept the thing going.

Chapter One
John McSherry

I probably first heard the sound of the uilleann pipes when I was five or six, but wouldn't have been aware of the actual instrument itself. I was born in 1970, so that would make it somewhere around 1975 or '76. In our house, my dad always had Irish music playing in the background, so I would have heard it without, I suspect, being terribly interested at the time. He would have been into the likes of Johnny McEvoy, The Chieftains, The Clancy Brothers – a lot of different styles of Irish music, from that period in the late 60s and early 70s when a lot of Irish ballads were making it into the pop charts. So, at that time in history at least, it wasn't exactly socially unacceptable to have an interest in such a thing.

My mum and dad first realised I really liked music when I went down to my uncle's in Dublin, aged about eight, and discovered his Beatles collection: three or four vinyl records, including the 'Red' and the 'Blue' ones. 'What is *this*?' I thought! I spent all day playing them over and over. Everybody else was out playing. *'Where's John …?'* Where indeed? I was just struck by the emotion each song was giving me, making me feel this way or that way, and I was kind of baffled by this. And that was the start of looking at record collections. It became a bit of habit. Wherever I went, anybody's house, the first thing I would have spied would have been the record collection – and I would have been over to it like a shot.

So what was it that turned me on to the pipes? People who suffer nervous breakdowns usually have a moment that triggers it, and I have a feeling it might be the same with people who throw themselves headlong into a lifetime of Irish piping. It's solitary, demanding, expensive and frustrating at first and, let's be honest, it's a bit odd. For me, the 'moment' involved my next door neighbour – God rest his soul, he later died in a car accident. I remember I was in his house – I think I was eight or nine at the time – and I was looking through his record collection. I came across Planxty. It was the second album, *The Well Below The Valley*. I saw Liam O'Flynn with this weird contraption wrapped around him in the picture on the cover, put the record on and thought, 'What's that instrument?' I was so struck by the sound. Even just looking at the picture was mesmerising.

I went straight to my dad and said, 'Dad, there's this instrument … this band called Planxty …' And he said, 'Oh, yeah, yeah … Do you like them?' And then he promised me he'd get me a set of pipes for Christmas. A practice set, obviously – you don't start with a full set, you get there bit by bit – but it was still a big investment. So I was promised them by Christmas and I think that was around early March. There was whistle playing on the Planxty record too, and it seemed to me a good idea to learn whistle before going on to the pipes. It was easy access to get a whistle. I had no idea it was similar fingering; all I knew was Liam O'Flynn played whistle and he played pipes – and the whistle looked a hell of a lot easier!

Liam has a lovely, sweet, contained style of playing now, but back in the early days he had a more raw, exciting sound. Yes, there was a kind of chamber music aspect to Liam's playing even in the Planxty days in the 70s, but the sound of the pipes and the way he was playing was really earthy, especially on a piece from *The Well Below The Valley* called 'An Phís Fhliuch', where his groove and bending of notes is something quite special. There's something magical about the C natural on the uilleann pipes but Liam's was particularly striking – a lot to do with the chanter, of course. Liam would make the most of this magical note by lengthening it, bending it and drawing it out for as long as possible – it was something that really resonated with me.

I didn't know of any kind of music scene in Belfast at that time, until my parents decided to send me to a whistle class run by the McPeake family at Clonard Monastery. They'd been a touring band in the 60s and they weren't touring as much by then, hence the school.

My older sister Tíona was going already – she'd been learning whistle for about a year by then – and I followed. There was a good club there running on Saturday evenings, with kids all the way up to about 17 or 18. I went for about a year or so before leaving.

So it started off as whistle for me, but I would have seen Francie McPeake III the odd time taking out a set of pipes and playing for us, which was great. Anyway, after leaving I continued on with the whistle, myself and Tíona swapping tunes that we'd learnt. By this stage Tíona was also expressing an interest in the pipes. I think this may have been two years after dad had promised to buy me pipes – two years of dad saving up the money. He was pretty convinced that I was going to take to it. I harassed him every week about it! So I got them the Christmas of 1981, just before I turned 12, on January 3rd.

Tíona: Noel Fitzpatrick, a shoemaker, had approached my dad in Clonard – he wasn't actually teaching there, he just wandered in – and said, 'There's not many girls play the pipes ...' He had a set of pipes and he wanted to know if I'd be interested in playing them, and my daddy jumped at the chance. I think that was about two weeks before I left, but Noel and my dad kept in contact and arranged that he would come up to the house with the pipes. So he came up on a Saturday night – just after Christmas, I think. He got the pipes out, it was a practice set, and I had a go on them. That night, I was playing away, or trying to, and John, who was outside, came in and wanted to have a go. And he did. Noel came back the next week and the week after that and the two of us, me and John, practised the pipes. Eventually he left the pipes with us.

Definitely in those days you had to be a bit unusual to take on the pipes, because there were so few pipers around, so few possibilities of getting a set of pipes. It wasn't one of those casual situations where you might think, 'I fancy taking up the pipes, I like the sound of them …' You really had to want to play the pipes – to be driven fanatically to do it!

My dad would have taken us to see Noel Fitzpatrick every other Saturday. He wasn't a great piper, by any means, but he just loved the pipes. We'd go down to his place, this somewhat careworn shoe shop with people walking in to get their shoes repaired, and there'd be this big Alsatian dog sitting there, Noel in his flat cap, his hands black with boot polish, constantly chain-smoking. My dad would be chain-smoking as well. The place would be just full of smoke! It was a foretaste of the session scene I'd discover a couple of years later: invariably, smoke-filled bars. *'Right, get the pipes out!'* Noel would say. He'd look forward to it every other Saturday. To any customers who'd come in he'd say, 'Have a listen to this …' He particularly loved slow airs. And he'd be walking around giving all these mad gestures, trying to pull out a performance like a conductor, 'Come on – *sing* it to me, *sing* it to me!' It was like a comedy, a real comedic situation. But he gave me the passion, a lot of passion. And it was Noel who introduced us to Seán McAloon.

> **Tíona**: Noel Fitzpatrick then brought us up to see Sean McAloon, one of the last of the gentlemen pipers who was living in St James'. He had known all the greats and was full of great tales. He made reeds and had a lathe out in his kitchen where he turned wood. One day he presented us with a boxwood chanter that he had made. He had painted it black so that it appeared like an ebony chanter – he was embarrassed that it was made of boxwood. For him, boxwood was the poor relation; it's beautiful.

Seán was another character: he was *so* eccentric, like a hermit. In fact, he was known as 'The Hermit'. There was nothing in his house; the place was bare apart from one wee sofa and one chair. He had no TV, but he had a wireless radio from the 1940s and it seemed to me that all he did was listen to folk programmes on the radio, listening out for the pipes. He would talk about Séamus Ennis a lot. He knew Séamus. Like Séamus, Seán was one of the boys who had kept the piping tradition going in the 40s, 50s and 60s. He told me stories, like how he had heard about this tune called 'The Crooked Road To Dublin' and he's thinking, 'I *must* have this tune, I *must* have this tune …' So he cycled down from Fermanagh, where he was living, to Athlone or somewhere equally implausible in distance, just to get this tune. He was a remarkable fellow.

Seán was like the guru, the wizard on the mountain top. My daddy would have brought me down to Seán's all but empty abode and Seán would say, 'Right, what tune have you learnt this week?' And I'd say, 'Well, I've learnt 'The Humours Of Ballyloughlin' …' I'd play it and he'd be walking around while I did so, and he'd be mumbling, *'Ah, Jeez, that's great … maybe try this here …'* – and then he'd show me something. So every other week, it seemed, I got a tip from the Zen master.

> **Tíona**: We shared the same bedroom, the four of us, and Saturday nights we just couldn't get into it – John locked the rest of us out! Basically, because I already had the flute, John was insisting, 'You play the flute, I'll play the pipes.' He was very persuasive!

All the time I would have been practising. I think it came naturally to me, but I did spend hours upon hours locked up in my bedroom. From the first time I heard Liam O'Flynn and then Finbar Furey, I'd have been thinking, 'What's he doing? How is he doing that? That *note* …' And this was even before I had a set of pipes myself. When I was learning the whistle I'd be learning these tunes from the records, so I would gradually have built up the technique of rolls on the whistle, and when it came to learning the pipes I would have used that, along with whatever I'd learnt from the McPeakes. My dad had a small Irish music collection, but he would've gathered tapes and recordings from his friends, and Finbar Furey's 1969 album of solo piping for Transatlantic was one of them. Tapes of The Bothy Band followed soon after.

Three months after I got my first set of pipes, I entered the competitions. It began with the Antrim Fleadh Cheoil 'Under 12s', around April 1982. I came first, but I don't think there was anyone else in for it! Then I entered the 'Ulsters' and I came first in that. This was about six months after I'd got my pipes. There were other people in for it this time, but I was improving a lot by then. Then came the All-Irelands in August, in which I came third. It was exciting stuff. 'This is for me!' I thought.

By then my interest in school was waning. I was practising about four hours a day. My parents were encouraging – though sometimes they were worrying, sometimes thinking, *'Jeez, he's been up there a long time, surely he needs a bit of a break?'* They wanted me to do well on the pipes, but they thought I was putting a bit too much time into it. But it's a solitary instrument, it needs the time, and perhaps also it needs the obsession. Tíona was making good progress on the flute by then too. We were learning off each other but I have a funny feeling I was the more dedicated. 'John, it's eleven o'clock at night,' they'd be saying, 'the neighbours'll be going mad!' And I'm afraid they sometimes were. There was music constantly in our house. I mean, God help them and fair play to them, but there were a few times when the neighbours just couldn't take it anymore. My dad would be the first line of defence when the enemy bombardments kicked off.

> **Tíona**: I think eight months – maybe a year – after meeting Seán McAloon, he gave us an ebony chanter. At some point over those couple of years there was another set of pipes in the house – one for John, one for me – and my daddy started to make bags and bellows. He went down to Seán's and used the lathe. He would have gone down religiously every Friday, bringing fish and chips with him …

My dad was amazing: he took us everywhere – down to Seán, down to Noel, anything we wanted. The reeds were maybe playing up, he'd sort it out. He'd find out how to make bags and he'd make them, and bellows, too. The first bags and bellows I played were made by my dad: these are expensive things, and there wasn't a lot of money around in those days, but he made them. The connection between us grew, there was a rapport there because of the pipes. My interest could have waned without him. If you don't have a set of pipes that you're happy playing, if you can't get driven somewhere to get them fixed, if your dad says, 'Ach, sure, they'll do …' – sooner or later you would lose heart. I owe him a great deal.

> **Tíona**: My Daddy met a fellow called Kieran Fitzpatrick who happened to be a flute player and he very generously made a tape of tunes for me to learn. It was through Kieran that we then met flute player Davy Maguire and through Davy that we met the flute maker Sam Murray. I have one of the first flutes Sam ever made, from a batch of seven, which I got around the same time the pipes came into the house. The night I got the flute Davy invited us down to Kelly's in the Strand for a session; I was about 14 or 15. From then on we were there every week till the place closed down. Tom Kelly was an absolute gentleman and did a lot for traditional music at that time.

As Tíona says, the first session I went to was following her lead, to Tom Kelly's in the

Strand. It was, of course, a smoke-filled atmosphere – just like Noel's shoe shop! Tom Kelly would sing a song, then we'd play some tunes. Mars bars and crisps and Coca-Cola would come down for myself and Tíona. Arty Lundy, a fiddle player, was the host. Up he would have stood, saying, 'Right, let's hear the young people play …' I must say, we were made very welcome. Perhaps we were lucky in that respect.

> **Tíona**: We walked there sometimes. There was one Saturday night that me and daddy – for whatever reason, John wasn't there – walked the whole way back. It was too late for the bus. Looking back, that was a golden period for sessions. Aside from Tom Kelly's on Wednesdays and Saturdays, there was the Cluain Árd on Hawthorn Street on Friday and Sunday. We also had The Rotterdam, Muldoon's, The American Bar and Pat's Bar, all down by the docks – you could have gone to a session every night of the week. When Tom Kelly's closed down, The American Bar was the place for a while, and then Tom got a new place, The Liverpool Bar, and then sessions happened there. And then sessions also started happening in the centre of town, in Madden's and Kelly's Cellars as well.

The first session we first went to away from Tom Kelly's was a year later, in Pat's Bar, where the welcome was somewhat frostier. In the same way as you might describe the Arctic as 'somewhat frosty'. The 'A Team', they were known as, which probably says it all – all these people who had a kind of snobbery about them. But we didn't know this at the time. Our dad brought us along, we took the instruments out and joined in with the tunes … and this palpable vibe descends. Just after we'd finished a set of tunes, they started tuning – tuning up to E flat. I didn't know what they were doing – I probably didn't even know there *was* another key! So they started playing another tune, I tried to come in … and, of course, couldn't. It was very bad mannered, but I felt too embarrassed to pack up and leave. The thing was, though, Marcas Ó Murchú, the flute player (and now Ard Comhairle in Comhaltas), was there, and he came over and started playing tunes in D with us. So we played a few numbers with him and then felt, okay, we can go now, our dignity still intact. It was a noble gesture from Marcas. I thought that was very good of him, and I developed a friendship with Marcas from there.

> **Marcas**: John had said to me, 'I'd like to hear more music, more pipers.' So one Saturday John came to our house, ten o'clock on the button, and stayed to six o'clock on the button. My mother made soup – she always had soup on for whoever came through the door, it could have been

Mícheál Ó Domhnaill or Clannad or whoever. I had all these records, I'd play something like Tommy Reck, and John would say, 'God, I haven't heard that type of playing before.' [Leo] Rowsome, [William] Andrews way back in the 20s, Billy McCormick, Dan Dowd I played. *The Breeze From Erin* [with Willie Clancy]. … Through the years, down in Dublin and in America, I'd picked up these records. I remember coming back from America with 36 records under my arm, coming back from a tour in 1983. I had two boxes of records with nothing but pipers on them. … It was up in my bedroom in the attic. John was so enthusiastic and so well mannered, my mum thought he was a lovely fellow. That's the thing about John, he's always been well mannered. He was very focused on what he was there for, and came away with many cassettes that he'd recorded [from my collection].

I knew this young and avid listener was destined for bigger things the way he respected the musicality of each performance. Within a short time, he had assimilated their repertoire and the best of the technique of the greats into his own in a creative and original fashion. He was well on his way to stretching the boundaries of possibility and imagination in the piping world, in Ireland and on the international music stage.

Marcas obviously saw something in me that he wanted to encourage. So he brought me up to his house, where we spent hours and hours going through tons and tons of old recordings. Anything that he thought I should listen to, he put onto cassette for me. It was a good process, great for learning tunes. He played me Séamus Ennis, Johnny Doran, Patsy Touhey – he had all of this stuff, which was far from easily found at that time, and it opened that world up to me. A continuum of piping going back the better part of a century.

The sessions were another way to learn new pieces of music. I was finding that I was picking up tunes even if I wasn't playing – you're sitting it out, listening to it, figuring out where it's going. The next week you hear it again, make an attempt at it while being careful not to mess it up for everyone else. Then by the third time you'd know it.

Marcas: From a flute player's point of view, I developed [a] strong style playing at Tom Kelly's, where people weren't necessarily there to hear traditional music; they were there for a night's craic. There's an argument to say that John's type of piping, which is strong, finds its roots at those Wednesday night sessions at Tom Kelly's – trying to be heard. People say to me, 'How come you play so loud? There's 24 fiddles and I can hear you playing over the top of them!' But every time I lift it up a gear I'm back in Kelly's on a Wednesday evening. The boys in Kelly's, arriving down after watching a Celtic match, couldn't have given a hoot if we were playing rock'n'roll, jazz or country, so when John and the family came in they were playing it 'out'. But the nice thing about it is, what he did was sweet, what he did was controlled, and it was perfectly in tune as well. And that, I'm sure, has moulded him.

There were a lot of interesting characters on the session scene in those days: 'The Brother Maguire', this great hippie character who called everyone 'brother' or 'sister'; Arty Lundy, whose son Marty fronted and still fronts to this day a popular Belfast pub rock band, Katmandu; Frankie Kennedy, who went on to form Altan; Sid Edwards; the Crickards; Billy McCormick; Brendan O'Hare … But all of those people were a lot older than us. There were very few our own age; everyone else was in their 20s or older. I don't know why that was.

Tíona: Billy McCormick actually got his pipes given to him by a nun when he was out busking. This nun came up to him, told him how much she loved it and that her father used to play the pipes. And then she asks, 'What's your name?' 'Billy McCormick,' says Billy. 'It's a sign from God! My father's name was Billy McCormick – you have to have his pipes.' And she sent over a Taylor set!* He lives in Clare now. He's a good piper.

Aside from Tíona I have two other siblings, Paul and Joanne. When we were all in our mid-teens we played as a band together and became 'The McSherrys', later to be called Tamalin.

Joanne had started off playing a wee bit on the tin whistle but didn't really take to it. So my mum sent her off to trumpet lessons. She wanted to go to fiddle lessons, but there were no fiddles available at the music school. So poor Jo had to learn trumpet for a couple of months until a fiddle became available. She hated the trumpet! But when she got the fiddle she loved it.

Paul played a bit of whistle but had no real interest in it either. He started getting into heavy rock music when he was about 14 and I was 13, and he introduced me to Led Zeppelin. I remember he had a tape with the song 'Whole

---

* Billy Taylor and his brother Charley were renowned pipe makers of the late 19th century, based in Philadelphia. They effectively brought the uilleann pipes to their modern state, in fixing the pitch and enhancing the volume.

Lotta Love' on it and I found it really exciting. I remember sitting underneath the bed sheets with a tape player, listening really closely over and over to this guitar solo. It blew me away. It was electrifying. I could imagine this being played on the pipes. It was very inspiring.

I won the Tommy Sands Co-operation North competition around this time, when I was about 14. I sent in a tape to his Downtown Radio show of me playing a tune, 'The Gold Ring'. The prize was a trip to Miltown Malbay. So I won it and went to Miltown Malbay for the 'Willie Clancy Week'. The 'Willie Clancy Week' is like a Mecca for Irish traditional musicians. I was being put up in a B&B and getting the chance to go to all these classes. The thing is, I think I only went to one or two of the classes. I was 15 by then and was far more interested in playing in sessions. I felt very comfortable in the pubs of Miltown, playing tunes all day long. After that, I used to go every year – I had great experiences in Miltown.

The Zeppelin record blew Paul away, too, and he wanted to learn guitar as a result. Luckily for the family band in waiting, he heard Moving Hearts' first album around that time, bringing this new rockier kind of style into Irish music, and fell in love with the idea of Irish music again. So there we were, the four of us, all into Irish music and all playing different instruments. Forming a band of some sort was inevitable. But, oh, what a shame Joanne didn't keep up that trumpet …

Tíona: Brian Moore and Fergus O'Hare had asked my daddy if we'd do a turn at this thing they had called the Oíche Airneál, which means a night of craic, storytelling, music, whatever. This was in a place called the PD Club and it was happening on a Friday night. Every Friday night there'd be all these Sinn Fein people – Bairbre De Brún, Gerry Adams, Alex Maskey … People got up and did their thing. Brian Moore and Fergus had a great passion for the culture. So we would get stuff together for that – a couple of songs and a couple of sets every Friday. So we had a regular deadline, a motivation, and were learning new stuff every week.

We were probably playing tunes that we learned off records – Bothy Band sets, Planxty sets – and Tíona started singing. It was a case of 'We need a singer – who's going to sing?' It was our good fortune that Tíona, who kind of drew the short straw, just happened to have such an incredible voice.

Thus it was that, without a brass section, the McSherrys became a band. We had this fellow from the Falls Road as our manager. He got us sound gear, was going to do this and that for us – but, of course, didn't. What he did do was get us a load of gigs in all these bars along the Falls Road. We supported Christy Moore a few times when he played there. We were singing Planxty numbers – 'The Blacksmith', 'Black Is The Colour' and so on – but in a lot of the places, all they wanted to hear were rebel songs.

We thought everyone had heard of Planxty. Seemingly not. I remember on one occasion we were booked to play in the Marty Forsyth. We went in, set up all the sound gear, did the first half of the gig, and I remember keeping my head down, thinking, 'Oh God, this is *so* bad ...' All these people were shouting, *'F***ing hell, why are you doing all that diddly-dee ...?'* We finished the first half, went outside for a breather ... and the door shut behind us. They locked us out! All you could hear inside was everyone singing rebel songs. We were kids, we were so disheartened, but we could see the funny side of it as well.

I continued on with the competitions. I came second in my second year in the 12-to-15 age group slow airs category and second in the dance tunes. I think the daughter of whoever was head of the Comhaltas won it that year. I remember people saying, *'Oh, it's a fix,'* but I wasn't that bothered. The next year, 12-to-15, I entered again and came first. And as soon as I came first I thought, 'Right, that's all I want – I'm off now'. I didn't care much for competitions after that: I'd won the All-Ireland. That was enough. Any time I went back after that, it was just for the craic, to meet friends and play tunes. The Fleadhs are great for that. I think it was shortly after this time that we played our first international festival in Italy.

Tíona: It was Marco Fabri who organised the first time we went abroad, in 1986. I was 18, I'd just started at Queen's University. Marco was playing in a band with Brendan O'Hare on the Belfast scene called Ultan. Through Marco we were invited out to Italy in July to play at Folkest, run by Andrea Del Favero, who became a good friend, and following that we played the Lorient Festival, which is in August. I don't know quite how we got that gig, but things just happened to us. We did a lot of stuff around that time, including a lot of TV work – *As I Roved Out* on BBC Northern Ireland and *Nós* on RTÉ – because people were phoning up my dad. It all just happened, we never had to look for anything.

There was one final competition that I would enter after that: the Oireachtas. The only people who could enter were All-Ireland champions and over 18s. I entered, though I was under 18, and won it. I think it was a kind of similar story for Finbar Furey 20-odd years before. As a result of that, I got to be a guest piper at the Lorient Inter-Celtic Festival and headline the international piping concert. The family band also got an invite to play the festival that year.

Tíona: On reflection, it was probably through RTÉ – one of their producers was involved in the Irish delegation to Lorient. So we got to go with Déanta and Killora – which was Niamh Parsons, Gerry 'Banjo' O'Connor, Steve Cooney, Dónal Murphy – on that first trip to Lorient, meeting people that we'd be tripping over for years to come. In fact, our Paul later married Kate from Déanta. So now he's tripping over her in the kitchen every day.

Meeting people from the international music scene at Lorient certainly helped The McSherrys/Tamalin. We were there for a week and I met all these people from all the Celtic regions – built up friendships with all these musicians from all over Europe, in particular Alfonso and Franky from Asturias in Spain. After the festival they invited me down to Asturias to play. I think I stayed there for a month and earned my keep by playing in the pubs every night – something I would do quite a bit of over the next few years.

While all this was going on, I had the inconvenience of attending school. I did O levels – I managed to get seven of them, though I don't know how. I loved Irish, I got an A in that; the rest I scraped by in. For some reason I decided to stay on and do A levels. I was at La Salle and A levels required a move to another school, St Mary's, where I'd put my name down for Irish, Politics and History of Art. I wanted to do Irish but you had to pick three: Politics and History of Art just looked the easiest. I stayed there for a year and a bit, but it was a new school, I didn't really know anybody and I didn't like it. After a while 'the boss' said, 'Get your hair cut or don't come back.' Need I say what happened next?

My mum wasn't too happy, but it was clear to me by then that hanging around school any longer was a waste of time: I wanted to do music anyway.

The conflict in the North was going at full tilt in the late 80s, and I remember playing in this Republican ballad band around this time with a great singer called 'Cruncher' (Terry O'Neil). I met him on the Belfast session scene, along with flute player Emmanuel McFarlane. We used to travel all around the North in a black taxi, going to these gigs. One night they picked me up in the taxi from my mum's house to do a gig in Lurgan. After the gig we decided to drop in on a friend, Barry Kerr senior. Mr Kerr was the proprietor of the Céilí House, a music pub in Lurgan. So we called into his house in the wee hours and had a bit of a session. His son Barry, about 10 at the time, who had been woken up by all the music and jollities, came downstairs to have a nosey. Barry Kerr's now a travelling musician himself, and he later told me that it was that session – with all these exotic characters arriving to play music and have a laugh in the middle of the night – that influenced him to become a musician. I hope he doesn't hold it against me! Anyway, we were there having a sing-song, playing tunes and all that, and we left about four o'clock in the morning. And, according to Barry, as soon as we left, the place was surrounded by police and army, guns pointing in all directions. And there was us tootling off to the Falls, utterly oblivious to this major security non-incident going on back at poor Barry's house.

> **Barry Kerr**: I was about 12, I'd just got a practice set of pipes, and these guys all landed round at our house in a black taxi, and it was a great night – despite the house being surrounded by about 200 soldiers. It was funny! It was a novelty for me to be up that late, and I remember John sitting me down with the pipes and saying, 'Who do you listen to?' And at that time the only pipers I knew were Paddy Moloney of The Chieftains and Finbar Furey. So I said, 'Paddy Moloney …' 'Hmmmmm …' '… and Finbar Furey …' 'Ah, good start, good start!' I never actually had a lesson from John at any time, but I was around him enough to pick a few things up. John would have been a hero of mine when I was younger.

This was pretty much the way Belfast was at the time. There were British soldiers everywhere. Belfast city centre at night was like a ghost town but still, traditional musicians from both sides of the community found a way of meeting up, playing tunes and having the craic.

My next move was the one that actually started the path I'm still on today, albeit there's usually some money involved these days. Back then, from about 1989 to 1992, I just went off and toured around Ireland on my own, very little money in my pocket, meeting up with people that I'd met at the Fleadhs. I would go from pub to pub, for months at a time – the Leitrim Bar in Sligo, Cryan's in Carrick-on-Shannon and lots more lost in the haze. The pubs would put me up, I'd play sessions nearly every night of the week. Other people I met would very kindly take me to their homes and look after me. I'd stay maybe a week and then someone might say, 'Come down to this place …' I'd go to that next place and stay there for a week. And I would travel all around the country like this. For about four years I did that, from when I was 19 to about 23, and it was perfect. I travelled the whole west coast from Donegal down to Cork – met all sorts of musicians, picking up tunes everywhere I went. It was a really carefree time for me.

Also, around this time, when I was about 19, I had a wee band on the go with fellow piper and friend Francis McIlduff and his brother Jack McIlduff, called Piping Hot – two sets of pipes and drums and a guitar player. We got a few gigs around Belfast and there was a bit of a buzz about it. I remember playing upstairs in Morrison's, the Hercules, etc. This was during the period when I was travelling around Ireland, and Francis would have come along with me on a few occasions, down to the likes of Drumshanbo in Leitrim where we stayed and played in Fox's pub for a week or more. Francis is the son of Kathleen McPeake, who was one of the extended 'McPeake Family' when they were an international touring and recording band during the 1960s.

I'd say travelling around Ireland in that free and easy way I did back then would be harder to do these days. The pub scene is very different; pubs that have sessions have regular people they pay to be doing that, and it's mostly based on money now. But I still get people saying, *'Do you remember the time you came down to …'* And usually I do.

My mum and dad were at their wits' end: 'Where's John off to now?' I would have been gone for months, coming back with no money in my pocket at all. But I paid my way with music.

> **Tíona**: John was always … special! But he was a great worry to our parents, especially during 'the troubles'. They were stressed about it. On one occasion he phoned my daddy and asked, 'Could you pick me up?' From Donegal. Which he did. There's a tune called 'The Wild Irishman' that was John. A wild streak runs in the family. If I hadn't been so sensible I'd have been away myself.

The family band thing was going on then as well. I'd come back every month or two, do the gigs with the band, in France or Asturias or wherever, then say, 'Right, I'm away off again, see you …' It didn't allow for too many practices, but luckily enough there had been plenty of that sort of thing a couple of years previously. I was getting around Ireland by myself, but the band was my way of getting around Europe, and every now and again I'd be asked to go to a piping 'tionól', like a weekend of tuition. I think I was 21 when I was first asked to do one of those in Germany.

We were doing McSherry arrangements to traditional tunes and songs. When we stepped out of the Falls Road scene we started doing the Irish 'folk circuit' – Belfast Folk Festival, Letterkenny Folk Festival, that kind of thing – as well as the international thing.

Being in a family group as well, there was the added bonus of family bickering. All water off a duck's back, of course. Our pal Kevin Dorris, known as Dod, was brought in, I think, to perform the same sort of function Billy Preston fulfilled when he arrived at The Beatles' *Let It Be* sessions in 1969 – suddenly a lot of over-familiar people start behaving civilly and manage to make some decent music together. I exaggerate, of course, but, well … Myself and Dod were like partners in crime. If there was a party or craic to be had somewhere, we'd be there. Dod plays bouzouki. He had been going out with our cousin for a while and felt almost part of the family.

> **Tíona**: We were all dead on, we always had great craic. John and Dod just seemed to have a bit more than everyone else – they were a wild pair. There was never any tension within the band because if there was a problem it was never hidden, it was out in the open, dealt with and then forgotten – like water off a duck's back. None of us have ever fallen out. Well, not for more than half an hour.

Drink was a big part of the scene back then. As a professional musician you have to be very sociable, and sometimes that can mean a drink or two. When you're travelling around a lot, there's a danger that the social aspect of it could get out of hand. You have to be careful and strike the right balance. I'm sure there were many occasions when I didn't.

> **Tíona**: Whenever we were on tour it was me looking after John and the others. If I was a mother hen figure it was because I definitely felt a pressure to be that. I didn't want anything to happen to them. Put it like this, if they had have been my friends, not my family, I wouldn't have felt such a strong responsibility. From my parents' point of view, all their children were going away and I was the eldest, and I had to keep an eye on them.
>
> Mudd Wallace, a local studio owner, was scouting round for young talent with his business partner around this time and consequently we were going to make an album. Neil Martin was going to produce it … It was all very traditional, it was our live set basically. I can't remember much about it, except that Mudd had a falling out with his business partner and the money disappeared. When we eventually did record a Tamalin album, for the Grapevine label in 1996, we had moved on several times, but we don't have recordings of every time we changed our music. It's a pity we don't have something to represent those developments. Because whenever the Tamalin album did come along we had moved a long way.
>
> **Neil Martin**: I forget what happened. I think we recorded it and mixed it, but it was never released. I remember listening to some of the rough mixes in America, so that would be 1987 or '88. I remember Joanne mitching off

school to come up and record. It had a very energetic vibe. It was very much their live set in a studio. We were *all* a lot younger! And I remember the inevitable tensions of being a family and making music – not in any severe way, but that tension and that family tautness also brought out incredible drive and punch in the music that was exceptional at the time.

Aside from the family group and Piping Hot, the first band I was in was Niamh Parsons' Loose Connections. My involvement came about through Dee Moore, a bass player from Belfast. I'd met Dee in Belfast. He was playing in a blues band called Boardwalk, a big band on the local scene at the time, with Rab McCullough on guitar. A great, great blues-rock band. Somehow I developed a friendship with Dee, and he'd invite me here and there and he'd come to the sessions then as well, and listen to me playing the pipes. He hooked up with Niamh Parsons – whom I had already met while playing in Brittany a few years before – they got married and then Dee said, 'Right, let's make an album …' Vinnie Kilduff was brought in to produce it. Dee was moving and shaking. Consequently I got called in on pipes on the record, titled *Loosely Connected* and released in 1992. When they needed a band to tour, that was the start of The Loose Connections. I was touring with Niamh Parsons & The Loose Connections for about two years, between 1991 and '93.

I met Vinnie Kilduff via the Loose Connections experience and we struck up a friendship. I'd meet him any time I went down to Dublin. Probably the most important person I met at that time, though, in terms of where my life in music went from then on, was Dónal Lunny. And I owe that connection (a very loose one indeed) to Dee Moore.

Dónal had been a member of both Planxty and The Bothy Band. I was down in Dublin in '93, a Loose Connection at the time, and Dee Moore says, 'Dónal Lunny's recording round the corner. Let's go and chance our arm and I'll introduce you …' So, fair play to Dee, we chanced our arm, he brought me round, I've no idea how we got into the studio – I don't think Dee actually knew Dónal – but we got in.

Dónal: I wasn't that close to Dee. We'd never worked together, we'd never spent any time together, so I wouldn't have known him that well. But I had heard about John, I'd heard from musicians that he was a wizard.

So Dee says, 'Hi Dónal, I'd like you to meet John McSherry. Maybe you've heard the Niamh Parsons album?' And Dónal says, 'Yes, I've heard it.' We were chatting away and he says, 'I might be giving you a call …' About a year later I got a phone call from Dónal about going down to Dublin for a studio session with Gary Kemp, from Spandau Ballet, who had a passion for Celtic music. I went down, hadn't heard the track beforehand, and Dónal says, 'Have a listen to this … See that space there? I want you to fill it with a solo.' So I was on the spot, but I went in and did it in the first take. I remember coming into the control room and Dónal Lunny and Gary Kemp applauding.

> **Dónal**: The Gary Kemp thing was brilliant. I loved Gary, a lovely man, and I really liked his music. I think he was just drawn towards the whole Celtic thing. I think I would have suggested people to play on the record. He would have expected pipes and fiddles. He wouldn't have known John. But it was to a very exacting standard: those recordings got the best of attention. … By and large, pipers are linear in that they play tunes and the variations are internal, and you don't often get extrapolation where people will leave the road and go parallel in terms of playing a harmonic part, breaking away. John is one of the few, and Davy Spillane likewise, who can play a harmonic line.

I did a tour of England with Gary shortly after that, when he released the album, but right there and then that was my introduction to a different world. I became a session recording musician. I got a phone call nearly every other month to come down to Dublin and record with all sorts of people – Clannad, Rod Stewart, Sharon Shannon and suchlike. Actually, one day after the tour with Gary, he was in Belfast on a visit and called in to my house. He was interested in seeing the Falls Road, so after one of my mum's special toasties and a mug of tea, we took him around sightseeing.

> **Dónal**: I wish I could remember sessions the way John remembers tunes! But I would say that John's delivery was always impeccable. I might have had a particular vision of a [given] piece of music that I would impart to John, which he would handle with ease. But, as well, starting so high up the scale with somebody like John who actually has the chops, has the ability and has the beauty in his playing already, it's not difficult to achieve the desired end. I would have characterised John, back then, as being totally lazy – but I would qualify that by saying that John would learn a piece of music in a few minutes that would take the average musician, if there is such a thing, 10 times as long. So what he lacked in application he made up for in sheer talent! I think he has a bit more of both now. John is a musical giant.

One of these 'other' tours I mentioned was a three or four week multi-artist 'Folk Festival' tour that travelled across Germany. Myself and Eamon McElholm (later in Stockton's Wing and Solas) were booked to do it. Eamon was living in Manchester at the time and Petr Pandula, who ran the tours, suggested that we both leave from there. We were to catch a lift with this Manchester band who were also doing the tour and were travelling in their own van to Dover and then on to Germany. I thought it would be a good way to get to know these lads. As soon as I got over to Manchester that night, all was revealed.

The band was 'Toss The Feathers', known fondly as 'The Tossers'. Mike McGoldrick and Dezi Donnelly were members and we struck up an instant rapport. In fact, as Mike reminded me only recently, he and I had actually met a few years before this, at the Lorient Inter-Celtic Festival in 1988:

> **Mike McGoldrick**: I went over there when I was 17. On the Sunday afternoon this lad walked in with a pipe case. I was playing wooden flute at the time. I asked, 'Is that a set of pipes?' He said, 'Yeah, yeah. Do you play music?' I said, 'Yeah. I play the flute. I'd love to have a go on the pipes – I've only ever heard them on record.' So he took the pipes out, then he realised I was left-handed, so I couldn't have a go. But he blew the bag up, handed me the chanter and he did the work on the bellows while I had a go at playing a tune on the chanter. It was about a year after that, at a festival in Shropshire, [that I met] a man called Dave Evans who made chanters. He had a stall and I'd just finished a gig; the bass player on the gig gave me his money, and with my money and that I bought a chanter, bag and bellows. And that was the start [of me playing the pipes].

The Tossers, Eamon and I hung out in Manchester and played tunes all night long, staggered into the van next morning and as soon as we got in, cans of beer were opened. It was one long party in The Tossers' van, and it must have been a two-day journey. There were another four weeks of the same, travelling around Germany from city to city. God knows how we survived it.

> **Mike**: When you're that age you don't hold back. We weren't earning a lot of money, but a lot of it was going on booze. [We were a] band of lads who had no inhibitions, living life to the fullest, mad about music, and who had invested in a PA and a van. We cracked open a beer, we hadn't even left Manchester, and John said, 'I think I fit in here.' I think when we were out in Germany we were both serving our apprenticeship in a way, kind of living

the dream. Because you've spent years and years practising, listening to the giants like Matt Molloy and Paddy Keenan and Liam O'Flynn. My hero was the wooden flute player Matt Molloy. And when I first heard John play, in Germany, I thought, 'Wow, I play like him.' Because we were both listening to the same records: The Bothy Band. So when we had a session later, it was easy – we just played a set of tunes off The Bothy Band albums. It was great, I'd met somebody the same age who was into the same buzz. And we'd both been to France, as well, and were being influenced by Breton music.

John [later] joined us for a week of touring in France. It must have been some week, for when we went back to this pub 10 years later and the landlord says, 'Great to see you again,' me and John looked confusedly at each other and said, 'Have we been here? Have we played at this bar before?'

Mike and I kept in touch quite a bit after that. After the German tour, he came over to Belfast to visit. I was working – the only job I've ever had – as a caretaker in an Irish language centre, the Cultúrlann.

Mike: John said, 'There's a great session scene in Belfast. Why don't you come over?' I'd never been to Belfast, so I flew in and his dad picked me up and then John said, 'I've got to go to work.' 'You work?' 'Yeah.' It was some kind of job scheme to keep him off the dole for a bit. So I went to work with John – and I ended up doing all the work! There were about six rolls of carpet and he says, 'This carpet needs to go into another room.' I said, 'I'll give you a hand.' And as the day went on I sort of realised it was just me moving the carpets. John was outside having a cigarette. 'We'll be finished about three,' he says!

I remember [later] going into the pub, Madden's, and ordering a pint. I was a short-haired, squaddie-looking guy with an English accent. I got a few funny looks until people realised I played the flute and was a friend of John McSherry's – *'Ah, what about ye, Mícheál?'* We had a great session there – Kevin Dorris [Dod], Joanne, Paul, Dezi Adams on flute …

So, somehow, without the slightest idea of a career plan, I had established myself pretty well by 1994/95. In retrospect, that was the point where I metaphorically crawled out of the dark corners and into the limelight as an artist of some sort, as opposed to a carefree chancer on the road.

It was around this time that I first met Dave Early, drummer to the stars. He was living in Belfast at the time and became a big presence on the Belfast music scene.

He had heard the family band Tamalin and became very interested in our music. He kind of got behind us and encouraged us to make an album. He was very passionate. We recorded *Rhythm & Rhyme* with Dave on drums and percussion. He was a great character whose enthusiasm for music was contagious. I remember anytime he was going to Dublin he would pick me up and we would drive down in his Saab for a musical adventure. Great times.

> **Tíona**: Dave Early had so much energy. He began to play with us – he was playing with the Mary Black band at the time; he'd also been playing with Sade and Van Morrison, and had played with John before in The Loose Connections. We had a number of gigs in The Rotterdam bar and so on, around Belfast. We actually recorded up the Shankill Road for a solo album that Dave was planning, which never appeared, which is a real pity. And then Dave died in a car accident.

*

On New Year's Eve, 1994, I had met a man called Seán Smyth at Matt Molloy's pub in Mayo. And that transpired to be the very beginning of a band called Lúnasa. Myself and Seán clicked immediately, both friendship-wise and musically. Dod had accompanied me down to Westport for the New Year's craic as well, so it was myself, Seán Smyth and Dod (among others) playing tunes all night. We were supposed to go back home the next day – Dod had a part-time job as a poster designer at the time, in between Tamalin gigs. Seán was urging us to stay: 'I'm going down to Galway – do you want to come along?' 'Yeah, no problem,' I said, 'I'm free …' And Dod was going, *'Shit, I have to get back for my work …'* But we convinced him to come down to Galway.

It was only supposed to be for a day; it ended up a week – we'd be stopping off at all these other places on the way to Galway. And every morning Dod would be fretting, *'I have to get back home …'* 'Ah, come on,' we'd say to him, 'we'll just go into this pub here …'

We'd play tunes all night, the craic would be great, and then the same thing happened the next morning. About a week later Dod eventually got home and, to his dismay, he found he had no job to go to. I stayed on in Galway with Seán, who suggested I join him on a tour promoting his forthcoming album, *The Blue Fiddle*, which was produced by Steve Cooney. So from that, The Seán Smyth Band was formed in early 1995: myself, Steve Cooney on guitar, Seán on fiddle. Jimmy Higgins would join us every now and again to play drums, along with Alan Kelly and Vinnie Kilduff. After that tour we continued on as a trio, as The Seán Smyth

Band for want of a better name. After a while I suggested that we bring in Mike McGoldrick to play flute. Mike was already a good friend from those tours in Europe with 'The Tossers', so I asked him if he'd like to come on board and he said, 'Yeah.'

> **Mike**: Seán Smyth was a doctor in London, and I met him [there] in 1995. He was telling me he was doing gigs with Jimmy Higgins and John. I played him some records, and some repertoire, maybe four tracks on the first Lúnasa album, came from those records.

We played a couple of gigs as a quartet in Manchester and then played a tour around Ireland. Most of the material for what would become the first Lúnasa album was developed on that tour, with Steve Cooney. Things were starting to gain momentum, but then Steve decided to bow out. Seán then went on a tour of Scandinavia, bringing with him Trevor Hutchinson and Donogh Hennessy from the Sharon Shannon band. When they came back, Seán, Trevor and Donogh got together with myself and Mike, and it was then that the band Lúnasa was born.

> **Mike**: The first gigs I did with the band were The Harcourt and Whelan's [in Dublin], and there was one in Manchester [before Trevor and Donogh joined], with Steve Cooney still in the band. It was the best-ever band. If I could turn the clock back, that line-up with me, John, Seán, Trevor and Donogh – I absolutely loved it. It was so exciting.

We toured around Ireland, and in the fall of '96 we recorded the debut Lúnasa album. A tour of Australia had been set up for February 1997 but myself and Mike were unable to go. For my part, I just didn't want to go. It seemed too long. It might seem a bit eccentric, but I always do things by instinct. I just felt I didn't want to do it, although actually I did end up going to Australia later that year with Tamalin. It's never premeditated, thinking about my career: 'Should I do this? Should I do that?' By and large, going by instinct has worked out for me.

> **Mike**: I'm still not a hundred per cent sure what happened, because they asked me to go to Australia for six weeks – which was six weeks doing one thing, whereas I was also committed to these other bands. It was just too long to be away. So I got my friend Kev Crawford to come in on flute. Financially it wasn't really working out for everyone to give everything else up and do Lúnasa full-time. John was in Coolfin and I was involved with

Capercaillie and also in Flook and the Afro Celt Sound System. So I was in four bands! I looked at my diary [recently] and there was one year I was away for eight months.

After that tour, Mike and Kevin swapped the flute playing role between them for another six months until Mike's departure. I stuck around for another year or so – but by that stage I was getting a lot more work with Dónal Lunny and Coolfin. It was time to move on, though Mike and I both played – as guests rather than members – on the second Lúnasa album, which was a transition into the career they've enjoyed ever since.

> **Mike**: If I was still the flute player [in Lúnasa], I think we would have made a different second album. I think more of our own compositions would have come into the equation. But things happen and that's the way it was. And if the split hadn't happened, me and John would never have made the *At First Light* album [a couple of years later].

*

Dónal Lunny had decided he was going to start a band, the Earth Celebration Band. He'd been invited over to Kodo Island in Japan for this Earth Celebration event, in 1996. The Kodo drummers are internationally renowned, and they love to collaborate with people from around the world – they're like The Chieftains of Japan! Dónal was one of those collaborators and the band he took was myself, Liam Ó Maonlaí, Sharon Shannon, Máire Brennan, Nollaig Casey, Máiréad Nesbitt, Ray Fean on drums, Fionn O'Loughlin on bass, Roy Dodds from Fairground Attraction on percussion. It was great. It really worked. We were there for five days. I'd never been to Japan before. It was a fantastic experience. The island was like a jungle with sweltering heat. My pipes were battling against the climate and the moisture.

The first time I had really played with Dónal Lunny, though, would have been at a gig maybe a year beforehand, at the annual Eisteddfod in Wales: Eoghan O'Neill on bass, Nollaig Casey on fiddle, Dónal and myself – just the four of us. This was whenever Dónal was composing a lot of stuff that ended up on the Coolfin album, like the mad hornpipe, 'Butler's'. He sent up a copy for me to learn it – a MIDI file actually, which was a bit of a nightmare for me, trying to pick out all those notes!

I think all of Dónal's subsequent connections to Japan came from that first visit – he fell in love with it. In my experience the Japanese are very humble and honourable. Dónal really found it a fascinating culture. He also met his future wife there.

Dónal: The band didn't have a name at the time – it was called 'Dónal Lunny & Friends' – but essential to it were Ray Fean on drums, Fionn O'Loughlin on bass and Graham Henderson on keyboards. Nollaig Casey, on fiddle, and John were also involved at that stage. So that was the heart of the band. I was asked [in 1996] by Hemisphere Records, which was a branch of EMI, to do the album *Common Ground*. A lot of the playing on it was by the future members of Coolfin [though not John].

We were calling ourselves The Wheels Of The World for a while. After that there was enough material there to make a Coolfin album. Up till then it was still 'me and friends' or whatever – we didn't have a name. So I called the album *Coolfin*, with the intention of shifting that onto the band. It's the name of a townland or a town. There was a song I remembered, years ago – when [my 60s band] Emmet Spiceland was finished, Brian Byrne, the lead singer, made an album and asked me to produce it. And one of the songs on it was 'The Lakes Of Coolfin', a lovely song. So when I came up with the notion of Coolfin as a band name I was trying to figure out where it was, and I didn't have any reference books to check. I met [RTÉ presenter] Ciarán Mac Mathúna and mentioned it to him and said, 'Do you have any idea where Coolfin is?' I didn't see him again for about two months, and when I did see him he reached in his top pocket, pulled out a little slip of paper and gave it to me and there were nine Coolfins on it, in different places round the country – none of which I can remember! I'm hoping I can find that piece of paper again.

When Coolfin started touring, that became another reason to leave Lúnasa. Francis McIlduff filled in for me on a few occasions and then Cillian Vallely got the job.

During the time I was playing with Coolfin in the late 90s, people were always telling me I should learn to read music. But I was always afraid to go down that road. There's a part of me that feels that I could lose whatever I have that may be special if I begin to learn those dreaded dots. I know what I want to get across musically in my own head, anyway. It's just a matter of communicating it. But I like the danger of spontaneous musical flight. It's exciting. There's an element of danger in piping, like a man wrestling a wild beast and trying to tame it. You can hear that in all the great piping recordings: Finbar Furey, Paddy Keenan, Johnny Doran. I want to keep that element of danger, but I can always keep it in a cage if the opportunity of a Clannad album comes along. And, in fact, one did.

Having met Máire Brennan through Dónal and the Earth Celebration Band, I was asked by her to do a tour with Clannad and to play on an album, *Landmarks*, which was released in 1998. It went on to win a Grammy as 'Best New Age Album', so I mustn't have played anything too visceral on it! I also went on to do a few tours with Clannad, squeezing them in between Gary Kemp, Tamalin, Coolfin and everything else.

One particularly interesting and rather hairy experience from that period was a session for Nanci Griffith in Abbey Road Studios. She was making an album called *The Dust Bowl Symphony* and her producer, Peter Collins, wanted a piper. I think it came through Dónal Lunny that I got the gig. Peter sent me over a MIDI file of what he wanted, but there must have been some kind of technical issue. For some reason I couldn't hear whatever he'd done to mock up the pipes. So I ended up going over to Abbey Road none the wiser. I met Nanci and Peter Collins, ready and waiting with the entire London Symphony Orchestra in this huge studio with the ghosts of The Beatles, Sir Edward Elgar and a century of legends hovering overhead.

'So, ready to go, John?' he says. 'Aye, okay,' I say. I'm directed into this little booth on my own, with a line of sight to the conductor who says, 'Okay, John …?' And I'm thinking, *'What am I doing here?'* I sat and waited, the orchestra plays for about 20 seconds then stops: 'John, John, John – you're supposed to be in there …' 'Oh, right …' The orchestra starts again and the same thing happens. At which point I say, 'Look, I really have no idea what I'm meant to be doing here!' 'Ah, right. Did you not get the tape? Orchestra, take five …' I'm sure my face was bright red.

Peter took me into the control room, explained where he wanted me to start and finish and I just went back in and jammed. And after that one take he said, 'Yep, that's it!' Nanci Griffith later said my playing brought her to tears. Well, I can tell you the session nearly had the same effect on me for wholly different reasons. But I can laugh about that now.

Having said that, I had actually recorded with an orchestra a couple of times before that, with Dónal Lunny as producer, and also performed one or two concerts with orchestra, including Dónal Lunny's 'Famine Suite' in 1997.

I'd also recorded in an orchestral situation with Shaun Davey around the same time, for the film *Waking Ned Devine*. I can't quite recall how I learned the music for this. Myself and fiddler Nollaig Casey probably picked it up once we got to the studio in London. I presume Liam O'Flynn must have been tidying his sock drawer that day. But Shaun really loved what we did – and lots of people loved his score for the film.

Every time I've played with an orchestra, I think the same thing: 'What the hell am I doing here?' But as long as I know where to come in, I seem to be able to deliver whatever it is that everyone requires.

People sometimes say 'never meet your heroes', but in the Irish trad world you're pretty certain to bump into them eventually. I actually met Liam O'Flynn for the first time long before I was a professional musician, at a Planxty gig in 1983 in Belfast. In fact, the whole family met him then, when we were all kids. Marcas Ó Murchú was on hand with a camera, as can be seen in the photo section herein. I've met him a few times since then and he always remembers meeting us! Liam is a quiet, mild mannered type of character, but even Liam, I'm sure, has had his moments: the heady days of Planxty in the early 70s. Dónal Lunny left them in 1974 – and then hit it even harder with The Bothy Band, which numbered among its alumni the great Paddy Keenan.

I met Paddy every now and again during the 90s, often at The Harcourt Hotel in Dublin, and would have had a drink with him. But the first time I really sat down and had some serious craic with him was, I think, around 1996. He's a great human being. We had great chats about politics, the North and all the rest of it. I would meet him on the road quite often after that.

He was in Belfast once for a gig, I think it was '98, at a folk club founded by Brendan O'Hare. The place was packed. Paddy got up to play but was a bit worse for the wear, shall we say. He got through the first 20 minutes, but then it all seemed to fall apart. Brendan O'Hare took to the stage and said, 'Can anybody play the pipes …? Is that John McSherry in the room …?'

So I got up to give Paddy time to sort himself out. I hadn't got my own pipes with me, so Paddy kindly gave me his pipes to play, and off I went – 'Rakish Paddy', 'Colonel Fraser's' and so on.

Paddy was living life on the edge at that time; that's what he was known for. You could never quite expect how Paddy would be. If he's on form, it'll be a good show; if he's not, at least it's an experience, you'll have a story to tell about it. I played for a while, but in due course Paddy got his act together and came back after the break, and the thing was rescued.

After the gig we headed off to a party at mine. I was living in Ladybrook at the time. So he and a couple of people who were with him got into the car, and he was driving. And he drove like a Formula One man – unbelievable! He drove the long way round, round the back roads of Dunmurry, then back to Ladybrook. I was like, *'Paddy, fucking hell …!'* We got round to the house and, after all this exhibitionist virtuoso driving, he slowed down to a snail's pace … and crashed into the driveway gates.

There would be two trips to Japan with Dónal, and the Kodo drummers later reciprocated and came to Dublin, where we were all filmed for a live DVD. Shortly after the first trip, as the Earth Celebration Band became Coolfin, there was money there for an album.

I moved down to Dublin around 1997/98 as a result of this Coolfin opportunity and the gigs started rolling in. I was still playing with Lúnasa and Tamalin at the time so there was a lot going on. It was a choice: Lúnasa or Coolfin. And I took the chance with Coolfin – a chance to play and record an album with Dónal Lunny.

We recorded the album in 1998 at Real World, in Bath, and Peter Gabriel was around – we all had dinner together on many an occasion. It was really good fun, and such an experience having the craic with Peter Gabriel. The album came out, got rave reviews, there were loads of gigs – big gigs, too. We toured America, Europe and Australia. We had guest singers in like Sinéad O'Connor, Eddi Reader, Maighréad Ní Dhomhnaill and Paul Brady. There were TV series like RTÉ's *Sult,* where Coolfin was the house band. It was all quite high profile stuff.

In the end, Coolfin petered out more than anything. We had started on a second album; we had four or five tracks put down, the bones of them anyway. We brought a portable studio into this big old hostel in Connemara and booked it out for a week – which turned out to be one big party, really. We got a bit done, but not as much as we'd hoped. I wasn't in the loop as to why it folded. We were still doing a few gigs here and there up to 2000/01. The Kennedy Centre Gala in Washington was one, an evening profiling Irish music with guests such as Emmylou Harris, Steve Earle and Elvis Costello. There's a DVD of it, *Gala Night.* Around that time we knew it was starting to slip away. It was a big operation, there were a lot of people to pay, seven in the band plus sound engineers and road crew, and maybe the balance sheet was moving in the wrong direction – I just don't know.

I don't actually have a copy of the Coolfin album, nor the DVD. In fact, I don't have lots of things I've played on over the years. I only really listen to the music I've recorded whenever I'm in the middle of it, and directly afterwards. I'd be very critical of what I've done, up until the point where I think, 'Oh, stuff it!' and move on, forget about it. Truth be told, I haven't really done an album I'm completely pleased with. With the *Soma* album, which has been the only one thus far released solely under my name, I wasn't really happy with the mix. I crammed it all into a single day, because of lack of money, and I'm sorry I did that now. But you live and learn.

I would have loved Coolfin to have stayed together longer. It was more challenging than Lúnasa. Lúnasa was great – it was traditional Irish music rocked up – but Coolfin was more sophisticated. There was more complexity to the arrangements, and I learned a lot from the experience. I didn't learn anything about the business end of it, unfortunately – I just wasn't interested enough at the time. That was all being looked after by Dónal's manager, John Dunford; I just turned up wherever and whenever. But the musicality of it, the way the rhythms interwove, blew me away.

*

By 2001, Tamalin, the family band, had ground to a halt, too. We'd had a crack at doing something four years earlier with *Rhythm & Rhyme*, our sole release, on the Grapevine label, with a title song by our old friend Eamon McElholm. Dónal Lunny had mixed it for us and one of Tíona's songs, 'In The Morning', had even been released in Britain as a single. But we were never the most 'together' of bands.

By this point Tíona was rearing a family, Paul was teaching, people were doing other things. We enjoyed playing together, but it had run its course. Maybe sometime in the future we could get back together again. Playing music with your siblings is something very special indeed and certainly something I would like to do again.

With Lúnasa, Coolfin and Tamalin all essentially 'played out' by the start of the new millennium, it felt like a new chapter was being opened in my personal life. My daughter, Áille, was born in 1999, when I was living in Dublin with my then partner, Karen. We lived in Dublin for about four years and had this lovely apartment in Kilmainham overlooking the Gaol. I can remember many times the van pulling up with Lunny & Co. – the gaoler's van! The craic in that van was great. Áille came on tour around Ireland with us once, when she was about six months old. It was great fun.

Unfortunately, my relationship with Karen broke down shortly after this period. I left Dublin and moved back to Belfast. With all this change, I thought, 'Right, I'd better get something together myself' – and I phoned my pal Mike McGoldrick.

The two of us chatted about doing an album together. Mike wasn't at that stage the big personality he is now, but his star was rising, and he had had a similar experience to myself of needing to shake things up, based on his family situation when his first child was born in 1995.

Mike: [By 2001, when John called], I was signed to Vertical Records and I'd been working well with Donald Shaw, as producer, who had worked on my first album, *Fused*, [the previous year], which was very successful. So I told John about Donald and his beautiful studio in Glasgow, and it felt like the right thing to do. There are two tracks which are dual pipes, but the main thing was to do a flute and pipes album. We did it in a week. It was good having Donald Shaw there, because he would sometimes say, 'Lads, you're going round in circles here … Listen back to the first take you did.'

We called the album *At First Light* – which has been the start of a whole saga of confusion ever since, which I'll come to. Donald Shaw released it on Vertical and, to our surprise and delight, it sold a hell of lot of copies. We had my brother Paul on guitar on it, we had Manus Lunny on a few numbers – whoever was around at the time. It got great reviews and we did gigs as a band under the name of the album: At First Light.

> **Mike**: We recorded *At First Light* at the end of 2001, and touring it rolled into 2002. We had a very memorable tour of the Highlands of Scotland. It was called 'Blas Ceoil' and we invited Dónal O'Connor [on fiddle], and Tony Byrne [on guitar] was also on that tour. We played the Hebrides, a massive festival there, and then all the village halls where you could bring your own booze. I remember taking John for a game of golf while there and after a while, with my right-handed clubs, he said, 'Hang on a minute, I'm left-handed – no wonder I'm no bloody good at this!'

We knew people would be interested – I had a bit of a following and Mike was very much up-and-coming. After we'd left Lúnasa we'd both helped out on their second album. A lot of people told us, 'Oh, the band's not the same without you' and suchlike – which was probably another reason we thought we ought to do something together.

I'd just met Dónal O'Connor, who was to become my regular musical partner from then on. Mike was involved in many other things, but if he was free over the next couple of years we'd do gigs; if he wasn't free, then myself and Dónal would do them – and Mike was cool about us using the name. So that was the start of the At First Light saga.

The first At First Light tour without Mike was an Irish Music Network tour, about 25 dates, and it was me, Dónal and Tony McManus from Scotland. Dónal was living in Belfast at the time. So for that first tour of At First Light he came along, on fiddle, and it was great craic. From then on, At First Light took off. Our Paul played guitar on some gigs, and then I met Tony Byrne around that time and he became involved on guitar, which I believe was his introduction to playing gigs. He's since become a very in-demand accompanist to many Scottish and Irish artists.

> **Dónal O'Connor**: It wasn't the first time I'd been on the road, because I'd toured Europe with my parents in Lá Lugh in the late 90s. But it's somewhat different touring with your parents to touring with boys like Michael McGoldrick and John McSherry.

I remember we did the 'Return To Camden Town' Festival in London, which turned into a wild night. John and I ended up in a road-sweeper's van, driving around Camden looking for an early house – which we found, a place called The Man Of Aran. The publican wouldn't let us in until half seven, but we started playing tunes on the street, so of course the door opens and he hauls us in. It was always interesting.

I don't think I thought, 'Yeah, this is the guy I should be in partnership with for the next 15 years,' but I wanted to play with John because I thought he was a great musician. We'd often meet at sessions in Belfast – I'd get a buzz from the sound we were making together. So when I did those early gigs with him I got a sense of what he thought a fiddle should be doing in a four-piece of that nature, and I agreed with it. We had similar outlooks in the music we liked, too – Breton music and all the Irish music that I liked, he liked, and certain things we didn't like would be the same as well. I wasn't in any way interested in Led Zeppelin in the way he was feverish about them, but I've come to like that band too. Almost.

At First Light is the closest I've come to an ongoing band, though it's a bit like Spinal Tap – the drummer always explodes. The thing about At First Light, after the album with Mike, is that that it's always been built around myself and Dónal and whoever else is in it at a given time. But then Dónal and I have made a duo album (*Tripswitch*) using just our names, a trio album with the late American guitarist Bob Brozman (*Six Days In Down*) where all three names were used, plus one album credited to At First Light as a band (*Idir*). So, in summary, at the time of writing there's one album called *At First Light*, by myself and Mike McGoldrick, and one album by the band At First Light, with myself, Dónal and Francis McIlduff comprising the band (plus some guests). Adding to the headache, Dónal and I have often performed together in various flexible incarnations – duo, trio, with other people – in recent years, but only sometimes as At First Light. At the time of writing we are actually finishing off a trio album with guitarist Seán Óg Graham from Beoga. Pete Frame and his *Rock Family Trees* would have a hell of a time making sense of the Irish trad world and its perpetual state of pragmatism and fluidity.

*

During the early 2000s I moved back with Karen and Áille, to Donegal, for about two years. If you're thinking that living in Donegal is not the most ideal location from which to sustain an international career in music, you'd be right – especially if you don't drive. I was trying to learn about IT at the time as well – I could foresee the importance of the Internet for cottage industry musicians. In fact, I built a website while I was in Donegal, about 2002/03. I was in Newtowncunningham, mostly just spending time with my daughter – not rushing anything, keeping my career ticking over, trying to build a website and make contacts. It was a kind of in-between time: in between the Dublin-focused days as a sideman for hire and then as a member of Coolfin and the start of a solo career proper. Dónal Lunny by this time had moved on to a reunion with Planxty, and after that a reunion of Moving Hearts. I needed to focus on building on what I'd started with the McGoldrick collaboration: doing something under my own steam.

I wasn't writing much music at this point. That really only started happening with *Tripswitch*, in 2006, which I suppose could be described as the starting point of my current career. In retrospect, not that much of importance, in terms of my musical path, happened between 2002 and 2006. In terms of my personal situation, I broke up again with Karen and moved back to Belfast. For some reason, in the middle of this personal trauma, that's when I started writing music. One of my earliest compositions from this new focus on composition, which I've sustained up to the present, was 'Áille's Arabesque', a tune for my daughter, which is on *Tripswitch*.

Tripswitch was a great creative release. Credited to myself and Dónal O'Connor, it was recorded in 2006 at Homestead Studios with Mudd Wallace, the scene of the lost Tamalin album of 20-odd years before. Dónal was still the 'junior partner' at that point, but his knowledge of music far surpassed his years. He's great to work with in the studio, and creatively we bounce off each other.

> **Dónal O'Connor**: *Tripswitch* was a great experience. We'd both worked before at Homestead, and working with John's brother Paul was a great experience. I noticed that John was really good at bringing the best out of Paul, though not necessarily knowing quite how to describe what he wanted, which is where I came in – having the musical and technical lingo to be able to filter and explain John's instinctive ideas. I became his interpreter! We brought Francis McIlduff in on that album. I didn't really know Francis – he was kind of like a mystery man. And nothing's changed there. John said, 'Wait till you hear him play the bodhrán …' 'He plays the bodhrán …?'

We wrote *Tripswitch* together. After its release in 2006, the two of us began getting lots of gigs in Europe. Luckily, I knew lots of agents from the days of Lúnasa and

Coolfin. The way we played was to just go out for a weekend, do a festival and come back – Spain and France were particularly receptive to what we were doing. We were doing a lot of that sort of work. No long tours. For me, that was heaven.

As an economic model, I don't think many people in Irish music could sustain big tours in Europe, anyway: Irish music has always been about festivals there, except for Germany, a seam that was mined exhaustively from the 70s to the 90s, where an artist might get 30 dates on a package tour but come away with a pittance. A tour like that might look great on the posters and on your CV, but financially it was time to stop messing around and put a realistic value on the sort of thing I was doing. In a sense, I was cashing in on the reputation I'd made as a musician in the 90s.

Myself and Dónal manage everything. We'd have agents in various territories, and typically they would ask, 'Are you free this date for this event?' And depending on their budget, we'd perform with the full band, quartet, trio or duo versions of the At First Light 'brand', although sometimes we wouldn't use the name if it was just a duo or trio. The pool of musicians that we drew from included Francis McIlduff on bodhrán and second pipes, Tony Byrne, Paul McSherry or Paul Meehan on guitar, Rubén Bada (from Spain) or Michael McCague on bouzouki and Ciara McCrickard on vocals and second fiddle. Alan Burke, a singer from Dublin, joined us for a while as well.

I'd known Francis for years. He never seemed to be doing much, but every time we played sessions together it was always really tight. Francis brings a lot of humour to the whole thing. We're all friends, and I think, from experience, it's really important to have friends around you on tour. The bottom line is that we all enjoy playing together and having a bit of craic. For me, it's never really been about the money – certainly not about making a fortune; just sustaining it and making music and having fun.

What could have been a stroke of genius was bringing Dónal on board: with regard to management, he's very organised. But that was just a bonus, because if he was a mediocre musician or we didn't get on so well, it wouldn't have lasted and I wouldn't have been interested. The two of us click as friends as well as musically. We both share the management and admin roles equally, depending on who's busy or free at a particular time. For my part, I have various performing and tutoring activities that don't involve Dónal, while in recent times Dónal has developed his own thing as a recording engineer and producer, co-owning RedBox Recording Studios in Belfast, as well as a sideline in Irish language TV presenting and as a sideman (on fiddle and keyboards) with other performing artists. Variety is the spice of life.

Dónal O'Connor: There's dovetailing in our relationship. In the early days, John was not in any way interested in the 'getting work' side of music. He has since become much more clued-in about that. From having watched my parents run a band from a tiny little office at the top of the staircase in our bungalow, I had a feel for that side of it. So with John's greater experience and age – he's almost nine years older than me – allied with my ability to follow through on things, we managed to get some work and make albums.

We did a four-week tour of Germany in 2006, and after that we both thought, 'I don't like being on long tours.' I remember John said, 'I don't like feeling like I don't know what the name of this town is'. So after that we purposely didn't target America and we didn't bother with any more of those long German tours. We just focused on getting some work in Spain, festivals in France and Italy – 'in and out' sort of things – plus a couple of short British and Irish tours here and there.

*

In July 2007, disaster struck: I had my pipes stolen. I was playing a gig in Zaragoza, Spain, and afterwards the organisers took us to a pub for food. We left all our instruments in the corner of the bar and by the end of the night – four or five o'clock in the morning, probably – everyone goes to get their instrument. And, to my horror, mine was gone. A Seán McAloon chanter, which I had played since I was 12, and a Dave Williams body.

Our flight was the next day. I told the lads I had to stay and look for my pipes – and they all delayed their flights, too, which was very decent of them. We booked into a hotel and I went round the town looking for the pipes, with no joy at all. I was in bits. I had no choice but to fly home the next day, leaving my pipes behind somewhere in Spain. That was devastating.

My girlfriend Trish – 'The Maid Of Murlough' – was a huge moral support and really helped me through a dark time. My confidence was broken. But I got a lot of support, both moral and practical, from within the worldwide piping community. A top-class pipe maker called Benedict Koehler got in touch from America. He'd heard about my plight – it was all over the Web – and he offered to make me a chanter. He immediately sent me over a spare chanter he already had, while he started working on making me a new one as close to the McAloon design as possible. I got a bag and bellows and for a while I played whatever gigs I had with what was essentially a practice set. Six months later he sent me over a really lovely chanter, made of boxwood like the McAloon one, and sounding pretty close to it.

Later, a young, up-and-coming pipe maker called Marcus Coulter also came to my rescue and made me a full body with drones and regulators – a very generous gesture indeed. I was also overwhelmed by the generosity and support of a lot of other people, in particular Tommy Shelton, an avid trad music follower (and great golfer) from America who has now become a dear friend of mine. My eternal thanks to all these guys!

Remarkably, five years later I got my original pipes back. This guy got in contact with me, saying, 'I believe I have your pipes …' I emailed straight back: 'Send me a picture!' He did so – at which point it became kind of weird. He said he was going away for two months and when he came back 'we'll talk about it'. The correspondence dragged on for seven or eight months. Eventually, at his request, I sent him over some whistles and he sent the pipes over in return. He might just have been an odd character, or maybe he was involved, who knows. He'd said he found the pipes in a flea market and bought them for a pittance. Whatever the story, I was thrilled to get them back.

Looking back, there was a plus side to all of this: when I got the full set from Marcus Coulter I became determined to make full use of the instrument, to really play the regulators. Beforehand, my focus hadn't been on the full instrument. So it gave me a kick up the arse. Every cloud …

*

One of the most interesting projects I've been involved with in the past couple of years is The Olllam. Yes, with three 'L's. It evolved out of a friendship I've long had with a young American piper, Tyler Duncan.

I first met Tyler in about 1998, in Miltown Malbay. I was standing at the bar and Karen says, 'John, don't look now but there's this young fellow staring at you. He hasn't taken his eyes off you for half an hour.'

Of course, when someone says 'don't look now', that's exactly what you do! I turned round and this fellow says:

'Are you John McSherry?'
'Yes …'
'I'm your biggest fan!'

He was about 13 at the time and was a particular fan of what I'd done in Lúnasa. He was over from America with his folks, Jeff and Barbara, immersing themselves in the Irish trad world, and we struck up a great friendship. The family would subsequently come and visit us any time they were in Ireland – in Dublin and later in Donegal. I used to teach Tyler piping on these occasions and he went on to win an All-Ireland title, so I suppose I must have been doing something right.

We kept the connection going by email. He came over with friends in 2006, and from that point on we started talking about doing something together, though we weren't sure what. About 2010 there was a window of time where we were both available. He was in Ireland then; we hooked up and spent two or three days writing material. He went back to America and hooked up with Michael Shimmin, a fantastic drummer and the third member of what became The Olllam. They worked up their parts and began putting the meat on the bones. Tyler has a jazz as well as a Celtic background and is also a great arranger, so this album was bound to take some new directions. I recorded my whistle parts at home and the piping parts in Dónal O'Connor's studio, RedBox, and they brought everything together at their studio in the States. We interacted a lot via Skype, passing files back and forth, arranging the tracks as we went. It was very efficient. The 'cons' are that you're not in the same room together, you can't really spark off each other so easily. But one of the 'pros' is that it focuses the mind.

The plan was to create something with a Celtic feel – which would obviously be dictated by the instruments – but we didn't want to use traditional material or follow the kind of structure that traditional tunes have. We wanted each track to be one piece of music, built to flow almost like a pop song, with verse and chorus parts. We wanted the mood to flow all the way through. We ended up using low whistles more than pipes on the album, although that wasn't planned – it just happened that we wrote the melodies using whistles. But the second album will make up for that …

The first album, titled *The Olllam*, came out in 2011, and the reaction was great: a lot of young people, especially, seem to love that album. It doesn't sit easily in any genre – not really Celtic, not really jazz, not really rock – so it can be difficult for festival bookers to get a handle on how to sell it. But, having said that, all the gigs we've done have been within the Celtic music world and we've had a universally great reception, especially from musicians. It seems to be a real 'musicians' band': if we're at a festival in America, the front row will all be musicians.

There are six people in the live band, but as with At First Light (which is myself, Dónal O'Connor and Francis McIlduff), the core of The Olllam is myself, Tyler and Michael. The rest of the band consists of top class session musicians – Joe Dart (bass), Woody Goss (keys), Sean O'Meara or Theo Katzman (guitar).

We've toured America twice at the time of writing, Ireland three times, and there've been gigs in Europe – festivals including Celtic Connections in Glasgow and Lorient in France. Logistically, it's a nightmare, having a six-piece band on the road, with members from two continents. And financially it's far from an easy option, but I'm happy to sacrifice profit in order to work with these fantastic musicians and explore this particular creative avenue. My 'rock' side is being satisfied in The Olllam.

*

Dónal O'Connor: When you're starting out, you're thinking, 'I'd love to be on an album.' And then you think, 'I'd love to have an album with my name on it – it'll be there for all time, I'll have made it.' But as you go on as a musician, you realise that time doesn't stand still and that you have to be continually productive. [In the] early days, it didn't feel like much of an effort. But it's a more thought-out process now: garnering your energy and ideas for months and then letting it loose.

Who you bring in around you in a studio makes a big difference, and I have to say that John in a studio is terrific. He never tires. Sometimes you're in a session for 14 hours and everyone else has fallen asleep on a sofa, left altogether or had a row with each other, but John will still be nit-picking away at getting it right. He's relentless in his energy in a studio, which is incredible. He doesn't get fed up or cynical in creative processes. He's not thinking, 'This has to be all about me' – it's just getting to the end point with the best ideas around, and creating a nice piece of music.

I think he's currently at the top of his game. He's at an age where the next 10 or 15 years will be really good for him, because the older pipers that he looked up to will be winding down. Most of them are doing that already. Liam O'Flynn doesn't seem to be gigging very much, Finbar Furey has more of less given up the pipes, Davy Spillane is coastguarding off the coast of Clare. Paddy Keenan is still 'out there', but inevitably even Paddy will wind down at some stage – though, having said that, he's a unique force of nature.

When the legendary progressive rock and jazz drummer Bill Bruford wrote his autobiography in 2009, he based his chapter headings on questions people regularly ask him. One of these was, 'So, what do you do in the daytime?' Any professional musician would cringe in recognition at that. Being constantly or substantially on the road is one way of working – and Michael McGoldrick, for instance, is very much at the road warrior end of things – but I try and limit the amount of tours I do these days, preferring to do short forays into Europe on a regular basis rather than seeking a month's worth of back-to-back dates. I think the live market at present reflects my preference, too: a series of long weekends is far easier to organise than three or four solid weeks.

So, what do I do in the daytime, as it were? Well, over the course of a year there are lots of different things that make up an income as a professional Irish traditional musician. Having looked through my diary for last year (2014), here are mine:

- Playing gigs throughout the world with various outfits: At First Light, The John McSherry Trio and The Olllam.
- Doing the admin for these gigs: correspondence with festivals/gig organisers, drafting up and sending out contracts, co-ordinating the gigs and the musicians involved.
- Booking flights, publicity, collecting invoices, receipts and so on for tax reasons.
- Being pro-active on social media (Facebook, Twitter and the rest) to keep the profile up and to advertise shows, TV/media appearances and so on.
- Keeping up a regular flow of creative output: tune composition, arrangement, tune-gathering – even though no records may be commercially released in a given year, as was the case in 2014.
- Recording and releasing of this creative output on CD. I like to try and release something new, under whatever banner/collaboration it may be, every other year. It's important to keep refreshing your ideas: to stay relevant, you need to be moving forward creatively all the time, and also to be *seen* to be moving forward – which means regular recorded output and regular live performing – for the sustained interest and confidence of not only your audience but also booking agents and the media.
- Collaboration projects with other artists: I believe it's valuable to connect with other creative artists to broaden your own outlook and also, potentially, to expand your own audience. Some people manage a career working with a small pool of musicians, but most Irish traditional players are almost predisposed, through the session scene, to playing with a wide range of fellow musicians. It keeps it interesting for both the players and the audience – and occasionally a collaboration that's really special will occur. It's what you aim for every time!
- Studio session work on other artists' albums/projects.
- TV and radio appearances: I seem to appear on BBC Radio Ulster, BBC Northern Ireland and RTÉ's TG4 channel pretty often, and occasionally there'll be foreign media requests when I'm gigging in Europe.

- Teaching: I run weekly classes for the Northern Pipers' Society (a not-for-profit organisation I've been involved in founding last year)* and give lessons by Skype to students worldwide.
- Bringing students to weekly sessions in Belfast (at Madden's, Kelly's and The Sunflower Bar) and encouraging them to participate. Sessions are part of any would-be traditional player's rite of passage, and however daunting they seem at first, they're a great way to learn tunes, build confidence and meet new people.

So much for last year (though many of the above points occur every year). What will I be doing this year, 2015? The big difference will be the amount of music I'll be releasing. There was nothing in 2014; there will be at least two and possibly three albums in 2015, plus the first one I've made as co-producer (along with Dónal O'Connor) for another artist, harpist/vocalist Susan Bates, which was an unexpected development but a very positive experience. There will also be two major commissioned pieces, for public performances in Derry and Dublin, which I'd better not wax lyrical about ahead of their completion and performances, lest fate be tempted! Suffice to say that they are creatively exciting opportunities.

The two albums that will definitely appear in 2015 are The Olllam's second, plus one that will be credited to the named trio of myself, Dónal O'Connor and guitarist Seán Óg Graham. Yes, it's another one of those Almost-But-Not-Quite-At-First-Light ones.

> **Dónal O'Connor**: Doing different stuff makes it more enjoyable when John and I do get together. At First Light hadn't done a gig for four or five months, so when we came together for a one-off gig in March 2015, you're halfway through a tune when you think, 'We make a good sound; I really, really enjoy this!' And sometimes when you're doing it every night you forget that – and you start hating the person beside you because they took the last scone at breakfast and you didn't get one. It feels like At First Light has a career of ongoing reunions – which isn't good for the head or the liver. But it feels like friends getting together every now and again, and that's great, and we feel the music's as good as it's ever been – and we'd just like to let more people hear it.

People have been encouraging me in recent times to think about a purely solo album:

---

* See the chapter *Piping In Ulster* for more on the Northern Pipers' Society.

a collection of solo piping. It's something I'm eager to do and lately, I've been shifting my focus from ensemble to solo playing which I'm really enjoying. So I'd say it's definitely on the cards.

In terms of live work, along with the usual weekend trips into Europe and odd shows in Britain and Ireland, there'll be an Olllam tour in December and a tour with Dónal and Seán Óg Graham in October/November. I'm also hooking up with Brian Finnegan, the flute player from Flook, for a festival in Spain, and we'll be bringing in some other musicians and hopefully setting up a tour around that Spanish gig. There's no point in doing all the work necessary and only doing one show.

Nevertheless, the professional music world I slipped into 20-odd years ago is a different beast today. Every Irish trad musician playing at a pro level needs to diversify to survive, and only the most committed will:

> **Dónal O'Connor**: There was an industry of bands who were touring more or less full time, from the 70s into the 90s: from Planxty up to Altan. Later on, when I was involved with Lá Lugh, you had the likes of Dervish, Nomos, early Lúnasa – bands that were able to get enough work in a year to justify giving up other jobs. But now there are almost no bands at that totally full-time level, maybe only Lúnasa. So that industry has changed. I don't know if that's having an effect on Irish traditional music; it's having an effect on the careers of musicians.
>
> Irish music is as popular as it ever was – but you can't survive on the gigs alone. You have to have a revenue stream that's working for you when you're not touring. So now that the revenue stream of physical music sales is completely eroded and the model of a record company paying an advance in order to create an album of music has gone, every artist needs to self-fund their next piece of recorded work, with the hope that that piece of work will spur another couple of years of live work. You still have to be seen to be creating new recorded work to help get live work, but ironically, the live work you get has to fund that recorded work – which totally flips the 1970s model of the record sales having the potential of being an artist's principal income stream. I call a CD an expensive business card now. Yes, you're still creating a body of work that you hope people appreciate, but as a business model the dodo is dead. Lots of people like the idea of the dodo, but nobody's found a way to resuscitate it yet.
>
> But I'm not totally cynical about it. One example of why John and I have lasted so well as a partnership happened just last month, on St Patrick's Day. We were booked to play a free access acoustic session for 90 minutes,

just fiddle and pipes, but we had such fun just playing together that we played for nearly four hours – and the people watching stayed with us for it, loved it, were electrified by it. That's why we do it: because we both love it. We love the moment of finding a common melody we haven't played in 10 years and it coming to us out of the blue in the middle of a tune and, bang, you're into it. There's a real thrill with that. As long as the thrill is there, there'll always be people, John and me included, who'll find a way to keep going out there and playing Irish music for people.

For me, there is still plenty more music to be made. I first picked up the uilleann pipes about 33 years ago. If anyone had asked me then if I thought I'd be making a living playing them in the 21st century, I don't believe I could even have answered that. Back then I didn't even know what a 'living' was, what a 'career' was – and I still don't! I didn't think about anything like that at the time. All I wanted to do was play the music. And, in a way, that's still at the heart of what I do. If you play music from the basis of loving it, ahead of any aspirations toward wealth or fame, you're in the best place to communicate that passion, and that music, to others. I've been privileged to have had an audience that has allowed me to play music for them over many years. That in itself is amazing. Yet still more amazing is the realisation that I'm a blink in the eye of the instrument's history, only the most recent chapter in a book that goes back 300 years. Not even Paddy Keenan is that old …

Chapter 2

Introducing Finbar Furey, Paddy Keenan and Liam O'Flynn

Uilleann piping is a continuum stretching back to the 18th century: the best players of every generation learn, directly or indirectly, from the best players of the one before. Through the extraordinary conduit of his (non-piping) father's memory, Willie Clancy, one of the four great pipers of the middle 20th century (alongside Johnny Doran, Leo Rowsome and Séamus Ennis), was able to draw from the playing style and repertoire of the long-dead Garrett Barry, a legendary figure of the late 19th century. Through the magic of recorded sound, such slender threads are no longer required. Any piper of the modern era has rich resources upon which to draw, all the way back to the ghostly sounds of Billy Hanafin and Mící 'Cumbá' O'Sullivan in the 1890s.

Not everything might be available at the click of a button, but with a little effort – deleted gems from eBay or Discogs online, digitised 78s streaming at the Internet Archive (archive.org), digitised non-commercial recordings available to hear at Dublin's Irish Traditional Music Archive – the curious student of pipers past can access over a century of music.

When John McSherry was learning the art in the 1980s, long before the Information Age, his earliest resources were a handful of LPs and second-generation cassettes of three great pipers who had come to prominence in the commercial recording world in the 1960s and 70s: Finbar Furey, Paddy Keenan and Liam O'Flynn. To Paddy Keenan's mind, the influence can be heard.

> **Paddy**: John's great, he's one of the few pipers, if not the only piper, who I'd give my pipes to in a concert. … I hear a lot of my dad's playing, or my dad's mind, in John's way of thinking on how pipes should be played, but it's coming through me from him, so I wouldn't take a lot of credit for that. But I will say that in all the technique [my dad] gave me, in all the wishes that he had to have a piper who would stand out – and nothing would do my dad but the best – there was a comparison once made by a Traveller and he said, 'There's Cassius Clay … and there's Paddy Keenan.' What a comparison!

As Finbar Furey recalls, Paddy reckoned that comparison (to a fighter who had power, finesse and charisma) was worth passing on to someone else:

Finbar: Paddy Keenan once caught my ear and said, 'You're the Cassius Clay of uilleann pipes!' I thought that was a lovely turn of phrase.

Cassius Clay, who became a world sensation as Muhammad Ali, combined skill at his art (boxing) with a star quality translated to actual stardom through an understanding of modern media. He needed television in the same way that Finbar & Eddie Furey, Planxty (with Liam O'Flynn) and The Bothy Band (with Paddy Keenan) needed the recording, touring and broadcasting infrastructure of the British and European popular music world of the same era. It required new ways of presenting and wielding what was a very venerable and still obscure instrument if it, and its players, were to thrive.

Leo Rowsome (1903–70) and Séamus Ennis (1918–82), in the early and middle years of the 20th century, managed to make a living largely as professional pipers, although Leo also had an income as a pipe maker, while Séamus had periods of salaried work as a folk music collector and broadcaster. Johnny Doran (1907–50), the greatest known Traveller musician of all time, also lived by his pipes. Across the Atlantic, Patsy Touhey made a living as a piper and comic performer on the American vaudeville circuit during the late Victorian and Edwardian era. Barring those caveats (of four exceptional people), the generation represented by Finbar Furey (b. 1946), Liam O'Flynn (b. 1945) and Paddy Keenan (b. 1950) was the first since the days of the itinerant pipers of the 18th and 19th centuries to coincide with a socio-cultural context that allowed for the possibility of uilleann pipers becoming professional touring musicians. In this case, their touring was not from town to town around Ireland on foot, finding a friendly 'big house' or crossroads at which to ply their trade, but around the stages of Europe and America.

While John McSherry learned the pipes through the traditional conduit of oral tradition, from personal contact with Seán McAloon and others, he also had ready access to three masters. Just as many other pipers 20 years younger than John, for instance, have learned from him or from his recordings, so John drew from, and aspired to, the music and mystique of Furey, O'Flynn and Keenan. In their turn, those three had drawn from the recordings and mystique of Johnny Doran and of Patsy Touhey, and from personal contact with the likes of Rowsome, Ennis and Clancy. But everyone's recipe for soup will be different – different seasoning, different measures of ingredients, sometimes different ingredients altogether.

While some instruments in Irish music tend to be prone to identifiably regional styles, each uilleann piper, certainly since the dawn of the recording era, has had more or less a style unto him or herself. And in every generation, perhaps because the masters of piping have always been so few, personalities and reputations become known, individuals become characters of legend and rumour, and devotees wonder aloud which one is best. It's a little like professional boxing in that respect. Was

Muhammad Ali really better than Henry Cooper? Arguments still rage on that one.

Liam O'Flynn, surely the mildest and most circumspect of all the great living pipers, explained his position on the matter in a 1978 interview, appropriately entitled 'The quiet man of the pipes':

> **Liam**: I always think of Willie Clancy as one of the greatest pipers, but I do not think there is much virtue or point in trying to draw up contrasts between different pipers, or other musicians. There is no sense in saying this one is the best of all, as there are so many different aspects to be considered. There are many styles and variations to be considered. Comparisons are unfair. … Willie always told me he was strongly influenced by Rowsome, Johnny Doran, Patsy Touhey and Séamus Ennis so that there is something of all of these in my playing, along with whatever I put in myself.[2]

All great musicians are products not only of their influences but of their innate musicality and instincts. For his part, Paddy Keenan's position is simple: 'I respect all pipers, from beginners to advanced players.' That said, he can point to differences between himself and others:

> **Paddy**: I believe I'm right in saying – I hope I'm right in saying – that if you hear Liam O'Flynn playing a tune, the pressure that the first note gets dictates the pressure of every note after that, which means that the tune is played very flowingly and beautifully. But if I'm playing it, every note gets a different pressure, to create a different mood and dynamic.

Finbar Furey and Paddy Keenan may superficially appear to be similar players, each capable of incredible fire and passion in their playing, each coming from the Traveller tradition, growing up together and learning the pipes together with the even-then legendary figure of the late Johnny Doran, whom their fathers knew, as the benchmark. To Paddy's mind, any similarity goes back to the influence of his father, John Keenan:

> **Paddy**: Finbar is a brother, in the fact that he came and lived with us for six or eight years, I can't remember – to the end of the 50s and into the 60s, and left in '66. My dad was very influential in his playing. He did tell him if he felt he was wrong or whatever. But then, I was his son and I was the 'dedicated piper' [in the family] and I was following the stature of Doran, the Cashes, the great people who held on to the culture when it might have been beaten out of them by the English. But the Traveller could not be stopped.

There is a spirit of wildness and danger in the playing of both men, certainly in their respective early recordings – and in concert to this day. Listen carefully and differences, even to the casual listener, will become apparent. To pipers, the differences, in technical aspects as well as in 'feel', should be glaring. Finbar has no doubt of it:

> **Finbar**: Sometimes people say me and Paddy Keenan sound alike. We don't! We're *completely* different! We know the difference between ourselves, but we can't describe it to you. You must understand the instrument. … I remember people saying to me, 'Listen to Paddy Keenan playing the pipes …' One great musician in particular said, 'I was afraid to go to the bar in case I missed something.' I wonder how many people have said that? There's an excitement: Paddy plays exciting pipes, there's fire in the air, you know. It's fantastic.

Both Finbar – determinedly representing the Traveller tradition – and Liam O'Flynn – representing (at least by default) the purity and control associated with the school of his tutor, Leo Rowsome – took part in Fleadh and Oireachtas competitions in the early 1960s. The two have very different personalities and backgrounds, and at that time Finbar's only goal in such events was the honour of the Travelling tradition. His perspective has changed with time:

> **Finbar**: I won [almost] every competition I went in for. I came second in one to Felix Doran, and that was in Clones … [In the Oireachtas], I was up against these great old pipers like Pat McNulty, Seán Seery, Mick Dowling, great pipers from The [Dublin] Pipers' Club … There were some great pipers out there, who had completely different styles of playing than I did … But in my eyes they played as well as I did. There was Liam Óg O'Flynn, who's still a beautiful piper and [has] a completely different style to what I play. Myself and Liam Óg would be pitted against each other. But we were kids, we never really got to know each other – we sort of kept away from each other, which was stupid. So when we did get to know each other and talk to each other, it was wonderful, because he has a great mind for music.[3]

*

John's three early heroes of piping happen to have had, with pleasing convenience for this narrative, an almost perfectly sequential impact on the wider world of music. Finbar Furey, in a ground-breaking duo partnership with his brother Eddie on guitar and vocals, toured heavily on the thriving British folk club scene from 1967 onward, switching his focus to mainland Europe from 1972. It was effectively two careers: the pair made five albums in Britain between 1968 and 1972, followed by four albums made in Germany between 1972 and 1976. In 1975, they created the group that duly became The Fureys & Davey Arthur, which was a third career in itself. Finbar left the group to pursue his own path in 1997.

In terms of creating an audience in Britain for Irish instrumental music, and for the pipes in particular, that 1967–72 period is hugely important. Similarly, their early touring in Europe opened the floodgates for a horde of Irish musicians (good, bad or indifferent) in their wake.

> **Dónal Lunny**: I'd say the work they did is underrated. There was an awareness that they were popular abroad – Germany, Holland, wherever. But people [in Ireland] wouldn't have been conscious of the profile they had [there].

During the same period, Christy Moore, a singer/guitarist from Ireland and an acquaintance of Finbar, was forging a career as a solo artist around the British folk clubs, especially in the north of England. His second album, *Prosperous*, recorded with English producer Bill Leader in 1971, begat Planxty – a band featuring himself, Andy Irvine, Dónal Lunny and Liam O'Flynn – which built on the platform created by the Furey brothers in Britain and Europe. In Ireland, Planxty were the right people at the right time, galvanising the young *en masse* into a new appreciation of their own country's traditional music.

> **Finbar**: It was great, because [Eddie and I] had just taken Britain apart, and [their producer] Phil Coulter was living in London at the time, so he would have heard [us on] John Peel every night, he would have understood it.

Bill Leader, a man of great taste but little acumen in business, had no success with *Prosperous* on his own label. Jack Fitzgerald, a Dublin retailer, noticed a demand in Ireland and bought the rights, creating a new label, Tara, for the purpose. Under John Cook's direction, Tara would go on to generate, itself, many more albums with significant piping content, from Séamus Ennis to Liam O'Flynn and Davy Spillane.

> **Bill**: It didn't sell for me at all. It sold for Tara, and we sort of gifted it to Christy, 'cos there was nothing we could do. … I think it was a glimmer in Christy's eye, which developed into whatever it is that glimmers in eyes develop into. It was an idea, and I think it probably exceeded the original intention. In fact, it did.

Planxty was building on existing foundations created by Irish musicians who had tapped into the British folk revival, but the band's success between 1972 and 1975 was based on a wholly new sound:

> **Liam**: Planxty had its own particular sound from day one. It wouldn't have been the first folk band with pipes – you had The McPeakes and The Fureys using pipes and guitars. But in Planxty, we were quite sure what we wanted to do from the start, and the really powerful, unique thing was the way in which we approached accompaniment – accompanying songs and tunes. Even though, when you listen to it, it sounds simple, it was really quite complex, with these lines from Dónal and Andy weaving together – which wasn't something that could be easily imitated.

From 1975, Dónal Lunny could be seen and heard in a new ensemble with international aspirations, The Bothy Band. Where Planxty had merged the vocal and instrumental traditions, The Bothy Band were more instrumentally focused, boasting a three-part frontline in Paddy Keenan (pipes), Matt Molloy (flute) and Tommy Peoples (fiddle, later replaced by Kevin Burke), with a three-part engine room consisting of Dónal Lunny (bouzouki), Mícheál Ó Domhnaill (guitar) and Tríona Ní Dhomhnaill (clavinet). It was an exciting and popular live act, releasing four albums and making numerous broadcasts on British and Irish TV and radio.

As Paddy Keenan concedes, though it lasted only five years (1975–79) and was financially a bittersweet experience for all concerned, the perceived success of The Bothy Band and the obvious success of its musical blend effectively made it the template for virtually all subsequent bands who have peddled Irish traditional music on concert platforms:

> **Paddy**: It was a timing thing, too. But, yes, you have Dervish who will say that, who'll admit that – it's near enough the same line-up. We had Moving Hearts afterwards, which Mícheál and I wanted, we wanted to move on and do something different with electronic stuff. When we got it, we weren't really happy with it. We'd have definitely taken it somewhere else – but I don't think we'd have ever lost the roots.

Formed in 1981 by Dónal Lunny and Christy Moore, Moving Hearts would be the next significant band innovation in Irish trad-influenced music, blending topical songwriting with uilleann pipes and a rock rhythm section, although it would devolve into an instrumental unit for their third and final studio album, *The Storm*. With

Paddy Keenan bowing out early, Davy Spillane was the piper in Moving Hearts, and it made his name.

> **Finbar Furey**: I remember Davy Spillane when he was a kid, learning. I can still remember Davy playing one of my tunes in Grafton Street for me, on a half set of pipes. And I can still hear the notes he played.

Finbar recalls someone saying to him, around the time Moving Hearts were formed, 'Ah, wait'll you hear this new piper!' At which point Davy, embarrassed, says, 'Sure, Finbar taught me all I know.' After which Finbar declares: 'Yeah, but I didn't teach him all *I* know …'

At the same time as Dónal Lunny was bringing the pipes into play with rock rhythms and political songs, one of his many associates, Shaun Davey (with whom Dónal had collaborated in a stillborn project between his stints with Planxty and The Bothy Band), was bringing the instrument into a European chamber orchestra setting with a ground-breaking instrumental suite, *The Brendan Voyage*, inspired by a then-recent recreation of St Brendan's legendary voyage to America. The featured piper would be Liam O'Flynn.

Released on Tara in 1980, and frequently performed around the world, it was the start of a significant compositional career for Davey and an additional career, alongside his more conventional solo and band activities, for Liam. Liam would be featured in many of Shaun's further suites, from *The Pilgrim* (1983) to *Voices From The Merry Cemetery* (2010), while Shaun would write for and produce two lavishly appointed solo albums for Liam. *The Brendan Voyage* would be as influential in its own way as Planxty and The Bothy Band had been:

> **Liam**: It was certainly ground-breaking, for sure, and it seems to me as time passes that the impact it made is an ongoing thing. It made a huge impact at the time, but it's growing, because [in] every new territory I go into with the piece, people are amazed by this new creature, as it were. … Insofar as Shaun was the most important person in fusing the idioms of European art music together with a little spice of modern rhythms and traditional instruments, I think he paved the way for a lot of the stuff we're hearing now.

*

Paddy Keenan and Liam O'Flynn remain giants in the world of piping. A casual listener at a concert by either might come away thinking that one is a chamber musician and the other a rock star. Their personalities, playing styles and lifestyles could hardly appear more different, and yet their roots and influences have a great deal of shared ground. Alas, Finbar Furey's relationship to piping nowadays can only be sporadic:

> **Finbar**: I had to get my arm literally taken out – the muscle was wasted, there was no muscle there. … And then I had a heart attack. I remember once coming home to Ireland and hearing that 'The Pecker' Dunne was dead.* It had gone all round Ireland. And then I got a phone call from him saying, 'Don't worry, I'm looking at myself in the mirror.' I remember I was in Australia one time, and this fellow had said, *'Oh my God, Finbar Furey is dead!'* And it turned out it was *Billy* Fury!
>
> So I have to be careful. I play the pipes now for about 20 minutes, then I've got to put them down. If I don't, it's like somebody taking a sword to my arm. Eventually I'll have to stop. … [So] I don't play the pipes for a living any more; I play the guitar and the banjo. The pipes is only a hobby with me now. If I never had to play them again, it wouldn't bother me. …
>
> [But] you know, I still love playing them, I really do. It's like a boxer who doesn't know his time is up, or an artist who can't throw the brush anymore. His mind knows what to do, but his body won't do it. And my hands are crippled with arthritis. It's just old age, you know … I'll still be able to play, but if I try and kick it into fifth gear now, I can go for about five minutes … My whole thing [now], I think, is I just enjoy playing them when I play them. Davy Spillane has a better idea. Davy says, 'You're not stopping: we're going to get you a set of electric pipes, so all you'll have to do is move your fingers.' …
>
> I was down in Clare a few months ago [with] Blackie O'Connell – a super piper. He's the next generation that's going to hold this instrument together. And I remember Paddy Keenan dropped in, and fortunately Davy Spillane did, too – he's just dropped out of the public eye, but he's not dropped out of piping. Davy's very much involved in Irish pipes and always has been – a great reed maker. Sure, we couldn't do without him. … I hadn't played the pipes [by then], because I have to be careful with my shoulder. Anyway, the boys decided, 'Get him to play a tune …' So I got the pipes and I played a couple of tunes. And Paddy says to me, 'You're getting older, but you don't get any worse, do you, Finbar?' I says, 'Wait'll I tell you, just because I don't play them, don't think I have forgotten how to!'

---

* 'The Pecker' Dunne (b. 1932) is a Traveller musician, best-known for writing 'Sullivan's John', recorded by The Dubliners (1967), Sweeney's Men (1968), Anne Briggs (1971) and many others.

Chapter 3
Finbar & Eddie Furey: A Dream In Their Hands

Finbar and Eddie Furey not only revolutionised the way Irish music could be performed, they effectively created a platform on which it could thrive in the popular music touring and recording worlds in Britain and Europe. They laid the foundations for an industry of professional touring units based on Irish traditional music that took root in the 1970s and which has lasted essentially unchanged to the present day.

By combining Finbar's virtuoso piping with guitar in instrumental sets, and by adding the pipes to folk and contemporary songs delivered with rare power by Eddie Furey, they not only opened up whole new worlds of possibility for the pipes as an instrument and for Irish music in general, but had a whale of time as young men – scraping by financially, yet giving pleasure to tens of thousands, cumulatively, in the heady days of the 1960s 'British folk revival'. When they began a second career in Germany in the early 70s, Finbar and Eddie would find themselves playing to audiences of thousands: not cumulatively but literally, every night. It undersells their rough-hewn brilliance as a duo to say that they were simply 'the right people at the right time', for it was only through determination and an unquantifiable, particular magic, individually and together, as performers and artists, that the opportunities they enjoyed were created.

In later years, when the duo had morphed into a full band, The Fureys & Davey Arthur, audiences would come to view Finbar (given his role as singer on the 1981 international hit single 'When You Were Sweet Sixteen' and on subsequent hit singles and albums) as the frontman. Nevertheless, during their original career as a duo, Eddie Furey was the public face of the act – bantering with audiences, introducing the songs, filling in while Finbar tuned the pipes, cracking jokes and sourcing material from fellow club performers like Martin Carthy and Gerry Rafferty. The emotional impact of Eddie's voice, declamatory in power yet resonant with yearning and sensitivity, maximised the duo's appeal, as did the accessibility of the songs they chose. The act provided a setting for Finbar's specialised musicianship that allowed it to be heard in a way that would not have been the case had he been plying his trade as a solo instrumentalist at that time.

Finbar took time to become the confident public personality he is today, focusing rather on delivering extraordinary instrumental performances during these early years of travelling up and down Britain, and later through Europe, with his brother. Eddie, however, was a great communicator and entertainer right from the start. He understood that audiences at a basic level want to be entertained; if great artistry can be built onto that base, so much the better – but the engagement has to be there first.

Finbar and Eddie brought different skills and personalities to the table. Combined, they were greater than the sum of their parts. If Eddie was the ringmaster and Finbar the star of the high wire, their circus needed each of them. As a duo, in the thriving heyday of the folk clubs, they were a lethal combination. The montage of photos on the gatefold sleeves of their German LPs from 1972 to '76 (records still largely unknown in Britain and Ireland) show two lads from Ireland as kings of the world: playing music, having fun and – in the guise of mass entertainment – bringing something of a venerable cultural tradition to the wider world.

While the brothers went their separate ways, professionally, in the mid-90s, their career as a duo has been underappreciated. To a very great extent Finbar Furey, in the duo with Eddie, was the man who first made the pipes visible in the modern era. They brought the instrument into public consciousness in Britain and Europe, bridging the gap between the mid-20th-century era of reverence by a limited cognoscenti for the great names of that time and the 1970s-onward era of Irish traditional music fully existing on a professional touring and recording level within a wider pop/rock context.

These were two young men from a well-travelled family with a long history of playing music and putting on shows, their father Ted and his performing partner Bully Ros being well known figures around Ireland. Nearly 50 years after Finbar and Eddie took a ferry to Scotland in February 1967, thinking they would be away for a fortnight, the pair remain significant figures in the music world. Eddie still tours and records on an international level with The Fureys, while Finbar pursues a solo career, having adopted banjo as his main instrument in recent years. To have forged 50-year careers in music is worthy of anyone's respect; to have essentially forged a whole industry within music – that of Irish folk and traditional music as a successful global entity – is an achievement still greater.

*

Eddie (b. 1944) and Finbar (b. 1946) were the eldest sons of Ted Furey (1914–79). Ted was a Travelling piper and fiddler who had worked all over Ireland, travelling with Johnny and Felix Doran amongst others. He would go on to make recordings in the 1970s and tour the European circuit that his sons had by then opened up, but in the 1950s and 60s he was a kind of underground figure, albeit well known among the traditional music cognoscenti in Ireland. He was, and would remain, a powerful force in the lives of his sons. Ted's family (his wife Nora and their four sons Eddie, Finbar,

Paul and George) made their home at 116 Claddagh Road, in Dublin's Ballyfermot area, in the mid-1950s. With Ted such a big figure in the traditional music and Travelling communities, the children had no shortage of inspiration to tap into.

> **Finbar**: My father always said, 'Be aware – with this music, you don't own it; this music is bigger than you. It's part of your heritage. I'll give you my music; you add to it. It's a circle that doesn't break. The minute you try to put that into a box, then you go onstage with an ego or a price on your head: one of them is going to explode. This music is bigger than you. Be clear on that, and you move on.' We're not there to please somebody else's ego in this business; we're there to play music, to pay our rent, to give it back as close to where we got it as we can for the next generation. … My father taught us more about music than you could ever learn in college. It's within you. You're either born with it or you're not … Meeting the pipes is like meeting the Pope. I'm serious. The pipes were sacred, and still are.

Fermanagh piper Seán McAloon (1923–98), a mentor to John McSherry 30 years later, played a similar role with the young Finbar Furey:

> **Finbar**: I was greatly influenced by two pipers, staccato players – Seán McAloon and Calum Moore. I remember Seán coming down from the North and winning the Oireachtas.* I was very influenced by this man – and what a great piper, too. I was only a kid, I wouldn't have known him; my father would have known him and played music with him. … Calum Moore was a Highland piper who played with the Fintan Lalor Pipe Band [in Dublin]. They won the world championships. Calum was infused with the Highland pipes, his fingers used to crack off the chanter: *'Teach me that, teach me that …'* [I'd say]. And I still play [based on that]. It's like a wheel, I can't describe it: I play 'within a wheel'. Johnny Doran was the same. It's like climbing a flight of stairs and never getting to the top.

Finbar was four when Johnny Doran died in 1950, but Johnny's brother Felix Doran and Clare piper Willie Clancy would be regulars among the musical visitors to the Furey household:

---

* The first Oireachtas na Gaeilge festival was held in Dublin in 1897 – an arts festival promoted by the Gaelic League, with prizes designed to celebrate the Irish language. Barring a fallow period in the 1930s, the event has continued annually ever since.

Finbar: Wake up in the morning and one of them would be lying in the bed beside you, snoring his head off, the pipes lying on the floor. ... They'd play the pipes all night. Someone was always in the house – you'd have dead bodies all over the place when you'd wake up in the morning to go to school, with fiddles and flutes and pipes and bottles of Guinness all over the place. You'd have to be very careful where you stepped. And my mother would say, '*Ssssh! The boys have just gone to bed an hour ago.*' And there'd be sheets of music on the table where they'd been scribbling out bits of music. They wouldn't have gone to bed pissed out of their brains – maybe a bottle or two bottles of Guinness, and a good chat about west and east and the music. That was the way of collecting our music. My father would have gone down to Clare or Galway, taken some tunes down – and that's the way it was passed around.[4]

A few years after Ted and his family had settled in Ballyfermot, Ted's great friend John Keenan and his family, including his piping son Paddy, moved in around the corner, on Oranmore Road.

Finbar: Both the lads [our father and John Keenan] shared us … I mean, we often sat at Johnny's table and Mary's table, having our dinner. They treated us the same; they wouldn't bat an eyelid, they'd just ask how my mammy was. I'd say, 'I haven't seen her for a couple of days …' '*What?! Get down there!*'

Eddie: When we met them first they only had a bag and chanter, really. There wasn't much money around in them days – it was a poor time for everybody. My father got Finbar's pipes from a fellow called Kennedy in Cork. [He] and Finbar had to hitch down to Cork to pick the pipes up and then hitch back with the pipes. My father, he saved all his money to get Finbar a set of pipes. I was [already] playing guitar by then. I started off playing the violin originally. [My father] couldn't afford to buy me a violin, so he made me a homemade fiddle. But I think Finbar had his pipes, maybe not a full set, by '61 or '62.

Finbar believes he was 12 or 13 when his father admitted he could teach him no more. Aside from music, Ted had also thought it wise to have his sons acquire some boxing skills. As Finbar recalls: 'We fancied ourselves from when we were 12 to about 14, and then we met our match and that was the end of it – we went back to music, it was easier!'[5]

*

Much of note that happened in and around Irish traditional music in the later 1960s and 70s can trace its roots back to gatherings at O'Donoghue's pub in Merrion Row, Dublin, owned by Paddy and Maureen of that name. Karl Dallas, for British music weekly *Melody Maker*, later recalled O'Donoghue's in the early 60s as 'one of the first places I heard someone play a jig on a 12-string guitar (it was one of the Furey brothers, as I recall, with his dad on fiddle), and I realised that there were more possibilities for the contemporary re-workings of traditional material than had been apparent till that moment.'[6]

The man whom Karl had seen accompanying Ted was Eddie. The Furey family were regulars at the pub, with Eddie dating their discovery of the place to 1961 or '62:

> **Eddie**: When we found O'Donoghue's pub first, Ciarán Burke brought us down there – myself and my father and Finbar. [As far as I know] there was no Dubliners then, there was no Chieftains. The only band I would have heard of would be The Clancy Brothers & Tommy Makem. That's where it all started. We played New Year's Eve at O'Donoghue's – a lovely old pub at the time, very clean. We were sitting in the back room with, say, about seven people – there was no one in the front room – and Ronnie Drew came in. Ronnie had been back that week from teaching English in Spain. We'd met Ciarán Burke in Gorey at the Fleadh Cheoil and he kind of befriended us.[*] We didn't realise that Ciarán's father was the pathologist for the Guards [Irish police]. He lived in a big house in Fitzwilliam Square in Dublin. We were invited down on New Year's Eve early in the afternoon, and he was all excited because he'd got the very first ever recording, long playing album, of Leo Rowsome, which had just come out.[†] No one had made a pipe album before that.

While Finbar was putting time into the solitary experience of mastering the pipes, during the early to mid-1960s Eddie was out dipping his toes into show business, playing guitar in a beat group:

> **Eddie**: [It was] a great little band. It started off as The Demons; they renamed it The Movement after I left.[‡] We were writing our own stuff. We wouldn't

---

* The Fleadh Cheoil at Gorey was in 1962.
† Leo Rowsome had been recording, on 78rpm, since 1926. His first LP record was released late in 1959: *Rí na bPíobairí (King of the Pipers)*, on the new Claddagh label. Ciarán may simply have purchased the LP late in 1962, having met the Furey family at Gorey that summer.
‡ The Movement existed between 1965 and '68 or '69, releasing two singles.

have been doing anything like The Beatles or The Rolling Stones. We'd try to keep away from that. But they weren't getting anywhere. I was out getting gigs here and there, and mostly we'd be playing in the middle of showbands.* But the clubs started up then. You got the Number Five Club in Dublin, the 72 Club and A-Go-Go and all that. We went across to Liverpool to buy clothes – reefer jackets and flower shirts and all that business. Couldn't get 'em in Dublin. Could have got 'em in Belfast, probably!

Eddie recalls a great camaraderie from the Dublin beat scene: 'There was a bar in the middle of Dublin, the Elbow Inn, at the back of the GPO. We all used to meet upstairs there, [including] people like Phil Lynott. Phil was in a band called The Black Eagles. He had a charisma about him all the time. When he walked in a room he had a presence.'

Phil Lynott, a future star with Thin Lizzy, joined The Black Eagles in 1965, clearly overlapping for a few months with Eddie's membership of The Demons, which expired that same year. The Demons would alternate with The Black Eagles on Saturday nights at the Number Five Club on Harcourt Street, the one band going down to cheer the other on. A similar arrangement happened at the Grove, off Clanbrassil Street: 'a kind of old tin shed like you'd see in the war, like a hangar!' Eddie would still always find time to accompany his father and Finbar when opportunities to play traditional music presented themselves:

> **Finbar**: The very first place we ever got as a professional gig, if you like, as kids – we got 30 bob – was O'Connell's pub, near St Stephen's Hospice. And then we got another place called Joe Ryan's, just beside the Labour Exchange at Christchurch. So he booked us for another gig and I remember he paid us 10 bob more. That was me and Eddie and [our brother] Paul – and Paul was only a baby, should never have been allowed into a pub in them days. And then I remember Mick McCarthy got involved when he built the Embankment.†

---

* The infrastructure of live entertainment in Ireland during the 60s was dominated by 'showbands' – groups with uniforms, a brass section and a personality vocalist. They performed sanitised arrangements of pop and country material from the US and UK, to accompany dancing, along with maudlin Irish songs, and operated within a vast network of alcohol-free ballrooms throughout the island. Visiting pop acts from the UK or local beat clubs or folk acts would play a half-hour set (the norm for the period) as a guest spot during a showband's interval, the showband itself playing for an extended period on either side.

† The Embankment would become a significant venue for the commercial end of folk music from the mid-60s onwards. Acts like The Bothy Band and De Danann were filmed there by RTÉ in the 1970s.

I used to play in the Embankment for Mick when I was 12 years of age. I'd made my confirmation and he kidnapped me from the house with my pipes – and my father found me at the Embankment at twelve o'clock at night, covered in sweat, playing the pipes and Mick shouting out [titles of] laments to me all night. But when I came into the house that night and put my bag down with a few bob in it, my father said, *'Jaysus, that Mick McCarthy's a decent man …'* He was going to kill him beforehand! But Mick was great, and that would have been Mick's first [promotion of music]. It was only a tiny pub; he built the big place round the back [later].[7]

Eddie: [Finbar] had a wild way of playing the music. The first ones to play that style of music were the Cashes and the Dorans, the Travelling musicians. My father was a good piper himself. So he taught him that way. Most of the pipers coming up in those days [were different] … Leo Rowsome, he taught a special way of playing the pipes, like, a 'perfect' way of playing, a 'drawing room' way of playing, kind of polite. It wasn't wild like Finbar. And then, of course, a load of people came in on Finbar's back, then. But that all came from the Cashes and the Dorans.

A surviving Telefís Éireann clip of Ted, Finbar and Eddie performing 'The Maid Of Mount Cisco' at the Abbey Tavern, filmed on November 4 1963, testifies to the skill of all concerned.* Another trio gig from the same month was memorable:

Eddie: I remember playing with Finbar and my father in St Anthony's Hall down the quay [in Dublin]. And Dan O'Dowd, the famous piper – he worked for the fire brigade in them days – he was on as well. Actually, the reason I remember that as clear as anything now is that it was the time that Kennedy got shot, the same day [November 22 1963]. And we were playing in that concert that night. And I remember going back to the Pipers' Club in Dublin – and funnily enough, they would let me in there with a guitar. Certain instruments weren't accepted in the Pipers' Club, including banjos and mandolins. But they let me in with a guitar, and I often got up and played slow airs behind Leo Rowsome in the Pipers' Club.

At some point during the first half of the 60s, Finbar and Eddie stumbled upon the sound that would soon define them as an act in Britain and Germany. The

---

* www.rte.ie/archives/exhibitions/1664-traditional-music/370213-the-abbey-tavern/

discovery would be made at a folk club in Trinity College run by one Frank Gyles:

> **Eddie**: He was president of the college, a North Wales musician. He used to bring us in there, and one night I sang a couple of songs with the pipes and guitar, and it just took off – the audience had never heard the sound before. I was singing a contemporary song with the pipes. There was no one [else] doing it. … I had two guitars: I had a 12-string [Epiphone]; the sound went well with the slow songs on the pipes. … At that time I used to urge Finbar to play a bit faster than usual, because I'd say, 'If this was a crossroads dance you couldn't dance at that pace there: take it up a bit.' We got the music out of the wardrobe, really, and made it hot!

*

Fleadh Cheoil competitions, run by Comhaltas Ceoltóirí Éireann (CCÉ), had begun in the 1950s with a mission to nurture traditional music around Ireland. Ted Furey entered Finbar into the Junior All-Ireland competition at the Mullingar Fleadh in 1963. He won it on pipes, but the trio with Eddie and their father didn't fare as well:

> **Eddie**: We got beaten by half a point because I wasn't playing a 'traditional instrument'. I was playing the guitar … They took a half point off. But we knew we had it won, because the crowd was still clapping when the other band was coming on. They wouldn't let the other band start, they wanted more from us. We never got our medals for that from the Comhaltas. But we didn't care about medals – we liked the music.

To Eddie's recollection, his brother had progressed very swiftly on his instrument: 'When he won the junior competition in Mullingar, he won it with 'Miss McLeod's Reel'. He included everything in it, doing a great job on the drones and the regulators, and I think everyone was amazed that a fellow who was only 13 or 14 years old could make the pipes talk at that age.'

In 1964, when he was 17 (technically a year too young), Finbar won the Senior All-Ireland piping competition. He won the Oireachtas piping event the same year: 'So I won the Junior, Senior and Oireachtas before I was 18 years old.'

The tunes he was using in the competitions included 'Sliabh Na mBan' and a difficult version of 'Róisín Dhu', 'and a take on 'The Derry Hornpipe'. I loved showing off.'

Accompanied by Eddie, Finbar would record 'Róisin Dhú' and 'Sliabh Na mBan' on two albums in 1968. He recalls winning every competition in which he was entered save for one, in Clones, in which he came second to Felix Doran. Winning competitions was a mixture of pride and discomfort:

> **Finbar**: I was always against the competitions. But Johnny Doran won the Oireachtas in 1947 or '46, and my father always said he was the first Travelling piper to win it. And he said, 'We'd better keep the tradition going.' I didn't want to, but I did. I remember I won the Oireachtas in '64 and the All-Ireland [for a second time] in '65, and then I won it again in '66 – that was the last time. But he asked me to do it. I was all for having a holiday; I'd won the thing twice already … My father was there, Eddie was there, we had banjos and all the boys were singing a few songs, and then he says, 'I've entered you for the All-Ireland.' And I said, *'Ffff … Where's me pipes?'* And I went in and I won it. I brought him out the cup and I said, 'If you want another one, you can win it yourself!'

In 1966, Finbar, Eddie and their younger brother Paul tried their luck in three categories of a ballad group competition at the annual Rose of Tralee festival:

> **Eddie**: There'd be a hundred other bands – some of them became quite famous afterwards. We won the first prize in the main event, and we won the pub prize and the street prize. We blew the whole lot out, and we won it with one song: 'I Know Where I'm Going'. It was in all the Dublin papers: 'Dublin band wins everything.' We were in the *Evening Press* and *Evening Herald*, on the front page. We came back to O'Donoghue's pub with a cheque. I remember it was £175. Paddy O'Donoghue cashed it for us.

Another part of the prize was a contract with Phillips (Ireland). It would be a first taste of the record business:

> **Eddie**: Instead of recording 'I Know Where I'm Going', which was a big hit in Tralee, they wanted us to record a Joe Lynch song. And we said, 'No. This song went down well with the crowd and that's what we want to record.' But they reneged on the recording.

*

One of Ted Furey's musical friends was Connemara *sean-nós* singer Joe Heaney. 'I loved Joe Heaney's company,' says Finbar. 'Of anybody who stayed in the house, Joe was very serious, very passionate. He'd be grinding his teeth, he'd shake while he told you how important something was to your heritage.' By chance, in February 1967, Joe's friendship with Ted and his sons would set in motion a chain of events that would define the course of Eddie and Finbar's lives thereafter. Joe had a tour of Scotland lined up, but circumstances had intervened and he needed to find a substitute act.

Finbar: Joe's brother was dying. It was the 5th of February 1967. I still remember when we left. It would have been a week previous to that [when] Joe had approached me. I was only a kid, you must remember. And Eddie was with a rock band. Me and Eddie had had a folk band and we'd just broken [up], and I wanted to go solo. And I did a few sessions with [flautist] Matt Molloy. Matt was only a kid then, but Matt had won the Oireachtas and I'd won the Oireachtas, so we used to team up and make a bit of that, and [also with] Johnny Keenan. But Joe approached one day and said, 'I'd love you to do the tour.'

'Joe, I can't …'

'Ah, come on …'

'Joe, I can't sing *sean-nós* – these people are going to lynch me!'

But I went up to my brother Eddie and said, 'Will you come?' And Eddie says, 'Yeah.' So I promised my mother I'd be home in 13 days – and I stayed away for nearly two years. When we got to Scotland we didn't know what to expect, trust me. You had all the 'pseudos', we called them, the purists: they didn't understand what we were about … But the boys were protective of their heritage, and that's cool enough. The Scots are very clannish, they were just particular about what was coming in. And we would be the same [in Ireland].

The first gig was in Aberdeen, and I'll never forget it. The place was *heaving*! Kilts and everything flying in the place. And when I played 'My Love Is In America', they'd never heard the pipes played like this, ever. Not since Johnny Doran. And they would never have heard of Johnny. So they'd *never* heard pipes played like this. They'd heard Ennis, they'd heard Rowsome, they'd heard Willie Clancy, but they'd never heard anything like this young kid on the pipes. And then Eddie produced the 12-string guitar and put that to it, and when he sang with his wild voice, the 12-string guitar, the pipes – wow! We also had the side flute; he had mandolin, which he used to play; and I had five-string banjo, though we didn't even use it. We carried it around, it was there. Loads of ammunition.

Eddie: We went down a storm [that first night] because they'd never seen anything like myself and Finbar playing. I said to Finbar, 'Look, you have to get your head up off your knees and look at the people. When you're playing they want to see what you're doing …' So after that … he got a bit more brave and he'd talk about [the pipes], and then he opened up more.

That first Aberdeen gig was at a club in the Royal Hotel, Bathgate Street, run by song collector Arthur Argo, who would introduce Eddie to the songs of Robert Burns. Right from the start of their professional career as a duo, Eddie shouldered most of the responsibility for interacting with the audience:

> **Finbar**: Eddie used to hate sitting down. He loved standing up singing. So he would always take the banter, because I'd be busy tuning the pipes or something. If he broke a string, I'd take over. So it was a great team. Eddie did all the singing back in those days, though I sang a bit of harmony with him, and I sang the odd track on the odd album. But that was his store, you know, and he kept it.

> **Eddie**: I could talk to the audience better. I could explain the song; people liked to hear what the song was about. And I'd say to Finbar, 'If you're playing a tune, tell them what the name of the tune is …' We met an awful lot of pipers in Edinburgh, playing all kind of pipes – Lowland pipes, war pipes – but there was no one playing the uilleann pipes in Scotland. [Finbar] got people interested. And he could copy the war pipes on the uilleann pipes, and all the people in the folk clubs loved that.

The pair found their feet onstage very quickly and easily. Offstage, a certain resolution, rare in the folk world at that time, ensured a level of professionalism and a fighting chance at longevity: they stayed away from heavy drinking. 'We'd have a pint, maybe, now and again,' says Finbar, 'but that'd be it. We never touched the top shelf and we never went near drugs. The auld fellow would never forgive us. We weren't religious about it, we were just very careful.'

The brothers made friends among the Scottish folk fraternity, which had been active as a club-based scene with its beginnings in Glasgow and Edinburgh, from the very early years of the decade. Roy Williamson and Ronnie Browne, known as The Corries, and already prominent as a concert and broadcasting act, became particularly close friends.

> **Finbar**: When we met, it was like meeting our brothers. We couldn't believe it. Myself and Roy, especially. I'd just left one of the greatest friends we

had in Ireland, Johnny Keenan. I missed him. We busked together, we did everything together since we were kids. And this fellow Roy took his place. He was an *incredible* musician, and I couldn't get enough of him, you know. And he played the Northumbrian pipes as well. There's one octave, but you can blow another half with the keys. It's like playing the tin whistle – with attitude! I remember Roy putting a few bob in our hands and looking after us when we moved to Edinburgh. And he got us interested in rugby. He used to watch the rugby every Sunday with us.

We did a trade. I wasn't a great guitar player, so I said [to Roy], 'I'll teach you to play the flute if you teach me to play the guitar.' When me and Sheila got married in Edinburgh [in 1968] he was best man, and I was very proud. … I remember when he'd written 'Flower Of Scotland', we were in Castle Terrace in Edinburgh. It was like a big commune. And 'Flower Of Scotland' was actually finished on the floor of that flat over a bottle of Bell's whisky one night. We watched Roy finish it. It was wonderful. And it's now the national anthem of Scotland.[8]

We had enough money after the tour, so we put the money on a deposit on a flat. But we didn't have any work then, although there was work coming up. So we went down the docks – they were digging out the docks – and I remember Eddie getting a job on a forklift, cos he didn't want to hurt his hands. And they gave me a job staking out stuff … So we worked for two weeks. You get your sub after two weeks. We worked one more week and told [the boss] we had to go home, that we had a funeral to go to and didn't know when it was.

Robin Dransfield, a Yorkshireman who would achieve widespread popularity on the English folk scene with his brother Barry from 1969 onwards, was in Edinburgh at the time and remembers Finbar and Eddie well:

We used to go into Sandy Bell's bar, as everybody did then. They were dossing about, living in 48 Forest Road, a flat where everybody used to go and stay, two or three doors from Bell's. They were working on the docks at Leith. They were playing a bit, but they hadn't turned professional, as it were. The pubs shut at ten in Edinburgh and we used to get a carry-out and go back to one particular flat, a guy called Graham Bell. Finbar did a tune later on one of their albums called 'Graham's Flat'. We'd be sitting in this place, all the lights would be out, and Finbar would sit and play the pipes for a couple of hours. Eerie stuff! He's always been a fantastic player, and he was then. And then one night everybody bailed out and there was no accommodation available. Eddie had a sleeping bag and it was split, all these feathers falling out it. We were in this kitchen and Eddie climbed into this feathery sleeping bag, leaned into a corner and slept there. Me and Finbar got under the carpet in the kitchen – the only place we could find, cos it was so cold! I probably didn't see them for six months or a year [after that] and then I heard this album had come out, this Transatlantic album. I bought a copy and was just blown away – fantastic.

Singer/guitarist Martin Carthy and fiddler Dave Swarbrick, touring the British clubs as a duo, would also meet the brothers in Edinburgh around this time.* Their album *Rags, Reels & Airs*, as a one-off trio with guitarist Diz Disley, had just been released. Understandably, Finbar and Dave clicked immediately:

Martin Carthy: I remember him and Swarb basically falling into each other's arms. I remember Swarb coming over to me and saying, *'God, he's bloody brilliant'* – except 'bloody' wasn't the word he used – *'I've suddenly met my soulmate.'* Cos the first thing Finbar said to Dave was, 'Do people go on to you about the speed you play, saying, "Why do you play so fast?" And Swarb said, 'Yeah, they do, all the time.' 'You know what I say? I say, 'I play fast because I can'.' And Swarb was ecstatic! He was so happy, so excited. People loved Finbar and Eddie, absolutely loved them.

Sandy Bell's pub was where Finbar met not only his future wife Sheila, during 1967, but also a generous soul from Belfast called Diane Halley, who would ease the transition from casual labourers to professional musicians:

Finbar: One of the most beautiful people I've met in my life. She didn't care about religion, we didn't either – because we come from a background [where] you're neither Catholic nor Protestant nor anything, we just are who we are. If I see a church and I need God I'll walk in there: it's God's house, nobody owns it anyway. That's the way we grew up. Diane saw who we were and she says, 'I've got an empty flat, you and Eddie come and stay …' And Diane wouldn't take a penny off us. She looked after Archie Fisher, us, The Corries – she took care of everybody. Without Diane Halley there would

---

* Martin Carthy and Dave Swarbrick would spend July 1967 to February 1968 in Denmark, with only a three-week trip back to England. Eddie recalls that they first met the duo in Edinburgh around the time *Rags, Reels & Airs* was released, which was June 1967.

have been no Billy Connolly, no Gerry Rafferty, no Finbar & Eddie Furey. She kept us all in the one place so we could bounce off each other.

The chronology is hazy but for a while, despite their plans to get a flat of their own, both Finbar and Eddie would stay with Diane before Finbar (with his new partner Sheila) moved out to a place of his own at Stobo, near Peebles, let by Roy Williamson. Eddie would stay on at Diane's apartment in Castle Terrace.

It was through Diane that Finbar and Eddie met Paddie Bell, an Edinburgh-based singer from Belfast, more than 10 years their senior and well established on the Scottish scene, having recorded and performed with The Corries from 1962 to '65. In 1965 she had released a solo LP, *Paddie Bell – Herself*, backed by Martin Carthy. Now recording a second LP, she invited Finbar and Eddie to be a part of it.[*]

The LP, *I Know Where I'm Going*, was released early in 1968 on EMI's Edinburgh-based subsidiary Waverley and was later reissued in Ireland as a Finbar & Eddie Furey album. Paddie, Finbar and Eddie only perform together on two songs; of the remaining 12 tracks, six are Finbar & Eddie pieces (four tunes, two songs) and six are Paddie Bell songs with Tom Smith on guitar.

Half an album on a regional label, perhaps, but a tremendous representation on record of what Finbar and Eddie had to offer. Finbar retains a great thankfulness for the help Paddie gave them:

> **Finbar**: You remember Millie, 'My Boy Lollipop'?[†] That was our first television show, and we did it with Paddie Bell. It was in Newcastle, Tyne Tees TV. I was actually playing the pipes with Paddie Bell, and it was amazing, and Eddie was singing harmony with her. And Eddie fell in love with Millie, she was the best thing he'd ever seen in his life, and went after her round the studio! Paddie Bell paid me and Eddie for that album, £120 each. She didn't have to do that, she could have given us 20 quid – we'd have done it for nothing, because we adored her. One hundred and twenty quid: that was a lot of money, and now we had something to go to England with.

---

[*] The LP's original sleeve-note writer, Scottish TV producer Gordon Smith – one of whose songs Eddie would sing on the duo's next LP – implied that a brief introductory note to himself from Paddy O'Donoghue, affirming Finbar and Eddie's qualities, was responsible for their involvement in the record.

[†] Jamaican singer Millie Small, aka Millie, had a UK No. 2 hit with 'My Boy Lollipop' in 1964. It was a standard career trajectory for successful female singers in 60s Britain to get their own TV show: e.g. Dusty Springfield, Lulu and Sandie Shaw on national TV; others, like Millie (who had a TV series in Finland in 1964), on the regional airwaves.

*

Two other beneficiaries of Diane's generosity were Ewan MacColl and Peggy Seeger: the doyen of the British folk scene and his banjo-playing American partner in life and music. By the time they came through Edinburgh, Finbar had moved to Stobo, but Eddie was still around:

> **Eddie**: MacColl and Seeger were playing that night in Edinburgh, and they came back to where I was staying and a session started in the apartment. And McColl said, 'When you're down in London, give us a shout and we'll give you a booking in the club.'

For any folk act at the time, a booking at Ewan's Singers' Club in London was a gateway to many other clubs around the country. Eddie recalls two bookings, but certainly the first, advertised in *Melody Maker*, was November 18 1967. It was rare for the Singers' Club to book an act with a heavy instrumental element.[*]

> **Eddie**: I remember we got the bus down overnight. We certainly had no money the next day – I had 10 bob or something. We arrived in Victoria Station and we rolled around in the Underground for about five hours to get a sleep on the Underground. [I] had my guitar between my legs in case anyone would rob it. So we walked around all day and that evening we went to the Singers' Club, and I got a pound off Peggy Seeger to get a drink, that's true.

Finbar and Eddie returned to Scotland, having gained a calling card to use when breaking into the English club scene – an activity they would undertake in earnest during 1968. The British folk scene, which had started from a handful of scattered clubs (in Glasgow, Birmingham, Bradford, Liverpool and London) in the late 50s, was at its peak in the late 60s. In May 1961, *Melody Maker* folk columnist Eric Winter could attest to the existence of nearly 40 clubs around Britain. By September, it was 47; by December, it was 70; by March 1962, it was 80. It would be several hundred within three or four years. As Martin Carthy notes: 'There was always

---

* Between February 1967 and April 1971 there were only three nights at the Singers' Club headlined by instrumentalists. London-Irish fiddler Martin Byrnes played the club on October 21 1967 and Februray 16 1968; on December 13 1969, Tom McCarthy (a piper from Clare) appeared with Bobby Casey (fiddle). Irish duo Margaret Barry & Michael Gorman, which featured both vocal and instrumental music, also guested in this period, on January 8 1969. If there was a second Fureys appearance at the club it was, unusually, not advertised in *Melody Maker*.

somewhere to work, cos it was a really, really diverse thing in the 60s and there was a *huge* number of clubs.'

Regional folk club scenes, such as the one in Scotland, could exist almost as separate entities. A popular Scottish entertainer like Hamish Imlach, for example, would rarely have any need to go to London, save to make a record. Similarly, The Corries would not tour England properly until August 1968 (with the Furey brothers as their guests).

> **Ronnie Browne (1970)**: There's a really strong, virile Scottish scene and there's a big range. The performers are either very good or very bad. There's not much mediocrity. The great thing about the Scottish scene is it gives you a good grounding. There's this feeling of old poetry and tunes in Scotland. It's really part of people's lives.[9]

> **Billy Connolly (2014)**: The Scottish clubs liked entertainers and English clubs liked educators. They seemed to like to be educated by the traditional unaccompanied songs. It was like Brussels sprouts, supposed to be good for you.[10]

Finbar and Eddie, combining world-class traditional instrumental music with a mixture of hard-core traditional ballads, the odd Beatles song and humorous banter from Eddie, were an unusual mixture of both aspects. He and Finbar had already made regional radio and TV appearances in Scotland before 1967 was out, and they were certainly having an impact on many younger musicians. One such was future Elton John sideman, guitarist Davey Johnstone:

> [I] absolutely adore Finbar and Eddie – they created such a stir on the Scottish folk scene when I was about 17 years old [in 1968]. I had a memorable New Year with Finbar, Roy Williamson of The Corries and me jamming all through the night at Roy's border cottage. The first time I heard Finbar playing 'The Fox Among The Hounds', I was totally blown away – like hearing Jimi Hendrix for the first time![11]

Future guitar virtuoso Martin Simpson had a similar experience:

> I still remember [hearing] Finbar Furey play the pipes at three feet away when I was about 17 [in 1970]. It was like watching Jimi Hendrix – he was just ridiculously good.[12]

The comparison is telling. Finbar himself attests to having the same feeling about the recordings of Johnny Doran: 'I think Johnny used to take music into Outer Space, and so did Jimi Hendrix.'

Dick Gaughan, the most significant Scottish troubadour of the coming decades, was another young acolyte of the Furey brothers. 'Dick was only 16 when we met him,' says Finbar. 'Dick followed me and Eddie around Edinburgh like a pussycat. I remember teaching him 'The Blackbird' and him picking it out on guitar. He still says it today, that his huge influence from Irish music was me and Eddie."

Dave Stewart, later successful as writer/guitarist with Eurythmics, was another devoted follower. 'I sat down with him and taught him the three or four chords I knew,' says Eddie.

Another fan was Ralph McTell, who was by then a rising songwriter/guitarist recording for Transatlantic. Finbar and Eddie would first meet Ralph on the fringes of the Cambridge Folk Festival in 1970, when the duo were putting on a show at a nearby Irish pub.

> **Ralph McTell**: I was working the clubs at the same time as Finbar and Eddie and only knew them by reputation, which was superb. The musicianship of the young Finbar was quite beyond belief.
>
> **Finbar**: When we met Ralph McTell, he was our total hero, like an English version of Gerry Rafferty – they had this 'groove', and we wanted to get in on this groove. And if you break the jigs and reels down you can actually groove them. And the boys wanted to get all these reel rhythms off Eddie, cos Eddie was great at backing the reels. Dave Stewart, for instance, sat with me with his guitar, and we'd be playing reels and jigs with the pipes – and they turned them into rock rhythms. So we were part of giving something back with it.[13]

*

During the first half of 1968, Nathan 'Nat' Joseph signed Finbar and Eddie to his label, Transatlantic, for which many of the key British folk acts of the era were already recording: Ralph McTell, Bert Jansch, The Humblebums, Archie Fisher, Pentangle amongst others. Nat assigned Bill Leader to record an album.

---

* Eddie recalls Dick Gaughan running a club on the Royal Mile in Edinburgh in 1967: 'There was three of them and they would sing a cappella songs, sea shanties and things like that.' As Dick puts it on his website: 'In 1966 or early 1967, Morris McPhillips, Phil Taylor and myself decided to start a folk song club called the Edinburgh Folk Centre, with more ideals and enthusiasm than sense.'

Finbar And Eddie Furey appeared in the Transatlantic catalogue in August 1968 as TRA168, back to back with the similarly self-titled *The Johnstons* (TRA169) and *Sweeney's Men* (TRA170): three Irish vocal and instrumental groups, albeit in differing styles. Finbar and Eddie would effectively break open the British and European market to the sound of virtuoso uilleann piping; Sweeney's Men would create the interweaving stringed-instrument template (bouzoukis, mandolins, guitars) that begat so many other Irish bands from the early 70s ever onwards (several also incorporating pipes); while The Johnstons, though barely a footnote in Irish music now, were at the time the most successful of the lot.*

While Bill recorded the Fureys and Sweeney's Men on the cheap, Nat produced The Johnstons' LP in a decent studio with John Wood engineering. His sleeve notes to their album gave a clear idea of why this was the case, and why Transatlantic were issuing three Irish ballad albums in quick succession:

> Ireland is a country of miracles, and one of the 20th century miracles that exists in Ireland today is that folk music is chart music. A large proportion of the singles that make the top 10 charts in Ireland are folk ballads. The Johnstons' first-ever record was a ballad, 'The Travelling People' by Ewan MacColl, which went straight to Number 1 in the Irish charts and was one of the best-selling singles in Irish record history. Since then The Johnstons have had three more hits and here now is their first LP …[14]

Anything seemed possible in the 1960s. Finbar and Eddie first met Bill Leader at the recording session for their first LP. They would meet him again around March 1969 for the recording of two further albums: a second duo LP, *The Lonesome Boatman*, and Finbar's solo LP, *Traditional Irish Pipe Music*.

Conflating the two experiences into one general memory, Finbar's view in retrospect is perhaps tainted by two things: a cultural difference with Bill Leader, a quiet, professorial Englishman; and a general feeling, common to almost every recording artist of the time, that they were in some way ripped off.

> **Finbar**: Bill Leader just recorded us. We stayed in Bill Leader's flat in the basement, me and Eddie, for three days when we made our album(s). A cup of tea and a sandwich in the morning: *'Thank you very much … Next*

---

* The Johnstons recorded four singles for Pye in Ireland (1966–67) and then six albums and five singles for Transatlantic (1968–72), four of the albums also being licensed for release in the USA. They tend to be referred to nowadays in the context of being the beginning of singer/songwriter Paul Brady's career.

please ...' I remember sitting in the back of a fucking pick-up van with no windows being driven to the studio, me and Eddie, in the morning. He was like the jailer, you know! And then in the evening that was it: there's a meal and good luck; going to bed at half eight at night. ... He was a nice man, but he wasn't a musician.

Nat Joseph had most likely heard of their reputation from musicians on his label or heard their early 1968 LP with Paddie Bell. While Bill Leader sometimes brought projects to Nat or played a mentoring role, on this occasion he was simply a hired hand: 'I didn't hear them before I recorded them,' says Bill. 'I [just] got the job of producing them, this bright young lad and his brother.'

Finbar: We were asked and begged to do these albums [for Transatlantic]. My father, he hated us recording stuff. ... We wouldn't have done those albums, only we needed the money. It was 60 quid we got for those two albums: £30 each. But £30 to me and Eddie was a lot of money in those days. So we don't look back with sour grapes: we needed the money, they paid us. ... We wanted somebody to help us build something, you know. ... [But] they didn't see. They couldn't see beyond the nose of a quick buck. It was as bad then as it is now.

With Nat Joseph not a man to splash money around if it could be helped, the first album was recorded quickly in a cheap studio. Nevertheless, Finbar and Eddie managed to overdub parts on a couple of tunes, which was quite an innovation in itself in the history of Irish instrumental music on record. For a duo with such multi-instrumental ability and arrangement ideas, the lack of time was frustrating:

Eddie: We wanted to get a bit more backing music on it for the songs. In those days you weren't doing stereo, it was mono. I was thinking of the studio being a studio and all the things we could do in it, you know. And we never did anything I suggested in it. ... We only ever got £40 altogether, each, off Nat Joseph. He wasn't a great man for paying out money.

Reflecting the solid success of the first album, the second session with Bill as producer, around March 1969, was at Livingstone Studios in Barnet and was engineered by Nick Kinsey. The sound they achieved was superb: natural but rich in vibrancy, placing the listener thrillingly close to the instruments and voice.

Finbar's seven-minute performance of 'The Fox Chase', the only 'descriptive piece' in the uilleann piping tradition, was extraordinary: a vivid piece of wordless storytelling and a stunning piece of music, surely as exciting as anything being performed in those heady days at the end of a decade that had birthed a global explosion of popular culture emanating outwards from London. Even here, in what had always been seen as a solo piper's test piece, Eddie's closely-miked guitar, with a handful of simple but carefully placed and exquisitely delivered major and suspended chords, lifted the arrangement, accentuating the pathos of the dying fox. There is, perhaps, no better example of the duo's instrumental teamwork and instinctive partnership. Certainly, if one were ever to wonder why Finbar was known among his folk scene contemporaries at the time as 'the Jimi Hendrix of the pipes', this bravura performance of youthful virtuosity and 'old soul' sensitivity provides the answer: he played fast 'because he could', but he could wring every drop of emotion from the slow movements of an existing piece of music like nobody else his listeners at the time would have been aware of. Even Jimi Hendrix never played anything from the 18th century.

Bill Leader had contributed lively sleeve notes to the first album but, having recorded Willie Clancy at a pub in Galway for a Topic LP in the summer of 1967, he felt the impact of Finbar's flash less powerfully than did the folk club masses:

> **Bill**: I don't think he compared at all. As a person, there was no comparison. Willie was a mature and quite wise person; Finbar was young and carefree – and that reflected in his playing, too. Finbar was a young man, proud of what he called his 'express train' style of playing. There was a careless virtuosity about the man – the faster he could play a tune, the happier he was.

Reg Hall, a veteran of the Camden Irish pub scene for over a decade by this stage, had a similar perspective:

> **Reg**: I was in their company on a number of occasions. [Finbar] came in, and he was accepted and liked by all the musicians. But he was a different sort of character. His music was flash in the sense that he played very fast – because he could! Aside from his Traveller background, which is different in itself, he represented the new wave of young Irish people, who weren't like the old-timers. They were flash in the sense that they built up technique, they could do Seán McGuire stuff, 'The Mason's Apron' and all that.* [But] I've seen him, in my opinion, ruin a session which was going wonderfully.

---

* Seán McGuire was a Belfast fiddle virtuoso and piper who had toured America in the 1950s and who enjoyed iconic status on the London-Irish scene in the 60s. See the chapter on 'Piping In Ulster'.

They say, 'Come on, play a tune' – and he gets the pipes out and the whole atmosphere changes. He just changed the mood. But then that's what happens in sessions.

The nature of Finbar and Eddie's Transatlantic recordings was, of course, different to that of Topic's Willie Clancy album. Not only were Finbar and Eddie operating within the commercial arena (touring British folk clubs, while Willie was a spare-time traditional musician in rural Clare), but the recording equipment was different.

Bill: Recording Willie, I did as a location recording in his native territory … whereas because Transatlantic were behind Finbar and Eddie, it was done in a studio. Immediately, instead of setting up some mics in a cosy, familiar situation, you've moved people into this strange atmosphere of a studio. Livingstone in Barnet was probably as friendly as you could get. Yet still, nevertheless, there's a load of gear, a load of technology, around you. I get the feeling that Finbar responded to this and it brought out the best in Finbar, but I think it creased Eddie up a little bit. … [But] I do remember Finbar saying [about 'The Lonesome Boatman'], 'We've got this great tune, it's going to be a huge hit, we should record it' – which we did.

The albums on Transatlantic may not have made the brothers any money, but they were crucial in launching and establishing long careers. The same could be said for so many albums by so many artists on the label during the 1960s. It was an era when records still had a cachet. They were a statement that somebody, some third party institution with resources, was endorsing you as an artist of quality and commercial possibility.

Tony Wilson, for *Melody Maker*, judged the first album, *Finbar And Eddie Furey*, 'a fine showcase for the talents of the brothers … Eddie has a slightly nasal, pleasantly rough voice that is always strong and confident … Finbar is a piper of great fluidity and feeling and, by the folk process of double tracking, duets with himself on both pipes and whistle. All the instrumental tracks are excellent …'[15]

*

In June 1968, the brothers had featured on their first national TV broadcast, as guests of The Corries, on the first episode of the series *Degrees Of Folk*. In September, they were guests of The Corries once again, along with English singer/songwriter Roy Harper, on a six-date tour of English city halls.

Following an appearance at the London Folk Music Festival at Cecil Sharp House in October, they would start to become periodically visible in *Melody Maker* adverts for gigs around London, usually in bursts of activity. Six London dates in November-December 1968 were followed by three in March 1969. Their modus operandi would be travelling from club to club with sleeping bags, hoping the promoter could find them a roof. Seán Cannon, later in The Dubliners, was operating a club near Coventry at the time and recalls their fee as £25.[16]

In March 1969, *Melody Maker* could announce: 'Finbar and Eddie Fury [sic] will tour Australia with The Clancy Brothers & Tommy Makem in the Summer. [The Fureys] have completed two albums for release later this year and until they go to Australia they will be playing clubs and concerts with a possible tour of Southern England in the near future.'[17]

The albums would be released in July: a second duo set, *The Lonesome Boatman*, and a solo instrumental set, *Traditional Irish Pipe Music* – a brave move indeed for a British record label. Reviewing both in *Melody Maker*, Tony Wilson gave equal praise to Finbar and Eddie, recognising the latter as 'a highly competent singer, with a fairly effortless style that has a pleasant touch of roughness that adds [to] rather than detracts from his singing.' Finbar's extraordinarily powerful rendering of 'The Fox Chase' was singled out for praise. *Traditional Irish Pipe Music* he viewed as 'one of the best instrumental albums of Irish music released to date.'[18]

The Lonesome Boatman was an impressive advance from the first Transatlantic LP, more confident and dynamic. But it might have been rather different:

> **Eddie**: I remember saying to Nat Joseph … with Martin Carthy and Dave Swarbrick, we done the very first festival up at Cleethorpes, and the four of us got up on stage at the end of the festival and I got the drummer and bass player out of The High Level Ranters from Newcastle – and that was the first time there was ever jigs and reels played with drums and bass.' And I thought

---

* While The High Level Ranters did not include bass and drums in their line-up normally, Eddie is certain that there were bass and drums involved in the Cleethorpes Festival jam – possibly from another act on the bill. A piece on The High Level Ranters in *Melody Maker* on February 14 1970 noted what Eddie confirms as another bit of fun on that Cleethorpes weekend: 'One of the classic moments for Alastair [Anderson] was when they were joined by Martin Carthy and Dave Swarbrick and Finbar & Eddie Furey for a busking session on the beach at Cleethorpes in order to raise beer money.' The Ranters were formed in 1964 and recorded their first album, *Northumberland For Ever*, with Bill Leader, for Topic in 1968. They pioneered the use of Northumbrian small pipes with guitar, just as Finbar and Eddie were pioneering the use of uilleann pipes with guitar. Forster Charlton and Colin Ross played the Northumbrian small pipes with the group during the 60s, while two other members (concertina player Alastair Anderson and guitarist Johnny Handle) later became proficient on the instrument.

this was a bit of a breakthrough. I went in and I said to Nat Joseph, 'The next album we make, can we have a lead guitar, a drummer and a bass player?' And he told me, 'Look, your last album's selling pretty good at the moment and we don't want to spoil that by bringing something different out.' Nine months later on, the Fairport Convention started and I went in and put my hand to my nose and said, 'Ah, you slipped up there, didn't you?''

Through the happenstance of being on Transatlantic, a label that has been bought over and mined many times since Nat Joseph first sold it on in the late 70s, the three 1968–69 Furey records are the most widely known of their duo career. The original notes to *The Lonesome Boatman* trumpeted the title track, 'which has proved a show-stopper on all their recent concerts.' It became Finbar's signature tune, and would be recorded again on *Four Green Fields*, the first of the duo's run of German albums, in 1972.

> **Finbar**: I couldn't get this image out of my head … it's this boatman who comes to take you from this life to the next. This boatman is there for millions of years. Don't ask me how I know. When I get in there [into the music], I can actually … I can see him. And I've no fear of him. He's to be pitied.[19]

'The Lonesome Boatman' featured Finbar on bamboo Indian flute. A chance purchase led to the invention of the 'low whistle', an instrument now entrenched in Irish music:

> **Finbar**: Roy Williamson had bought me this thing … We were walking through the Ideal Home Exhibition in Edinburgh. There was an Indian department there, and they had these bamboo flutes. They were half a crown each and I went, 'Wow! I've never seen one of them things before.' And he picked one up and said, 'If you can play it, I'll buy it for you.' And I played a reel on it. It was like playing the tin whistle. I'd been writing 'The Boatman' on the banjo, so I thought, 'I wonder if this would fit on the flute?' I had it for about a year, I had it bandaged up – you'll see it on *The Dawning Of The Day* [1971 LP] cover – and it was just after we'd done that album. I put it on

---

* Fairport Convention formed in 1967 as a West Coast American-influenced rock band. Fiddler Dave Swarbrick joined after guesting on a one-off experiment with an English traditional song on their third LP, *Unhalfbricking* (1969). The group, with Swarbrick, then embraced more fully this new 'folk-rock' direction with their next album *Liege & Lief*, released in late 1969.

a wooden seat in a pub and this guy came along and sat on it and flattened it. We did everything we could to put it back together. When I was a kid I used to make tin whistles out of old television aerials – using scissors, just keeping at the aluminium till I got through it, and I made the whistle [part] out of a piece of cork. So I knew that the aluminium would work, although I made a first one out of copper.

Bernard Overton was a steel worker, a lathe turner, a great craftsman, and he played jazz on the piano. And I said to him, 'Can you make me one of these?' And he looked at me and said, 'What is it?' I said, 'It's a flute.' And I stood out with this copper flute and we made a model, and then we made a jig that we were going to fit this aluminium in. And we spent the whole night at it. I remember I was covered in aluminium dust! [The first one] was round and I said, 'We should copyright it.' But we couldn't – that had no copyright, that type of flute [design]. We didn't know this at the time. So my young fellow, Martin – I had the flute at home with me and I heard this crunch. He was, like, three, and he was hitting ants with this flute. I thought, *'Aw, Jaysus…'* So I phoned up Bernard, as I'd be using it that night, and he said, 'Bring it over, we'll clean it up.'

So we cleaned one side, we cleaned the other side, and we looked at it and thought … 'Jesus!' It was a total accident [that it was flat on two sides]. I said, 'You'll get the copyright now.' And he said, 'I'll share it with you.' I said, 'No. You've no money, you've no work; I'm doing okay, I don't need it. Just make me a flute now and again if I need it.' And we shook hands on it. And before he died he said, 'I made a lot of money out of that flute, so I'd like to give you some of the money.' I said, 'No, it's okay. A deal is a deal. I'm just happy to have the flutes.' I didn't actually want anybody to know [that I was involved], because people would say, *'Oh, we need to make a flute, let's call on Finbar Furey!'* So I could say, 'No, it's Bernard's.' I invented it, but he made it. It wouldn't be there without him.*

One of the features of Finbar's 1969 solo piping album is a dominant percussive pulse played on some tunes, using the regulators with his wrist. A similar technique can be heard on vintage recordings by Leo Rowsome (and also on Willie Clancy's earliest surviving Radio Éireann recordings):

---

* Finbar had the idea of making the thing in different keys: 'Because with the pipes I was stuck with the one key, while Eddie could change keys all over the place. We did a load of stuff with the flute, and it opened up a whole new style of playing.'

Finbar: Felix Doran would have been my influence on regulators: watching Felix. Felix was a master on the regulators; so was Leo. Pat McNulty was another great master ...* It's like only playing two strings on a guitar: regulators are a part of the instrument, they're supposed to be played. But you don't get that style from anybody – you just play around with what you're doing yourself.

There was a piece of music called 'The Bluebells Of Scotland', when I was a kid, and I learned it. My father had learned it from the Stewarts of Blairgowrie. He travelled with them and played the banjo with them and sang with them. My father learned lots of tunes from John and from Belle Stewart, and songs, and vice versa. And they travelled here in Ireland with my father. My father and mother were on their honeymoon, and so were they on their honeymoon – two Travelling families who got together, young kids, different backgrounds, but the same. He taught my father how to pearl fish, and they played music at night. For about a year or two years they travelled, until they had to go back to Scotland and my father came back to Ballyfermot. He got a lot of great music from John and Belle, and one of them was 'The Bluebells Of Scotland'. And if you think about that [rhythm, you can tap it out with the wrist while playing the melody].

Finbar's percussive technique was purely there for its musical value, not as any kind of strict-tempo aid to prospective dancers:

I'd nothing to do with dancers! Oh Jaysus, there's nothing worse than some eejit standing up and throwing feet around the place. It happened a lot in the Irish folk clubs. The English were more timid. But in general you don't want to be playing for some fellow who's louder than the pipes!

*

The Clancy Brothers reference in that March 1969 *Melody Maker* news item, on a prospective Australian tour, would be the first signs of an intrigue which would ultimately lead to Finbar and Eddie joining the group. A hugely popular act in America, comprising three brothers from an acting background and their friend Tommy Makem providing the musical backbone, with a repertoire of rousing

---

* Martin Carthy recalls that Pat McNulty, a non-professional player based in Glasgow, made a couple of club appearances in England during the 60s. He also played pipes in a BBC Home Service radio drama, about the adventures of St Columba, in 1963. He was one of those involved in the 1968 Bettystown meeting that led to the formation of Na Píobairí Uilleann.

balladry and matching sweaters, the popularity of the Clancys in Britain during the 60s should not be underestimated. They could sell out two-week tours of city hall venues, always including the Royal Albert Hall, more or less annually, and they enjoyed extensive coverage in the British press.

In 1968, Tommy Makem had revealed that the group were going to pare back their commitments to allow time for individual ventures. He himself had a parallel solo recording career. But he was grateful for having been in the right place at the right moment:

> Most of our work is colleges. Twice a year we play Carnegie Hall in New York, Boston, Chicago, San Francisco, all through Canada up into the Maritime Provinces. The circuit where we play is civic auditoriums. The college appearances are great, because the kids know what's going on … We were lucky. We got in as folk was starting and built up a terrific following, which now enables us to do concerts.[20]

By April 1969, Tommy had left the group. *Melody Maker* announced that the three Clancys would still tour with the Fureys: 'They have all been rehearsing together in Tipperary in preparation for the trip downunder.'[21]

A month later, it was announced that brother Bobby Clancy (who had worked as a duo with sister Peg in Ireland, and was currently running a pub in Kilkenny) would also join the group. Recording sessions were scheduled for London in June, and the Australian tour was now due to begin in Brisbane in September. In the event, the Australian jaunt was cancelled, and instead the four Clancys and two Fureys arrived in London in August to record two LPs – one a Christmas album, one of contemporary material – with renowned producer Teo Macero, better known for his work with Miles Davis.*

Tom Clancy warned British fans to expect something different: 'Fat, more of a pop sound … Eddie and Finbar have supplied the music that Tommy Makem used to supply. Their kind of sound fits in with us well and, of course, they're in our tradition.'[22]

In the same interview, Eddie was quoted as saying: 'We're not going back to the old Clancy sound. What we're doing on record is more commercialised.'[23]

The Furey brothers, however, had already recorded an album, uncredited, with the Clancys towards the end of the previous year: Bold Fenian Men. The

---

* In a *Melody Maker* piece published on September 20 1969, Joe Kennedy reports on visiting Liam Clancy's summer house in County Waterford, where Finbar Furey was among those present. The visit isn't dated, but was presumably within a month of the publication date.

discretion over crediting Finbar and Eddie's involvement was due to their existing Transatlantic contract:

> **Eddie**: I think we signed a contract for a couple of years and we couldn't get out of it. When we recorded the albums with The Clancy Brothers we were uncredited, and that's why. Liam Clancy said to me, about a year before he died, 'We should have told them to fuck off and put your names on the albums, for all the work you did on them.' That's including the last one that Tommy Makem made with them, *Bold Fenian Men* – we're on that album as well, doing backing vocals and playing various instruments.

The two albums recorded in August 1969 were *Flowers In The Valley* and *The Clancy Brothers' Christmas*.* The title track of the former was part traditional, part Eddie Furey. For Eddie, it connected to the first time he had met Liam Clancy:

> **Eddie**: I sang it once at the Fleadh Cheoil in Clones, the All-Ireland. I was walking by a pub and there was a fellow singing 'The Bonnán Buí', and I went in and this fellow was singing a verse in Irish and a verse in English, and after he'd finished I was having a drink at the bar and I said, 'You know, you're probably singing that song better than Liam Clancy.' He said, 'I *am* Liam Clancy!'

While the secrecy of the Fureys' involvement in *Bold Fenian Men* had been wholly successful, the balloon had surely gone up by the time these two appeared: they were not credited on the albums' performer lists, but they had composed two songs on *Flowers Of The Valley*, were referred to obliquely by the sleeve-note writer and, as seen above, had been implicated in various issues of *Melody Maker*, the biggest selling music paper in Britain. Their names appeared in glowing terms several times in the paper's review of *Flowers Of The Valley*:

> There's not much doubt that The Clancy Brothers get better with each album. Or maybe it's just their choice of material which improves. … Fin and Eddie's 'Jennifer Gentle' is a wonderful new song in the traditional fashion.[24]

---

* The albums seemingly took a couple of weeks to record, with Teo Macero adding string arrangements to some of the tracks on *Flowers Of The Valley*. Finbar and Eddie nevertheless found time to play at least one gig during this period: the Topic Folk Club in Bradford on August 22. They may possibly also have recorded a session for John Peel's BBC Radio 1 show *Night Ride* on August 27, although evidence is contradictory (see the discographical appendix).

Shortly after a return appearance as a duo (sharing the bill with The High Level Ranters) at the annual London Folk Music Festival at Cecil Sharpe House in October 1969, Finbar and Eddie arrived in New York for their first concert as members of The Clancy Brothers.

> **Finbar**: I remember we walked into The Lion's Head in Greenwich Village and Joe Heaney was sitting waiting there at the counter, and he put his arm around me and he gave me the biggest kiss I ever got off any man – on my lips – and he looked at me and he says, *'Jaysus Christ, the music has come to America at last!'* And Liam Clancy says, *'Ah, shaddup!'* But he was just messing and it was lovely to see him. I spent the whole day talking to him.* He should have been minded, he was a treasure to this country – he should have been teaching in the universities, teaching kids, instead of chasing shadows around the world.† His place was in Ireland. Any time I saw him in New York it was awful to see – the beautiful background he came from, and what he had to do for a living.[25]

Finbar had been lucky to get to New York at all:

> I'd lost my passport. Liam Clancy decided that we'd left it in W.B. Yeats' brother's restaurant down in Cobh [County Cork]. We'd been there the night before. It must have fallen out of my pocket. Liam decided he'd drive back, so off he went all the way back to Cobh, we got the passport and he drove all the way back. So we arrived [in New York] the *next* day. The boys

---

* An RTÉ news clip, purportedly from 1970, with presenter Proinsias Mac Aonghusa chatting in Gaelic to Joe Heaney, Finbar Furey and two of the Clancys in a New York bar can be seen at www.youtube.com/watch?v=pBR56qxfbdM

† Joe Heaney was the cousin of Colm Ó Caodháin, Séamus Ennis' most prolific source of songs during his time with the Irish Folklore Commission in the 1940s. Séamus recorded Joe on acetate disc in 1945, in Dublin, proximate to Joe winning an Oireachtas event. In June 1946 Séamus encountered Joe during a collecting trip in Connemara. As he wrote in his field diary: 'He had to have his collarbone removed recently in hospital and he says he is finished singing for ever. I feel very sorry for the poor man – he is only young, not much more than 20' (*Going To The Well For Water*, 2009). In fact, Joe was 28 at the time, and he would return to singing. He would spend 14 years as a lift operator in a New York apartment block in the 1960s and 70s. Eventually his knowledge was recognised as a teaching resource: in the late 70s he had part-time positions as a visiting professor teaching folklore at Wesleyan University in Middletown, Connecticut, and then at the University of Washington in Seattle, before returning to Ireland and receiving coverage in British music magazines as a kind of legendary figure.

were already there. And we had a soundcheck the *next* day. Of course, there was no pipes in this set, and I was mad to play the pipes – I was playing the banjo with them, and guitar.

Anyway, that [first] night I met this mad blues singer who was playing guitar, and I said, *'Hang on till I get my pipes …'* So I got my pipes out and started this session, and I ended up in the middle of Harlem. It must have been half eleven in the morning, my tongue was sticking to my palate from drinking beer all night and dehydration from the flight. The flat was empty, the first thing I thought, *'My pipes …!'* [But] I found my pipes sitting beside me, and I looked out the window and the *only* white face in the place was me! I walked out into the middle of the street. There was a cop there on duty. I says, 'Excuse me …'

He says, 'Take your hands off me, buddy! Stand back on the sidewalk! Stand back on the sidewalk!'

I said, 'I'm lost!'

He says, 'Stand back!'

So, anyway, another guy came along and took his place and he came over and says, 'What's the matter?'

So I showed him the passport.

'I'm playing with the Clancy Brothers,' I says, 'tonight at Carnegie Hall.' And I says, 'I'm supposed to be there in half an hour from now for a soundcheck. I was at a session last night, a jazz session. Man oh man, we played great music …'

He says, 'You sound like a good kid …'

He was a big Puerto Rican guy. So he just got on the blower, black-and-white comes up, two white fellows get out: 'You're with The Clancy Brothers?'

They had tickets for The Clancy Brothers, these cops! When they came to pick me up they thought I was one of the Clancys. By the time we got to Carnegie Hall they'd found out I was a piper – they'd heard of me, which was nice. They were in the police pipe band. So we're talking about uilleann pipes, having a cigarette, and I says, 'Drop me about 20 yards from the Clancys …' All the boys were outside the door, waiting for me. And I come up and, of course, the boys said, 'Oh God, he's been arrested for something …' And Paddy says, *'Aw, Jaysus, not on his first night in New York!'* And then the two cops, I give them a wave and they drive off, and Paddy says to me, 'What's going on there?' I said, 'Ah, Paddy, they heard I was in town, so they gave me a lift.'

The Carnegie Hall show was on November 1 1969. The rest of the month included further concerts and at least three television appearances with the group.* Finbar and Eddie were back in Britain by December 1, when they had a gig at Enfield Folk Club in London and a string of further London-area gigs up to December 14, at the Tower Hotel, Walthamstow, advertised as their 'last London appearance for a very long time'. As well as performing on BBC Radio 1's *Country Meets Folk*, they squeezed in an interview with Jeremy Gilbert at *Melody Maker* for their first significant piece of national press:

> Fin and Eddie have just returned from the States after a highly successful tour with The Clancy Brothers, Irish traditional airs in the Carnegie Hall with Finbar strapped to his treasured Uillen [sic] shoulder pipes. Who would have thought it possible? Certainly not Fin, for when the audience of 5,000 stood to the Fureys stamping and clapping furiously (if you'll pardon the pun) Fin and Eddie were shaking in disbelief.[26]

Headlined 'Bringing Irish Music To The People', the feature revealed that the duo were going to continue as such, in between Clancy commitments, but that things had looked shaky for a while. Pertinently, perhaps, Eddie was now living in Dublin, with Finbar still based at Stobo, in Scotland.† Finbar conceded to Gilbert that, as a duo, they had considered splitting:

> I want to play traditional Irish music and I found that I wasn't getting the chance to play Indian flute and penny whistle on stage [in the duo]. When

---

* *David Frost Tonight*, November 4 1969; *The Mike Douglas Show*, November 10 1969; [syndication programme], Channel 13, November 13 1969 (with the US moon-landing astronauts). Clips of the Clancys with the Fureys performing 'The Wren Song', 'Flowers In The Valley' and 'Beer, Beer, Beer' on *The Mike Douglas Show* and 'Beer, Beer, Beer' on *David Frost Tonight* can be seen on YouTube. 'Beer, Beer, Beer' was released as a single in America, with Eddie Furey's 'Jennifer Gentle' on the B-side, albeit miscredited jointly to Finbar and Eddie. At some point, possibly on a subsequent tour, they also appeared on *The Dick Cavett Show* with the Clancys.

† The residential arrangements of Finbar and Eddie in the late 60s are difficult to pin down. Eddie believes that he was living in Coventry and Finbar 'somewhere in Daventry' when they met the Clancys in May 1968, but this appears incorrect. Information gleaned from BBC Written Records shows that in February 1969 Finbar was based in Scotland and Eddie in Coventry; in July 1970, Eddie is based in Dublin and Finbar still in Scotland; by December 1971 the BBC contact address for both is 52 Birchfield Road in Coventry; by June 1972 the address for both is c/o Sheila Furey (Finbar's wife, essentially the duo's manager) at 14 Quillitty Close, Coventry.

people heard, they begged us not to split, saying it would be an awful shame for Ireland. The Clancy Brothers nearly went mad when we told them, so we don't think we'll split now.[27]

Aside from that passing glimmer of doubt, Finbar was brimming with enthusiasm for the American experience – the Clancys' show having included a feature spot for himself and Eddie – and for his mission with Irish music:

> American audiences love The Clancy Brothers … but we had to pick our stuff carefully, because we knew that pure Irish traditional music dies the death in America at the moment. But we felt great after the first night. We did 'Lonesome Boatman' and 'Madame Bonaparte' and the audience listened silently. Then they let rip, and we were shaking with embarrassment.
>   We are pleased that audiences over there took to the pipes so readily. We just stood dumbfounded, then Liam Clancy told us to bow, and we ended up bowing for 15 minutes. We even received a police escort in Chicago!
>   We want to introduce Irish music to everyone [in Britain], as the Clancys have done in America. The pipes seem to be dying out. The uilleann pipes are a beautiful instrument, but it seems to be exclusive among old people only … It's great to come across to England and find people playing the pipes and singing Irish material.[28]

In January 1970, the Clancys with Finbar and Eddie undertook a 13-date British tour, including the Royal Albert Hall, promoted by Irish property mogul Bill Fuller. The Fureys continued with the arrangement during 1970, learning a great deal about stagecraft along the way. It's hard to be certain when the Clancys/Fureys combination went their separate ways. Certainly, there was Finbar & Eddie duo activity in Britain in late April and May 1970; a Scottish TV show in July; and a full tour in November 1970. There was also a unique Finbar solo gig at a Northumberland Pipers' Society event on 20 October in Newcastle. Nevertheless, at some point Finbar decided that enough was enough:

> **Finbar**: There was only so many times you could sing 'I'll Tell Me Ma When I Get Home', and I had a pain in my ass because I wanted to play my pipes and I wasn't playing any pipes – and I was losing my piping. The singing was great, but I missed the music and I missed moving on.
>   We had a spotlight on us and it was switched off, at this show, and I knew: I said, 'This is going nowhere.' I looked at the pipes and I looked at

the five-string banjo, and we did two songs – and I just picked the pipes up and walked off the stage! The management ran backstage and I said, 'I want a ticket tonight, there's a flight to London …' Anyway, he got me on it, and I went back on and finished the concert. And that was it … I knew if I'd have stayed there, I would have died inside, cos I wasn't playing what I wanted to play.[29]

Finbar had not set aside his pipes completely during his Clancy Brothers sojourn. The Fureys had a 15-minute spot within the show, while the pipes were an occasional texture throughout:

Eddie: During the show, he would play the pipes [as a backing instrument]. Liam would play the concertina and I could play guitar, or Bobby would play the guitar and then I could play mandolin, and Finbar would play the pipes or the whistle. [But] I suppose his heart was always in playing the pipes freely.

He wanted to go home cos he had a family at home – his daughter was born. I wanted to stay with the boys forever in America, because I loved America and I was getting on all these big TV shows.

*

In February 1971 Finbar and Eddie toured the clubs in the south of England, including four dates in London and a spot on BBC Radio 1's *Country Meets Folk*, with their old friends The High Level Ranters and Yorkshire band Mr Fox also on the bill.[*] This was all routine stuff by now, but a booking on February 6 1971 – a radio concert in Frankfurt alongside English folk-rock bands Fotheringay and Fairport Convention[†] – would open the door to the next phase of their career.

Eddie: That was the first show we ever did in Germany. I was wise enough on that show – there was a man who was going to be [translating onstage]

---

* The *Melody Maker*'s 'Raver' column reported on May 29 1971, about another shared bill, that Mr Fox 'were threatened by Irish heavies who demanded that they shut up in favour of local idols Finbar and Eddie Furie [sic] …' The Ranters would share another bill with Finbar & Eddie (along with Ted Furey, and also with singer Ray Fisher, cumulatively representing England, Ireland and Scotland) at a traditional music festival in Verdun, France, in August 1972.

† Only Fotheringay and Finbar & Eddie were referred to in *Melody Maker* news on the Frankfurt event, but both Finbar and Eddie recall only Fairport Convention.

into German. I told all my funny stories, and he was off to one side telling the audience these stories in German and the two of us went down a storm. Finbar went down a storm. Fairport Convention were a great band at the time, but I'd say we went down better than they did on the night – because we talked to the audience. And I think being Irish, they were more accepting to Irish people than they were to English. We met a fellow in the audience who became our manager out there, Carsten Linde. He asked us to do a tour of youth clubs.

Finbar: We went to Germany with Fairport Convention – and we *wrecked* it! We just did one concert with them, in Frankfurt. It was a huge response. So we readied ourselves for a tour of Europe, a university tour. And we never looked back. We knew exactly where we were. There was a bit of friction between the Germans and the British all the time, so of course the Germans loved us. All we did was just enjoy having a bit of craic with the Germans.

The brothers would alter their act a little for the German market, singing more traditional material than they would in England. But it was the attitude and openness they came with that endeared them to the German audiences:

Finbar: We never once, ever, dictated to the Germans how to play their music. We were going over there from '71 to 1976, which is when we stopped. But when we went there in '71, it was great. Because we would go to a town and say, 'Okay, where are we playing tonight, Walter?' And Walter would say, 'You are playing Weisbaden …' 'Okay, what is Weisbaden famous for?' And he'd tell us what Weisbaden was famous for. And when we played we had a translator and we'd talk about all this, and people would be interested in what we do. And when we came back [on the next tour], the place'd be mobbed, because now they knew we didn't just come to play, they knew we were interested. We asked about Hitler and the war, cos we didn't know anything about it, but these guys could teach us about it. And I loved the food and so on …

We were just very down to earth, we didn't try to get anything out of them, and they absolutely adored us. They lost their beautiful folk music through propaganda that Hitler put out there, a war that destroyed their heritage. I remember these two old men, though they'd only have been in their 50s when we met them, and I says, 'Give us one of them soft German folk songs …' He sang this amazing song. And I asked him what it was about and he said, 'It's just about a kid playing in a playground …' And it was so lovely. I said, 'You can't lose this. This music didn't belong to Hitler, it belongs to you …' So we started to help with the revival. We didn't go in there to take the money and run.

For a couple of years the duo's new German opportunities were balanced with work on the British club scene. Indeed, 1972 may well be the high water mark of Finbar & Eddie Furey as an act within the British music world. Seemingly in the same month, February, they would record two albums: *Four Green Fields*, the first of four duo albums to be released solely in Europe, recorded in Hamburg for the Plane label; and *The Dawning Of The Day*, recorded in London for British label Pye's new 'progressive music' imprint, Dawn. As the *Melody Maker* reported in February 1972:

> Ed and Finbar Furey have completed two albums for Dawn, the first of which is due for late March release. Said Finbar: 'We're calling it *Everyone Can Share* and it's all our own work apart from Gerry Rafferty's 'Her Father Didn't Like Me Anyway'. And it's all contemporary. The other LP is very traditional.'[30]

Finbar was jumping the gun somewhat: the album would be titled *The Dawning Of The Day*; would be released in June or July rather than March; and nothing would ever be heard of any second album again. Possibly, the best of both prospective albums were combined into what became *The Dawning Of The Day*, though it featured mostly traditional material (Scottish, English and Irish) alongside the Rafferty song and a new version of Eddie's 'Jennifer Gentle'. It also featured a powerful, dynamic recorded sound, with the brothers playing many instruments between them – making great use of the extensive overdubbing and arranging luxury they felt had been denied them with the Transatlantic albums – and with Brian Brocklehurst, who had often accompanied them on BBC radio shows, on double bass.

The album had been produced by Dawn staffer Barry Murray, who had recently produced a series of hits for Mungo Jerry including the No. 1s 'In The Summertime' and 'Baby Jump'.

> **Finbar**: This man wanted to put me and Eddie on a weekly wage of £100 a week – we weren't allowed to work anywhere until he told us. Well, 'Fuck that,' you know. … He wanted us to do support, first of all, for big acts [like] The Moody Blues. Ray Thomas was a great friend of mine. … Barry sat down and said to me, 'I want you to think about the offer.' I'd been to Carnegie Hall with The Clancy Brothers, I'd done *The Dick Cavett Show*,

The Johnny Carson Show with the Clancys, and I saw how hard these guys had to travel, and how hard they had to work. And I said to Eddie, 'You know, there has to be an easier way than this.' So I shook his hand and I said, 'No, I've two children now and I've another one on the way.' I wanted to go home. I'd had enough.

As had been the case with the Clancy Brothers membership, Eddie was presented with a *fait accompli*:

Eddie: Finbar didn't want it. But I wanted it, of course: anything to get up the ladder a bit. I mean, I was the one who brought a PA into the duo. Finbar didn't want to use a PA. 'I don't want to put anything through a microphone,' he'd say. 'Well, it's a big mistake,' I said. 'If you're wanting to get to a wider audience, you've got to be heard!'

The Dawning Of The Day, the first time the brothers would actually earn any royalties from recorded music, was trailered by the release of a single in May, coupling 'Her Father Didn't Like Me Anyway' with 'Reynardine', a haunting Irish song that was already a favourite of the British folk-rock bands. If there can have been any doubt about Eddie's quality as a singer and guitarist, it was surely addressed by these two tracks: visceral, windswept and totally compelling deliveries of both songs. Finbar's musicianship in the rich arrangements effectively occupied the space and roles that lead guitar and Hammond organ would have taken in a rock band.

At this point, Finbar and Eddie found that they had a fervent and influential supporter in BBC Radio 1 'progressive music' taste-maker John Peel. He played the single A-side at least eight times between May and early July before moving on to other tracks from the album.* The pair would record two studio sessions for Peel's show that year: one in June, the other when they were back in Britain working the club circuit during November-December.

Strangely, they never performed 'Her Father Didn't Like Me Anyway' during these sessions, nor on two subsequent sessions for the show. Perhaps they all reckoned the Dawn recording couldn't be bettered. Certainly, Peel had an evangelistic fervour for it. Towards the end of the year, Peel had some kind of single or song of the year competition or playlist running over several weeks on his programme – a precursor to his annual 'Festive 50', begun later in the decade. It was exciting stuff:

---

* Detailed information can be found at the remarkable John Peel fan site: peel.wikia.com/wiki/Finbar_%26_Eddie_Furey (Accessed: 15/1/15). Peel also played the Fureys' single on his Radio Luxembourg shows in 1972.

Finbar: I remember we were going up against The Beatles. Each week he'd say, 'This week, so-and-so has gone and we have The Beatles and Finbar & Eddie Furey and we have blah blah …' And it went all the way down to ourselves and The Beatles.' I remember we were parked under the motorway in London, listening to the radio. We were driving this big old Daimler, myself and Eddie, we were going to a gig someplace, down in Croydon I think it was, so we pulled in to hear what the result was. And I couldn't believe it: 'Number Two …' and he played 'Jo-Jo' ['Get Back']. Then he says, 'My single of the year: Finbar & Eddie Furey.'

I remember Gerry [Rafferty] phoned us. It was fantastic. The Beatles had won everything for years. For two Ballyfermot kids and a Glaswegian kid to come in and shake it up a bit, it was lovely. Of course, everyone was going, 'Who the fuck are those guys? Paddies with a set of pipes and a 12-string guitar? *Come on!*' [31]

While the duo would continue to revisit the British club circuit (doing so, for example, during April 1973 and January-March 1974), the Peel sensation at the end of 1972 was less of a door opening than two people going out with a bang. The seed they had planted with one concert in Frankfurt back in February 1971 was beginning to blossom. Germany and mainland Europe would now become their prime focus for both record releases and live performances.

*

Finbar and Eddie's recording career in Germany had begun with *Four Green Fields* on Plane, recorded by 'kraut-rock' pioneer Conny Plank. While successfully adding a few sound effects and a cellist to the mix, it lacked the power and clarity of the British albums.

As it was a release for a new territory, the brothers could revamp a few numbers already featured on their British albums: 'Lark In The Morning' (previously heard on the Paddie Bell record); 'Roy's Hands' (from *Traditional Irish Pipe Music*); and 'The Lonesome Boatman'. There may also have been more licence to bring in songs referencing England's involvement in Ireland, but it's still a well balanced set: mostly traditional, a couple of originals (Finbar's instrumentals this time) and two or three songs gleaned from their British folk peers. In the latter category were Robin

---

* Why The Beatles' 'Get Back' was in competition with anyone, if the competition really was to do with single releases in 1972, is a mystery. 'Get Back' was released in Britain in 1969 and not re-released until 1976. Whatever the nature of the competition, it undoubtedly put Finbar & Eddie Furey on the British music map.

Williamson's immortal 'October Song', Tommy Makem's 'Four Green Fields' and Alex Campbell's version of 'Night Visiting Song'. Finbar also made his lead vocal debut with 'Four Green Fields'.

Finbar and Eddie's progress in Germany was triumphal. Their second German album, *A Dream In My Hand,* was recorded in January 1974 for Intercord. The sleevenote writer could declare of the duo that 'after The Dubliners they are the second Irish group the Germans have taken to their hearts. … Clubs like the Sinkkasten in Frankfurt are bursting at the seams when the Fureys perform on consecutive evenings, and the brothers are having to switch over to larger concert halls in order to satisfy all their 'Irophile' fans.'[32]

> **Finbar**: In Germany I'd say we played for 60 people the first night. I think the next night it was 100 people. Before we came home it was a thousand people, because the name was spreading all over the place. So we got Germany; in two years we had it.

> **Eddie**: We brought our own PA when we were playing round the clubs, the big clubs. We came out of the youth clubs into a bigger club scene. It was before we got into the halls. We only got into the halls about two years [before we stopped as a duo]. … We had an awful lot of friends in Germany helping us getting into bigger places, getting work for us, getting us onto different TV shows. We done TV shows in Munich with several big German stars. We did an awful lot of hard work to get to where we were going. We roughed it a good bit till we got on our feet. And an awful lot of people befriended us, and got us on radio, explaining what it was like in Ireland and so on. … I don't remember getting a penny off the albums [though]. We got put up in a hotel, all right, while making them, but that's as far as it went.

A Dream In My Hand was sonically an improvement on *Four Green Fields*, a return to the raw, vibrant sound of *The Dawning Of The Day*. It was mostly traditional (both Irish and English) in content and instrumentally less 'flash' than its predecessor. Finbar demonstrated with his magisterial solo piping lament 'The Plains Of Waterloo' that just 'because he could', he didn't need to. He also contributed two songs to the album, 'Pollution' and 'Life Is Just That Way', though both were sung, as were all the vocal items this time, by Eddie. Martin Carthy was the source of one song, 'Peggy And The Soldier'.

The third German album, *I Live Not Where I Love* (Intercord, 1975) had a smoother production sound which, in retrospect, pointed toward the mixture of refined backing and gritty vocals that would characterise the subsequent career of The Fureys & Davey Arthur. The album was roughly half traditional and half contemporary in content. One of the highlights was 'Lord Lovell', traditional text with an elegiac tune from English singer Dave Burland.* Finbar took to the microphone on two songs: his own 'Wounded Knee', based on Native American experiences; and Jim McLean's minor-key lullaby 'Hush, Hush', on the theme of the Scottish Highland clearances. It was effectively the same theme of repression on two sides of the Atlantic. He also performed a lament and reel of his own, 'Tribute To Leo Rowsome', in honour of the great piper and pipe maker from Dublin who had recently passed on.

During May 1974, a year before *I Live Not Where I Love*, Finbar & Eddie Furey had helmed an 'Irish Folk Festival' tour of Germany, based on the model of the 'American Folk Blues Festival' tours of the mid-60s. They brought along a few friends: singer/guitarist Bobby Clancy; tin whistler Miko Russell; their father Ted Furey, backed by their brother George; and The Buskers, being their other brother Paul with Davey Arthur and Brendan Leeson. A double LP, *Irish Folk Festival – Live 1974*, resulted. Though it would be the only one to feature Finbar and Eddie, it would herald many tours and live albums under the 'Irish Folk Festival' banner.

> **Finbar**: [In] 1974 we were taking Germany apart, myself and my brother Eddie. So [to] Carsten Linde, who was taking care of us then [as manager], and a fellow called Walter Gunnas [at] Intercord, I said, 'Look, why don't I bring more Irish acts over here? Cos it's ridiculous: all they know is The Dubliners. There has to be more.'

Ted Furey had recommended the brothers check out Clannad, a new family group from Gweedore in Donegal who sang in Irish. They subsequently took Carsten Linde to a fleadh in Bundoran and on to Gweedore to hear them:

---

* Dave Burland didn't know his song was on the album until much later. He did meet the brothers on the road in 1976, though: 'I was in a folk rock band called Hedgehog Pie, with my two best mates Mick Doonan and Jed Grimes. We were touring Belgium and staying at a bar called The Mallemolen outside Brussels. There was dormitory accommodation, and another great band called Ossian were also in residence. The Furey family arrived later that night – Finbar, Eddie, George, Paul, and Davey Arthur, breaking their journey before a tour of Germany. When everybody rose in the morning there was an impromptu pipes workshop, as we had three pipers under the same roof: Mick Doonan, Billy Jackson from Ossian and Finbar. Finbar's pipes seemed huge, and as he sat down to play a selection of his greatest hits, you could have heard a pin drop. A masterful performance – the Jimi Hendrix of the pipes.'

Finbar: We did the first tour, me and Eddie, and we ripped the place apart. So the next tour, we come over and did just the first three or four nights and then we backed off and let Clannad go, and Clannad did the rest of the tour, and then the whole thing exploded.*

*

Back in Britain, where Finbar and Eddie would also champion Clannad, readers of *Melody Maker* in October 1975 were brought up to date on recent and forthcoming developments in the Furey camp in an interview with Colin Irwin. He painted a picture of Finbar in confident form:

Finbar, much more relaxed and easy-going than you'd ever imagine from looking at him, offers no false modesty about his abilities, and doesn't argue when his brothers claim he revolutionised Irish pipe playing. Finbar said: 'A man once said to me, 'The pipes were a dying art until your brother started playing guitar with them'; and he was right.'[33]

Finbar and Eddie had formed a band. Their brother Paul and Davey Arthur, being two thirds of The Buskers, had joined them in a new quartet called Tam Linn. Listeners in Britain could have heard them in session on John Peel's Radio 1 show back in March, and during the summer Tam Linn had played at the Cambridge, Bracknell and Thurso folk festivals.

Finbar (1975): It's a magic group and I think Tam Linn is going to be an awful long time on the go. It'll take a good group to shift us. I remember the first morning we had a practice – Eddie and me have never practised in our lives – and everybody was a bit shaky from drink the night before. Anyway, we tried to do it and we came to a dead stop, so we went and had a drink or two and relaxed, and it worked. It came together very quickly.[34]

It was reported that Finbar & Eddie Furey were returning to tour Germany in late 1975 as a duo to promote a new LP (*I Live Not Where I Love*), while The Buskers were also still continuing. As Irwin explained:

---

* The *2nd Irish Folk Festival* tour and double LP featured Ted & George Furey, The Buskers, Miko Russell, Jerry Bourke and Clannad. Finbar believes that over the next 12 years or so the German market for Irish music was milked too heavily and too often by artists who didn't have enough respect for the audience: 'And then it died on its ass. It was absolutely destroyed. Me and [my] brothers went back in about 1987, I think that was the last one we did.'

Financial rewards for Tam Linn now are minimal and they can make much more on the Continent as individual acts, so it's a matter of cash to keep the separate acts going although these are eventually likely to be phased out. A further change is the probable addition of the youngest Furey brother George, who is still in Dublin playing with his father.[35]

When the 'phase-out' finally came for Finbar & Eddie as a duo, it came as something of a surprise to Eddie. A new double album recorded in Germany – half live, half studio, with the live disc featuring their brothers Paul and George as well as Davey Arthur – was to be called *The Farewell Album*:

Eddie: I didn't want to knock it on the head. I went over to do a tour and found out we were doing a 'Farewell Tour' – and I knew nothing about it. Finbar took it upon himself to put this out. He tried to do the same thing with the band before he left [in 1997] – he was going to put an Australian tour out as a 'Farewell Tour'. But I said, 'You're not doing that. At the end of the day, *we're* not saying 'farewell'.'

Instinctively, as had been the case with leaving The Clancy Brothers and turning down Barry Murray's plan for stardom, Finbar felt it was time for a change:

Finbar: I wanted to move on. I love music, I can't do without music, I can't sit still. And eventually we reached 2,000, 2,500 people a night, and I didn't like that. It moved too fast. And the tours were getting longer and longer; I felt they should be getting shorter. And it affects the music; you're on automatic pilot.

In the middle of this, my brothers had a crash – Paul and George, and Davey. We had two more concerts to do in Belgium, me and Eddie, and I said, 'Eddie, you'd better see if they're all right. I'll do the gigs on my own.' So Eddie took the train – we were in Denmark when we heard – and I drove, a long drive, to finish these two gigs. Eddie [later] phoned me at the hotel. 'The boys are okay,' he says, 'they were very lucky, but the car's a write-off.'

'Aw, shit …'

I'd hooked up with Martin Carthy, who was staying in the same place I was staying, and John Martyn – we were doing three different gigs [in the same town]. I loved John's music, he was incredible, another genius. John said: 'Will you come and play the pipes for me?'

'Sure, I'll play them …'

So me and Martin Carthy joined him at his gig, and then he came and joined in at Martin's gig, and we finished the three gigs together, the three of us – it was a fucking great time! So the whole story was my brothers were okay, we got a brand new car out of it, and when I came home I said to Eddie, 'I'm forming a band. … I'd like to work with the whole family so we know where we all are. I don't want my brothers to die in a car crash.'

The first time we got together as The Furey Brothers, Davey [Arthur] was sitting there. I really didn't want Davey in the band. But he was Paul's best friend, and I remember turning to Davey and I said, 'Do you want to join the band?' And he said, 'I'd love to.' And the rest is history.

*

While the new band, The Fureys & Davey Arthur, would continue to work across Europe, the German-based recording career came to an end with *The Farewell Album* (1976) and a one-off album for Intercord the following year, *The Furey Family*, featuring all four brothers with their father Ted in various combinations. 'It was lovely,' says Finbar, 'and we did it just before my father died.'

The Fureys & Davey Arthur would base their new career in Ireland, releasing a series of albums on Polydor Ireland, Dolphin and their own label Banshee* before achieving an international hit single in 1981 with an old music hall ballad, 'When You Were Sweet Sixteen'. Reaching No. 1 in Ireland, No. 9 in Australia and No. 14 in Britain, it saw the group on BBC TV's *Top Of The Pops* – a year before their friends in Clannad repeated the trick with their 'Theme From Harry's Game'. It was a big deal for Irish music, let alone Irish folk music.

Finbar sang lead and played very distinctive, elegant banjo on the track, which he had learned from his mother, and his voice became, to a new audience of millions, the 'sound' of The Fureys. Ballads rather than piping became the selling point:

'It was amazing when you think about it,' said Finbar, 'with my father, with the pipes … But in the end it's ironic that it was her banjo playing and singing that took us to *Top Of The Pops*.'[36]

For Eddie, the success of the single 'changed our focus, [it was] a complete new direction.' It was one more change in a career that was already longer and more diverse than those who first encountered the group on mainstream TV shows and radio would have known:

---

* The albums were *Emigrant* (1977), *Morning On A Distant Shore* (1977), *Banshee* (1978) and *The Green Fields Of France* (1979). Several songs and tunes from the previous German albums were newly recorded for these releases. A new recording of 'Her Father Didn't Like Me Anyway' was also released as a single on Polydor Ireland in 1977.

Eddie: We weren't too much a heavy traditional band, nor a traditional duo, really. Finbar had his traditional music; I backed him. And then I was doing some middle-of-the-road stuff myself, but with the pipes, and then I was getting given songs and doing them with pipes and whistle – a new kind of [sound]. You have to move forward. Certainly, I knew we had to move forward in the 60s. We didn't want to be just a traditional duo or a traditional band. Most traditional bands out at the moment – they're great bands, but they're playing the music like they're playing typewriters. Our stuff was raw.

Now it was time to be smooth; or, at least, not quite so raw. Further hit singles followed in Ireland, and two albums entered the UK Top 40. The Fureys & Davey Arthur became a solid international concert hall attraction, with music that resonated around the world.

Within time, Finbar became restless and wanted to move on again. Aware of his importance in the group, having become the voice of its biggest songs, he remained longer than he would have liked, finally leaving in 1997 to pursue a solo career. Eddie, George, Paul and Davey continued on as The Fureys, with Eddie, George and Davey continuing in the band to this day – touring internationally and recording new albums, blending traditional music, old ballads and contemporary songs, on a regular basis. I saw their show in March 2015 and it was a joyous experience. Their skill as entertainers was a pleasure to watch, and Eddie's voice retains its commanding character and presence.

Finbar: When Paul died [in 2002], I was absolutely devastated ... For 10 years I went around being lost, literally lost. Everything was hitting me. I wasn't doing anything – I was running off to America, doing two weeks in pubs ... and picking up a heap of cash, spending most of it before I came home, drinking a lot. And then I got very sick.[37]

Finbar had an operation on his shoulder in 2005, followed by three months of recuperation that were both a dark night of the soul and an epiphany, a re-engagement with his muse. Focusing on banjo as his first instrument – the pipes being now almost off limits, given his shoulder weakness – Finbar released *Colours* in 2011 as a mission statement of where he was as an artist. What happened next has the air of a fairy tale.

In August 2013 Finbar took part as a mentor on the RTÉ series *The Hit*, in which unknown songwriters were paired with established artists to create something the public could vote for. After hearing a few bars of 'The Last Great Love Song', Finbar chose writer Gerry Fleming. He was given 3,000 euro and tasked with arranging and recording the song:

> **Finbar**: In the end I had five hours to record it, because I didn't set myself enough time. I got a really terrific guitar player, we got the studio and I played every [other] instrument on it bar the bass and shakers. I played guitar, banjo, pipes, whistles, flutes; I sang it, I arranged it, I produced it. And when I handed it over to the lads in RTÉ they freaked: 'Jesus, this is fantastic!' It was No. 1 on the Wednesday. They knew it was No. 1, it went straight in, but I couldn't tell anybody [for a couple of days]. That was the hardest thing!

His TV performance of the song in the series final, with the RTÉ Concert Orchestra, has an aura of the heroic: 'I played the pipes with the orchestra and without thinking about it, without worrying about it. It was probably one of the most perfect things I've done in my life. The magic was there.'

The magic was still there. It had been there for 50 years. But people easily forget.

Chapter 4
Liam O'Flynn: The Quiet Man

'It was a glimmer in Christy's eye, which developed into whatever it is that glimmers in eyes develop into,' says Bill Leader, the man who recorded *Prosperous* (which, as a title for anything related to people hoping to make a living in folk music, is beyond parody). 'It was an idea, and I think it probably exceeded the original intention. In fact, it did exceed it.'

Christy Moore, an Irish singer/guitarist who had been making a solid living on the thriving folk club scene during the late 60s, primarily in the North of England, had made one album thus far, produced by Dominic Behan, which had not been a satisfactory experience. He had an idea to bring together, as his backing band, Andy Irvine and Dónal Lunny on double-course stringed instruments and Liam O'Flynn on pipes. Three others would contribute to the sessions, but this would be the core quartet.

> **Liam**: Christy and Dónal are originally from Newbridge, which is about eight miles from where I'm from originally, but growing up we didn't have any contact. But there was a little pocket of musical activity centred around the village called Prosperous in County Kildare, and in later years a gang of us used to meet there every Wednesday evening – sometimes Christy would be there, sometimes Dónal.

'I can't say exactly what was in my mind,' Christy admitted many years later. 'But … it had to have pipes … Liam was the first piper I ever got in close to, and I've always found a deep and moving soulfulness about his playing. Even as a young man, I heard that, and without knowing much about the instrument or its history, it still touched me deeply.'[38]

Christy had also been deeply inspired, in 1968, by the first of two albums for Transatlantic by Sweeney's Men, recorded in London by Bill. With Andy Irvine on mandolin and Johnny Moynihan on bouzouki, the first Sweeney album would be the wellspring of the interweaving double-course instrument sound that would be resurrected on *Prosperous*, with uilleann pipes added to the gumbo for the first time.

Christy Moore's loose vision and Bill Leader's similarly vague but noble progress

– neither man terribly well suited to the business of making money, but each one digging deeply into something that seemed to have a higher purpose – would coalesce in a London pub on the recommendation of Mike Harding, a Northern comedian with a guitar:

> **Bill**: Mike Harding was the connection. Christy spent a lot of time in the mid-Pennine area between Manchester and Halifax. He was not that happy with [his first LP] *Paddy On The Road*, and talked to Mike about it. And Mike, who I think had just finished recording his own album for Trailer, said, 'Get in touch with Bill Leader, see if you can't do something there.' So he did that. We met up in some Irish bar in Fleet Street – Mooney's, that was the place – and by the end of the conversation I'd agreed to go across to Ireland.

Bill Leader had been producing folk and traditional records for Topic, Transatlantic and Decca from the late 50s onwards. Based in London, living in Camden Town, he had been sucked into this hand-to-mouth profession through the London-Irish music scene, with the duo of Margaret Barry & Michael Gorman his earliest prey. As of 1969, Bill had established his own binary star of labels: Leader (for pure traditional music) and Trailer (for folk club artists). He had a vague idea that the one would pay for the other.

'I would like eventually to have the whole of the traditional culture on record,' he had mused in 1970.[39] Over the next decade he would give the ambition a serious attempt. With the recording of *Prosperous*, at a rambling old house of that name, in the summer of 1971, Bill had unconsciously notched up his fifth uilleann piper in 10 years.

From one end of the 'long 60s' to the other, Bill had recorded: the McPeakes in 1962; Willie Clancy in 1967; Finbar Furey in 1968–69; Séamus Ennis in 1969; and now Liam O'Flynn in 1971. He'd notched up a few Northumbrian pipers during that period, too. The albums by Willie Clancy (*The Minstrel From Clare*) and Séamus Ennis (*Masters Of Irish Music Vol. 1*) remain the best albums they made in their lifetimes. The album with Liam would be the appropriately subdued starting point of a stealthily illustrious career.

> **Bill**: I wanted to produce some of the things that were happening around that seemed to be important. The economical way of doing it was to sell directly to the customer by mail order. That way, we could cut out the retailer and the wholesaler and all the people who took the money for doing little or no work. Our first two releases, simultaneously, were: one Leader, *Jack Elliott of Birtley*; and one Trailer, [*The Fate o'Charlie: Songs of the Jacobite Rebellion*, by] Archie Fisher and Barbara Dickson.

Neither of them sold particularly well. We did have a lucky break because – having set all this up and [having] thought, 'Right, if we sell them direct to the public we can get enough to finance the next release' – as soon as we started releasing, Transatlantic wanted to take over the distribution. Well, we could have happily said no to that, because we'd just have been paying them to do the good or bad job of distribution, but they'd just done a deal with HMV/EMI. Transatlantic were going to retain their own wholesale distribution, but EMI were going to press the records.

One of the problems that we'd suffered at Topic, and looked as if we were going to carry on suffering as a small label, was the inability to get competent presses to press the records. We were always driven to backstreet abortionists to press out records, with inferior materials and no technique at all. So the opportunity of being pressed [properly], the records actually sounding like they should sound, was terribly attractive. So we fell for that. And of course immediately we lost our margin – but we did sell in reasonable numbers into Transatlantic's wholesale section, and an early bonus was that EMI said to Transatlantic, 'Well, we've never handled this sort of crap, er, product, before – how many do we order?' They came to the conclusion that how many they would take on and put into the warehouse at Hayes, Middlesex, or wherever it was would be the same as what Transatlantic ordered. So if Transatlantic ordered 1,000 copies, EMI would order 1,000 copies. So there was a honeymoon period when we were selling bloody loads of these things – only at wholesale price, of course, but at least we were selling in quantities. Then EMI woke up one morning and realised that they were heavily overstocked with all this folk nonsense, and they started unloading. And I think you can still find warehouses in the depths of the Indian subcontinent where you can buy boxes of Leader/Trailer records for bugger all, if you know who to ask.

Christy, luckily, had approached Bill less for his business acumen than for his availability and his reputation: 'There's more to him than meets the eye,' he reflected.[40]

'I liked Bill a lot,' says Andy Irvine. 'I always thought Bill was a very wise man – because he didn't say very much.'

'He made the business of recording, for an inexperienced recording musician like myself, a very enjoyable thing,' said Liam. 'There was something of the Ciarán Mac Mathúna* about him.'[41]

---

* Ciarán Mac Mathúna was the presenter of *A Job Of Journeywork* on Radio Éireann from 1955 onwards, actively seeking out and broadcasting regional traditional musicians.

Bill: [Prosperous] was a reasonable bit of space where they could rehearse and we could record them without being disturbed. Actually, we didn't realise it then, but we were on the verge of being disturbed by the Garda, looking for an illicit still. … It was done on virtually no equipment. I carried my trusty Revox to Ireland with a couple of not terribly expensive, nor particularly good, microphones, strung them up the best I could to capture the sounds … The trick was, it was a sort of vaulted cellar we were doing it in and it had a rich acoustic, so the natural sound … We messed about a bit, but not too much; we didn't need to. … That may be the secret, you know. Less is definitely more. I discovered later when having to teach this as a subject that it goes in phases. There was a time when you put as many microphones around a drum kit as you possibly could, but I've come to the conclusion that 'the fewer microphones, the better' is actually quite a good slogan.

Dónal Lunny: The way Bill balanced it was by moving us around. He put Liam down the back, because his pipes were louder than any of the guitars or bouzoukis or other instruments. … Then it was just a recording of a situation, of an environment, really. … He actually got a great result.[42]

Andy was working with Dónal as a duo at the time and saw no particularly fabulous future with the album to which they had all contributed: 'I enjoyed it very much, but I didn't see the potential in it.'

Liam was quietly confident, however: 'I knew it was going to make a huge impact. I really did. It was a different sound.'[43]
Released on Trailer, in Britain, in March 1972, it might have been a different sound – the opening track alone, 'Raggle Taggle Gypsy/Tabhair Dom Do Lámh', daringly marrying the Irish vocal and instrumental traditions – but nobody was listening.

'It didn't sell for me at all,' says Bill. 'It sold for Tara [to whom we sold it on], and we sort of gifted it to Christy, cos there was nothing we could do.'

Prosperous was 'gifted' to Christy by being sold to Jack Fitzgerald, who owned Ireland's Golden Discs chain of record stores. Jack and Bill each gave Christy £1,000. It was the most money he would see from music for years. Tara Records was initially a store on Dublin's Tara Street; they used the name as the label for their vinyl acquisition. The retail end was at that point transitioning into a chain called Golden Discs. Over in the Rathfarnham Shopping Centre, John Cook, a former hotel industry accountant, had been running his own independent record store. Cook would become involved with both Tara Records and, before the 70s were out, the band that had debuted on *Prosperous*.

John Cook: [Young people in Ireland at the time] were not particularly buying Irish music. I think the youth of Ireland were buying your end-of-60s rock, and buying it in preference to any Irish music at all. Jack Fitzgerald did very well – specialising in American imports. There was maybe up to a two-month delay between an American release and UK release and … he would bring in the likes of Charley Pride and Elvis Presley stuff and built up his business that way. I knew Jack all through those years [in the 60s] while I was in the hotel business and he was in the record store, for no other reason than [that] I used to be a particularly good customer.

[*Prosperous*] was only available in Ireland as an import. … But [it] was continually going out of stock as demand was increasing. It was the breaking album, if you like, that started to turn the whole direction of Irish music around, because the four members of Planxty were on that album and it was the precursor of the band. Jack Fitzgerald did a deal with Bill Leader … and released it as the first album on the Tara label, in 1972.

In between the album being recorded and appearing on Trailer and then on Tara, Liam O'Flynn had spent five months in America, memorably gigging on one occasion with blues icon John Lee Hooker and singer-songwriter Patrick Sky, who would himself take up the uilleann pipes and enhance the discography of Séamus Ennis in due course – as would Tara Records. Ennis, for his part, would be a notable influence on the band that became Planxty: Christy Moore, Andy Irvine, Dónal Lunny and Liam O'Flynn. But whether there would be any band at all was a moot point. Andy Irvine, running a weekly gig with Dónal Lunny at Slattery's on Capel Street at the time, recalls being doubtful:

Andy: Liam's always been an enigmatic fellow. I remember when Christy said, 'What about forming a band?' after we'd made *Prosperous*. And I'd been playing with Dónal. I said, 'What does Dónal think?' 'Oh, he's heavily into it.' And I said, 'Ah, yes, but what about Liam?' And he said Liam was in, and I was really surprised because Liam was a teacher. I would not have foreseen that he would give up a safe job to take to the road. He has a certain reserve. But he was very much into Planxty at the time.

Christy was interviewed by *Melody Maker* in March 1972 ('I'm fed up with being a solo singer … I think Andy feels the same way'), on the cusp of both *Prosperous* being released on Trailer in Britain and a first Planxty single, 'Three Drunken Maidens', on Des Kelly's label, Ruby Records, in Ireland. The new band was clearly exciting him:

Christy: This is really a solo LP, although from the solo LP we got the idea for the group. ... I think that Dónal particularly will make a big impact over here. I think the two most important members of the group will be Liam and Dónal, and [yet] it's Andy and myself that are best known. ... Liam has received some criticism from fellow musicians for coming into the group. The other three of us were a bit worried that Liam wouldn't become immersed in the group, but he has done. We don't want to lower his standards. We don't want him to do anything that would go against his musical ideals.[44]

Liam (2002): We had one rule in the band: if there was any one individual within the band who really didn't want to do this, that or the other, that was respected and there was no further argument about it. And that was, to me, a terrifically important thing.[45]

Forever doomed to be described as 'mild-mannered', 'cautious' and, yes, 'enigmatic', Liam O'Flynn may lack the braggadocio or colourful lifestyles of other 'big characters' involved in Irish traditional music, but his decision-making has always been daring, and over nearly 45 years he would accumulate a discography both eclectic and immense. If uilleann piping were a race, one would be tempted when talking about Liam O'Flynn to cite the fable of the tortoise and the hare. Other people have done a lot of haring around; Liam has quietly and consistently covered the ground – and not always the ground one might expect.

Planxty had debuted live at Slattery's in Dublin on January 30 1972. Within weeks, they had a single out on Des Kelly's Ruby Records – Des being a former manager of Sweeney's Men and an old friend of Andy's. Despite their ramshackle stage presentation (similar to that of Sweeney's Men before them), Des could see the magic. As he explained to Planxty biographer Leagues O'Toole: 'Put the four of them on stage and I believe there's a presence there they don't have individually.'[46]

It was just like The Beatles: the 'folk Beatles'. More or less single-handedly, with perhaps a little help from Horslips (also formed in 1972, a rock band with traditional music overtones as opposed to Planxty, a folk/trad band with a kind of rock music appeal), Planxty created a sizeable youth market for Irish traditional music. Their music – drawing from Liam's Irish instrumental repertoire, Christy's wealth of songs from the British folk scene, Andy's cache of intriguing confessionals from a sojourn in the Balkans during 1968–69 and compound rhythmic ideas from the same region, plus a dash of Americana – was a unique and exotic concoction, yet still felt passionately 'Irish'. It had the air of authenticity about it whilst simultaneously feeling wholly new.

Neil Martin, then a young piper who would go on to work with Liam O'Flynn from the mid-80s onwards, puts his finger on the intangible as well as anyone:

> **Neil Martin**: I think they made traditional music 'cool'. And part of that was the rhythm instruments, what Dónal was doing, the songs Christy was singing and Andy's glorious filigree work on his machine. It broadened it. It wasn't the standard straight melodic thing. The bandwidth had got bigger. Planxty brought a particular colour to it.

In one sense, black was the colour. The Beatles had had their 'White Album'; within a year of starting, and kicking off with a re-recording of 'Raggle Taggle Gypsy/Tabhair Dom Do Lámh', as heard first on *Prosperous*, Planxty had their 'Black Album'.*

'The arrangements are identical,' wrote one commentator shortly after the 'Black Album's' release in 1973, 'and in both they manage the tricky bridge from the song to the harp tune, changing tempo from 2/4 to 3/4 so smoothly that Liam's pipes are well into the first phrase of the second tune before you're aware of it. Nevertheless, the second recording has a togetherness that was not there the first time round. The first is obviously a pick-up group of musicians who have got together for the occasion, playing supremely well but with all the rough edges showing. The second is a band. That is the difference.'[47]

> **Liam**: When we started Planxty, we said we'd give it three months and if nothing was happening, then fair enough. By three months, the thing had really taken off. It was like a runaway train. You couldn't get off.[48]

*

'Wherever you go in the burgeoning Irish contemporary folk scene, where electric folk bands are springing up all over like shamrocks in the night,' wrote Karl Dallas in August 1973, 'you will find one bunch of musicians have the unanimous approval of all, whether you are talking to the most conservative of traditionalists or the most electric of folk rockers. The band is Planxty …'[49]

Planxty had begun touring in Britain by April 1972, Christy having worked his contacts on the British club scene to string together a number of club dates shared with Mike Harding, Martin Carthy, The Watersons and others. They would make their first of many live and in-session appearances on BBC radio on *Country Meets Folk* on May 6. As he was with the Furey brothers, John Peel was a particular

---

* 'The White Album' was actually called *The Beatles*, a name by which no one ever refers to it. Likewise, 'The Black Album' was called *Planxty*, and no one ever refers to it as that, either.

supporter. Back home, RTÉ were similarly supportive, with appearances on the prime-time Saturday night *Late Late Show* at both the beginning and the end of their first year, the December appearance being on a bill with The Chieftains and Séamus Ennis, the chaotic godfather of Irish piping, with whom Liam O'Flynn was by then sharing a domestic environment.

The 'Black Album' had been recorded in London in September 1972. Under a production deal with Eurovision songwriter Phil Coulter and his business partner Bill Martin, it would – like the subsequent two albums of the band's original lifespan – be leased to Polydor for Ireland, Britain, Germany and France.

'I reckon that Bill Martin made more money out of Planxty than I did,' said Christy in 1979, 'and y'know something? If he walked in now, I wouldn't know what the fuck he looked like.'[50]

They may all have come to regret the long-term financial implications of the production deal, but partly through it, Planxty had very swiftly become an international act.

'One of the most significant comments upon Planxty's development of their music,' concluded Dallas, 18 months in, 'is the way that piper Liam O'Flynn has retained the respect of his fellow pipers, possibly the most conservative of the guardians of the Irish tradition. … [T]hey have had to acknowledge that he still remains the master they thought he was before he joined the band.'[51]

By that point the group's second album, *The Well Below The Valley*, was in the can. It would be released before the year was out.

> **Christy**: The pressure on the second album was ridiculous. We finished an Irish tour and we went over to England to record, and at the time it wasn't even rehearsed … and yet that second album is my favourite.[52]

'Once a band becomes a permanent operation, it's immediately limited,' Liam mused, wisely, during the same interview session, in 1979. Those limitations – constant travelling, little time to develop new repertoire and remain interested as musicians – soon caught up with Dónal Lunny. Not long after an appearance at the Cambridge Folk Festival in July 1973 (with Breton folk-rocker Alan Stivell's fiddler René Werneer standing in for an ill O'Flynn), Dónal decided to move on. He wanted to work with singer-songwriter, Fine Art graduate and future orchestral composer Shaun Davey, who had enjoyed the British release of a duo album, *Davey & Morris*, with James Morris, future founder of Dublin's Windmill Lane Studios, in 1973. While the venture failed to yield any recorded work, with Dónal moving on again to create a new unit, The Bothy Band, it would not be the last time a Planxty alumnus would work with Davey.

Andy's former Sweeney's Men colleague Johnny Moynihan came in on bouzouki, and a 'difficult third album', *Cold Blow And The Rainy Night*, was recorded at Island Records' London studio in August 1974, not long after another appearance at the Cambridge Folk Festival.* A singular character, Johnny brought a fresh wit and *joie de vivre* to the band, coupled with an exasperating obsession with lengthy tuning-up sessions onstage and indecision about arrangements. Dónal Lunny was asked back in temporarily to help pull the third album together. Pressures of the road and resentment over the financial arrangements with Coulter and Martin were taking their toll. By the end of the year – after a couple of months of transition, with singer/guitarist Paul Brady as a fifth member – Christy had bowed out.†

> **Liam**: I remember a period of time when it seemed desperately difficult to just continue, because the lifestyle was affecting everybody. But it didn't really affect performance. There was tremendous pride in the work, and for that reason the notion of going on stage plastered was a no-no.[53]

> **Andy**: When Paul joined the band, we got the 'engine room' back [which Dónal had been]. But just the three and a half years of permanent gigging began to get to us … Liam called a meeting and we knew what it was going to be: 'Aha, this is it …' When we were all there, he said, 'I've called this meeting because I want to leave the band.' And everybody else said, 'Yes, I do too! Me, me, me, me, me!' So we all left the band and came over here [to O'Donoghues] and got plastered, I'm sure. And by the end of the night we were probably saying, 'Oh God, it was a great band – should we *really* do this?'[54]

Planxty played a final British tour in October 1975, followed by a tour of France. Their last gig was in Brussels, Belgium, on December 5. A huge tax bill hadn't helped, but everyone was just exhausted. It was time to do other things, with fewer people and overheads. For Liam, that was easy: he got an agent and became an entirely solo performer.

*

---

* Planxty were filmed for BBC2's *Old Grey Whistle Test* at the 1974 Cambridge Folk Festival, with 'The Blacksmith' being broadcast in late September. Anglia TV filmed a documentary on the festival that year, although Planxty were not featured.
† The five-piece Planxty of September-October 1974 made no commercial recordings but did perform a TV concert for BBC Northern Ireland.

'I'm not really very interesting to talk to,' Liam had said, having just given an interview to the man from *Folk News* in 1978. The interviewer, Tomás Mac Ruairí, begged to disagree:

> He is in reality most interesting to talk to. He is somewhat unique, being one of very few, if not the only, full-time professional Irish traditional musicians (not including singers) working a solo career. ... Seven years a full-time musician, he is optimistic for the future, not only of the music, but of his own career and admits to no over-riding personal ambitions, other than that everything should keep going as at present for him. ... His advice to young pipers is to first of all become 'good listeners to good music' and to strongly 'resist all attempts to be spectacular by playing too fast'.[55]

A prospective solo LP on promoter Kevin Flynn's Ogham label had been mentioned, but nothing came of it. Nevertheless, in 1979 Liam was the featured performer on a Decca single, 'David's Song', by composer Vladimir Cosma, from a series called *Kidnapped*. It would be the first of many soundtrack and session recordings, across diverse genres, over the coming years.

Artistically, by this point Liam was on the cusp of two significant developments: one, a daring orchestral project with Shaun Davey; the other, a more obviously lucrative reunion of Planxty.

Andy Irvine explained the situation to Colin Irwin at *Melody Maker* in March 1979, ahead of two months' worth of major concert hall dates across Britain, Europe and Ireland, beginning at London's Hammersmith Odeon and finishing at Dublin's National Stadium:*

> **Andy (1979)**: After we broke up I thought, 'Thank Christ that's over,' and then the next moment I thought, 'Jeez, I wish Planxty were still together.' I can remember talking to Liam about it a couple of years ago and being amazed to find he was into it. I was into it five minutes after we broke up.[56]

Being an enigmatic fellow of few and careful words, Liam had given his own view on the reunion subject to Colin Irwin a year before: 'I don't really have any feelings about whether it should or shouldn't happen.'[57]

Nevertheless, by September 1978 the four original members of Planxty plus, at Liam's suggestion, flautist Matt Molloy from the then-crumbling Bothy Band

---

* The National Stadium had been the scene of an atmospheric televised concert for RTÉ, viewable online, a mere six years earlier.

(in which Dónal was also involved) convened to rehearse. Rumours went quickly abroad, and this time round there was no problem getting record labels interested.

John Cook, who had been running Jack Fitzgerald's Tara label, was determined to acquire the inevitable Planxty reunion LP. The label had released a handful of albums in the intervening period, some licensed from other labels and some originated, most notably two Séamus Ennis albums, but it would only build a head of steam as an active originating label during 1978–79, with releases including two albums from Christy Moore, the first Stockton's Wing album and the Paddy Glackin & Paddy Keenan album *Doublin'*. A new Planxty album would put it on the map:

> **John Cook**: Planxty started a whole strain of Irish music that was coming more into the centre, was more crossover. When the band decided to get back together, they put themselves up for a record deal, and we were basically competing against Polygram and some other major. We decided that if we were going to start a label [in earnest], the best way to do it, even if it's costly, is to get a big album and a recognised artist. So after protracted negotiations we got a two-album deal with Planxty.

After The Break was recorded in June 1979, straight after the reunion tour. The gigs had started off shakily, but the omens were still good. After rueful reminiscences of past struggles, and the determination to get it right this time round, Colin Irwin painted an upbeat picture of the new five-piece. He concluded his piece, with layers of portent and metaphor (intentional or otherwise):

> A few of us make it back to O'Flynn's flat. 'Fancy a drink?' says Liam, pouring himself a generous red wine and playing Eric Clapton's new album rather loudly. A picture of Willie Clancy shudders on the wall. 'It's great to be back with the boys,' muses Liam. 'It's already good crack.'[58]

After The Break (1979) would be followed by *The Woman I Loved So Well* (1980) before things became complicated. Christy and Dónal, wanting to work with a rock rhythm section and to have a vehicle for politically charged material, formed Moving Hearts in 1981. They remained simultaneously in the essentially part-time Planxty for a period. Other people began coming into the ranks. A 12-inch single on WEA in 1981, of new member Bill Whelan's 'Timedance' – performed by Planxty as the interval music to that year's Eurovision Song Contest – began the new era. Bill would have monstrous success a few years later, in the same slot, with 'Riverdance', which had as its ultimate origin the marriage of Balkan rhythms with the flavour of Irish music birthed on the 'Black Album' back in 1973. A third and final album, *Words & Music* (WEA, 1983) followed. Christy and Dónal left, more people came in and the band limped on for a period, earning the Irvine sobriquet 'Planxty-Too-Far'.

'History will tell you it was a mistake to call it Planxty,' Andy mused to the band's biographer, 'but it wasn't a huge mistake, because no one remembers it and it didn't do very well, so that's okay.'[59]

Andy summarised the whole Planxty experience in a 2002 RTÉ documentary, which ironically itself inspired a third and surely final reunion during 2003–05:

> **Andy**: The first three albums have a lot of youthful energy about them, a novelty, etcetera. … I prefer the second three albums. Musically they're more intricate. We had evolved musically quite a long way by that time, and I just prefer the music, I think it's more interesting to listen to. But when I think of the times we had, 1972 through to the end of '74 was magic; '74 till Brady joined the band was kind of a struggle; and then it was great for a while with Brady until we were just too tired to continue. '79 onwards was okay. … The music was better, but more was expected of us at that point. There was more responsibility to do well, and when we didn't get the reaction we wanted there was a slight feeling – with me, anyway – of paranoia.[60]

Everything has its season. Even if The Beatles had succumbed to pressure and reunited, it would never have been the same. Why should the folk Beatles be any different? Yet during all this initial excitement and gradual fizzling out, Liam had been quietly pursuing a typically unexpected path with a man who wrote jingles for a living and had form for failed projects with Planxty people: Shaun Davey.

*

> **John Cook**: *The Brendan Voyage* (1980) was the next album [on Tara] after the second Planxty album [*The Woman I Loved So Well*]. At that time Shaun and Bill Whelan had the advertising market cornered – they did an enormous amount of jingles for radio and TV, and that's how both of them got their first experiences of orchestration. *The Brendan Voyage* came about by Shaun being approached by Harry Bradshaw from RTÉ, who asked him to write a piece for the RTÉ orchestra and base it on Tim Severin's book, which Shaun had just read. It was a kind of commission, performed by the RTÉ orchestra, after which the question of recording it came about. There was a gap between performance and releasing a record, and Shaun was actually talking to a couple of different companies … Looking back at

the catalogue, it was the album I agonised over more than anything else, as it was such a departure from anything else that had been recorded up to that date, in putting pipes together with an orchestra and with a rhythm section, plus one [that] had very high costs [involved]. I agonised for many days over that, but of course I don't regret it. We went ahead and recorded it, and it's still a great album. In fact, it's interesting that its 10th year of release was its second highest year of sales within those 10 years, so that's a good example of a consistently selling album. Liam only performs it maybe once or twice a year, but it doesn't date.

Tim Severin had spent part of 1976–77 (re)-enacting the legendary sixth century voyage of St Brendan from Ireland to Newfoundland in a small currach, writing a best-selling book on the adventure in 1978. It provided Shaun Davey with a subject to get his teeth into, bringing together the uilleann pipes with an orchestra to create a musically descriptive suite. It would be Shaun's first of several suites on Celtic themes, all of which would feature Liam O'Flynn and most of which would be recorded for Tara. The key works, which, like *The Brendan Voyage* have all been performed periodically and to consistent acclaim in the years since, are *The Pilgrim* (1984; revised and expanded in 1994), *Granuaile* (1986) and *The Relief Of Derry Symphony* (1990).

Shaun Davey: That year [1973], when I formed a band called Bugle with Dónal Lunny – we only did four gigs, in Dublin, and we did some demo recording. It was a very experimental band. He took a year out of Planxty to pursue these things, and it was very good of him to have done that. … But there was only one way for me to go at that stage: a combination of formal composition and a lesser amount of music by ear. … I was very keen to cross certain boundaries and arrange meeting points between certain instruments and traditions, [and] that had to be thought out on the page.

When I was working on *The Brendan Voyage*, I figured that I was trying to write music for people like me, who wanted to hear something like it but who hadn't, up to that point, heard it. … In a sense, I'm not qualified to write just for an orchestra, because I have no formal training, and I've largely made it up as I've gone along. What I'm equipped to do is arrange meeting points between what I can do for an orchestra – which is by no means everything an orchestra can do – and what I can enable other people to do, who don't normally work with an orchestra. This is typically what I've done, and it's typically what I've enjoyed doing most – staging these meeting points.

Liam O'Flynn: Shaun was very much in love with the sound of the uilleann pipes, and when he first approached me with the idea of writing a piece of music for the pipes based on *The Brendan Voyage* [book], we sat down and discussed the instrument and the difficulties and strengths that a composer would come up against. During the whole process of the writing Shaun learned very well indeed, as he says himself, the 'inner workings of the instrument' – what was possible and what wasn't.

I had a basic knowledge of [music notation], but I would never be comfortable having to perform music and reading it at the same time – coming from the tradition, you learn music by heart. So I would only be comfortable with these pieces once I'd committed them to memory and had a bloody good idea what the orchestra were up to as well. [There's room for improvisation], but you wouldn't want to overdo it – otherwise the conductor would begin to wonder what the hell your man was up to! It would throw a serious spanner in the works.

One of the biggest difficulties I found with *The Brendan Voyage* wasn't a musical thing; it was finding oneself within a totally different performing environment. The formality of the concert hall, an absolutely quiet audience out there in front of you – that puts some pressure on a traditional musician.

The whole concept of *The Brendan Voyage* was wonderful, with the pipes telling the story of this little boat and the orchestra telling the story of what the little boat encountered. It was certainly ground-breaking and it seems to me, as time passes, that the impact it made is an ongoing thing. It made a huge impact at the time, but it's growing, because [in] every new territory I go into with the piece, people are amazed by this new creature, as it were.

The ongoing partnership between Liam and Shaun effectively also created the solo career Liam currently enjoys. His first solo album, *Liam O'Flynn*, was released by WEA Ireland in 1988, but his current career as a solo artist – with lavishly arranged albums on the one hand and live performances, replicating the luxuriant sound of the albums, as far as possible, in a trio context, on the other – really began during the 1990s, with a series of solo albums on Tara, produced by Shaun Davey: *Out To An Other Side* (1993), *The Given Note* (1995) and *The Piper's Call* (1998). Along with traditional material, the albums would include some of Shaun's music for Trevor Nunn's Royal Shakespeare Company stage productions:

Shaun (1995): I put my heart and soul into something, whether it's ephemeral [like theatre music] or not; otherwise, the whole thing is pointless … Some things are going to have an extended life and other things are not. The very good tunes I think it is possible to have recorded. For example, the big tune in *The Winter's Tale* RSC 1992 production Liam took for *Out To An Other Side*. It's a grand tune and it actually has, funnily enough, been recorded by at least two other artists [since]. Similarly, Liam has taken the main theme from [1995's] RSC production of *Romeo And Juliet* to record for [*The Given Note*].

The quality of Shaun's material, alongside his skills as an arranger and producer, contributed hugely to the longevity of Liam's albums for Tara. I recall once meeting Liam by chance at a bar in Donegal, where the notion of a solo 'best of' was on his mind. I mentioned it, as Liam had suggested, to John Cook, but he was having none of it: a 'best of' would immediately mean the rest of an artist's catalogue becoming redundant to retailers. While Tara has become semi-dormant as an originating label in recent years, as music retail outlets have all but disappeared, it remains pro-active in keeping existing catalogue available online. The 1990s works of Liam O'Flynn, now including a period video release of *The Piper's Call* band upgraded to DVD, are consequently enjoying the same 'long tail' as the works of Shaun Davey.

In 2003, *The Poet & The Piper*, released on Claddagh, saw a smaller-scale collaborative recording between Nobel Laureate Séamus Heaney and Liam, with a version of his live trio (Steve Cooney and Rod McVey). Since then, Liam has contributed to two further orchestrated Shaun Davey albums, both on Tara: *May We Never Have To Say Goodbye* (2006), mopping up several of Shaun's hitherto unrecorded pieces; and *Voices From The Merry Cemetery* (2010), a suite inspired by Romanian grave inscriptions.

There have, since the mid-80s, been numerous guest and session appearances on a remarkable array of albums, from Kate Bush to a Led Zeppelin symphonic tribute by a man from Killing Joke via Mike Oldfield, Elmer Bernstein, Sinéad O'Connor and The Everly Brothers.

There have also been a few appearances on 21st century albums by Andy Irvine, most recently Andy's CD/DVD release *70th Birthday Concert At Vicar Street 2012* (2014), performing with the band LAPD. Named, as Planxty almost was, after the initials of its members (Liam, Andy, Paddy Glackin and Dónal Lunny), LAPD was an occasional spin-off from the 2003–05 Planxty reunion, which had been somewhat happier than the 1979–83 comeback.* It was, in effect, a valedictory parade. This time, when Christy stopped, the job having been done and done well, the name wisely stopped with him.

---

* Planxty were almost called CLAD: Christy, Liam, Andy, Dónal.

LAPD was a happy solution to the three others wanting to keep playing, hampered only by Liam's desire by now not to tour abroad. Andy's birthday album would be its only record, for Liam decided to call it quits at the end of 2014. With the admirable pragmatism of a man who never tires of the road, and never runs out of people to join him on it, Andy (with Lunny and Glackin) recruited piper/flautist Michael McGoldrick and guitarist John Doyle:

Andy: When Christy decided he couldn't play with Planxty anymore, Dónal and I thought it a real shame to let the whole shooting gallery go down the drain. Dónal had been playing quite a lot with Paddy Glackin, and of course Liam and Paddy knew each other from way back. Dónal suggested the name LAPD, and we played, off and on, for a couple of years – festivals and biggish concerts. It was a great success, and we three were very sad when Liam decided to call it a day. I suggested John and Mike as replacements, as I had played a bit with John and [had] always admired Mike's playing. After numerous attempts at finding a name, we finally settled on Usher's Island, the name of a quay in Dublin. We played a couple of warm-up gigs in Ireland and then Celtic Connections in Glasgow [in January 2015]. The acclaim was very promising, and we hope for a rosy future.

At this stage in the game, Liam O'Flynn – now aged 70 and purportedly comfortably off – can pick and choose what he wants to do. He grew up learning from the best; he became one of the most prominent uilleann pipers of the 1970s; he brought the instrument into the orchestral world in a significant and thrilling way; and he has graced dozens of albums by artists far beyond Irish traditional music, aside from creating a body of solo work in the 1990s that will remain amongst the most sumptuous and polished settings for the instrument in an era that will come to be seen as the last hurrah for a well-funded record industry. The rustic solo instrument of the baroque era finally became, at the end of the 'rock era', the lead voice in a new kind of chamber music, however briefly. Liam O'Flynn's recorded works stand for themselves, and he can be assured of an audience wherever and whenever he chooses to perform. As he put it to Leagues O'Toole in *The Humours Of Planxty* (2006):

To this day when I'm on tour people continually come up and say that it was through Planxty that they were first introduced to Irish traditional music. Or that their first contact with uilleann pipes was through Planxty and it changed their life. To me, that's fantastic. That's the greatest reward any musician can be given …[61]

Chapter 5
Paddy Keenan: Rakish Paddy Blues

Paddy Keenan: In the beginning, it was my brother Johnny who put the whistle in my mouth and forced me to learn it. And he was like my dad – he probably got it from my dad – a fierce, tough tutor. He would use all sorts of methods to get you to play what he wanted to hear. If he hadn't have done that maybe I wouldn't have taken up the pipes. One day, when my dad returned from fishing – He caught me with his pipes. And I was terrified he'd be mad at me for having his pipes out – not that he was that rough with us. [But] in those days you wouldn't even give your pipes to another piper.

That reminds me of something in London, at 'A Sense Of Ireland' festival, when I handed my pipes to a curious young lad. He was of African origin. Some people were very hostile towards me later, not only for giving my pipes to someone else but giving them to a black lad. To me, this big festival thing was [supposed to be] an awareness of the Irish and their culture and their music and whatever else, but when I saw the reaction it really, really shocked me.

And there, in one illustration, is the essence of Paddy Keenan: scion of a proud family, pre-ordained keeper of the Traveller piping tradition, and in the end a truly free spirit – not in the sense of a catch-all description of the Travelling community ethos, but in a more specific way. Paddy Keenan is an individual, a one-off, with an inspirational, gentle soul. He's a mixture of Irish Traveller heritage and the values of the 1960s counter-culture. For a long time he wasn't so much a combination of these ideals as a conflict: 'I'm a Traveller – which I was very, very ashamed of years and years back, because it was like being black in Ireland.'

He does what he likes, when he likes, with whom he likes and with as little negative impact on the world around him as possible. 'I'm not a rock star, I'm a piper,' he quipped when I suggested that he would be, inconveniently, mobbed by fans directly after a 2014 gig in Belfast, a time he had reckoned suitable for an interview (albeit only if he felt like it). And yet, of course, the show ended and he was mobbed by fans, just like a rock star. For he is the closest thing Irish traditional music has to one. Everyone wants to shake Paddy Keenan's hand or pass him a jazz woodbine. It is the worst time and environment possible for an interview – and yet, after an hour of glad-handing and with the faithful milling around expectantly, hoping to take him off to a pub session, he can, instantly, apply total focus to the embattled interviewer's questions. His answers, during the 45 minutes of what he had said would be five, were almost all nuanced, sensitive and sometimes profound. He was in the moment, leaning in close to the microphone, while the event horizon of the crowd's plan for a late night's fun hovered a few feet away. Other people might grasp at the opportunity to feature in a book; Paddy Keenan doesn't really care. It holds no sway over him.* The sublime fiddle player Martin Hayes once told me, 'The muse has no interest in press cuttings.' Paddy Keenan is a man in constant search of that muse.

If you hire him for a concert, it might be the best thing you've ever heard … or it might, although this is much less likely now than was once the case, be a shambles. He does the unexpected. He wears a cowboy hat, all the time. He's never been much good at turning his genius into a career as big and as financially successful as it might have been. But then, if he could do that, he would lose his essence.

> I do excite myself with mistakes! For me, it's happening automatic – I sometimes don't know split seconds before what's coming next. I really need to find change, for me; I'm not trying to change Irish music. *Riverdance*, The Chieftains – they're all brilliant, and there's a reason why they should be there. They're creating work for the likes of me, for people who want to see the platform where it came from. I don't hate commercialism – because it helps people who are not so well known.

Solid people have solid careers; geniuses have lives that career all over the place but leave a monumental footprint of influence and affection in their wake. He is, in a way, a living last hurrah – or, at least, is perceived as such – for a lifestyle and spirit in music that we associate with the 1960s and 70s. Like most musical heroes of those times, his fame outstrips his wealth. He has, though, despite sceptical views on the pension prospects for Irish cultural ambassadors, no really obvious hang-ups around this dichotomy, which is probably as good a way as any of dealing with the ongoing weight of people's expectations: 'I'm really lucky and rich in health – in health!'

His slender discography notwithstanding, Paddy's impact in the piping world has been immense.

---

* Having said that, Paddy asked to see this chapter in draft form. He rephrased or removed very little of what he had said during the interview but, rather, expanded on a few points. He sought to change nothing of what I had written nor what any other interviewee had said.

John McSherry: I remember hearing The Bothy Band for the first time, on tape. I'd already been introduced to The Chieftains, The Fureys and Planxty, but this was something quite different: raw energy and power wrapped up with a great sensitivity. It was fresh and exciting. And, of course, Paddy was right at the centre. His piping was smooth, intricate, precise and full of soul. It drew me in. Whether in a band or [in a] solo setting, Paddy is always exciting to listen to. You never know what he's gonna do next.

Paddy's performances are capable of being as electrifying today as they were in the 70s, his 'moment' as a member of The Bothy Band. The key word is 'capable' – for, as many well-travelled anecdotes attest, there have oft been times when he wasn't. He admitted as much, and highlighted the consequences of being a larger-than-life figure, back in 1997, when we met during what was perceived as a comeback period, after some years spent trying to find something to do outside of music:

> I do have a bit of a reputation, I know. And the more you're known, of course, the bigger the reputation grows. If something happens, it might be minor, but by the time it gets back to you, it's huge! Here's an example: I was over in Los Angeles with Dolly Parton, Emmylou Harris and Linda Ronstadt, and when I came back, maybe six months later, this guy came up to me in the street and said, 'Hey, Paddy, is it true that when you were over with Dolly that you ran up and felt her boobs to see if they were real?' Another one was when this guy came to me and said:
> 'Hey, didn't we have a great time in Lisdoonvarna?'
> And I said, 'Well, I wasn't there …'
> 'Aww, you were – sure, we were drinking together!'
> 'Damn it, I wasn't there!'
> And you know something? The worst part of it was, when this guy was finished and I was blue in the face [from] saying I wasn't there, he walked away saying, 'Ah, well, you must have had a better time than I did if you can't remember it!' I mean, what can you do?

*

Paddy Keenan was born in 1950, to a Traveller family. Around 1956, the family settled in Ballyfermot, Dublin, near the Furey family – the two patriarchs, John Keenan senior and Ted Furey, being firm friends. John Keenan had also been a friend of the late Johnny Doran:

> Keenan subsequently was determined that he would have a piper in the

family, such was his infatuation with Doran. He designated Paddy as the piper, but Paddy readily admits that his brother Johnny was a better piper. The Doran mantle, however, fell to Paddy simply because Johnny was quicker on his feet getting out to play when not prepared to dedicate the time required to learn the intricacies of the instrument.[62]

Paddy was nine when his father decided that he was to become the keeper of the Doran flame. He was already schooled on tin whistle and had tinkered with other instruments.

> **Tomás Ó Canainn**: His father made him a bag, bellows and chanter and gave it to him one morning, saying: 'If you can play a tune when I come back tonight, I'll see what I can do about getting you the full set of pipes.' Paddy could play part of the reel 'Rakish Paddy' on the chanter that evening and his piping career started forthwith, under his father's tuition.[63]

Ó Canainn went on to quote at length, in *Traditional Music In Ireland* (1978), a neighbour of the family, John Connors, describing how uncompromising John Keenan's teaching regime was. It was a tough time, and molly-coddling was no friend of ambition:

> **Paddy**: I wouldn't like to magnify it out of proportion. My dad was a gifted musician, [a] multi-instrumentalist, who's responsible for a lot of young pipers today through tutoring or inspiring. They loved him for it. The one lad who'll come out and say that, and I'm really proud of this lad, is Martin Nolan from Dublin. He'll say, 'I learned everything I have from Johnny Keenan.'

According to Paddy, Finbar Furey (four years older) had moved in with the Keenans around 1961–62 and would stay for a few years, until Finbar and Eddie Furey made their fateful trip to Scotland in 1967. Finbar has a slightly different recollection:

> I didn't live with Paddy, Paddy didn't live with me. He lived about 300 yards up the road. It was sort of that we had two fathers and two mothers. My best friend, of all time, was Johnny Keenan, his brother – he was a month older than I was. Johnny was a great Travelling piper. To this day I've yet to meet his equal. He was incredible. Not just as a player but talking about it, understanding exactly what he's playing. Paddy is a

brilliant musician, but Johnny was something special. My father would have helped Johnny [senior] get the house in Ballyfermot when they moved there first. Mary [Keenan] was my mother's best friend. The two families were always locked together.

Paddy: Our house was called at one time Radio 116 Oranmore Road, because the music was going all through the night. There was the Sweeneys, the Ryans, some of the Fureys, and we'd be playing till school time in the morning. I'd have a plate of porridge, my mum would be doing my homework – that's how it was. And then, of course, the neighbours would sometimes complain about so many of us being in there playing. That's why I got into making elder reeds for the pipes, just to soften the sounds so we didn't bother the neighbours.

Fortuitously, there was an elder tree in the Keenans' garden. John senior had been as good as his word and had bought his son a set of pipes:

Paddy: I first had a John Clark set – and I never found much out about John Clark, I'd love to find out more. They were lovely pipes, very much like the Crowley pipes [I later acquired], so he was probably influenced by Crowley. I later got a full set of Rowsome pipes, when I was 12: 1962.

Curiously, John Keenan senior, who knew Leo Rowsome, never took Paddy to Leo's Pipers' Club; nor did he introduce his son to the great man. There were, though, a couple of Rowsome-related incidents during the period of Paddy's apprenticeship as a piper:

Paddy: My dad [had] me under pressure once to record for him a reel-to-reel tape. And he spent days with me to get, as he thought, the best. And this was his introduction of me to the Rowsome club, to the Pipers' Club in Thomas Street, in '64. I remember it well. I was 14. It was a tough thing to do, to sit in front of him and try to give him what he wanted – he was such a perfectionist. He wanted what he believed was going to impress those people, and eventually he did. He brought the tape in and gave it to Leo – for Leo had been asking my dad to take me in one night. [Our neighbour] Johnny Connors, actually, was with him. He was husband of Johnny Doran's sister, he used to bottle for Johnny Doran when busking; he also played the whistle.

So he brought the tape to Leo Rowsome and all the students were coming in – like, Garech de Brún was there, Paddy Moloney, Peter Browne, maybe Ronan Browne, probably Brendan Behan and Maggie Barry and all those old characters were there. Rowsome put it on, it's playing, he's listening to it, the students are saying, 'Leo, who's that?' And Leo goes quiet and says nothing. After a while he finished the tape – which my dad was over the moon with, that he'd even listened to the whole thing – and he turned round to his students and said, 'That's this man's son, and I haven't heard piping like this since the late, great Johnny Doran.'

But do you know what the weird thing was? Sometime later, many years later, in the 90s, in Belgium with Peter Browne and Mícheál [Ó Domhnaill] we did this benefit for the relatives of the Omagh bombing victims. And during my time there I mentioned this thing happening and I'm thinking to myself, 'Shit! Did that really happen? Did Rowsome *really* say that?' So I spoke to Peter and he said to me, 'Paddy, I remember that well. I was one of the students. But here's the thing: when your dad and John Connors went out of the room and down the stairs, someone said: 'Isn't that amazing? There's two Travellers who have a tape recorder…' which many settled people couldn't afford. 'And not only that, but they have recordings of Johnny Doran that we never knew existed …' Now, if my dad had heard that, he'd have been over the moon! But at the same time he'd be pissed that they didn't believe him!

Garech de Brún, one of Leo's students, had been born (in 1939) into the Lordship of Oranmore, and would marry into the wealthy Guinness family.[*] A devotee of traditional music, he had co-founded Claddagh Records in 1959, specifically to record Leo Rowsome. By the mid-60s, the business had Dublin retail outlets – one of which, in Capel Street, would be significant in the Paddy Keenan story:

> **Paddy**: Walking up Capel Street one day, I saw these pipes hanging on the wall inside the shop. My dad and I went into the shop to inquire. The guy took the pipes off the wall, I put them on and said to my dad, 'I like them'. After battling for a while, my dad said, 'I'll get them for you'. But he had no money. He wasn't working at the time, he was on the dole. The following morning my dad was at the door before opening! Went into the shop. He wasn't too sure they were for sale. It was a record outlet. My dad's there first

---

[*] The death in 1966 of Garech's brother, Tara Browne, in London partly inspired The Beatles' 'A Day In The Life'.

thing, goes inside and the man's there on the phone talking to someone who we later found out to be no other than Garech de Brún and he's going:

'But the gentleman's here … he wants to buy the pipes …'

I didn't know who he was talking to, but of course Garech is going, 'The pipes are not for sale!' They were only on display.

Meanwhile the shopkeeper and my dad are whispering with the phone cupped in hand:

'Well,' my dad said, 'it's surely better to have someone play them? And not only that, didn't I leave a deposit yesterday?'

Garech supposedly asked, 'Well, does he *play* the pipes?'

The shopkeeper says, 'I don't know, but his son is making reasonable sounds with them….'

'Okay,' says Garech. 'Sixty pounds.'

John Keenan's chutzpah had gained his son a set of pipes from the renowned Crowley brothers, of Cork, which had been made for Garech himself.[*] Paddy retained the chanter from his Rowsome set, preferring its sound, and this would be the set he would use for the remainder of the 20th century, before commissioning Dave Williams to make him a new set modelled exactly on the Crowley set. The acquisition of the Crowley pipes probably happened around 1966, when the Keenan family's circumstances changed:

> **Paddy**: My dad had left the house after we'd been there for maybe 10 years. We moved in when I was six, he moved out when I was 16. So we moved out to the side of the road, Ring Road – my dad had a bought new van. He'd had an accident at a job, got some money out of it – back then £1,500 was like a million today, and he did well with it. He bought a new bus, started really seriously working, on a new business, with John Connors, and they made a great living out of it. But he was too generous. He was giving away and giving away. Whatever he had, he'd be helping people. After some couple of years in our barrelled tops, square tops, etcetera, we moved into the first settlement ever for Travelling people. It was a chalet, a one room prefab, one big room, a toilet and a Belfast sink! They christened the site St. Labre Park.

---

[*] Tadhg Crowley (1899–52), with his brother Denis (1908–66), came from a war piping/pipe band background before developing an interest in uilleann piping. Tadhg established the pipe making business in Cork in the late 1920s.

In 1967, aged 17, Paddy finally rebelled against the expectations that had been placed on him (and, as with most teenagers, the strictures of his parents) and went to London:

> I really wasn't interested in Irish music in the late 60s. I left home at about 17 and my father was very strict about music, especially the fact that I was a piper and I believe now that he wanted to mould me as the piper of the future. I loved the pipes in the beginning, then rebelled and ran away. So I wasn't in touch with Irish music for a while. I actually went off the pipes altogether. I fell in love with the blues and for next three years I spent my time back and forth on the B&I ferry from Dublin to Liverpool and hitching to London. I tried to pawn my pipes in London and went as low as a half crown at the time: they wouldn't take them. I just couldn't get rid of them – they are Irish uilleann pipes, once owned by the honourable Garech de Brún! In the end I got so frustrated I dumped them in a trash-can outside a pawn shop!*
>
> I was playing more guitar at the time, and harmonica and singing – I was making a living busking. Then about two years later a friend of mine wrote to John Lennon. She was a singer-songwriter, married to Grattan Puxon, who is now president of the World Gypsy Council. She knew of The Beatles' search for new instrumentation – she saw this as a way not only to get me back on the pipes, but also a positive way to save a dying instrument, even at home in Ireland! It was on the way out, really, 'cept for a handful of pipers in Dublin, and of course the few younger students, under the tuition of the great Leo Rowsome. The Beatles were recording their final LPs and were all looking for new instruments, new religion, new whatever. [So] Venice Manley, wife of Grattan, wrote to John Lennon: 'I've got this friend who plays a very unusual instrument and he's the top guy at it', and so on.
>
> I was to go to [Grattan's house at] 14 Princes Ave, Finchley, to stay over and meet John next morning, show him the Irish pipes. But I was a Pavee, hippying around London, having a great time and was very reluctant to meet him. I went to Grattan's house and stayed over along with my hippy girlfriend. I swear to God I was kind of embarrassed about going to meet John Lennon, being a Pavee and with my pipes that had been out of action for a couple years. I chickened out! Left early next morning to where I'd been staying – 144 Piccadilly, a commune that became quite famous in later years.

---

* As Paddy explained in the notes to *The Long Grazing Acre* (Hot Conya, 2002), a friend retrieved them and kept them safe until his world view changed.

After three years I did take out the pipes, took them into St James' Park, and after a while tuning them up a crowd of people gathered round me, throwing money in the box. I thought, 'God, what have I been thinking?' I later found out that around that time John and Yoko were taking an interest in the Traveller caravan schools, known as Romano Drom Schools. They paid for one out at Dunstable (later moved to Barking). If I'd known this back then, I may not have been so insecure!

During the mid-60s Paddy had been playing with his father (pipes), brother Johnny (banjo) and others, including Liam Weldon (vocals) and George Furey (guitar), in The Pavees. This continued whenever he was home from London during 1967–69 and into the 70s. Several reels of tape privately recorded in Dublin during November and December 1967 by Alan MacWeeney, in domestic settings, are preserved at the Irish Traditional Music Archive (ITMA), featuring Paddy playing pipes with his father and in combinations including his brother Johnny and Liam Weldon. Similarly, amateur recordings of The Pavees proper, at Slattery's on Capel Street during 1968–69, all involving Paddy on pipes, are also preserved at ITMA, as is a Radio Éireann concert recording made at O'Connell's Hall, Dublin, on November 22 1969.*

> **Paddy**: For years we played together, and actually did some professional recordings for an Irish-American company, but they were never released. They're still there waiting for my 'okay', so you never know. Liam Weldon was one of the first members of the band, himself and Johnny Flood. That went on for a couple years. Later, my dad decided to join in. We played mostly local. The instrumentation was pipes, banjo, fiddle, mandolin, guitar and vocals.

Putting guitars as an accompaniment to uilleann pipes was still a novelty, with only the Furey brothers and The Pavees known to have been doing so during the 1960s. The guitar was the instrument of the present, and Paddy, culturally, was immersed in that present, much to the potential embarrassment of his father:

> **Paddy**: I'd just come back from London. … And my dad actually passed me

---

* The line-up on the RÉ recording is: John Keenan (pipes), Paddy Keenan (pipes), Johnny Keenan (banjo), Mick Moriarty (flute, vocals), Liam Weldon (vocals) and George Furey (guitar). Guitarist/vocalist Johnny Flood had previously been a member of the band and is present on one of the 1968 Slattery's recordings. A handful of undated photos at ITMA, taken at the Slattery's club by organiser Chris Corlett, add Paul Furey to the Pavees' fluid line-up.

walking down the street with Leo Rowsome, myself and my brother. I had a top hat and an old leather case for the top hat – I used to sit on it when I was busking in subways in London, with a guitar. So I'm walking with that, with pink cords, top hat, hair to my arse, possibly barefoot or colourfully shod? Of course, he didn't want to introduce me to Leo Rowsome like that. So he passed us in the street! We passed him out of respect as well, cos we knew … I remember sometime later at the door of Matt Kiernan's house – I was having some repairs done on my pipes, my dad arrived the same day – Matt came to the door: 'Hi Mr Keenan!' 'Hello Matt! And what do you think of that?' Pointing at me, in more or less the same gear! 'Well John, I don't know anyone more entitled to wear tails than your son.'

Paddy did, however, meet Willie Clancy. Once again, John Keenan wanted to show his son off to one of the greats of the older generation:

Paddy: I was up the canal line with my 60s long hair, drinking a few beers with the lads, and one of the kids came up and says, 'Daddy wants you, there's people there to see you …' I was 18. I wandered down and it was Willie Clancy and Martin Talty. I had always been used to people calling, to hear the family play. As I said before, the house in Ballyer was Christened 116 Radio Oranmore Road! There were people like John Molloy along with other actors and musicians from the Gaiety Theatre, the Irish Life, etcetera. I played a few tunes and they seemed to like it very much! I was 18, I was shy and I'd had a couple of beers, but I did what I could to please my dad, with offering a little of myself. Even though I was that age, I still had this thing of using music to present myself. Cos being a Traveller, having lived all those years in a house, being made feel a lower class by the not so well off, as one can read in *Angela's Ashes* for that matter, insecurities [of] feeling inadequate towards the educated and stuff like that – at the time I would keep my mouth closed and the music was my language, really. So that may be the reason I experiment and move around so much with music.

*

At some point in 1970 Paddy returned to Dublin, fully re-engaged with his pipes, and set about the path that would lead, by 1975, to The Bothy Band. As he looks back on it: 'I came back to Ireland and got together with Tríona and Mícheál [Ó Domhnaill] and then Tony MacMahon and Paddy Glackin, and that was the beginning of The Bothy Band.' But it was, naturally, rather more circuitous than that. The people

Paddy mentioned above came together in 1974 in a seven-piece grouping known as Seachtar (of which, seemingly, no recordings survive), but there had been a kind of false start even before that:

> **Paddy**: In 1969 or 1970, Tony MacMahon asked me if I'd like to join a band called 1691 with Peter Browne, Matt Molloy, Tommy Peoples – most of the people who ended up in The Bothy Band, actually!* I remember touring with Mícheál Ó Domhnaill and Mick Hanly around that time. They were playing in Brittany in 1972. Liam Weldon had asked if I would come to Brittany to stand in for Peter Browne, so I went along but Peter arrived some days later so I never did play with 1691. Mícheál and Mick were starting a month long tour around Brittany at this time, and I'd decided to hang around with them for a month. And I suppose that's where I got to know Mícheál. After returning to Ireland we played a while, with Paddy Glackin, Tony MacMahon and Tríona. Soon after came the name Seachtar and, later, The Bothy Band.

Even at that time, there was occasional Pavees activity.† By 1974, though, the two focuses of Paddy's attention were Seachtar and the opportunity of a solo album with Gael Linn. The album, Paddy Keenan, was solo by credit and features some purely solo piping, although Paddy opted for sonic variety by involving his brothers John and Thomas, on banjo and whistle respectively, and Paddy Glackin on fiddle. Séamus Ennis provided a fulsome sleeve note, comparing Paddy's style and repertoire often and favourably with Johnny Doran, whom he had known. The album remains a cornerstone in Paddy's slim discography.‡

---

* The band 1691 (or Sixteen Ninety-One) made one LP, issued only in France: *Irish Folk Songs* (Arfolk, 1973). The personnel: Tríona Ní Dhomhnaill, Matt Molloy, Tommy Peoples, Liam Weldon and piper Peter Browne.

† There is one stray 1972 amateur recording of The Pavees at Slattery's held at ITMA, along with a January 1971 domestic recording by Alan MacWeeney of four of the members (Paddy and Johnny Keenan, Liam Weldon and Mick Moriarty).

‡ Paddy's discography was unwantedly expanded in 1974, in the wake of his solo album, as he explains: 'I'd recorded an album a year or two before [the solo album] with a skiffle band who were busking around Grafton Street. They called themselves The Blacksmiths, because we couldn't think of a better name in the studio … [It's not a lost gem], it's a load of crap! The guy who had us do it was a freelance producer and we'd signed a contract for one album, and he went on and sold it to EMI. I released [the] solo album of piping on Gael Linn in 1974, that got great reviews, and then of course EMI brought out *The Blacksmiths Featuring Paddy Keenan*, which was terrible. But I was having a load of fun drinking, playing, having a great life, and in fact that's really the way it continued with The Bothy Band. We were having such a great time, we didn't think enough about money.'

While the album was almost entirely traditional in content, Paddy had still debuted one of his own compositions, 'Paddy Keenan's Jig'. 'Far be it from me to praise or criticise it as a piece,' wrote Ennis, 'but that I like it very much.'[64]

Nevertheless, Paddy's immediate future lay in a group setting. Seachtar, sponsored by Diane Hamilton, also featured Paddy Glackin (fiddle), siblings Mícheál Ó Domhnaill and Tríona Ní Dhomhnaill (guitar/vocals and clavichord/vocals, respectively), Roscommon's Matt Molloy (flute), Clare's Tony MacMahon (accordion) and Planxty veteran Dónal Lunny (bouzouki).

> **Tríona**: Mícheál was the one who enticed Paddy into the band, and it was a really big thing, from the Travellers. Mícheál went out to Ballyfermot and officially asked John Keenan – like asking for his hand in marriage – could we spirit Paddy away to join us, settled people, in the band. That had to be done. They sat down and talked, and he convinced John. It was unheard of at the time. We were lucky to get Paddy on board. We took the risk because we didn't doubt it for a moment. The music was so strong and so special. There were certain moments where you almost levitated.

Mícheál Ó Domhnaill had recently worked as a collector for the Irish Folklore Commission, as Séamus Ennis had 30 years earlier, and had recorded an Irish language album for Gael Linn with the Pentangle-influenced Skara Brae in 1971. From Seachtar initially getting together loosely to play at a week of Gael Linn 21st anniversary events, things took on a momentum of their own:

> **Mícheál**: Interest in the band was immediate, and things began to escalate. It was at the back of our minds to become full-timers, but the commitment was slow in coming because nobody wanted to leave what they were doing already. I was with RTÉ and so was Tony, who was very much tied to his production work. Tommy was doing craft work down in Clare, Matt worked for Aer Lingus, Dónal was producing and Tríona was working in a shop.[65]

> **Tríona**: Tony McMahon encouraged me to phone around: 'Where, this weekend, could we do a small gig and meet other musicians?' I organised a few like that, like in Clare. It was [for] whatever we took on the door. I'd get in touch with somebody who was good at making tea and sandwiches, and we'd invite the audience afterwards to stay for a chat and then, of course, repair to the pub with the [local musicians]. Of all of us, I think it was Matt who had the most to consider, with his job. The rest of us were just surviving on air!

When it came to the crunch, Paddy Glackin opted to marry a succession of day jobs (with RTÉ and the Irish Arts Council) with recording and performing opportunities on his own terms. Tony MacMahon, similarly, prioritised his RTÉ job; indeed, he initiated the series The Long Note – a radio programme for which Paddy Keenan was recorded performing solo, in Slattery's, in November 1974, promoting the solo album.

Thus, seven became five. Donegal fiddler Tommy Peoples came on board and five became six. With Seachtar translating as 'the seven', the name had to change. Sé being Irish for five, and both incomprehensible and unpronounceable to non-Irish speakers, it was surely wise to seek an English name if the band aspiration was to take their music beyond Ireland (and it was). 'The Bothy Band', as a name, referenced informal gatherings of musicians in rural Scottish communities, a bothy being a cottage in which such sessions might happen. It captured something of the spirit of this particular gathering of earthy, tradition-hardened warriors. For Matt Molloy, looking back, none was earthier than Paddy Keenan:

> **Matt**: What a great player, an earthy player! Even if you'd never heard or understood Irish music and you heard Keenan on a hot night, you knew there was something special happening. He had that power! He could be temperamental at times and the music would be okay, but on a night when the stars aligned and Keenan bag, bellows, chanter, drones and regulators immersed into one … magic happened! He was a force to be reckoned with, a powerhouse player. Music coming from the soil in the great Travelling piping tradition … An earthy, passionate player who had learned from the playing of those masters [the Cashes and the Dorans] and made it his own. He took no prisoners. *We* took no prisoners. Everybody just got fired up! They were some of the nights I remember.

The Bothy Band, sometimes known as 1975, was recorded in Dublin in October 1975 and released on Mulligan Records before the year's end. It was the second release on a label newly established by Dónal Lunny with business partner Séamus O'Neill. Throughout the band's life, Dónal would give close involvement, as player or producer, to many of the records by other artists on the label. In November, The Bothy Band took the plunge and became professionals.

> **Matt**: I got leave of absence [from my job]. The group was very powerful. We gelled very well, in spite of all the pundits and critics who said it was going to blow apart at any given moment. It lasted four or five years, though we never really got ourselves organised from a managerial point of view. We

were too busy having a good time. I was new to the whole thing, fresh out of a secure, pensionable job, and I didn't know what hit me. I thought I was on permanent holidays for the first two years.[66]

In early April 1976, Polydor released the album in Britain and in France; the recently launched Green Linnet released it in America. The whole thing seemed to spiral within weeks. As Colin Irwin, at that time a staff writer at *Melody Maker*, would later recall:

[My] memory of their first British appearance is … vivid and treasured. It took place at Hammersmith Town Hall, and their impact was staggering – when they let rip, the effect was like being in a jet when it suddenly whipped into full throttle along the runway. I just couldn't believe the ferocity with which Paddy Keenan attacked the uilleann pipes … Tommy Peoples was equally startling. I've still never heard a fiddle performance like he played that night in Hammersmith: unorthodox, unpredictable and utterly breathtaking.[67]

That first appearance, along with a few dates at Irish clubs, took place in November 1975. On February 22 1976, the band headlined a concert, supported by Scottish 'revival singer' Ray Fisher, at the end of a week-long traditional music festival at Trinity College Dublin, Éigse na Tríonóide.* Earlier that week Paddy Keenan, along with Liam O'Flynn, played solo at a piping concert and lecture with Breandán Breathnach.

During March 1976 the group toured Britain seriously, returning for a handful of dates in mid-April. On March 9 they had recorded their first (of three) studio sessions for BBC Radio 1's John Peel. It was the start of a significant relationship with the BBC: there would be at least six broadcasts of exclusive session and concert material on BBC radio during 1976 alone.†

Tommy Peoples would not last long with the touring lifestyle. Nevertheless, for Paddy this line-up of The Bothy Band, with himself, Tommy and Matt as the front line, was the most special. Having said that, he never thought at the time that it was, or would become, the stuff of legend:

---

* Ray's husband, the High Level Ranters' piper Colin Ross, had given a talk on the Northumbrian pipes at the festival a couple of days earlier.
† The Bothy Band's BBC broadcasting history is detailed in the 'Discographies & Sessionographies' appendix.

Paddy: We didn't do harm to the musical root of the tunes. The lovely thing about it is it's very, very rare that you would get a collaboration of musicians – lead musicians – who could sit onstage and work off each other. It wasn't even work: we gelled in moods and answered and spoke to each other through the music onstage. You didn't have to listen to the musician beside you, because you knew for a fact that guy was capable of playing straight with you, staying with you. No matter what I did musically, Matt or the fiddle was there, giving me great confidence. And between the three of us we thought the same way – well, most of the time. So one never had to worry about, 'What should I do with this or that?', musically. You had the freedom to do what you wanted – and the three moods miraculously met. Well, you don't get that very often.

Matt: Tommy Peoples [on] one side of Paddy and I [on] the other, we just went for it – no quarter given or taken. Then you had the rolling thunder from Tríona, Mícheál and Dónal's mesmeric accompaniment. Though accompaniment is the wrong word – it was integral to the music, it was different and unique at that time. It was new, and it appealed to a younger audience who would not normally have listened to traditional music. That was The Bothy Band.

The print media in Britain were as responsive as the BBC. With promotion by Polydor, the group was afforded substantial coverage during that first 1976 tour in both *NME* and *Melody Maker*, from Fred Dellar and Colin Irwin, respectively.* Fred Dellar's piece, published in April, put their rapid rise in context:

> For some considerable time now, a new "underground" music situation has been developing. Not one concerned with any aspect of rock, but rather one that's found its way into this country via such Guinness-stained record labels as Gael-Linn, Claddagh, Mulligan and Tara.
>
> There's always been a fair sized market for Irish traditional music here, and in recent years bands like Planxty have acquainted us with a whole range of Shamrock-tinted jigs, reels and beautiful slow airs – while fringe benefit units such as Horslips and Spud have also played their part.
>
> But the real breakthrough has been a long time coming, witness the years it's taken for The Chieftains to be accepted as a major band.

---

* Colin Irwin's piece, from *Melody Maker* (May 1 1976), is reproduced at the end of this book by kind permission.

And though Paddy Maloney and his minstrels have managed to reach a wide public through a couple of enterprising record and film deals, plus some prestigious concerts, general acceptance of Irish music in its traditional form still has some way to go.

However, there's no doubt that the audience is steadily growing and the current tour of The Bothy Band must be adding converts by the hundred if the scenes at some of their concerts are anything to judge by.[68]

Tellingly, Dellar observed (during his interview with Mícheál and Dónal) that 'the remarkable Paddy Keenan … plays pipes with the kind of dexterity John McLaughlin demonstrates on guitar.' Too often and too easily, pipers are referred to as 'the Jimi Hendrix' of their instrument.* But the comparison between Paddy Keenan and John McLaughlin, at that time at the pinnacle of his art in The Mahavishnu Orchestra, visiting worlds of rhythm and mood with virtuosity beyond mere speed for the sake of 'flash', was more apposite. There was, and has remained, great subtlety and sensitivity in Paddy's playing, as well as huge rhythmic complexity and improvisational brilliance made to sound effortless. Dónal agreed with Dellar's observation:

> Yes – his style is full of fast playing. But though it sounds very wild, everything is totally controlled. Paddy nearly gets to the brink with his improvisations, but he never quite crosses it because he's always thinking about one-eighth of a second ahead. The skill is in retaining the character of a tune throughout such an improvisation.
>
> Some players will play a tune a customary couple of times and leave it at that, but there are other musicians, such as Paddy, who can take a melody and play a reel five or six times, embellishing it differently on each occasion. But the thread must never be lost, the tune must always survive the embellishments, as far as we're concerned.[69]

Being perceived ever since as a speed merchant, like a gunslinger riding into town, makes Paddy a magnet for young guns, which can be somewhat wearying:

Paddy: Some of the young kids today believe, as it was with Finbar, [that they should play fast] 'because I can'. And in the end they couldn't. Because

---

* Dónal Lunny referred to Paddy Keenan in this way in at least one interview during the band's tenure. Finbar Furey would earn the comparison before him, John McSherry has earned it after. See the chapter on Johnny Doran.

there's very few people who can do that, very few people who can play at record speed and hold the tune. And I've had competition people competing with me in that [in sessions], and I could see that they would even split a phrase of the tune to pass me! It was a really highly competitive thing. I'm thinking, 'This isn't fucking music – it's a race!'

Whenever I play fast, you'll find that the tune is held onto – nothing is lost from the tune. Everything is happening faster in my head, so you'll get a very different representation of me, simply because it's happening faster. If I'm playing at normal speed, normal rhythm – and my rhythm is a very new thing; before that, it was a mood, like [Clare fiddle maestro] Martin Hayes. Martin doesn't play rhythm, he plays mood – not to say that he cannot play rhythm – and that's why [his accompanist] Dennis Cahill has to be very sparse so as not to interfere with Martin's mood, as opposed to rhythm. If you were to play a straightforward rhythm with Martin Hayes, you'd ruin him – and it's the same here [with me]. But then, if you're playing with people, they can't climb inside your mind and find out what you're going to do next, because you don't know yourself, for that matter.

The decades during which Paddy Keenan could explore mood and subtlety, after the fiery music of those early Bothy Band days, lay ahead. Back in 1976, that first Bothy Band album appeared to lay down a gauntlet. The members, though, were thinking of reining it in a little for their next record, as Dónal Lunny mused at the time:

> We produced *The Bothy Band* album together – but if we did it again tomorrow, it would turn out very different. It wouldn't be so frantic. It's all very high-pressure, and not really balanced from a material point of view. Ninety per cent of it goes at 90 miles an hour. But we'll just have to take the long view and temper things with the second album, which we'll probably do around May or June.[70]

Shortly after those aspirations were expressed, something happened that would ensure the next record really would sound different. The Inverness Folk Festival show on April 18 was to prove Tommy Peoples' last with the band.[*]

Colin Irwin: Kevin Burke slotted in smoothly in his place, though his

---

[*] Presumably the one scheduled show after this – at Dingwall's, London – was cancelled.

inclusion gave them a softer, more mellow approach, which pleased as many as it disappointed. Initially, their second album *Old Hag You Have Killed Me* seemed weaker as a result, though it stands up well in retrospect … The stage favourite 'Fionnghuala', a nonsensical burst of Scots Gaelic mouth music, even momentarily threatened to be a hit single.[71]

*

Kevin Burke was born and raised in London, and had been brought up with a European art music education and a fondness for the London-Irish music scene. Having debuted dazzlingly on record, through a chance meeting with Arlo Guthrie in 1973, he had then played in a band called Lazy Reel in England before drifting into Christy Moore's loosely organised road band in Ireland, which occasionally included Dónal Lunny. Kevin and Dónal had also both played on the Pumpkinhead LP, which had launched the Mulligan label. Being influenced by the Sligo fiddle tradition and having had formal training, Kevin certainly had a slinkier, more lyrical style and a sweeter sound than Tommy's visceral Donegal tones.

> **Matt**: Kevin was a great addition – a laid-back, easygoing character with a lovely, lilting Sligo style. I particularly liked his style, influenced like myself by the great Sligo fiddle players, especially Paddy Killoran who was a family friend. But make no mistake, when the fire was up, Kevin was in there to be reckoned with. A great, talented player and a gentleman!

> **Kevin**: There was no animosity to me in the band about taking [Tommy's] position, but I don't think that was the public perception. I think people felt it was much more hostile than it really was. I heard rumours that Matt had said, 'Well, I'll play with Kevin Burke, but don't expect me to talk to him.' But it was actually Matt who came round to ask me to join!

As Kevin admitted a couple of years in: 'I was a bit nervous about it, because I was a real fan of the band, and then I thought, 'Jesus, it's just a matter of playing the bloody tunes as I thought best,' and after about three days it was mighty.'[72]

The band was back in Britain for three folk festivals in late July and early August: Cambridge, Sidmouth (their set recorded for Radio 2) and Durham. Before those shows, on July 15, there was a BBC Radio 1 concert broadcast from the Paris Theatre, London, revealing six sets of tunes and songs that would appear on the second album, Old Hag You Have Killed Me – which was itself recorded that same month at Rockfield Studios in Wales. It was a productive time. Peter Browne was filling in on pipes for Paddy at the Paris Theatre concert, though Paddy would be back for the Festival shows.*

Shortly after this, the band embarked on what would be their only tour of America:

Tríona: It was great. It was organised by a friend of Matt's, Mick Casey, who probably said, 'If you were to come out, I'm sure I could get you a few gigs.' We began in the States in, I think, Chicago, and then New York and then into Canada. I think we played a university in New York. [But] it was [mostly] to Irish-American audiences.

Paddy: We visited St Paul and worked up to Montreal with a major concert in Chicago, some members of the band staying with the then 17-year-old Michael Flatley – I think his dad may have had something to do with the gig. If I remember rightly, we did a house concert where there were people hanging from the rafters, or so it seemed. That venue later became known as the Ark Theater [Ann Arbor, Michigan].

On reflection, Kevin Burke has more a sobering view of both the American expedition and the band's free-and-easy approach in general. He also had a canny instinct that there was a potentially great untapped market:

Kevin: At the time I just went along with what was going. I didn't really feel there was a proper direction – we just went along with whatever presented itself. That was part of the problem. There was no one to steer us. We had a couple of people who gave us great advice. But we didn't take it!

[The American tour] was very, very amateurish. We used a friend of Matt's, a really great guy, but he didn't know the music business at all. We were playing, say, St Mary's Church Hall, organised by St Patrick's Hurling Club, and stuff like this. If we'd had someone more established, we'd have been playing different venues and thinking in terms of a second tour.

I had played in America previously with Arlo Guthrie, and I met a bunch of American musicians, saw what they did with their folk music – what the Byrds did, what Ry Cooder did, what Arlo did. The folk music was altered to contain contemporary sounds. And I remember thinking at the time, 'I wonder if there would ever be an Irish band to do that?' And then, of course,

---

* Kevin Burke: 'There was a period where Paddy had hurt his ankle, and there was another time he'd hurt his wrist, and both of those injuries knocked him out for a while. Peter was the natural choice to fill in.' Paddy believes he had hurt his hand on this occasion.

five or six years later, there am I, doing exactly that. When I was over that first time, I was amazed on two levels: one, I was amazed that these people seemed to have no idea that this kind of music even existed. Irish music to most of them was The Clancy Brothers; they had no idea of the instrumental tradition – outside of the Irish communities, the American version of Kilburn. There seemed to be no knowledge of it even among bluegrass players. My other amazement was how much people seemed to enjoy it when I played, even though they'd never heard it before. I was convinced American people would really enjoy Irish music if they only got to hear it.

Old Hag You Have Killed Me would be released in the UK in November 1976. The group had headlined at the Queen Elizabeth Hall in September, supported by Paul Brady.[*] They were back for a full tour spanning mid-October to at least December 12 (a show at the Shaftesbury Theatre), recording two more BBC radio sessions on the trip. A week before the tour, Matt Molloy had performed at a Comhaltas Ceoltóirí Éireann silver jubilee concert at the Royal Albert Hall. This was all a long way from the boozy back rooms of pubs.

A single with, unusually, both the arresting close-harmony 'Fionnghuala' and the 'Music In The Glen' tune set on the A-side was released on Polydor on November 26. It would be a few years yet before a Gaelic hit single in Britain.[†]

Where The Bothy Band had been gritty and straight-ahead, Old Hag had seen greater thought go into the arrangements and production values, with greater variety of mood and dynamics throughout. Mícheál's Gaelic song 'Farewell To Erin', backed with great sensitivity by all concerned, was a masterpiece. Elsewhere, there was plenty for fans of Paddy Keenan's piping to savour.

The Bothy Band had made remarkable progress in their first year. To an extent, they must have been pushing at an open door – a question of the timing being right for a predominantly instrumental band playing Irish music to excite the British media so much and to gain such traction as performers, moving from clubs to concert venues within the year. Nevertheless, the impression is sometimes given, with the broad brush-stroking of hindsight, that The Bothy Band swept all before them. This wasn't the case: they would always, certainly in Britain, be less successful (and viewed as less successful) than The Chieftains.

---

[*] Brady's first solo LP, *Welcome Here Kind Stranger*, had been produced by Dónal Lunny and would be released on Mulligan the following month. How Dónal was managing to be apparently everywhere at once remains a mystery, but the recorded history of Irish music is surely the better for it.

[†] Clannad's 'Theme To Harry's Game', 1982.

One snapshot, however imperfect, of the way things were is found in the results of *Melody Maker*'s first 'Folk Poll' at the end of the year, with The Bothy Band third in the 'instrumental band' category behind The Chieftains and Scottish band Five Hand Reel. While The Bothy Band are surely more influential today on other musicians than either of these, at the time they were still in the 'fast rising' or 'almost breaking through' stage. The trouble was, they would never quite get beyond it.

> **Kevin**: We were never comfortable with any of the managers or agents we worked with. … [But] we managed *ourselves* very badly, it's not simply that the managers or agents were at fault. At that time we were an anti-capitalist group of people, just like every other person wearing jeans and playing music. And yet we wanted to enjoy the fruits of capitalism!

There was a feeling in those days, however true, that the international market for Irish music groups could only sustain two or three at any time. In Britain, 1977 would be a breakthrough year for Galway instrumental group De Danann and Donegal vocal/instrumental group Clannad. It was perceived that they were after The Bothy Band's market. Still, as Colin Irwin observed in *Melody Maker*:

> The rise in popularity of De Danann over here is likely to be less spectacular than that of The Bothy Band, in that they don't have quite the same sense of drama or immediacy. For one thing they don't have a piper.[73]

*

In February 1977, The Bothy Band played at an exciting new venue on London's Kilburn High Road: the National Club, run by Kevin Flynn. Gabriel McKeon, future head of Na Píobairí Uilleann, then a London-based solo piping sensation, was one of several support acts. The venue would feature in the group's itineraries thereafter. In *Melody Maker*, this first performance was judged 'an unqualified success both commercially and artistically, for despite the absence of Tríona Ní Dhomhnaill, due to the death of her father, the Bothies played exceptionally well, returning to top form after the marginal disappointment of the Shaftesbury Theatre concert in December.'[74]

The group headed off to Germany and worked extensively in Europe for the next few months. One press report in May promised possible British dates in late summer, also revealing that work was soon to begin on filming a Bothy Band documentary for the BBC's Omnibus strand. It was to be a project of much gestation.

Come June, the group were among a dazzling line-up of mostly British and Irish artists at a week-long Dutch Festival, 'Rotterdam Folk '77'.* They had played the event's predecessor (specifically then a 'Celtic' festival) the previous year, alongside a possibly unique European appearance by Séamus Ennis. On this second occasion they shared a concert with English unaccompanied vocal group (and 60s legends reunited) The Watersons and the duo Andy Irvine & Paul Brady. For *Melody Maker*'s Colin Irwin, it was 'the most magical event of the week'.[75]

July 12 saw a return to the National, on a bill that included Midnight Well and, once again, Gabriel McKeon. 'The Bothy Band brought the evening to a fitting climax with a rousing performance,' wrote Mary Hardy in Folk News. 'They also managed to completely silence the [very noisy] audience, no mean achievement.'[76] A few days later, in and around working on a third album, they were back in Dublin for a week-long festival of Irish music, playing at Liberty Hall with special guest Séamus Ennis. A couple of weeks after that, it was off to Sligo for the first 'Boys Of Ballisodare' Festival, a new event run by Kevin Flynn from the National Club which would, along with a similar festival at Lisdoonvarna, come to define this late 70s/early 80s boom era in Irish folk and traditional music. It was almost as if the youth culture and festival bug that had gripped England for a few years at the end of the 60s was arriving, 10 years later, in Ireland.†

The band returned to Holland on September 4 1977 for an Irish-themed festival in Leiden with The Boys Of The Lough, The Woods Band, Clannad, Liam O'Flynn and others. Back in England, late-night listeners to classical music station BBC Radio 3 might have been surprised to encounter a half-hour programme on The Bothy Band from Tony McAuley, who had produced a TV concert featuring the band for BBC Northern Ireland earlier in the year. Towards the end of 1977 they appeared

---

* The Rotterdam 1977 bill was a virtual Woodstock of the British Isles folk world: The Watersons, The Bothy Band, Fairport Convention, Five Hand Reel, The Battlefield Band, Martin Carthy & Dave Swarbrick, Andy Irvine & Paul Brady, The Tannahill Weavers, Albion Dance Band, Ralph McTell, June Tabor and more. Alan Stivell, from Brittany, seemed to be there representing the rest of Europe.

† Low-key folk festivals, of which Cambridge was one, had emerged in Britain early in the 60s, but I'm referring here to a more general explosion of music festivals between 1967 and 1970, culminating in the colossal third and final Isle of Wight Festival in 1970 (subject of Murray Lerner's epochal film *Message To Love*). The National Jazz & Blues Festival, beginning in 1961 in Richmond, then relocating to Windsor, Sunbury and Plumpton before moving to Reading in 1971 where it became the 'Reading Festival', was the template for all the late 60s English festivals. Mostly a rock and blues event by the late 60s, it gave platforms to a number of acoustic-based performers, including Pentangle, Donovan and Roy Harper. The Lisdoonvarna and Ballisodare Festivals were like an inversion of these: beginning as purely folk festivals but bringing a handful of rock acts onto the bills after a couple of years. By 1981, even Chuck Berry was playing Ballisodare.

on Broadsides on Harlech Television, serving Wales and the West Country, although they would be absent from the British touring scene in the latter half of the year. Still, if The Bothy Band were struggling financially, it wasn't for any lack of publicity.

Warning signs could be found in an interview Dónal gave in February 1978:

> We found all the business stuff completely overwhelming, simply because we weren't interested in it. We couldn't summon up the interest to organise the tours or make decisions about gigs. Two years ago, things were pretty frantic anyway. It was like … *frenzy*. Kevin's a much more laid-back person and a more laid-back player – I think his playing has become more positive, more aggressive since he's been in the band. …
>
> Essentially it's still about just playing an instrument, and you do it for enjoyment. Having to get up for soundchecks with a hangover and all the peripherals can be hard, but it's a question of self-discipline. You use up a lot of energy outside the gigs.[77]

The third album, *Out Of The Wind, Into The Sun*, had been released towards the end of 1977. In Britain, it would be promoted with a tour during February-March (coincidentally, at the same time that Liam O'Flynn was touring folk clubs), with Peter Browne standing in for Matt Molloy who was hospitalised with TB. Matt managed to recuperate enough to re-join the band for the tour climax at London's prestigious Rainbow Theatre. The Rainbow was a rock temple, and playing there represented a wider aspiration within the band to broaden their market. During his February '78 interview, Dónal had conceded as much:

> The policy of the whole band is not to stay in the confines of traditional circles. Personally I like aggressive music, I like a lot of rock music. I like to think that the same elements are contained in traditional music – it's just that a lot of … people don't bring it out. We're still playing pure music, but we're putting a lot of balls into it.

Dónal also revealed that the band had made a conscious decision to up their game as performers as well, with the addition of a light show and a synthesizer:

> We're pretty static on stage. Two years ago we were a non-show, it was just f****** music. But people like to see something visual. We're using lights to accentuate the subtleties of the music more and make things more memorable for people. We're not the sort to leap around on stage – I can't

see a time when Paddy leaps about with the pipes – there's plenty of leaping about after the show, though.[78]

Being back in Britain allowed for the opportunity to record another session for John Peel's Radio 1 show. This time, they featured two pieces from the new album but also a couple of items that indicated the constituent parts of the band: 'Lord Franklin', based on the 1970 Pentangle recording, would become Mícheál Ó Domhnaill's signature song, released on the album *Promenade* and as a single in 1979, both credited to himself and Kevin Burke as a duo (within the lifespan of The Bothy Band, with Tríona and Dónal also contributing); and 'O'Neill's March', which would feature on Poirt An Phíobaire, an album released by Paddy Keenan in 1983.

The solo and duo capacities within the band were, in a way, both an asset and a constant low-level tension: there was no reason people couldn't enjoy solo or duo recording opportunities outside the band while the band still remained the mothership, as had been the case with Pentangle;[*] but likewise there needed to be a clear incentive to keep that mothership afloat, rather than members going off to pursue such solo or duo opportunities more fully. Matt Molloy had already released a solo album, Matt Molloy, on Mulligan in 1976 (with both Dónal and Mícheál involved), and would follow this up early in 1978 with Matt Molloy, Paul Brady, Tommy Peoples, also on Mulligan.[†]

Shortly after Matt's trio album, it was Kevin Burke's turn for a Mulligan album: If The Cap Fits … (with Dónal and Mícheál involved) was released in May 1978, gaining UK release on Sandy Roberton's Rockburgh label.[‡] Colin Irwin, at *Melody Maker*, had Kevin in for an interview on the back of it, during which Kevin made an observation that seems prescient and profound:

---

[*] Pentangle members Bert Jansch and John Renbourn had each enjoyed a series of solo LP releases within the lifespan of the band, 1967–73, often featuring other members of the band, while dedicating almost all of their time as performing musicians to the band. The Bothy Band followed this template exactly, although Kevin recalls that in Ireland duo and trio combinations would occasionally take bookings when a promoter's budget could not stretch to the whole band. The default duo would usually be Mícheál and Kevin, who conveniently shared a house at the time.

[†] The *Melody Maker* of May 28 1977 reported that Matt had signed a solo deal with RCA and planned to record an album with European art music maestro James Galway. While Matt and James, with Dónal Lunny accompanying, did make at least one Irish TV appearance in 1977, the RCA deal seems to have disappeared. Ten years later, as a member of The Chieftains, Matt finally got to make a record with James. And, funnily enough, it was for RCA.

[‡] Presumably the cap did fit: Kevin seemed to traverse the 1970s with one on his head, usually at a raffish angle.

I've a feeling a lot of the kids starting now do so because they want to do tours of Europe and make records ... You go on the telly in Ireland and they think you're a star and earn millions. I just hope that kids today are learning the music because they like it, not because they like the life, or at least what the life looks like.[79]

A couple of weeks after Kevin's wise words appeared in print, life began to look very strange indeed to grass-roots Bothy Band fans: their heroes were on prime-time British television with a man in a rocking chair, crooning to swaying lovelies sat around him. For an act determinedly hoping to connect with rock audiences, The Bothy Band's appearance on *The Val Doonican Music Show* flirted with serious Light Entertainment cheese. But it could have been so much cheesier:

> **Dónal**: I remember the Val Doonican show rather vividly. Val wanted to tootle along with us on his tin whistle for our closing number, which we found unthinkable, and we declined as graciously as his punctured vanity would allow. The very formidable – female – producer [Yvonne Littlewood] appeared, and assured us we'd never work in London and/or on the BBC again.

The idea of Val Doonican's producer exerting any sway over the booking policies of John Peel, Kevin Flynn or anyone else certainly raises a smile, but this was merely a momentary oasis of kitsch in a touring regime that was not for the faint-hearted, as Kevin had affirmed in his *Melody Maker* interview:

> I tell you, the touring gets me down. If The Bothy Band broke up and I was asked to join another group, the touring might put me off. English f****** highways. Your head's in bits after a week, and you've got to go out and do a show.[80]

By June 1978 the band were back in Britain, in concert at BBC Broadcasting House for Radio 2. During the same month they recorded for a prospective live album in Paris. On July 7 they appeared, with Paul Brady, Liam O'Flynn, De Danann and Christy Moore, at the Royal Albert Hall. A couple of weeks later they were in more familiar territory, recording a concert at the National (broadcast in March 1979). Paddy Keenan's pipes solo on the night, comprising 'Garrett Barry's/The Bucks Of Oranmore', remains tremendously exciting in its rhythmical twists and rough-edged beauty, however much alcohol may have been consumed beforehand.

In early August some members of the band could be seen around the Dublin Folk Festival: Dónal Lunny, for instance, performed in a duo with Andy Irvine. The BBC Omnibus documentary received a debut screening during the festival. In fact, it was so popular that it received three screenings, the third 'in front of an audience that included a wise-cracking running commentary from Kevin Burke'.[81]

The documentary was eventually broadcast in edited form as an Arena film in 1980, with Paddy's moments of the limelight being a solo 'Bucks Of Oranmore' and a trip through 'Rakish Paddy' with his family. While every other member of The Bothy Band speaks in the film, Paddy is silent throughout. It was a trait that sometimes led to frustration in the band:

> **Kevin**: More communication would have been better. He was a quiet guy until he had a few drinks, and then he'd get very talkative – often in the wrong way or in a way that was surprising. And you'd think, 'Why didn't you say that last week?'

On August 13 the band headlined (above De Danann, Andy Irvine, Liam O'Flynn and Tom Paxton) the Sunday afternoon bill at Kevin Flynn's 2nd Ballisodare Festival. Clannad headlined the Sunday evening; Matt and Kevin had also performed in a Sunday morning concert of Sligo music. As one reviewer put it: 'The Bothy set was nostalgic, considering current doubts about the band's future.'[82]

The following weekend, August 18–20, The Bothy Band gave what was all but envisaged, though not publicised, as their final concert, at an anti-nuclear power free festival at Carnsore Point, County Wexford. Organised by Christy Moore, the bill included all the key names at the professional end of Irish traditional music: De Danann, Clannad, Paddy Glackin and many more.

For all the acclaim, all the airtime and all the perceived success, The Bothy Band were not succeeding in a financial sense. They were also frayed at the edges from the lifestyle.

> **Dónal**: I think it was like being on a rollercoaster. We were touring, then coming back to Dublin and trying to live a normal life. And that was difficult because sometimes it was like a non-stop party. ... We were touring without making much money from it. So there was no incentive.'[83]

Indeed, as Andy Irvine later quipped: 'I would've loved to [have been] in The Bothy Band, but I'm not quite sure I could have afforded it!'[84]

As a member of Planxty between 1972 and 1975, Andy had already experienced the difficulties in making ends meet, while trying to attain a sustainable level, in an Irish music band. The 1970s was an era without an existing textbook for this sort of thing: the nature of professional, full-time bands playing Irish music was itself new; the international touring business was still in its infancy; and the 'Eureka' moment of professional Irish traditional musicians realising that they should be splitting their time between a number of different performing units on an overlapping, ongoing basis (the norm in subsequent decades) rather than grinding one act into the ground had yet to be happen.

The lure of cracking England, an idea that was a kind of left-over from the notion of the 1960s pop industry (where Irish bands like Them and Éire Apparent would take a ferry over and sleep in vans around London, waiting for something to happen in the crucible of the world's popular culture), could be particularly merciless on the pocket. As Christy Moore reflected, in an interview coincidentally given just as The Bothy Band were embarking on their open-ended sabbatical:

> The big thing that happened to Planxty – and the same that happened to various bands – is that everyone said how important it was to do well in England. So you do tour after tour without getting any money, just to try and establish yourselves in England. Planxty went over to support Steeleye Span at the Royal Albert Hall and got £50, and it cost £250 or something just to travel across ... Do one good tour in Germany and that's it, you'll get established and you get good money, but in England you [can] do tour after tour and still not earn any money.[85]

Mícheál expanded on the decision to take a break, for six months before then assessing whether to bring the group back, in an interview later that year:

> The whole impetus for getting new material and keeping the set fresh is very different if you're having problems in other directions. I think we realised last Easter that it was time to stop, and Carnsore was to be our last gig. And once we'd decided to take a break the difference was amazing. I think the best gigs we ever did were the last couple of things, at Balllisodare and Carnsore. There was a big sigh of relief from everyone when we took the decision to break and we could get back to playing music again.[86]

The Bothy Band didn't announce the sabbatical at the time, but it didn't take long for rumours to fill the void. Even in the week before their Ballisodare appearance, the *Melody Maker* could report on 'widespread speculation' of a split:

[Nevertheless] official sources have denied any knowledge of the split, and attempts to get a concrete statement have failed. However Molloy … is thought to have grown tired of the trudge involved in touring and the restrictions on playing to a disciplined set. … This isn't the first time rumours have spread about an intended departure by a member of the band, though this time there would appear to be more substance in these than most.[87]

The next few weeks brought bits of news that appeared to support this. Firstly, it was announced under the headline 'Solo tour for Molloy' that Matt's two Mulligan albums were being distributed in the UK and that he would be taking part in a 'Mulligan Roadshow' tour before the end of the year. Then in mid-September it was reported that, while an expected 'farewell' announcement hadn't materialised at Ballisodare, 'the group have … come off the road for the time being perhaps to consider their future.'[88]

While all this conjecture was going on, back in Ireland on September 19, the four original members of Planxty (Dónal Lunny, Andy Irvine, Christy Moore and Liam O'Flynn) met at Matt Molloy's house for a first rehearsal toward a planned comeback as a five-piece. Under Kevin Flynn's management, it would involve a huge tour of Britain, Europe and Ireland spanning April to June 1979, although, for the moment, everyone's individual activities continued. Nonetheless, an 'anonymous caller' to *Melody Maker* spilled the beans in early October, fuelling more speculation that The Bothy Band would surely have to cease, given that two members would be Planxty-bound.

Over at Karl Dallas' monthly *Folk News*, the forthcoming Planxty resurrection was being referred to as 'strictly a once a year thing' rather than a full-time reunion: '[R]eports that The Bothy Band is about to cease operations are premature, to say the least. Although Matt's future with the Bothys is still uncertain, mainly because of health problems …'[89]

In late November 1978, Kevin Burke, Mícheál Ó Domhnaill and Matt Molloy joined guitarist/vocalist Paul Brady on a UK tour named, as *Melody Maker* had foretold, 'The Mulligan Roadshow'. Kevin, Paul and Matt were all promoting their recent solo albums on Mulligan, and the tour was a one-off grouping. Sponsored by *Folk News*, the tour generated substantial publicity: aside from print coverage, there would be a concert recorded for *Folk 78* at Broadcasting House and sessions for Radio 1's *John Peel Show* and Radio 2's *Folkweave*. The last date of the tour was at the National on November 28:

Matt: I was having a drink [there] with Kevin [Flynn] and telling him the sad story of The Bothy Band. I quoted fees that we were getting for gigs, and he was shocked and he said, 'Jaysus, I know I could do ten times better than that.' So he did some costings and booked a tour. The Bothy Band ended the break after four months and, true to his promise, financially it was the best tour of Ireland and England that we ever did. That was our last-ever tour.[90]

Flynn wasted no time in getting the news out. *Melody Maker* could report on November 11 1978: 'The widely held belief that the Bothies would never play live again has been dispelled with the news that a tour is being set up in Britain and Ireland next year.'[91] Camden Town Hall was already confirmed, on March 3 1979. The writer, Colin Irwin, speculated that Polydor would surely now issue the live album recorded back in June in Paris, held back during the sabbatical.

Colin lanced the boil during the Mulligan Roadshow tour when Matt Molloy ('currently a somewhat reluctant centre of attention') and Mícheál Ó Domhnaill swung by for a chat. Matt's position was that The Bothy Band would continue but in 'a much looser arrangement', as a part-time entity: 'We've been confined to one another for four years and it can get a bit much.' Mícheál talked of expanding things through writing original material and possibly adding electric instruments. He revealed that one step toward this had happened at the Paris concert from which the forthcoming *After Hours* live album (now edited down to a single LP) was derived. One piece had been performed with organ, synth, drums and three bombardes:

Mícheál (1978): That was a *big* sound … On closer scrutiny, it was perhaps a bit *too* heavy to put on the album. But certainly I think more could be done in that direction. … I think somebody will eventually crack it.[92]

Tríona (2015): There was so little time to work anything out [in Paris]. It was literally a few hours before we played. There wasn't time to work out all the kinks. That was the direction, maybe, we were headed.

Kevin (2015): The drummer didn't really work out. He was the wrong kind of drummer – actually we might have had two drummers, four-square rock'n'roll drummers. Everything was too strong on the down beat. Dónal moved on to Moving Hearts and Coolfin, and I'm sure we'd have all been up for that. We were willing to try anything and if it didn't work we'd toss it, like the drums. We didn't reject drums; we just rejected the way they were played [in Paris].

After Hours would be released early in 1979. A single from it, 'The Death Of Queen Jane', a vocal feature for Mícheál, was a tentative step in the direction he spoke about. It was unusual in being an original composition, from Mícheál's former Skara Brae colleague Dáithí Sproule, and was a stately piece. Paddy's solo fitted its vaguely baroque feel perfectly – the uilleann pipes being a child, after all, of the last days of the European baroque age in the 18th century. The song had been Mícheál's featured piece on the Roadshow quartet's *John Peel Show* session, with Kevin airing his stunning version of 'Farrell O'Gara', previously recorded in 1973 as a cameo on Arlo Guthrie's Last Of The Brooklyn Cowboys.

Mícheál reckoned, in 1978, that Irish music might yet still 'hit the jackpot':

> I'm surprised it hasn't happened yet. At one stage I thought it was going to sweep the whole thing and be as big as reggae. Maybe it's something to do with the make-up of the people involved in it. When you consider it's only seven or eight years since Ó Riada was doing his stuff How long was reggae going before it broke out?' And the whole music industry is so unspecified, and it's such a young industry there are no hard and fast rules about making it. I don't even know what that means.[93]

By January 1979, Dónal Lunny was reported to be busy working on the music for a Turkish film, and he and Matt were putting in time on Planxty rehearsals. The Bothy Band tour, not advertised as a swansong, had taken shape and would now begin at Belfast's Ulster Hall on March 1, finishing at Dublin's National Stadium a couple of weeks before the rejuvenated Planxty tour began at London's Hammersmith Odeon on April 15. Kevin Flynn had secured venues at city hall level up and down the country. All it took was one man with the right amount of energy, ambition and nous.

People in the band were already setting out their stalls for future careers. Aside from his forthcoming Planxty adventure, Matt Molloy was announcing a duo tour of Britain, with Liam O'Flynn, for October. Mícheál Ó Domhnaill and Kevin Burke's duo LP *Promenade* would be out soon, heralding a move to the USA to continue

---

* Seán Ó Riada (1931–71) was an art music composer, broadcaster and advocate of traditional music. His music for the 1959 film *Mise Éire* made his name. He ran an Irish traditional music chamber ensemble, Ceoltóirí Chualann, during the 60s, from which emerged The Chieftains, while his 1962 Radio Éireann series *Our Musical Heritage* was influential in stoking the popular revival of Irish music. Reggae, in its earlier guise as ska, was an influence on some British pop acts (e.g. Georgie Fame & The Blue Flames) during the 1960s and, with Millie Small and Desmond Dekker, enjoyed a couple of British hits on its own terms. Nevertheless, it took an individual with singular charisma, Bob Marley, for it to 'break' as a significant international genre within popular music. Irish traditional music has not produced a figure of similar appeal.

that partnership. Tríona Ní Dhomhnaill would also move to the States in due course to pursue a musical path of her own. Paddy Keenan, meanwhile, had a duo album, Doublin', with fiddler and old friend Paddy Glackin, coming out on Tara.

'Undoubtedly, both players are not just the finest, but the most exciting young musicians in Ireland,' wrote Colin Irwin in his review. 'Hearing Keenan play you get some measure of the discipline that working in a band context has imposed on him … Such is the fervour stirred between them that it transcends the normal limitations in appeal of instrumental albums.'[94]

Keenan had used the opportunity to record as duets two piping favourites that he had only ever performed, sometimes on radio, with The Bothy Band – 'Garrett Barry's Jig' and 'The Bucks Of Oranmore' – as well as a piping solo on 'The Bunch Of Keys', forever associated with Johnny Doran. Stepping down a rung in the billing, he promoted the album with solo performances in July and early August at the Dublin Folk Festival and the Ballyshannon Folk Festival – the latter with his oldest friends The Fureys topping the bill.

The Bothy Band bowed out at the Ballisodare Festival in Sligo, August 1979, on the Friday night. They had squeezed another year out of the wounded beast. Colin Irwin, travelling by boat from England, missed their set. He caught the 'amazing' Keenan and Glackin, as a duo, the next day: 'Supreme musicians … there's undoubtedly an empathy, a spark between them that lights fires all over the place when they start playing.'[95]

Even this Ballisodare event wasn't necessarily the last hurrah; it's just that nothing more happened and everyone drifted off on their own paths:

Kevin: I wasn't sure that it *was* the last gig. I seem to remember Mícheál and I went to the States and we came back to the realisation that the band had finished. We were completely disorganised. . I was definitely disappointed when The Bothy Band wound down, but I wasn't depressed. It was just a realisation of opportunities lost. But on the other hand, you do what you can and move on.

Tríona: It was mixed feelings. We were tired, we were broke, but we still loved playing together. It kind of was inevitable. It wasn't a falling-out, it just kind of petered out. We were all thinking of fresh pastures, other things.

*

'There was money made all right,' said Paddy, 20 years after the heyday of the band; 'someone was making it. The record company, Mulligan – shares were passed around.

But I wouldn't hold my breath for the rest of my life, waiting for some rewards to come from it. I still do have that share in the company, but royalty-wise I haven't seen a statement let alone a royalty since 1975. Obviously a breach of contract many times over … The point is, it did leave a sour taste about the record business, and I felt sorry not just for myself but for the other musicians who'd put so much work into it, trying to build a company to facilitate other musicians who wouldn't have got a chance. That was the purpose of Mulligan: to record good music and music that wasn't necessarily commercial.'

> **Kevin**: Dónal and Mícheál put [Mulligan Records] together and they needed a business person, and they knew Séamus [O'Neill] from his work at Gael Linn. And then as time went on, Dónal and Mícheál kind of threw their hands up in the air at trying to make business decisions and be in the band. They kind of capitulated to Séamus' suggestions, which resulted in Séamus taking over, and then the rest of the story is very murky. From there on, Dónal and Mícheál were saying, 'It's nothing to do with us.' Séamus proceeded to work in his way, and we still don't really know what happened.

> **Paddy (1997)**: With The Bothy Band, I was always shouting at them to try writing our own stuff. It never really happened, although we tried it once in Paris for the live album. [But] a lot of that was scrapped. After the band split up, about a year later, Dónal and Christy [Moore] came to me and Dónal said, 'Paddy, you've always been looking for something new: well, we've got it.' And that was the beginning of Moving Hearts. So I spent a month with them at the Baggot Inn, listening more than playing. But I decided no, I couldn't go ahead with another three or four years of my life doing the same thing. I'd had such a bad time, financially, with The Bothy Band. But I did recommend Davy [Spillane], who was down the country playing in pubs.

At that time, in 1997, around the release of what was perceived to be a comeback album, *Na Keen Affair*, Paddy was pragmatic about the reputation of The Bothy Band, which all of the former members (but perhaps he most of all, having not found a sustained collegiate vehicle since) carried on their shoulders:

> A lot of the reason for The Bothy Band being recognised as one of the great bands is because it's finished! But I know that a lot of them in the band would love to reunite, do an American tour with contracts up front,

of course … so you never know. If someone comes and offers us a huge amount of money, we might just do it.

The death of Mícheál Ó Domhnaill in 2006 put a stop to that chimera. The remaining members of The Bothy Band reunited once in concert, a year later in Dublin, as a tribute to Mícheál, with the proceeds being given to the Irish Traditional Music Archive.

*

Paddy Keenan made one more record, *Poirt An Phíobaire*, with guitarist Arty McGlynn, in this phase of his life as a professional musician, but his heart wasn't really in the lifestyle any more:

> **Paddy**: Since The Bothy Band split I played a lot on my own – solo stuff, occasionally with another musician if we could afford it, a guitarist or a singer. I did some tours of Europe and then I decided in 1982, I think, after doing a short stint with a group called Last Night's Fun, with Johnny Moynihan, Tommy Peoples, Eddie Stack and myself, to get away from the music altogether. I renamed that Tomorrow's Hangover. But it was a great time. We spent a month or two in the States and then I came back to Ireland and took a couple of courses – one in general engineering, one in furniture restoration – and I got into antiques.
>
> So I bought a place in Clonakilty, West Cork, and opened an antiques shop where I bought and sold stuff. The reason for that was to get away from the whole club scene – the booze, the hangovers … And also so I would have some other business to fall back on, so I could pick and choose what gigs I wanted to play. Because, before that, some of the bread-and-butter gigs were becoming a bit strenuous. Also, after a number of years with The Bothy Band and various other bands and various situations with record companies and bad management, financially it just wasn't that great.
>
> Around 1989–90 I went over to Germany and did a tour with Oisín, and then I travelled around Europe for a bit and went [back] down to West Cork and lived for a year on my own, to get away from everything. … It's difficult to settle down … when you're travelling all the time and it's in your blood. … I get itchy feet all the time. In 1991 I went to the States, did a short tour and it went so well, with venues asking me back, that I stayed six months. I did have an indefinite visa, so I could stay on if I wanted, and I had a Green Card for work reasons. So then I decided I'd move to the States and live there for a while …

Paddy moved to Boston and gradually got back into performing music. *Na Keen Affair* was his most personal statement to date: co-produced, arranged and mixed by himself, released on his own label and including his own 'Johnny's Tune', a tribute to his late father John Keenan. The album was largely an ensemble project, featuring several musicians from Newfoundland and Ireland – Tommy Peoples amongst them.

Paddy was hoping to put together a small band, make more records and get back to live performance in a more concerted fashion: 'I'd rather do something that I'm happy with than worry about it selling even one copy,' he said at the time. 'I hope I can make it in the next three years, cos that's about all I've got left in me, I think!'

Paddy was wrong on several counts: he never did get a band together; his rate of recorded works did not increase; and he had, and has, much more than three years left in him. A 2002 album, *The Long Grazing Acre*, self-released as a duo project with guitarist/vocalist Tommy O'Sullivan is, at the time of writing, his last commercial release. Recorded, in terms of the pipes, with a less processed, more vibrant and natural sound than its predecessor, the album's instrumental content ranks among Paddy's best on record and hinted toward how a truly Keenan-focused album with 21st century recording technology might sound – not air-brushing or compressing the pipes, but capturing in rich ambience every nuance of the instrument's qualities, in the hands of a master.

The album debuted Paddy's new pipes, commissioned from Dave Williams as a faithful copy of his Crowley set, although he still used his Rowsome chanter. It also boasted more original pieces of music than any of his previous recordings, and bore witness to a reflective mood – thinking about his time in London in the 60s, his late brother Johnny (who had passed on in 2000) and saluting the fortitude of his mother when times were hard. His notes to the album also reflected his pride in the Traveller heritage which had once sat uncomfortably on his shoulders.

Like Na Keen Affair before it, The Long Grazing Acre included many other musicians, which has always appeared to be the context in which Paddy feels most comfortable, however much people might wish to hear him perform or record solo. The man himself remains pragmatic on the matter: 'People say, 'If Paddy played solo we'd have him tomorrow, and we'd fill the place for him.' But, do you know something, will it fill the next place?'

*

Interviewed for this book towards the end of 2014, Paddy made a passing reference to having wished he had recorded more, but it's hardly something, one felt, that would keep him awake at night.˙ Paddy Keenan's towering brilliance as a performing musician is in direct disproportion to the frequency of his recorded output. But that's just the way it is. He is a free spirit, with a mind uncluttered by the mundane and capable of assailing, in the moment, the gates of ecstasy.

> **Kevin Burke**: Just to stand beside him and hear the pipes start with the strength of tone, the clarity, the precision, the strength of the rhythm, the mental strength. The tune is presented in a way that's unquestionable, unassailable. When you hear other pipers there's hesitation, there are certain weaknesses here and there. There's very few people who give you the comfort that Paddy does – from the first few notes of a tune, you can rely on it completely.
>
> **Tríona**: There's other pipers, but there's something wild and free and unpredictable and lonesome [with Paddy] – it's hard to put into words. It's more a feeling. It could be only coming out in one or two notes. I've heard him play to the point of almost collapsing on the floor. It's not the speed of it. He's one of a kind, a gorgeous guy. I can't even put into words what he means to me as a friend. There's a special connection between us all from those days [in the 70s].
>
> **Kevin**: We bump into each other now and again. The last five or six years or so, it's always been really nice to see Paddy; the previous five or six years, I couldn't really say that. You'd never know if you were going to meet Paddy the good guy or Paddy the difficult guy. The last few times I've met him, it's been great.

Paddy may never have become a rich man through music, but he knows that his association with The Bothy Band is to an extent his meal ticket, a reputation with a long tail.

> **Paddy**: I remember Paul Simon said once, 'The song I'd like to see make it to No. 1 is the beautiful 'Streets Of Derry', sung by Tríona Ní Dhomhnaill in The Bothy Band, with that haunting pipes solo.' Now, when you hear something like that from someone who is as huge as he [is], then you have

---

˙ Paddy played in Belfast in late 2014 accompanied, for the first time in many years, by guitarist Steve Cooney (a similarly brilliant, mercurial musician). Afterwards, Paddy mused that the pair of them should perform again and record it. A splendid idea.

to start realising the influence that band had in America. The children today are still, through their parents of course, looking at that and following that.

What those people are following is a body of work and a way of doing things that were in no small part created by Paddy Keenan: the man in the middle of the stage who never said much, never stood up and played better than anyone had a right to expect.

To an extent, the 21st century Paddy Keenan is burdened by a certain weight of responsibility, given his unique knowledge and skills as a traditional musician, reed maker and innovator of piping techniques*, let alone his image as a kind of last great gunslinger from the pioneer days of Irish music's 'Old West' in the 1970s.

Paddy: It's sometimes a little overbearing. It's hard to take all this [adulation]. … [But] I would say it's water over a duck's head. … The good thing for me is no matter how subtle the tune, no matter how many times I play it, five minutes later there's going to be something else in it, because my mind is thinking differently. It's purely an expression of me at that moment. And it's that individuality that stands out.

Tríona: I can remember the first time we got him to speak into a microphone, to introduce a set – and probably nobody heard it. He leaned forward, his head almost to where the mic was, in front of the drones, and muttered. But that was Dónal and Mícheál pushing him to do that. He would have been terrified. He was very shy of the mic. We got to know him bit by bit. It was very funny. Now, of course, he's been all over the world. He called me once, out of the blue, a good many years back. I was surprised to get the call:

'It's Paddy here!'

'Jesus, where are you?'

'I'm in Timbuktu.'

'You're joking?'

'No, I am. I'm sitting at the base of an oul' monument. There's some kids here and I'm playing a tune …'

You could just imagine it! He had that knack – he could take off and never be lost.

Part of Paddy's irrepressible freedom these days is his unapologetic favouring of a

---

* Detailed descriptions of Paddy's technical innovations can be found in Tomás Ó Canainn's *Traditional Music In Ireland* (Routledge & Kegan Paul, 1978).

cowboy hat, as totemic to his image in recent years as Kevin Burke's raffish cap was in the 70s:

> **Paddy**: I like wearing a hat. But the other side of it is I have tinnitus, I have this buzzing in my ear constantly. And I drive a bike as well in the States. I'll have to get a quieter bike. Any piper who doesn't believe it should wear a hat, and the wider the brim, the easier it is to hear the drones and the regulators and the easier it is to tune up. You'll get a better buzz from everything with a hat than you will without a hat.

As we made our way out of the venue, with a crowd of acolytes arranging to meet Paddy at a late-night pub session nearby, I asked one last question: 'Do people still expect you to turn up and be the riotous character you were in the 70s?' To which Paddy answered: 'It's quite possible. But you know what? I couldn't do it again – if I did, I'd be dead!' And with that, we left the venue and dropped Paddy after midnight at Madden's, where he was welcomed with open arms. As John McSherry, already lining them up at the bar, told me the next day, Paddy pressed the flesh, had the craic … and then wisely drew the line at one pint. But with Paddy Keenan the excitement, the frisson of danger, is that you just never know.

Chapter 6
Three Kings: Leo Rowsome, Séamus Ennis, Willie Clancy

On August 6 1977, British rock weekly *Melody Maker* had exciting news, of a rarefied kind, for devotees of traditional music:

> Séamus Ennis, the king of them all when it comes to uilleann pipes, is coming to Britain in September for an extremely rare folk club tour.
>
> A legend who has inspired many of the pipers who have sprung to prominence in the upsurge of Irish bands playing traditional music, Ennis' excursions to Britain in recent history have been sadly few, and this tour will cause great excitement amongst anybody remotely interested in the pipes. Paddy Moloney and Liam O'Flynn are just two of the names directly influenced and inspired by him.
>
> In his late 50s, his public appearances became somewhat infrequent after a serious illness, but without question he's still regarded as the greatest living piper, and comparisons between him, Leo Rowsome and Willie Clancy, both now dead, as to who was the greatest of them all, have caused many arguments in Irish bars.[96]

And therein lies a tale. While the likes of Paddy Moloney and Liam O'Flynn (then in between incarnations of Planxty) were at the forefront of pipers operating within the modern popular music world – generally in bands, experiencing more or less the same management, publishing, broadcasting, marketing, touring and recording infrastructure as anyone else involved in professional popular music – Séamus Ennis (1918–82), Willie Clancy (1919–73) and Leo Rowsome (1903–70) represented, in different ways, the bridge back to the piping tradition as it was in the 19th century and beyond.

> **Liam O'Flynn**: I've been fortunate enough in having known probably the three most important names in piping this century – Leo Rowsome, Willie Clancy and Séamus Ennis – and having known them very well. They had a very direct contact with the tradition that was untainted, if you like, and what I am is a synthesis of those people's styles, I suppose … I still play a set of Leo Rowsome pipes.

Rowsome, Clancy and Ennis were very different people, experienced life and conducted themselves in different ways and were a loosely associated trio of individual voices in the wilderness for much of their lifetimes. All three enjoyed recording careers, but not in the sustained album-tour-album sense of the music industry that was essentially created during the 1960s, in the wake of The Beatles as a global phenomenon. Rather, like the great pipers of the 18th and 19th centuries, they were, even in their lifetimes, almost characters of legend who needed to be seen and heard in person. Recorded artefacts were tantalising glimpses of their magic, not the foundations of their celebrity.

While Leo Rowsome had pursued a recording career in the 1920s, 30s and 40s, on 78rpm discs for a series of labels in Britain, with the Indian summer of an LP and EP for Irish label Claddagh in the 1960s, one has the impression that Ennis and certainly Clancy almost exist on record by luck. Forging careers based on vinyl was never a priority for either. We must be grateful, especially, to English producer Bill Leader for determinedly creating long-playing records of both Clancy and Ennis in the late 1960s: *The Minstrel From Clare* (Topic, 1967) and *Masters Of Irish Music Vol. 1* (Leader, 1969). They are albums that stand as the greatest single snapshots of each man's respective genius.

The imperfections of Clancy's and Ennis' respectively modest and chaotic discographies have been firmly addressed with the release of two decades-spanning CD sets curated by Peter Browne: Clancy's *The Gold Ring* (RTÉ, 2009), sourced from private tapes and broadcasts spanning 1949–72; and Ennis's *The Return From Fingal* (RTÉ, 1997), broadcast recordings spanning 1940–80.

Peter Browne: The reason we did the CDs of Willie and Séamus was because I was in a particular position: first of all [as] a piper who had learned from both, and there was also a lot of personal family contact with both, so I knew them well. And then being in RTÉ I became aware that the material was there, and the opportunity and the will existed to do it in the various different sections of the organisation necessary to bring it to a good conclusion. So you could describe it as self-propelling!

In Séamus' case, the fact that the recordings were so early in his life and so good was a revelation – they were all from within RTÉ. For Willie, it was slightly different in that we selected the best of what was in RTÉ but also trawled as far and wide as we could to produce what would be a comprehensive collection 'under one roof'. But in both cases the quality of the piping is exceptional and iconic, and its availability does actually have a 'hearable' bearing on present-day players' (not just pipers') styles, repertoire, et cetera …

> For Leo, it is different in that while he broadcast so much on Radio Éireann, it was mostly in the era before tape recording and his performances were (almost) always live.

Of the three players, Rowsome might be characterised as the rock at the heart of piping, a Wexford man in Dublin, quietly focused on maintaining and rebuilding the piping tradition from the threadbare vestiges of the post-Gaelic League/post-Irish Civil War era through tuition, broadcasting, pipe making and restoration. He represented discipline, tenacity and perfection.

> **Seán Reid (1975)**: Much of his extraordinary pre-eminence stems from the fact that in contrast to all other pipe makers during the last three quarters of a century, he alone devoted his whole lifetime solely to the uilleann pipes … Other great pipers and pipe makers came and went, but to all of them the pipes was but a sideline or a hobby, whereas with Leo it was his whole life, and indeed for 50 long years he lived by the pipes alone.[97]

Professional pipers and pipe makers had, of course, existed in previous centuries, but Leo Rowsome re-forged the template for a new and less generous age. The amount of dedication he applied to his running of the family pipe making business (after his father's early death), in tandem with a hugely proactive performing and tutoring career, is extraordinary.

> **Helena Rowsome**: Ever since his sudden and untimely death on September 20 1970, whilst adjudicating the Fiddler of Dooney Competition, six weeks after my marriage, I have tried to tell people as best I could through magazine articles, et cetera, how much he contributed to the survival of the uilleann pipes. It is almost 44 years since his death and I still wonder how on earth he did so much for so many! My great-grandfather, Samuel, and grandfather, William, and great-uncles are all well documented by Captain Francis O'Neill in *Irish Minstrels And Musicians*. I have often wished that Captain O'Neill were alive during my father's working life, as I know that he would have written of him with equal appreciation. He would have been fascinated at the third-generation Rowsome who did it all – manufactured, performed and taught!

Willie Clancy was a labouring man from Miltown Malbay, in rural West Clare, a magically gifted spare-time player, only taking up the pipes at 20, but inspired directly by Johnny Doran and, from beyond the grave, by legendary piper Garrett Barry, whom his father had known well. Willie was recorded for Radio Éireann by Séamus Ennis, whom he admired greatly, in 1949, and during the early 50s was a student of Leo Rowsome (and an occasional member of his piping quartet) in Dublin. In the mid-50s he was a presence on the Irish pub scene in Camden, whilst working in London as a carpenter – during which time he was recorded commercially for an LP released in America and an EP released in Britain – before returning to Miltown Malbay. He would find, thereafter, that he didn't need to go anywhere: people interested in music, drawn by his reputation, came to him.

> **Liam O'Flynn**: He was a man with a real roguish sense of humour, and that all came out in the playing as well. People had great warmth towards him. I don't think I ever heard anyone say anything derogatory about him.[98]

Séamus Ennis was more controversial: a maverick, a one-off. His piping was of a style essentially his own, and his professorial character was a combination of mischief, charm and idiosyncrasy. At times in his life a professional folk music collector and broadcaster, he was also at times homeless, marginal and reliant wholly on his piping, his extraordinary knowledge of folklore and his voice. He alone, of the three, was a presence, albeit a mercurial one, on the British club scene and Irish festival scene during the 'folk revival' era of the late 50s and onwards into the early 80s. He must have seemed, by virtue of personality and wayward musical brilliance, like a manifestation of the mystical soul of Irish music made real.

> **Paddy Keenan**: Séamus was the granddad of pipes and piping. Séamus did more for not just piping but for Irish culture and tourism than anyone could ever, ever imagine was possible – taking an instrument that was on its deathbed and having it on the BBC when it was unheard of … travelling by pedal bike to Connemara and Donegal, collecting. If it wasn't for him … it wouldn't be there. [And] Rowsome should be up there on a pedestal the height of Nelson's Column.

While piping is a solitary discipline, any suggestion of rivalries between Rowsome, Ennis and Clancy is very largely false, although some stories attest to Séamus Ennis having a peculiar tendency towards vainglory in later years. NPU Archivist Terry Moylan has often heard repeated a tale involving a man in O'Donoghue's pub who asked Séamus his view on the best three living pipers. Séamus replied, 'Felix Doran and Willie Clancy.'

The questioner asks, 'But who is the third?' to which Séamus responds, 'You mean the *first* …'

Clare fiddler Junior Crehan (1908–98) knew Séamus for over 25 years and was a little surprised to find a streak of envy in the man shortly after Willie Clancy's passing in 1973:

> He was jealous, I'd say. He believed that there was no piper as good as himself. I wrote a bit of a song, a lamentation for Willie Clancy. When he [next] came to Miltown: 'Ach, that was a grand job you did for Willie,' he said. … 'The lads asked me to do another one, so I did another one.' … 'How did it go?' he said. 'Well, the first line was, "Lament ye musicians, the king of our music is dead …" He didn't listen to any more of it. He walked away. Of course, he was a king himself. [But] he was serious.'[99]

During Willie Clancy's lifetime there was no such problem. People can recall sessions at Friel's pub in Miltown Malbay with the pair at either end of the room, swapping slow airs with friendly banter, every so often Séamus saying, 'That's the best pupil I ever had,' or Willie saying, 'Séamus, you're a credit to me.'[100]

'Willie and I got on very well,' said Séamus. 'Willie was quite a character, it turned out, in later years. He was able to do repairs on his own pipes and to make reeds. He made some reeds for my pipes, too. By trade he was a carpenter and joiner – and perfectionist.'[101]

'He is one of my best friends,' said Willie of Séamus, 'and a most knowledgeable man on Irish music and *seanchas* [lore]. He has done more to promote our music than any other man I know of. … It would take too long to examine all the good work Séamus has done for traditional music, but to round off I will say that he is a fine storyteller and a most entertaining host, a man who has charm and *blas* [taste].'[102]

Willie had reportedly 'unshaken devotion to … Ennis as the 'complete' piper, the one who had fused in his music the idiom of the pipes with that of the language and the songs.'[103]

> **Liam O'Flynn**: Willie Clancy and Séamus Ennis … were the pipers I travelled miles to see in my summer holidays. … They were very different personalities: Willie was a great character, very witty, and he had a great philosophy of life. Séamus was a larger-than-life figure. He could play to the gallery at times, but his piping was so deep. I listened to him playing slow airs, and I couldn't make out what he was up to. Then he told me the stories behind the tunes and, through him, I discovered the words to the airs, and

his piping began to make perfect sense. That's where his genius was – in bringing the words into the music.[104]

Willie Clancy, though never fluent in the Irish language, felt, like Séamus, that it held the key to understanding and interpreting the music. He gave this advice to young musicians:

> Get a grasp of the Gaelic tongue and develop a love for it. Go to the Gaeltacht and the old people who have it and learn it. I feel that a knowledge of our language is essential if you are to express the true spirit of our music and, as the saying goes, 'Don't settle for the skim milk when the cream is at hand.' … The Irish language is the greatest music of all. If I were to choose in the morning between my music and a knowledge of the Gaelic tongue, I would settle for the latter.[105]

With Willie the youngest and least 'public' of the trio, debates around the two elder statesmen, Leo and Séamus, back in the 60s were fuelled not only by their very different personalities but by perceived differences in their techniques. Leo was believed to play in an 'open' style, while Séamus was believed to play in a 'closed' or 'tight' style. Na Píobairí Uilleann (NPU) Archivist Terry Moylan was a student of Leo's from 1968 to 1970, knew both men and observed their approaches at close quarters:

> **Terry Moylan**: It's a kind of a canard, really, that there's an open and a closed style. Some of the people who claim they want to sound like [Johnny] Doran accompany this by saying they prefer the open style, but Doran did not play in an open style. Leo didn't really, either. They both played in a mixed style. The only person who you could point to and say it's a real closed style is [Richard] O'Mealy: if you listen to his [1943] BBC recordings, it sounds like Northumbrian piping, it's totally pippity-poppity. Andy Conroy used to do it as a kind of party trick. It's something you would listen to with fascination but not enjoyment. All the good pipers – Leo, Johnny, Paddy Keenan, Finbar [Furey] – all of them played in a mixed style. No piper of any repute ever played in a totally open or a totally closed style.

> **Helena Rowsome**: I have fond memories [as a child] of Willie Clancy in our house both when practising for Leo's Pipes Quartet and when he came for lessons, instrument maintenance and chat. We were all fond of Willie.

I can see the big smile on Dad's face as he cranned and popped the chanter along with Willie. They simply had fun playing together. My father had huge respect for Séamus Ennis, too – they had a great rapport.

Paddy Glackin: I saw Leo Rowsome and Séamus Ennis in each other's company and they seemed quite comfortable. A lot of this stuff [about rivalries] is fed by people from the outside, people who quite frankly couldn't strap on a set of pipes for either man. To hear Séamus playing a 12-minute version of 'The Fox Chase' – a stunning piece of work. But then to go back to the old recordings of Leo Rowsome – fantastic. It's all music.

Terry Moylan: There was an invented rivalry between Rowsome and Ennis. I don't think Willie partook of [that kind of talk]   I remarked to Leo once about Séamus – the only time I ever did – and all he did was compliment him on the wonderful long fingers he had for being a piper! He never said anything denigratory about him. On one occasion I asked for a particular tune, 'The Frieze Britches', and I remarked that Séamus played it – and Leo remarked that he had more parts of it than Séamus had.˙

From 1963, Andy Irvine was resident in Dublin and hanging around the kind of bars where discussions on pipering priority were taking place. At that stage, before the foundation of Na Píobairí Uilleann, Leo was a less prominent figure to casual observers:

Andy: Leo Rowsome was better known, really, [by then] as a teacher and a maker of pipes. The two pipers – they were never in contention themselves, I'm sure, but they were in contention with listeners – were Willie Clancy and Séamus Ennis. Every so often some idiotic person would say, *'Who's the best piper, do you think – Willie Clancy or Séamus Ennis?'* In the minds of a lot of people who listened to music, there was a kind of 'who's the best?' thing, but that's ridiculous. Now that one sees it with a little bit of distance, one realises how stupid that remark is. [They're] both different and both brilliant.

Séamus and Leo played on the same bill, albeit neither together nor one following the other directly, at a concert at O'Connor's pub in Doolin, Co. Clare, in August

---

* Séamus had five parts of the tune, which appears on his album *The Wandering Minstrel* (Topic, 1974).

1959. Recorded by Radio Éireann, the concert was very likely viewed by Séamus as an occasion to re-establish his presence after seven years in London. The atmosphere has been recalled as electric.[106] The performances by both players are magisterial.*

Perhaps the most famous occasion on which we glimpse these three giants together is a meeting in Bettystown, Co. Meath, in April 1968: the first ever piping *tionól* (a pipers' gathering), run under the auspices of Comhaltas Ceoltóirí Éireann – which, as Séamus Mac Mathúna noted in a lively report of the event for *Treoir*, was 'at last doing something definite to promote piping'. His account reads, at times, like the gathering of the denizens of 'Old Narnia' in C.S. Lewis' *Prince Caspian* – dwarves, fauns, talking beavers and the like, magical creatures who had been hiding in forests for generations – finally coming into the light to try and rebuild a former ascendancy. The Bettystown event led directly to the formation of Na Píobairí Uilleann ('The Uilleann Pipers'), which would galvanise pipers into the effective salvation and rebirth of their tradition.

Mac Mathúna's tale is worth quoting at length:

> 'The race of pipers is doomed,' wrote Francis O'Neill in his book *Irish Music – A Fascinating Hobby* – 60 years ago, and pessimists over the past few years have been echoing his words. So it was with no little trepidation that we (Breandán Breathnach and I) approached the idea of gathering the pipers of Ireland together for a weekend, just to see how things stood. Everyone knew of a score or so, but there must be others
>
> Finally a list of 56 pipers was drawn up and a circular issued. The response was gratifying: 32 replies, ranging from interested to very enthusiastic From Armagh came news of a recently formed Pipers' Club. Pat McNulty, of Glasgow, would come Tommy MacCarthy, of London, would be there too with two more pipers; Belfast rallied strongly too: 'If we jist knoo whire the dom thing was gooin' to be'; Séamus Ennis would be delighted to attend, give lecture, demonstrations, etc. By April 2nd, our list of pipers had grown to 88, 47 of whom would attend the Tionól
>
> At 6pm on Saturday, April 6th, they finally came together – each man with his pipes, wondering Séamus Ennis, one might say, called the tune with a short talk on piping in general. He followed this up with a demonstration on the tuning of the pipes, and then, as we had all hoped, he went from reeds to reels. Tape recorders and mics sprouted on all sides

---

* The entire Doolin concert is digitised and can be heard by arrangement at the Irish Traditional Music Archive (ITMA), Dublin. Two of Séamus' three tunes have been released commercially, on *The Return From Fingal* (RTÉ, 1997).

like magic and 47 pipers listened in rapt attention. Rí na bPíobairí [the king of the pipers] was in great form, backing up great piping with a running commentary (bi-lingual) and with a few verses thrown in for good measure.

After a short hour or so, Séamus handed over to Willie Clancy, who, not to be out-done, showed us some of the tricks from the Clare bag. Liam Ó Floinn [O'Flynn], a grand young piper, was not to be overshadowed either By midnight the sound of piping could be heard from different rooms, with one man practising a trick he had just seen demonstrated, another man having a go at a borrowed low-pitched set, and another half-a-dozen 'blashting away' in a typical session. How the hours flew. By four o'clock many had finally played themselves to a standstill, but Séamus Ennis, looking better and fitter than for many a day, was still piping away to a dozen eager listeners.

[The next day] Leo Rowsome arrived bright and early, in great form after his American tour [By the end of the day] a lot of music had been played, and now there was time for a chat and a drink. Arguments and discussions were in order – how did Clancy, Rowsome or Ennis compare with the immortal Touhey or Doran? – How about young Ó Floinn … ? – was there a great piper in the making among the many young ones we had just heard?

Brian Vallely, who had founded Armagh Pipers' Club two years earlier, was one of those present:

> **Brian Vallely**: The music was really dying in the rural areas in the 60s. But the thing is, it wasn't a dying tradition; you had some of the greatest players of the century there. … It was the age of the tape recorder, and I'll always remember when Ennis started to play he was surrounded by people pressing 'record'. And with Rowsome it was the same. And then you'd these huge groups of pipers playing together – music all night. … We all wore suits, that was the dress code in those days. We had a laugh about it a few years later about it all going to the dogs with people in jeans and long hair and all that! But it was timely, because in three years [looking at the famous group photographs from that weekend], most of the front row were dead.

'That evening is the stuff of legend,' wrote Planxty biographer Leagues O'Toole, on the basis of Liam O'Flynn's recollections. 'Séamus Ennis sat back as his younger colleagues displayed their talents, and, after a couple of hours, he prepared his famous 130-year-old Coyne pipes, reportedly testing the patience of onlookers as he spent some 20 minutes tuning the drones. Of course, once he was up and running, he soon had Ireland's finest assemblage of pipers mesmerised by his unique flair. He finished his set with 'The Bucks Of Oranmore' and, in an unusual gesture, passed the pipes to a surprised and reluctant Willie Clancy. After a couple of tunes, Clancy attempted to pass the pipes back to Ennis, but was instructed to pass them on to Liam O'Flynn, their esteemed pupil of the next generation.

'I remember being handed the pipes to play and being absolutely gobsmacked,' admits Liam. 'I also knew that the pipes were extremely difficult to blow because the bellows weren't completely airtight. I used to watch Séamus playing them and the physical effort involved. It was a major business just to keep air in the thing. I remember Clancy's remark: 'Séamus,' he says, 'the bellows, they wouldn't hold hay!''[107]

Within two years, Rowsome would be gone; within five, so would Clancy. Séamus Ennis remained until 1982. As Andy Irvine recalls, by the time he performed at the Lisdoonvarna Festival, near the end of his life, 'he was like a god.'

Chapter 7
Leo Rowsome: Keeper Of The Flame

Francis O'Neill: Mr Samuel Rowsome, a 'strong' farmer of Ballintore, Ferns, County Wexford, was a fine performer on the Irish pipes, by all accounts. His sons, William and Thomas, of Dublin, need no introduction to the lovers of pipe music in this generation.[108]

Such was the Captain's view, expressed in *Irish Minstrels And Musicians* in 1913. William and Thomas were each noted musicians and instrument repairmen of their time; a third son, John, was also a noted piper profiled glowingly in O'Neill's book. William established his pipe making and repair business at 18 Armstrong Street, Harold's Cross, Dublin, in the early years of the 20th century. His eldest son, Samuel, was born in 1896 – early enough to get a promising nod in O'Neill's book. Leo, the third son, was born in 1903. Francis O'Neill was friendly with William and describes him in typically florid terms as having eyes 'sparkl[ing] with animation and his whole anatomy ... vibrat[ing] with a buoyancy which found suitable expression in the clear tones of his chanter.'[109]

Seán Reid would later describe similar characteristics in Leo, whose performance exhibited 'the sheer exuberance and joy that rose in his heart as he played, as was clear from the animated movements of his body and the way his face lit up.'[110]

Leo Rowsome: My grandfather was very much associated with the Cashes and the Byrnes of Carlow. There was a wonderful tradition around that part of Ireland, and I had the honour of remembering my grandfather and playing with him. ... When he came to Dublin, [my father] was known as a fiddler; his brother Tom was the piper, a brave piper, and his brother John. John emigrated to America ... [and] none of [his family] followed on the pipes. Tom Rowsome was famous everywhere, all over Europe, he played concerts here and there. He was a bachelor. He was better known as a piper than my father. My father took up the pipes after he came to Dublin. He started making pipes and about four or five years afterwards' he went back to Wexford, and everybody was astonished to find Willie Rowsome the fiddler playing the pipes.[111]

O'Neill had applauded William for being 'commendably circumspect in his language and reference to others in his profession', noting that it was no doubt his 'artistic temperament' which 'may be accountable for many little misunderstandings which sensitive natures magnify into grievances.'[112]

Yet, as he went on to note, there appeared to be very few others *in* William Rowsome's profession by then. Barring a few mechanics in America who could turn out a serviceable chanter, only William Rowsome and Richard O'Mealy of Belfast (a man 'liberally endowed with the artistic temperament') were alive and well and skilled in the art at that time. 'In the vicissitudes of human life,' he concluded, 'the pipe makers … have dwindled almost to the vanishing point.'[113]

William Rowsome died in 1925. Leo, who had learned the pipes from both his father and his uncle Tom – winner of the 1899 Dublin Feis Ceoil in piping and adjudged by some to have been even better than William[†] – had also learned pipe making. The premises were by now at 125 Harold's Cross Road. Aged only 22, Leo became the family's breadwinner.

> **Seán Reid**: Times were bad, money scarce, payments slow, and the price of a set of pipes bore little relation to the length of time and cost of materials involved. Undeterred, however, by such difficulties, young Rowsome carried on to such good effect that not only did he put the business on a sound footing, but he found time to make a new concert-pitch set of pipes for himself, which for quality of tone and brilliance was never equalled in his lifetime.[114]

---

* Francis O'Neill describes this return visit to Wexford as occurring in 1911, during a time when he knew William Rowsome well. If we take Leo's 'four or five years' reference as correct, that would put the establishment of William's Dublin business – or at least the beginning of his piping – at 1906. O'Neill visited William at his premises in 1906. We might move it back a year or two from this, but we can hardly move it back to 1895 – the establishment date for 'Wm Rowsome & Sons, Irish Union Pipes & Reed Makers', as it appeared in letter-headed paper used by Leo from 1931 on. William did not, in fact, *have* any sons in 1895. Possibly Leo chose this date to reflect the year in which his late father began to make and repair instruments professionally.

† Francis O'Neill claimed no personal acquaintance with Tom, as he had with William, but cited the testimony of mutual friends in *Irish Minstrels And Musicians*. Intriguingly, among Tom's piping qualities he mentioned, with a little criticism implied, a 'flute-like' tone – the same description used later by some in relation to Leo's playing. O'Neill noted as well, in a delightful turn of phrase, that Tom was 'also accused of being both genial and kindly, yet apparently insensible to female charms.'

Leo had something of a head start in earning: he had been appointed pipes tutor at Dublin's Municipal School of Music, aged 16, in 1919 (a post he held for more than 50 years, during which it became the Dublin Institute Of Technology); and he had also been teaching at Dublin Pipers' Club between the death of its first tutor, Nicholas Markey, around 1920 and the club's closure around 1922.*

During the early 1920s, Leo established himself as a pre-eminent piper with a series of wins at the Dublin Feis Ceoil and its successor, the Oireachtas competition. No doubt building on this notoriety, he began to make records. A series of four 78rpm discs on the Winner label was released in 1925.† There would be further blocks of releases in 1926 (on Columbia), 1928 (Broadcast), 1933 (Imperial), 1935–38 (HMV and Decca) and 1944–48 (HMV and Rex). These were early days for commercial recorded sound, and as Leo's contemporaneous correspondence with the BBC confirms, he was not a man content to wait around, hoping for opportunities to come his way; he created those opportunities himself through determined networking. He was the first solo piper to perform on Radio Éireann (during its first month, January 1926), and had remarkable success in vaulting institutional barriers against minority-interest instruments and regional 'turns' on the BBC airwaves (detailed in the next chapter).

The tone of Leo's pipes and the fluidity of his playing on his 1930s recordings, especially, are extraordinary. While Leo was known for his use of regulators, his focus was melody.

> **Seán Reid**: The sheer economic necessity of impressing audiences and getting engagements with subsequent orders for new sets compelled him to present his music in the most brilliant manner possible. He therefore

---

* Various dates between 1922 and 1926 have been given, including in testimony from those around at the time, for the closure of the Pipers' Club. In *An Píobaire* Vol. 6, No. 2 (April 2010), Terry Moylan probably nails it: 'The first Dublin Pipers' Club had been established in 1900. It had been preceded by two years by the club established in Cork in 1898 … The Dublin club ran out of steam after a decade and had ceased to exist by the outbreak of the First World War. A tentative re-start in 1919 was cut short by the repressive measures implemented by the 'Black & Tans', who deliberately targeted Irish cultural activities. A new club was established at a premises in Thomas Street in 1921 under the name 'The Irish Union Pipers Club', but this was again disrupted by military activities and political tensions, this time in the context of the Civil War [in 1922].'

† A London company called G&T (The Gramophone & Typewriter Co.) recorded some solo uilleann piping 78s prior to 1920, purportedly by one Thomas Caroghan, though details are obscure. The key pipers on 78 prior to Leo Rowsome's prolific recording career were from America: Patsy Touhey and Tom Ennis, the latter often heard in tandem with fiddler James Morrison.

gave less prominence to the finer points of staccato ornamentation, most of which would have been lost on a lay audience anyhow. He concentrated instead on letting the melody flow out, clearly and sweetly, controlling the tone by clever tricks of fingering and momentary raisings of the chanter, using just enough closed (staccato) fingering to impart the essential phrasing and making the utmost use of the regulators.[115]

Leo's command of the regulators is splendidly illustrated on his 1937 recording of the slow air 'Savourneen Deelish', providing flowing chordal accompaniment throughout, alongside incredibly disciplined chanter work – a sustained and controlled sound, harmonium-like in effect. Another four sides cut in England during 1937 revealed further innovation, this time in setting the pipes in trio context with violin and drum (from unknown but skilled players), the parts apparently arranged on the day of the session by Leo himself.* Back home, he was broadcasting regularly on Radio Éireann in first a pipes/flute/fiddle trio (up to 1930) and then in a piping quartet format – from the 30s to the 50s, drawing from a small circle of fellow pipers including, in later days, Willie Clancy.

Leo married Helena Williams, a primary school teacher from Wexford, in 1934. The following year he resurrected the Dublin Pipers' Club.† It came to be almost inevitably, after he had assembled around 30 of his piping pupils for a Gaelic League event that summer in the Phoenix Park. It was a quantity of uilleann pipers never before known to have come together in one place and time.

> **Leo**: When we finished, I called the leaders – the senior pupils – together, about six of us. I said to them, 'Why not re-float the Pipers' Club?' We held a meeting and issued a circular, sent it to people interested … and formed a provisional committee. That was the foundation of the Pipers' Club.[116]

One of Leo's pupils at the Municipal School of Music at this time (enrolling in 1935 and 1936) was Tommy Reck, subsequently a great name amongst piping connoisseurs.

---

* Any Irish musician wanting to record 78rpm discs before 1937 (from which point record labels began to establish offices in Dublin) was obliged to travel to London.

† Seán Reid, in a 1974 interview in *Dál gCais*, said: 'Tommy Reck and I discussed the possibility of reviving [the club] and eventually we went ahead with our plans. Leo Rowsome joined us and our idea became reality about 1936.' Seán may have been a year out in his recollection (in the same piece he is a year out on the founding of NPU), but it affirms that Seán and Tommy had been pondering the idea seemingly simultaneously to Leo. The new Pipers' Club began in premises on Ely Place, then on Molesworth Place and finally, in 1946, at 14 Thomas Street. Leo was its president until his death in 1970.

Tommy had been inspired into piping through admiration for John Potts – like himself, a Dublin-raised scion of a Wexford family – and the 2RN broadcasts of James Ennis (father of Séamus), and would later become an alumnus of Leo's piping quartet.

Seán Reid, who went on to become one of Leo's firmest friends, was another great-name-in-waiting for piping connoisseurs of the future. Seán met Leo in 1935, at a concert in Thurles. He found the great man to be 'simple, warm-hearted, jovial, happy, a fund of anecdotes and in general the very best of good company'.[117] For the next three years Seán took lessons from Leo, amazed at the quality of his teaching and his ability to attend to great numbers of students, many of them juveniles, in a class situation.

> **Seán Reid**: Not many of the other pipe makers were also great pipers, for the simple reason that their work cut into their practising time. Leo somehow continued to achieve phenomenal proficiency as a piper despite long hours at his father's old treadle lathe and the time-consuming business of repairing and tuning derelict sets, making reeds, teaching some five nights a week and [heading] off on a long journey nearly every weekend to [a] concert, feis or Fleadh Cheoil.
>
> Johnny Doran, one of the greatest pipers of all time, swore by Leo, and his brother Felix Doran put him at the top of the list. Willie Clancy admired his playing intensely and used to maintain that he was a lot better than he was given credit for. There must be few better qualified to judge him than these three – now all, alas, gone to their eternal reward. Of course, the first two had their origins in the same school of piping as Leo, but Clancy's background was that of the greatest school in the world, Clare and Galway, [the one] that produced such great pipers as Patsy Touhey and Garrett Barry.
>
> Leo, like his father before him, never had an unkind word to say about anyone, least of all another piper. He just went on his own serene way: topping the bills, broadcasting, teaching, pipe making, and building up his business and reputation until it was worldwide and he was in demand for the most important functions on both sides of the Irish Sea.[118]

Between 1930 and '39, Leo performed annually at the Royal Opera House, Covent Garden, around St Patrick's Day. He had already given concerts in London, Glasgow and Manchester by the mid-1920s, and would return to these cities and to Liverpool, Birmingham and elsewhere in Britain in subsequent years, while somehow managing to keep all of his other commitments active. Not least among these was family. Leo had four children: Leon (1936–94); Liam (1939–97); and twins Olivia and Helena

(b. 1946). All would receive a musical education defined by their own interests. Only Leon pursued piping, although Helena gave it a go:

> **Helena**: I took piping lessons from him at Dublin's School Of Music (where I also learned violin and harp). My journeys home with him on the bus after my pipes lessons were interesting and joyful. We had a great rapport – he knew how much I respected his amazing gifts and how proud I was of him. When I would bring droves of friends back to the house after a late music session, he would (at my request) actually come downstairs at an unearthly hour and play for them. I think I may have been the apple of his eye for some reason! My mother, a primary school teacher, was very hospitable and would provide supper for all.* She was a huge support to my dad. I just loved the humble, quiet and efficient manner in which he conducted his business. I consider myself to be very fortunate to have realised at an early age the phenomenal person he was.

Leo never had a car and relied on public transport to get him to the music college of an evening, after a day in his workshop, with lifts to the Pipers' Club for Saturday tuition – concert appearances and frequent radio broadcasts being squeezed in wherever else he could manage. He retained the 'Wm Rowsome & Sons' name on the pipe making business for many years after his father's death, also keeping the increasingly archaic 'Union Pipes' on his headed stationery.† By 1947 the family had moved to 9 Belton Park Road, Dublin, and Leo's stationery now declared: 'Leo Rowsome: Uilleann Pipes Maker and Expert'.

---

* In a magazine piece entitled 'In My Father's Time', undated but online, Leon Rowsome recalled one occasion, a visit from Brother Gildas (a Belfast piper), when his mother's hospitality was unsatisfactory: 'My mother asked him if he would have an egg for his tea … and he replied that he knew a man that ate two that was alive still.' Leon's sister Helena is certain he was conflating recollections: 'My grandfather, William, told my father of a lady who was 'sparing with the food'. Whilst visiting her house, she asked him if he would have a boiled egg and he replied: 'I know a man who ate two and he is still alive.' My mother was extremely hospitable and generous. She would never have offered a visitor a boiled egg!'

† His 1936 publication *Leo Rowsome's Tutor For The Uileann Pipes* [sic] made the move from union to uilleann before his stationery. Along with Tadhg Crowley's *How To Play The Irish Uillean Pipes* [sic], also published in 1936, this was the first tutor since those by O'Farrell and Colclough over a century before. Tadhg and his brother Denis made pipes in Cork from 1926 onwards – with Rowsome in Dublin and O'Mealy in Belfast, the third of the only three serious uilleann pipe makers in the world at that time. Tadhg died in 1952, Denis in 1966. Tadhg's son Michael maintained the business, including a general musical instrument store, until his death in 2010.

His publicity material of the time stated: 'Proffessor [sic] Leo Rowsome of Dublin is acknowledged to be the world's leading exponent of the Uilleann Pipes, and has Broadcast to many parts of the world. … He is the most popular recording artist in Ireland …'[119]

Leo had worked hard to obtain a handful of broadcasting opportunities in Britain prior to WWII, but by the late 40s he was clearly accepted as a significant international artist, securing a number of performances on mainstream BBC programmes *Variety Bandbox* (one seemingly with orchestral or band backing) and *In Town Tonight*. His piping quartet performed for BBC TV in 1953. On paper, he was in a perfect position to have moved his performing career forward with further international broadcasts, concerts and releases in the new-fangled vinyl era. But the pressures of a young family and his other responsibilities, teaching the next generation of pipers, curtailed that option.

At least two of Leo's students would enjoy sustained international performing careers. Paddy Moloney, future chieftain of The Chieftains, had (aged four) first encountered Leo as a man on a bus giving him a word of encouragement on his whistle playing. With Paddy being at the same primary school as Leo's son Leon, and being enthralled by the sound of Leon's playing, enrolment at the Municipal School Of Music duly followed. Paddy would make his public debut, aged 10, at one of Leo's Phoenix Park summer events in 1947. From 1956 to 1960 and for a couple of years later on, Liam O'Flynn attended lessons with Leo, his father driving him up from Kildare every Friday night:

> **Liam**: Even though it was a teacher-pupil relationship, there was nothing formal about it, unlike having my piano lessons. This was almost more like a father-son relationship. I was so excited to have him as my teacher, and he was so excited to have a young lad who showed promise, as they say, and who was obviously keen. When I was sent off with my couple of tunes after a lesson, I came back the next time and I really knew them because I wanted to … play them well for Leo.[120]

Helena believes that most of today's surviving historic sets of pipes were restored by her father. He was effectively keeping not only the art of piping but the pipes themselves alive, as physical entities, with his performing career taking second place (or third, behind his family). Something had to give.

Seán Reid: In 1956, he had a very serious illness from which he nearly died. This took the fine edge off his technique, and while he remained a great piper and made two excellent records for Claddagh, he had to be wary and use conscious control of his fingers. So well did he succeed that only the sharpest critic could detect the difference.[121]

The two Claddagh recordings, Leo's only artefacts of the vinyl era, were *Rí Na bPíobairí/ The King Of The Pipers* (1959) and a much rarer EP, *Piper's Choice* (1966). The LP was the debut release on the Dublin-based label, which would go on to record many more commercially marginal traditional performers. Getting Leo onto the new format and available to the masses had been the impetus behind it. Claddagh's co-founder was Garech de Brún, then aged 20, a scion of landed nobility and pupil of Leo.

> **Garech de Brún**: I set out to make something happen. None of the major record companies believed that two sides of 20 minutes each of pipering was something that anyone would listen to. But we didn't think that this was the case, and indeed we were proved right. … Somebody wrote that Leo's record was a foible and that I was merely slumming it. There was a lot of prejudice against me by people who had no idea of my motives and what I was trying to accomplish. I started Claddagh Records to make money for the musicians and other people concerned and [to] turn around their image – and also that of traditional music.[122]

Leo also appeared in two Irish-made films in 1959: *Broth Of A Boy*, in which he plays 'The Heather Breeze' in a short scene set around Irish dancing auditions; and *Home Is The Hero*, shot at Ardmore Studios in Bray.˙

Leo Rowsome's name as a performer may have faded from the consciousness of the O'Donoghue's generation by the 1960s, but no one listening to *The King Of The Pipers*, then or now, could come away thinking that this was a man past his best.

'An aptly titled set of recordings' was the *Melody Maker* view when copies appeared in Britain on import from EMI a decade later. 'His precise fluid style on even the most intricate tunes is a pleasure to listen to … highly recommended and worth obtaining.'[123]

Back in 1951, Leo and his Pipers' Club colleagues had been instrumental in establishing Comhaltas Ceoltóirí Éireann ('Society Of The Musicians Of Ireland') to promote and nurture Irish traditional music generally. Leo was its chairman. By 1968

---

* Back in 1934, Leo had appeared, uncredited, in *Irish Hearts*, the first Irish 'talkie' – albeit filmed at Cricklewood Studios in England, with only exteriors shot in Ireland – playing 'The Rakes Of Kildare' in a piping duo with Seán Dempsey. Trinity College Dublin holds a print of *An Irish Journey* (date unspecified), a travelogue fronted by Bing Crosby, in which Leo is credited as a musical performer.

it was time to look after piping – still marginal within Irish music. A gathering was arranged for a weekend in May 1968 at the Neptune Hotel, Bettystown. Just before this, Leo enjoyed the trip of a lifetime, to America: performing to over 6,000 people at New York's Carnegie Hall and appearing on US television while there.

On his return, and referencing previous trips to the annual Northumbrian Festival Of Piping, Leo addressed the Bettystown faithful with a tangible passion:

> I'm teaching the pipes for 48 years, I'm proud to say it, and in that 48 years I helped in large measure – others kept it going the same as I did. I'm very glad to be alive to tell you of how proud I am to add this achievement to my credit … You're never good enough, you can be always better. I am learning, myself. You can always improve. The time has come, from now on, unfortunately – the hardening of the arteries and so on – [that] in another few years I possibly might fade out of the picture. But if I live long enough I might be able to play again. … I only hope, and I know in my heart and soul, that [this gathering] will have fruitful results … The pipes have been downtrodden long enough and looked down upon but thank God the time has come when they're ascending.[124]

This critical mass of 47 pipers was the galvanising factor in the creation of Na Píobairí Uilleann (NPU). Seán Reid pushed through the notion of a new organisation, under the auspices of Comhaltas, at a meeting of the latter later in the year. It came not a moment too soon:

> **Seán Reid**: [T]he art of piping, of tuning and [of] pipe making was dying out. There were but few left who were competent to teach the art, and the only sensible solution seemed to be a body that would collect and transmit, through workshop and discussion, the knowledge already available.[125]

Leo, of course, had a huge amount of knowledge to pass on – though time, as it transpired, was running out. In March 1969, he performed 'The Fox Chase', arranged by A.J. Potter, with the Radio Éireann Light Orchestra, at Dublin's RDS – foreshadowing the work that would bring Liam O'Flynn and Shaun Davey so much success in the 1980s and beyond.* On September 20 1970, aged 67, adjudicating

---

* A.J. Potter was one of four arrangers used by Radio Éireann from the mid-50s onwards to create ensemble settings for traditional music. RÉ was committed to traditional music as part of its remit, but felt the need to vary its presentation away from the then-prevailing standard of solo/duo performers and céilí bands.

'The Fiddler Of Dooney' competition at Riverstown, Sligo, Leo passed away.

'There is no need to name out the achievements of the late Leo Rowsome because his name is a household one,' declared an appreciation in *Treoir*. 'His tunes bore the stamp of a great musician and craftsman.'[126]

For piping and pipe making, Leo Rowsome had almost single-handedly held the fort during decades in which the soldiers were few and scattered. He was an artist and an entertainer whose energy, patience and will over many years were extraordinary. Perhaps uniquely for a traditional musician, he became a genuine household name in Ireland through his extensive broadcasting from 1926 onwards. Many people who knew him speak of his amiability.

> **Helena Rowsome**: I know well that my father's success was in no small way due to the type of person he was. He was a thorough gentleman of great character … He played music to make people happy! When playing at a midnight show in the Grafton Cinema, he would play what the audience wanted to hear and would change the tempo often in order to captivate them entirely, as he often told me: 'At first they were a bit noisy, but halfway into the performance, I had them all eating from my hand …'

> **Leo Rowsome**: I myself inherited what I have from my father … It's him I thank for anything I've done. People say to me, 'You're a great man, you've done great work' – where would I [be], how could I do it without him? Well, I had the honour of playing with my grandfather also, in his ancestral home. Unfortunately, my father died young … but I was very proud to do what I could to keep his tradition going.[127]

Leo's refined, exquisitely controlled style of piping drifted out of fashion during the 1970s, with younger players like Paddy Keenan (from the wilder Johnny Doran tradition) coming to prominence and the singular Séamus Ennis remaining a hugely charismatic figure.

> **Seán Reid (1974)**: The stature of Leo Rowsome as a piper has undergone some changes, and opinions are varied. I feel that he does not get sufficient credit, and this is a viewpoint that Willie Clancy shared. … Leo Rowsome made a very considerable contribution to Irish music. Without him it would be less varied, and certainly less popular.[128]

> **Terry Moylan**: An earlier generation had been influenced by Leo because of

all the radio broadcasts and so on, but by the early 70s Ennis was the person to follow. By the mid-70s, Willie [Clancy] had died, but his recordings were becoming very influential as well. Willie was perceived as kind of an unspoiled country style, whereas Ennis was the austere, classic style – very clean and considered.

But fashion tends to be mitigated by quality over the long term, and Leo's qualities as a player are probably better appreciated today. 'Quite a lot of people sound like Leo,' says Terry Moylan of pipers today. 'Willie Reynolds, Peter Carberry, the Brophys, Tommy Carney …' There is, nonetheless, a relative paucity of commercially available recordings, surely necessary to stoke renewed interest in his playing, which will perhaps be addressed in due course.*

Leo's most obvious legacy was his pipe making. Good sets of uilleann pipes are not prone to sell-by dates:

> **Liam O'Flynn**: Leo Rowsome was, I believe, the greatest maker of uilleann pipes during the 20th century. And you could argue that maybe he was the greatest of all time. … He was completely in love with the instrument.'[129]

> **Terry Moylan**: He was the only show in town, really, when you take into account performer and maker. There were a few other makers, but they were nowhere near Leo's league at all. There was Kennedy and Crowley in Cork, though Crowley made more war pipes than uilleann pipes. I only know of one set of Kennedy pipes knocking around, and that was the set that Willie [Clancy] had. O'Mealy [in Belfast] made a few sets, but nothing like the output of Leo. And Leo was the one who constantly performed – and he took his performing seriously.

Reg Hall, doyen and later chronicler of the 1950s London-Irish scene, found in his own research that Leo really had been 'the only show in town' at a certain point in time:

> I spoke to lots and lots of old country players whose only experience of piping was Leo Rowsome on the radio. At the end of the 30s and into the

---

* In contrast to their extensive collections of recordings by Séamus Ennis and Willie Clancy, RTÉ have very few Leo Rowsome recordings. There is surviving Radio Éireann material from Fleadhs in 1954 and 1964, plus nine fabulous pieces – near perfect in execution – from the 1959 Doolin concert. No doubt further high quality 1950s and 60s recordings can be found in private sources.

war, musicians that I knew living in London, who were living in Ireland then, only knew of uilleann pipes from the radio, from Rowsome. [Only] some of them experienced the Travellers. I knew about five or six musicians who used to hear either Johnny Doran or Felix Doran when they were on their rounds.

Leo represented the thin red line between his instrument's survival and its oblivion. And yet he was more than a lone figure raging against the dying of the light. He actually did something about it. Aside from his own recordings and broadcasts and the many sets of pipes he made with his hands, Leo co-founded two organisations which have sought to sustain aspects of traditional music, its practitioners and its public: the organisation that became Comhaltas Ceoltóirí Éireann in 1951; and Na Píobairí Uilleann in 1968.

As Terry Moylan has observed: 'Like any art, piping, while performed by individuals, must be related to a social context or it withers. Before 1968, piping had not much of an audience.'[130]

That there were any pipers at all in 1968, enough to at least seek out an audience, was in large part down to the unrelenting and good-natured efforts of Leo Rowsome over the previous 50 years.

*

Before his death, Leo had been working on a book of his music. On the centenary of his birth, his daughter Helena completed the task with the publication of *The Rowsome Collection Of Irish Music* (Waltons, 2003), with a biographical introduction and an appendix re-printing his piping tutor of 1936. She has since been working towards a full biography:

> **Helena**: The main reason I am writing Dad's biography is to make present and future generations aware of the full impact Leo Rowsome made, not alone on the piping world but that of Irish music in general. … He was a great ambassador for Irish music and for Ireland. … I saw him doing this. He was a national treasure.

But it's not all about history. The Rowsome tradition of piping lives on into a fifth generation with his grandson, Kevin Rowsome, a touring and recording musician of the present. For any musician, having the name of an illustrious forebear might carry a burden of responsibility and audience expectation. For Kevin, it's 'more of a blessing than a curse':

Kevin Rowsome: Uilleann pipes and pipe making have been a part of my life for as far back as I remember. Even though I was very involved with music from an early age, I didn't really play the pipes much in my teenage years. I was in my early 20s before I developed a love for the instrument and started to play on a regular basis, developing an appreciation for different aspects of piping by listening to recordings of other pipers.

I revived the Rowsome Quartet a few years ago and we played at a few concerts and festivals. [Also], I have two daughters, Tierna and Naoise, who play many instruments including the uilleann pipes. Some of their cousins also play pipes, so the sixth generation of piping in the Rowsome family is going strong!

Leo lived in an era where the pipes were in danger of dying out. He undoubtedly would be over the moon with the popularity of the pipes and the standard of playing today.

Ciarán Rowsome: A Memoir On Leo

Colin Harper: During the course of writing this book I attended an 'International Uilleann Piping Day' event, run by Helena Rowsome, at Northern Ireland's parliament building. Among those I was delighted to meet there – Wilbert Garvin, Robbie Hughes, Kevin Rowsome, Sheila Friel and the redoubtable Helena herself – was Leo's nephew Ciarán Rowsome, a cheery time management consultant with a clearly affectionate memory of his uncle. I asked Ciarán to contribute a few recollections, which he was very happy to do. They provide another perspective on an extraordinary man.

My personal involvement in the world of Irish music began in 1951. Thus, only six weeks after I was born was the launch of the inaugural All-Ireland Fleadh Ceoil in Mullingar, Westmeath: the culmination of years of preparation on the part of the Comhaltas Ceoltóirí Éireann committee. There had been a preceding event in Glendalough in 1948, which, by those involved, was viewed as a tester for the ultimate All-Ireland showcase three years later in Mullingar.

So, all through the early part of 1951, my father Tom Rowsome, as inaugural President of the fledgling Comhaltas, was immersed in the organisation of the event. There were regular visits to Mullingar, negotiating with local public and private sector bodies in terms of what possible venues could become available and then the myriad of other considerations associated with making such an ambitious gathering a success.

Leo was, of course, a huge part of the process – but very much on the musical side. So, while my father was also a piper by that middle stage of his life, he was well experienced in the organisational element – having, for instance, run two renowned men's and boys' clothing shops in Dublin's Thomas Street since 1932. The family recall how he planned aspects even as detailed as writing speeches for others to deliver at the opening event.

So all was well on plan until a few weeks after I arrived on the scene in mid-April. The problem was that just before the event was due to begin, I contracted double pneumonia, aged only five weeks. As the time grew nearer, it seems I ended up in intensive care in Temple Street Hospital and some feared the worst.

It was with this backdrop that my father had to proceed with his involvement in what was the biggest event with which all on the committee had ever been involved. Needless to say, it was a great success; I managed to pull through; and forever after, the members of the committee called me 'Comhaltas' Rowsome!

Of course, I have no personal memory of all the fuss back in 1951, but growing up, I quickly became conscious that my family was immersed in the Irish traditional music movement and that in our midst we had the crown prince, my uncle, the immensely talented Leo Rowsome. As we all now know, he was more accurately titled the 'King of the Pipers'.

Leo's own background was influenced by the pipe playing of his father William and his uncle Thomas who, like Leo, had become a celebrity, regularly playing at important events in the early part of the 20th century.

My earlier memories of Leo were a mixture of Leo the famous uilleann piper and Leo as our uncle. In terms of the famous uncle, we would hear him play regularly on Radio Éireann and at the annual Fleadh Cheoils, each held in different parts of Ireland. There were other settings: for example, in our family sitting room in Terenure and also in his own house over in Donnycarney.

In those cosier domestic settings, he sometimes liked to lighten things. On one occasion, in the late 50s, maybe sensing that the younger folk also had other musical interests, he really surprised us when launching into playing 'Jailhouse Rock'. Elvis meets Leo!

To me, that was indeed Leo. He seemed instinctively to know what was in the other person's mind. This is what made him an exceptional teacher. He showed, during many years of tirelessly imparting his knowledge, that he was a man of unique generosity. His mission when it came to pipe playing was to ensure that as many people as was possible could learn what he had learned before them. There was no holding back, and many of the current generation of pipers and piping in general were the beneficiaries. He had that same generosity in his role as an uncle – for instance, always arriving to our home with a massive brown paper bag filled with loose sweets of every variety.

At the Fleadh Cheoils we might expect Leo to play in the town's concert halls – and undoubtedly he did – but my more vivid memories were of him captivating large audiences in more unusual venues. This often included the local department or hardware stores, with the stock removed to allow for maximum audience space. Even the largest pharmacy in town was expected to get in on the act! Indeed, these choices of venue were no accident. One consideration that Leo and my father and others on the Comhaltas committee had was that, before the organisation's emergence, music tended to be played mainly in pubs and other drink-related venues, which they had no problem with. However, with the emergence of Comhaltas and the Fleadh Cheoils, there was a conscious effort to offer a choice of such alternative musical settings, where drink didn't always need to play a part. The focus was on the playing.

It was remarkable how Leo was so immersed in traditional music at so many levels. This was not just as an uilleann pipe player, but also as a teacher, pipe maker and repairer, let alone his involvement in Comhaltas. Leo must have felt a huge sense of responsibility to keep the music alive at a time when Ireland was losing tens of thousands of people through emigration. Not alone was he down the country, regularly playing in village and towns around Ireland, he also played to emigrant groups over in the UK. I can also recall my father's pride in his brother playing at those illustrious locations such as the Royal Albert Hall in London and Carnegie Hall in New York.

I always felt that Leo had an unusual type of fame. In the fledgling years of the Irish state, citizens experienced many difficulties and challenges. So, while the population most likely were experiencing a sense of pride in belonging to Europe's newest state, for many, life was run at quite a basic level. Often, outside of the urban areas, communication with the outside world was dependent on radio. The new national station 2RN opened in 1926 and Leo played during its first month. From then on, from the 20s to the 60s, he was featured on the successor to the 2RN station, Radio Éireann, more than most other artists.

The fact of being heard so regularly on the only medium that most people had access to, combined with the attachment many people in rural areas had to the feelings of nationhood, of which Irish music played a huge part, resulted in Leo having an almost mystical appeal. Personally, I most noticed this in my work in the 1970s and 1980s when many of my contacts were rurally based. This was either when meeting people when working outside of my Dublin base, or when in the city, in conversations with those from the country, working in civil service departments. Often, on hearing my surname and realising the connection, the tone of the person's voice would change, expressing hushed admiration of 'Leo'. Many would recount memories of Leo from their childhood, saying that their entire village would turn out see and hear Leo when he appeared. It has to also be remembered that in those early days, relatively few people had fame – which in some way heightened the respect for those who did have it. Indeed, on the night of my introduction to my girlfriend's (now my wife's) parents, that relationship was properly sealed once it became known that I was related to Leo. So he came in handy sometimes!

My brother Tomás gave me a good example of how readily people knew of Leo. It was when Tomás was once standing in a row of 50 award winners at a sports event in Dublin, back in the 1970s. They were in the process of receiving the congratulatory handshake from the Irish President, Cearbhall Ó Dáilaigh. When my brother's surname name was announced to the President, he instantly pronounced: 'Tomás, you're in the wrong place, surely – where are your uilleann pipes?'

Another memory of Leo was his many visits to our father's shop in Thomas Street. It was a venue where pipers and Comhaltas committee members regularly converged, with Willie Clancy being a regular visitor. There, stories of piping and points concerning upcoming events would be discussed and debated in great detail. Of course, the Pipers' Club was located right across the road.

The three great pipers, Leo, Willie Clancy and Séamus Ennis, were true friends. Leo, being quite a bit older than either Willie or Séamus, was probably viewed as a father figure. Our family not only admired their piping, but in the case of Séamus we were also in awe of his abilities in folklore archiving. Séamus was a constant and major contributor not only to the Irish national archive but to the BBC's also. My brother recalls how upset Séamus was when Leo died. Like all of us, he knew that we had lost a very special person.

Chapter 8
Leo Rowsome At The BBC

'Mr Rowsome wishes to play upon the Irish Pipes in our programmes …'
  – BBC internal memo, June 29 1937

Listed amongst various other achievements in Leo Rowsome's promotional material of the 1950s is a passing declaration that he was the first Irish artist televised by the BBC. It was a bold claim, and there was no reason to disbelieve it. From the testimony of those who knew him, Leo's integrity was beyond question. But it is the duty of an historian to seek evidence. The BBC would never have given Leo Rowsome a certificate saying *'Congratulations – you are the first Irish artist to appear!'* There would be no formal mechanism to notify performers from this or that nation of their priority. It would be the sort of information that might be casually mentioned by a producer, as in, *'Thanks for doing the show – you know, I do believe you're the first Irish [or Venezuelan or Portuguese or whatever] act we've had …'* Nevertheless, the means to verify Leo's claim would perhaps be found at the BBC Written Archive Centre (WAC) in Caversham.

Anyone examining the (tantalisingly incomplete) surviving contracts and correspondence there might come away thinking, *'Well, it can't be proved, but it just might be true …'* Such an individual would certainly come away knowing that Leo was likely *among* the first Irish traditional musicians to broadcast on BBC radio. It would seem hardly credible that any other uilleann piper would have been there before him. The days when Leo was hammering on the BBC door were days in which there were few other players of the instrument around.

The surviving correspondence between Leo and various producers and executives at mostly London-based BBC departments between 1926 and 1952 – a period mirroring his early recording career on commercial 78s almost exactly – reveals a great deal about the way things were, and how things were done, at that time.

It was an era of mass wireless (radio) listening and overwhelming deference towards the BBC as an institution, as the communications wing of 'the Establishment'. It connected the Empire and the regions with numerous home (Home Service, Light Programme and Third Programme) and overseas Services, each run independently. Within the home-based Services there was regional segregation. In an era of 'BBC

English', it was rare to hear regional British voices on the national airwaves, let alone Irish ones. Many 'Northern' English comedians, latterly household names, including Morecambe & Wise, struggled with this uneven playing field – able only to get broadcast engagements on the Northern frequency of the Home Service. It was a kind of genteel prejudice – the notion that only Northern audiences would understand either the accent or the humour of a Northern comedian.

Leo Rowsome's gentle war of attrition over four decades of indefatigable correspondence reflects this *realpolitik* implicitly: he repeatedly focuses on securing a broadcast around St Patrick's Day, clearly believing that this was probably the only opportunity (and even then a slender one) for an Irish traditional musician to get through the door. And he was surely correct in this belief.

Leo was, to the BBC producers and listenership, a novelty act. His piping competition credentials counted for little. It was an age of applying for – and, if lucky, receiving – a BBC audition. After that, it was a case of waiting and hoping that you might get a call (or more likely a letter). The BBC audition process continued well into the 1970s, with many subsequently legendary names in pop, rock and jazz obliged to impress an anonymous panel of airwave guardians who might deign to let them loose on *Saturday Club* and the shows that came in its wake as the Light Programme gave way to Radios 1 and 2 in September 1967. The patrician aspect of the Corporation was long in lingering.

There was little concept of music as an 'art' during the period in which Leo Rowsome was trying to be heard. Beyond European art music ('classical music'), any performer was obliged to be filed under 'Variety' and, if seeking a broadcast, to have a 'turn' lasting a few minutes, preferably bright and breezy in nature. These years were the heyday of Variety: a catch-all entertainment term that encompassed musical acts, comedy acts, animal acts, circus acts and myriad novelty performers. It was a kind of cleaned-up, grown-up progeny of the Victorian music hall. A network of theatres up and down the country supported the Variety industry, with multiple artists packing the bill on any given night. The gradual rise of one's name up that bill, with bigger lettering on the posters, toward the coveted spots of closing the first half or topping the second, was the mark of success. Some acts could sustain a career for years with a single routine lasting a few minutes. Wilson, Keppel & Betty's Egyptian Sand Dance is but one example: a newsreel film of a 1933 performance can be viewed online, and they were still doing it when they retired (having replaced several 'Bettys' along the way) in 1963.

Leo's live work in Britain, mentioned periodically in his BBC correspondence, seems to have been a smattering of Irish-focused concert events in any given year. His 1948 appearance on the BBC's *Variety Bandbox* – a hugely popular show which launched the careers of Terry-Thomas, Tony Hancock and Frankie Howerd amongst many others in the 1940s – would appear, to the researcher reliant on BBC WAC resources, to be his only foray into this milieu of British Variety. Leo had a business to run back in Dublin and plenty of opportunities to at least sustain his career, performing and teaching, within Ireland. But if his promotional campaign with the BBC confirms anything, it is that Leo was seeking not to sustain a career but to build one, to expand from his base in Ireland. His efforts and resolve in trying to do so were heroic.

To what extent Leo viewed piping as an art or an entertainment remains moot. It had developed as a functional instrument, to accompany dancing, yet it had the aura of magic and nobility. Leo Rowsome's life and career – however he may have viewed his vocation in the pre- and immediately post-war years – represents, perhaps, a bridge between the notion of the pipes as purely an instrument of entertainment, albeit a rarefied one whose players tended to attract or exude enigma, and the status of piping today as the 10th *dan* pinnacle of a hallowed tradition, venerated and protected by public subsidy.

Pioneered by the BBC in the 1930s, following a couple of years as a privately run concern by inventor John Logie Baird, television was an expensive novelty with a very limited reach in the pre-war era. By 1939, there were only 10,000 sets. It was only in 1953, with national interest surrounding the coronation of Elizabeth II, that television sets became widespread in Britain. The BBC written records are incomplete, but it seemed from close reading that Leo just *may* have participated in a pre-war television broadcast. Typically, given that a piper is involved, enigma still shrouded the possibility.

Radio would still, nevertheless, dominate home entertainment in Britain for some years to come. During the period in which Leo was pitching his services, a BBC radio broadcast was not only a significant notch on one's CV (of value in securing live bookings) but an endorsement of one's quality. If Leo was seeking to bring uilleann piping to the masses, as well as to promote his own career (a perfectly valid aim in itself), he recognised that he would have to adapt to the medium. His suggested repertoire of audition material from a letter of July 20 1926 reflects this: popular light tunes leavening the traditional music.

It would be easy to misunderstand Leo's compromising before the God of the Airwaves as some kind of sell-out, but that would be wholly anachronistic. It was simply the way things were, and Leo displays canny pragmatism, mixed with deference, courtesy and a vexatious determination, in his desire to be heard. Even as late as the 1970s, black Midlands-born comedian Lenny Henry understood that to build a career via British TV meant accepting racial stereotyping and delivering what was required within that context on the platforms available at that time.

During the 1960s, the concept of non-classical music as an art form began to gain currency even at the BBC, with traditional music possibly getting into this realm of perception a little earlier than pop/rock. The McPeakes, for example, were able to appear on BBC TV arts programme *Line Up* in 1967, while also gracing Light Entertainment shows such as ABC TV's *Eamonn Andrews Show* around the same time. Finbar & Eddie Furey, in the same period, straddled British TV and radio shows associated with Light Entertainment, rock music and Scots Gaelic culture. The Bothy Band, in the mid-70s, similarly managed to traverse the airwaves between *The Val Doonican Show* at one end and *The John Peel Show* at the other.

By that stage, in the 1960s and 70s, opportunities to broadcast generally came to such artists without the relentless velvet-gloved push and shove (as reflected in the Leo Rowsome correspondence) of earlier times. An Irish traditional act of quality no longer had to bow and scrape (not even the fiddlers): there were enough sympathetic producers around the BBC by then who could see value, in terms of art and entertainment, in such people – and who could provide platforms to suit both them and their audience. Crucially, attitudes were by then changing within the BBC from 'what the BBC thinks its listeners want' to 'what our listeners probably want based on what is demonstrably popular out in the world beyond our studios'.

By the 1960s, Leo's remarkable competition credentials would have carried more weight. 7Ironically, however, he had stopped offering his services. Focused on family, teaching and pipe making in Ireland by then, why would he need to? It had become a more professionalised industry – bookings tended to be made through agents – but it was still one in which who you knew could make life easier. The 26 years' worth of correspondence retained at the BBC's Caversham archive is a reflection on Leo's persistence, and its results are a triumph against the odds of his times. It may have taken him a long time, but if Leo Rowsome didn't quite manage to kick the door in for Séamus Ennis, the McPeakes, the Fureys and all who followed, he certainly put a few dents in it.

A Note On The BBC

Launched in October 1922, pre-war BBC radio comprised a network of 11 local stations (including Belfast) and a further eight relay stations around Great Britain. Broadcasts originating from most or all of these stations began at various times over the next two years. In July 1925, the Daventry Station – the first to which Leo Rowsome offered his services – became the first to achieve near-national coverage, beginning a two-year process toward what became the BBC National Service (broadcasts originating in London for the whole country) and the BBC Regional

Service (local stations broadcasting their own content on a different frequency). The two services were merged to become the BBC Home Service on the outbreak of war in September 1939.

Following the war, the single Home Service returned to a regional structure, with regional Home Services operating from Belfast, Glasgow, Cardiff, Bristol, Manchester and Birmingham in addition to the 'National' Home Service broadcasting from London. During 1946–47 the Light Programme and the Third Programme, two new national services with distinct programming identities, were launched. In September 1967, BBC Radios 1, 2, 3 and 4 were launched: Radio 2 replaced the Light Programme; Radio 3 replaced the Third Programme; Radio 4 replaced the Home Service; while Radio 1 was designed to replace the pop music 'pirate' stations (Radio Caroline, Radio London and others) which had thrived, broadcasting to Britain from international waters, between 1964 and 1967.

The Leo Rowsome BBC Written Archives Files

11/1/26 *Letter from Leo to BBC Station Director, Daventry*

> I take the liberty of applying for an engagement at your station and attach a leaflet showing some of my qualifications … I might mention that I have appeared – with success – in London, Glasgow and Manchester concerts. Our local station director has given me a trial, with excellent results, and an engagement for 2RN. Your esteemed consideration is earnestly sought …

The enclosed leaflet promotes four 78rpm discs by Leo on Edison Bell Winner Records. His competition wins are listed, including 1st prize at the Dublin Feis Ceoil (1921, 1922, 1924, 1925).

Note: Leo had wasted no time in getting broadcasting opportunities at home: 2RN, the government-run forerunner of RTÉ, only began on January 1 1926, initially broadcasting for three hours a night. He uses headed notepaper: Wm Rowsome & Sons, Irish Union Pipes, Reed Makers, 125 Harold's Cross Road, Dublin.

?/1/26 *Reply from the BBC Station Director, Daventry, to Leo*

> Your best plan would be to apply to the Director of the Belfast Station for an audition. We can then obtain a report as to your transmission and write to you in the event of our being able to offer you an engagement in London …

10/7/26 *Leo replies to the BBC Station Director, Daventry*

> The Belfast station is taking only <u>local</u> turns on the Union pipes … I expect to be in London about the end of this month, and respectfully apply for a turn. I have broadcast on several occasions from 2RN with excellent results [underlined in red] and if you require any references as to my suitability, I can admit same if necessary …

Note: In fact, the local BBC station, 2BE, was at this point only featuring one local turn on the instrument: Richard Lewis O'Mealy. Even then, from Radio Times listings evidence, the presence of pipes on the station was limited: O'Mealy performed on three 2BE programmes on 30/9/24, a further three on 25/11/24 and two on 4/9/25. As far as one can tell, no uilleann piper was then heard on the BBC NI service until Liam Walsh on 8/8/30. After that there is nothing until O'Mealy reappears on 9/1/34. He broadcasts fairly frequently thereafter on the regional airwaves until 30/4/43. Aside from O'Mealy, Fermanagh piper Philip Maxwell was most prolific on NI airwaves: 12 broadcasts, 1934–40. Three other 'local turns' on the pipes – Frank McFadden, William Andrews and Patrick Maxwell – are heard on four local programmes between them during the late 1930s.

14/7/26 *The BBC Station Director, Daventry, replies to Leo*

> Before discussing the possibility of an engagement to transmit from our London studio, it will be necessary for you to submit to our Variety Producer a short 7 minute act consisting of material which you consider would be suitable to our public. We regret that this must be done in all cases, but you will realise readily that the standard of our London programmes is considerably higher than that in the provinces …

20/7/26 *Letter from Leo to the suggested Variety Prod*

Leo suggests dates when he would be in London, available for a BBC trial (giving 10 days' notice as requested): August 7–10 1926.

> Our pipes is [sic] used chiefly for our National music, but (in capable hands) is an excellent exponent for any class of song. Having due regard for the various tastes of your 'listeners in' I respectfully submit herewith a possible selection which I propose to offer at my trial …

The tunes he suggests are: 'Annie Laurie' (air); 'Miss McLeod' (reel); 'Home Sweet Home' (air); 'The Irish Washerwoman' (jig); 'Marsellaise [sic] / The Men Of Harlech' (march). A BBC trial is duly offered for Monday August 9.

2/10/26 *Letter from Leo to John F. Barham, BBC*

> Having submitted a short item on August 9 to your Variety Producer, in the nature of a trial, I am now prepared to make the following offer. I am free to travel any weekend you wish to suggest i.e. Broadcast from your London studio on a Saturday evening, and from any of your stations on the Monday following at a fee of £12/12 [12 guineas] inclusive …

Note: This is a rather bold figure: the equivalent of over £600 today. An average farm labourer in Britain in 1926 could expect to work around 10 weeks for such a sum.

A note from a producer is appended to the letter in the BBC file:

> I regret nothing doing – will let him know as soon as I can offer a date.

6/10/26 *Letter from John F. Barham to Leo*

> At the moment we are unable to offer you a broadcast date … In the event of our being able to offer you a date, we will again communicate with you …

Note: There is no correspondence extant between 6/10/26 and 17/9/30, though there must have been communications in 1927 as the letter below suggests.

17/9/30 *Letter from Leo to the BBC*

> I have not been to London since March 1927, when I gave an audition from the Irish bagpipes in your studios … I will be crossing again in about three weeks. Can it be possible to give me a booking then? I have broadcast from Dublin and Cork on last Saturday and Sunday, September 13th and 14th respectively, and will be doing something from Belfast in a few weeks and am anxious to do Glasgow also. I sincerely hope you will kindly see your way to offer me an engagement from London and Cardiff or any other of the British studios …

Note: The Cork broadcasting station 6CK had opened in 1927, as both a relay station for the Dublin-based 2RN and (though briefly, as it transpired) as a contributor of original programming to the network.

19/9/30 *BBC reply*

> We regret to say that as we make up our programmes some six weeks ahead, I am afraid it will be impossible to include you on your arrival in London …

16/1/31 *Letter from Leo to the BBC*

Leo acknowledges the six-week lead time and says he will be in London for an engagement on March 17. He asks for a 'double booking', to broadcast from London and Manchester on consecutive days.

Note: Leo has new letter-headed paper: 'Wm Rowsome & Sons, Irish Union Pipes & Reed Makers, est. 1895'.

12/1/31 *BBC reply*

> We will let you know …

14/2/31 *Letter from Leo to the BBC*

> Should the opportunity arise for including me in your programmes I shall be very grateful … I will be performing at the Queen's Hall, London, on March 17 and have broadcast from Dublin frequently …

Note: There is no BBC reply.

17/2/31 *Letter from Leo to the BBC*

> Kindly let me know at your earliest convenience if my services are required …

20/2/31 *BBC reply*

> We regret that we have been unable to include you …

18/2/32 *Letter from Leo to the BBC*

> I expect to be in England performing on the Irish bagpipes at concerts about the middle of March. I respectfully beg to apply for a Broadcast engagement … I may add that I broadcast frequently from the Dublin station on the Irish Pipes, my next dates are February 21st (next Sunday) and March 17th … Trusting you will kindly see your way to include me in your programmes …

26/2/32 *BBC reply*

> We are afraid … it will be impossible to avail ourselves of your services when you will be here in the middle of March …

6/12/32 *Letter from Leo to the BBC*

> I am engaged to perform at the Queen's Hall on March 17 next …

Leo then embarks on a career resumé, mentioning concerts at London, Liverpool, Manchester, Glasgow 'and all the chief towns in Ireland' and that he is 'well established on Gramophone records'. He declares that he broadcasts frequently in Ireland, with his next bookings being December 21 and January 10, 21 and 22:

> I may possibly be joining a concert party to the USA next summer and I would like to tell the folks out there I have performed for the BBC.

19/12/32 *BBC reply*

> We thank you for your letter … from which we note that you will be coming to London [around] March 17th … It is too early to make any definite programme arrangements for March but if you care to send us a reminder about the beginning of February we will certainly keep your name in mind.

23/1/32 *Letter from Leo to the BBC*

> I am now placing the matter again before you and I sincerely hope you will kindly see your way to offer me a few evenings during my visit. I will be free to broadcast on March 16th, 18th, 19th and 20th from any of your studios …

27/1/32 *BBC reply*

We will keep these dates in mind …

20/2/33 *Letter from Leo to the BBC*

Having already acknowledged their reply (on 2/2/32), Leo reminds the BBC of his available dates in March.

Note: No BBC reply is extant, nor is any further correspondence until January 1936.

21/1/36 *Letter from Leo to Eustace Robb, BBC*

Leo explains that he is coming to London again for March 17 and, once again, seeks an engagement:

> I am sure you will agree that a selection of Irish airs and Dance music on the old Irish Bagpipes would prove a very interesting and unusual Broadcast and would be very appropriate about the time of my visit for the National Festival of Ireland. … I am also desirous of making some further Gramophone records and perhaps you may also kindly put me in touch with some of the companies who would be interested … I must apologise for giving you so much trouble but when I recollect your courtesy in the past, I am sure you will not fail to answer this letter with the necessary particulars.

Note: Any letters attesting to previous cordiality between Mr Robb and Leo are no longer extant in the BBC archive.

From Leo's letter it is also clear that he has already applied for a BBC television transmission and has received a letter of refusal. The letter of application and the BBC letter of regret are no longer extant.

Note: Leo's tenacity in trying to get on television before, in any meaningful sense, there even was television is remarkable. BBC TV would not officially begin until November 2 1936. A very limited, experimental service – broadcasting to just a few hundred people in London – ran between August 1932 and September 1935, at which point it was suspended until the higher-definition re-launch a year later. In August 1936 there was a kind of trial session for the forthcoming BBC TV service. Being thought of as radio with visuals, the first programme to be broadcast (live) was, of course, a Variety show: Here's Looking At You. It was performed twice a day for 10 days and featured The Three Admirals (singers from a musical revue), Miss Lutie & Her Wonder Horse Pogo, a pair of tap dancers and singer Helen McKay. Leo Rowsome was not involved. By the outbreak of World War II in September 1939, transmission was suspended. By then the BBC television service was reaching an estimated 25,000–40,000 homes.

23/1/36 *Internal Circulating Memo from Eustace Robb to 'Variety Booking' and 'Music Booking'*

Mr Robb attaches Leo's latest letter to the memo.

> I do not know if this interests you. He is a good Irish piper, and has appeared in several St Patrick's Day programmes for Television and given satisfaction …

Note: Robb's reference to 'several television programmes' is enigmatic. Is it a misunderstanding (meaning to say 'radio programmes') or could there really have been pre-1936 BBC television broadcasts now beyond the reach of surviving documentation? Leo has already acknowledged, in his previous letter, that BBC TV in London have turned him down, and at this time there was no other television service operating in Belfast, Dublin or anywhere else in the British Isles.

There are several hand-written ponderings from booking personnel on the memo, but nothing concrete. On 24/1/36 a Variety booker scribbles:

> My nearest date is Saturday 14th. I do not suppose for the sake of a small fee we could offer for *Saturday Magazine* that this man would come to London on 14th as it would presumably mean two extra days expenses at least. [But] I will write and enquire whether he would be interested.

Another Variety booker, a Mr Hanson, scribbles that he will take a note of Rowsome's name and address for future reference. On 27/1/36 the first booker writes: 'On second thoughts I don't feel inclined to make use of him.'

1/2/36 *Letter from Leo to the BBC*

Leo acknowledges that no TV opportunities are available, but asks again about March 15–19 radio possibilities.

song. Would you kindly arrange for this. Apart from the above we would probably like two or three numbers from you and would be glad if you would send along your suggestions …

10/2/37 *Contract for* Irish Variety

> Fee (Performance): 4 guineas, all expenses
> Fee (Mechanical Reproduction to Empire): 1 guinea

15/2/37 *Letter from Leo to Miss Eales*

> I have selected three groups of items, each will take about 5 or 6 minutes to perform. You can choose any of these groups … You will notice I have chosen 'The Last Glimpse Of Erin' for the fading in and fading out. This is a fine old traditional air and is also known as 'The Coulin'.

Leo's suggestions are: 'O'Donnell Abú/St Patrick's Day/The Heather Breeze'; 'Parnell's March/The Copper Plate/The Connacht Men's Ramble'; 'Haste To The Wedding/Pigeon On The Gate/The Londonderry Hornpipe'. A signed contract is enclosed.

17/3/37 *Irish Variety* (Empire Service, 8.00–8.30am)

Leo's first BBC broadcast.

22/6/37 *Letter from Leo to A.H. Brown*

Leo informs Brown he will be in London in early August.

> You will recall my recent Empire broadcast on 17th March, which I trust was satisfactory. The Garryowen Ceilidhe Band [sic], with whom I broadcast from Dublin recently, would also like to broadcast from London during my visit …

24/6/37 *Reply from A.H. Brown*

> If it is possible to arrange an engagement for you during [your visit] I will write you further. These remarks also apply in the case of the Garryowen Ceilidhe Band.

28/6/37 *Note from Dance Band Producer attached to above circulated letter*

I don't think we could make satisfactory use of this suggestion in the Dance Band Schedule.

29/6/37 *Internal Circulating Memo 'to all producers'*

Mr Rowsome wishes to play upon the Irish Pipes in our programmes. There might possibly be a spot for him with the Theatre Organ recital, or he could be used in the *ABC* [series] for 'U' under Uilleann Pipes.

Scribbled note from well-informed producer: "U' falls on September 4th!'

Twenty producers acknowledge the memo, the only other comment being: 'No use for *ABC*.'

29/7/37 *Internal Memo from Peter Montgomery (BBC NI Region's Assistant Music Director) to Arthur Wynn*

We have heard from Mr Leo Rowson [sic] (Dublin Piper) who claims to have broadcast from London. If this is so would you please send us a report of his work.

Written note on memo from R. Little (secretary to a Mr Pifford, upon whose desk this memo has fallen): 'Mr Pifford is away on hols at the moment but from shorthand notes I have found Mr Pifford thought what he did [on *Empire Programme – Irish Variety* 17/3/37] was good. He also has a very large repertoire.'

19/8/37 *Reply to Peter Montgomery from Variety Booking*

I have a report to say that they were quite satisfied with his performance and that he has a large repertoire. They would be quite prepared to offer Mr Rowsome another engagement as soon as the opportunity arises.

17/1/38 *Letter from Leo to A.H. Brown*

I expect to be in London on March 17th next, performing at Irish Festivities …

18/1/38 *Internal Circulating Memo*

> Mr Leo Rowsome, the Irish Pipe player, writes to say he will be in London on March 17th … He is asking whether he can have a broadcast engagement on that date …

Scribbled notes on the memo confirm nothing is available.

28/1/38 *Reply from A.H. Brown*

> We are sorry to inform you …

6/1/39 *Letter from Leo to A.H. Brown*

> I expect to be in London on March 17th … Thanking you for past kindnesses and wishing you a Happy New Year …

9/2/39 *Letter from Leo to A.H. Brown*

> I wrote to you a few weeks ago …

13/2/39 *Reply from A.H. Brown*

> We are very sorry your letter of the 6th January was not acknowledged. Unfortunately …

Note: There is no correspondence during the war years.

30/1/47 *Letter from Leo to C.J. Meehan, BBC*

Note: Leo has new letter-headed paper: Leo Rowsome: Uilleann Pipes Maker and Expert: 9 Belton Park Road, Dublin

> I am engaged to perform in Birmingham on March 16th and in London on March 17th (the Irish Festival) and am wondering if you can kindly fit me in your programme on this night …

A note from a producer (presumably of a St Patrick's Day themed programme) is scribbled on the letter:

> As this bloke is performing in Birmingham on the 16th I can't fit him into the show. Besides, pipes are not too popular.

Leo encloses with his letter a promotional leaflet for a Dublin Ceilidhe [sic] event, including the text:

> Proffessor [sic] Leo Rowsome of Dublin is acknowledged as the world's leading exponent of the Uilleann Pipes and has broadcast to many parts of the world. He was the 1st Irish artist to be televised by the BBC …

Note: Was Leo ever televised by the BBC? The mystery continues … BBC Television, which had closed down in September 1939 when war was declared, reopened in June 1946. Its first day back included a Mickey Mouse cartoon, which was the last broadcast in 1939, and a performance by Light Music maestro Mantovani's orchestra – which had been booked to play the day after the shutdown. On day two of the comeback, BBC Television broadcast live from the VE Day parade in London. There is no evidence in BBC Written Records to show that Leo Rowsome was squeezed into the schedule between June 1946 and January 1947, nor that he ever secured a pre-war TV broadcast. Still, records are incomplete, and given Leo's tenacity with a pen it is just possible that he did. Oral tradition around Leo (reflected in, for example, his Wikipedia entry) has it that 1933 was the year of his BBC television broadcast. As discussed above, the BBC had an extremely limited TV service operating from London for half an hour a day between 1932 and 1935 prior to its suspension and re-launch in 1936 with a higher-definition and more widely accessible service. In Leo's letter of 12/1/37, he refers to having previously broadcast from Broadcasting House – and this may be a tantalising clue to the veracity of his claim. For between August 1932 and February 1934, Broadcasting House was used as the base for the BBC's prototype television service – a system using a vertically-scanned image of 30 lines, which was just enough for a close-up of one person, and with a bandwidth low enough to use an existing radio transmitter. Is it really possible that Leo Rowsome somehow convinced the same institution which would only give him a radio broadcast after 11 years of badgering to give him a television spot in the days when the medium barely existed? You wouldn't have put it past him.

6/2/47 *Reply from C.F. Meehan*

> Dear Mr Rowsome, I am sorry to say …

24/5/48 *Letter from Leo to Peter Duncan, Aeolian Hall (a BBC London studio):*

> I expect to be visiting London again [in July] … I wonder if you could do anything in the way of getting me fixed up for a Broadcast … I enjoyed my last date with you and hope to be at your service again for next year's National Festival …

Note: Could Leo have been featured on a previous programme produced by Peter Duncan? Peter Duncan was producer of the BBC radio magazine/chat show In Town Tonight *(which ran from 1933 to 1960, with a TV version simulcast from 1954 to 1956). Opening to the sound (and later vision) of Piccadilly Circus, the presenter would begin: 'Once more we stop the mighty roar of London's traffic and, from the great crowds, we bring you some of the interesting people who have come by land, sea and air to be 'In Town Tonight'.' Among regular outside broadcast spots in the show during the 1940s was 'Standing On The Corner' with a man named Michael Standing. Genius. Leo's addressing of his letter to Peter at Aeolian Hall is suggestive: the premises had only been acquired by the BBC for broadcasting in March 1943. As it seems unlikely that Leo would have been in London during the 'Emergency' of the war years, we are left with the possibility that he may have broadcast under Peter Duncan's patronage during 1946, or more likely in 1947 or early 1948. If so, the paperwork is no longer extant. Alternatively, it remains possible that Duncan had been involved in Leo's confirmed Empire broadcast of 1937. Nevertheless, the feeling grows that something important is being missed through the incomplete surviving documentation.*

26/5/48 *Reply from Peter Duncan*

> I suggest you get in touch with Joy Russell-Smith who is the producer of *Variety Bandbox*. I know that this programme is pretty heavily booked up and you may find it difficult to break in, but I think it is your best bet. Wish you success in this matter …

[Leo apparently did write to Joy Russell-Smith – of course he did! – but the letter is not extant.]

4/6/48 *Letter to Leo from J.E. Sheffield (Variety Booking):*

> I understand that you will be in London next month, and Miss Joy Russell-Smith, the producer of *Variety Bandbox*, would like to include you in her programme on Sunday 25th July 1948, from 8.00–9.00pm with a

rehearsal on the same day at Golders Green Hippodrome. We can offer you a fee of 7 Guineas …

8/6/48 *Letter from Leo to J.E. Sheffield*

I am willing to accept your offer of 7 Guineas for my engagement to appear on *Variety Bandbox* … Whilst I appreciate same I would be better pleased if you will kindly make it 10 Guineas. When advising me time of rehearsal, please state what part of London is Golders Green Hippodrome …

Note: Leo was not being greedy: it was the norm for artists, or their agents, to negotiate for higher fees from the BBC in the 'Variety' era. In general, it was simple supply/demand, albeit negotiated within the gentlemanly BBC atmosphere of commerce and Reithian values dressed in tweedy conviviality that will by now be apparent. Comedian Terry-Thomas became particularly noted for demanding, and receiving, eye-watering fees from the BBC in the 1940s and 50s – because he knew his popularity and worth. Leo Rowsome, of course, had no such pre-existing popular base to stand on. His additional guinea was really a token reward for having the gumption to ask. By 1948, aged 45, Leo would surely have had a solid understanding of his own worth as an artist.

11/6/48 *Reply from J.E. Sheffield*

We regret we are unable to increase the fee to 10 Guineas but we have, however, made it 8 Guineas and I am enclosing a contract herewith. You can reach the Hippodrome by tube from Piccadilly Circus …

The enclosed contract adds the possibility of further fees in various circumstances: 4 guineas for mechanical reproduction (repeat broadcasts in the UK); £1/13/8 for the first five mechanical reproduction broadcasts overseas; 16 shillings and 10 pence per broadcast overseas after the first five. (A shilling equalled 12 pence.)

Note: As Graham McCann notes in his biography Frankie Howerd: Stand Up Comic (Harper Perennial, 2005): 'Established in 1944, Variety Bandbox had soon become the radio show on which every popular entertainer in the country craved to be heard … It was the most listened-to programme of its type – overheard coming from most of the houses in most of the streets in Britain each Sunday night, and discussed in countless workplaces each Monday morning.' Howerd, whose career was effectively launched on the show, was receiving around 18 guineas per appearance on it in 1948.

25/7/48 *Variety Bandbox* (Light Programme, 10.00–11.00pm)

Radio Times confirms that this episode will feature Leo on a bill with Revnell & West, Billy Munn, Bill Kerr, The Peterson Brothers, Billy Tennent & His Orchestra, The Three Monarchs and future comedy legend Bob Monkhouse.

26/8/48 *Letter to Leo from the BBC Transcription Service*

The Transcription Service is proposing to record Leo's episode of *Variety Bandbox* on LP for distribution to overseas stations. They offer Leo an additional £4/4. Naturally, Leo signs the contract.

Note: The BBC Transcription Service began as part of the General Overseas Department in the 1930s. Its staff selected domestic programme content to record onto disc for sending to overseas stations for local broadcast. Generally, only 100 copies of each disc were pressed, often with instructions to each overseas radio network to destroy the disc at the end of the licence period. The early discs were 12-inch 78rpm records capable of holding three minutes per side, meaning that several discs were required to contain a whole programme. By around 1947, the 12-inch 78s were superseded by 16-inch discs running at 33⅓rpm. These could hold around 10 minutes per side. Leo's performance on Variety Bandbox *may conceivably survive, although it is not in the British Library catalogue of BBC transcriptions. One complete one-hour episode of the series, from 1950, survives and at least 16 transcription discs – certainly eight from 1948, though not including Leo's episode – are known to exist. The one-hour UK show was edited to 30 minutes for transcription disc distribution.*

7/9/48 *Letter from Leo to Joy Russell-Smith*

> A few lines to state I am now tentative booking for your *Band Box* [sic] on November 21st. I expect to be performing in Leicester on November 20th at the Folk Dancing Festival there … Rory O'Connor, Ireland's champion step dancer, is dancing in Leicester to my accompaniment on the pipes, and he would also like an engagement in your *Family Band Box* [sic] on the date in question …

30/9/48 *Reply from Jan Roland (current producer of* Variety Bandbox*)*

Ms Roland tells Leo she will pass his letter on to Brian Sears, who succeeds her the following month (Joy Russell-Smith having moved on herself some time previously).

25/1/49 *Letter from Leo to Mr Connell, Music Bookings Manager, Broadcasting House*

> I would like to offer my services to the BBC for some broadcast engagements during the Irish National Festival from March 16th to 18th. I have already been featured in Empire programmes in recent years …
>
> Anxiously awaiting an early reply which I trust will be in the affirmative …

There is a scribbled note on the letter, which has clearly been passed on to an Overseas Services producer:

> Thank you – we've already had one addressed to 'Overseas Booking Manager' – no doubt there are more to come!

Note: Neither Leo's letter to the 'Overseas Booking Manager' nor a subsequent letter to Peter Duncan, producer of In Town Tonight (see below), is extant.

22/6/49 *Letter to Leo from Patrick Newman, Variety Booking Manager*

> Your letter to Mr Peter Duncan of the 15th instant [May 15] has been passed to me as I am afraid that he cannot fit you into his *In Town Tonight* programme. We will keep a note of your particulars … should you ever be coming to town for your own purposes …
>
> However, I am afraid your suggestion of making a special journey for which you would need three or four dates in one week would not be practicable …

There is a handwritten note on the (circulated) letter from one producer (Patrick Newman) to another (Miss Lyons):

> Haven't we done all this before? (Yearly?)

15/2/50 *Letter from Leo to Head of Features, Broadcasting House*

> I am wondering if you can possibly feature me in any programme of the BBC around March 17th for the Irish Festival … I have often taken part in Irish programmes before during this period …

17/2/50 *Internal memo to Pat Newman from 'N.L.' (Miss Lyons)*

> This man broadcast in *Variety Bandbox* in 1948 and did an Empire broadcast (*Irish Variety*) in 1937. These are the only two bookings shown on the cards, but he may, of course, have taken part in programmes relayed from Belfast or Dublin. Can we just circulate his name in case producers are interested and tell him that we have done this? We might, perhaps, also say that … we will keep a note of his qualifications for future reference?

The memo is circulated and acknowledged by 29 producers.

Note: Intriguingly, given the tantalising possibility (discussed above) of a previous now-undocumented radio broadcast for Peter Duncan's In Town Tonight *and the enigma of a possible pre-war television broadcast, it's valuable to note that even in 1950 the available documentation only listed the two radio appearances that can be validated from paperwork 64 years later.*

21/5/50 *Reply to Leo from Patrick Newman, Variety Booking Manager*

> We have made a note that you are available in the event of any of our producers requiring an act such as yours …

24/7/50 *Letter from Leo to Patrick Newman*

> I expect to be in Liverpool on a short holiday from August 27th to September 4th and would be very glad to accept a broadcast during this period.
>
> PS I gave a performance on *Variety Bandbox* two years ago about August …

No reply is extant.

17/7/52 *Letter from Leo to 'The Producer',* Variety Bandbox*:*

> I expect to be in England during the holidays for August 13th to 22nd or so, and would like to do a spot on your programme …
>
> PS I appeared on *Variety Bandbox* three years ago [sic] at Golders Green Hippodrome with the Uilleann Pipes and orchestral accompaniment …

Note: Orchestral accompaniment? Could Leo Rowsome have, in the last days of the British Music Hall tradition, inadvertently foreshadowed the innovations of Seán Ó Riada and Shaun Davey?

29/7/52 *Reply from Bill Worsley (Variety Department)*

> Dear Mr Rowsome, Thank you for your letter. I am afraid *Bandbox* is almost certainly booked up to the end of its run, but I won't forget you if the opportunity occurs …

Denouement

And there the surviving documentation in the BBC Written Archive Centre runs out. We come away with the certainty that Leo Rowsome made two BBC radio broadcasts in his 26 years of trying: one to the Empire on St Patrick's Day 1937, which was very likely recorded with delightfully arcane technology for rebroadcast; and one for *Variety Bandbox* on the Home Service, July 25 1948. But we also come away with a suspicion of things just outside the edge of vision: vague passing references to previous broadcasts; an apparent convivial familiarity with certain producers that would appear to suggest relationships beyond the extant correspondence.

In being aware, from the internal evidence of the paper trail, that there are certainly some letters missing, we must ask: could more letters, even contracts, be missing? Perhaps there were contracts and correspondence that were never even filed. From the BBC's own trawl of contracts relating to Leo in 1950 – in the light of his passing reference to 'several' previous broadcasts – we know that at that point, a mere 24 years after his first dealings with the Corporation, there were only the two contracts extant which we have, still, in the file 64 years later.

Shortly after finishing a draft of the present chapter, I contacted Kevin Rowsome, Leo's grandson and a celebrated piper in his own right. Kevin was intrigued by the material and put me in touch with his Aunt Helena, Leo's daughter. Aunt Helena, who is (as has already been mentioned) herself engaged upon a biography of Leo, was, in the manner of Miss Marple, able to conjure up a *denouement* as thrilling as it was unexpected. And there was not a butler in sight.

Leo evidently retained a great deal of his correspondence and Helena had, among these papers, a contract for a BBC TV broadcast (from the experimental television era of 1932–35) on March 17 1933. The time of the broadcast was stated as 11.00–11.30pm.

As remarkable as this was, Kate O'Brien at the BBC WAC had decided to investigate the matter further, in response to a query from myself as to the likelihood that very early BBC TV records, in general, might not have been retained at the time. She found not only confirmation of Aunt Helena's contract but a repeat booking the following year. Subsequent research revealed a third TV appearance in this first decade of British television.

The *Radio Times* listings for these transmissions is as follows:

17/3/33 *Television Transmission By The Baird Process*, National Programme (also listed as Regional Programme, Midland, 11.00–11:30pm)
Leo Rowsome (Irish Piper). Wilfred Shine, Cathleen Drago and Billy Shine in 'A Helpin' Hand' by Wilfred Shine. Sara Allgood (Irish songs). Mario Lorenzi (Harp solos). (Vision, 261.6 m.; Sound, 398.9 m.).

16/3/34 *By The Baird Process*, BBC Television (11.05–11.35pm)
A St Patrick Eve Programme. Denis O'Neil (songs). Liam Cuffe and Mary Hogan (Irish dances). Leo Rowsome (Irish piper). Michael Dunne (Irish violinist).

17/3/37 *St Patrick's Day Irish Dances*, BBC Television (3.00–3.10pm)
Liam Cuffe and Mary Hogan accompanied by Leo Rowsome, pipes.

Note: Leo also made his Irish Variety radio broadcast to the Empire on this date, at 8.00am (see above).

Thus, surely beyond reasonable doubt, Leo Rowsome really *was* the first Irish traditional musician broadcast on BBC Television. Aunt Helena dug deeper and was able to reveal an amount of information on further broadcasts missing from the BBC written record. There was, for example, a letter inviting Leo to appear at 11.00am for a rehearsal prior to the 1934 TV broadcast. Further broadcasts Leo took part in, evidenced by his own copies of contracts or in some cases solely from billings in *Radio Times*, are as follows:

17/3/38 *European Concert From Eire*, Regional Programme, London (8.00–8.40pm)
The Orchestra of the Irish Broadcasting Service with a Vocal Quartet ... and Leo Rowsome (piper).

Note: A radio broadcast. Leo appears to have accompanied one of the (five, not four) singers, John Lynskey as well as performing two instrumental pieces – whether solo or with orchestral backing is not stated: 'The Dear Little Shamrock' and 'St Patrick Was A Gentleman/St Patrick's Day'.

26/12/38 *Irish Airs*, London, Empire broadcast

Note: Another Overseas/Empire broadcast (of solo piping) from London. Perhaps this was produced by A.H. Brown, hence Leo's otherwise obscure reference to 'past kindnesses' in his letter to Brown of January 1939.

17/3/41 *St Patrick's Day*, Home Service (9.00–10.00pm)

Note: Leo's only BBC broadcast of the war years – presumably recorded at Radio Éireann's studios in Dublin.

From *Radio Times*:

> An all Irish entertainment, produced in collaboration with Radio Éireann, including a performance by the company of the Abbey Theatre, Dublin and a performance by Jimmy O'Dea's pantomime company, which has been appearing in Belfast. Leo Rowsome's Pipe Quartet and the Ulster Amateur Flute Band; The Belfast Queen's Island Choir and Culwick Choral Society Choir; James McCafferty (Derry) and Máire ní Scolaidhe (Galway). Presented by Nicholas Barron, of Dublin, and Alan McClelland, of Belfast.

8/5/46 *[Programme title not stated]*, BBC Belfast, Northern Ireland Home Service

Note: In Leo's correspondence at BBC Written Records, he states in September 1930 that he will be broadcasting from Belfast 'in a few weeks'; and, in January 1937, he states that he has broadcast 'frequently' from both Dublin and Belfast. There is no doubt about Dublin (2RN). While not even Leo's own copies of contracts and correspondence appear to hold anything to confirm any Belfast (BBC) broadcasts between 1930–37, the integrity of his claims elsewhere, as measured against the accumulated documentation, should leave us in little doubt that if he says there were Belfast broadcasts, then there surely were. The prejudice he referred to in his letter of July 1926, with BBC Belfast 'taking only <u>local</u> turns on the Union pipes' (his underlining), had clearly passed by 1930. Nevertheless, this broadcast of May 1946 is the first BBC Belfast broadcast for which there is contractual confirmation. The contract originally stated 'London' but was amended at source to 'Belfast'.

30/7/46 *[Programme title not stated]*, BBC Belfast, Northern Ireland Home Service

Note: Obviously, Leo's broadcast two months earlier was not a disaster. The contract states the broadcast time to be 7.45–8.25pm. It was a solo piping engagement.

17/3/48 *St Patrick's Day Variety*, BBC Television (9.00–9.30pm)

From *Radio Times*:

> Professor Leo Rowsome (the world's leading exponent of the Uileann Pipes [sic]); Maurice Keary (baritone); Comerford Irish Dancers (Feis Gold Medal winners); Frank O'Donovan and Kitty McMahon (comedy couple). Compered by Joe Linnane. Augmented Orchestra conducted by Eric Robinson. Produced by Richard Afton.

20/3/48 *In Town Tonight*, BBC Home Service

Note: At last, an answer to the suspicions raised by Leo's letter of May 1948 to producer Peter Duncan, including his words 'I enjoyed my last date with you and hope to be at your service again.' It likewise explains the congenial familiarity of Peter Duncan's reply to Leo, which led directly to his appearance on Variety Bandbox *in July 1948. In keeping with* In Town Tonight'*s ethos, Leo was, of course 'in town' to appear at a St Patrick's Day concert – and appear on BBC television (above).*

17/3/52 *In Town Tonight*, BBC Home Service

Note: The lack of an extant reply to Leo's letter of July 1950 to Patrick Newman had already suggested at least one missing document in between that and the next BBC-archived communication exchange, in July 1952. The existence of a contract, in Leo's collection, for another appearance on Peter Duncan's In Town Tonight, *again coinciding with Leo's presence 'in town' for a St Patrick's Day concert, confirms that there was more than the one missing document. This show, with Leo piping solo, was broadcast from the BBC's Aeolian Hall studio.*

23/8/52 *In Town Tonight*, BBC Home Service

Note: Leo's becoming a regular on the show! This appearance can be inferred from a letter to Leo (in his collection) from producer Peter Duncan, dated Monday August 25 1952, *in which Duncan says:* 'Dear Leo, Very many thanks for coming along to take part in In Town Tonight *once again on Saturday evening. I thought the broadcast was most successful …' Perhaps also, by this time, with the growing familiarity between Leo and at least some BBC personnel, and the growing accessibility of telecommunications, more was being done by telephone than by letter. Helena, for example, has a letter to Leo from* In Town Tonight *producer Peter Duncan dated 19 August 1952 in which he says,* 'I would be glad if you could ring me as soon as you arrive in London so that I can arrange for you to have a chat with my scriptwriter. Looking forward to seeing you again …'

16/3/53 *[Programme title not stated]*, BBC Glasgow

Note: Tele-recorded at Broadcasting House, Glasgow, two days earlier (14 March 1953), this was a piping quartet engagement. Presumably the quartet was also playing a St Patrick's Day concert in Glasgow this year. This was almost Leo's final BBC appearance, for reasons outlined below. Nevertheless, he continued to perform regularly on Radio Éireann.

With Aunt Helena's evidence and the evidence of the *Radio Times* listings, we can now say that Leo Rowsome, between 1933 and 1953, appeared on at least five BBC TV broadcasts (three of these being extraordinarily early) and at least five BBC Home Service national radio broadcasts, two British Empire radio broadcasts and three BBC regional broadcasts. There is also a high likelihood of one or more earlier BBC Belfast broadcasts. That door is beginning to look more kicked-in than merely dented.

Helena has no doubt about it:

> Leo Rowsome opened doors for all. He did so when many doors were creaking and in urgent need of lubrication by several drops of 3-in-1! That indeed was done by a 1-in-3 – Leo Rowsome: Piper, Manufacturer and Teacher, and much more besides!

There was to be one last BBC booking, a straggler after the years of sustained effort, at the end of 1957, in the form of a TV celebration of Irish talent:

3/11/57 *The Irish In Us*, BBC Television (7.30–8.00pm)

From *Radio Times*:

> The Grand Order of Water Rats, the Variety profession's most famous confraternity, presents *The Irish In Us*. Starring Jimmy O'Dea with Jack

Cruise, Maureen Potter, Josephine Lesley, Leo Rowsome, Jack Daly, Dave O'Gorman, George Doonan, The Television Toppers and members of the Grand Order of Water Rats. Dance direction by Larry Gordon. Orchestra conducted by Eric Robinson. Produced by Richard Afton.

Aside from his BBC adventures, Helena can confirm that Leo was *almost* the first uilleann piper to appear on Irish station 2RN, the precursor of Radio Éireann. Strictly speaking, he was the first piper to give a solo performance on the station, on January 30 1926, live from Dublin's GPO. Séamus Mac Aonghusa (also known as James Ennis, father of Séamus Ennis) and William (Liam) Andrews were the first to play the instrument on 2RN, albeit in duo performance, on January 1 1926. While Leo, to Helena's recollection, always had a great rapport with Séamus Ennis, he had been a youthful rival at piping competitions with Ennis senior:

> In 1925, Dad got first place at the Feis Ceoil and Séamus' father (listed then as James Magennis) came second. Suffice to say that the young Leo was not congratulated!*

At the time of writing, Helena's biography of her father is forthcoming. It will be a most welcome addition to the literature on Irish music. In the meantime, her recollections can at least explain why this most tenacious of champions for the uilleann pipes and Irish traditional music so suddenly disappears from the British broadcasting scene in 1953, after 27 years of fervent knockings on the door.

Within 10 years the 'British folk revival' was exploding, with artists of Leo's vintage and calibre – among them Irish singer Joe Heaney, English singer Sam Larner, Scottish Travellers Jeannie Robertson and Belle Stewart – being afforded reverential status in the folk club scene up and down Britain. In that world, Séamus Ennis became an iconic figure: he and Felix Doran were the only solo uilleann pipers of venerability in age and experience who moved, even occasionally, in that new world. Leo Rowsome, whose commercial recording career had stalled in 1948 but was revived by his LP for Claddagh in 1959, was known by reputation among the cognoscenti in the British 'folk revival' era, but remained a distant figure.

As Jenny Barton, booker between 1958 and 1964 for London venue the Troubadour, where Séamus Ennis performed in 1959, puts it: 'He would have been too expensive for the average folk club by the 60s.' And she would most probably have been right.

---

* *The Leo Rowsome Collection Of Irish Music* (Waltons, 2002) mistakenly references Séamus Ennis rather than his father James as Leo's rival in 1920s piping competitions.

As Helena explains, Leo, by then, had done his bit:

I was born in 1946 and remember well from early 1950s that he was away every weekend in London, Birmingham, Glasgow et cetera. He would always check with the BBC well in advance of his trips for broadcasting opportunities. Dad told me that his trips to the BBC were so frequent at one time that the taxi men on the route got to know him well, as did the customs officers at Dublin Airport. A couple of letters I have from the BBC indicate great trust in him, both as a person of good character and [as] a businesslike and well presented performer. He certainly won their respect.

The explanation I can offer as to the reason the BBC broadcasts stopped is as follows. Firstly, there was constant demand on his time at home to broadcast regularly (sometimes twice each week) with Radio Éireann – as a soloist and with his Pipes Quartet. So, apart from the occasional trip to Glasgow and Edinburgh – he was Ireland's representative at the Edinburgh Festival for years – he remained at home. Secondly, his work making new sets of pipes and repairing and restoring all makes, from clients worldwide, was essential to ensure the survival of the instrument. This work was continuous. Most of today's surviving historic sets were restored by him.

There was also his regular teaching at Dublin's School Of Music and Pipers' Club. As President, he was also involved in the organisation of the Club and its fund-raising. Added to that, again, was adjudication and performance at Fleadhanna country-wide.

I believe that Dad had so much work at home that he stopped asking the BBC for work, as he knew he was needed to service the home market. It was for that reason that his own father, William Rowsome, dissuaded him from availing of the many invitations he was given to tour in the US. Finally, in 1968, he agreed to a programme of concerts and TV appearances in New York, including playing to a packed Carnegie Hall. He thoroughly enjoyed being in the US and vowed to return again. Unfortunately, he died two years later.

Chapter 9
Séamus Ennis: The Master Outside

Ciarán Mac Mathúna (1982): Séamus Ennis was unique. Of course, every person in the world is unique but to twist a phrase of George Orwell's, some people are more unique than others. Séamus was the complete individual; he was the uilleann piper *par excellence* who owed nothing to any school of pipering. He was the master in the truest sense, not because of age, for indeed he was comparatively young, only 63, when he died this week. He was master for the reason that his brilliant performance of music and his extraordinary personality attracted young musicians around him from far and near. They worshipped at his feet and followed him in the way medieval students followed their Abelard. And all this he enjoyed because there was no false humility in Séamus Ennis. He knew his own worth.[131]

There is no single character in the history of Irish piping greater than Séamus Ennis (1919–82). For 'character', one takes into account his commanding physical presence, his extraordinary memory and accumulation of knowledge, his singular musicianship, his role as both keeper of flame (as a traditional music collector for three institutions in the 1940s and 50s) and spreader of fire (as a broadcaster on the BBC and RTÉ), his chameleonic capacity with language, his demeanour (a curious flux between the measured professorial and the irascible Dickensian), his ability to both charm and annoy people (at will) and all the flaws that made the magic.

With a peripatetic lifestyle during much of his life – initially as a salaried collector, subsequently as a freelance drifter from a failed marriage – he was a man who existed within a context of legend and rumour. He didn't quite fit into any walk of life, career or scene, but was held in some awe by many who did. His private life sometimes appears to have been conducted in a kind of shabby-genteel chaos. Alcohol was a fairly constant companion, with odd periods of abstinence, but he had many friends upon whom he could rely for board and lodging. He began his working life when traditional music in Ireland was a fading activity, only beginning to attract the attention of State-funded preservation machinery; he ended it as the central icon of a musical community that had become an industry, a viable big-stage appendage to the popular music world.

He had become, to the 1970s generation, a pre-eminent carrier of tradition, while simultaneously remaining a man on the margins of life, like those he had documented in Connemara, the Hebrides and elsewhere in the 1940s and 50s.

By the late 70s, after decades of wandering, Séamus was living alone in a caravan at Naul, County Dublin, on a piece of land that had once belonged to his grandfather. He preferred the country. He was a loner within a traditional music world built on communality:

> **Ciarán Mac Mathúna**: Even though he loved an audience, and the bigger the better, Séamus was a very private person and had all the detachment of the artist. He chose to live alone, and though he had many friends his circle of intimates was quite small.[132]

He was, in short, an enigma – and he rather enjoyed it. As Ríonach Uí Ógáin observes, in a scrupulously dry Introduction to *Going To The Well For Water: The Séamus Ennis Field Diary 1942–46*:[*]

> Over time, Séamus Ennis has attracted a wealth of anecdotal material … Those who remember him inevitably recall a tall, dark, striking-looking man who always wore a dark suit and tie. His exceptional height and long fingers impressed everyone … Stories are told of his cleverness, his music and his good looks. It is said that he related very well to women and that they liked him very well. People also recalled periods of time and events for which no diary account appears to exist … Ennis was blessed and cursed with these legends. Be that as it may, the anecdotes contribute to the popular perception …[133]

'Séamus had an enormous store of knowledge, of folklore and stories … which connected to the music he played,' says Dónal Lunny, who occasionally saw Séamus around Dublin in the 1960s. 'He would tell stories about every second tune, so Séamus' presentation would be about 50 per cent talk and 50 per cent music. He was unique – unique in the 20th century. He was the tallest piper, physically and musically, and he has not been replaced. People would unapologetically try and do what he did, there's no doubt about that. But I would draw a comparison between the great pipers and [the] great painters. The style would be as singular and distinctive as that. And it was down to personality and outlook.'

---

* The text in this quote has been reordered.

Finbar Furey also encountered Séamus in 60s Dublin, but remains less impressed by his singularity:

> Johnny Doran's piping came from an historic source – it may be a slightly different technique of playing that style, but it's the same style. Séamus Ennis just invented his style. It came from nobody else but Séamus Ennis.

'I don't know what planet he lived on, I really don't,' says Jenny Barton, who knew him in London in the 1950s and kept in touch with him until his death. 'I was very fond of him. I still am. He was magic in so many ways … He was fascinating to listen to, but you knew there were always one or two bum notes hidden in it. Did it matter? No, it didn't! If you wanted perfection you got Leo Rowsome, who didn't play bum notes but who, as far I was concerned, wasn't Séamus. Leo was very good indeed, but Séamus had his own particular magic, bum notes and all.'

Séamus never exactly had a recording career as such. Rather, he periodically converged with recording opportunites, did his thing, pocketed the cash (if there was any) and moved on. Neither did he really embrace a touring career in the way we now understand it. There was no concerted touring in support of particular albums. He travelled America for five months in 1964 on the back of a Newport Folk Festival booking (playing mostly universities and some clubs) and agreed to a tour of UK folk clubs in 1977, although this would be cancelled due to illness. Generally, he appeared to operate in an ad hoc fashion – a festival here, a broadcast there, a piping *tionól* as required. Often, part of the problem for prospective bookers, as his BBC Written Archive files attest, was finding out where he was. He was a man of many postal addresses, several of which would be c/o licensed premises.[*]

For all that, he was a man of inspirational qualities, a specialness that exists outside of fashion and outlasts it. Sooner or later, in a manner akin to other fervently individual or 'outsider' personalities in the arts – within or beyond that person's lifetime – a kind of unbreakable status adheres to the reputation of that person. They become heroic figures, celebrated for their integrity and individuality and (if still with us) their longevity. Séamus Ennis ploughed his furrow both before and during the 'folk revival' era, and drank from its well on his own terms. He never built, nor wanted to build, a more mainstream performing career from it in the manner of, say, Paddy Moloney with The Chieftains. But he did live to see his ascension to Olympus.

---

* Among various addresses in his BBC files are: c/o O'Reilly, Galway; c/o George Bennett's, Wine & Spirit Merchants, Fishguard; and c/o O'Donoghue's, Dublin

Andy Irvine: Because of the time when he lived, I don't think there was a great position open to him as a piper. He was very well respected by the community that enjoyed that kind of music, but I don't think he would ever have become a household name …

[But] right at the end of his life he did become kind of famous. When he took the stage at the Lisdoonvarna Festival, he was almost a god by that time – because bands like Planxty had created a much bigger audience [for traditional music].*

Séamus Ennis was an inspiration of his time, and that inspiration seems unlikely to fade or tarnish. Only a few years after his death, his 'unforgettable fire' was playing its part in the creativity of a new generation:

The Edge (1986): There are times when we run ourselves dry, when probably the best course of action is to acknowledge the fact that we're not being productive, but we tend to push on doggedly. During the *Unforgettable Fire* sessions, Brian [Eno, our producer] was very quick to spot when we were in that mode, and he would suggest that we take a walk or listen to some Séamus Ennis! In that mundane sort of way, you can encourage creative moods.[134]

That being said, there was nothing mundane about Séamus Ennis.

*

'My O! How I yearn at times to have pipes playing around me again!' wrote, purportedly, Mary Josephine Ennis, widow of James and mother of Séamus, in September 1969. 'We lived in the townland Jamestown where I bore and reared my family, in the district of Fingal … It was a place of large farms and widely spaced homes. My husband cycled to his civil service office in Dublin city each morning. We had no other transport but the pony-and-trap for Mass on Sundays, week-end shopping and outings.'[135]

As Séamus described it, his grandfather was a descendent of a stable boy from Scotland who had eloped with his employer's daughter and her jewellery and bought

---

* Séamus performed at the 4th Lisdoonvarna Festival, July 10–12 1981, sharing the bill with Planxty (including Andy Irvine) and many others: Chris De Burgh, The Beat, John Sebastian, Lindisfarne, De Danann, John Martyn, Steel Pulse, Moving Hearts, The Roches, Clannad, Country Joe McDonald, Dr Feelgood, Roy Harper, Home Service, Stockton's Wing, Chris Smither, Hank Wangford Band.

a farm at Naul. The grandfather had a family of 13, of which Séamus' father, James, was number 12.*

In spite of cycling 18 miles each way, every day, from Jamestown to the Department Of Education and later the Department Of Agriculture in Dublin, James Ennis (1885–1965) became actively involved in the Irish language and culture revival promoted by the Gaelic League at the end of the 19th century and into the next. It was at a Gaelic League meeting that he met his future wife, Mary McCabe, from Greaghlass, Monaghan. James became proficient at war pipes, whistle, fiddle, flute and step-dancing, and subsequently took up the uilleann pipes and Northumbrian small pipes. Pat Ward of Drogheda was an influence, and James took lessons from Nicholas Markey, star pupil of US-based pipe maker Billy Taylor and tutor at the Dublin Pipers' Club, founded in 1900.

Not one to enter competitions himself (though many of his pupils became winners), Markey warranted an honourable mention in Francis O'Neill's *Irish Minstrels And Musicians*:

> Even though we cannot subscribe to the opinion of his friend, Mr Deegan, the honourable secretary of [Dublin Pipers' Club], that Mr Markey 'is the best living piper', we can readily concede that for an Irish piper his modesty is truly refreshing.[136]

Pat Mitchell, editor of *The Dance Music Of Séamus Ennis* (NPU, 2007), notes a programme for a concert in 1913 in which James attributes the source of one piece, 'The Pigeon On The Gate', to a recording by Patsy Touhey. 'You couldn't fault Patsy Touhey,' Séamus later declared. 'He was the greatest I've heard of the men before my father's time.'[137]

James built up a collection of piping records, which formed the basis of his style alongside exposure to Markey and the older pipers from the oral tradition heard at the Gaelic League's Feis Ceoil competitions.

> **Séamus**: My father met most of the old pipers of his day because at that time the Oireachtas used to pay pipers' expenses to come to the competition. He took from them a synthesis of all their styles, particularly anything that pleased his own taste. His playing was perfected by Nicholas Markey.[138]

---

* Séamus' father is generally referred to as James Ennis, or James Magennis, although he was sometimes known in its Gaelic form: Séamus (or Séamas) Mac Aonghusa. Very occasionally, in his early professional life, Séamus was referred to as Séamus Óg Mac Aonghusa, the 'Óg' denoting the younger bearer of a name in a family. Similarly, Liam O'Flynn has often been referred to as Liam Óg O'Flynn (or Ó Floinn).

In a 1975 RTÉ documentary, Séamus elaborated further on Markey: 'Late in life he was the curator of a men's lavatory on North Circular Road, behind the Mater Hospital. He rented an office in this emporium, where he gave my father tuition.'[139] Helpfully, the documentary included footage of these premises.

> **Breandán Breathnach**: The pipers and fiddlers who attended the Feis Ceoil in its first years were the last in a line of professional performers. Men in their sixties and seventies, they would have acquired their skills and repertoire from musicians born in the previous century.[140]

Some of the old pipers involved in the early competitions, the last of the 19th century troubadours, were Turlough McSweeney of Donegal, blind Denis Delaney of Galway and Mící 'Cumba' O'Sullivan of Kerry. It was believed that these people likely possessed a store of hitherto uncollected tunes, and efforts were made to collect the material thought rare. *The Feis Ceoil Collection Of Irish Airs* was eventually published in 1913.

Breathnach observed that one piece therein, 'When The Cock Crows It Is Day', is identical to the version later popularised by Séamus Ennis, and surmises that he or his father picked it up here – or perhaps in person, at a Feis Ceoil, from the player who had performed it.

All this is pertinent because Séamus Ennis, consistently, would credit his father as the source of all his technique and much of his repertoire: 'My style is identical to my father's style,' he said in 1973. 'I can't think of any movement that I do on the pipes that I didn't get from him …'[141]

As Terry Moylan notes: 'Markey had been taught by the Taylor brothers [of Drogheda], so you can trace the Ennis style back as far as the pre-Famine days in County Louth.'

James Ennis' energy and interest in music was remarkable. He was involved in starting a (war) pipe band at Naul in the early years of the 1900s, and came second on uilleann pipes at the 1912 Oireachtas competition. He came second again, this time to Leo Rowsome, at the 1925 Feis Ceoil. A few months later he beat Leo by a matter of days to the claim of being the first uilleann piper to broadcast on 2RN, Ireland's first national radio station, on January 1 1926 – appearing in a piping duo with Liam Andrews. James Ennis also performed in trio format as The Fingal Trio, with a flautist and a fiddler. It was in this context that he made his only commercial recording, a Regal-Zonophone 78, in 1931, coupling 'The Battle Of Clontarf' (a medley featuring 'Brian The Brave', better known in the rock era as 'March Into Trouble' on Horslips' *The Book Of Invasions* LP) with a set of hornpipes.

Wilbert Garvin: It is difficult to assess James' prowess from that recording alone, but it is significant that piping connoisseurs such as Tommy Reck and Peadar Broe marvelled at James Ennis' piping. Breandán Breathnach also thought extremely high[ly] of him, although he considered Séamus to be a better piper.[142]

James Ennis and Mary McCabe were married in 1916. 'By the time Séamus was born, on 5 May 1919,' wrote Pat Mitchell, 'the heyday of the professional piper was over, with most of them by then in the grave.'[143] Séamus would be the second of six siblings, his sister Angela being the eldest.

Séamus: When I was young, my father used to play the pipes to me to put me to sleep at night. I'd ask him for tunes by name, trying all the time not to fall asleep. I remember one time asking him for the 'Munster Buttermilk' and cursing myself the following morning for having fallen asleep in the middle of it.[144]

During a trip to London in 1908, aged 23, to take part in a flute competition (which he won), James had found a set of pipes, in pieces in a sack, in a pawnbroker's shop. He bought them for £5. Rather like a character in an episode of *Bagpuss*, James took them home to John Brogan of Harold's Cross, where restoration revealed them as the work of the great Dublin pipe maker Maurice Coyne.[*] In due course these would be bequeathed to Séamus and, after his death, to Liam O'Flynn. As the Coyne pipes were a flat set, somewhere between C and C sharp, James later procured a modern concert-pitch set from Brogan, to play with his Fingal Trio.

Séamus: I remember well – one dreary, drizzly Sunday afternoon [aged 13], I put on these pipes and started to play.[†] That night I was able to play 'The Bard Of Armagh'. My mother told me that I had a wrong note. I was playing a C sharp instead of C natural, and my father showed me how to play it right. I

---

* Coyne had premises listed in Dublin street directories between 1839 and 1861, although he may have been active before that. A pipe making J. Coyne was also active earlier. The Ennis pipes are generally referred to as circa 1840.
† It's been said that Séamus began on a full set of pipes. Yet his mother, in the sleeve notes to *Masters Of Irish Music* (1969), stated: 'He remembers getting child's size bag, bellows and chanter (the beginner's set) from Santa Claus, but played no note till he had churned 13¼ years' music, so rich that it must out. One wet August Sunday afternoon (he tells me), on a spare set of pipes, he found some 'outs' – some notes encouragingly musical.' One has to suspect that these sleeve notes were probably ghost-written by Séamus himself.

had no formal lessons on the pipes, but my father would explain any difficult bit. He wrote out the scale for me, and from that I was able to go to O'Neill's book and take a turn I knew, and that was how I learned staff notation.[145]

'Séamus asked later and got several hours grinding on music manuscript paper and was told to take it from there,' his mother later recalled. 'Practical tuition soon followed, in advancing stages. When he was 16 he played on radio in *Children's Hour*. His father never allowed him to enter for a competition and seldom let him play outside home.'[146]

Nevertheless, in 1934, he played his first known gig: at an Irish Youth Hostel Association (IYHA) conference. James Ennis danced to accompaniment from Séamus on pipes and a pianist. Pat Mitchell: 'His playing must have been acceptable, because Ennis senior was himself a superb musician, and by all accounts, a hard taskmaster …'[147]

Séamus would often declare that it took seven years' learning, seven years' practising and seven years' playing to make a piper. A somewhat demanding amount of time – to which Séamus himself clearly had an exemption, as 10 sets of tunes recorded for Radio Éireann across four sessions in 1940, when Séamus was 21, attest. Collected on *The Return From Fingal* nearly 60 years later, and including complex regulator work and the test piece 'The Bucks Of Oranmore', this doesn't sound like a man with much to learn. His next recordings on pipes, also for Radio Éireann, would be eight years away.*

> **John McSherry**: When I first began playing, I must say I wasn't particularly drawn to Ennis's piping. I couldn't quite see what all the fuss was about. I have come to appreciate it a lot more over the years, though. There are some recordings where his playing really grabs me. His 1948 Radio Éireann version of 'The Gold Ring' is great. His style was certainly very unique back in the day and he was one of a kind, though I never understood the whole worshipping thing with him. Some accomplished players would rather mimic his playing (warts and all) than try to develop their own personal style. Kind of a waste, I think, cos there'll only ever be one Seamus Ennis.

Nevertheless, as Séamus maintained in 1973: 'After 21 years I wasn't as able as I am now, and if my father were alive today I would still be learning from him … [But] after all that, I'm afraid pipers are born, not made.'[148]

---

* He recorded five songs for the BBC Permanent Library before this, in August 1947.

*

Séamus was educated at several establishments, the last two being Dublin Irish language schools: Scoil Cholmcille and Coláiste Mhuire. In 1937 he undertook a course at Darragh's Commercial College, designed to prepare students for office work, and subsequently applied to the civil service: 'As I remember it, 44 were called and I had 45th place. I was waiting for the next call.'[149]

His father's friend, Colm Ó Lochlainn, offered Séamus a job on 10 shillings a week at his printing and publishing business, At The Sign Of The Three Candles, in Fleet Street, Dublin, which specialised in Irish text and music. In time, this rose to 32 shillings per week.

Ó Lochlainn had been a presence in Séamus' life for some time, taking piping lessons from James Ennis and in return coaching him in the Irish language and entertaining the children with drives in the country. Ó Lochlainn had also performed, singing in Irish, at the 1934 IYHA concert.

Musical notation was handwritten before being transferred to plates for printing and, as practice for such work, Séamus reputedly copied by hand all 1,001 pieces from Francis O'Neill's *The Dance Music Of Ireland* (1907). He became adept at staff notation and capable of elegant script – skills that would come in handy.

> **Séamus**: I learned more and more about music and song from Colm Ó Lochlainn, now gone to his reward. He taught me how to write tunes of the slow songs so well that when I hear a song sung I'd automatically visualise it on paper. This, in turn, qualified me for the post of Folk Music Collector with the Irish Folklore Commission.[150]

With supplies of paper inconvenienced by the Second World War (in which Ireland remained neutral), Séamus was among several staff let go by Ó Lochlainn in 1941. After some months, pondering upon joining the British forces, Séamus (through Ó Lochlainn's influence) was given a six-week trial and then offered a job, beginning June 1 1942, as a full-time collector with the Irish Folklore Commission (IFC). The Commission had been founded in 1935 by James Delargy, a man 'inspired with the burning desire to rescue Irish tradition from oblivion', who 'compared the situation to watching a house burn and stated that he was trying to rescue pieces of furniture from the burning mass'.[151]

Aside from his practical and linguistic skills, Séamus had a 'feel' for the music in question and an easy way with people. He was a perfect fit for the job, and perfectly fit as well: travel, given the wartime rationing of petrol, would be largely by bicycle. Most of the other collectors employed at that time lived and worked in particular counties, but

Séamus was based in Dublin and would be sent on field trips to various regions for a few weeks or months at a time, followed by periods of admin work back in Dublin. He would start on £150 per annum plus postal expenses – almost twice his previous salary.*

During his first year with the Commission, Séamus spent a lot of time at the organisation's Dublin office, transcribing from Ediphone cylinders song material that had already been collected under IFC auspices, plus all that was retrievable from the early 20th century cylinder collection of Father Luke Donnellan.†

Séamus' first field trip, aged 23, was to Connemara, spanning July-September 1942. He had first visited the area in 1927, during a family holiday. He was drawn to the place: 'In Connemara I felt myself nearer to God … There's something in the atmosphere out there, definitely.'¹⁵²

A regular attender of Mass, Séamus also had a predilection or sensitivity toward the mystical. His later repertoire would be full of delightfully rambunctious stories about fairies, magic, talking ravens and suchlike, but there may have been a little more to it than pure whimsy for the tale-teller. In one personal aside in his IFC field diary for September 1945, while collecting in Clare, he recounts meeting, by a castle, 'a small, calm, quiet man [who] is very jolly', called Darby Griffy:

> Darby Griffy comes from the old life, and I thought when he left me that I had returned into the world in which you and I live today. This was not due to the topic of conversation that we had, but because of some aspect of Darby that I do not understand.‡ Darby is not the first person with whom this has happened, in my experience, because others in whose company I have been in many places in Ireland have been the same. I walked westwards, turning this question over in my mind, but [when I reached my lodgings]

---

* From summer 1943, Séamus graduated to £250 PA (pro rata) when engaged in fieldwork, £150 PA when based in Dublin. It was still a very meagre salary for the work, and the specialist skills, involved. Although government funded, the IFC was on hand-to-mouth finances for its first 20 years or so. The 1930s and 40s were a very fragile time for the Irish economy in general.

† As Mícheál Briody notes, in *The Irish Folklore Commission 1935–1970* (2007): 'Ennis' transcription … was opportune as much of it would not have been possible to transcribe later due to deterioration of the wax cylinders. His transcriptions of this material constitute a valuable source for southeast Ulster song tradition.'

‡ Curiously, in Seán Ó Súilleabháin's *The Handbook Of Irish Folklore* (Folklore Of Ireland Society, 1942), 'Darby Rós' is mentioned as a common fairy name: 'Belief in fairies was very strong in Ireland in former times as it was in most countries throughout the world. In Ireland, however, it flourished to an unusual degree owing to the highly developed imaginative powers of our ancestors. It is very difficult to draw a clear line of demarcation between the kingdom of the dead and the fairy world in Irish popular belief.'

it was as unsolved as it had been when Darby had shaken hands with me.[153]

Although he visited several counties during his four years with the Commission,[*] Connemara (in Galway) and Donegal would consume most of Séamus' time and attention:

> The greatest repository of songs and tunes and their background in facts and fables I found in a little pocket of North Connemara, a place known as Clearwater in English … I know that these people enjoyed my visits to them. I sang strange songs for them, and it seems they couldn't do enough for me when I played my pipes for them.[154]

Séamus' friend and fellow IFC collector Seán Ó hEochaidh described in his diary one such occasion, when Séamus entertained a Donegal family and their neighbours in January 1944:

> Séamus started playing the pipes and I heard the best night's music ever. Séamus plays to perfection, and only a very heavy heart would not find his music uplifting. The man of the house, Micí Mac Gabhann, who is 80 years old, was … scowling at the young lads there who were not up dancing. He said a few times in the course of the evening that in his younger days he would not ignore such fine music! … Séamus played old music that was truly Irish. I thanked God that there was at least one man left who was able to play our ancestors' music in such a melodious, true way that I cannot describe here in a few words. May God leave him health, agile fingers and his hearing. … Long life, Séamus! If you were to give Ireland only what music you have, we need have no fear.[155]

Séamus remained friends with everyone from whom he collected. He swiftly mastered regional dialects, and his sources in turn 'included him in every aspect of their daily lives'.[156] He would return to many of the same people when employed later in collecting roles for both Radio Éireann and the BBC. On one occasion, he arrived at the house of a regular source, Mrs Elizabeth Cronin, to find that she had already written out a number of songs for him, as she would much rather spend the time talking with him than dictating songs.

Séamus did not collect a great deal of music from the Travelling community during his time with the Folklore Commission, although his notes to Paddy Keenan's

---

* Séamus visited the following counties during his time with the folklore Commission: Galway, Mayo, Donegal, Clare, Kerry, Cork, Longford, Leitrim, Cavan, Waterford and Wexford.

1975 debut LP confirmed that he was well aware of the great Travelling piper Johnny Doran, who died in 1950:

> I recognise the music of Johnny Doran clearly in the piping of this record. John [Keenan] need not have told me, for I myself spent nights in the caravan of Doran, comfortable and cosy, drinking and playing – tea and carding [and] pipering – and exchanging tunes.[157]

Doran is not mentioned in his surviving field diaries – and, indeed, it is notable how few pipers are. He notes in his entry for January 26 1944 how pleased he is to have encountered the priest who gave last rites to the great 19th century piper Turlough McSweeney, to whom Turlough had left his pipes, which Séamus inspected. It was not a common instrument by this time, even in communities with a strong oral tradition of music and song.

Séamus remained with the IFC until July 31 1947. Field diaries exist for 98 weeks of his collecting, spanning 1942–46. Edited by Ríonach Uí Ógáin as *Going To The Well For Water* (Cork University Press, 2009), they provide a glimpse into Séamus' quirks and lifestyle:

> He went swimming in summer and winter, much to the amazement of many local people. He appears from the diaries to have been extremely fit and athletic and thought nothing of cycling long distances. He frequently rowed a boat, sometimes the smaller timber-framed canvas boat or *curach* and also even a sailing boat when a calm settled and he was compelled to row long distances. This occurred in 1945 on a return trip from the Aran Islands when he wrote in the diary that the blisters on his hands were still healing.
>
> He appears to have been mechanically minded and was able to overhaul and repair his bicycle and Ediphone machine* whenever necessary, and even

---

* From mid-1944, Séamus had access to an Ediphone wax cylinder machine, which was clearly a major help when transcribing tunes and words – although Séamus (with perfect pitch) was exceptionally adept at catching a tune on one hearing, words on two or three. Some material would be collected on cylinders, which were then posted back to HQ, transcribed there and posted back to Séamus for re-use. Only very occasionally, and not before 1945, would Séamus record a 'performance' on cylinder while in the field with the intention of it being kept by the IFC. Most 'permanent' IFC recordings were created using an acetate disc machine, acquired in 1945. Séamus made (often in collaboration with Kevin Danaher) a total of 147 recorded performances for the IFC between 1945 and 1947, 42 of which were made while in the Hebrides. The majority of his IFC recordings date from 1947. Those he recorded include singers Elizabeth Cronin and Colm Ó Caodháin, fiddler Denis Murphy and lore from Peig Sayers.

the clock in one of the houses in which he was staying ... He repaired his own shoes on a number of occasions ... His ability to name the direction from which the wind was coming is impressive ... Ennis would do in a day what others would do in a week. He might work without taking a break and would then take a few days' rest.[158]

In one day, Séamus apparently cycled from Finglas to Carna (close to 180 miles), taking a week to recover. The purchase of a car in April 1946, when petrol was again available, would put a stop to such madness.

Much of Séamus' correspondence with the Commission while in the field relates to financial matters. It would be a trait notable in future correspondence with the BBC over many years.

Over the winter of 1946–47, from November to Easter, and thanks largely to his skill in mastering the myriad Gaelic dialects, he lived on Canna in the Hebrides (a region to which he would return as a BBC collector), on secondment, notating the collection of Scotsman John Lorne Campbell. While there, he would transcribe 168 pieces from Campbell's collection and collect music on his own account as well. Reputedly, to the amazement of locals, Séamus swam in the sea every day of those five months. It is a sea that, from personal experience, is shockingly cold. By the time he left, to become an Outside Broadcast Officer with Radio Éireann (RÉ) in August 1947, Séamus had collected around 2,000 items – 212 from one prodigious fellow in Glinsk, Colm Ó Caodháin, a non-English speaker who could neither read nor write.*

Éamon de Buitléar, who made a documentary on Séamus in the 1970s, recalled the tale of the pair's first meeting, which illustrates well why Séamus became 'the most successful collector of folklore in the Irish language':[159]

> Séamus told me that the first time he had gone to visit Colm Ó Caodháin in search of music, Colm thought he was just another one of those individuals who regularly came to bother him. He decided that he would discourage Séamus by singing for him one of his most difficult tunes. When he began to sing he closed his eyes, as is the fashion with many traditional singers. Séamus immediately began writing down the notes, which he was well accustomed to doing. When Colm finally came to the end of his piece he

---

* Uí Ógáin gives August 1 1947 as Séamus' start date with Radio Éireann; Peter Browne, who quotes from the job description, gives it as August 18 1947 in his notes to *The Return From Fingal* (RTÉ, 1997) – confirmed by Reg Hall's recollections. Mícheál Briody's *The Irish Folklore Commission 1935–1970* also gives the date as August 18 1947. Presumably Séamus was paid to this date but had an amount of leave to use up.

opened his eyes and exclaimed (in Irish), 'Have you got it?' Séamus replied that he thought he had, and promptly took a tin whistle out of the inside pocket of his jacket. The piece of paper was still on the table where Seamus could read it and he played the tune straight through. Colm stared at him wide-eyed, exclaiming, 'You're a ghost!' After that episode Séamus had no problems and they became good friends.[160]

As Mícheál Briody observes: 'The Commission had been extremely lucky to get music collectors of the calibre of [Ennis' predecessor Liam] de Noraidh and Ennis. It was not to be as lucky again. The vacancy left by Ennis' departure was never filled.'[161]

*

Séamus had a window of 18 days between the IFC job and the Radio Éireann job, which was to prove fortuitous to his future. As Reg Hall, an English musician who would be active as a chronicler of Irish music within Britain from the mid-50s onwards, recalls:

> Brian George was a BBC producer and he was from County Donegal. In 1947 he took a mobile unit – a van, an acetate disc recording machine – to Ireland to record Irish music. Séamus Ennis was between jobs. In a fortnight's time he was going to join Radio Éireann. So in that fortnight the BBC hired him to go with Brian George – and Brian, in actual fact, only recorded people who Ennis introduced him to.
>
> **Séamus**: When I went to take up my new job as Outside Broadcast Officer in Radio Éireann, I was asked had I got a motor car and I said, 'Yes.' And I was told, 'You're to join a BBC unit in Galway.' This was Brian George, whom I had just left at Galway. I got into my car and went back to Galway again. And I remember Mrs George was there, and she said, 'Are you happy in your new job?'[162]

Brian wanted this tranche of material as an exemplar to help his cause toward getting BBC funding for a full-scale collecting programme across the British Isles. For the moment, some of the material collected on this Irish trip – a remarkable 400 acetate discs' worth – was used in a BBC programme called *Songs From The Four Provinces*. Additionally, one of five songs Séamus himself recorded for Brian would turn up a year later in a BBC radio documentary, *The Irish Storyteller*. A connection had been made that would lead to greater things in due course.

In the meantime, his job with Radio Éireann – which had not yet acquired Outside Broadcast vans but which was employing, in Séamus and Seán Mac Réamoinn, two characterful individuals to get the show on the road – was to seek out material from the regions suitable for broadcast. It was a development that had not been possible during the war years of severe petrol rationing. This was to be field recording not for purely archival purposes, but rather with a view to exemplifying the various counties of Ireland within broadcast documentary formats. Even in this, though, RÉ was ahead of the BBC in representing regional voices and culture on the national network.

Writing in 1967, in *Forty Years Of Irish Broadcasting*, Maurice Gorham noted Mac Réamoinn's appetite for all aspects of culture and Ennis' skill in drawing the best out of other musicians. Indeed, he asserted that 'the present-day revival of Irish traditional music really stems from him.' He describes the modus operandi of the OB unit in their pioneer days:

> Together or separately, but always accompanied by one of the invaluable outside broadcast engineers, these two toured the remoter areas of Ireland – their first sortie was to Valentia Island, off the Kerry Coast, their first control room the snug off the bar of the Royal Hotel, and on the same trip they visited … Peig Sayers' house in Dunquin. That was in 1947, when they had to transport the gear in Séamus Ennis' car, but once the vans arrived in 1948 they were able to tour far and wide, and their visits included Gaelic-speaking occasions in Scotland, Cornwall and Wales.[163]

Interviewed in the 70s, Séamus recalled not Valentia Island but the rather more banal setting of Leitrim as his first Radio Éireann road trip:

> **Séamus**: At the beginning they had no mobile unit, but they had transportable recording gear, which was transported in the back of my Model ABF and ruined the bloody upholstery on it … You went to a district and you started making your enquiries, perhaps in the bar of the hotel you stayed in … you'd be told 'You should go and have a chat with so-and-so,' and you'd do that and see what happened … [W]e sent rough notes and a bundle of discs back to Norris Davidson to write a script and present the programme. That's the way those two half-hour programmes were done. And behind the scenes we were told it was the greatest pile of tripe that was ever bundled into Radio Éireann![164]

Radio Éireann felt that programmes based solely on an area's music would not be good listening:

Séamus: I got very disheartened about the whole thing, although I did [make music programmes] whenever I got the chance. I recorded interesting items both instrumental and vocal, with the result [that] there was quite an archive built up of disc-recorded material.[165]

RTÉ producer Peter Browne has heard a couple of surviving programmes on *sean-nós* (unaccompanied) singing that Séamus slipped through the net in this period, revealing him as a 'a naturally skilled presenter'.[166]

*

Late in 1950, Alan Lomax, a driven man from America whose father, John, had begun the family dynasty in field recording, arrived in England. Being a socialist, he was effectively on the run from the House Un-American Activities people back home*, but was also pursuing – using his own money in tandem with a commission – an ambitious project to document the traditional music of the world for a series of releases on Columbia Records: *The Columbia World Library Of Folk & Primitive Music*.

Alan didn't take long to get his feet under the table, with Brian George an ally, at the BBC, presenting his first of many BBC series, *Adventures In Folk Song*, in February 1951 – with himself and a female sidekick, Robin Roberts, singing and presenting field recordings from the BBC Library. The previous month, with an Irish volume of the Columbia series in mind, Alan and Robin had loaded up a car with a heavy Magnecord tape recorder and travelled to Dublin, heading straight to Jamestown on Brian George's advice. As Robin later noted: 'We found a long, young greyhound of a fellow with mischievous sharp eyes and a low, measured brogue, always combining drollery with seriousness.'[167]

John Szwed (Lomax biographer): After a night of drinking and singing in the Ennis family kitchen the next day, Alan was convinced they could collaborate. There were still songs to be heard that had not been recorded, Séamus said, and he could find the people … Before they set out, Alan tested his equipment by recording Séamus' piping, and the tape recorder broke down on the first try …[168]

They ended up borrowing a mobile recording unit and a man to operate it from

---

* Lomax was never formally charged with Communism, but he was investigated by the FBI for years, with agencies in the various European countries he visited being asked to monitor his activities. The idea of Scotland Yard listening to his BBC broadcasts on folk music, hoping to detect revolutionary plots, is both absurd and amusing.

Radio Éireann, with whom Séamus was still employed. Over six weeks they recorded all over Ireland, using Séamus' contacts, from Elizabeth Cronin in Cork to fiddler Mickey Doherty in Donegal. A sizeable number of items from Séamus himself were also recorded.˙

Released as one of the first 14 volumes in the series in December 1954, the Lomax/Columbia double LP on Ireland would also include eight performances by Séamus, including three items on pipes: 'The Bucks Of Oranmore', 'Were You At The Rock?' and 'The Woman Of The House'. They were his first commercially available recordings.

Over the next four years, as he continued with his somewhat frustrating RÉ career, Séamus had several more encounters with the BBC. He recorded a couple of spoken and musical contributions for BBC programmes at RÉ studios in Dublin in 1947–48 and then, in September 1949, he was recorded in Dublin over four days, probably during Brian George's second visit, for the BBC Permanent Library: at least 28 songs and seven tune sets on pipes and whistle. Many of the songs had been learned from his sources during IFC days, although a few he credited to Colm Ó Lochlainn (as source or translator). Once again, 'Were You At The Rock?', a hauntingly beautiful piping air, was among the pipe tunes.

Séamus was flown over to London three times in late 1950 and 1951 for BBC broadcasts, on one occasion providing a further Permanent Library session, this time at Broadcasting House. Most or all of these early BBC bookings had been for producer David Thomson. Thomson's next booking, reuniting Séamus with Alan Lomax for *The Stone Of Tory*, an 'Irish Ballad Opera' to be recorded in Dublin, would be a turning point in Séamus' career and the beginning of a major repositioning for the BBC's involvement with the traditional music of the British Isles.

With Alan writing it and Séamus hired as both researcher and participant, the programme was the first in a series of 'Ballad Operas' Lomax planned, involving different cultures of the world. The exuberant American went on a collecting trip to Scotland that summer, involving the then similarly freelance leftist writer and collector Hamish Henderson. Along the way, Alan's force of personality helped to galvanise the beginnings of the Scottish folk song revival and the beginnings of the Edinburgh Festival Fringe. These were also having an effect in London:

John Szwed: Once they saw the results of Lomax's collecting, the BBC

---

* Extracts from Alan's recordings of 55 items from Séamus from this trip and two later sessions, in June 1951 and in 1953 (probably in London), can be heard here: research.culturalequity.org/rc-b2/audio-ix-recording.jsp?d-446288-p=1 Michael Lydon's 2012 Galway University paper 'Lomax In Ireland: Fieldwork, Commercial Recordings And 'Great Remembers" looks at the trip in detail and is also available online.

created a folk music project under the direction of Peter Kennedy and Séamus Ennis.[169]

*

Brian George, who had been trying to promote a more active BBC involvement in folk music since his Irish adventure in 1947, finally got a green light in 1951:

> **Reg Hall**: In 1951, Brian George got very serious promotion in the BBC. He was now head of a big department with a hundred people working for him, and he head-hunted Éamonn Andrews, a radio presenter, and Séamus Ennis – head-hunted both of them from Radio Éireann. I've got that from Bob Copper, the [English] traditional singer, who worked with both of them. Brian George got together a budget, £10,000, and hired two field recordists – Ennis and Peter Kennedy – on contract. He had the money for three collectors, but he only ever hired others casually. So that brought Ennis to London.

Séamus would be earning twice his Radio Éireann salary, with an apparently lavish expense account on top. The opportunity to collect from the whole of the British Isles was an incentive in itself. Based in London, Séamus would visit a particular area – from Sussex to the Hebrides – for a few weeks at a time to collect material for the archive. 'We expected that it might last three, maybe four, maybe five years,' he reflected. 'In fact, it lasted seven years.'[170]

As it had been with the IFC, Séamus' departure from Radio Éireann was a devastating blow. Referring to him as one of 'its shooting stars' in his fascinating 1967 book *Forty Years Of Irish Broadcasting*, Maurice Gorham (a former RÉ Director Of Broadcasting) went on to note:

> The post that had been vacated by Séamus Ennis was still empty [over two years later] – no successor had been found who had his gift of extracting traditional music from amateurs all over the country and weaving it into radio programmes.[171]

Séamus was hired on a series of rolling short-term but full-time contracts, spanning January 1952 to March 1957.* He would also enjoy prolific opportunities to earn

---

* Séamus' contract periods were as follows: 6/1/52–2/2/52; 3/2/52–29/3/52; 30/3/52–31/12/52; 1/1/53–31/3/53; 1/4/53–31/12/53; 1/1/54–31/3/54; 1/4/54–31/3/55; 1/4/55–31/3/56; 1/4/56–31/3/57 and then 'contract not renewed'.

substantial freelance fees in a speaking, scripting or performing capacity with various BBC radio programmes during this time of his employment as a roving recorder, and to take concert bookings: 'And if it happened on a work day and I had to travel, I just took a day's annual leave.'[172]

Brian George was a very flexible boss. On one occasion, Séamus dutifully turned down a television appearance because it clashed with a field trip. When George heard about it through the grapevine, he told Séamus to put the trip back a day and do the show. In 1952 he met and married Margaret Glynn, a teacher turned air hostess. Not one to miss a trick, Séamus advanced a proposal to *Woman's Hour* on the BBC Light Programme in November 1952, which reads:

> Séamus Ennis recently married an attractive air-hostess, and she is frequently asked by passengers who notice her ring: 'What is your husband?' This is not an easy question to answer. He is a collector of folk music and in this talk will explain exactly how one goes about making such a collection.[173]

Seven guineas later, the listenership of *Woman's Hour* had their answer. Unsurprisingly, Séamus later viewed his BBC years as the happiest period in his life.

The most resonant series with which he was associated was *As I Roved Out*. Running for six series between 1953 and 1958, it was in effect the national shop window for the work Séamus, Peter Kennedy and others were doing as folk song collectors for the BBC. At least two episodes were broadcast from rural pubs, and in many of the episodes Séamus also got an opportunity to perform.

The programme would be a touchstone for a whole generation of British folk music performers who would come to prominence in the later 50s and 60s.

Séamus: The programme went so well that I think pressure was brought on Radio Éireann … to do such a job … And their first programme of this nature was *The Job Of Journeywork* [presented by Ciarán Mac Mathúna], which was the name of a tune – more or less a direct copy of my title … *As I Roved Out* … It was an achievement to get Radio Éireann broadcasting this material … Another direct result of *As I Roved Out* was the forming of all these ballad groups, of which I think The Clancy Brothers were the first.[174]

Pat Mitchell: Somewhat untypically, Séamus later modestly suggested that the proximity to the very popular Wilfred Pickles quiz programme *Have A Go* played a part in their popularity.[175]

Throughout the 50s, Séamus found an outlet on a wide variety of on-air platforms: dramas, discussion programmes, religious programmes, light entertainment, documentaries. Fittingly, the last series begun while he was still a BBC employee was a reunion with Alan Lomax. If *As I Roved Out* had been a regular update from the BBC's collecting project, *A Ballad Hunter Looks At Britain* – broadcast over eight episodes in November and December 1957 – was a kind of summation. The project's funding had run out, although there was a luxurious £800 budget for this programme (most of which went to Lomax). Séamus made 103 guineas for his contributions – which was just as well, as his Permanent contract had expired back in March.

*

Séamus' old friend Willie Clancy had been working in London, as a carpenter, during the mid-50s. Aside from Willie, notable musicians in London's Irish music scene at the time, based around certain pubs in Camden Town and Cricklewood, included fiddlers Bobby Casey and Martin Byrnes and songster Margaret Barry with her fiddle partner Michael Gorman. Reg Hall, a keen participant in this scene who later interviewed many of its doyens for a PhD, has intriguing observations of Séamus' involvement, or not, during the period:

> **Reg Hall**: I met Séamus Ennis five times, I reckon. I was introduced to him – and every time, he took me for a stranger! I think he bloody knew who I was. It was his way of putting me down – not that I was worth putting down. I was insignificant. But I think that was just his manner. He had this instant charm he could turn on – which would also put you down. *'Oh, how very nice to meet you …'* Okay: I met you last week. It was like, 'I don't really care who you are; I'm just going to be charming to you, because that's the way I do things.'
>
> In my experience, he didn't go very much into the Irish pubs. I saw him in Irish pubs, I was in his company in Irish pubs, but [not often].* I don't think he knew how everybody functioned. He borrowed money off people, off Irish musicians – he'd borrow a tenner, then never come back. He had a bad reputation, eventually. I think all [the musicians] accepted

---

* Remarkably, Séamus was recorded by Ewan MacColl in an Irish pub, seemingly in the mid-50s. His performance of 'Twisting The Hayrope' appears on *Irish Music In London Pubs*, released on Folkways in 1965, alongside performances from Joe Heaney, Margaret Barry & Michael Gorman and the constant hubbub of drinking and chat. One is left with the impression that Séamus popped in, played a tune and swiftly cleared out again.

him at face value in the beginning. But they eventually saw him as a doer of dirty tricks.*

All the Irish musicians were from farming or labouring backgrounds. They were country people. And Ennis was middle-class, articulate, and mixed in middle-class circles, and he showed it – he almost let it be known. I didn't necessarily see this or feel this at the time, but I knew he was different, I knew he had a foot in another camp.

It's interesting that he recorded no Irish music, except three singers, in London – and [yet] he had *entrée* to everybody. Bob Copper would have known him, as they bumped into each other at the BBC. ... Bob said he was just a lazy bugger. He used to booze with personalities at the BBC – every lunch-time he was boozing with BBC characters, and essentially he was lazy.

It's hard to imagine the same man who was cycling Olympian distances and swimming daily in terrifyingly cold Hebridean seas in the 1940s as 'lazy', but a complacent aspect may have crept into Séamus' lifestyle by this time. Certainly, a boozing aspect had. One former colleague recalled, on RTÉ's *The Séamus Ennis Story* in 1988, that the BBC era was the beginning of his serious drinking, with a loyal secretary often covering for him when he was down at the Stag's Head.

Ewan MacColl's partner by the late 50s, Peggy Seeger, recalls Séamus from visits to their mutual friend Alan Lomax's house in Highgate, where he would sometimes be recorded, and also from great but hazardous performances at Ewan's clubs:

Peggy Seeger: He was very dicey, because he drank – and he couldn't control it. You could never tell when he was going to be capable. ... But when Séamus played freely, when he played the slow tunes, he was just heartbreaking, he really was. ... He was a total and complete character. When he arrived at your house, you knew he was there. He invaded every room, had to be waited on hand and foot, did nothing – didn't have to, because he played the pipes!

One might suggest that institutional policy was a factor in Séamus' disregard of the London-Irish players – after all, this was a BBC-funded survey of folk music from specific regions, untainted by city life. Brian George already had hundreds of

---

* Reg Hall: 'I went to his memorial in London, in Cecil Sharpe House. Bobby Casey, who didn't think ill of anybody, was there. A lot of other musicians turned up, but none of them had a good word to say about him. I interviewed loads and loads of musicians when I was doing my PhD, and none of them said anything warm about Ennis.'

examples of Irish music from his trips to Ireland in the late 40s. Séamus may have felt that there were greater untapped sources out there in the wild than in the pubs across town.

'He was selective in the things he did, extremely selective,' says fiddler Paddy Glackin, who knew Séamus well in later life. 'I would say that Séamus had a particular standard, and that was where he wanted to operate. I don't think sessions in Camden Town or Kentish Town were going to float his boat.'

On a personal level, Séamus didn't care for cities: he found 'rural England okay, urban England absolutely dreary'.[176] Perhaps he may simply have felt that once he had returned to London from lengthy collecting trips to Galloway or Norfolk, he was entitled to a breather – he was off duty. By the spring of 1957, however, with the end of the BBC collecting project, he was off duty for good.

> **Séamus**: I was probably the strongest cutter of my own throat, let me say. But I voted that I thought we had the job finished now. What I was getting now was mostly variant[s] of something I had before. It's a matter of conscience as well as common sense ... You have to justify your existence, justify it with your own conscience.[177]

*

By now, Séamus and Margaret had two young children, Catherine and Christopher.* They were living at Flat 2, 65 Alexandra Road, NW8. English traditional singer Bob Davenport, who first went to the Bedford in Camden Town in 1957, was a neighbour:

> **Bob Davenport**: He lived close to me. His wife had dark hair and blue eyes, his son and his daughter were beautiful and he was a very handsome man. He was known as 'The Ennis' and when he used to walk into the Bedford, it was like watching a cowboy film where the marshal walks in and everybody looks round. When he played, there was nobody ever comes close – it stood your hair on end, it was just absolutely devastating. He was absolutely at his height. But then things went really wrong for him.

Around this time Margaret, who had accompanied Séamus on some of his BBC collecting trips, went back into teaching. Séamus would later describe his freelance career as unrewarding, although he threw himself into it. He hung around the pubs

---

* Christopher was born in October 1953, Catherine in January 1957.

where producers gathered and cadged for opportunities. He pitched five proposals at a BBC Talks Department producer in December 1957, although when one was accepted and a fast delivery requested, he took nearly three months (blaming 'other chores') before delivering a script that was far too long.

On February 7 1958 he recorded another session for the BBC Permanent Library: 10 items of piping and a handy 35 guineas.* A week later, he was recorded live at Ewan MacColl's Ballads & Blues club at the Princess Louise, for a programme by producer Charles Parker. That same month, Séamus signed a 30-guinea contract to provide scripts and select music for a three-part series called *The Rambler From Clare*. On March 20 he arrived at the recording session with no scripts and no preparation. Peter Kennedy was swiftly drafted in to helm the first two programmes, while Séamus was offered a reduced contract for the third episode – but only if the script could be in producer Harold Rogers' hands in six days. Even then, his delivery was late.

It's tempting to read a frisson of chaos, certainly disorganisation, between the lines in Séamus' BBC Artist and Contributor files. Nevertheless, he had many skills, many good and loyal contacts among the producers and enough energy – certainly during his first year with freelancing as his primary income – to keep pitching script ideas at people and, along with various one-off spots in dramas and the like, to keep appearing semi-regularly on the music and discussion programmes *A Golden Treasury* and *Today* (occasionally recycling material he'd used on Overseas Service broadcasts). Many of his bookings would be for storytelling.

Regrettably, very little of Séamus' 1950s BBC radio work survives. Almost the only significant item which does is *Eileen Aroon*, broadcast in June 1959. A 60-minute dramatisation of an old Irish folk tale, it was scripted (from a translation by James Delargy) and co-produced by Séamus, and featured him in the acting and performing role of a piper. No doubt aware of the *Rambler From Clare* fiasco, co-producer Francis Dillon wrote to the Contracts Department in mid-May, when the script was delivered, to say that it was 'very satisfactory indeed' and that they could now pay Séamus the second half of his 100-guinea fee.

By chance, the next two BBC radio productions involving Séamus complete the trio of survivals from this era. *Song Of A Road*, broadcast in November 1959, was the second in a series of eight 'Radio Ballads' by Charles Parker with Ewan MacColl and a revolving cast of emerging personalities from the Scots, Irish and English folk revival scenes. Curiously, MacColl only required Séamus to sing on

---

* Many years later, Peter Kennedy released this BBC Library session on his own cassette label, Folktrax, disguising the provenance. Kennedy's activities around ownership and copyright remain controversial.

the broadcast, asking Belfast's Francis McPeake (in his national radio debut) to play pipes. Two months later, Séamus wrote and presented a half-hour tribute to 19th century collector Patrick Weston Joyce as one episode in a series titled, in a doff of the cap to the illustrious forebears of the BBC collectors, *As They Roved Out*.

Performing live would now become, necessarily, a renewed focus in Séamus' life. Over the next three years there would also be a burst of activity on the commercial recording front. As well as recording several vocal and piping tracks which would appear across four volumes of US label Caedmon's *Folk Songs Of Britain* Series in 1961 and contributing to a HMV album of British sea songs (*A Pinch Of Salt*, 1960), he would make three records under his own name. These would be solo recordings released in America, Britain and Ireland respectively, with no overlap in material: *The Bonny Bunch Of Roses* (Tradition, 1959); *The Ace And Deuce Of Piping* EP (Collector, 1960); and *Ceol, Scéalta agus Amhráin* (Gael Linn, 1961).[*]

*

A concert at O'Connor's pub in Doolin, County Clare, on August 3 1959 was Séamus' first appearance in Ireland for many years and featured him on a bill with Leo Rowsome and the London-Irish fiddler Martin Byrnes amongst others. Séamus had something to prove – and, luckily, Radio Éireann recorded it. Nearly an hour into the show, after a superb textbook set of five pieces from Leo Rowsome early in the proceedings and a mixed bag of other acts – including a man with an appallingly out-of-tune melodeon and a priest singing in the drawing-room style of John McCormack – Séamus came onstage and unleashed three pieces of magical playing. Two of these, including 'The Silver Spear/The Dublin Reel', played at atypically blistering speed, were later released on *The Return From Fingal* (RTÉ, 1997).[†]

If the Doolin 'comeback' was important for Séamus' soon-coming permanent return to Ireland, a Saturday night performance at the Troubadour, pillar of London folk clubs, on February 28 1959 was to have far-reaching consequences for the British folk revival.

Jenny Barton, running the folk nights for Troubadour owner Mike van

---

[*] The EP remains a covetable rarity in Séamus' discography. Collector Records was an offshoot of Jazz Collector. Founded in the late 40s, Jazz Collector reissued rare 1920s American records. Reg Hall: 'It was run by a bloke called Colin Pomeroy, who ran a tiny little shop in Kensington. When the folk revival began to get a little bit of steam up, Paul Carter – husband of Angela Carter, later a novelist – approached Colin Pomeroy and said, 'What about folk records?' So on the strength of that they recorded Jeannie Robertson, Dominic Behan, Joe Heaney (for two EPs) and Ennis.'

[†] The full 80 minutes of the RÉ recording can be heard at the Irish Traditional Music Archive (ITMA), Dublin.

Blumen, had created a thriving scene largely through a 1958 residency by Ramblin' Jack Elliott.

Jenny Barton: I was still fairly new to folk music. I hit it about '58, [the] year of my 21st birthday. Most of the time, then, if there was a folk thing going, I tried to be at [it] – and you could be at every one [of them] then [in London]. I'd heard it first on the *As I Roved Out* programmes, and I'd heard Séamus a year earlier on a programme called *Sons Of The Sea*. I have the script that Séamus wrote for himself. When I [later] told [him] that that's where I'd first heard him, he rummaged in his pipe box and said, 'Jenny, I think you'd better have this …'

In the audience on February 28 1959 was Martin Carthy, a 17-year-old who would be galvanised by the performance into a career as one of the most pivotal artists in English traditional music for the next 50 years and counting:

Martin Carthy: Our local hero was Robin Hall, when I was 16 [or] 17. I got talking to him. He was a funny bugger, but basically he said, 'If you want to hear proper folk music, you've got to go down to the Troubadour in Earl's Court. And I thought, 'Okay, I'll go to the Troubadour.' I didn't go down straightaway; it was sort of in the back of my mind until one Saturday, for absolutely no reason, I walked into the tube station and got the train down to Earl's Court. The ceiling and the walls of the Troubadour were all hung with old instruments. It was fashionably gloomy. The whole place was low lighting, lots of candles. I thought this place was absolutely wonderful. And as I walked down the stairs – the club was downstairs – I heard these pipes playing, and I thought, 'Oh, bagpipes, I know what bagpipes are.' I walked in and there was this bloke – and he wasn't playing the bagpipes properly! I knew about the Scots bagpipes – you stood up – and I'd *heard* about the Northumbrian pipes, but there he was, this man sitting down in this gloomy light, and I always say he looked like he was wrestling an octopus. I was just absolutely stunned. He played the pipes and it was absolutely beautiful, and then he sang a song and he played the whistle and he told stories – and I was completely mesmerised. What was his name? Séamus Ennis. And it stayed with me. I went away with this feeling I had in my head after that – it was just a fabulous evening.

I went and bought that record he made for Tradition, *The Bonny Bunch Of Roses*. I still have it, I love that record. And I loved his whole approach, his whole attitude. He was such a beautiful player – a lovely, relaxed style. He could be very, very funny. And very, very informative – a very clever man, and highly opinionated, and very, very kind. I met him later on, when he was staying with Jenny Barton. I went round when I thought I could play a bit and played a couple of tunes, and he was very patient and he sat there, and he played a couple of tunes. We didn't play together because, frankly, I didn't know what to do. I was completely unable, I had no technique – I just wanted to hear him talk. And he talked. He talked about music, and he was fascinating.

Séamus' encyclopaedic memory for matters of folklore was not matched by similar skills in personal organisation:

Jenny Barton: When we organised for him to come down, I made sure his wife knew where he was meant to be going. [But] when we had to get him home, he couldn't remember what bloody street he lived in! He was not noticeably drunk, but very absent-minded.

Three months later, on May 29, Jenny and Martin heard Séamus again, this time headlining a concert compèred by singer/guitarist Steve Benbow:

Jenny Barton: I can remember Martin taking what I thought was a school bag – and he says no, it wasn't, it was a bag of music stuff – and balancing it against a chair leg. And I remarked to whichever girl was sitting beside me, *'Who on earth is this kid? Is he old enough to be here?'* Séamus, shall we say, had drink taken. Steve Benbow seemed to be compèring the thing. As he was playing, Séamus started to keel over [in slow motion]. And Steve Benbow fielded him, very gently pushed him back up. And he never stopped playing!

Reg Hall: He was a big romantic. I always found him entertaining, any of his concerts I went to. I saw him at one or two things, and he had a huge charm in his presentation. There was a point where the pipes would go wrong and he wouldn't be piping much – there was a time in London when his pipes didn't work – and then he had this notion that he was the only tin whistle player in the world. I actually heard him say, 'I introduced the tin whistle to London.' *'What the hell are you talking about?'* I thought. *Everybody* could play the tin whistle!

On one occasion he went on in an Irish concert at Hammersmith Town

Hall with [fiddler] Jimmy Power. They worked out what tunes they were going to play in duet, and they go up on the stage to play, and then Ennis said, 'Now, Power, when we do those reels, when we go into the second reel, you lay off – don't you play, I'll break into it, I'll play it through once, then you come in.' So they're on the stage, and 10 minutes later they go into this routine, they come to the second tune and Jimmy stops playing, Ennis goes on a little and then says, *'Power! God, I would have thought you knew that tune!'* And Jimmy Power was absolutely livid, furious – would never play with him again.

Early in 1960, Séamus took part in loose ensemble sessions at Cecil Sharp House, recorded by his former colleague Peter Kennedy for a series of three themed albums of skiffle-ish folk songs – *A Jug Of Punch*, *A Pinch Of Salt* and *Rocket Along* – for HMV. Among the cast were Steve Benbow, Shirley Collins, Jimmie Macgregor, Bob and Ron Copper, Cyril Tawney and Isabel Sutherland. It was a fair snapshot of that part of the nascent British folk revival which would have been vaguely apparent to people from radio and TV, several of the artists being already known from broadcasts. Séamus was present on the first two albums, singing two songs on each and playing whistle on songs by others, but *A Jug Of Punch* is especially interesting in being the only occasion when Séamus released commercial recordings backed by a band: his 'Football Crazy' and 'Brian O'Lynn' feature combinations of guitar, mandolin, banjo and bass along with his own vocals and whistle.

Séamus' luck with BBC commissions, however, was beginning to run out: 'It was a complete change after affluence. I've known what it is to be hungry.'[178]

One of his projects involved a performance 'not passed for broadcast'. At times he took work as an electrician's assistant, with a friend from Limerick, at four shillings an hour. Bob Davenport, who feels that Ewan MacColl and Alan Lomax had also frozen him out of their circles, was a witness to the decline:

> **Bob Davenport**: I was passing by this pub on the way up to the tube at Swiss Cottage and I heard this voice, 'Bob!' and it was Séamus. It was a lovely day, and he said, 'What are you doing?' I was going down the West End for something. He said, 'Come with me, I'm going down to the George' – this BBC pub. There was a man called Francis Dillon who was producing Irish things. ... I said, 'No, I don't want to go down the George, it's lunchtime,' you know. 'Oh, come on, come on, come on ...' So I got in a taxi with him, which he couldn't afford, and Francis Dillon was at the bar, talking to three or four cronies, and Séamus says, 'The usual, Francis!' He looks at

him and sends a whisky over to him, and then Francis just continued to talk to these people and blanked Séamus. And Séamus tried to buy himself in. Somebody else there in the same circumstances said to me, 'He's drinking at the wrong producer.' The BBC then, I'll tell you, if you thought Florence was a place where you had to guard yourself from a knife in the back, the BBC in the 1950s made Florence look like a bunch of amateurs. It was sad. He was drinking more and more. … Séamus was too innocent, in a way. He fell out of favour, and they stabbed him.

Séamus: One day a senior producer in the BBC said to me – you know, I used to drop into the local at lunchtime, looking for work – he said, 'Do you know, Séamus, this is the British Broadcasting Corporation, not the Irish Broadcasting Corporation.' So I said, 'Thanks for the hint,' and I came home.[179]

Séamus returned to Dublin. He had no correspondence with anyone at the BBC for six years. He had separated from Margaret and the children before the end of the 50s, perhaps being simply unsuited for family life. He would have no contact with his children for 10 years.

'His wife had thrown him out, I think,' says Jenny Barton. 'She was making a living as a schoolteacher, coping with two children, and Séamus was just no help. He may have been charming and exciting and all that but, God, you wouldn't want to be married to him.'

The final BBC radio appearance in this phase of his life was in June 1960, telling the story of 'The Bold Fisherman' on *Monday Night At Home*. And where his home was, at this stage, had become a moot point.

*

Séamus' *Ceol, Scéalta Agus Amhráin*, in 1961, was one of the earliest releases on the new record label of Irish cultural organisation Gael Linn.* It was still rare for anyone to be making solo uilleann piping records at all. Radio Éireann was doing something new as well: Telefís Éireann, the first Irish television channel, began in December that year. Séamus, with unassailable broadcasting experience, would find himself in demand.

Paddy Glackin: I first became aware of Séamus in the very early 60s, as a

---

* The first Gael Linn record release was a one-off LP by the Radio Éireann Light Orchestra with Seán Ó Riada in 1958. The label proper launched in 1961.

child, watching him presenting a children's programme – '63, maybe '64. I forget what the name of the programme was, but he would have all these kids, and he would play the whistle, tell stories, play the pipes and kids would get up and dance and so on.

The show was almost certainly *Séamus Ennis Sa Chathaoir* ('Séamus Ennis In The Chair'), which ran from October 1963 into at least December and featured young musicians and dancers and the odd guest, including Dubliners banjo man Barney McKenna.*

'He was so wonderful with children,' Séamus' daughter Catherine said many years later. 'He created a magical world of his own and told stories and was completely devoted to them. In the time he was with them, he created mystery and fun and magic. When I met him again [as an adult, having not seen him since I was four], I slightly resented the fact that he'd deprived me of it … It took a bit of getting over.'[180]

Little of Séamus' 60s TV work survives, but he can be seen leading a hearty Gaelic sing-along in a 1962 episode of the series *Ballad Session*, presented by his old colleague from the RÉ Outside Broadcast days, Seán Mac Réamoinn. That same year, he completed a translation, from an idiosyncratic version of Gaelic, of *An Old Woman's Reflections* by Blasket Islander Peig Sayers.† It is still in print. Around the same time, he was writing a piping tutor – potentially the first since Leo Rowsome's in 1936. He would revise his early 60s work on it in 1968, but still never saw it through to publication.‡

He became an enigmatic presence around Dublin during the decade. Andy Irvine, a future member of Planxty, had moved to Dublin from London (after a period working for the BBC repertory company) in 1963:

> I remember hearing *As I Roved Out* when I was in London – that was a big influence on me. In those days, a lot of people [in Ireland] listened to the BBC, because Radio Éireann was fairly young. The first time I remember seeing him was at Slattery's in Capel Street. He hadn't been living in Dublin for some time, he'd just come back from somewhere, and he got up on stage and said, 'I'm going to play a couple of reels now, and the first one is

---

* Séamus also had another TV music programme around this time: *An Ceoltóir Sí* ('The Musician').

† BBC Radio's Third Programme broadcast a four-part series of readings from the book in December 1963. Séamus was not directly involved.

‡ It was eventually published as *The Master's Touch*, edited by Wilbert Garvin and Robbie Hannon, in 1998.

called 'The Master's Return'!' It was always hard to tell how much the drink was having an effect on him. He used to enjoy drinking a large bottle of Guinness, which he referred to as a 'sergeant'. But he would also be drinking what looked like tomato juice – but it might be heavily laden with vodka.

Andy recalls Séamus playing fiddle duets with Ted Furey at O'Donoghue's around this time. When Séamus came for a session at Ted's house, though, he brought a different instrument:

> **Finbar Furey**: I remember there'd be Willie Clancy and my father, there'd be Séamus Ennis – it'd be a few of them. Séamus Ennis, especially, would come in. And Séamus would pop himself down with a set of C pipes, which you couldn't tune to the rest of us cos we were playing concert pipes. So, of course, we'd be playing a few tunes, and then Séamus would decide to sing a song – and it would be *War And Peace*! The song would go on and on and on. And my father would say, 'I'll have to go and shave shortly ...' And when Séamus left, we all went, *'Whew! Thanks be to Jaysus!'* And then we'd get back to playing pipes. He was a character.

During 1963 or '64, Jenny Barton and her husband came to Dublin to try and find Séamus. They succeeded without great difficulty:

> We went to O'Donoghue's, and there he was, sitting there with Joe Heaney, and they were singing, verse about, a macaronic song – one sings it in English, the other in Gaelic, and then they swap. And they trailed through this – and it was the last time I heard Séamus really sing well – because, actually, the alcohol had really eaten his voice. Joe could always sing. I don't know that my husband had been *that* impressed with Séamus [before], but he said, 'My God, they can sing, can't they?' Anyway, Séamus took us home and was giving us some supper, and mother appears, [shouting] *'How long are these people staying, James?'* And we thought we'd better scuttle! She was a fierce lady.

Séamus was a perhaps unlikely guest at the July 1964 Newport Folk Festival in Rhode Island, USA, but his old friend Alan Lomax was on the organising committee that year, with a brief to enhance the traditional music content, and he was surely behind Séamus' invitation. It was an impressive bill: from rediscovered blues legends Sleepy John Estes, Mississippi John Hurt and Skip James through jug bands, hillbillies, Southern gospel groups and up to stalwarts Pete Seeger, Joan Baez and a bunch of hip young protest singers like Phil Ochs, Tom Paxton and Buffy Sainte-Marie. Several live albums from the event were issued by Vanguard the following year, with a medley of songs and piping from Séamus on one (*Traditional Music At Newport 1964 – Part 2*). It would be his only trip to America.

He stayed there for five or six months, one other engagement being a residency for a week or two at the Ash Grove, a folk and blues club in Los Angeles, in September, supporting Hispanic guitarist/vocalist José Feliciano. A recording of one of the Ash Grove sets provides a fascinating, almost unique, opportunity to hear Séamus working with an accompanist – 'Country' Al Ross, a young American bluegrass guitarist and Doc Watson protégé.* Tailoring his act to the West Coast crowd, Séamus sings and plays whistle in the duo format, tells stories and plays only one piping solo (his pipes clearly malfunctioning in the heat). He parries a request for a song in Irish, singing one verse before reverting back to the English that his audience could deal with.

Al Ross: Ed Pearl, the owner [of the Ash Grove], called me and said, 'I'd like you to come down and accompany this guy: he plays the kind of music that's maybe at the roots of what you do.' … The Ash Grove was a great, great venue. Ed brought in acts that nobody else would bring in. The average nightclub owner doesn't bring in somebody like Séamus Ennis. Maybe a rarefied not-for-profit folk music foundation some place might have brought him in to play for 12 people, but Ed brought him in as a real act. … Part of the reason Ed wanted me to play with him was he was afraid Séamus would bore people, and I was a fancy-dancy guitar player who would counterbalance that. … [But] as I recall, people liked him.

If you were tuned into him or you took the trouble to get tuned into him once you found yourself part of an audience watching him, he *was* mesmerising. The stuff that he knew was absolutely spellbinding. It happens that the big university in Los Angeles, UCLA, had a really serious Anglo-American Folk Music department. And at that point in time [I was there], studying Irish lore, mythical history, and he talked about that – he talked about Cú Chulainn. We never thought we would hear anybody first-hand who could, and here was this guy who was part of it, who believed it.

---

* Séamus had performed on Telefís Éireann in whistle/banjo duo with Barney McKenna in 1963. He can be seen in photographs taken circa 1968 at Slattery's, Dublin, playing whistle, pipes on his knees, with The Pavees, including George Furey on guitar and Johnny Keenan on banjo. His only official recordings with stringed accompaniment are three songs on the 1960 HMV LPs *A Jug Of Punch* and *A Pinch Of Salt*. The Ash Grove set can be found online at the subscription site Concert Vault.

He was a storyteller as much as a player. So a great part of every set was about stories … he was in the fabric of Irish and Scottish storytellers. So, in that sense, he wasn't eccentric; that said, he *was* eccentric! Seamus would pretend to fall asleep as part of his act, except occasionally he *would* actually fall asleep.

Al was 23 at the time, on the UCLA postgraduate course alongside John Fahey, the godfather of 'American Primitive' guitar. He would later work with many of the top names in country music and, later still, would pen a series of richly entertaining reminiscences online. In one such, he paints a picture of one night, during the Ash Grove run, when José Feliciano's combative manager was heckling him throughout his set with Séamus to play faster, while Séamus, bemused, was happy to let the duelling between his sidekick and the Latino lady carry on.*

If American audiences were intrigued by Séamus, in Al's opinion, 'for the most part, he thought [Americans] were boorish. I just had the feeling that he thought that he wasn't appreciated as much as he was in Ireland. [But if so], he kept it to himself.' What was obvious, though, was Séamus' style of dress being a kind of counterculture all to itself:

> **Al Ross**: I remember him wearing a harsh tweed suit, night after night. I remember that it was so different from everybody else. You knew you were seeing somebody from another time. Who the hell wears a tweed suit in 60s Los Angeles? And it would have been hot. Here was a rangy guy that came on and told these stories and told them in a voice that was very different from what else we were hearing and, yes, that had the effect of mesmerising some people.
>
> And yet he did seem to understand what he was. He did know there was a cadre, however small, of people who 'got' him. Just the fact that he could sit on a stage for 40 minutes and tell stories meant he was not uncomfortable. He may not have liked us, [but] he was charismatic and he came alive on stage – as much as he came alive – and he was 'the alternative'. I don't see him as being actively 'anti' the 60s. [But] he was not part of a revival, he was part of a continuous thing, like the last person alive doing this.

The duo's typical set (played to two houses a night at weekends) was around 45 minutes. After the Ash Grove run, they did a series of one-nighters at universities ('a

---

* Al's piece is worth reading: www.power-pickers.com/jose-feliciano-guitar-duel

more selective audience … they liked him a lot'). Al doesn't recall the broken ankle Séamus refers to on the live recording, but he does recall a lot of drinking:

> Not to make too big a deal of it, he was a serious alcoholic. I had the feeling that it was pretty much his modus operandi. I don't think that he particularly picked on the Ash Grove to act out his drinking career. He didn't slur his speech: he just got deeply into what he was talking about.

Al and Séamus got on tremendously well. There was even a possibility, or at least an idea that appealed to Séamus, that they might take the partnership further:

> **Al Ross**: I do remember [that] he talked about, 'We should really record together.' I don't know how serious that was, but he seemed to think that there was something worth mining there. I felt good about that. Then again, he was so much in his cups that I'm not sure how much he *really* wanted to. But I think he liked me; I think we got on.
>
> You knew that you were in the company of – and I don't mean this in any negative way – a real relic, that you were listening to somebody talk and play who was from another time. He was the real deal. I really loved playing with him, I loved his stories, I loved his music and I thought he was terrific. I really hoped that we could have done an album together.

*

Towards the end of 1965, Séamus became the unexpected guest of an old friend at 126 Portland Road, London:

> **Jenny Barton**: He'd come over to do a programme or two. His hotel had not wanted what they thought was a 'fluey man' on their hands and had handed him back to the Beeb. Someone had grabbed a doctor to him, who said, '*But he's got TB* …' So they bundled him off to a TB sanatorium in Aylesbury or somewhere. He'd had it since he was a teenager, but not eating, drinking too much – all those things didn't help. He was in there, I suppose, for months. I started visiting him because Mike Smythe, Seán O'Boyle's [friend], was doing the visiting and Séamus was driving him nearly cuckoo. So I dumped my child on my sister, spent the whole bloody day trailing out then trailing back again – [but] he did enjoy being visited. When he finally came out he went to the O'Boyles, who were out at work all day, so he went to the pub – which is not what anyone intended. So I got a panicked phone call saying, 'Séamus

says you *did* say he could come and stay with you …?' I said, 'Yes …' 'Can we bring him round this evening?' They didn't actually say that he'd be wrapped in a blanket, with the DTs, but that was the reality of it!

It was the tail end of '65 – Séamus was there for [my son] Sandy's birthday. He very much did have a drink problem. We slowly got him onto food. I had him three months in my house. We rationed him: he got one half pint in the evening – walked down to the pub with my husband in the evening, and back again. And finally the hospital said he was as near cured as he would be and he could go home. He left us in very early '66.

Séamus recorded some tin whistle for a BBC Home Service programme, *Pionair Disaster*, in February 1966 – seemingly the only BBC work he would do between 1960 and 1969. The fee was 12 guineas, hardly worth travelling over for, but there is no surviving record of any other commission from this period. Perhaps Séamus felt it would be a foot back in the door. An internal memo of March 1 1966, the date on which Séamus returns his signed contract, reveals 'Mr Ennis is most anxious to get his money as soon as possible.'*

In due course, he made his way back to Dublin. As Jenny Barton recalls, 'Florrie Brennan had him [to stay] in Liverpool, and I'm sure there were others.'

Brian Vallely, a young piper in Armagh, in Northern Ireland, had started a Pipers' Club there in 1966, and on occasions in the late 60s brought Séamus up for a concert, which would entail a week or two of hospitality at Brian's parents' house:

Brian: I grew up in a very fundamentalist, teetotal, no-smoking household, and I brought Ennis up to it … My mother got worried, cos he never seemed to eat any food. He never got slobbering drunk, but he was never totally sober.

Brian recalls with affection how Séamus could spend a whole day in an Armagh pub, amazing people with card and matchstick tricks. He also recalls being horrified on one occasion to see Séamus bringing out his pipes in the Charlemont Arms, in an era when people on those premises would have been ejected for even talking too loudly.

---

* Séamus is credited as 'Adviser' on a film made independently in 1965, *The Irishmen: An Impression Of Exile*, directed by Philip Donnellan with editing by Charles Parker, the folk-friendly BBC producer. Séamus' trip to London in 1965 may have had something to do with this. The BFI database gives this synopsis: 'Documentary following the journey of a young Irish fisherman from Carna in Connemara, as he travels to London to work on the Victoria line tube excavation. During the journey the film reflects on the social situation of Irish people in Britain. The soundtrack features songs specially written by Ewan MacColl.'

He recalls the proprietor descending the stairs as onlookers gazed with bated breath. Amazingly, the fellow was delighted, bought everyone a round and great music ensued.

In April 1969, *Melody Maker* writer Tony Wilson visited Dublin and reported back from a night at the Traditional Club at Slattery's in Capel Street, where he'd heard Ted Furey and Séamus Ennis 'who played some great music on Irish pipes'.[181] 'There is plenty of folk music of all kinds every night' in Dublin, he declared. Most of it, indeed, was happening at Slattery's, on several floors:

> **Andy Irvine**: I once played all the clubs in Slattery's. There was one on Monday, one on Tuesday, two on Wednesday, two on Friday, one on Saturday ... There were something like seven gigs in a week [that] I played, in Slattery's, upstairs and downstairs. Séamus would have played at the Traditional Club, which I think was on a Wednesday. But he ran a club, briefly, in the basement. I'm not sure whether I was booked there, but he asked me up to sing [once], and so I impressed him by singing, unaccompanied, a very little-known Child ballad called 'Young Reedon', which is a version of 'Young Hunter'. And he *was* impressed. '*A not very often heard ballad, that, from the Child collection ...,*' he said.

Perhaps, though, Séamus Ennis' most lasting achievement in the 1960s was his involvement, after the Bettystown gathering of May 1968, in the founding of Na Píobairí Uilleann (NPU). Both Séamus and Leo Rowsome were given joint Patron status in the new organisation. There were those within it who sought to promote Séamus' style of piping as the benchmark for future tuition, a position that contributed to Brian Vallely leaving, after three years as Secretary:

> **Brian**: Some people did try to standardise uilleann piping, almost like Highland piping, based on [the playing of] Ennis. But none of them came near Seamus Ennis: Seamus Ennis wasn't up for cataloguing or quantifying. He wasn't a one-dimensional man. He would play whatever the hell he wanted to. He would play 'Freight Train' or anything.' That was one of his favourite party pieces – he'd make the noises of the train and all that.

It might seem odd to see Séamus Ennis, the arch-solitary, involved in an organisation, but it wasn't the case that Séamus had aligned himself to it:

---

* 'Freight Train', by Elizabeth Cotten, was a UK No. 5 hit for the Chas McDevitt Skiffle Group featuring Nancy Whiskey in 1957. Séamus playing it for laughs 10 years later was still the closest he would come to popular culture.

Paddy Glackin: It was aligned to *him*. I don't think Séamus was *able* to align himself to anything. It would have been unthinkable not to have had him [involved]. Séamus was a legend even in the 50s and 60s. But there were various schisms in piping – there was this nonsense about open piping versus closed piping. His piping at a particular time would have been championed by NPU, whereas Comhaltas [Ceoltóirí Éireann] were championing the piping of Leo Rowsome. Within the piping community, depending on what side of the fence you were on, you either loved Séamus Ennis or you didn't particularly go for it. … [But] he used to go to the pipers' convention at Bettystown every year and do a midnight concert. That was the highlight of the weekend.

*

Barring his by-default appearance on one of the torrent of 1964 Newport Festival live albums, Séamus Ennis managed to traverse the 1960s – between 1961's *Ceol, Scéalta Agus Amhráin* and 1969 – without enhancing his discography. It might have been otherwise. In February 1968, a former BBC colleague, H. Rooney Pelletier, newly appointed General Manager of BBC Radio Enterprises, wrote to Séamus offering to release an LP culled from his 1958 piping session for the Permanent Library. His letter, sent to Séamus at 3 Home Farm Park, Dublin 9, was returned by the current occupants with the news that Séamus had left the address in 1965. Pelletier then wrote to him c/o Donoghue's pub, but his offer went apparently unanswered, and consequently no such record appeared.

Before the end of 1969, Bill Leader had decided to pretend he had some money and to put it where his mouth was. Launching a binary star of labels, Leader and Trailer, he was going to record the best of 'traditional' and 'revival' artists, and in many cases give a chance to people who were falling between the cracks of Topic, Transatlantic and the other independents (such as the folk-rock friendly Island Records) that were emerging at the time. His first release on the Leader imprint would profile the English traditional singer Jack Elliott of Birtley. The second would feature a man he almost recorded in the 50s and who, to his British public, had all but disappeared by this point: Séamus Ennis.

As Bill puts it, he 'wanted to produce some of the things that were happening around that seemed to be important'. An album by Séamus would be followed directly by albums featuring fiddler Martin Byrnes and flautist Séamus Tansey, all three releases entitled *Masters Of Irish Music*. Reg Hall would accompany the latter two on piano, but the Ennis record would be a glorious solo showcase.

Bill Leader: I first met Séamus around 1957 or so, through Jean Jenkins, ethnomusicologist and political activist. Topic was going to record an LP of Séamus and Jean. It was to be an Irish/American song swap. The venture eventually fizzled out. It was early on in my career as producer/recorder/organiser, and I failed to keep up the impetus of the idea.

I next saw Séamus during a period when I made frequent trips to Dublin. It was in O'Donoghue's. He was sitting at the bar, explaining that his doctor had told him that he must drink milk, which was why he was adding it to his vodka.

An arrangement was made for Séamus to record in Bill's flat at 5 North Villas, Camden Town, in July 1969. Bill's flat had already birthed several great British folk revival records, and this one would equal any of them. It is Séamus' greatest single recording – a magical mix of piping, songs and stories.

Bill Leader: Séamus needed no direction, coaching or encouragement. He was fully professional – after all, he'd worked both for the BBC and Radio Éireann. So the session consisted of his playing, singing and storytelling.

We were trying to get a fairly total picture of the man. That's the way I pretty well always worked. It got a bit difficult sometimes. I hadn't realised early on that if you just let, [say], Margaret Barry and Michael Gorman record what they wanted to record, they would record what they had recorded for the last record company.

Obviously, that's what record companies wanted [they thought] – that particular song or that particular tune. But other than that, as a general principle, I just let the artist speak.

Interestingly, after the record's release, we got an angry letter from Leeds demanding a refund on account of the fact that they didn't buy folk records in order to get a load of talking.

Séamus tied his recording trip in with an appearance at the Keele Folk Festival, July 11–13, and a booking at Rod Stradling's strictly traditional club at the King's Head, Islington, on July 16. 'Séamus was a great hero of anyone interested in traditional music: singer, astonishing piper and a wonderful storyteller,' remembered Rod. 'That night, there were more people in the club room than you would believe possible!'[182]

Reg Hall: The interesting thing about that was that Ennis came and did what appeared to be a totally spontaneous show – absolutely wonderful –

and he recorded the next day for Bill Leader, in Bill Leader's house, and did exactly the same spontaneous show! So it was a rehearsal!

More than 40 years later, the King's Head Club's 1968–70 run would be commemorated with a double CD release of selected amateur recordings from the venue. Of the four pieces from Séamus included, only one was not featured on *Masters Of Irish Music*. Bill Leader had hired a man with a camera to shoot Séamus at the recording session the following day, for the LP cover:

> **Bill Leader**: I hadn't realised that this lad didn't want to take posed pictures, but wanted to capture Séamus candidly. It was awkward, because he was waiting for a candid moment, while Séamus, for whom showbiz was not a strange occupation, was constantly moving into poses – he would actually interrupt his conversation at some point with his hands extended in such a way that most photographers would have given their eyeteeth to have taken the snap, and this fellow ignored him! So we ended up with a session with no pictures of Séamus.

In the event, one of Rod Stradling's imperfect but hugely atmospheric photos from the King's Head (Reg Hall just behind Séamus with a pint in his hand) became the LP cover.

Séamus was certainly back in Dublin by October, when he recorded (at Radio Éireann) a by now rare commission for the BBC: writing, narrating and performing music as a 10-minute show based on East Anglian folk song, for a BBC Radio 4 regional opt-out. Not so much a comeback as an oddity. Five tracks – none of them repeating the Leader material – were also recorded in 1969 for a various-artists LP on Gael Linn, *Seoda Ceoil 2* ('Musical Treasures 2').

'Of late they write and speak of him as the Ard-Rí or high king of Irish pipers,' wrote Séamus' mother, purportedly, in the notes to the Leader LP. 'Maybe he is. He grew a bit taller than any of our folks, on both sides.'[183]

If all this activity gave the impression that Séamus' career was in some way back on track, or at least moving purposefully towards something, it wasn't reflected in his lifestyle. Somewhere between nomadic by choice and destitute, he spent some months around this time being looked after at Ted and Nora Furey's house in Ballyfermot:

> **Finbar Furey**: My mother looked after him. He wouldn't have had much back in those days. He was very sick. It was when we were with The Clancy

Brothers – '69, '70, '71. And he would have been there for six months or so, because he had no place else to go. He was an awful man for the drink, Séamus was. Most of the lads drank, you know, but trust me, Séamus ... I think he had TB, I'm not sure. But I remember when he was as thin as a rake – Jesus, you'd be afraid to touch him in case you'd break him. My mother took him in for six months and minded him, [then] somebody else would take him in for six months and mind him.

Paddy Glackin, a young fiddler who became close to Séamus from 1970 onwards, isn't so sure that this seemingly chaotic lifestyle was due to alcohol. For, despite being dressed immaculately in a suit, Séamus Ennis was inherently far more of an outsider than the generation then coming to prominence in Ireland with outwardly bohemian traits like long hair and denim trousers:

> **Paddy Glackin**: I think it's just that inability that a lot of artists have to get settled and to be content, to be able to be organised and have a normal life. And I think Séamus had that problem. He was different – that's the only way I can put it. And people in the 'establishment' found that difference very, very difficult to deal with. And he found it, in turn, equally difficult to deal with. I think people understood that he was apart.

*

'A wave of consternation and dismay swept through the ranks of Irish music lovers,' declared the May/June 1970 issue of Irish music magazine *Treoir*, 'when the news was heard that Séamus Ennis was in a critical condition in the regional Hospital, Galway, after being involved in a car accident on 1st April. He was travelling to a session in Conamara [sic] at the time. Séamus was very ill for some days, but gradually rallied, and at the time of going to press (April 20th) we are glad to report that he is making a steady recovery. Willie Clancy, Tony MacMahon ... and many more friends and admirers were at Séamus' bedside in the critical hours, and the exchange at the hospital was kept busy answering calls from all parts of Ireland, England and further afield – a testimony, if one were needed, of the esteem in which the towering piper from Jamestown is held.'[184]

Seán Mac Réamoinn later observed that 'Séamus died seven or eight times before his death.'[185] He was either reckless or prone to misfortune on the roads. As early as December 1954, BBC colleagues had feared the worst, as glimpsed in a surviving letter from *As I Roved Out* producer Harold Rogers (although the precise context remains mysterious):

> So glad to hear that everything is now well – sorry if I sounded shaken, but I was convinced that you would not have returned to Fishguard, and it was like hearing the voice of a ghost – ghost Ennis.[186]

Seán Mac Réamoinn recalled that one of the major problems after the 1970 accident was getting him to eat properly:

> When he did sit down, he had a wonderful appetite and could eat us all under the table ... It was getting him to take time off for this matter, which was 'not as important' as his other activities ... Sadly, I mean physically, he never came back to us, to that flower of the days that I knew him ... But I think his musicianship remained remarkably strong.[187]

While Séamus never gave any formal tuition on the pipes, he became a periodically available resource to other pipers and traditional musicians throughout the 70s, with appearances at the annual NPU *tionól* and, from 1973, at the Willie Clancy week at Miltown Malbay:*

> As the week progressed, the faithful would be looking out for the long black Zephyr parked literally at the door of Friel's public house, which would signal the master was in town.[188]

If this all seemed like God coming down from the mountain to dispense enlightenment, it was a perception with which Séamus would have been perfectly happy. Paddy Glackin confirms that there was an aspect of Séamus' personality that revelled in the legend around it: 'When Séamus Ennis entered a room, the room stopped. He had an amazing presence. He'd fill the room. You knew you were in the presence of somebody from another world.'

Reacquainted with his children by the late 60s, Séamus surprised his daughter, Catherine Ennis, by failing to attend an important organ recital she was giving in Dún Laoghaire, near Dublin. He later explained: 'I didn't want to steal your thunder.'[189]

Paddy Glackin and Liam O'Flynn were among the few who benefited from Séamus' knowledge and wisdom in music over a sustained period:

> **Paddy Glackin**: [From 1970], as my view of life, and musical life, began to change, I became aware of Séamus again, and I began to see his music as

---

* Amateur recordings from many of these events are accessible at the ITMA, Dublin.

being quite different to the mainstream. And as a result, then ... I just kind of got to know him bit by bit and I started to visit him. He was exceptionally generous to me. That was the thing about Séamus: if Séamus thought you were serious about music, he opened the door. He didn't suffer fools. I got to know him because I had a particular interest in Frank Cassidy, a Donegal fiddle player, and Séamus had recorded him. We became very good friends. He was not the easiest man to get to know, and when you got to know him you began to realise that there were these other sides to his personality. ... He was an exceptionally articulate man. Even the way he wrote. He had a phenomenal memory, a phenomenal gift. The way he could write stuff down, the way he could tune his ear into different dialects of Irish – quite extraordinary. And if you got involved in a joust with Séamus, you'd lose!

During the period when he was a member of Planxty (1972–75), Liam O'Flynn, a young piper with a distinctly more reserved personality than the Master's, shared living space with Séamus:

> **Liam O'Flynn**: He got very ill – self-inflicted. He got in touch with me and told me he was coming out of hospital and asked if I knew of any place he could use as accommodation. And as it happens, I was sharing a place with my brother Mícheál in Mount Street and we had more space there than we needed. ... Séamus moved in. ... Then we moved from there to a flat in Pembroke Road, and from there to a house in Templeogue, again with my brother. All in all, I was around him a lot for two to three years. They were the early Planxty days as well, and I was doing a lot of travelling. He was – to say the least – a fairly demanding sort of person. If my brother was alive today, he'd have the funniest stories to tell about Séamus.[190]

For a fellow piper, though, living with Séamus Ennis had a silver lining:

> **Liam O'Flynn**: Any time I took out the pipes to play – I would just be playing for minutes – a door would open very quietly, and this vision [would] appear in the doorway in the form of Séamus. And he'd just sit and listen, offer advice and whatever – not wanting to be critical or anything. He was just interested in helping.[191]

Friendly also towards Christy Moore, Planxty's guitarist/vocalist, Séamus became a source of material for the band, and always expressed an interest in what they were doing – although he had no aspirations to follow an ensemble path himself, amplified or otherwise. His concerts were akin to chamber recitals, on his own terms:

> **Paddy Glackin**: The music scene wasn't set up to accommodate someone like Séamus Ennis, and he certainly wasn't wired up to accommodate it. He wouldn't have survived on the [touring] circuit. He wasn't equipped. There's also the nature of Séamus' music – it wasn't commercial. The audience he had was a very refined audience. They were going in to hear *him*.

Kevin Burke, future fiddler with The Bothy Band, occasionally encountered Séamus at Slattery's on Capel Street 'and probably played with him here and there':

> He knew lots of people I knew [from the London Irish scene]. He was good friends with Joe Heaney, he knew Martin Byrnes. … Funny, just thinking about it, all of those guys – Joe Heaney, Martin Byrnes, Séamus Ennis – I was just enthralled by their voices, the way they spoke. Rich-sounding voices, an unusual way of speaking, an interesting turn of phrase. It just made everything entertaining, even if it was just ordering another round. And when they were together …

Doubtless aware that his 'great work', as a preserver of vast tracts of musical and storytelling traditions, was behind him, Séamus gave a series of very substantial interviews to Mícheál Ó hAlmhain between 1970 and 1973. Five themed pieces from these interviews were published in sequential issues of *Treoir* in 1973, covering his own career, songs, storytelling, slow airs and piping techniques – including information on several piping notes originated by himself (the 'ghost D' harmonic, and E and F sharp in the third octave).* Séamus was merciless towards those who used E flat when not in the mode of the tune, those who used the regulators for percussion and those who reckoned themselves any good without 21 years at the coal-face: 'There are far too many pipers who think they have it, and they haven't even started yet.'[192]

Séamus, however, clearly recognised the talent and dedication in his flatmate:

> **Liam O'Flynn**: It was palpable [that] he really wanted to pass on as much as he could, of what he had, to me. I think a lot of people imagined that I had known Séamus Ennis all his life – and, of course, I [only] knew Séamus for the last 10, 11 years of his life. His work had been done, his collecting,

---

* The full interview recordings, some extracts from which were used in RTÉ's *The Séamus Ennis Story* in 1988, are available to be heard at the ITMA, Dublin.

and I suppose in a sense I was kind of lucky in having known him those 10 years, because I was getting the benefit of all his work … [But] I'd love to have known the Séamus Ennis of the 1950s. He must have been an amazing character altogether.[193]

While he was still a periodic presence on RTÉ television during the 70s – sharing an episode of prime-time magazine *The Late, Late Show* with The Chieftains and Planxty in 1972, for example, with further appearances on Irish language programmes and in several documentaries about himself – much of Séamus' focus was now on live performance:

> **Séamus**: I really do put my heart and soul into my playing, and I really do enjoy playing well and doing my best in playing. I never look on a performance as a chore. If I find one person in the audience who's all ears, I'm pleased; a full, rapt audience brings out the best in me.[194]

> **Paddy Glackin**: I remember [one] night he did a gig without a note of music – just talk. Now, I believe he was worse for wear, couldn't get the pipes on him, so he got up on the stage, fiddling with the keys, but he spoke. And he got other musicians up to play. But he got a standing ovation at the end of the night. It was an extraordinary night.

> **Andy Irvine**: I did a gig with him somewhere – I don't know where it was – but I well remember I was scared stiff. It was just after I'd got the hurdy-gurdy. He went on first – I was really embarrassed by that. It must have been after Planxty, and I suppose I had a bit of a name because of Planxty. He went on first, then I went on, then he came on again and we played a couple of tunes together. I think he must have felt a little bit pissed off, having opened the show for me – so as soon as I finished he was on the stage, he took over! I remember talking to him afterwards. He wanted to see the hurdy-gurdy. He was quite interested in it, had a little go at it and said, *'If I had one of these I would play it while sitting on the toilet.'* And I couldn't tell whether that was a derogatory remark or not!

By the 1970s, Séamus occupied a very rarefied, if not unique, position within Irish culture. *Treoir* had described him as a 'household name' in 1970; and the television airtime given to him on RTÉ throughout that decade and up to his passing in 1982 would seem to bear that out. The tale of how one RTÉ documentary, *Miles And Miles*

Of Music, broadcast in 1975 and directed by noted wildlife filmmaker Éamon de Buitléar, came to be illustrates this.*

Éamon de Buitléar: During the 1970s, Ennis' health was deteriorating, and I was anxious to record some of his material on film before it was too late. I telephoned his doctor, Ivor Browne ... He was naturally delighted to hear of my plans and advised me to make the film as soon as possible. I approached RTÉ with the proposal and consulted Liam Ó Murchú, who was in charge of Irish music programming, but his response was that they had no money available for such a programme. My immediate reaction was to say to him, 'Look, Liam, Séamus Ennis is not all that well. Supposing I were to come in to you in the morning and announce that Ennis had died, what would you say then?' 'O, Jaysus!' replied Liam. 'Go and make the film!'[195]

Séamus transcended the traditional music world, although that in itself was now in a more vibrant state than it had been during the previous decades of his life. In practical terms, within the traditional music scene, Séamus' notoriety meant that he was unassailable. If he turned up somewhere and was awkward or irascible, he wasn't shown the door; he was tolerated, listened to, and the incident merely added to the growing store of anecdotes about him. Typical of such is the riposte he is supposed to have given when asked for advice on the best way to play a bodhrán: 'With a penknife.'

Paddy Glackin: There are all these stories told of him in Miltown Malbay. He was upstairs in Friel's one night and someone was downstairs trying to play the pipes, and Séamus couldn't get to sleep, started banging on the floor with his shoe and then came down and said, *'Would somebody put that cow out of its misery!'* And on another occasion, again at Friel's, there was a session outside and he opened the window and roared out, *'Would you stop and let your betters get some sleep!'*

I remember one night being out and about in Dublin and there was a session going on and Séamus was sitting there, and some guy was

---

* De Buitléar, an accordion player and member of Seán Ó Riada's pioneering Irish music ensemble Ceoltóirí Chualann in the 60s, had known Séamus from the 1950s. Work began on *Miles And Miles Of Music* on March 8 1973, when Séamus came to Éamon's studio to discuss sequences for the film; these included a scene in University College Dublin, with the IFC archive he had helped assemble, and another in Connemara with his old friend Colm Ó Caodháin, the last time the pair would meet.

playing a piano accordion – and Séamus wasn't happy. In fact, he officially complained: *'Can we stop this?'* He didn't care. That's just the way he was! He was one of those individuals who was 'outside'. He was on the margins, and he was quite happy to be on the margins.

He was selective in the things he did, extremely selective. But he did have a problem in terms of staying with something. I think he got bored easily. … The thing is with Séamus, a lot of people don't get it – pure and simple. I remember I would see people in Slattery's, at the Traditional Club, years ago and they would just blank over, because it wasn't the way they wanted to hear the pipes. So his music was an absolute challenge. Séamus did not conform. I don't know why, but that's the way he was and you had to respect that.

*

Having shared living space with Liam O'Flynn and his brother Mícheál for two or three years, by the middle 70s Séamus clearly needed his own place:

Liam O'Flynn: Séamus wasn't the most domesticated man. I suppose he didn't lead a regular type of life. He was much happier being up at night and sleeping through the day. At the time my brother had a day job and was also studying for a degree in university at night, so there was a conflict of timetables. Gradually, Séamus' health began to fail, and eventually it just wasn't practical for us to continue. The responsibility was large.[196]

After renting a flat on his own in north Dublin for a period, Séamus arranged a more permanent solution:

Jenny Barton: He ended up living in a caravan out at Naul. There was a piece of ground there that had been part of his grandfather's farm and he had a caravan on it, and his sister [Pixie and her husband Tom] had a caravan on it – and in theory the sister looked after him. I visited him down there once and it wasn't as bad as it sounded, but it still wasn't good. It wouldn't have helped. The time I went [there], he said, 'You know Jenny, my liver's gone.' 'Highly probable, the way you live,' I said. He didn't look wonderful, and I think he was probably fairly accurate.

Séamus moved into his caravan, near to his by now demolished family home, Jamestown Lodge, in 1975. 'Very cosy, very comfortable and very happy,' is how he described the situation. 'It's a big change to be in a nice, quiet place by yourself now, with nice quiet neighbours who don't interfere. To play your music there and eat what and when you like, sleep when you like and more or less lead your own life, please yourself.'[197]

By now, he doubted there was a permanent job that would suit him and was stoic about his lot:

> When you think of going out at night and doing a job and being paid what would amount to a pretty good week's wages in Ireland – for one night's work – and then a job that wouldn't be so well paid … well, [even] two of these would amount to a pretty good week's wages. And then you haven't got to be under the thumb of some petty boss.[198]

Paddy Glackin: I spent many's the night in Séamus' caravan, drinking till four in the morning, talking about music and playing music. Even with a good amount of alcohol on board, he could still focus. When he wasn't drinking, he was extremely lucid. But then he'd have his relapses. [But] I had very good moments in the caravan with him where we'd just sit and drink and talk about the state of the country or talk about football.

If Séamus didn't want you in his space, you knew very, very quickly. Now, equally, if you were in his space, it was all-embracing and it was intense. I can remember sitting in his caravan, going through tunes – *'Wrong! That's wrong,'* he'd say. I'd be asking him for his particular take on tunes, based on his recording. So when I asked him, say, for Frank Cassidy's version of 'Lord Mayo', Séamus would be able to say, *'No, that's not the way Cassidy did it – this is what you need to be doing …'* … I remember another occasion being with him, doing a radio programme, and there was a bit of tuning up going on, and someone said, 'It's grand.' And he said: *'It's not grand! It's still not in tune.'* He was kind of exact.

And then Séamus did the notes for my first album for me, which I regard as a wonderful honour.* The first date I was ever on with my wife was to Séamus Ennis' caravan – to pick up the notes, which he hadn't done. I brought her out to meet Séamus Ennis because she was interested in him, because he had recorded her aunt. This was around '76. I remember we went out that night for a drink into Balbriggan with Séamus and bought some drink and came back to the house, and he said to my wife, 'How are you at

---

* The album is *Glackin*, released in 1977 by Gael Linn. Two years earlier, Séamus had annotated piper Paddy Keenan's eponymous debut, also on Gael Linn.

typing?' And she said, 'Well, not very good …' He said, 'Well, we'll try it anyway.' So he sat her down at the typewriter and started dictating the notes to her. I remember halfway through it he said to her, 'How did you spell that?' She told him. *'Wrong!'* he said. I didn't go to bed at all that night – left my wife straight into work the next day. That was my first date with my wife. So Séamus looms large in my life!

Alongside his performing and television appearances, Séamus managed a minor frenzy of record releases in the mid-70s: *The Pure Drop* (Tara, 1973); *The Wandering Minstrel* (Topic, 1974); *Féidlim Tonn Rí's Castle, Or The King Of Ireland's Son* (Claddagh, 1977); and *The Fox Chase* (Tara, 1978) – the Tara and Topic releases comprising piping, the Claddagh record being a long tale with musical interludes. In amongst these, two compilations of old recordings appeared: *Music At The Gate* (1975) on Peter Kennedy's low-circulation Folktrax cassette label; and *40 Years Of Irish Piping* (1974/76) on Innisfree (US) and Free Reed (UK). How much involvement, if any, Séamus had in the Folktrax release is a matter of conjecture. For the latter release, he supplied the compiler, Patrick Sky, with a letter of introduction and let him get on with it – tapping associates for anything of use.

Séamus' performing work during his later years was almost entirely in Ireland, where he was a revered figure among the cognoscenti. On July 19 1977, for instance, he was special guest of The Bothy Band at Liberty Hall during the Dublin Folk Festival. As the festival's programme put it:

> Even though one would never tire of listening to his pipes, his mode of conversing with his audience adds a strange charisma to his whole performance. The Dublin Folk Festival is indeed privileged to have such a genius in one of our major concerts.[199]

The previous year, in late June 1976, Séamus had performed at a 'Celtic' festival in Rotterdam, alongside other artists from Scotland and Brittany. This may have been his only performance in mainland Europe. Even in England he had become notable for his absence. *The Wandering Minstrel*, for Topic, had been recorded on a now rare visit. He had appeared at a traditional music festival, 'Folkmeet '70', at Liverpool University during October 1970, sharing the bill with Bert Lloyd, Shirley & Dolly Collins and others. He had then been contracted to appear at a Radio 1 concert recording at Loughborough University in February 1971, but the contract was unfulfilled, without explanation in the surviving paperwork. More worryingly, in September 1977, during which he was due to undertake a much-trumpeted short tour of Scottish and English folk clubs, he was booked to perform for BBC Radio 2 at Broadcasting House. The contract was annulled with the words 'Artist Indisposed'.

The tour had been organised by *Folk News*, edited by Karl Dallas, and was to have included an appearance at the National Club in Kilburn supporting Five Hand Reel. As the paper's October edition reported, 'a virus infection caused the last minute cancellation' of the tour.'[200] Liam O'Flynn flew in for a day to deputise for his friend at the National. *Melody Maker* later reported: 'Ennis is very disappointed at missing the gigs, which have aroused much interest, and has vowed to rearrange them as soon as possible.' Seemingly this rearrangement never happened.

Séamus did, however, turn up for what were to be his last British and BBC appearances, in February 1980: a World Service interview with John Amis and a concert at the Royal Albert Hall, recorded for Radio 2's *Folk On 2*.*

> **Paddy Glackin**: He stormed the Albert Hall. There was a festival called A Sense Of Ireland held in London. It was put on by the Foreign Affairs department as a showcase for Ireland. Pipers had a piping exhibition in Battersea … but the finale was this concert with Planxty, De Danann, Tony MacMahon & Peader Mercier, myself and Paddy Keenan – and Ennis. And I remember Ennis arrived into the dressing room at the Albert Hall with this navy suit on, an absolutely elegant coat with a white silk scarf. He had been in Harrods that day. He went out on the stage that night and he stormed the place. He was on his own, that place was full to the rafters, and they were standing. It was an extraordinary night.

As well as attending every Willie Clancy Week from its inception in 1973, Séamus had a regular booking at the Lisdoonvarna Festival: not at the first event in 1978, but he was present every year from 1979 to 1982. He can be glimpsed going onstage at the 1980 event to warm applause, a besuited figure in a sea of rain-soaked hippies, in *Hand Me Down*, an RTÉ documentary profile first broadcast the following year.

It was around this period that some felt it was time to bring Séamus in from the cold, in a literal sense:

---

* While the Albert Hall concert was recorded, and while Séamus signed a contract and received payment for such, it's unclear whether any excerpt was actually broadcast. *Radio Times* listings confirm only that the sets by De Danann and the reunited Planxty were broadcast, although excerpts from the other artists on the bill could of course have been featured in the programme throughout the year without specific *Radio Times* billing.

Paddy Glackin: I started [working for] the Arts Council in September 1980. And one of the first tasks I set myself was to see if we could do something for Séamus. And it was very difficult. ... He was living in the caravan, the caravan wasn't in good nick, and we were kind of worried about him being out there in the cold and the damp. But that's where he wanted to live. We all felt, 'This here's a guy who we regard as a national treasure, and he's living on the margins.' I got him an apartment, but when it came to actually move into it he wouldn't go – he just wouldn't do it.

On Sunday July 11 1982, Séamus Ennis walked onstage at the 5th Lisdoonvarna Festival – headlined that year by Jackson Browne, UB40 and Wishbone Ash – for his by now customary slot opening the final day. A couple of slots further along were Martin Carthy and his new band, Brass Monkey:

Martin Carthy: I remember seeing him ... He could still play. They wanted him to do an encore, but he said, *'Nobody ever does anything after 'The Connaught Heifer'!'* It was a lovely tune – and he played it beautifully.

Jenny Barton was also there, another friendly onlooker from the past: 'His performance was still pretty good. Singing he couldn't do: the booze had buggered his voice, but the playing was still fine.'

Paddy Glackin: It would have been his last big performance. He walked onto that stage, with a field full of people, and filled that space – it's very difficult to put words on it.

It wasn't apparent to Séamus' friends until relatively late in the day that Séamus had cancer, but even then, it didn't seem terminal.

Paddy Glackin: Liam O'Flynn and myself were with Séamus a week before he died. We brought him for his last medical appointment. He was quite low at that stage, but we didn't think he was in any imminent danger. But he was dead the following Tuesday.

Séamus Ennis went to his reward, as he himself would have put it, on October 5 1982. For all that his great work was behind him, he surely had more to offer, more wisdom to impart, more music to make and more stories to tell – even if he would always be the curious fellow rattling around on the fringes of the folk music revival that he himself had done so much to foment in the lonely years before, the dangerous years for the survival of Irish tradition.

The real triumph was not that, by the end, he was opening the bill for Wishbone Ash and UB40, but that he had been both an engine and a key link in a chain that had led to a situation where, by the 1980s, pure Irish traditional music could share stages with the popular music of the day, with an audience just as eager to hear both and with no sense of embarrassment about what would once have been the preserve of elderly, unschooled, rural people. Séamus Ennis, perhaps more than anyone, had brought traditional music in from the cold. He just couldn't do the same thing for himself.

Paddy Glackin: It was a very hard life he had. But it was absolutely self-imposed – an absolute shame. He had that inability to be tied down, to compromise. He was an extraordinary man.

Chapter 10
Séamus Ennis At The BBC

All the information below has been distilled from the contents of six large files relating to Séamus at the BBC Written Archive Centre (WAC) and from the following sources: the BBC Sound Archive database (SA); BBC Transcription Service materials at both the Irish Traditional Music Archive (ITMA) and the British Library/National Sound Archive (NSA); *Radio Times* national broadcast listings, sourced from the Project Genome online resource; and, in a few cases, *Radio Times* regional editions, *London Calling* (the listings magazine for Overseas Services) and other resources at the WAC.

The Radio Éireann Employee Era: 1947–51

Séamus was permanently employed by Radio Éireann (RÉ) during this period, but after making a positive connection with BBC producer Brian George during the latter's 1947 field recording trip to Ireland, Séamus made periodic contributions as performer, speaker and adviser on BBC programmes. He was loaned by RÉ to assist Brian on a further BBC collecting trip in Ireland, and RÉ was similarly relaxed about Séamus making occasional recordings in Dublin or London for the BBC. Aside from programme contributions, Séamus recorded on several occasions during this period (in 1947 and 1949) for the BBC's Permanent Library. This material can be heard at both the ITMA and the NSA.

'Irish Folk Songs', Permanent Library session
Rec: 30/8/47, Jamestown, Co. Dublin
'When Pat Come Over The Hill' (2.40); 'The Rocks Of Bawn' (3.06); 'Seventeen Come Sunday (When Cockle Shells Make Silver Bells)' (3.36); 'The Mary Ann McHugh' (3.13)

The above four songs were recorded by Brian George at Séamus' home in August 1947. While no documents relate to the session at the WAC, all four songs exist across three 78rpm discs. The first three also exist, curiously, on tape in the BBC SA. 'Cockle Shells' from this session appeared, along with items from other Irish singers and storytellers (all recorded by the BBC Recording Unit in Éire, August 1947), in a 63-minute programme called *The Irish Storyteller*, transmitted on 13/6/48. Written and produced by W.R. Rodgers and narrated by Cyril Cusack, this programme included stories told by Peig Sayers (whose memoir Séamus would later translate) and also survives in the BBC SA.

Country Magazine: Irish Number (No. 140), Home Service
Rec: 29/8/47, Dublin / Tx: 7/9/47 / Prod: David Thomson
Fee: 6 guineas

Séamus is booked for a talk.

***The Hidden Ireland*, Third Programme**
Rec: ?/48, Dublin / Tx: 17/3/48; 22/3/48; 25/3/48
Fee: 2 guineas

The recording date on the contract is 30/3/48, but this can't be right – more likely it's the date of a contract in retrospect for work done. These were three 20-minute talks on the theme of Gaelic culture and its preservation given by James Delargy, Séamus' former boss at the Irish Folklore Commission. Séamus is booked to play pipes.

'Irish Folk Music (Uilleann Pipes And Tin Whistle)', Permanent Library
Rec: 19/9/49, 20/9/49, 21/9/49, 22/9/49, Dublin
Fee: 40 guineas

Three recording sessions of three hours each were mooted. The contracts state Broadcasting House, London, to be the venue, but the transcription discs give it as 'Dublin'. Four sessions eventuated, at 10 guineas each. The contract was for 16 songs and approximately six record sides of uilleann pipes plus six of tin whistle. In the event, around 23 minutes of piping with some whistling was recorded (all on the final session), and 27 songs (across the other three sessions) seem to have been recorded. Material from the piping session was recorded onto a 10 inch vinyl disc, with material from the other sessions spread across 12 shellac 78rpm discs. The music recorded, with timings where known, is given below. Those marked with an asterisk, all from the third session, are 'copyright Colm Ó Lochlainn', Séamus' old mentor. Presumably Colm had collected or translated the versions sung here by Séamus of what were surely all traditional songs. 'Twisting The Hayrope' appears twice, as both song and instrumental.

19/9/49: *'Uncle Pat' (1.38); 'Cuc-A-Nandy' (1.34); 'The Old Man Rocking The*

Cradle' (3.00); 'The Herring Song' (1.25); 'Paul And The Football Club' (1.39); 'Colleen Ruadh' (3.10)

20/9/49: 'The Soft Deal Board' (3.49); 'Young Mary Barry' (3.05); 'Rise Up Woman Of The House' (3.21); 'Young Donald' (3.25); 'Johnny Joyce' (2.34); 'Fair Nancy' (2.39); 'Twisting The Hayrope' (3.05); 'I Wonder What's Keeping My True Love Tonight'; 'The Bonnie Boy'

21/9/49: 'Mrs McGrath' (3.15)*; 'Bench Of Rushes' (2.08); 'The Limerick Rake' (2.43)*; 'Van Diemen's Land' (3.10)*; 'The Deserted Wife' (1.42); 'The Banks Of Roses' (2.03)*; 'The Red-Haired Man's Wife' (2.55)*; 'Molly Bawn' (3.27); 'My False Hearted Lover' (3.34); 'Brian O'Lynn' (2.03)*; 'There's Whiskey In The Jar' (2.12)*

22/9/49: *Reels: Tuning Up & Improv/'Dublin Reel/Leitrim Lilt'* (4.26); *Hornpipes: 'Kelly's Hornpipe/Ballymanus Fair'* (3.08); *'Were You At The Rock?'* (2.10); *'Twisting The Hayrope'* (2.21); *Jigs: 'The Cavan Brigade/When The Cock Crows It Is Day/Sixpenny Money'* (3.03); *Reels: 'The Rainy Day/The Merry Blacksmith/Miss Lane's Fancy'* (3.31); *Jigs & Reel: 'Tipperary Wedding/The Dark Girls In Blue/Humours Of Lisheen/The Sligo Maid's Lament'* (4.20)

Six of the songs from these sessions (plus one other, 'The Frog And The Mouse', from the same sessions but apparently not extant on transcription disc) also exist on tape, for reasons unknown, in the BBC SA, where they are catalogued with notes by Séamus. These, with the notes, are as follows:

'Cuc-A-Nandy': 'Children's dandling song (in Gaelic & in English). Learnt from Mrs. Cronin.'

'The Frog And The Mouse': 'A song for children. Origin probably English. Universally known. Learnt from Mrs. Cronin, Ballymakeery, Co. Cork. The English version is usually: 'A Frog he would a-wooing go'.'

'The Old Man Rocking The Cradle': 'The tune is interesting in that Irish tradition says that it was used by Our Lady when putting the child, Jesus, to sleep. As far as I can trace them, the words are of some antiquity. This has been learnt from Michael Doherty, travelling tinsmith, Ballybofey, Co. Donegal.'

'The Herring': 'Simple folk song type. Heard only in one instance from Denis Murphy (fiddle player), Lisbeen, Gneeveguilla, Co. Kerry, Feb. 1949.'

'Paul And The Football Club': 'A modern humorous song. Probably composed in the district in which I heard it. Sung by Patrick Cronin, Gneeveguilla, Co. Kerry, Feb. 1949.'

'Caoine Na Baintrighe (The Widow's Lament)': 'The lament of a woman whose three sons were killed fighting in a foreign war. An abridged version of the words as learnt from various singers in Connemara.' [Séamus also provides a full lyric translation.]

'Johnny Seoige (Johnny Joyce)': 'Learnt from Colm Keane, Glinsk, Cashel, Connemara. A song of the famine times. Johnny Joyce was in charge of the distribution of Indian meal in Carna Parish. The song was composed by Thomas Shiunach.' [Colm Keane aka Colm Ó Caodháin.]

Music Magazine, **Home Service**
Rec: live broadcast? / Tx: 20/11/49 / Prod: Anna Listore
Fee: 5 guineas

Three of the pieces recorded on the fourth session were broadcast here, alongside selections from Bartok and settings of Goethe lyrics, plus other Irish pieces by Denis Murphy (fiddle) and John Barratt (lilting), which had been recorded to disc for the BBC library in 1947 and 1943, respectively. The producer asked Contracts to offer Séamus extra money for providing further information towards an introductory talk for the broadcast. Séamus was contacted c/o Radio Éireann and accepted an additional 5 guineas for the BBC 'to use the material in any way desired'. The three pieces (erroneously listed as four) used in *Music Magazine* were noted on the contract as: *'Tuning Up & Improvisation (Dublin Reel)'* – pipes; *'The Corn Brigade'* [sic] & *'When The Cock Crows'* – pipes; *'It Is Day'* [sic] – pipes; *'Tipperary Wedding'* – whistle.'

Irish Street Ballads, **Home Service**
Rec: ? / Tx: 14/12/49; repeated 3/4/50 / Prod: Brian George

From *Radio Times*: 'Humorous songs from the towns and villages of Ireland. Singer: Séamus Ennis.' A 15-minute show introduced by Brian George. No contract extant.

The Enchanted Islands, **Third Programme**
Rec: 5/9/50 / Tx: 6/9/50; repeated 8/9/50 and 28/9/50 / Producer/Writer: David Thomson
Fee: 12 guineas and £17.9.6 expenses

'A [60-minute] programme about the legendary lands that by tradition lie beneath the sea off the coasts of Ireland, the Hebrides, Scandinavia, and Brittany.' Séamus is flown in from Dublin to advise on traditional music, to play examples (five minutes) and to read a traditional folk tale (five minutes).

His contact address seems to be a public house: c/o O'Reilly, Ely Place, Galway. Séamus has asked to be paid in cash on the day of the broadcast, as he'll be fronting up his travel expenses (airfare and hotel). This is agreed, but in the event he returns his signed contract too late and has to wait for a cheque in the post.

Sons Of The Sea, Third Programme
Rec: ?/11/50 / Tx: 20/11/50; repeated 12/12/50 and 17/1/53; repeated on Home Service 9/1/52 / Producer/Writer: David Thomson
Fee: 12 guineas (plus travelling and subsistence expenses) per programme

Séamus travels from Dublin to advise on traditional music, play examples and read a folk story. Memos in the WAC suggest that there were two separate broadcasts – 6/11/50 and either 20/11/50 or 23/11/50 – with Séamus contributing to both. 'Live repeats' were not unusual. However, information with the transcription disc held at the NSA gives the broadcast date as 20/11/50.

He returns to Dublin on 21/11/50. *Radio Times* confirms 20/11/50 as the first broadcast, plus repeats listed above. The one-hour programme was billed thus: 'I am a man upon the land I am a selchie in the sea … Tradition, Songs and Stories of the Grey Atlantic Seal.' Séamus was among a cast of 17 actors and musicians, with Owen Brannigan the chief singer accompanied by a harpist. Séamus is credited solely with uilleann pipes.

'Five Irish Folk Songs', Permanent Library session
Rec: 21/11/50 / Commissioned: Ms M.A. Room
Fee: 15 guineas
'*The Pup Came Up From Claodach*' (3.08); '*The Tailor Bawn*' (4.34); '*Going To Mass Last Sunday*' (2.58); '*My Lost One*' (2.51); '*The Road To Kilaloe*' (3.44); '*Johnny Mó Mhíle Stór*' (3.36)

Séamus records a two-hour-15-minute session at Broadcasting House (just before returning to Dublin). The contract states 'Five Irish Folk Songs'; six are recorded. The contract names only the first four listed above plus a fifth, 'My Home In Sweet Glenlee', which seems not to have been recorded.

***Francesco Landini*, Third Programme**
Rec: live? / Tx: 8/3/51; repeated 11/3/51 and 16/4/52 / Commissioned: 'Music Booking Manager'
Fee: 10 guineas, plus third-class Dublin-London return (rail or sea) and subsistence

Séamus is brought from Dublin to play pipes in a 45-minute programme of music by Landini – a 14th century Italian composer (mostly of vocal works). A curious booking, in which Séamus joined an instrumental ensemble comprising himself on pipes with the great Julian Bream on guitar, Michael Dobson (oboe), John Alexandra (bassoon), Bernard Davis (viola), Basil Lam (harpsichord and regal), Charles Spinks (organ), Jack Lees (glockenspiel) and Gilbert Webster (triangle and tabor). Séamus asks for the music in advance, in case it needs transcription, but says he can transcribe it on rehearsal day if necessary.

***The Stone Of Tory: A Ballad Opera From The West Of Ireland*, Home Service**
Rec: 19/5/51, Royal Irish Academy of Music, Dublin / Tx: 1/8/51 / Prod: David Thomson
Fee: 20 guineas (artist fee), 30 guineas (research fee)

David Thomson asks Miss Gray (Copyrights) to arrange a fee with 'Seumas Ennis' [sic] of Jamestown Lodge, Finglas, for consulting on the above 60-minute programme, to be recorded in Dublin. Alan Lomax has travelled to Dublin to work on the script with Séamus – whom he recommended to Thomson as the major contributor required. 'I understand from Mr Lomax,' writes Thomson, 'that Ennis will supply us with most of the musical material for the programme and will do a considerable amount of research.' Thomson suggests a fee of 30 guineas.

On 7/5/51, Séamus writes to Mrs Gray: 'I am already at work on *Irish Ballad Opera* with Mr Alan Lomax who arrived the day after I received your letter. I am satisfied with the fee … and I understand the fee does not include the acting, singing or piping it is proposed I do during recording. Mr Lomax tells me the contract for that part of the work is issued by another department.'

Séamus' script fee is paid on 28/5/51. As a performer, Séamus is contracted to play the leading part, which will involve singing several ballads and solo performances on pipes, fiddle 'and possibly accordion'. The high fee of 20 guineas also reflects his speaking/acting role (usually contracted separately to music).

The plot explored attempts by a land agent to collect rent by gunboat on Tory Island, off Donegal, and his thwarting by magic. The production combined a cast from Dublin's Abbey Theatre with rural Irish singers. In his biography of Alan Lomax, John

Szwed declares that the project was 'the first time that professional singers and actors had joined forces with singers who had never performed for audiences other than their own families and neighbours, and it often took great skill to get them to appreciate and make room for each other's very different senses of time, movement, and art.' After three weeks of intense writing and two days of rehearsal, it was recorded.

The BBC Employee Era: 1951–57

During this period, Séamus is employed as a folk song collector for the BBC Permanent Library, along with Englishman Peter Kennedy, on a series of medium-term but rolling full-time contracts. He nevertheless enjoyed the opportunity to make a secondary income as both an occasional live performer, often in events associated with Ewan MacColl, and a freelance broadcaster – incidental musician, featured musician, speaker, script-writer, researcher – on various BBC Services. Occasionally, as internal memos indicate, there is confusion as to how to book Séamus (i.e. through which department – eventually standardised as via Music Bookings), and occasionally someone will ask whether this or that broadcast, or the time of a recording, should be regarded as falling under Séamus' existing salary/remit. Invariably, the decision is that it doesn't.

Curiously, on those occasions when Séamus is making an on-air appearance to discuss his role or lifestyle as a folk music collector – which might well be considered a public relations exercise for the BBC project that already employs him – there are no such questions raised. The impression gained of the BBC culture at this time is of an institution with scrupulous administration and record-keeping processes, yet one within which things can generally be resolved by bumping into a useful colleague in the corridor or by a bit of paper from someone saying 'Don't worry, it's all fine.' It would appear to be an era before external auditing, and Séamus did very well in finessing the sale of his considerable knowledge and skills to the broadcasting platforms available.

From the evidence on surviving contracts, Séamus' BBC freelance income, not including expenses and not including fees for contributions to Series 1, 3 and 4 (1953, 1955 and 1956) of *As I Roved Out* (for which relevant paperwork is missing), for 1951–57 is as follows:

- 1952 (including December 1951): 236 guineas
- 1953: 71 guineas
- 1954: 321 guineas 12 shillings and sixpence
- 1955: 42 guineas
- 1956: 91 guineas
- 1957: (up to and including *Ballad Hunter*): 323½ guineas

Possibly the modest figures for 1953, '55 and '56 reflect his busiest times as a collector, away 'in the field' in the Hebrides or elsewhere. Another caveat is that there are no contracts extant for at least seven national broadcasts to which he contributed between 1949 and 1957, known from *Radio Times*. There may be a further few regional and overseas service broadcasts for which contracts have not survived and that do not appear within the searchable Project Genome online database of *Radio Times* national broadcast listings. Ironically, the one programme with which Séamus is most closely associated during this era – *As I Roved Out*, essentially a shop window for the BBC song collecting project he was engaged upon and hugely influential on the nascent 'British folk revival' – earned him very little freelance income (for example: 39 guineas for the 1954 series). An external auditor, on that occasion, would surely have been satisfied.

The Gaelic West, **Third Programme**
Rec: 20/12/51 (piping) and 29/12/51 (narration, singing and other instruments) / Tx: 16/4/52; repeated 28/12/52 / Prod: Alan Lomax/Douglas Cleverdon
Fee: 8 guineas (first session), 17 guineas (second session), 30 guineas (script)

Séamus narrates, plays the pipes and sings Gaelic folk songs in a 60-minute programme on Gaelic music devised and produced by Alan Lomax, although Douglas Cleverdon's name appears as producer on some documents. On 10/12/51, Séamus is offered and accepts 30 guineas for assisting Lomax with the script and research. The title in the contracts is given as '*World Folk Song – Alan Lomax*'. As billed in *Radio Times*: 'A programme of folk songs and music recorded in Scotland and Ireland.'

Folk Song With Variations, **Home Service [regional?]**
Rec: ?/52 / Tx: ? / Prod: Francis Dillon
Fee: 60 guineas in two instalments – first half paid 23/1/52, second half paid 5/11/52

Séamus is contracted in January 1952 to write this 45-minute programme (an analysis of decadence in folk song) for a broadcast date TBC. Francis Dillon attests to the Contracts Department that 'Ennis is an expert on world Folk Song with a particular knowledge of Irish Folk Song' and that there will be 'rather more talk or script than the title suggests. Ennis will have to augment his knowledge with at least 10 days' research.'

Séamus is also to take part as a singer – usually a separate booking. The fee agreed suggests it was all-in. Curiously, while Séamus was paid well, no transmission date for this programme – nor for any remotely similar-sounding programme – can be found via *Radio Times* online listings (albeit national only). Though the titles are similar, and the producer the same, this programme seems unlikely to be *Variations On A Folk Song Theme*, broadcast 10/2/54, as Séamus was paid again for script and performance.

Blame Not The Bard, **Third Programme**
Rec: live? / Tx: 4/2/52; repeated 6/3/52 and 2/4/52 / Prod: Douglas Cleverdon and W.R. Rodgers
Fee: 8 guineas

Séamus is contracted on 30/1/52 to sing some Thomas Moore songs in this 60-minute programme – presumably broadcast live or recorded a day or two beforehand. It was a portrait of the 19th century author of *Moore's Irish Melodies*, written by H.A.L. Craig. C. Day Lewis appeared as Moore and sang, with piano and harp accompaniment, alongside Séamus, Joseph Tomelty and opera star James Johnston. *Radio Times*: 'Moore left one enduring memorial, his Irish melodies. In this centenary programme they can be heard both as he himself sang them in the Regency drawing-rooms and as they are sung in Ireland today.'

Piper's Meeting, [**North Of England Home Service?**]
Rec: ?/52, Newcastle-upon-Tyne / Tx: 1/2/52
Fee: 12 guineas plus London-Newcastle expenses

Séamus will be playing 11½ minutes on the pipes, singing two folk songs and taking part in a discussion with Mr J.H. Miller and Mr. J. Armstrong (presumably pre-eminent Northumbrian piper Jack Armstrong). The contract is requested by the Northern Programme Executive at BBC Manchester. Séamus is by now working on a permanent contract with the BBC Recorded Programmes Department in London (this booking being outside of that contract) and is staying at the home of BBC producer Brian George in Sonning-on-Thames, Berkshire.

'Séamus Ennis, Ballad Singer' [**probably Permanent Library**]
Rec: 10/2/52, Alexandra Palace, London
Fee: 20 guineas

It's unclear whether this is a session for the Permanent Library or a programme called *Séamus Ennis, Ballad Singer*. A session for the Permanent Library may seem likelier, although the fee is twice that for the Library sessions recorded only three years earlier – hence suggesting a programme involving both singing and presenting. Séamus is on a full-time contract with the Permanent Library as a collector at this time, so it seems curious that he would be allowed to make a freelance recording for his own department. Surviving documentation cannot resolve the matter.

***Séamus Ennis*, BBC TV**
Rec: live broadcast? / Tx: 10/2/52; repeated 6/3/52 and 6/5/52?

From the days when BBC television was something that happened between only 5pm and 10.30pm, this was billed in *Radio Times* as: 'SÉAMUS ENNIS in a programme of Irish and American folk songs and stories. Presented by Robert Barr.' A 15-minute mid-evening programme, this was apparently repeated on the two occasions above (although tele-recording was rare at this time), given that the exact same blurb was used in *Radio Times*. Alternatively, Séamus may simply have reprised his presentation as 'live repeats'. There are no contracts extant.

SERIES: *Crime Is Our Business*, [North Of England Home Service?]
Rec: live from Manchester / Tx: 17/4/52; 15/5/52 / Prod: Tom Waldron
Fee: 12 guineas per programme plus travel/subsistence

Séamus is booked by the Programme Executive in Manchester through the Talks Booking Manager, London. From *Radio Times*: 'A series of dramatised programmes of the constant fight against crime waged by the C.I.D. of police forces in the north of England with John Slater as the storyteller.' The shows are Episodes 1 ('A Night Job In Salford') and 5 ('East Meets East In Liverpool') in the six-part series, rehearsed and broadcast live on the days in question.

[St Patrick's Day programme], North American Service
Rec: 14/3/52 / Tx: 14/3/52 / Prod: Peggie Broadhead
Fee: 10 guineas

Séamus is to write and narrate, play some Irish recordings and sing for around six and a half minutes (two Irish folk songs, unaccompanied). Even though St Patrick's Day is March 17, this show was recorded on 14/3/52 and broadcast later that day, at 10.20 GMT, on the NA Service, programme title unknown.

London Column: 'Folk Music In Britain', **North American Service**
Rec: live broadcast? / Tx: 7/5/52 / Prod: Charles Parker
Fee: 15 guineas

Séamus is to write and narrate this 15-minute programme, and create recorded inserts. His fee covers writing and performance. His current address is c/o Room 508, Rothwell (BBC premises).

Alexis Benoit Soyer, **Home Service**
Rec: ?/52 / Tx: 10/6/52 / Prod: Francis Dillon
Fee: 7 guineas

Séamus sang one song in this programme about a celebrity chef from the Victorian era, with links to Famine-era Ireland. The contract for it is arranged retrospectively.

Kerry Fair, **Home Service**
Rec: 26/9/52 / Tx: 16/10/52 / Prod: Maurice Brown
Fee: 10 guineas

Again, the contract is arranged retrospectively – a week after Séamus' contribution. Séamus supplies technical advice and records a five-minute insert for this programme on 26/9/52, consisting of the following tunes on tin whistle: 'Trim The Velvet,' 'The Lament For The Fox', 'The Fox Hunters' Jig', 'The Master's Return'. From *Radio Times*: 'A wicker-work of talk, song, and dance woven out of the events leading up to, into, and out of a cattle fair in County Kerry in the month of January by W.R. Rodgers and Maurice Brown.'

Woman's Hour, **Light Programme**
Rec: 7/11/52 / Tx: 12/11/52 / Prod: Marguerite Scott
Fee: 7 guineas

Séamus submitted a proposal on 24/10/52 to give a talk on *Woman's Hour* (a 'daily programme for women at home') about being a folk music collector. (See previous chapter for proposal details.) Personal anecdotes and illustrations from his recordings are promised. The talk is billed as 'Song Hunting'. Séamus submits by post a draft script ahead of recording, having failed for a couple of days to bump into Marguerite around the BBC (with the script on his person), as he'd expected to. He invites her to change whatever she wishes and gives her approval over the discs he'd like to use as illustrations. His BBC address is now 311 Rothwell House.

Gaelic Magazine, **Scottish Home Service**
Rec: live broadcast? / Tx: 18/11/52
Fee: 8 guineas

Séamus sings two traditional Irish songs and plays two tunes on the pipes.

Twelve Days Of Christmas, **Home Service**
Rec: 3/1/53 / Tx: 6/1/53 / Prod: Louis MacNeice
Fee: 7 guineas

Séamus recorded a three-minute song in Gaelic and played pipes for this 60-minute programme. The contract is arranged two weeks in retrospect. However, a handwritten note from one Stella Hillier notes that Séamus' recording was not used in the programme, and that action has been taken on late bookings for Séamus: 'Miss Sheffield [?] has been suitably reprimanded for this one!'

Possibly this need for 'action' also reflects the late bookings for Séamus in the two mid-1952 programmes (above) to which he contributed without enough time to arrange contracts beforehand. One might imagine Séamus, multifariously talented, being based on BBC premises in London and naturally bumping into BBC producers – and consequently getting himself involved in their programmes.

Jazz Folk Song, **North Of England Home Service**
Rec: live broadcast? / Tx: 11/1/53
Fee: 7 guineas

Séamus is contracted to sing two songs on one episode of this series.

Mass On St Patrick's Day, **North American Service**
Rec: ?/3/53 / Tx: 17/3/53? / Prod: Kenneth R. Wright
Fee: 15 guineas

Séamus is requisitioned on 10/3/53 to provide a script and presentation at the microphone, with illustrations, for this programme. He notes that Miss Room (presumably representing Séamus' full-time employment duties) has given permission for Séamus to do this. The contract is issued on 13/5/53.

***Ben Bach*, Welsh Home Service**
Rec: ?/53 in London / Tx: 24/2/53
Fee: 7 guineas

A month after broadcast, the Welsh Programme Executive confirm to BBC Music Bookings that Séamus recorded two ballads for them in London for the above programme, and request a contract be agreed – which is signed on 30/3/53. A Miss Joyce Rainbow had pointed out to them that Séamus should be paid. Again, the inference seems to be that Séamus' permanent employment in one branch of the BBC results in a certain vagueness about what he is or isn't entitled to in terms of on-air/performing fees.

***Just A Year Ago*, Light Programme**
Rec: live broadcast? / Tx: 8/5/53 / Prod: Harold Rogers
Fee: 3 guineas

Séamus is to supply a three-minute script and present, describing his job as a folk music collector. Presumably this was to give context to a re-broadcast of some material from his BBC work in 1952, as the *Radio Times* blurb for this weekly half-hour show says: 'David Lloyd James looks through the BBC Recorded Programmes Diary for 1952 and invites you to listen again to some of the broadcasts that took place during this week last year.'

***Summer Pasture*, Third Programme**
Rec: live? / Tx: 8/7/53; repeated 11/7/53 and 15/10/53 / Producer/Writer: David Thomson
Fee: 7 guineas

Thomson requests Séamus the day before broadcast to be booked to take part as a speaker and to play uilleann pipes. A contract for 8 guineas is proposed five days after the broadcast, but revised down to 7. The final contract only references Séamus playing incidental music on the pipes.

From combined *Radio Times* blurbs: 'A dramatized [sic] account [starring Laurence Payne] of the shieling system in Sweden, Ireland, and Scotland, with the music and customs traditional to the annual movement of cattle to and from the summer pastures With traditional music on cowhorn, ox-horn, goathorn and fiddle. Uileann [sic] pipes played by Séamus Ennis.'

SERIES: *As I Roved Out* **(Series 1), Light Programme**
Rec: 1953 / Tx: 27/9/53–27/12/53 (13 weekly episodes) / Prod: Harold Rogers
Fee: ?

This series of half-hour shows – running between 1953 and 1958 and generally broadcast on Sunday mornings – would become the programme most associated with Séamus' BBC era. It was, in effect, a rolling report on the work Séamus, Peter Kennedy and others were doing as folk song collectors for the BBC during this time, and was hugely popular with audiences. In 1978, Peter Kennedy – a man who became deeply controversial within the British folk world for his business dealings and his approach to copyright – wrote to *Folk News* to outline the programme's history and his role in it:

> I was recording folk music in England three years before the BBC scheme came into being ... The scheme owed its beginnings to Alan Lomax, the American collector, and to Brian George of the BBC in particular. Until she retired, Marie Slocombe was the Librarian of BBC Recorded Programmes Library (now BBC Sound Archive) and was responsible for putting our field recordings into the Permanent Library. I suggested *As I Roved Out* and with Séamus Ennis presented the programmes weekly on Sunday mornings. The producer was Harold Rogers, now Director of Radio Medway. After the scheme ended, and Séamus and I had left the BBC, Marie Slocombe presented some follow-up programmes called *As They Roved Out* ... We owe her a deep debt of gratitude for all she did over the years in encouraging Séamus and myself in the field and in persuading the BBC to process hundreds of recordings of British Isles folk music and customs ...[201]

Whether Peter Kennedy was declaring that he suggested the programme itself or just its name is unclear. (Kennedy later suggested that he had introduced The Quarrymen to George Martin – a claim rendered absurd by decades of Beatle-ology.) Séamus maintained that the name was his, and would reference the programme fondly in interviews in the 1970s. Indeed, for all the 1950s broadcasting with which he was involved, much of it concerned with traditional music, *As I Roved Out* would be the only programme widely recalled in later years. Along with Ewan MacColl's *Radio Ballads* (1958–64), *As I Roved Out* stands as the most significant influence on the 'British folk revival' of the coming decade.

Curiously, the production team seems to have been lax in filing paperwork:

Séamus Ennis' files at the WAC only have contracts for the 1954 series and some of the 1957 and '58 episodes; Peter Kennedy's file is similar. While each man did not necessarily appear in every episode of every series, there is no paperwork whatsoever for the 1953 series – the existence of which can be confirmed from other sources (the Radio Programme Index microfiche at the WAC and, of course, *Radio Times*).

> **Séamus Ennis (1972)**: Each programme would be 30 minutes, of which about 14 minutes would be me. Peter Kennedy or some other part-time collector would do another 12 to 14 minutes … I would say, yes [this period was the height of my career]. That would be because of the programme. Every Sunday morning for most of the year – nine months of the year, anyway.[202]

There may be exaggeration in what Séamus was recalling about both the airtime he enjoyed on an ongoing basis and the prolificity of the programme itself. Each series of 12 or 13 episodes would have had to be repeated twice in the same year to accumulate nine months. He went on to explain one of the reasons he felt the programme resonated with a wide audience:

> I tried always to paint a word picture of the district, the person singing and the house he lived in – just little unimportant details about my visit there, like 'At that moment the dog came in,' for instance.[203]

According to *Radio Times* listings, Séamus was involved in 11 of the 13 episodes of Series 1 (all bar the second and fourth). Across these 11 episodes he: recalls Amos Becket, a singer from Buckinghamshire; recalls his first visit to Skye; goes collecting in Pembrokeshire; talks about a visit to Buchan in North-East Scotland; introduces his old friend Colm Keane from Glinsk, Connemara; introduces Togo Crawford, a shepherd from Kirkcudbrightshire; meets some fiddlers from Donegal; introduces Andrew Thomas from Pembrokeshire; goes collecting in Buckinghamshire; and discusses the lore around the 'Christ Child Lullaby'.

An off-air recording of the final show in Series 1 exists, being a get-together of the show's presenters and production team plus traditional singers Bob and Ron Copper, with Séamus performing several songs and tunes solo and in collaboration. The introductory music for the series was Armagh singer Sarah Makem singing a few lines of the song 'As I Roved Out', with the tune then taken up by the band of jazz/light entertainment man Spike Hughes – by coincidence or otherwise, the son of Irish song collector Herbert Hughes.

SERIES: *Ballads And Blues,* **Home Service [regional]**
Rec: 3–4/53? / Tx: 10/3/53–14/4/53; three episodes repeated in 6/53 on *Light Programme* / Prod: Denis Mitchell
Fee: ?

From *Radio Times*: 'A series of programmes in which folk singers and jazz musicians find a common platform in modern and traditional folk music from both sides of the Atlantic.' According to his biographer, Alan Lomax returned to Britain in April 1953, after more than a year in Spain collecting material for the Spanish volume of the *Columbia World Folk & Primitive Music* LP series – spun out into several BBC radio shows to help keep the wolves from the door. His return must, however, have been the previous month, for Alan was involved in Episodes 4 and 6 of Ewan MacColl's series *Ballads And Blues*. This series, airing British and American folk songs on a weekly theme, would inspire, a few months later, MacColl's new London folk club of the same name – one of the first in the country.

There is, strangely, no record of Séamus' participation in these shows in Séamus' own files at the WAC, but *Radio Times* lists him as being involved in Episode 5, on the theme of Soldiering. This episode was repeated on the Light Programme on 21/6/53 (one of three to be repeated thus). The cast on Séamus' episode consisted of Humphrey Lyttelton's band, A.L. Lloyd, Jean Ritchie, Isla Cameron and Neva Raphaello. (The six original Home Service regional broadcasts are absent from the BBC's online *Radio Times* digitisation, which only covers 'Home Service Basic'.)

The episode titles, with transmission dates, were: 1. *Singing Sailormen* (10/03/53); 2. *Bad Lads And Hard Cases* (17/03/53); 3. *Song Of The Iron Road* (24/03/53); 4. *The Hammer And The Loom* (31/03/53); 5. *Johnny Has Gone For A Soldier* (07/04/53); 6. *Big City* (14/04/53).

Later that year, Lomax fronted a six-part BBC TV programme, produced by David Attenborough, entitled *Song Hunter: Alan Lomax*, which included numerous 'source singers' from around Britain – among them a full Gaelic choir from the Outer Hebrides whose travel expenses used up the budget for three episodes in one fell swoop. A landmark programme which, tragically, does not survive.

Ceilidh, **Third Programme**
Rec: 8–9/52? / Tx: 8/10/53; repeated 14/10/53 / Prod: Douglas Cleverdon
Fee: 15 guineas (script), 10 guineas (transcription fee)

Séamus is to edit and script, in collaboration with Scottish collector Hamish Henderson, this 30-minute programme based around the recording of 'the 1952

Ceilidh of the Edinburgh People's Festival'. Featured performers are: Kitty and Marietta MacLeod of Lewis; Arthur Argo of Fyvie; Jimmy Macbeth of Elgin; Blanche Wood of Portknockie; Frank Steele of Banff; and Piper Calum Johnston of Barra. The BBC Transcription Service subsequently takes an interest and offers Séamus a further 10 guineas (and Henderson likewise) for permission to transfer the tape to disc for potential rebroadcasting on overseas services. The programme subsequently *is* rebroadcast (to the USA) and the BBC Transcription Service, English (Overseas) Unit, gives Séamus a further fee of £2/12/6 in February 1954. Whereas original fees would often be negotiated, these fees for transcription/rebroadcast were standard.

SERIES: *As I Roved Out* **(Series 2), Light Programme**
Rec: 1954 / Tx: 3/1/54–28/3/54 (13 weekly episodes) / Prod: Harold Rogers
Fee: 39 guineas

For all the notoriety of *As I Roved Out*, Séamus would make very little money from his direct on-air contributions to it. While there is missing paperwork for Series 1 and for most of the subsequent series, the contracts in Séamus' BBC Artist File for Series 2 appear complete. *Radio Times* confirms that he had a presentational role in nine of the 13 episodes; his Artist File confirms that he gave musical performances in six (detailed below), earning a total of 39 guineas. Nevertheless, the best material he had collected, on a BBC salary, from source singers and musicians across the British Isles would have been aired on the series, which was obviously a reward in itself. A note from an unknown person on the first Séamus-related memo around this series asks whether Séamus will be recording during office hours, as this may affect the fee. The programmes seem to have been recorded roughly three or four weeks before broadcast.

The information below is what can be gleaned from the WAC regarding Séamus' contributions to the episodes broadcast on the dates given, along with further information from *Radio Times*:

Tx 10/1/54 (Episode 2)
Séamus to record two folk songs, five minutes' duration. Fee: 5 guineas. On this episode he also talks about his collecting in Wales.

Tx 17/1/54 (Episode 3)
Séamus 'to play folk music on Uilleann pipes with Peter Kennedy (violin)'. Fee: 5 guineas. He also paints a verbal portrait of Annie Johnston from Barra.

Tx 7/2/54 (Episode 6)
Séamus to sing one song with instrumental accompaniment. Fee: 5 guineas. He introduces some songs and tunes he found in North-East Scotland.

Tx 28/2/54 (Episode 9)
Séamus 'to sing two songs with orchestra as arranged'. Fee: 5 guineas. A 'Children's Edition' of the show, with Séamus also telling two Irish fairy stories.

Tx 21/3/54 (Episode 12)
Séamus to sing two songs and play one pipe tune (recording in Suffolk). Fee: 7 guineas. This episode comes from The Butt & Oyster Inn in Pin Mill, Suffolk – an area noted for sea shanties.

Tx 28/3/54 (Episode 13)
Séamus recorded one song for this episode, on 8/3/54. Harold Rogers apologises to the Contracts Department two days later, saying he didn't realise they needed this item 'until the last moment', and asks them to sort something out for Séamus. Fee: 5 guineas. Séamus and Peter Kennedy also recall on the episode some of the singers they've introduced during this series.

On the three other episodes from this series in which he participated (as a presenter only), Séamus: introduces Donegal fiddler Frank Cassidy (24/1/54); compares collecting notes with Peter Kennedy, with illustrations on record (31/1/54); and introduces some music from Ireland (14/2/54).

An additional contract exists for a show titled 'Episode 8', apparently to be broadcast on (Saturday) 29/5/54. Harold Rogers asked the Contracts Department in mid-April to issue Séamus with a contract for one short piping solo in this episode. The fee was 7 guineas. One assumes that this was part of a Saturday re-run of the series and that Séamus' on-air piping performance had been missed for payment first time around.

***The Changeling*, Third Programme**
Rec: Ireland 12/53–1/54, edited in London 1/54 / Tx: 4/1/54; repeated 6/1/54 and 17/6/54 / Prod: David Thomson
Fee: 7 guineas for piping, 15 guineas for script and research

'Traditional stories and music arising from the belief that people can be stolen by the fairies and that fairy changelings can be put in their place.' Séamus was contracted in mid-December 1953 to play pipes on this programme, which was fine, but the producer's request for payment for Séamus' other contributions yielded a series of memos. David Thomson declared that Séamus had contributed about 20 minutes (airtime) of translation, had given advice, made contacts and acted as interpreter while the production team was in Ireland. A Miss Wakeham at Contracts thought that surely Séamus' work in Ireland was covered by his normal salary, which he continued to receive while working for the Features Department. Séamus initially agreed to waive any claim on an extra fee, but a few days later the producer weighed in again: 'I did not make clear that Mr Séamus Ennis worked with me on the script during his spare time after my return from Ireland …' Included in this work was the 20 minutes' worth of translation, two folk tales written from memory and musical advice. 'As he was fully engaged on work for Recorded Programmes Dept during normal working hours, I had to ask him to work with me on *The Changeling* on the evenings of Thur 31st December, Fri 1st and all day Sat 2nd January.' Miss Wakeham then offers 15 guineas 'all in' for Séamus' own-time work on the programme, to which Séamus, a month after broadcast, replies: 'This offer is quite satisfactory to me …'

London Column, North American Service
Rec: live broadcast? / Tx: 13/1/54
Fee: 7 guineas for piping, 11 guineas for script and presentation

An edition on folk music. Séamus is contracted the day before broadcast 'to sing and play pipes' and, in a separate contract, for provision of script, presentation at the microphone and research for a folk song extract.

Variations On A Folk Song Theme, Third Programme
Rec: late 2/54? / Tx: 10/2/54 / Prod: Francis Dillon
Fee: 10½ guineas for musical performance, 10 guineas for script, presentation and rehearsal

A couple of weeks before broadcast, Séamus is booked to play four tunes on the pipes and to sing three or four unaccompanied Gaelic songs (the latter to be recorded with the other artists – whose names are not given). A separate contract requires Séamus to narrate the 30-minute programme and provide a 12-minute script, with rehearsals all day on February 7. Séamus' BBC address is now 508 Rothwell House. From *Radio Times*: 'Irish pipe tunes and songs that became popular ballads in Britain and the USA compared and set for instruments and voices by Spike Hughes with Rita McKerrow (soprano), James Johnston (tenor), Trefor Jones (tenor), Robert Irwin (baritone). Written and narrated by Seumas Ennis [sic] who also plays the Uileann pipes [sic] and sings the Gaelic versions of the songs.'

***Weekend Review*, [Service unknown]**
Rec: live broadcast? / Tx: 5/2/54
Fee: 5 guineas

An edition on Welsh folk songs. Duration five minutes; Séamus' duties not mentioned. Hard-copy editions of *Radio Times* giving regional listing for Wales and some other regions were checked, but the Service remains elusive.

***Radio Theatre: The Law And The Prophets*, Light Programme**
Rec: ?/54 / Tx: 14/3/54; repeated 29/8/54 / Prod: Charles Lefeaux
Fee: 7 guineas

Séamus is contracted in early February to sing 'about five Irish songs to melodeon accompaniment', of approximately six minutes' duration, in this play by Donagh MacDonagh starring Joseph Tomelty and Liam Redmond. The melodeon playing is provided by Peter Kennedy. In April, Séamus agrees to an additional 7 guineas to allow the distribution of transcription discs of the play overseas.

***St Patrick's Day Party*, North American Service**
Rec: 6/3/54 / Tx: 17/3/54? / Prod: Victor Menzies
Fee: 7 guineas

Séamus pre-records two songs with spoken introductions and one pipe solo (total duration: 4.02). His contract is sorted out five days later.

***Seelkie*, Third Programme**
Rec: 31/3/54–3/4/54 / Tx: 4/4/54; 5/4/54 / Prod: Douglas Cleverdon
Fee: £11.0s.6d

Usually spelt 'Selkie', these are sea creatures from Scots and Faeroese myth. Written by James Forsyth with music by Brian Easdale, Séamus played pipes either solo or along with a section of the Royal Philharmonic Orchestra in this 85-minute drama. From *Radio Times*: 'In November 1950 a programme devoted to the 'tradition, songs, and stories of the grey Atlantic seal' was broadcast in the Third Programme under the title *Sons Of The Sea*. The story of Seelkie is based on one of the folk tales heard in that programme. It describes the arrival of a seal-woman on the Island of the Tree in the Western Isles, and her meeting with Hewan, the fisherman. He gives her the name Seelkie.'

SERIES: *Music Of The Commonwealth*, **Parts 3, 4 & 5,** **[Service unknown]**
Rec: mid-3/54 / Tx: c. 4/54–5/54 / Prod: Harold Rogers
Fee: 36 guineas (12 guineas per programme)

Harold Rogers requests (post-recording session) on 24/3/54 that Contracts sort something out for Séamus for writing and presenting the half-hour Episode 3 in this series. Research was done by Mary Slocombe, so the scripting only involved linking the recordings with material already prepared. It seems his subsequent requests for payment to Séamus for similar contributions to Episodes 4 and 5 were made ahead of the sessions happening. The programme may have been on a regional Home Service, as no trace can be found in online *Radio Times* listings. *London Calling: Western* WAC files for April-May 1954 were checked with no luck. Four shows broadcast in Britain around Christmas 1954 entitled *Commonwealth Of Song* are purely choral presentations.

SERIES: *Folk Music Of The British Isles*, **Parts 1, 2, 3 & 4,** **[Service unknown]**
Rec: ? / Tx: ?
Fee: 120 guineas (30 guineas per programme)

Four 'proposed contracts' exist (spanning 31/3/54 to 15/6/54) for Séamus to write and present these four programmes and to sing and play pipes therein. Presumably, given the spread of dates on the proposed contracts, the series actually happened. No other documents on the series are extant. No trace can be found in online *Radio Times* listings. Possibly it was for an Overseas Service but, without more date information, finding it via *London Calling* would be a Herculean task.

SERIES: *Traditional Songs,* **[Service unknown]**
Rec: 6/54? / Tx: 1954? / Producer/Commissioner: Laurence Stapley
Fee: 30 guineas (5 guineas per programme)

On 9/6/54, Stapley advances a requisition to Contracts for Séamus to make a series of six talks, illustrated with singing and pipe playing. The duration of each will be approximately 4.30. A 'proposed contract' a week later offers 5 guineas per show. Whether the series happened is unclear.

Scottish Anthology: Ane Sang Of The Birth Of Christ, **North American Service**
Rec: 10/54? / Tx: 11/54? / Prod: Kenneth Buthley
Fee: 4 guineas

Séamus has translated and written out the music for 'Christ Child Lullaby', an 'old Gaelic song'. Again, this seems to be a case of a producer getting Séamus to do something and sorting out a fee afterwards. Séamus signs the contract on 2/11/54.

Intermediate German: O Du Lieber Augustin, **Schools Programme**
Rec: live broadcast? / Tx: 3/2/55 / Prod: Duncan Taylor
Fee: 5 guineas

Séamus is to play a short piece on the pipes. There is an exchange of correspondence discussing whether the work falls outside Séamus' normal BBC duties before a decision that it does.

The Ass Thy Servant, **Home Service**
Rec: ? / Tx: 3/4/55 / Prod: Charles Parker

From *Radio Times*: 'A browse through the music, prose, and poetry by which men have expressed the inspiration – or exasperation – of the donkey. Devised for Palm Sunday by Kenneth Bird with Felix Felton, Alan Bridges, Ronald Baddiley, Doreen Aris, Séamus Ennis. Introduced by Deryck Guyler.' No contract extant.

SERIES: *As I Roved Out* **(Series 3), Light Programme**
Rec: 1955 / Tx: 03/4/55–26/6/55 (12 weekly episodes – no episode on 22/5/55) / Prod: Harold Rogers
Fee: ?

There is no paperwork in Séamus' BBC files for this series, and the very brief information from the Programme Index only refers to him co-presenting two episodes. From *Radio Times*, however, we can be sure that Séamus was involved in at least five episodes: 2, 3, 5, 8 and 10. *Radio Times* gave no information at all for Episode 1, but the Programme Index says 'narrated by Brian George'. Seán O'Boyle was guest presenter on two episodes about Ulster.

    Séamus' known contributions to this series were as follows: introducing, with Francis Collinson, songs from Galloway and Skye (10/4/55); telling the story of a song from Arranmore (17/4/55); reporting, with Peter Kennedy, on song-hunting visits they made to Wales in 1954 (1/5/55); introducing Thomas Moran from County Leitrim, in an episode in which Marie Slocombe recalled a trip she made with Séamus to Connemara the previous year (29/5/55); talking about songs he heard in Norfolk earlier that year (12/6/55).

Going Places … Meeting People, **Light Programme**
Rec: 4/55? / Tx: n/a / Prod: Ronald Gibson
Fee: 7 guineas

Séamus has apparently recorded 'The Girl I Left Behind Me' as signature tune for the above series. However, in a letter to Contracts (subsequent to the recording and early use of the music on air) the producer explains that it was recorded at very short notice and is no longer being used. Nevertheless, Séamus is paid 7 guineas at the end of April. The series began on 9/5/55, running for 10 daily episodes. It reappeared from October through to December, with a pool of presenters – including, on a couple of occasions, future TV personality Alan Whicker. From *Radio Times*: 'One man's view of people and places that make the wheels go round in the world's biggest city.' One might conjecture that with a series due to go on air, either no one had sorted out theme music or some issue had arisen with it – and then the producer bumps into Séamus in a BBC corridor.

[Unnamed programme, referred to only as 'Folk Music'], Home Service
Rec: 5/55? / Tx: 27/5/55
Fee: 30 guineas

A 'proposed contract', dated 12 days after the supposed transmission date, exists for Séamus to sing, play pipes, write and present the programme. No other relevant documents survive. Conceivably, the programme was *Children's Hour*, which on this date was featuring part of a serial, 'Kate And The Gypsies', involving music and singing around a campfire.

The Devil's On The Prowl, **Home Service**
Rec: ? / Tx: 4/7/55; repeated 21/7/55 / Prod: R.D. Smith

A 90-minute play, from Carl Zuckmayer's *Schinderhannes*, translated and adapted for radio by folk revival godfather A.L. Lloyd, with a cast of 25 including Lloyd as narrator. Lloyd also arranged the music. The players are: Séamus (whistle), James Blades (percussion), Alf Edwards (concertina), Harvey Webb (violin). No contract extant.

***In Sand*, Third Programme**
Rec: 2/56? / Tx: 19/2/56; repeated 24/2/56 and 7/5/56 / Prod: Frederick Bradnam
Fee: 7 guineas for piping, 5 guineas for arrangement and presentation

A 30-minute play by Jack Yeats. Séamus is paid for his musical performance without controversy, on 30/1/56. He must have asked the producer for further consideration, however, resulting in an exchange of memos between various BBC departments in February.

One memo from a Miss Layton to Séamus reads: 'I am sorry there has been a muddle about the booking for you to work in connection with *In Sand*. I now understand that this consists merely of reading the script and selecting suitable tunes and some very slight rearrangement for players on the pipes, but not apparently sufficient to qualify for an 'arranger's fee'. I feel that a fee of 2 guineas would be appropriate.'

A few days later, no doubt after a robust exchange of views in person or over the phone with Séamus, Miss Layton writes to Frederick Bradnam to say: 'I have now agreed to pay Séamus Ennis a fee of 5 guineas.' The *Radio Times* credit reads: 'Music for the Irish pipes arranged and played by Séamus Ennis.'

***Folk Song Forum*, Northern Ireland Home Service**
Rec: live broadcast? / Tx: late 2/56?
Fee: 15 guineas plus one night's subsistence

Séamus is booked for this regional show on 22/2/56, with the fee to include provision of script and presentation at the microphone.

***Calling Newfoundland*, [North American Service?]**
Rec: ?/3/56 / Tx: 12/3/56 / Prod: Kay Sharman
Fee: 3 guineas

Séamus receives a contract two days after broadcast for this three-minute talk. North American Service programmes are never titled in *London Calling*, but are merely listed as 'special programmes'. As there is no mention of this programme on 12/3/56 in the general listings or attributed to any of the other Overseas Services, it was probably for the North American Service.

Golden Treasury, **Home Service**
Rec: 5/56? / Tx: 26/5/56; 9/6/56; 23/6/56 / Prod: Neil Sutherland
Fee: 6 guineas (2 guineas per programme)

Séamus would contribute to many episodes of this weekly series between May 1956 and December 1958. The appearances tend to clump together and are here given in these clumps chronologically rather than as one long entry. In these three episodes, Séamus is to play the pipes 'as arranged with Mr Neil Sutherland'. An original offer of 7 guineas was amended down to 6. From *Radio Times* for the 26/5/56 episode: 'An album of music and song with contributions by Philip Hattey, Séamus Ennis and the Granville Singers and Players. Directed by Cecil Woods.' Two other episodes are referred to in the contract, but without broadcast dates given. They appear, from *Radio Times*, to have been 9/6/56 and 23/6/56, both of which feature 'recordings made by Séamus Ennis during his travels'.

SERIES: *As I Roved Out* **(Series 4), Light Programme**
Rec: 1956 / Tx: 20/5/56–8/7/56 (seven weekly episodes – no episode on 10/6/56) / Prod: Harold Rogers
Fee: ?

As with Series 1 and 3, there is no paperwork for this series in Séamus' BBC files. From *Radio Times*, Séamus appears to have been involved in four of the seven episodes: 2, 4, 6 and 7. His contributions were described thus: introducing an episode themed around 'songs of the land' (27/5/56); 'an Irish journey with Séamus Ennis, song hunting through Cork, Kerry, Connemara, Donegal and Leitrim' (17/6/56); talking about 'cumulative songs' with Peter Kennedy and playing examples they have collected (1/7/56); 'Séamus Ennis and Peter Kennedy are joined by American folk-song collector Jean Randolph' (8/7/56). During the series, 'musical interludes' were provided by The Haymakers, 'directed by Peter Kennedy'.

Impavidi Progrediamur, **Third Programme**
Rec: 11/9/56 / Tx: 19/12/56; repeated 21/12/56 / Prod: D.G. Bridson
Fee: 10 guineas

An early September memo from Music Bookings to the Assistant Head Of Features' secretary asks for Séamus to take part in this 'unscheduled programme', provisionally titled *Hugh MacDiarmid – Unpublished Poetry*, which will be pre-recorded on 11/9/56. A proposed contract is then issued to Séamus, although what he is required for is unspecified. The *Radio Times* billing says only: 'Selections from an unpublished poem by Hugh MacDiarmid. Read by James McKechnie, Ewan MacColl and Séamus Ennis.'

A Party For Hallowe'en, **Home Service**
Rec: live broadcast? / Tx: 31/10/56 / Producer/Writer: Francis Dillon
Fee: 12 guineas

As *Radio Times* puts it: 'to which your hosts, James McKechnie and Séamus Ennis, have invited a few Scots and Irish exiles in London (and such pagan spirits as are able to attend), to dance, sing, tell stories, and play the old games.' Séamus is contracted (a week ahead of broadcast for a change) to play pipes, sing and speak on this 30-minute show.

A Golden Treasury Of Music And Song, **Home Service**
Rec: (probably two days during 11/56 and 12/56) / Tx: 10/11/56; 24/11/56; 8/12/56; 29/12/56; 12/1/56; 26/1/57 / Prod: Neil Sutherland (1956), Travis Thorneloe (1957)
Fee: 2 guineas per programme for 1–3; 5 guineas per programme for 4–6

Another block of fortnightly appearances on this weekly series (see above), now with a longer title. From *Radio Times*: 'Séamus Ennis brings a recording of another musical 'character' discovered in his travels round Britain'. His fee increases for the later three episodes, so presumably his contribution/time on air also increases. Curiously, Séamus' name is absent from *Radio Times* 26/1/57 billing. While the recording dates are unknown, one memo reveals that episodes were generally pre-recorded three at a time: three in one day (see below).

Postmark UK, **North American Service**
Rec: 12/56? / Tx: 12/56?
Fee: 5 guineas

A contract dated 12/12/56 requires Séamus to provide a five-minute insert (nature unspecified). The broadcast date can't be pinned down.

From Bard To Busker, **[Service unspecified]**
Rec: live broadcast? / Tx: 30/12/56 / Producer/Writer: Louis MacNeice
Fee: 12 guineas

Séamus is booked to play pipes and tell a two-minute story in this 'dramatised anthology'. From *Radio Times*: 'Since the time of Homer and in many countries, entertainment – good, bad, and indifferent – has been provided by wandering minstrels and storytellers, including such varied types as the medieval goliard and the Irish travelling man. Today, inevitably, this race of artists has dwindled, yet it is still represented in England by the buskers. In this programme buskers in the persons of Bill and Wyn Cutler, well known in the streets of London, are used as a modern link and chorus in the long chain of history and poetry.'

A Golden Treasury Of Music And Song, **Home Service**
Rec: 2/2/57 / Tx: 2/2/57 (plus two nearby episodes?)
Fee: 5 guineas

A memo of 3/1/57 reveals that a recording session for three episodes of *Golden Treasury* has moved from 26/1 to 2/2/57. A contract to Séamus follows eight days later, for 5 guineas. Possibly a payment is made for the day of recording and then another fee given for each episode when broadcast. The contract states three unspecified episodes, but *Radio Times* includes Séamus' name for only one (2/2/57) in this period.

Ready The Band, **Home Service**
Rec: 2/57? / Tx: 15/2/57 / Prod: Francis Dillon
Fee: 7 guineas

Séamus is contracted on 15/2/57 (the day of broadcast, so possibly he had recorded his contributions prior to being contracted) to play two tunes on pipes in Episode 3 of this three-part series, subtitled '200 Years Of Marches And Songs Of The British Army' – Episode 3 covering the 19th century. Presumably Séamus plays war pipes repertoire on the uilleann pipes. *Radio Times* credits John Buckland with arrangements and Charles Mackerras with conducting orchestra and chorus, but doesn't mention Séamus.

Children's Television, **BBC TV**
Rec: live broadcasts? / Tx: 25/2/57; 4/3/57; 11/3/57 / Prod: Peter Newington

From *Radio Times*: 'Vera McKechnie in Studio E introduces …' In between programmes entitled *Mainly For Women*, *Watch With Mother* and *Cliff Michelmore's Tonight* ('for all the family'), this was a dedicated hour of TV for older children, mixing lightly educational items with entertainment. 'Séamus Ennis with a song, a story and a penny whistle' was the billing for Séamus' first appearance; 'Séamus Ennis leaning on a gate' is the enigmatic descriptor for the other two. He was joined by singer Isla Cameron for the second show. Legendary TV personalities Clive Dunn and Tony Hart were among those also involved in these episodes. No contracts are extant.

A Golden Treasury Of Music And Song, **Home Service**
Rec: ? / Tx: 4/5/57 / Prod: Travers Thorneloe
Fee: 5 guineas

Séamus 'brings recordings of more musical characters discovered in his travels'. The contract erroneously gives 4/4/57 as the transmission date.

This Is Britain, **[Service unspecified]**
Rec: 5/57? / Tx: 29/5/57 / Prod: John Laird?
Fee: 25 guineas

A contract issued on the same day as the broadcast declares that Séamus is to provide '30 minutes of material as arranged with John Laird'. Presumably he is scripting and presenting, and presumably it is for a regional service, as it doesn't appear in the online *Radio Times* database. John Laird was a producer with the Pacific & South African Service, so one imagines this would have appeared on the General Overseas Service or its associated special services. Unfortunately, there's nothing that fits the bill in the listings for this day – the transmission date having been given in the contract. Conceivably, the transmission date may have changed or, alternatively, Laird could have been moonlighting with the North American Service, whose programme titles remain absent from *London Calling*.

A Golden Treasury Of Music And Song, **Home Service**
Rec: ? / Tx: 1/6/57
Fee: 8 guineas

For this episode, contracted six weeks before the transmission date, Séamus is to play one instrumental item and introduce one record.

Writing For Radio: The Homing Of Roberts, **Home Service**
Rec: 6/57? / Tx: 14/6/57 / Prod: David Thomson
Fee: 12 guineas

Séamus is to compose or improvise approximately five minutes of music, 10 items in all, for this 45-minute drama described in *Radio Times* as 'a variation upon three fables of parricide: Spanish, Welsh, and Greek by Martin Shuttleworth'. In a memo to Contracts, David Thomson also mentions needing two conferences of two hours each with Séamus. The contract is issued on 7/6/57. This was one of a series of eight dramas, all written especially for radio, the previous episode of which had been written by and starred, as a 'ballad singer', Brendan Behan. There will be an enhanced 'live repeat' of *The Homing Of Roberts* two years later (see below).

Count Rumford, **Home Service**
Rec: 7/57? / Tx: 21/7/57 / Prod: David Thomson
Fee: 7 guineas

Séamus is booked to sing ballads. From *Radio Times*: 'Soldier, statesman, scientist, secret agent, and founder of The Royal Institution: a radio biography by Martin Chisholm based on *An American In Europe* by Egon Larsen.' A contract is issued by Miss Penty on 19/7/57. Two months later she writes to Séamus to point out that they still haven't received his signature on it. If this suggests he is too busy to remember to collect monies owed, it will be in contrast to his forthcoming freelance career.

A Golden Treasury Of Music And Song, **Home Service**
Rec: 6/57? / Tx: 27/7/57; 29/7/57 / Prod: Travers Thorneloe
Fee: 14 guineas in total

There is one contract for Séamus' contribution to these two shows, issued on 19/6/57, specifying '1 or 2 items tin whistle and possible introduce disc' – from which one may infer that Yoda from *Star Wars* was then employed in the BBC Contracts Department.

SERIES: *Turkey In The Straw*, **Light Programme**
Rec: 6/57? / Tx: Séamus' six episodes broadcast 2/7/57–13/8/57 (no episode on 9/7/57) / Prod: Humphrey Burton
Fee: 67½ guineas

Humphrey Burton's requisition to Contracts for this weekly series, subtitled 'songs and dances of the American people', declares that Séamus is to 'introduce records as a 'disk jockey''. The programmes are to be 15 minutes long, but a memo from Burton on 20/6/57 explains that Episode 5, for reasons unclear, will now be 30 minutes long. He invites Contracts to enhance Séamus' fee (originally 10 guineas per episode) accordingly. An offer of 15 guineas for Episode 5, from Miss Penty in

Contracts, elicits a letter from Séamus on 4/7/57. He says the producer agrees that the 30-minute programme entails more than double the amount of work for the other 15-minute programmes, and suggests the fee of 15 guineas is not fair: 'I trust I am not causing you undue trouble in this hot weather!' The following day a further 2 ½ guineas is offered. Judging by *Radio Times* information, Episode 5 was certainly packed: guests were Burl Ives, Jean Ritchie, Peggy Seeger, Alan Lomax, The Swaneers, The Choraliers and Howard Cable & His Orchestra. With all of these people getting airtime, one would have thought that Séamus would have *less* work to do. Alan Lomax and Jean Ritchie joined Séamus for Episode 1; Peggy Seeger for Episode 2; Episode 3 featured Dick Cameron and Kenneth Schoen; Episode 4 included records by Lead Belly (wellspring of the skiffle craze at that time sweeping Britain); and Episode 6 featured Burl Ives along with Séamus talking about 'The Ballad Of John Henry' – another skiffle staple. Immediately following the six episodes fronted by Séamus, Peter Kennedy helmed a further six, with most of the same people guesting.

SERIES: *As I Roved Out* **(Series 5), Light Programme/Home Service**
Rec: 1957 / Tx: 31/7/57–28/8/57 (five weekly episodes) / Prod: Harold Rogers
Fee: 32 guineas

This series of *As I Roved Out* was broadcast on Wednesday afternoons, simultaneously on both the Light Programme and the Home Service. Contracts exist in Séamus' BBC files for this particular series – requisitions from producer Harold Rogers dated 1/7/57. Séamus was involved on air in all five episodes in this run. 'Musical interludes', which had been provided by Peter Kennedy's Haymakers in the previous series, were provided this time by The Moonrakers. The format had been rejigged, too, with each episode featuring a 'Collector's Corner', a 'Song Snapshot' and a 'Roving Report'. From *Radio Times*, Séamus' contributions to each episode were as follows:

> 31/8/57 Song Snapshot: Séamus tells the story of a well known folk song. (The Programme Index file tells us that Episode 1 featured Séamus in Scotland as one of its items – possibly the location of said song.) Fee: 3 guineas

> 7/8/57 Collector's Corner: Séamus introduces singers and players he met during his travels in Scotland. (The contract states 'Visit To Vatersay'.) Fee: 12 guineas

> 14/8/57 Song Snapshot: Séamus tells the story of a well known folk song. Fee: 3 guineas

21/8/57 Collector's Corner: Séamus introduces some of the people he has met during his journeys in Ireland. (The contract describes this as 'Irish Fiddlers', being a 12-minute piece including a recording Séamus has already made for the BBC – although the transmission date is given incorrectly as 12/8/57.) Fee: 12 guineas

28/8/57 Song Snapshot: Séamus tells the story of a well known folk song. Fee: 2 guineas

If I Had A Million, **Light Programme**
Rec: 7/57? (at Séamus' home in London) / Tx: 19/8/57? / Prod: Marguerite Cutforth
Fee: 10 guineas

The name and address on a requisition of 11/7/57 is 'Mrs Séamus Ennis (and 2 children), Flat 2, 63 Alexandra Road'. It seems unlikely that this programme, the content of which is self-explanatory, involved an interview with Mrs Ennis rather than with Séamus. The contract gives the transmission date as 12/8/57. While no programme of this title can be found in *Radio Times* online, a one-off show titled *If I Were A Millionaire* was broadcast on 19/8/57 on both the Home Service and Light Programme – a revival of a similarly one-off show with the same title from BBC TV in 1939, which had featured 'a scientist, an Irish poet, a woman novelist, a sculptor, and a taxi-driver' discussing imaginary wealth.

One Good Turn Deserves Another: The World Scout Jubilee Jamboree, **Light Programme**
Rec: 8/57 / Tx: 27/12/57 / Prod: Charles Parker
Fee: 15 guineas

A memo from Charles Parker's office to Miss Penty (Music Booking) on 12/7/57 requests that Séamus be booked to introduce this programme, sing folk songs and perhaps play the pipes. They suggest Séamus will need a research fee, performance fee, travelling expenses and two days' subsistence. The contract (15 guineas) seems rather low for all this; possibly there were separate contracts for some of the above which do not survive. The contract gives the broadcast date as 6/8/57. However, a programme of this title was broadcast on 27/12/57, produced by James Pestridge (not Charles Parker) and presented by Wynford Vaughan Thomas (not Séamus), 'with the aid of recordings made during the Jamboree at Sutton Park, Sutton Coldfield in August'. Whether Séamus made these recordings but then pulled out of the project or, perhaps likelier, turned down the small fee and heavy workload is a matter of conjecture.

***A Golden Treasury Of Music And Song*, Home Service**
Rec: 8/57? / Tx: 2/9/57; 16/9/57 / Prod: Travis Thorneloe
Fee: 8 guineas per programme

There are separate contracts for these two shows, but each specifies that Séamus is to play pipes and introduce one record. *Radio Times* only bills Séamus as appearing on the first of the two shows.

SERIES: *A Ballad-Hunter Looks At Britain*, Home Service
Rec: 10–12/57 / Tx: 1/11/57; 8/11/57; 15/11/57; 22/11/57; 29/11/57; 6/12/57; 13/12/57; 27/12/57 / Prod: Stella Hillier/Sasha Moorsom
Fee: 75 guineas (research/script), 28 guineas (musical performance and presentation)

Alan Lomax had proposed this series of eight 30-minute programmes. After seven years of intense, hand-to-mouth collecting work around Europe, it would be, with *Sing Christmas And The Turn Of The Year* (see below), his last major work for the BBC. It was a summation of Alan's collecting in Britain and the BBC's own collecting project (with Séamus Ennis and Peter Kennedy), which had just lost its funding.

On 8/10/57 Stella Hillier, Features Dept, circulates a memo stating:

> The proposal is that [Lomax] shall be assisted by Séamus Ennis and Peter Kennedy, both of whom have been collecting material throughout the UK while under BBC contract, the results of their efforts now being lodged in the BBC Permanent Library. Séamus Ennis and Peter Kennedy will be working with Alan Lomax on the selection of recorded material and in the completion of the script, and Peter Kennedy in particular will be giving a great deal of background advice … Our feeling is, therefore, that his contract shall be for a larger fee than Ennis', although Ennis will appear in voice more frequently in the programmes. We have £800 overall for the eight programmes and I should say that at least half of this will go to Lomax …

On 10/10/57 an additional contract is requested for Hamish Henderson for his work on Episodes 5 and 6 of the series.

On 14/10/57 a memo from Miss Rainbow, Contracts, states that Séamus Ennis and Peter Kennedy, though previously on salary with the BBC, 'are freelance now' and will 'have to be engaged ad hoc for any spoken contributions to the programmes later on'. The next day, Séamus is offered a fee of 50 guineas outright (with no repeat fees) for research on *A Ballad-Hunter Looks At Britain*. A separate contract will be issued for his spoken contributions to the programmes.

Two days later, Séamus writes to Miss Wakeham (Contracts): 'Further to our conversations yesterday and this morning I agree to accept the revised fee of 75 guineas for research and script collaboration with Mr Alan Lomax in his series *Folk Song Hunter Looks At Britain* [sic]. I understand half of this fee is to be paid for work undertaken to date and I look forward to calling upon you instantly, if not sooner …'

The following day, 18/10/57, Miss Wakeham writes to the 'Features Organiser'. She points out (doing well not to reveal exasperation) that until it is decided in which programmes Séamus is to take part as a speaker and/or as an artist, they will be unable to issue a contract for this aspect. However, the rest has been sorted out:

> I have now seen Mr Ennis, and in view of the amount of work involved, I have agreed to pay him an inclusive fee of 75 guineas, which will cover selection of recorded material, background advice and assisting with the scripting and compilation of the final programmes. This fee also includes the use of any of his recordings, other than those belonging to the BBC, which may be included in the programmes. It does not, however, cover his performance at the microphone if he is asked to take part as a speaker or performer (other than on the recordings referred to above) for which a separate contract must be issued. No further fees will be payable to him for any repeat performances of the programmes which may be given.

Over the next few weeks, several further contracts are issued to Séamus for various bits of musical performance and presentation at the microphone, as the information becomes available. A memo relating to Séamus' contribution to Episode 8 reveals that he recorded his part on 29/11/57 – which would imply that each episode was completed roughly a month ahead of broadcast. Séamus' artist fees are as follows:

- Episode 1: 3 guineas for a two-minute talk (an introductory episode)
- Episode 3: 5 guineas for a four-minute spoken contribution (episode titled 'From Cornwall To Yorkshire')

- Episode 7: 10 guineas for seven minutes of narration plus 'singing as requested' (Séamus relating the story of Margaret Barry)
- Episode 8: 3 guineas for two minutes of narration (episode on Ireland 'North and South')

On 26/11/57 – by which stage it would appear that work on the series is virtually complete (three days ahead of Séamus' narrator contribution to the final episode being recorded) – Miss Wakeham is given the green light to pay Séamus the second half of his fee for *A Ballad Hunter Looks At Britain*. (Occasionally, BBC fees for freelance work on programmes were paid half on signing the contract, half when the programme/programmes are broadcast. Four *Ballad Hunter* episodes had now been broadcast.)

The London Freelance Era: 1957–60
Séamus would later describe his freelance career as 'unrewarding', but for the year 1958 (plus December 1957) he earned 390 guineas from his freelance activities with the BBC. This was notably greater than his freelance BBC earnings for any of the preceding six years – although, of course, he no longer had his BBC salary on top. Nevertheless, by way of comparison, figures given to Parliament by the Minister of Labour in November 1960 give the average annual salary for a London-based journalist as £1,118 and for a London-based Civil Service clerical officer as £789. Séamus' freelance broadcasting earnings would start to slide after 1958, clearly prompting his move back to Ireland. His 1959 BBC earnings were 245 guineas 9 shillings and sixpence; the 1960 (January-June) figure was a meagre 46 guineas 15 shillings and ninepence.

One Morning Early – **the first freelance proposals**
On 13/12/57 Marguerite Cutforth forwards to a Miss Benzie (Talks Dept) a proposal written by Séamus for a series titled *One Morning Early*, comprising five short pieces, detailing various adventures, to be broadcast at certain points in the year. The pieces are called 'Herring Longshore Netting', 'My First Wild-Goose Chase', 'Spinning The Minnow For Trout', 'An Irish Cattle-Fair' and 'Hebridean Boating Adventure' – this last named being marked 'January'.

Marguerite gives Miss Benzie an endorsement of Séamus:

> Harry Craig's recent success has caused a flurry among the ex-patriot [sic] Irish in London, I'm afraid! I don't suppose you'll want any more yet, but if you

do, Séamus Ennis is a very experienced broadcaster and folk-song collector.

This is Séamus' proposal for *The Hebridean Boating Adventure*:

> One island is short of whiskey, whilst I am on another island. I am commissioned to bring the whiskey and in a friend's boat we run into a gale. His boat is two tons short of ballast and is rolling like a cork. Sky is down, wheel-house windows are open for visibility. As he is wiping his spectacles the boat lurches again and they snap in his fingers. He has only one weak eye! He crawls the desk for charts, which I have to read – everything saturated. By a miracle we get the boat in at nightfall and are complimented by local fisherman who are all on the quay awaiting the whiskey. (Sing 'Whiskey In The Jar').

Miss Benzie writes to Séamus, wondering if he 'would care to write the Hebridean Boating Adventure fairly quickly for me?' Séamus delivers a script to Miss Benzie on 6/3/58, apologising for the delay (caused by 'other chores'). Miss Benzie replies 11 days later saying: 'How nice, but how far too long? How long do you feel it will take you to read in its present form?'

There is no record of a reply from Séamus, or of any further correspondence on this proposal, and no record of *The Hebridean Boating Adventure* – probably based on an incident during January 1947 when Séamus was in the Hebrides for the Irish Folklore Commission – having been broadcast.

Sing Christmas And The Turn Of The Year, Home Service
Rec: live broadcast (in Birmingham) / Tx: 25/12/57 / Prod: Charles Parker
Fee: 10 guineas (plus expenses)

Alan Lomax's very last BBC project, this would be a typically ambitious venture – a Christmas morning regional round-up programme, following the Queen's Speech, presenting folk music from around Britain and involving live links and exchanges of greetings in local dialects between seven BBC broadcasting regions. Alan Lomax held it together as presenter; stalwarts Ewan MacColl and Peter Kennedy appeared, along with a cast of thousands – from a skiffle group to brass bands, carollers, a mummers' play, a trad jazz ensemble and more besides. Séamus was booked to play tin whistle, pipes and sing in chorus. There is a rehearsal in Birmingham on Christmas Eve. An off-air or master copy of the programme survives, from which a CD was issued on Rounder in 2000.

Lullabies And Baby Play, **Third Programme**
Rec: 12/57 / Tx: 28/12/57 / Prod: David Thomson
Fee: 12 guineas

A memo from David Thomson to Miss Penty (Music Bookings) on 17/12/57 asks her to arrange terms with Séamus for a programme provisionally titled *Children's Lullabies*. He has already recorded eight traditional songs and rhymes (approximately 20 minutes' worth) for Thomson to choose from. Séamus has also provided translations and background material for these and other Gaelic and Irish items in the programme. The notion of contracting Séamus before he does the work still hasn't quite taken hold.

The Last Cornfield, **Third Programme**
Rec: live broadcast? / Tx: 1/1/58; repeated 2/1/58 and (on the Home Service) 13/7/58 / Prod: Rayner Heppenstall
Fee: 7 guineas

Séamus is contracted (two days before the broadcast) to play tin whistle. From *Radio Times*: 'An episode in the future by Edward Hyams. The date is 2038. The scene alternates between Whitehall and Northumberland.' The running time, oddly, varies between 55 and 65 minutes across its three broadcasts.

Session for BBC Permanent Library
Rec: 7/2/58, Maida Vale Studios
Fee: 35 guineas
Demonstration & Tuning; 'Connaught Heifer' (with 'The Braes Of Busby'); 'Lament Of The Fox'; 'Tatterjack Welch (& Patty-No-Rafferty)'; 'Mountain Of The Women'; 'The Morning Thrush/The Dublin Reel'; 'Jockey To The Fair'; 'The Groves'; 'Dark Lady Of The Glen'; 'Chief O'Neill's Favourite' (with 'The Boys Of Blue Hill')

The Permanent Library wish to get approximately 25–30 minutes of recorded material on uilleann pipes from Séamus. A memo requesting a taxi is later amended by hand to reflect Séamus driving there himself. A contract issued on 5/2/58 for 12 guineas is replaced two days later by one for 35 guineas. Clearly, Séamus' negotiating skills are reaching new heights.

Hootenanny, [Service unknown]
Rec: 16/2/58, Princess Louise, High Holborn / Tx: 'TBA' / Prod: Charles Parker
Fee: 10 guineas

This is a live recording to be made at Ewan MacColl's Ballads & Blues Club at the Princess Louise (although neither MacColl nor the club appear in the requisition). Parker plans to record Séamus, described as the 'guest artist', singing three songs and playing whistle and pipes. It's unclear if this is a case of Séamus' having already been booked as club guest that night or if the whole show is 'radio led'. The specification of 'three songs' suggests that the contents will have been pre-arranged between Parker and the performers.

Presumably other performers on the night will also have received contracts. Parker was based in Coventry, so this was likely a Home Service Midlands regional series, as nothing can be found in the online *Radio Times* listings. Print copies of *Radio Times* Midlands edition were checked for two weeks after the recording date, but nothing was found.

Famous Trials: 2. The Parnell Case, **Home Service**
Rec: ?/2/58, Langham / Tx: 11/2/58 / Prod: Nesta Pain
Fee: £8.5s

Séamus is booked a few days before broadcast, as a flautist, to play 'Three Flowers'. His signed contract is returned two days after broadcast. This was a series of five fortnightly 60-minute programmes 'introduced by the Rt. Hon. Sir Norman Birkett' – who had become Lord Birkett by the time four of the five episodes (the missing one being Séamus') were repeated in the middle of the year. By the end of the year, Birkett was fronting a new series called *The Verdict Of The Court* – fully dramatised (as opposed to the narrated *Famous Trials*), but based on the same idea as its predecessor.

Britannia Mews, **Light Programme**
Rec: 2/58? / Tx: 9/3/58; repeated 29/10/58 on the Home Service / Prod: Wilfrid Grantham
Fee: 7 guineas

Séamus is booked a month ahead of broadcast for Episode 5 of this eight-part drama series, based on a novel by Margery Sharp, 'to play a tin whistle'. His contribution doesn't merit a credit in *Radio Times*.

***Saturday Night On The Light*, Light Programme**
Rec: 14/3/58 / Tx: 15/3/58 / Prod: John Bridges
Fee: 6 guineas

Two days after broadcast, Bridges asks Miss Penty (Music Bookings) to sort out a fee for Séamus, who recorded a three-minute item for this show that included 'a recording he made for the BBC some time ago and which is now in the Permanent Library'. A contract for three guineas is replaced three days later with one for six. Séamus continues to offer a robust defence of his worth – even though his 'act', on this occasion, seems to have been simply introducing a record he made in the 1940s, for which he has already been paid by the same organisation with whom he is now haggling! From *Radio Times*: 'Three hours of words and music introduced by Charles Richardson and Tim Gudgin with Stars – Interviews – Features – Short Stories – News – Comedy and Personalities, featuring the recorded music of the BBC Northern Dance Orchestra conducted by Alyn Ainsworth with Sheila Buxton and Jimmy Leach at the electronic organ, Charlie Katz and his Novelty Sextet'.*

***The Horns Of Plenty*, Home Service**
Rec: ?/4/58 / Tx: 13/4/58 / Prod: Francis Dillon
Fee: 10 guineas

Dillon writes to Miss Penty (Music Bookings) on 1/4/58 to book Séamus for this drama – described as 'a fairy-tale for businessmen based on an anecdote by W.J. Turner' – to sing and to play the violin and tin whistle. He asks her to make sure Séamus is not booked for any other performance that day, perhaps reflecting a previous incident where Séamus' prolificity or lapsing memory caused headaches.

***The Rambler From Clare*, Light Programme**
Rec: ?/4/58 / Tx: 16/4/58 (Episode 3) / Prod: Harold Rogers/Humphrey Burton/Elizabeth Johnson
Fee: 10 guineas

Here we come to quite a saga. This episode in a travelogue series was originally to have been broadcast in December 1956, but was cancelled 'because of IRA and

---

* Charlie Katz, free of his Novelty Sextet, later emerged as the most ruthless 'fixer' on the London session work scene in the 1960s, controlling the lives of numerous studio musicians including, for a while, such legendary guitarists as Jimmy Page, John McLaughlin, Vic Flick and Big Jim Sullivan.

1. At First Light at Balve Cave, Germany, 2012 L-R: Francis McIlduff, Ciara McCrickard, Dónal O'Connor, John McSherry, Michael McCague. (Colin Goldie)

2. Dónal O'Connor, John McSherry and Neil Martin: live at the William Kennedy Piping Festival, 2013. (Paul Eliasberg)

1. McSherrys in order of height, early 1980s (it's changed since then). L-R: Joanne, John, Paul and Tíona. (Courtesy John McSherry)

2. John and Joanne McSherry, 1985, with the Leo Rowsome Cup, after winning the All-Ireland piping competition. (Courtesy John McSherry)

3. John and Tíona McSherry, early 1980s. (Courtesy John McSherry)

4. John McSherry, Germany, live in the mid-90s. (Courtesy John McSherry)

1. The McSherrys, late 80s. L-R: Paul, Joanne, Tíona, John. (Courtesy John McSherry)

2. John and Áille, early 2000s. (Courtesy John McSherry)

3. John & Dad (Denis), Ladybrook, Belfast, 2001. (Courtesy John McSherry)

1. The Earth Celebration Band (proto-Coolfin) at the airport, circa 1996. (Courtesy John McSherry)

2. Dónal Lunny and John McSherry, Edmonton Folk Festival, 1999. (Courtesy John McSherry)

3. Michael McGoldrick, Paddy Keenan, John McSherry, in the Herschel Arms, London, during the Dave Williams memorial weekend, 2005.
(Courtesy Tom King)

4. John McSherry and Michael McGoldrick, Belfast, 2011. (Courtesy John McSherry)

1. Finbar & Eddie Furey, mid-70s in Germany (detail from *I Live Not Where I Love*).

2-4. Finbar & Eddie Furey: the first three British LPs 1968-69.

1. Planxty performing at Dublin's Old Shieling Hotel for RTÉ/BBC Scotland's *Capital Folk*, February 1972. L-R: Liam O'Flynn, Dónal Lunny, Christy Moore, Andy Irvine. (Roy Bedell/RTÉ Stills Library)

2. LAPD, 2012. L-R: Dónal Lunny, Andy Irvine, Liam O'Flynn, Paddy Glackin. (Dónal Glackin)

3. Planxty comeback tour ad, *Melody Maker*, 1979.

4. The McSherry family with Liam O'Flynn, 1983. L-R: Tíona, Paul, John, Liam, Joanne, Mrs McSherry. (Courtesy John McSherry)

1. Seachtar, Dublin 1974. L-R: Tony MacMahon, Paddy Keenan, Matt Molloy, Tríona Ní Dhomhnaill, Paddy Glackin, Donal Lunny, Mícheál Ó Domhnaill. (Robert Dawson/Courtesy Dónal Lunny/Diane Hamilton Estate/ITMA)

2. Paddy Keenan, early 2000s.

3. Paddy Keenan (with Kevin Burke), Cambridge Folk Festival, 1976. (Val Wilmer)

4. Paddy Keenan and John McSherry, The Crosses of Anagh, Miltown Malbay, 1998. (Courtesy John McSherry)

Bothy Band ad, 1977 (Courtesy ITMA)

1. The Bettystown meeting of May 1968. Front row: Séamus Ennis, Leo Rowsome, Willie Clancy (sixth to eighth from left). Second row: Wilbert Garvin (fourth from right) and Breandán Breathnach (second from left). (Courtesy NPU)

2. Leo Rowsome: detail from *King Of The Pipers*, 1959. (Courtesy ITMA)

3. Leo Rowsome, 1950s. (Courtesy Helena Rowsome)

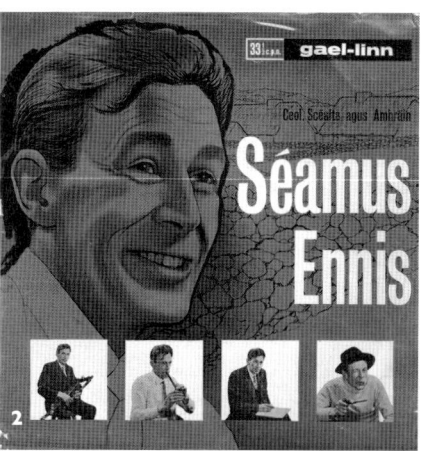
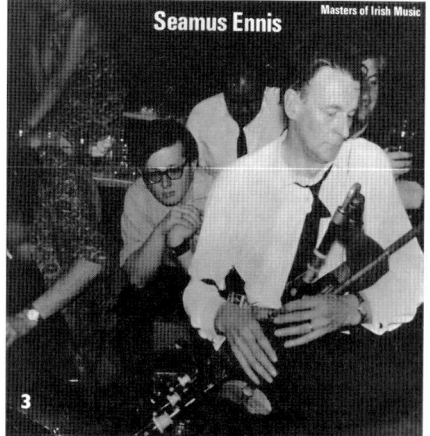

1. Séamus Ennis, RTÉ Studios, Dublin, January 1963. (Roy Bedell/RTÉ Stills Library)

2. The rare original cover of the 1961 Séamus Ennis LP *Ceol, Scéalta agus Amhráin*. (Courtesy ITMA)

3. Séamus Ennis LP *Masters Of Irish Music*, 1969.

1. Séamus Ennis on *Séamus Ennis sa Chathaoir*, Telefís Éireann, circa October 1963. (Roy Bedell/RTÉ Stills Library)

2. The Pavees with Séamus Ennis, Rebel Folk Club at Slattery's, Dublin circa1968. L-R: (seated) John Keenan senior, Paddy Keenan, Séamus Ennis and George Furey with guitar. (Chris Corlett/ITMA)

3. Séamus Ennis with Jean Ritchie, 1952. (NUI Galway: James Hardiman Library Archives: Ritchie-Pickow Collection)

1. Johnny Doran (right) with Pat Cash, 1941. (John McCaffrey/Courtesy NPU)

2. Willie Clancy, early 60s. (Courtesy NPU)

3. Liam O'Flynn with Willie Clancy, early 70s. (Courtesy NPU)

1. Turlough McSweeney. (Courtesy ITMA)
2. John Cash. (Courtesy ITMA)
3. Micí 'Cumbá' O'Sullivan. (Courtesy ITMA)
4. Patsy Touhey, early 1900s. (Courtesy NPU)
5. Captain Francis O'Neill, Chicago PD: the man who saved Irish music from extinction. (Courtesy ITMA)

A HIVE OF HONEYED SOUND

1. The McPeake Family at the 1960 Eisteddfod, Llangollen. (NUI Galway: James Hardiman Library Archives: Ritchie-Pickow Collection)

2. R.L. O'Mealy, circa 1940s. (Courtesy Ken McLeod)

3. Brian and Eithne Vallely, 1972. (Courtesy Brian Vallely)

4. Seán McAloon, detail from *Drops Of Brandy* (1970).

5. Wilbert Garvin, as seen in *Irish Bagpipes: Their Construction And Maintenance* (1978). (Wilbert Garvin)

1. Brian Vallely, founder of Armagh Pipers' Club, with his first piping student (in 1966) Eamonn Curran and his most recent (in 2015), Miadhach Lughain O'Donnell. (Paul Eliasberg)

2. Barry Kerr. (Courtesy Barry Kerr)

3. Sheila Friel. (Courtesy Sheila Friel)

1. The Olllam, on stage at the Lorient Inter-Celtique Festival, France, 2014. (Courtesy John McSherry)

2. John McSherry and Seán Óg Graham in Red Box Studios, 2015. (Courtesy John McSherry)

3. Piping session in the Sunflower Bar, Belfast 2014. (Courtesy John McSherry)

Northern Ireland'. A memo of 18/12/56 declares Séamus to have completed the script. There was a proposed fee of 30 guineas, although whether this was delivered is unclear.

In March of the following year, it was tentatively re-commissioned in a different format. Humphrey Burton puts through a request to Miss Penty (Music Bookings) for Séamus to prepare a seven-minute script, to include phrases of songs and a snatch of melody on the pipes. A proposed contract of 10 guineas is created; again, it's unclear whether this was actually paid to Séamus.

Another year goes by until, in late February 1958, another requisition goes to Contracts requesting that Séamus be booked to provide a script and selection of records for *The Rambler From Clare*, which has by now become a series of three 15-minute shows with transmission dates 2/4/58, 9/4/58 and 16/4/58. A contract is issued for 30 guineas: 10 per programme, although a handwritten note (from someone doubtless aware of Séamus' tendency to negotiate) reveals 'we could go to 15'.

On 20/3/58, a memo asks Miss Penty to cancel Séamus' contract for Episodes 1 and 2 of *The Rambler From Clare*. Séamus had arrived for the recording session, but without any scripts, and was therefore unable to honour this commitment: 'He had done no preparation on these programmes [and the recording couldn't go ahead as a result].' Peter Kennedy will be used instead for Episodes 1 and 2. Séamus will be issued with a new contract for Episode 3 – presumably giving him enough time to deal with whatever complications are going on in his private life and actually write it.

Miss Penty writes to Séamus to explain that a new contract for Episode 3 will be issued on 27/3/58 'providing the script for this programme is in the hands of Mr Harold Rogers by 26/3.' A contract for 10 guineas is eventually issued (the script presumably having been delivered) on 1/4/58. One might conjecture that Séamus felt he was in no position, on this occasion, to negotiate on his fee.

From *Radio Times*: 'Séamus Ennis introduces singers and players he has met on his travels around the British Isles.' *Radio Times* also introduces the name of Elizabeth Johnson, which appears on none of the internal paperwork, as producer.

***A Golden Treasury Of Music And Song*, Home Service**
Rec: 4/58? / Tx: 5/5/58 / Prod: Travers Thorneloe
Fee: 10 guineas

Séamus is contracted in early April to 'play tin whistle and Irish Bagpipes and introduce items in a programme with the Granville Singers and Players'.

SERIES: *British Folk Songs*, **Network Three**
Rec: 11/5/58 / Tx: 26/5/58 (Episode 4) / Prod: Roger Fiske
Fee: 30 guineas

Roger Fiske writes to Séamus on 28/3/58 to say that he is producing a series on British folk song. He hopes Episode 4 will feature Séamus dealing with British folk songs in America: 'Although we would hope that you would use a good many of the BBC recordings, you might like to have Jean Randolph in the studio with you to sing and possibly to speak too.' He invites Séamus to record the programme live on 26/5/58. A further letter suggests a pre-recording date of 11/5/58 – possibly reflecting a concern, after the *Rambler From Clare* fiasco, that having Séamus front a live programme might be too much of a risk. Roger invites Séamus to his office to meet with himself and Jean Randolph over a cup of tea to discuss the programme. A contract is signed two weeks before broadcast. The episode is duly titled 'American Relations'. From *Radio Times*: 'Séamus Ennis talks about British folk songs taken by settlers to America, and compares versions that survive there and in this country. Illustrations on records and by Jean Randolph and Séamus Ennis.'

The series ran for six 30-minute weekly episodes beginning 5/5/58 and featuring a different presenter on each: Maud Karpeles ('Collecting In The Past'); Brian George and Marie Slocombe ('Collecting Today'); Peter Kennedy ('Regional Variants'); Patrick Shuldham-Shaw ('Accompaniments'); A.L. Lloyd ('Folk Song Today').

Today, **Home Service**
Rec: live / Tx: 14/5/58; 13/6/58 / Prod: H. Olsson
Fee: 10 guineas

Séamus was booked to talk about Irish folk music and give a demonstration on tin whistle. Many items on *Today* went out twice during the same edition of the programme (or, rather, as two editions the same morning, split by 25 minutes of news and weather). These would be broadcast live both times, rather than using a recording of the first. Thus a contributor would be paid twice for his or her efforts, rather than receiving a (smaller) repeat fee for the second broadcast.

Curiously, perhaps as a result of listener demand, Séamus was booked for a repeat of his contribution a month after his first appearance. This seemed to cause an administrative crisis. A memo from a Miss Rowley, from *Today*, on 3/7/58 sets out their position in the matter:

> On May 14th and again on June 13th, Séamus Ennis broadcast and played

the tin whistle on *Today*. It appears that Music Bookings take the view that, as he broadcast the same material, he is entitled to a repeat fee only [he has received a fee of £5.5s for 1st edition and £3.3s for the 2nd edition, rather than the same pay for both]. Apart from the fact that his 'tootles' between items were not always the same, it is, as you know, our practice to pay double to a broadcast who is 'live' in both editions – whether he broadcasts the same material or not.

After further memos, involving the Talks Department, Séamus' fee for the second broadcast is bumped up to 5 guineas.

Rejected Script Proposals
On 22/7/58, Miss Rowley's secretary writes to Séamus to thank him for three scripts Séamus had given her in person the previous day. Presumably these scripts are being pitched at *Today*. They are politely declined as unsuitable, although Miss Rowley has passed two of them to a Mr Cradock and returns the other, on 'Kwela', to Séamus.

Dateline London, **North American Service**
Rec: live broadcast? / Tx: 18/6/58
Fee: 7 guineas

Séamus is hired 'to speak on Kwela and illustrate on tin whistle', for approximately two minutes. This overseas broadcast on the topic (whatever it may be) precedes Séamus' submission of a script on it to Miss Rowley on *Today* (see above). Probably Séamus was trying to have two bites of the cherry, hoping to re-use ideas across two networks.

The Tragedy Of Nan, **Home Service**
Rec: ?/6/58 (in Birmingham) / Tx: 16/6/58
Fee: 7 guineas (£11.6s with expenses included) plus £3.13s.6d for rehearsal

Séamus is contracted to play 'one or two folk tunes on violin' in this adaptation of John Masefield's play. The recording will be in Birmingham, with a rehearsal in London.

Towie Castle, **Third Programme**
Rec: 6–7/58 / Tx: 12/8/58; repeated 15/8/58 / Prod: Frederick Bradnum
Fee: 7 guineas + £3.13s.6d

Séamus is to accompany singers on the pipes for five minutes approximately in this

25-minute drama by Gordon Bottomley. There are two contracts issued for Séamus' contribution (dated 10/6/58 and 1/7/58), for the two amounts above. Presumably the latter reflects a rehearsal day, although details are not given – only the information that it will be a pre-recorded rather than live broadcast.

A Golden Treasury Of Music And Song, **Home Service**
Rec: 6/58? / Tx: 7/7/58 / Prod: Travers Thorneloe
Fee: 10 guineas

Séamus is contracted in early June for this episode, a contemporaneous memo revealing it to be recorded at Maida Vale studios and instructing Séamus that 'Mr Thorneloe would like you to tell a story and play the Irish Pipes.'

Lots Of Fun At Finnegans Wake, **Third Programme**
Rec: 7/58? / Tx: 9/9/58; repeated 12/9/58, 30/12/58 and 4/6/60 / Prod: Sasha Moorsom
Fee: 7 guineas

Séamus is contracted on 9/7/58 to sing 'Brian O'Lynn' unaccompanied. The 30-minute programme is billed thus: 'Matthew Hodgart introduces some of the Dublin street ballads that James Joyce knew, and shows how Joyce used them symbolically in *Finnegans Wake*.' Wilfred Brambell reads extracts from Joyce's novel, with Dominic Behan (singing four songs) and Isla Cameron (singing one) completing the cast. Both Séamus and Dominic appear in a follow-up programme a year later (see below).

Today, **Home Service**
Rec: live / Tx: 5/8/58; 7/8/58
Fee: 12 guineas

Séamus is contracted to tell an Irish folk tale and play 'Illyan [sic] pipes' on each programme. It's not clear whether this is to be two distinct presentations or whether the second will be a live repeat of the first (see above).

SERIES: *Dateline London*, **North American Service**
Rec: seemingly transcription disc recordings / Tx: 6/8/58; 19/8/58; 25/8/58
Fee: 5 guineas, 28 guineas, 21 guineas

The first broadcast is an item on Morris dancing; the second is 'four talks on Irish folk songs with musical illustrations' (7 guineas per talk); the third is 'three talks on Irish folk songs with musical illustrations' (7 guineas per talk).

SERIES: *As I Roved Out* **(Series 6), Light Programme**
Rec: 1958 / Tx: 17/8/58–7/9/58 (four weekly episodes) / Prod: Denys Gueroult
Fee: 20 guineas

After the one-series move to Wednesdays, this final hurrah for *As I Roved Out* is back to Sunday mornings, introduced by former producer Harold Rogers but produced by Denys Gueroult. The BBC collecting project that had employed both Séamus and Peter Kennedy full time has concluded the previous year, so both men appear in a freelance capacity. These four final episodes were titled 'The North', 'The South', 'The East' and 'The West'. Séamus was involved only in the episodes on East and West: introducing 'music from farm, fair and prefab' and songs and music from Belfast, Connemara, Galway and Clare, respectively. Musical interludes in this series come from four different ensembles (cf. the previous two series' resident ensembles). Only one item in Séamus' BBC files relates to this series: a requisition dated 25/7/58 for Séamus' contribution to Episodes 3 and 4 – specified as a 10-minute talk in each, illustrated with BBC Permanent Library recordings, with the fee set at 10 guineas per programme.

The Scots And Irish Ballad Makers, **Home Service**
Rec: ?/8/58 / Tx: 26/8/58; repeated 31/10/58 / Prod: Francis Dillon
Fee: 12 guineas

Francis Dillon asks Miss Penty (Music Bookings) to arrange terms with Séamus, who will contribute one song to the above programme, with commentary on its origin and possibly other comments. He suggests a fee of 12 guineas, 'since he is an authority on the subject'. Miss Penty complies. From *Radio Times*: 'Some ballads and a discussion on the people who wrote them with Seán O'Boyle, Hamish Henderson and Dominic Behan.'

Today, **Home Service**
Rec: live broadcast / Tx: 28/10/58 (twice) / Prod: Robert Cradock
Fee: 10 guineas

Séamus is booked to sing and play tin whistle, specified as a double performance in the one broadcast (i.e. two editions split by news and weather).

A Golden Treasury Of Music And Song, **Home Service**
Rec: 12/58? / Tx: 12/12/58 / Prod: Gareth Walters
Fee: 15 guineas

Séamus is contracted in late November to introduce two discs and play pipes. The original fee of 10 guineas is subsequently increased, on 1/12/57, to 15 guineas, for reasons unclear. Show stalwarts The Well-Tempered Singers and The Granville Players also appear.

On The Feast Of Stephen, **Third Programme**
Rec: early December 1958 / Tx: 26/12/58 / Prod: David Thomson
Fee: 8 guineas

David Thomson confirms to Miss Penty on 9/12/58 that Séamus has already attended a rehearsal and pre-recording for the above. He is issued the next day with a contract for 7 guineas 'to sing as arranged' – although this is replaced, the same day, with a contract for 8. Perhaps Séamus had phoned in and suggested a movement upwards. From *Radio Times*: 'Rhymes, legends, and music belonging to the custom of Hunting the Wren as it has survived in Ireland and the Isle of Man, with something about the cult of bird sacrifice as it was practised in Great Britain.' Written by Leslie Daiken and narrated by Séamus Kavanagh.

Today, **Home Service**
Rec: live broadcast / Tx: early February 1959 (twice) / Prod: Elizabeth Brewer
Fee: 10 guineas plus transport

On 21/1/59, Elizabeth Brewer writes to Séamus to say that she has had four of his scripts passed to her. She wants to accept 'The Fairies' Hornpipe'. She mentions liking 'Raising The Wind', but says that it is far too long and would be spoilt by cutting. She rejects 'Monday, Tuesday And Wednesday' and 'The Magic Mist'. A subsequent requisition says that Séamus will illustrate the talk with intermittent playing on his pipes. The script is roughly two minutes long but will be about three minutes with music.

Rejected Script Proposal
On 12/3/59, Elizabeth Brewer writes to Séamus to reject a script (not mentioning its title): 'We did suggest it to *Roundabout* but it wasn't quite what they wanted. Perhaps you have other ideas for it.'

The Homing Of Roberts, Third Programme
Rec: ?/2/59 / Tx: 24/2/59 / Prod: Louis MacNeice
Fee: 15 guineas (plus £1.16s expenses)

This is an enhanced 'live repeat' of the programme first broadcast in 1957 (see above), with Séamus reprising his 1957 role along with two of the original three actors, under new producer Louis MacNeice.

A letter from Miss (Margaret) Penty to Séamus on 2/2/59 confirms that he will be attending a conference with Christopher Holme, who will be producer (David Thomson had produced the original). For the meeting, Séamus is offered a fee of 1½ guineas. A contract is prepared, offering Séamus 6 guineas for his role in the programme. This is swiftly upgraded to a 'special fee' of 12 guineas. Perhaps someone had noticed that this was the fee Séamus had received first time around.

On 9/2/59 Louis MacNeice informs Miss Penty that he has replaced Christopher Holme (who has flu) as producer. Louis has decided that Séamus will be required to produce more music than on the original occasion, and more than is indicated in the script. He also says he will need Séamus for an extra day, which will, naturally, affect the fee. A contract for 15 guineas subsequently appears. Séamus sends in an invoice for expenses on 24/2/59: three taxi journeys from Hampstead to Grafton, on three rehearsal days. He explains that a taxi is necessary because he's carrying his pipes.

The Good Journey, Third Programme
Rec: ?/3/59 / Tx: 1/8/59 / Prod: Francis Dillon
Fee: 8 guineas (performance), £3.13s.6d (rehearsal)

Séamus is contracted on 24/2/59 to 'sing a short snatch of song unaccompanied, and to speak a line or two' in this 50-minute item. When an additional rehearsal is required (this is probably a play), Séamus is issued a supplementary contract for £3.13s.6d on 7/3/59. This is almost certainly a new recording of a 50-minute item of the same title, also produced by Francis Dillon, which had aired on 31/12/56 – seemingly then a narrated story by Gerard McLarnon.

Dateline London, North American Service
Rec: live broadcasts? / Tx: 1/4/59; 4/4/59
Fee: 7 guineas, 6 guineas

The first programme involved Séamus 'taking part in an illustrated interview with

Lee Hamilton about the difference between Scots and Irish pipes', for roughly three minutes. The content of the second broadcast is not specified. Seemingly recorded on transcription discs.

Monitor, BBC TV
Rec: 4/59? / Tx: 4/59?
Fee: 5 guineas per talk (15 guineas)

This could be another example of Séamus spreading his ideas across two BBC services (see *Dateline London*, above). All that remains is a 7/4/59 Transcription invoice for three four-minute talks, with illustrations, on the following: a comparison between Scots and Irish bagpipes; Irish fiddles; tin flutes. *Monitor* was an arts magazine series hosted by Huw Weldon and produced by Peter Newington – presenting, as per *Radio Times*, 'people, events, and controversies on film and in the studio every fortnight'.

Séamus' name, alas, doesn't appear in any of the detailed *Radio Times* blurbs for the 21 episodes of *Monitor* during 1959. Microfiche resources on *Monitor* transcriptions at the WAC were checked, but to no avail. Some bits of *Monitor* from 1959 survive, including director Ken Russell's short film *The Guitar Craze*, shown on 7/6/59 and featuring the earliest known footage of future guitar icons John Williams and Davy Graham.

More Fun At Finnegans Wake, Third Programme
Rec: 4/59? / Tx: 23/5/59; repeated 14/9/59 / Prod: Sasha Moorsom
Fee: 10 guineas

Séamus is contracted on 13/4/59 to 'rehearse and record Irish Ballads'. As before, the show is billed thus: 'Matthew Hodgart introduces more of the Dublin street ballads that James Joyce knew, and shows how Joyce used them symbolically in *Finnegans Wake*.' Irish harpist/vocalist Mary O'Hara and singer Dominic Behan also appear (performing two and four songs, respectively), with reader Éamonn Keane (reading four Joyce extracts) completing the cast.

Séamus performs 'The Rocky Road To Dublin', first on pipes and then as a song. A note with the transcription disc states: 'Selected as an outstanding programme at Annual Review 1962.' Sasha Moorsom had previously produced *Lots Of Fun At Finnegans Wake*, circa July 1957, also with Séamus' involvement (see above). The contract states that the first transmission was on 18/5/59, but the transcription disc and *Radio Times* both state it as 23/5/59.

Eileen Aroon [aka The Gift Of Music], **Third Programme**
Rec: 5–6/59 / Tx: 10/6/59; repeated 30/7/59 and 19/9/59 / Producers/Writers: Francis Dillon and Séamus Ennis
Fee: 100 guineas (script), 10 guineas (tin whistle), 3½ guineas (unknown), 2 guineas (rehearsal), 3½ guineas (probably for piping)

A 2/1/59 memo from Francis Dillon to Miss Wakeham (Contracts) explains that this, originally titled *The Gift Of Music*, is to be a 60-minute programme for the second quarter of 1959:

> Seumas Ennis [sic] is to adapt the old Irish folk tale of this title for radio. It will be a fully dramatized [sic] show, with no narrator. Seumas Ennis will play the Eullain [sic] pipes and take the part of the piper but his performance should be the subject of a separate contract. In addition to writing the show he will provide the composer with the ancient tunes proper to the lute … I should think something like £100 would cover his work.

Séamus' address is provided as Flat 2, 65 Alexandra Road, NW8. A contract is issued on the same day, not for £100 but for 100 guineas. Miss Wakeham subsequently informs Francis Dillon:

> I did in fact offer him less than [£100] as I thought it sounded rather high, but he asked for 125 guineas, and in view of your recommendation I agreed to pay 100 guineas.

As is typical of BBC contracts of the period, there are provisions for further fees payable under a series of circumstances:

- If broadcast on Overseas or Singapore Services (in English): £35 (for up to seven broadcasts)
- If broadcast in a foreign language: £17 per language (for up to two broadcasts per language)
- UK repeats: £70 per repeat broadcast

A series of memos and contracts from April and May reveal that Séamus negotiates for and receives several additional payments for musical contributions. An original fee of 7 guineas for a tin whistle session is upgraded to 10 (seemingly a second session was necessary). A further 3½ guineas is given in April for reasons unspecified – possibly a rehearsal fee.

In late May, a fee of 2 guineas is paid for a rehearsal session and a further 3½-guinea fee follows for an unspecified reason, though almost certainly for an open-air piping recording session, as mentioned in a memo from Francis Dillon to Miss Penty. (This piping session is later revealed as having happened on 29/5/59 – see below.) Dillon argues that 'It will be necessary to go into the country to avoid traffic noises and get the right effect.'

By 28/5/59, the show is confirmed as being retitled *Eileen Aroon*, with some earlier contracts being amended in pen to reflect the new title. On 19/5/59, with the programme now scheduled for transmission on 10/6/59, Francis Dillon writes to Miss Wakeham:

> I have now received the completed script of this programme from Séamus Ennis, and it is very satisfactory indeed. I should be glad if you would arrange to pay him the second half of his fee.

Eileen Aroon, with a cast of 21 including Séamus (and Dominic Behan, acting), is repeated on the Third Programme on 30/7/59 and 19/9/59. Séamus receives a repeat fee of £70 on each occasion. There is, additionally, correspondence expressing interest in the programme from the Australian Broadcasting Commission on 3/8/60, suggesting that overseas broadcasts may have eventuated.

Eileen Aroon is one of the few Ennis-related items still preserved in the BBC Sound Archive. (The tape-based SA catalogue does not include material preserved on transcription discs.) The SA catalogue provides further information on the programme: it was the story of Carroll O'Daly and Eileen Kavanagh, based on translations made from Gaelic by J.H. Delargy (Séamus' former IFC boss), with incidental music composed by Tristram Cary.

***Voyage In A Bowler Hat*, [Service unspecified]**
Rec: ?/59 / Tx: 8–9/59 / Prod: Francis Dillon
Fee: ?

Francis Dillon confirms, in an 11/9/59 memo to Miss Penty, that Séamus Ennis had recorded Irish pipe music on 29/5/59 for *Eileen Aroon*, and that he has used one minute from this session, 'The Dark Lady Of The Glen', in the above.

This was a six-part series describing the travels of one Hugh Malet along the waterways of Britain and Ireland. The Irish-based episodes were broadcast on 3/9/59 and 17/9/59. A handwritten note states that no action is necessary, as the music has been broadcast already – a reproduction fee only will be paid.

Song Of A Road, **Home Service**
Rec: 4/10/59, 23/10/59 / Tx: 5/11/59; repeated 29/12/59 / Prod: Charles Parker
Fee: 17 guineas

This was the second of the innovative 'Radio Ballads', combining music and actuality, created by producer Charles Parker with British 'folk revival' pillars Ewan MacColl and Peggy Seeger – a series of eight themed programmes broadcast between 1958 and 1964.

Assembled from 90 hours of vox pop material recorded from workers during the building of the M1 motorway in England, plus specially written music reflecting the multiple nationalities involved on the road, *Song Of A Road* was first transmitted three days after the first stretch of the M1 was opened. The production team felt it their weakest Radio Ballad, and consequently it was one of two not released on LP in the mid-60s (but released on CD by Topic in 1999).

> **Ewan MacColl**: We found ourselves asking questions about road-building, about running a concrete-batching plant, about prefabrication techniques. Worse, we found ourselves incorporating the answers in the programme itself. In short, we were behaving as though our intention was to create a programme which would inform the listeners how to build their own motorway … The consensus of opinion among those who worked on *Song Of A Road* was that the programme was an uneasy compromise between a typical feature programme and a radio-ballad, and a not particularly good example of either.[204]

Séamus was recorded on the two dates above (the second contract says 'The Circular Road', specifying that he is to play tin whistle and sing – it seems likely this was a second session towards *Song Of A Road*) for 10 guineas and 7 guineas, respectively. In the broadcast programme, he sings 'Hot Asphalt', claiming that he will 'eat his hat' if the road surface doesn't last forever.

If 'The Circular Road' was a song title, it didn't make the cut. Among the other singers involved were Scots Isla Cameron and Jimmy Macgregor; Ulsterman Francis McPeake; Englishmen A.L. Lloyd, Louis Killen (from the North-East) and Cyril Tawney (from the South-West). Francis McPeake (though not Séamus) also played pipes on the broadcast.

***As They Roved Out*, Home Service**
Rec: 6/1/60? / Tx: 21/01/60 / Prod: Harold Rogers
Fee: 30 guineas (script), 5 guineas (music)

Written and narrated by Séamus, with musical contributions from him, this was an appreciation of 19th century Irishman Patrick Weston Joyce: the fourth in a six-programme series on pioneer British Isles folk song collectors. Others profiled in the weekly series, which began on 31/12/59, were Alfred Williams, Lady Herbert Lewis, Lucy Broadwood, Gavin Greig and Marjory Kennedy-Fraser.

Harold Rogers writes to Séamus on 12/11/59, having apparently bumped into him in the street and discussed this programme idea (whether it came from Séamus is unstated), saying he has the green light for it. He asks Séamus for a script in a month's time:

> The idea is to use as many of our own recordings as possible; to have one or two songs sung in the studio, and here I suggest yourself, all linked together with the life of the man concerned. In this series we do want to bring out the character of each collector as best we possibly can. Could you also let me know which Joyce you're going to do.

It's a curious question, as there *is* only one Joyce associated with folk song collecting.

Séamus is seemingly booked for an all-in fee of 30 guineas – although, after a representation from Harold Rogers to Miss Penty on 15/1/60, he is paid a further 5 guineas for musical contributions: two short pieces on the pipes, four items on the tin whistle and two short vocal items.

A 29-minute programme, this is one of the very few Séamus Ennis BBC radio works extant in the BBC Sound Archive.

***House Under The Hill*, trial recording – not broadcast**
Rec: 21/1/60, Maida Vale Studios / Tx: n/a / Prod: Sheila Anderson
Fee: 25 guineas (£19.13s.9d in advance, the rest if/when broadcast)

Séamus is asked to present five minutes of continuity, to read a two-to-three-minute folk story and to sing and/or play if required. An undated memo from a Miss Boxall to Miss Penty (Music Bookings) asks her to advise Séamus that 'the records he made have not been passed for broadcasting, therefore no further payment is due to him.' Presumably he received the £19.13s.9d.

East Anglian Highlights, **Midlands Home Service**
Rec: live? / Tx: 18/3/60?
Fee: 8 guineas

Séamus is contracted on 18/3/60 for a five-minute talk, including illustrations. The Midlands edition of *Radio Times* describes this series as 'a weekly topical magazine, introduced by Tom Wisdom'. An edition of the show went out on 18/3/60, so possibly it was a live broadcast with the contract sorted out on the day, or possibly he was booked a week ahead for the next edition on 25/3/60.

Monday Night At Home, **Home Service**
Rec: ? / Tx: 28/3/60 / Prod: Francis Dillon
Fee: 5 guineas

A weekly programme described as 'a selection of music and humour', usually presented by Richard Hurndall and regularly featuring the likes of Ivor Cutler, Jonathan Miller and Alan Bennett. Séamus is booked for one item on uilleann pipes. However, a memo from Francis Dillon to Miss Penty confirms that he played two pieces in this programme, 'Slievenamon' and 'Westering Home'. He will probably have received a supplementary fee, although no contract for such is extant.

Monday Night At Home, **Home Service**
Rec: ? / Tx: late May 1960 / Prod: Francis Dillon
Fee: 7.5 guineas

A 27/5/60 memo from Francis Dillon to Miss Penty confirms that Séamus read a four-minute-45-second story, 'The Little Red Caps', on this episode. He asks that Séamus be contracted for this, for 5 guineas, in retrospect. A handwritten note says: 'Paid by copyright for collecting story and translating it from the Gaelic.' Four days later, perhaps after a nudge from Séamus, a supplementary contract is issued for 2½ guineas.

Monday Night At Home, **Home Service**
Rec: ? / Tx: 20/6/60 / Prod: Francis Dillon
Fee: 7½ guineas

Séamus is contracted on 7/6/60 to translate from Gaelic 'The Bold Fisherman', a five-minute folk tale, for an episode provisionally scheduled for 20/6/60. The only one of Séamus' three appearances on the show to be billed in *Radio Times*.

The Dublin Freelance Era: 1962–1980

Séamus appears to have moved back to Dublin in June 1960. Bar one item in February 1966, there is no 'Artist' correspondence between the BBC and him between May 1960 and February 1968.

Country Dancing, Home Service
Rec: 10/62? / Tx: 31/10/62
Fee: £10

Séamus was not personally involved in this. The contract relates to a performance of 'Tree In The Bog', noted as having been collected by Séamus. The fee seems to be a copyright payment. Séamus' address is noted as 2 St Michael's, Sarsfield Road, Inchicore, Dublin, although BBC correspondence for him is, curiously, sent to 60a Alexandra Road, London NW8 – possibly the family home (it is the third of three different addresses in Alexandra Road associated with Séamus during his BBC era). Séamus is by now estranged from his wife and two children.

Pionair Disaster, Home Service
Rec: 15/2/66 / Tx: 17/2/66 / Prod: Tom Wisdom
Fee: 12 guineas

From *Radio Times*: 'The loss of LT 245 – the trawler Boston Pionair – with all hands, on February 14 1965, led to the North Sea's biggest search operation. Music arranged by Alf Edwards and Séamus Ennis.' Séamus receives his fee for 'arranging and playing whistle'. Alf Edwards was a concertina player involved in a huge number of BBC radio programmes during the 1950s and 60s – cornering the market for his own speciality instrument in rather the same way that Séamus had with his. They had worked together previously on a few occasions. An internal memo of 1/3/66 (on which date Séamus returns his signed contract) reveals 'Mr Ennis is most anxious to get his money as soon as possible.'

BBC Record Contract – unfulfilled
H. Rooney Pelletier is the former Controller of the BBC Light Programme and is now General Manager of BBC Radio Enterprises, in which capacity he writes, on 26/2/68, to Séamus in very convivial terms, hoping to rekindle a former association with an exciting offer of a record project: 'I want to make a commercial record of your playing of the Uilleann pipes which you recorded for us on 7/2/58.'

He explains that the BBC have rights to these and could proceed without further payment but 'this is not the Corporation's way'. He later adds, however, that if necessary they are prepared to go ahead without Séamus' permission. A £10 fee against royalties is offered, with the proviso that Séamus writes a 400-word sleeve note and supplies a photograph. A contract is enclosed and a list of titles given, being seven of the 10 pieces recorded (the ones not selected were: 'Demonstration & Tuning', 'Connaught Heifer/The Braes Of Busby', 'Mountain Of The Women').

The letter is sent to Séamus at 3 Home Farm Park, Dublin 9. Pelletier is told by the current occupants that Séamus 'left this address 1965'. He then writes to Séamus c/o Donoghue's Pub, Dublin. No BBC record with any of Séamus' Permanent Library recordings ever appeared. We can only guess at whether the letter ever reached Séamus or whether the project stalled for other reasons.

It's All Yours, **Radio 4 East Anglia**
Rec: 10/69?, Radio Éireann, Dublin / Tx: 18/10/69 / Prod: 'Mr Wisdom'
Fee: £25 all-in

Séamus is to write, read the script, sing and play instruments for this 10-minute show based on East Anglian folk song. The contract offered is supposedly inclusive, but a note from Séamus scribbled beneath the details of the fee says: 'Details of tape purchase, postal registration and taxi fares are with Mr Wisdom. I submit these items be deemed necessary extra.'

Folk On Friday Special – Loughborough '71, **Radio 1**
Rec: 15/2/71, Loughborough University, Main Hall / Tx: 9/7/71 / Prod: Francis Line and Peter Pilbeam
Fee: £12

Séamus was contracted to appear as a performer at this concert. However, the contract is scored through as 'cancelled'. It erroneously gives the transmission date as 17/7/71.

Both Sides Now, **Radio 2**
Rec: 18/9/77, Broadcasting House, Concert Hall / Tx: 24/9/77 / Prod: Bill Bebb
Fee: £35

Séamus was booked on a by then rare tour of British folk clubs in September 1977. He was to perform 'three or four songs' on this programme, presented by Wally Whyton, whose other studio guests were Na Filí, featuring piper Tomás Ó Canainn. The tour was cancelled due to illness. The contract is annulled with the words 'Artist Indisposed'.

***Music Now*, World Service**
Rec: 17/2/80 / Tx: 14/3/80
Fee: £13

Séamus is interviewed by John Amis.

***Folk On 2*, Radio 2**
Rec: ? / Tx: 31/3/80
Prod: Ray Harvey and Peter Pilbeam

Séamus is a guest along with The Califians and Cyril Tawney. The contract is not extant.

***Royal Albert Hall Concert*, Radio 2**
Rec: 28/2/80 / Tx: ?
Fee: £40

Séamus performs solo piping at this concert – the 'Sense Of Ireland' event recalled by Paddy Glackin (see Séamus Ennis chapter) at which Séamus shone. After years away, this was a fitting last hurrah for the great man in Britain and a farewell nod from the BBC to one of their greatest on-air characters – if, indeed, it was ever broadcast. *Folk On 2* broadcast De Danann and Planxty from the event in November and December 1980, but no trace can be found in online *Radio Times* listings of any broadcast for Séamus' set. On 24/3/80, an internal memo circulates, saying that Séamus' contact address was now c/o O'Donoghue's pub, Dublin. No one at the BBC would ever use it again. On October 5 1982, Séamus Ennis was dead.

Note: Extant BBC Recordings

There are three sources for surviving BBC recordings involving Séamus Ennis: on tape in the BBC SA; on transcription disc in the British Library/NSA (BBC Permanent Library recordings and programmes recorded for overseas broadcast); and off-air recordings of some programmes, given low-level commercial circulation by the late Peter Kennedy on his Folktrax cassette label. Most of the Permanent Library recordings of songs and tunes (but not the radio programmes) can also be heard in NSA copies given to the ITMA in Dublin. Material held by the NSA and the ITMA is available to be heard by the public.

1. BBC Sound Archive (Tape)

The SA holdings comprise seven songs from Séamus' September 1949 Permanent Library sessions (including one, 'The Frog And The Mouse', missing on transcription disc), plus three radio programmes:

- *The Irish Storyteller* – Tx: 13/6/48
- *Eileen Aroon* – Tx: 10/6/59
- *As They Roved Out: Patrick Weston Joyce* – Tx: 21/1/60

2. National Sound Archive (Transcription Disc)

The NSA also holds copies of the three programmes listed above under BBC SA. In addition, there are copies of the following three programmes:

- *Sons Of The Sea* – Tx: 20/11/50
- *Lots Of Fun At Finnegans Wake* – Tx: 9/9/58
- *More Fun At Finnegans Wake* – Tx: 23/5/59

The NSA (with digital copies at the ITMA) also holds transcription discs of Séamus' Permanent Library recordings of August 1948, September 1949 and November 1950 (all detailed above). There is no sign of the mysterious possible Permanent Library session of February 1952 or the definite session of February 1958, although this latter session was commercially released (its provenance disguised) as a Folktrax album (see below), presumably from a copy of the acetate or tape acquired by Peter Kennedy when he was employed by the BBC. Indeed, he may have taken the only copy.

The NSA also holds several items catalogued as radio programmes but which are clearly field recordings by Séamus, possibly indicating their having been cut to disc for use in radio programmes. Several are dated to the mid-50s (the period when Séamus was working as a BBC field recordist) – but, curiously, some are dated to August 1960, when he was no longer in BBC employ. Most likely, this date is simply the date on which the material in question was cut to transcription disc. The list below is not exhaustive:

- 6/9/54 John Martin (street singer) – interviewed by Séamus Ennis and Seán Haughey at a cattle fair, Gortshork, Donegal.
- 1/6/55 Morag McKinnon (singer) – recorded by Séamus Ennis on Vatersay, Hebrides, singing 'A Chailein Oig A'Stiuir Thu Mise?' (O Young Girl Will You Guide Me?).
- 1/6/55 Neil Gillies (singer) – interviewed by Séamus Ennis on Barra,

Hebrides, talking about sea birds (Barra and Vatersay are linked by a causeway, so this date and the previous one are not a mistake!).
- 1/7/55 Nan McKinnon (singer) – interviewed by Séamus Ennis on Vatersay, Hebrides, talking (in Gaelic) about the song 'Tha Seathan aAnochd 'Na Bhalbhan' (Seán is dumb (dead) tonight).
- 1/8/60 Tom Lenihan (singer, Co. Clare) – 'The Potken Song', collected by Séamus Ennis. [Surely a misprint for 'The Poteen/Poitín Song'. Film of Tom Lenihan performing the likely candidate at the Kilrush Fleadh in 1967 can be viewed online.]
- 1/8/60 Bartley Conneely (singer, Carna, Co. Galway) – 'The Rocks Of Bawn', collected by Séamus Ennis. A note says that Conneely 'was about 65 years old at the time of this recording'.
- 1/8/60 Colm Keane [Colm Ó Caodháin] (singer, Co. Galway) – 'Ceann Gan Árann' (Head Without Sense), collected by Séamus Ennis.
- 1/8/60 Patrick Egan (singer, Tulla, Co. Clare) – 'When Sarsfield Sailed', collected by Séamus Ennis.
- 1/8/60 Dolly McMahon (singer, Co. Galway) – 'The Trees They Do Grow High', collected by Séamus Ennis.
- 1/8/60 Jimmy Ward (Miltown Malbay, Co. Clare) – oral whistling and interview, collected by Séamus Ennis. A note says: 'This performer is a building and decorating contractor by trade. He has never played an instrument but followed music from childhood, being an accomplished whistler until teeth and short breath troubled him. At the time of these recordings he was about 52 years of age.'
- 1/8/60 Willie Clancy (uilleann piper/singer, Co. Clare) – several pieces by Willie, collected by Séamus, are in the NSA with that troublesome August 1960 date (but almost certainly collected in the early 50s). These include: 'The Humours Of Glynn' (pipes); 'The Red-Haired Man's Wife' (song); 'Tom San Catty' (whistle) with interview; 'The Bright Lady' (whistle) with interview. A note with one of the pieces says Willie was recorded in the same month as Bartley Conneely.

3. Folktrax Cassette Releases

In addition to four albums of music and storytelling by Séamus, released from the mid-70s onwards (one comprising BBC recordings in disguise and at least one other featuring recordings purloined from elsewhere), Séamus' former BBC colleague Peter Kennedy also circulated off-air recordings of several radio programmes involving himself and Séamus. The Folktrax archive is now co-owned by Topic Records and the British Library. As far as one can tell, the label's Ennis-related off-air cassettes (all 'released' in 2002) were as follows:

Radio Programmes
Wassail Wassail (Folktrax 253), 2002
This comprised two episodes of *As I Roved Out* (not otherwise extant), from Series 1 and 2:

- Programme 1: 27/12/53 – a Christmas party from the Central Club, Peacehaven, Sussex: Bob and Ron Copper (landlords of the nearby Queen Victoria pub in Rottingdean) as hosts with guests Isla Cameron, Peter Kennedy (fiddle), Séamus Ennis (pipes), Brian George (Head of Recorded Progammes), Marie Slocombe (RP Library) and Harold Rogers (Producer)
- Programme 2: 3/1/54 – in the studio with Spike Hughes with his sextet and Isla Cameron, Ewan MacColl, Frances Kitching, Peter Kennedy and the Coppers

Séamus was not involved in the second programme. His contributions to the first programme are: *'The Merry Blacksmith/Mrs McLeod's' (pipes, with PK on fiddle) (2:34); Untitled Jig (whistle) (1:24); 'The Mountain Dew' (song) (2:06); 'Jennie Jenkins' (song, with Brian George) (1:51); 'Kelly's/Off To California' (pipes, with PK on melodeon) (3:03).*

The Gaelic West – The West Of Ireland & The Western Isles (Folktrax 275), 2002
The Folktrax blurb states: 'Presented by Séamus Ennis; compiled and produced by Alan Lomax 1951. An outstanding study of Celtic music in which Séamus wonders why the Irish have not preserved, except in Donegal, any of the rhythmical chorus songs he encountered on his visit to the Hebrides. He also gives an account of his work for the Irish Folklore Commission in the 1940s when he transcribed hundreds of songs from phonograph records – he himself sings and ends by playing a lament followed by a reel on his handed down set of Uilleann (bellows-blown) bagpipes.'

This is the programme recorded for the BBC Third Programme in December 1951. As well as presenting many other musical recordings, Séamus himself performs: *'Soldier, Soldier' (song with fiddle) (2:01); 'Were You At The Rock?/The Bucks Of Oranmore' (pipes) (4:12).*

Alan Lomax Presents Sing Christmas 1957 (Folktrax 950), 2002
This is a recording of the Christmas Day 1957 programme *Sing Christmas And The Turn of the Year*, on the Home Service. Séamus' contributions are playing whistle in a

mass choir/skiffle version of 'Good King Wenceslas' and pipes on 'The Dublin Reel' (played in a medley with two other tunes by two other performers). The broadcast, sourced/licensed from Kennedy, was also released on CD by Rounder in 2000 as *Sing Christmas And The Turn Of The Year: The Live Christmas Day 1957 Broadcast On BBC Radio* (Rounder 11661–1850-2). One can only conclude that by releasing his own Folktrax version of the BBC broadcast a couple of years after the more widely distributed Rounder CD, Kennedy was essentially pirating his own bootleg.

Séamus Ennis Album
The Morning Brush aka *The Mountain Of Women* aka *The Pied Piper Of Dublin* (Folktrax 374), 1982
'The Mountain Of The Women' (3:20); 'The Lament Of The Fox' (4:02); 'The Morning Brush/The Dublin Reel' (4:32); 'Chief O'Neill's/The Boys Of Bluehill' (2:18); 'Jockey To The Fair' (1:44); 'Tatter Jack Welch/Paddy O'Rafferty' (3:22); 'The Groves' (3:51); 'The Connaught Heifer/The Braes Of Busby' (3:12); 'The Dark Lady Of The Glen' (3:03); 'The Leitrim Lilt' (1:05); 'Kelly's/Ballymanus Fair' (3:13); 'Were You At The Rock?' (2:15); 'Twisting The Hayrope' (2:26); 'Cavan Brigade/When The Cock Crows/Sixpenny Money' (3:07); 'Rainy Day/Merry Blacksmith's/Miss Lane's Fancy' (3:32).

Purportedly recorded by Peter Kennedy in London, 22/3/58, this is in fact almost all of Séamus' two piping sessions for the BBC Permanent Library on 22/9/49 and 7/2/58. The only items missing are 'Tuning-up/Dublin Reel' and 'Tipperary Wedding' from the 1949 session. *The Morning Brush* appears to have been the original title of this release – owing to a mis-crediting of 'The Morning Thrush' (composed by Séamus' father). Online information suggests the above alternative titles for the cassette may have been used.

Appendix: Extant RTÉ Television Appearances
A full inventory of Séamus' Radio Éireann and Radio Telefís Éireann work would prove challenging, due to the lack of a publicly accessible RTÉ equivalent to the BBC WAC and NSA. A manual trawl through broadcast listings in old newspapers would be the obvious route. The current RTÉ archive database is itself somewhat imperfect, making it difficult even for an RTÉ insider to ascertain exactly what survives of Séamus' Irish TV work. The Ennis-related episodes of the shows *Ag Déanamh Ceoil*, *The Humours Of Donnybrook* and *Ballad Session*, for example, did not appear in a search of the database, although (as attested by clips online) they clearly survive. Nevertheless, through a combination of odd items on YouTube and gleanings

from the database, what follows is a listing of surely most of Séamus' surving RTÉ appearances.

Ballad Session
Tx: 1/1/63 / Prod: Kevin Sheldon / Presenter: Seán Mac Réamoinn
Duration: 23:04

Presented by Séamus' erstwhile RÉ Outside Broadcast colleague, this seems to be a stray survivor from a series. Featuring The Ronnie Drew Ballad Group (subsequently The Dubliners), Bobby Clancy and others, Séamus leads the audience in 'An Poc ar Buile' ('The Mad Puck Goat') which Seán Ó Riada with Ceoltóirí Chualann had recently released on an EP. The show can be viewed online.

Ag Déanamh Ceoil
Tx: 1972 / Presenter: Tony MacMahon

(Translation: *Making Music*) Séamus' blistering performance of 'The Bucks Of Oranmore', viewable online, apparently derives from this show. Another online clip of Noel Hill playing concertina flanked by Séamus is from the same programme.

The Late Late Show
Tx: 23/12/72 / Presenter: Gay Byrne
Duration: 27:23

An Irish music special edition of the long-running talk show, featuring Planxty, The Chieftains and Séamus Ennis. It was rebroadcast on RTÉ on 17/6/02 in a series of six *Late Late Show* specials. A stunning performance of 'Were You At The Rock?' from this show, with Gay Byrne and The Chieftains visible toward the end, can be viewed online.

Rogha: Séamus Ennis
Tx: 5/11/72 / Prod/Dir: Agnes Cogan, Noel Ó Briain
Duration: 15:42

(Translation: *Choice*) This was a weekly series in which noted performers presented their choice of stories or poems in Irish. In this episode, Séamus talks about Labhrás Ó Cadhla, from whom he had collected music. He also performs a number of relevant items: 'Bean Dubh An Ghleanna' and 'Amhrán Na Leabhar' on tin whistle; and the songs 'A Mhichíl Naofa, Glaoimse Ar T'Ainm', 'Bean Dubh An Ghleanna', 'Ar A Ghabhailt Dom Trid An mBaile Beag'.

Miles And Miles Of Music: Séamus Ennis
Tx: 17/3/75 / Prod/Dir: Éamon de Buitléar
Duration: 31:40 / 25:45

A kind of documentary travelogue on Séamus, including scenes revisiting the site of his family home at Jamestown, the IFC archive and Colm Ó Caodháin, the Connemara farmer from whom he collected 212 items in the 1940s. Séamus is also seen in performance on the pipes: in a three-minute sequence with a small audience in a pub he plays 'The Kid On The Mountain' (his father's arrangement) and 'The Mist On The Mountain', a tune he collected in the 40s from Pat Cannavan – one of the very few pipers he met during his IFC collecting days.

Later, in footage from a more formal recital, we see two more pieces in full, including 'Pat Ward's Jig'. The RTÉ database gives this programme's duration as 31:40, although a rebroadcast within the traditional music series *Come West Along The Road* (viewable on YouTube) lasted only 25:45. The master copy retained by the de Buitléar family is also the 25-minute one, suggesting an error in the RTÉ database.

An Fear Agus A Chuid Ceoil: Séamus Ennis
Tx: 20/9/75 / Prod/Dir: Seán Cotter / Presenter: Riobard Mac Góráin
Duration: 22:00

(Translation: *The Man And His Music*) One of a series profiling traditional musicians (Tomás Ó Canainn, piper with Na Filí, was also featured in the series). Séamus and Riobard talk in Irish and Séamus performs three piping pieces: 'An Leanbh Sí' (4:00), 'Port Na Giboga' (3:20), 'Fáilte Sinéad De Cathal' (1:55). The episode was filmed on September 5 1975.

Fonn
Tx: 8/7/77 / Prod: Peter Canning / Presenter: Ciarán Mac Mathúna
Duration: 26:45

(Translation: *Eager*) This was Episode 5 in a series and featured Séamus plus The Enniscorthy Group, The Enniscorthy Set Dancers, Jimmy Sinnott, Dónall O'Connor, Denis Doody, Séamus Carroll, Donny Murphy, Máire Claire Breathnach. Séamus has roughly six minutes of airtime, talking about a Pat Phelan painting of himself (Séamus), talking about his pipes and playing two pieces: 'An Gamhain Geal Bán' and 'The Flax In Bloom'.

Proinsias Mac Aonghusa Ag Caint Le: Séamus Ennis
Tx: 11/8/77 / Prod/Dir: Aindreas Ó Gallchoir / Presenter: Proinsias Mac Aonghusa
Duration: 25:40

(Translation: *Proinsias Mac Aonghusa Talking To …*) A studio interview programme, in Irish, with Séamus talking about his life and revealing that he wished he had written a book about it. It was tele-recorded on 20/6/77. Séamus plays a number of items on the pipes throughout, including 'Duke Goran' and 'Bean Dubh a'Ghleanna' and sings 'The Trees (My Bonny Boy Is Young But He's Growing)'.

An Tráchtaireacht: No. 5 – Séamus Ennis
Tx: 3/11/79 / Prod/Dir: Michael Murphy / Presenter: Liam Mac Con Iomaire
Duration: 29:34

(Translation: *The Commentary*) A discussion programme in Irish, with Séamus playing short pieces on the pipes at the beginning and end.

The Humours Of Donnybrook
Tx: 24/1/79 / Presenter: Ciarán Mac Mathúna

One of a series, this episode featured Séamus, Liam O'Flynn and Chieftains fiddler Seán Keane. The episode was recorded on August 1 1978. Whatever else he did on the show, Séamus performed the air 'An Gamhain Geal Bán', which he had collected in the 1940s from Elizabeth Cronin. Rebroadcast at some point on the retrospective RTÉ series on *Come West Along The Road*, this air and 'Fasten The Leg On Her', a tin whistle tune involving Séamus, Seán and Liam, are both viewable online. Donnybrook is the location of the RTÉ studios.

Unidentified solo performance
Tx: ?
Duration: 22:34

This is apparently a solo performance in black and white in an empty studio, dating from some point in the 1970s. It was found in 2011 in an RTÉ regional studio (Colonnade). There is picture up to 10 minutes 24 seconds, then sound only for the remaining 12 minutes.

Hand Me Down
Tx: 21/4/81 / Prod/Dir: Agnes Cogan / Presenter: Doireann Ní Bhriain
Duration: 54:17

The first in a series of six documentaries on Irish traditions and musicians. Séamus is seen in Co. Dublin, Co. Clare and Connemara, talking and making music with a number of his friends, including Liam O'Flynn, Seán Mac Donncha, Martin Talty, Jeaic Mac Donncha and his own daughter Catherine. Séamus is seen performing at the 1980 Lisdoonvarna Festival (around six minutes' worth, at the beginning and end of the programme), at his caravan at Naul, guesting at a piping *tionól* run by Liam O'Flynn at the Willie Clancy Summer School and also playing fiddle in duet with Liam on pipes. There's around 10 minutes' worth of additional footage of Séamus piping throughout the programme. The show was rebroadcast on 10/10/82, in the wake of Séamus' death.

News Dublin
Tx: 8/10/82
Duration: 0:48

Séamus Ennis' funeral: footage of Liam O'Flynn playing at the graveside with Seán Mac Réamoinn and other mourners present.

Ó Bhéal Go Béal: Séamus Ennis, Ina Rothaí Óg Ag Bailiú Ceoil
Tx: 2010 / Prod: Kevin Cummins
Duration: c. 26:00

(Translation: *Word Of Mouth: The Bicycle Diaries Of Séamus Ennis*) A new documentary on Séamus, in a mix of English and Irish (with subtitles), made for RTÉ Irish language channel TG4. Short clips from a number of Séamus' RTÉ appearances and previous documentaries are interspersed with 'dramatic reconstruction' clips of a man wearing 1940s clothing on a bicycle and various talking heads, the most interesting of which is Séamus' son Christopher. Most of the programme is viewable online.

Chapter 11
Willie Clancy: The Minstrel From Clare

During the early 1960s, within the context of the 'folk revival' in America, a number of venerable acoustic blues musicians, legendary by virtue of recordings made in the 1920s or 30s, were tracked down and 're-discovered' by young enthusiasts. Skip James, Son House, Mississippi John Hurt and others were given Indian summers as performers in the new world of vinyl records and college, coffee-house and folk festival gigs. They were bearers of tradition, living links back to the beginnings of a culture that was massively impacting the sound and structure of mainstream rock music at the time.

To a degree, something similar could be said to have been happening, during the same decade, to a rather younger man quietly going about his business in Ireland's equivalent of the Deep South: West Clare. Though born on Christmas Eve 1918, Willie Clancy was a rich resource of traditional music and its lore linking back through oral tradition to the middle of the previous century. Through what Seán Reid described as 'an almost unexampled deed of salvage',[205] Willie had reconstructed – from the flute playing and lilting of his father – much of the repertoire and style of Garrett Barry, who had died nearly 20 years before Willie was born and nearly 40 years before he took up the pipes:

> **Willie**: My father was always talking about the pipes to me and trying to explain the pipes and their various sounds, even while he taught me the whistle, started me off on the whistle when I was about five years old, he was always preaching Garrett Barry. Garrett was the St Patrick of music as far as people in West Clare were concerned. He was the great apostle of the music there. As well as being blind, he was a very talented man. Along with being a great piper he was a wonderful singer. My father used to say, *'As well pleased as I'd be to hear him playing the pipes, I'd prefer to hear him singing'*. … [But] he thought the pipes were the closest thing to the human voice – not so much concert-pitch pipes as the flat-toned pipes. … [He] thought there was something wrong with a fellow's ear if he didn't like the sound of the pipes, he was so fond of them![206]

Willie Clancy would make a small number of commercial recordings in the 1950s and 60s, but his own fame as a piper, singer, whistler and tradition bearer was a word-of-mouth phenomenon. And, like Mississippi John Hurt, much of what resonated across the generations was the gentle, playful, warm and philosophical nature of the man. It was the man as much as his music that would leave such a huge hole at the heart of the Irish traditional world when he died, aged only 54, on January 24 1973.

*

The Willie Clancy story really begins with Garrett Barry and the culture of the travelling piper in the post-famine days of the 19th century. Barry, blinded by chicken pox at the age of four, was born in Inagh, West Clare, in 1847.[*] He played music for his living – one of the few options open to a blind man in the rural Ireland of his time and before – and was a frequent guest at the houses of both Willie's grandparents. He was also a regular guest of the grandparents of Willie's contemporary and friend, fiddler Junior Crehan:

> **Junior Crehan**: [H]e used to travel around to all the towns and villages and people loved him, he was a lovely musician, and they'd keep him for a week. And then he'd go to the country houses and the country pubs … He'd be well looked after everywhere he went. [Even when he was playing during the working day, sitting on a bridge wall by a roadside], people would stand listening. Whatever work they were doing, they would stand listening to the music.[207]

Garrett Barry, strangely, is not among the many noted pipers profiled in Francis O'Neill's *Irish Minstrels And Musicians* (1913). Willie's knowledge came from both his father, who 'could never speak unemotionally about Garrett',[208] and from Hugh Curtin, a piper who had been a pupil of the great man.[†] Tellingly, Willie recalled a maxim his father used, related to Barry, in the context of giving him advice as a youngster learning music:

> **Willie**: His saying was, 'Some of the finest tunes are the simplest; so are some of the finest people,' and to reinforce his point he would refer to Garrett Barry, who could turn a jig into a lament. Indeed, Garrett's saying was, 'My music is not for the feet but for the soul.'[209]

---

[*] Garrett's forename is sometimes given as 'Garret' but more often as 'Garrett'. For the sake of clarity, all references herein will use the latter spelling.
[†] Hugh Curtin's surname is sometimes given as McCurtin or even as Curtain.

A couple of others who knew Garrett Barry, and were by then in their 80s, were interviewed by enthusiasts around 1960. One man, Jack Donoghue, recalled the animated bonhomie between Garrett and a man named 'Mad' Culligan, a shell-shocked veteran of the Crimean War, whose favourite tune was 'Bonaparte's Retreat'. The pair would then talk at length with Jack's father about military history. Jack also recalled that Barry 'was as popular in Kerry as he was in Clare' and had been apprenticed to an unnamed piper in Kerry, who had several pupils and quickly became jealous of Barry's aptitude at learning – 'so he wouldn't give him a chance to hear him play much.'[210] Willie had heard a version of this tale himself, although in his version the jealous piper was Frank Cleary, a Limerick man who lived in Ennis, Co. Clare.

Other fragments of first-hand memory relating to Garrett Barry come from Michael Cunningham. Interviewed by Eugene Lambe in 1961, he recalled the piper as 'a dark black man, thin and worn and little whiskers, and you wouldn't like to be looking at the two eyes he had – like they'd be turned inside out, the Lord save us!' Later, he described Barry as 'a sizeable, clean, hardy man'. Michael recalled throngs of people listening to him at house dances – playing solo reels rather than the ensemble 'flings and polkas' played by the other musicians who would be present.

After Willie Clancy (who was present at the interview) had played for a while, Eugene asked Michael: 'Would that put you in mind of Garrett Barry's playing?' To which the reply was, not unreasonably, 'How the heck could you remember?'[211]

'Politically, he was very emotional and national-minded,' Willie explained of Barry. 'His favourite song – he sang in English and Irish – was one called 'We'll Not Give Up The Old Land Yet Without Another Fight'. His music was his nationalism.'[212]

Willie's father, Gilbert Clancy, who became a noted flautist and singer locally, also playing concertina, had been entranced by Barry's music as a child and would remain so.* Gilbert spent time in America in the 1890s but had returned to Clare a few months before Barry died of cancer, aged 52, on April 6 1899. Spending his last years at an Ennistymon workhouse, Barry was buried at Inagh in an unmarked grave, albeit in a coffin made by Gilbert Clancy. A hundred years later a headstone would be erected.

Tony Kearns and Barry Taylor, in *A Touchstone For The Tradition* (2001), note that there were three other pipers in the area during the late 19th century: John Carroll, Pat Burke and Tom Hehir, the first two of whom were of Gilbert Clancy's generation and all three of whom 'spent many an evening together' with Garrett

---

* Pat Mitchell, curious about how Garrett Barry's repertoire had passed from Barry via Gilbert Clancy to Willie, once asked Willie if his father had been a piper. 'He played them in his head,' Willie replied. 'He could never afford to buy a set.' (*The Dance Music Of Willie Clancy*, 1993)

Barry.[213] John Carroll died a year after Barry, and piping in Clare became a thing of rarity. Traditional music, however, was still a thriving facet of community life:

> **Willie**: Since I was a youngster I was surrounded by music – being in the family, my father and mother, several of the neighbours at the time, played the music. Old people, of course, had told us the old stories associated with the great pipers, the travelling pipers, and fiddlers. Maybe I gave a little too much time to the music and not enough to the book![214]

*

West Clare in those days was far enough away to be an adventure for any willing traveller, but close enough to be attainable. The geography of Clare meant that not only was it relatively isolated in terms of transport links from the rest of Ireland, but even within it there were distinct pockets of population, separated by difficult terrain, and consequently distinct strains of traditional music.*

House dances, where musicians from miles around could gather, were the major platform for music in Clare at that time. Willie had moved on from tin whistle to concert flute and was keen on step-dancing.

> **Willie**: These country dances, where the youth learned from their elders, kept the art of music, dancing, singing and storytelling alive. But what really gave these gatherings the spark of life was the competitive spirit; people tried to best each other in the traditional arts; and as well as this, there was strong competition between the different localities. It all added up to a flourishing musical life.[215]

The Public Dance Halls Act of 1934, bolstering the nefarious influence of the church on Irish life, was designed to stop unlicensed gatherings such as house dances. As Seán Reid observed, it 'practically broke the tradition altogether … the Act broke a link between the generations, and the skills of the older generation were largely lost to the younger, with unfortunate results. … Traditional music was in real danger of extinction.'[216]

Commercially run céilís in parish halls replaced the informal gatherings, encouraging the rise of céilí bands – a controversial substitute for less formal groupings. Growing emigration was another problem. At one point, as Junior Crehan

---

* The fiddle tradition of East Clare, for example, informs the most magical of Irish fiddlers of the present era, Martin Hayes, whose own father, P.J. Hayes, was at one time a member of The Tulla Céilí Band alongside Willie Clancy.

recalled, 'there was no one but myself … I used to nearly cry. Nowhere to go, no one to meet, no sets in the houses, nothing left but the hall!'[217]

Willie's epiphany with the uilleann pipes (by then a very rare and expensive instrument) came in 1936, on the road not to Damascus but to Spanish Point, on the Clare coast, for the annual local horse races. Travelling piper Johnny Doran was plying his trade among the crowds, and it is sometimes said that this was the first time Willie Clancy had actually heard the sound of the instrument.* Hearing Johnny playing, Willie and his friend Martin Talty ran up the road toward the sound. Entranced, they came back to Johnny's caravan near Quilty that night, then borrowed bicycles, bought a tent and started followed him around as he travelled elsewhere in the county.

Martin, who had known Willie from childhood, recalled the occasion as if it had been fated:

> **Martin Talty**: It was obvious from the beginning that he was destined to be a piper, as for years before he ever saw the instrument he would talk for hours on Garrett Barry and all the stories his father … had told him about the great piper of the last century. I was with him when he first saw the pipes being played by the late Johnny Doran, and straightaway a friendship was struck up between boy and man, which culminated in Johnny becoming his first teacher – and what an apt pupil Willie turned out to be. In a very short time he had incorporated the intricate virtuosity of the master with the flowing, meaningful and racy music of his father, and produced an almost super-human expression of music, which embodied everything that is really part of the true Gaelic soul of Ireland.[218]

At that time there were still people alive who had heard both Garrett Barry and Johnny Doran, the new kid in town.

> **Junior Crehan**: I used to hear the old people talk about Garrett, the

---

* This may not be entirely true. In his 1972 *Dál gCais* interview, Willie says: 'All this time, of course [between the age of five and losing his teeth, thus losing the ability to play flute effectively], I had been listening to the pipes, and with the tradition of piping so strong in the locality, and so many good players around, it was natural that I should take to playing them.' While the Garrett Barry-era tradition of piping in Clare was still fondly recalled in the 1920s and 30s, no other piper from the area immediately prior to Willie Clancy is ever referred to, bar Hugh Curtin, who lived near Miltown Malbay and played several instruments to a certain degree. It seems likely that Willie was referring to itinerant pipers like Johnny and Felix Doran as the good players 'around'.

wonderful player he was. Lovely at airs and mostly slip jigs, hop-jigs. He'd play a lot of them. There was a blacksmith over here, Jack Tracey. Jack used to follow Garrett all over the country. Jack was at the races when Johnny Doran [played], and he was mad about Johnny. So I asked him:

'Jack,' I said, 'you heard both of them. Which would you say was the best piper?'

''Tis very hard to answer that question,' he said, 'but there was more *gramhár* sound in Garrett's pipes. I think the low chanter made a more lonesome sound, like.'

That's the only point he made on it.[219]

Seán Reid, a Donegal-born traditional music enthusiast who had been working in Dublin since 1934 – befriending pipers Leo Rowsome, John and Tommy Potts and Tommy Reck – took a job in Ennis, West Clare, in 1937. He was soon acquainted with the area's musicians, helped by some introductions from Leo Rowsome. One of his work colleagues, Joe Leyden, told him of the legend of Garrett Barry and also had interesting news of piping in the land of the living:

Seán Reid: He mentioned the fact that a travelling piper regularly visited West Clare, and that he was 'in a caravan parked near Crow's Bridge, between Kilmaley and Inagh'. This was Johnny Doran, whom I was to meet sometime later at Joe's house. During the course of our conversation, Johnny Doran spoke of 'a young fellow in Miltown Malbay, the likes I have never heard as a flute player'. This was the first I heard of Willie Clancy, whom I was to meet the next year at a feis in Miltown Malbay. So I began my friendship with two of the best pipers this century has seen. Almost 10 years later, I was to go with Willie Clancy and Tommy Potts to the bedside of a seriously injured Johnny Doran. We brought with us the proceeds of several benefit concerts and there, by the bedside, Willie Clancy buckled on the pipes and played some farewell tunes for Johnny Doran.* The matron, a rigid disciplinarian type, who didn't take kindly to the music of the pipes, cleared us from the place, but not before Tommy had given her some abuse.[220]

While Johnny Doran was not a good teacher – 'Willie had to deduce a lot of what Johnny was doing,' Seán Reid recalled[221] – his influence was profound:

---

* Johnny Doran died in Dublin in 1950, two years after a wall had collapsed on him.

Willie: He made the greatest impact on me. It was the pure beauty of his music rather than his piping that impressed me. In Johnny Doran, feeling was all-important; he could get into the spirit of a tune and put it across beautifully. As someone said of him, 'He had nothing less than a shower of fingers.' He came from a long line of pipers, and could play the full set by the age of seven. He was always very welcome in West Clare, especially around Quilty. There, the people used to collect enough money to keep him for a week whenever he came around the area. He was a truly professional musician; piping was his life; nothing else mattered. ... I'm sure he had an influence on many pipers, but who could hope to imitate him? It was a common saying among pipers that he was put into the world to discourage all other pipers.[222]

Fiddler Bobby Casey, who would later make his reputation on the Irish pub scene in London, was another of Willie's friends from Clare. Bobby's uncle Thady, who had danced to Garrett Barry as a child, had taught Willie step-dancing, while Willie would credit Bobby's father, Scully, also a fiddler, as another significant influence on his own playing: 'His style had a flow and melancholy about it, very like that of Doran. His playing was full of feeling.'[223]

At this stage Willie's first instrument was still flute. He could only become a piper if he had a set of pipes. In 1938, Johnny's brother Felix Doran, also a travelling piper, would deliver the missing piece of the jigsaw:

Willie: I was waiting for them for about 10 years before that, but of course there was no option in those days – too expensive, couldn't afford it. ... Felix gave me a practice set when he was camped out near the graveyard outside Miltown. And I was the happiest man ever came in that road that night with the auld practice set, tattered though it was![224]

The chanter of this tattered set had been made by Leo Rowsome. Most of the old sets around Clare had been made by the Moloney brothers, Thomas and Andrew, of Kilrush, who had operated around the middle years of the 19th century. Willie acquired the remnants of a Moloney set from Hugh Curtin. The first full set Willie acquired was in 1942 or '43, a set made by another 19th century great, Maurice Coyne – although, never entirely satisfied with it, he later traded it in to Leo Rowsome for a new concert-pitch Rowsome set.

Junior Crehan: As a direct result of listening to Johnny Doran, Willie

Clancy took up the uilleann pipes. ... He followed Doran a lot, and I suppose Doran gave him a good few tips, because Willie used to be in the caravan with him day and night. I remember [how I happened] to break a bolt on the mowing machine, and I untackled the horse and went to Miltown on a bicycle to get a new bolt. Up from the crosses of Annagh there was a kind of a little bit of commonage, and Doran was set up there. There was Willie, sitting on the steps going up to the caravan, and Doran sitting up higher, and they having a set of pipes each. And my trouble was to have that strip of hay cut before nightfall. I laughed and said: 'Fine it is for you, Willie, that the hay doesn't bother you, or the cows or anything.'[225]

Pat Mitchell, who knew Willie well, noted that he voraciously absorbed influences: 'At one time he fell in love with Ted Furey's banjo playing, to the extent that he left Johnny Doran to follow Ted round Dublin.'[226]

Testifying further to Willie's fascination with the music itself, as opposed to purely piping, and with getting at the soul of it rather than focusing on technical aspects, Seán Reid later observed that, 'satisfied with nothing short of perfection, Willie could get the ultimate from any musical instrument he handled. I can recall him playing a slow air on his violin before he had made much headway as regards technique, and the tone he extracted and the delicate shades of expression were remarkable.'[227]

Willie would develop a keen interest in piping archaeology, both for the instruments themselves and, later in life, for historical recordings of their players. When he eventually heard the c. 1899 Gaelic League wax cylinder recordings of Kerry piper Mící 'Cumbá' O'Sullivan, for example, he 'declared that if he had heard such playing in his youth, he would have spent his life trying to make all his music sound like it'.[228] In the meantime, as a fast-learning piper in the 1940s and 50s, he would often scour junk shops, particularly during the 1950s when he lived first in Dublin and then London, for old sets of pipes. He would also borrow sets from friends, including a Moloney set and a Rowsome set, both from Seán Reid. Consequently, a great variety of pipes in a variety of keys can be heard on Willie's recordings.*

It has sometimes been said that Séamus Ennis was the first person to record Willie Clancy, but this seems not to be the case. Willie was recorded for the Irish Folklore Commission (IFC) in 1947 by Kevin Danaher – the man who would

---

* For example, on the superb 1947–72 double CD anthology *The Gold Ring* (RTÉ, 2009), Willie can be heard playing: Seán Reid's Moloney Brothers set and Leo Rowsome set; an Egan set; a Taylor Brothers set; and others of uncertain provenance. The pitches range between B flat and D.

record, that same year, the only session by Johnny Doran.* According to Willie's own testimony, he didn't meet Séamus Ennis until Séamus came to the area as an Outside Broadcast Officer for Radio Éireann (RÉ), collecting material for a programme called *Behind The Cliffs Of Moher*. Séamus recorded Willie on that occasion, which was November 5 1949.

We must presume that Séamus was unaware of Willie during his tenure as an IFC field recordist (1942–47). In one interview, Willie casually dated the RÉ programme meeting with Séamus to 1947, but we cannot doubt the accuracy of Peter Browne and Pat Mitchell's November 1949 date, obtained via access to RÉ archives, in their notes to the posthumous Clancy anthology *The Gold Ring* (RTÉ, 2009). Mitchell notes that *Behind The Cliffs Of Moher* was 'almost certainly the first time Willie was recorded for broadcast purposes'.[229] It would not be the last: much of *The Gold Ring* comprises sessions recorded, often by Ciarán Mac Mathúna, for RÉ and its successor RTÉ, spanning 1960–72.†

Following Danaher's 1947 session, the IFC recorded Willie again in 1954; Séamus next recorded him in the mid-1950s, while collecting for the BBC. Some of the IFC material and one piece from *Behind The Cliffs Of Moher*, 'The Plains of Boyle', can be heard on *The Gold Ring*.

If we accept that Ennis and Clancy did not meet until November 1949, Pat Mitchell's speculation that one of the four IFC 1947 recordings on *The Gold Ring* ('The Groves') had come to Willie direct from Séamus must be incorrect. Mitchell noted that 'The Groves', a hornpipe, closely resembled the standard setting in Francis O'Neill's *Music Of Ireland*, while the piping techniques suggested Ennis. Regardless of who Willie's source may have been, the tune stood out among these four early pieces (the others being sets including 'Garrett Barry's Jig', 'Garrett Barry's Reel' and 'The Gold Ring') in *not* bearing the obvious DNA of Garrett Barry.

Indeed, Mitchell goes on to mention from his own experience an amusing aside from Willie's father, Gilbert – who, after hearing Ennis play his version of 'The Gold Ring', akin to the 'standard' O'Neill setting, 'turned to Willie and asked, 'What's that oul' thing he played?"[230]

For a couple of years during the late 40s, Willie played flute with The Tulla Céilí Band, with Seán Reid on piano and Paddy O'Donoghue (an East Clare man, 10 years

---

* Willie won the Oireachtas competition on pipes in 1947. As Ríonach Uí Ógáin notes in *Going To The Well For Water* (2009), recordings were often made at Oireachtas events by Danaher and other IFC staff.
† Mac Mathúna's first recording trip to Clare was in 1955, and his frequent broadcasts of Clare musicians have been credited with establishing the notoriety and national reputations of Clancy and others from the county.

younger than Willie) on pipes. The Tulla won the céilí band competition at Féile na Mumhan at Cork in 1948. At the same event, a one-off unit of Willie (flute), Paddy O'Donoghue (pipes) and Bobby Casey (fiddle) won the trio competition. Willie gave up the flute, seemingly in the early 50s, when the loss of his teeth made playing effectively impossible. He gave his flute to Martin Talty, but not before making a rather ignominious broadcast with the band for Radio Éireann.

> **Seán Reid**: It was in the summer of 1948, after winning the céilí band competition at Féile Luimní [in Limerick] for the third time in a row and Corn Na Mumhan in Cork, that the Tulla band decided to seek a broadcast. Accordingly, I got in touch with Radio Éireann and the audition took place in Cork. … In due course I was notified that we had passed … and a 15-minute broadcast date was set in the middle of September. … [When we got to the RÉ studio in Dublin], Fathna Ó hAnnracháin, Director of Music, did not like the look of us. He complained that this was not the band he had auditioned, that the inclusion of an accordion [accordionist Joe Cooley having been unavailable to audition] would give it a completely different sound, et cetera, et cetera. He set about arranging us in a wide semicircle around one large microphone. Here was another problem. I realised that this would make us lose contact, as we had been in the habit of a compact group, so I took charge and arranged them all beside the piano, facing the microphone, with the four fiddles [in] front, the four flutes immediately behind and the accordion in the rear. At this stage, Mr Ó hAnnracháin voiced his displeasure and assured us in no uncertain terms that if we did not do it well, it would be a long time before we got another broadcast. Fair play to him, he kept his word and [it] was all of 25 years before we got in again.[231]

Radio was a powerful, proprietorial and prescriptive institution in those days, both in Ireland and in Britain. The Tulla Céilí Band were far from being The Rolling Stones of East Clare, turning up to urinate in the car park of Radio Éireann: these were respectful men from the country in the dark suits and severe haircuts of the day, simply looking to deliver their best performance at a privileged opportunity. It would be some years yet before the national broadcaster broadcast much of any culture reflecting the nation.

> **Willie**: Back in the 40s, you would be lucky to hear 15 minutes of Irish music per week on our national radio. But then Séamus Ennis, together

with Seán Mac Réamoinn and Aindreas Ó Gallchóir, began to get to work … That was the first step forward, and this pioneering work was followed up by Ciarán Mac Mathúna, who scoured the country in search of tunes and ballads. The work of these people made Irish music more accessible to the people who were interested in it.[232]

*

A carpenter by trade, Willie moved to Dublin to work in 1951. He had already, though, been learning from Leo Rowsome at the Dublin School of Music. Surviving roll books from Leo's classes show that Willie was enrolled in 1950 (presumably travelling in from Clare), 1951, 1954 and 1955. The inclusion of the latter two years is curious, given that Willie had moved to London in 1953, but conceivably he returned home for a month or two each year and fitted in tuition.

'I went to school to him, in a sort of way,' as Willie later put it shortly after Leo's death. 'He ran a piping school in Dublin, and I used to go in for the last half hour and we would play a few tunes together. He was one of the finest players I have known.'[233]

A surviving letter from Willie to Leo dated February 27 1948 shows that the pair were already friendly by then. It would be entirely natural that Willie would have sought Leo out for advice, given the latter's prominence through his frequent RÉ broadcasts. Indeed, around this time Willie was an occasional member of Leo's piping quartet, along with Tommy Reck, Seán Seery and Leo's son Leon. While the letter is mostly concerned with Willie enquiring after reeds and discussing a chanter that needed repairing, it reveals a familiar tone and shows Willie to have been bowled over by Leo's playing the night before, presumably on a broadcast:

Dear Leo,

It is about time I wrote you a line. Well Leo you know I don't like this job of writing – Anyhow, how are you going on – There is no cause to ask from the playing you did last night. I never heard anything like it in my life before, or can you account for it yourself. We were all listening here – We said the march and the air and jig were beautiful, but by God, when you struck up 'The Bucks' and 'The Fermoy Lass', I don't know what to say to you after this and the pipes were going grand to crown it all.[234]

Willie was interviewed and recorded (piping, whistling and singing) in Clare, probably in 1952 or '53, by Séamus Ennis, who had by now moved on from RÉ to become a folk music collector for the BBC.* Willie and Séamus would have more opportunities to spend time together when, in 1953, following in the footsteps of his friend Bobby Casey, Willie moved to London to work in the construction industry.

Writing a profile of Willie based on an interview shortly before he died (though containing no direct quotation), Séamus Mac Mathúna noted:

> He has many interesting recollections of the London period, and of music at 'The Laurel Tree' and 'The Bedford Arms' with Michael Gorman, Martin Byrnes, Bobby Casey, Roger Sherlock and many more fine musicians who had to take the boat.[235]

Sadly, we don't get to hear any of these recollections. For a couple of years he shared a cramped room in Camden Town with Bobby Casey, Sligo flautist Roger Sherlock and Galway fiddler Martin Byrnes, for an exorbitant rent of 30 shillings a week each, as recalled by Roger Sherlock.[236] Glimpses of Willie's time in London, however, are recalled by English musician Reg Hall.

Born in 1933, Reg would go on to become involved as both a musical participant (on piano or melodeon) in and historian of the London-based Irish music scene, as well as being active in the English country dancing world, recording throughout the 60s and occasionally beyond as a member of Bob Davenport & The Rakes (specialising in Northumberland music), accompanying the Bampton Morris and holding down

---

* Several pieces by Willie, collected by Séamus, are held on disc at the National Sound Archive/British Library, but bear the date 'August 1960' (as do various other of Séamus' field recordings, from both Ireland and the Hebrides) which is patently wrong, probably reflecting an administrative date relating to the library filing of the items. See the 'Séamus Ennis At The BBC' chapter for details. The BBC Written Archive Centre holds a single contract for 'William Clancy', dated 23/2/61. It gives Willie's correspondence address as c/o 'Tom Quailey esq., Miltown Malbay' (presumably publican Tom Queally). The contract affirms payment of 20 guineas for 22 items, 36 minutes' duration, of 'Irish folk songs' for the Recorded Programmes Permanent Library. The troublesome aspect of this is the 1961 date. The BBC Permanent Library folk music recording project, to which Séamus Ennis and Peter Kennedy as full-time field recordists had been the principal contributors, ended in 1957. There being no separate contract extant for the 78rpm discs of BBC-recorded Clancy material at the National Sound Archive (to which Séamus' name as collector is attached), one must conjecture that the 'August 1960' and 'February 1961' dates on the discs and contract, respectively, refer to the same recording session – which can only have taken place in the early 50s, surely before Willie moved to London. Séamus certainly collected in Clare for the BBC before the end of the Permanent Library project, as *Radio Times* notes that he talks about this during an episode of *As I Roved Out* in 1958. We know from another *Radio Times* reference that he and the series' editor, Marie Slocombe, collected in Connemara (in the next-door county, Galway) in 1954.

a day job as a probation officer. He and Bill Leader – a freelance recording engineer who was introduced to traditional music through Reg and the London-Irish scene – would collaborate on several Irish and London-Irish music projects in the 1960s, including Topic Records' 1968 LP *Paddy In The Smoke*, documenting several of the key people on the scene.*

Having been a jazz fan since his early teens, Reg was aware of the American music collector Alan Lomax. Following his arrival in England in 1950, Lomax swiftly became a regular presence on the BBC, with broadcasts focusing on indigenous music.

> **Reg Hall**: I was very surprised to find out that he was interested in the traditional music of these islands. At the same time, there was what has now been called the 'square dance boom', which was the English Folk Dance & Song Society (EFDSS) putting on country dancing all over the country, and I got caught up with that. So by 1955 I'd heard traditional music on the radio, which Alan Lomax, Hamish Henderson [and] Peter Kennedy had collected. I'd heard Irish music on the radio – Johnny Doherty, Mickey Doherty, these people who were recorded in the 40s and 50s. So by 1955 I was actually seeing Irish musicians in London, and I started playing with them.
>
> Me and my mate Michael Plunkett … we both were accepted and we were essentially the only English people who took the slightest bit of interest in Irish music. We'd go into a pub and be the only English people in the pub all night – probably the only ones to be in that week. We went to Camden Town; we also went to Cricklewood, to Kilburn. We followed the music round, we hunted it out. In the end I was hunting music out in Woolworth, Wandsworth, Plumstead …

The Bedford Arms in Camden Town, especially, was an intriguingly otherworldly place at that time, with a frisson of danger about it. Jenny Barton, who ran folk nights at the Troubadour in Earl's Court from 1958 to 1964, went there once only:

> A girl on her own in those days didn't go to those places. They were fairly rough. Somebody got pitched out on his head one night and died. If you said you were going on your own to the Bedford, there'd be looks – somebody would say, 'No, no – I'll come with you.' So someone took me to the Bedford.

---

* Among Reg Hall's achievements is Topic's ongoing *Voice Of The People* series of richly annotated thematic CDs of traditional music from around the British Isles. He was awarded the Gold Badge of the EFDSS in 1987 and the Gradam Cheoil musician's award from the Irish language broadcaster TG4 in 2009.

Willie Clancy, labouring in London during the mid-50s, would often play at a neighbouring Irish pub, the Laurel Tree, favoured by pipers – what few there were. The instrument and its players were a rarity in London at that time:

> **Reg Hall**: In my subsequent interviews [with Irish musicians], I spoke to lots and lots of old country players whose only experience of piping was Leo Rowsome on the radio. I'm talking about before the war. At the end of the 30s and into the war, musicians that I knew, living in London, who were living in Ireland then, only knew of uilleann pipes from the radio, from Rowsome. But some of them experienced the Travellers. I knew about five or six musicians who used to hear either Johnny Doran or Felix Doran when they were on their rounds.*

Bill Leader, living in Camden during the 50s and similarly fascinated with Irish music, would go on to make a splendid album with Willie Clancy in 1967 – by which point he (Bill) had become a prolific and skilled recorder of folk and traditional music of all shades – but, unlike his friend Reg, he never met Willie during his 1950s period in London.

> **Reg Hall**: I went and heard him in the Laurel Tree playing with, I suppose, [fiddler] Bobby Casey. I can't remember – but I remember going in [to] the Laurel Tree and hearing him play. And we saw him playing in the Soho Fair, which was playing in the street with Michael Gorman, and we followed him round.

His experience, however, was not to be limited to that of a listener only:

> **Reg Hall**: Willie was the best Irish musician I ever played with. I played the melodeon [in 1956] for a little group of dancers in North London who were run by Ewan MacColl's wife Jean, Kirsty's mother. I went and played two or three times on the understanding that they sometimes had Irish musicians

---

* Reg Hall: 'Willie Clancy was inspired by seeing Johnny Doran; Martin Byrnes, the fiddle player, saw Johnny Doran; Tom Sheridan, who played the pipes in London, was from Mullingar and he saw Felix Doran, as a boy of 13. Paddy McLynn, my great pal, who was in London from 1950 and played more or less every night of the week for years and years – he lived in a village in County Longford where Felix Doran used to come and used to play in the village, and then he'd be invited in the McLynn house and be given bread and jam and a cup of tea, and he'd play some tunes on the pipes.'

play for them. So I'd been going three or four weeks, and one day she said:

'Oh, we've got a little concert coming up, we're going to be playing a social for the Labour Party in East Ham Town Hall.'

It was a dance, but essentially we were a cabaret act.

'And by the way,' she says, 'we've got some Irish musicians playing. You'll play with them, won't you?'

And I said yeah. So when I turn up the day before for the rehearsal, Michael Gorman turns up, who I was on nodding terms with; he vaguely knew who I was. And in comes [fiddler] Martin Byrnes and Willie Clancy. I didn't understand a word they said! Martin Byrnes more or less ignored me, and I think Willie Clancy couldn't understand how my melodeon would be in tune with his pipes. Anyway, we sat down and we played the required tunes for the dancing. And the next day we did the show – but then Margaret Barry turned up! So, sitting in the middle of the floor, in this whacking great big dance hall, was me on the left, Michael Gorman, Martin Byrnes, Willie Clancy, then Margaret Barry – and we just played for 20 minutes. They were highly suspicious of me the day before – well, Michael Gorman wasn't – but the next day we got on fine, had drinks together. But, significantly, when I met both of them years later, neither of them remembered me!

While Willie would only remain in London for three to four years, with regular trips back home, the period would bring him into the world of commercial recording, albeit in a suitably homespun fashion. In 1955, Ewan MacColl recorded both Willie and Margaret Barry & Michael Gorman – a hugely popular banjo/vocal and fiddle duo on the Camden scene – at his home in Croydon, using a huge Ferrograph machine he'd obtained from the BBC. The notes to the ensuing 10-inch album credited to both men, *Irish Jigs, Reels & Hornpipes*, issued in the USA on Folkways Records in 1956, hogwashed the public by claiming that it been 'recorded in Ireland'. Though it contained no solo piping, this was Willie Clancy's first record release. Two further Clancy solo tunes and two duets with Gorman from the same Croydon session would slip out on a Topic EP, *Irish Pipe & Fiddle Tunes*, in 1963.

Kearns and Taylor speculate that the presence of Willie's two solo pieces ('Hardiman The Fiddler' and 'The Chanter's Song') were 'perhaps the first solo commercial recording to be made by a Clare-born traditional musician'.[237] This might be true – although, as far as release dates go, it would be beaten to the marketplace by three sets of tunes Willie would record in Dublin for Gael Linn in 1957 (see below).

Séamus Mac Mathúna (1973): [T]he music and the musicians were held in greater esteem in Cricklewood and Camden Town than in Dublin or most Irish towns, where gombeen publicans were wont to 'show the door' to any musician who dared to strike up a tune. But the Fleadh era was already bringing a change. 1956 saw Willie back in Ennis for Fleadh Cheoil na hÉireann, and the following year saw him back home, to stay, in Miltown Malbay.[238]

*

Willie's impetus to return, in 1957, had been the death of his father in August. But, as Mac Mathúna had pointed out, things were beginning to change in Ireland for traditional music in general and for music in Clare in particular. Comhaltas Ceoltóirí Éireann (CCÉ), founded in 1951, had introduced the concept of regional and national *fleadhanna*: competition events designed to promote and nurture traditional music and musicians. In 1956 the All-Ireland Fleadh (Fleadh Cheoil na hÉireann) was held in Ennis, Co. Clare; in 1957 the first County Clare Fleadh was held. Radio Éireann personality Ciarán Mac Mathúna had, in 1955, begun making trips to Clare to record its musicians for programmes including *A Job Of Journeywork* – a feature on indigenous music inspired, apparently, by the success of Séamus Ennis' BBC series *As I Roved Out*.

Added to all this was a surge in the popularity of céilí bands. These were controversial amongst commentators on traditional music both at the time[*] and subsequently, because they combined flutes, fiddles and occasionally pipes with non-indigenous instruments including the piano or the accordion, the banjo and – worst of all – the drum kit. Barry Taylor (historian of Clare's Tulla Céilí Band) makes the argument that it was a case, in the wake of the Dance Halls Act, of necessity being the mother of invention:

> When traditional dance and its music was as its lowest ebb in the late 1940s and early 1950s, it was not Radio Éireann or Comhaltas Ceoltóirí Éireann who were its saviour. Rather, it was the musicians and dancers who carried on their traditions, albeit under different social conditions, and in a manner suited to the epoch. Ultimately, it was the céilí band and céilí dance which ensured that the tradition maintained its purpose, integrity and vitality. It is not overstating the case to say that it was the tenacity of a few musicians, often vilified by supposed experts, who ensured that Irish dance music has survived as a living force and not simply an object in a museum.[239]

---

[*] Séamus Ennis, for example, writing in his field diary entry for 14/11/45 (while in Limerick collecting for the IFC), makes a couple of passing remarks about the then new trend, lamenting 'the breakneck speed of present day céilí bands' and the new-fangled dances associated with them, at the expense of older, traditional dance styles. (*Going To The Well For Water*, 2009)

In Clare, the 1950s and beyond saw an exciting rivalry between The Kilfenora Céilí Band and The Tulla Céilí Band, who would regularly fight it out for first and second places in the fleadhs. A series of 78rpm discs recorded by The Tulla Céilí Band for HMV in 1956 (including one tune delightfully titled 'The Quarrelsome Piper') were reputedly the first commercial recordings of traditional music made in Ireland since the 1930s. Two years later, the band recorded an LP, *All Ireland Champions '57*, for the New York based Dublin Record Company.

Miltown Malbay, not to be outdone, formed its own unit, The Laichtín Naofa Céilí Band, which came third to the two usual suspects in its first event, a Fleadh at Loughrea in 1955. Willie Clancy joined his friends Junior Crehan and Martin Talty in the band on his return from London. Although lasting only into the early 60s, the Laichtín Naofa also had the opportunity, after winning 1957's Oireachtas competition, to record an LP for the Dublin Record Company, *Come To An Irish Dance Party*.

Commercial recordings never seemed to be much of a priority with Willie. That said, between 1957 and 1961, Dublin label Gael Linn released a series of 20 purely traditional 78rpm discs, with performers mostly from the west of Ireland, and Willie was among them. He was featured solo on three sides, on discs split with three other performers, all released in 1960 but seemingly recorded in 1957. These discs are probably his rarest releases.

*

Unlike Leo Rowsome or Séamus Ennis, Willie's livelihood was not music. He made his living around Miltown as a carpenter from the late 50s until his death in 1973, but a huge amount of his spare time was spent making music and entertaining the increasing numbers of traditional music enthusiasts who sought him out.

'There must have been times when he was annoyed at invasions on his privacy,' wrote one commentator, 'but he said that he always tried to be courteous because he was conscious of all the help the visitors were to the town of Miltown Malbay.'[240]

Willie married Dóirín Healy in 1962. They had a son who died in infancy the following year. Some have suggested that, behind his famous playfulness and good humour, there was a sadness. It would be remarkable if the various hardships in his life had not left some scars, however deep. Breandán Breathnach later wrote, in the notes to Willie's Topic LP of 1967, that the qualities in Clare music which had so captivated the 19th century collector George Petrie were its combination of sorrow with buoyancy of spirit, a vigour in the face of adversity. These qualities can certainly be heard in the music associated with Garrett Barry and his champion, Willie Clancy.

The incessant string of cold-callers on Willie's doorstep, however, came not to share in sorrow but to be uplifted. And Willie always did his best to meet that expectation. One periodic visitor gave back as much as he received:

> **Dóirín Clancy**: Willie'd be thrilled to see him – he'd even know his knock on the door. One morning he came with Finbar Furey ... about nine o'clock. I think it was a Saturday morning and Willie wasn't up, wasn't out of bed. And the door knocked and he said to me, *'That's Séamus Ennis!'* And he hopped out. He was usually pretty slow, but he wasn't that time – down the stairs to welcome Séamus and Finbar.* Of course, I didn't appear at all, knowing what was in store ... But as I went down, I heard Finbar saying to Willie, 'She's coming down the stairs!'[241]

During the mid-60s, Bill Leader had been recording a huge amount of pure English, Irish and Scottish traditional music for Topic, Transatlantic and occasionally other labels, in tandem with recording artists of a more fashionably bohemian, commercial nature. On the Irish side of his recording activities, there were a couple of Paddy Tunney albums for Topic; albums with 1966 All-Ireland winners The Glenside Céilí Band and Manchester-based Irish vocal group The Grehan Sisters for Transatlantic; a torrent of records involving The Dubliners (before they defected to Major Minor and started having UK chart hits) for Decca and subsequently Transatlantic; and an album of dance tunes by fiddler Jimmy Power on the Bounty label. And then, in 1967, Bill took his portable Revox machine on a field trip to the west of Ireland:

> **Bill Leader**: Field trip is a rather grandiose term, but [the idea] was to travel around. Bert Lloyd [at Topic] had set up one or two people who should be visited and recorded if possible. So we went along the north coast of Galway Bay for a bit and on into Clare, and we recorded singers, mainly singers, and also Willie Clancy.

In visiting Willie Clancy, even with a tape recorder, Bill Leader was but the latest in a line of piping pilgrims:

> **Reg Hall**: In September 1965, [fiddler] Jimmy Power and I went to stay with his mother in Waterford, for a week. And one night he said, 'Tomorrow we'll go and see Willie Clancy.' So we drove from Dublin to Miltown, and

---

* Finbar Furey: 'Willie Clancy, to me, was one of the greatest pipers I ever heard. He was like a hybrid between the settler style, if you like, and the Traveller style. ... He developed this beautiful style, which is now known as the Clare style of piping.'

unexpectedly arrived on Willie's doorstep at six o'clock at night. His wife was a bit angry about it, but Willie was lovely. He said, 'Give me a chance to have a meal, and I'll see you in the pub at eight o'clock.' And so we went to the pub and it was Jimmy, me, Willie Clancy and another piper, his pal who played with him locally in the céilí band. The four of us sat in this back room of the pub for the whole evening. I'd had correspondence with him over that EP on Topic [*Irish Pipe & Fiddle Tunes*, 1963] – I wrote the notes – and he remembered the letter. But he didn't remember playing with me all those years before. But then, all English people look alike, don't they!

Bill Leader: I contacted Willie, and he explained that his mother had just died [in May 1967]. He realised that I'd come all the way from England to record him, so he had decided that it would be more seemly to do the recording away from the town, and avoid people thinking he was not respecting his mother's memory. Willie played the tunes that he wanted to play, while I tried to find the best mic placement to pick up [the] sound of the beast ... You've just got to figure out where you're going to put [them] – if you've only got one mic, particularly, which a lot of my other recordings were, or two if it was stereo. The pipes had a particular problem, because there are so many mechanical valves and things going on, you've got to be careful not to get much mechanical noise in – as much reed noise and as few flapping valves and wheezing bellows as possible.

The trick was to capture the instrument's character, but not too much of it:

Bill Leader: There's a difference between being in a room with someone, when you can sort out what you want to pay attention to, whereas on a recording you get what you're given. And if the perspective of what you're given is out of true, then there's no easy way of [dealing with it].

The recording was made at a pub in Carraroe, Co. Galway, a two-and-a-half-hour drive from Miltown:

Reg Hall: It would have been very disapproved of if Bill had gone and recorded Willie in Miltown, or if it was known. So they had to get in the car, and they drove to somewhere in Galway – 30 or 40 miles out of the area, somewhere he wasn't particularly known.

Most of the recordings of Willie Clancy made by Bill were released in September of the same year as *The Minstrel From Clare*.* It was essentially Willie's first album – his first solo release and his first long-format release of any kind in Britain – and a superb representation of his magic and artistry. A Topic advert in *Melody Maker* declared him: 'The 'Compleat Musician', virtuoso performer of the Uillean [sic] pipes, superb tin whistle player and no mean singer.'[242]

Six of the album's 14 tracks were piping tunes, four were songs (largely whimsical, and occasionally with the sound of chickens in the background) and four were whistle items.

> **Reg Hall**: When we went to see him in Miltown, he and Jimmy did the playing, but he saw I had a tin whistle, and it was an old one with a metal fipple at the end. He took a fancy to it, so I gave it to him. I assume ever after that he was playing that tin whistle.

The Minstrel From Clare would be the only Willie Clancy solo album released in his lifetime. While Bill Leader remains extremely modest about his contribution to traditional music, he admits to a certain feeling of stoicism and pride during his efforts, which must surely include those recordings of Willie Clancy at his free and easy best, in that Galway pub during the 'Summer of Love':

> **Bill Leader**: There were occasions when you were quite convinced that what you were doing was worthwhile, whether anybody else would ever agree with you. It happened quite a lot, travelling around and recording singers from Scotland, for instance, who would perform particular feats of genius, and you'd be thinking, 'I'm glad we managed to capture that.' If nobody else really hears it, it is *there*, it will be heard by someone sometime.

Seemingly a month or two after Bill Leader's visit,† Robin Dransfield, a great young English traditional singer from Yorkshire (who would end up recording for and even, briefly, working for Bill in the early 70s) also made the pilgrimage to Miltown:

---

* Three further tracks from the session were released in May 1969 on the Topic 'Various Artists' LP *The Breeze From Erin: Irish Folk Music On Wind Instruments*: two piping tracks ('An Phis Fhliuch' and 'Táimse Im Chodladh') and one set of reels on whistle ('The Morning Dew/ The Woman Of The House'). Although the LP's catalogue number implies that it appeared in 1968, it was mentioned as a new release in a May 1969 *Melody Maker* news item.
† There is still the problem, with Robin's tale, of the appropriate mourning period for Willie's mother. It's not impossible that Robin's trip could have been a year earlier.

Robin Dransfield: Me, my brother Barry [a multi-instrumentalist and singer] and three of my mates, we all came over to Dublin in two cars. We camped at Dún Laoghaire and went into Dublin, went to O'Donoghue's and the usual places. We met up with [singer/guitarist] Al O'Donnell, who we knew from England. We had heard some 'real' Irish traditional players coming to do bits in England in the early 60s – there was one or two legendary pipers around like Felix Doran, the McPeakes and others. Talking to Al, he said, 'There's only one place to go: you've got to go to Miltown Malbay in Clare.'

So off we went down to Clare and there was a bit of synchronicity, cos we arrived at what I think they used to call 'August weekend', what we would call August Bank Holiday weekend in England, I suppose. So we're driving in and there's more donkeys and carts going in than cars, it was amazing. We were very lucky to hit that place at the right time. So we went into Miltown, went into one or two bars, and there was people playing, wild-looking geezers playing fiddles – it was incredible. One particular bar, Mrs Cleary's Bar I think it was, Willie Clancy was there – and he was playing with a young fiddle player, Seán Keane, who apparently had come down on holiday for two weeks and ended up there for two years or something. So they were playing and we had fiddle and guitar and we played a bit, over the weekend in that bar, and did a couple of songs now and again, and we heard all this amazing music – especially Willie Clancy, who just was out of this world.

Now it's changed a lot: you've got the Willie Clancy Memorial School and Swedish backpackers coming in, instead of one or two nutters from the English folk clubs, which is what we were at the time. So we were virtually the only non-Irish people there that weekend. It was incredible. I've actually got some recordings of that. … The recordings I've heard of Willie don't do him justice. I think he was a much better piper than you would think when he was recorded.

Robin recalls an entire Cornish Morris dance troupe making the trip around the same time. 'Calling upon Willie Clancy', especially given the awkwardness of his location, became a most curious and widespread phenomenon. In an appreciation of the man published during his lifetime, which captures the essence of Willie's appeal, Séamus Mac Mathúna practically printed his address and rounded up a coach party there and then:

> Surely Miltown's greatest attraction visitor-wise – even in winter, not a week

passes without its quota of callers to the Clancy home – collectors, students from England and the Continent, Professors and scholars from the US, or just plain tourists and, of course, lovers of piping from all parts of Ireland. In the summer this trickle swells to a flood …

Clancy's music and humour go hand in hand. … Indeed Clancy, the man, is as interesting and complex a study as Clancy the musician. Whether on his own hearth, or over a glass at his favourite pub, he is as entertaining a companion, for an hour or a month, as you could find. He is the most approachable of men, as many young musicians who have had the benefit of his advice will tell you. But music-lore is his speciality, and I'm sure he could tell some tall story for every tune he plays.

Willie Clancy, and his charming wife, Dóirín, live in their comfortable home at Flag Road, Miltown Malbay, where Willie has spent many a late night and early morning making music, singing, and talking piping. With Willie on the pipes, and that other renowned Miltown man 'Farmer' Moroney – singer, step-dancer and wit – helping to keep everyone in good humour, the hours fly, and the cocks are oft arching their necks for the first morning call ere the instruments are finally put away. When it is all over, Willie gets down his plane and saw, and gets back to the serious and relevant business of making a living in Miltown Malbay.[243]

One regular pilgrim, though less forward than many, was London-born Irish music enthusiast Andy Irvine. Andy would form Sweeney's Men with Johnny Moynihan and Joe Dolan (later replaced by Terry Woods) in 1966. By 1968, after a couple of Irish chart singles on Pye Ireland, the group had an album out in Britain on Transatlantic, coincidentally recorded by Bill Leader.

Andy Irvine: I didn't have a lot of personal connection with Willie, because I was awestruck by him. He was a shy man and I was shy, too, so I wasn't going to barge in and say, 'Ah, Jeez, Willie, I love your music …' Over the years that we visited Miltown Malbay to listen to him, I always hoped that he'd say, 'Ah, Andy! You're back again, how nice to see you …' But the nearest I got to that was when he said once, *'You were here before …'* The high point of my life at that point, in '68, when Sweeney's Men had made our album, [was that] we played a gig in Miltown Malbay. And in Queally's pub, in a room with a shut door, which I passed, I heard Willie Clancy learning to play 'Dance To Your Daddy' on the tin whistle – having heard us play it at the gig!

Sweeney's Men featured, at that point, bouzouki, mandolin, guitar, tin whistle and concertina, with an eclectic repertoire – which all made sense when presented together with this ensemble of double-course stringed instruments and this trio of particular personalities – encompassing British, Irish and Appalachian traditional songs and a few whistle-led instrumentals. In a 1972 interview, Willie lamented that the *fleadhanna*, begun in the 50s as a platform for purely traditional music, had deteriorated, partly through the spread of non-traditional instrumentation:

> **Willie**: [T]he undesirable element crept in and we were subject to an abuse of tambourines and guitars, and a display of showmanship with little or no sincerity. This type of attitude is not good enough if we are to preserve what's valuable.[244]

He had expressed similar concerns in a 1962 interview with Sligo fiddler John Vesey and American piper Tom Standheven:

> **Willie**: I heard a man say something one time, and I think it was very wise: he says that jazz was the folk music of the Negro before it became 'tin pan alleyed'. That is what is happening to our Irish music today – that's a very sad case. You have men taking up their fiddles and just because they got a classical knowledge of the fiddle, they try to apply that classical knowledge to folk music, which is a sacrilege. They can play Italian music, too, but they try to put Italian touches into the traditional Irish fiddle, and it's a catastrophe, in my opinion! … It is something that Mother Nature gave us and unfortunately, some have gone astray from it.[245]

A devil's advocate might point out that the drums, pianos and accordions of the céilí band world, of which Willie was an alumnus, were hardly native, let alone desirable. Willie would have conceded the point:

> **Willie**: Even the best accordion players will admit that the pipes, fiddles and flutes are the best to bring out the real quality of traditional music. Personally, I feel that more stress should be laid on the pipes because they are really traditional …[246]

He was surely right in believing that the uilleann pipes were the only instrument associated with Irish traditional music which could realistically claim to be truly indigenous. Everything else – violins, flutes (and concert flutes were what Willie was referring to, rather than the wooden flute common in Irish trad today), bouzoukis, mandolins, guitars, accordion et al. – were the progeny of other cultures.

Yet it would be wrong to give an impression that Willie was po-faced about these things. If he appreciated something of the raggle-taggle ebullience of Sweeney's Men, he can hardly have been a man to impose rules. While his friend Séamus Ennis would take an active interest in Planxty – direct successors to Sweeney's Men, in continuing with the concept of presenting Irish music (this time with uilleann pipes) accompanied by double-course stringed instruments – Willie would have no direct interaction with such 'rock era' touring trad bands of the 70s. In truth, he would never have the chance.

Sometime in the early 70s, Wilbert Garvin, a piper from mid-Ulster who had often visited Willie in Clare, facilitated a concert for him at Queen's University in Belfast. It was a very rare 'formal' public performance for Willie, undertaken purely through friendship. To Wilbert's recollection, Willie performed a set of solo piping with little onstage banter, but held a very appreciative audience. The next day, a couple of Willie's friends in tow, they went on a field trip in Wilbert's car to see the flashpoints of 'the troubles', and were not disappointed. It's an adventure that Wilbert recalls with much hilarity.

In 1972, Willie expressed some concern about the price of the burgeoning mass appeal of the once-endangered music he had grown up with:

> **Willie**: Certainly, there is far more traditional music and dance broadcast today than ever before, but unfortunately there is still not enough of the genuine thing. … I learned music for the pure love of it, and I think people who are really serious about it will do the same, no matter whether they are playing on television or before the open hearth.[247]

Nevertheless, Liam O'Flynn believes he was more likely to have been pragmatic than prescriptive, particularly if the right spirit could be maintained:

> **Liam O'Flynn**: Willie Clancy knew that the pipes had the potential to move out of strict traditional music. He might not have agreed with everything the pipes have done, but I think he'd be pleased they are so well received now.[248]

*

Shortly before Christmas 1972, a French TV crew filmed Willie for a documentary on Irish music. He disliked making television appearances – which is, perhaps, why there are only a few short fragments of moving image on the man, none of them filmed in a TV studio.* Nevertheless, he was now known as a 'keeper of the flame'. Asked by myself as to how he felt about his own status as such, in the 1990s, Liam O'Flynn took his cue from the master:

> **Liam O'Flynn**: It's great craic! You can't let it get to you. Actually, when one talks about 'burdens of responsibility', it reminds me of Willie Clancy being interviewed by some French TV outfit in Miltown Malbay. 'Well, Mr Clancy,' they said, 'where did you get your piping from?' And he told them his mother was a plumber.

Yet despite this outward sense of fun, all was not well. Of the more recent years up to this point, Dóirín would recall that 'he stayed at home a lot and … liked to listen more than play.'[249]

Pat Mitchell recalls braving the icy roads with a few friends in December of 1972 to visit Willie in Miltown:

> **Pat Mitchell**: The high point of the weekend was the session of music after Sunday Mass. Old and unusual tunes were dug out of the recesses of memory and played and delighted over. In the middle of it all out came – 'Pity, pity we can't roll back the wheel to hear Micí Cumba and Garrett Barry and all of them!' In words as rich as his music, Willie evoked memories of the great pipers whose names had lasted through generations. Words inspired by the conversation, hindsight bestows a ring of prophecy to them; a few short weeks later, we too were wishing we could 'turn back the wheel' to meet and hear and be inspired by Willie himself. Universally loved by all those who responded to his openness, his humanity, his sharp-edged – and frequently

---

* Willie did perform in a TV studio situation at least twice, on two 1967 episodes of the RTÉ programme *Bring Down The Lamp*, which are not extant. There are surviving short outside broadcast RTÉ TV clips of the following: Willie playing pipes in the street, with fiddler Joe Leary, at the Kilrush Fleadh, 1963; playing the pipes solo in the street at the Kilrush Fleadh, 1967; playing the pipes at Seán Ó Riada's funeral service, 1971. The only foreign TV clip currently online is an amusing interview with Willie in the company of friends at O'Connor's pub in Doolin, conducted, apparently, by a German, following which Willie plays the pipes. Though only two minutes long, it captures a good glimpse of his personality. Most of these clips were used in the 2009 TG4 documentary (in Irish and English, but with subtitles) *Cérbh É – Willie Clancy*, presented by Peter Browne, which can also be found online. The 1963 Kilrush clip, a full performance of 'The Flogging Reel/Sligo Maid', is commercially available on the DVD *Come West Along The Road Vol. 3* (RTÉ, 2010).

ribald – wit, his singing, his whistle playing and, of course, his piping, he drew us to his warmth like moths to a flame.[250]

Willie Clancy suffered a heart attack over the Christmas period and, after a short stay at hospitals in Ennis and then Galway, died on January 24 1973.

Ivor Browne, a noted Dublin-based psychiatrist who was a friend of the piper, recalled the situation in a documentary:

> **Ivor Browne**: He went into a very depressed state just some months before he died. And I'd arranged an appointment for him to come up to Vincent's [St Vincent's University Hospital, Dublin], to the Cardiology unit. … But he just died before he reached that appointment, which I felt very sad about. People would tell me, I'd been getting the word, that he wasn't well, and I think he'd been drinking too heavily – and he wasn't always a heavy drinker. But unfortunately the appointment he got was just one week too late.[251]

On January 26, the funeral was held in Miltown, with large numbers in attendance despite heavy rain. The Seán Ó Riada Mass was celebrated, led by the composer's son Peadar. Willie himself had played at Seán's funeral two years earlier. Luminaries from the traditional music world were there in force, pipers Séamus Ennis, Paddy Moloney and Liam O'Flynn among them. Ennis played the end of 'The Fox Chase' at the service and spoke at the graveside:

> **Séamus Ennis (1973)**: I knew him as a young man and watched him become one of the top pipers in Ireland. Yet even when he became internationally known, he still remained one of ourselves.[252]

Within weeks, plans were afoot – led by his friends Muiris Ó Róchain and Séamus Mac Mathúna, with the involvement of both CCÉ and Na Píobairí Uilleann (despite tension between the two organisations) – to honour Willie with a traditional music summer school. The Willie Clancy Summer School opened its doors in Miltown Malbay that very July, and continues to do so to this day – a central event in the Irish traditional music calendar, for the passing on of knowledge, for the playing of music and for the good of the human spirit.

Giving a memorial address at the graveside of his old friend during the School's fourth year, Seán Reid had this to say:

> **Seán Reid (1977)**: His name and fame continue to spread, and through him

as well as through a few other great pipers, the pipes are becoming known and admired all over the world. It is comforting to reflect that nowadays a musician's music lives on after they are gone, whereas in the past it died with them. …

While we have a permanent record of his playing and singing, we have no literary record, and in this latter he was quite capable of making a unique and invaluable contribution. I know that in his latter years, being troubled by insomnia, he used to pass the sleepless hours going back in fancy to West Clare as it was at 50 to 100 years before and meeting and talking to the pipers and other musicians and characters of those days, imagining the conversations word for word. As no one was more capable of doing this with full authenticity than Willie himself, it is a great misfortune that he did not get to put some of it on paper, or at least on tape. But perhaps he felt it was too personal and he may have feared ridicule.

He could very well have been a noted literary figure if only he had made a start or been nudged in the right direction, as he had sensitivity and creative imagination, a flair for fluent and vivid expression and an inexhaustible store of material upon which to draw.[253]

But perhaps to Willie the music was mightier than the pen, or perhaps he could only give his energy to the one. A year before he died, he was asked what direction he thought traditional music would take, in an era of high-profile professional groups. He was admirably pragmatic, playful and profound to the last.

Willie (1972): Who knows what direction it will take? Times change and people change. All I know is that I was often told, 'Lave down that tin whistle and take up your book.' I never did, thank God. To the parents of would-be musicians today I would say that it is important to encourage the younger folk. We have to rely on them to keep our music alive.[254]

Chapter 12
Johnny Doran: Along The Road Forever

Michael McGoldrick: One evening, me and John sat and listened to the old recordings of Johnny Doran – and we were pretty freaked out, actually. We were hearing things which Paddy Keenan had totally lifted – 'Colonel Fraser', 'The Bunch Of Keys' – but also these back D triplets, these unique techniques that were being done by Johnny on the only recording that he ever made. And apparently he wasn't feeling very well at the time. Imagine him on a good day: endless possibilities. I remember John jumping out of his seat, saying *'That's … that's … did you hear that? That's exactly the way Paddy plays it!'* So it's all been passed down.

John McSherry: I remember sitting in a hotel room with Mike McGoldrick after some Lúnasa gig. We were listening to the recordings of Johnny Doran, and we both had the biggest grins on our faces with the sheer joy and exuberance of his playing. I think Johnny was way ahead of his time. He was a free player with no restraints or confines: very creative. I'm sure he was influenced by the jazz sounds of the day emanating from his wireless. If he were alive today, he'd surely be taking the pipes down all sorts of musical avenues. The purists mightn't be too happy with him, though. I know he had a great influence on Paddy Keenan, who in turn had a great influence on me.

Paddy Keenan: I didn't hear Doran till I was 18 or 19. Johnny died in January 1950. I was born two weeks after he died – which is why old John Connors used to say, 'He's back!' I didn't think much of it back then, but that sort of compliment would be huge today. There'll never be nothing like Johnny again, because anyone who uses an art as a way to express themselves is an individual. If people like you and what you're representing as yourself, that's a bonus.

*

As war raged across Europe in the summer of 1942, out on the far western edge of the continent – on the sand hills at Spanish Point between Quilty and Miltown Malbay

– the annual Miltown Races were taking people's minds off the hardness of life. A young man called Michael Falsey, aged around 12, heard something that would stay in his memory forever. He remains, perhaps, one of the last men alive who has a vivid memory of Johnny Doran, the most celebrated of all recorded pipers:

> As we entered the 'enclosure' at the race-course, which was the place where all the amusements and refreshments were, a small, hardy, neat-looking man came in behind us, carrying a brown wooden case. His wife was with him, a stocky, dark-complexioned woman with a light scarf tied at the back of her head. He opened the case near a marquee and put the pipes together. He stood the case on the grass and put his leg on it to balance the chanter.
>
> I didn't see much of the races that day as I was near the piper wherever he played, and when his wife moved around with Johnny's peaked cap we gladly threw our few coppers into it. On other occasions I saw him on an old bicycle with the case on his back going to some fair or sporting event and again as I came from school in Quilty I'd see him with his wife and young children going by in the pony and 'flat cart'. I didn't know Willie Clancy at this time, but he used to cycle from his home in Miltown to meet Johnny near the 'metal bridge' of the now defunct West Clare Railway. …
>
> I have a fond memory of the Dorans [Johnny and his brother Felix] and a lot of other travelling musicians who often came our way during the war when food and other commodities were rationed and emigration was the order of the day. …*
>
> Most of their tunes were played for years after they left, as the travelling musician was a great help to the local player for learning tunes. My father … spoke well of Johnny Doran and was very anxious that I'd play the pipes. He didn't live long enough to hear me play and go on to win the All-Ireland

---

* There are at least three published first-hand versions of Michael's recollection of meeting Johnny Doran at the 1942 Miltown Races. He wrote the account above in 1984 for *An Píobaire*. He was interviewed in 2008 for the NPU DVD *Traveller Piper* (2009), and was interviewed for Fegan and O'Connell's book *Free Spirits* (2011). Michael recalls in *Traveller Piper* a few details additional to his 1984 account – Johnny wearing collar and tie, Mary Doran passing Johnny's hat around, people requesting tunes, Johnny polishing his pipes' keys with his handkerchief before playing – all of which ring true. Michael stated that he stayed for about one hour and gave Johnny two of the four pennies he had in his pocket. In *Free Spirits*, he recalled Mary Doran passing the hat with the entreaty 'Assist the musician,' and money flowing into it. Fegan and O'Connell mis-attribute the tale to 1943. While their book is valuable, some of the dating is imprecise, e.g. dating Doran's recording session to 1948 (a year out) and John Cash's death to 1906 (three years out).

at a Fleadh in Thurles in the mid-60s. I have vivid memories of all those things, particularly the great piper Johnny Doran. … I still have the original account of Johnny's accident, which I cut from the *Clare Champion* in 1948.[255]

Johnny Doran, born in 1907 or 1908, would die in January 1950 from injuries sustained, in January 1948, from a wall falling on his horse-drawn caravan parked near Christchurch Cathedral in Dublin. Only weeks prior to this freak accident, he had been recorded, for the first and only time, in circumstances that now seem almost miraculous. The resulting 43 minutes of sound are not only what separates Johnny Doran from Garrett Barry (a piper from an earlier age who enjoyed similarly legendary status within his own lifetime); they are what now defines a whole school of piping. Whatever the 'Traveller piping' tradition was before Johnny Doran, it is now *wholly* Johnny Doran: he has cemented it for all time. He remains both the wellspring of a tradition and a benchmark for all those who come after.

The man had wildness and control balanced in perfect, exhilarating equilibrium; he simultaneously delivered the gravitas of a venerable music and the *joie de vivre* of reforging it anew, in the moment, with every performance; he was a master of improvisation and technical innovation, who still gave his listeners what they wanted to hear and thought they knew; he made a living, and a good one, in hard times, as a busker on the street among people with little to spare; and he left behind nine fragile acetates of art music that transcend his time.

Of all the people who have been called 'the Jimi Hendrix of the pipes', the only one for whom the phrase is truly meaningful, as a cross-genre comparison or metaphor (rather than simply as an easy descriptor for someone perceived to be fast or exciting on his or her instrument), is Johnny Doran. Jimi Hendrix, in the late 1960s, from an unschooled background, revolutionised the sound and style of his instrument, the electric guitar, bringing both virtuosity and soulful, original expression to it along with new techniques of playing and a rare charisma as a stage performer. In a five-year career, before an untimely death in 1970, Hendrix changed both his instrument and the nature of popular music. Johnny Doran, in a life similarly cut short and in a recording career of one session, likewise engendered a seismic shift in the perceived capabilities of his instrument and the nature of the music associated with it.

As both an entertainer and a virtuoso within traditional music, the man was a one-off in his time, celebrated and anticipated wherever he went as a technicolour magician, a joy-bringer, in a monochrome age of austerity: the post-Civil War era of the 1920s, the worldwide Depression of the 30s and the World War 'Emergency' of the 40s. Had Johnny Doran never recorded at all, his legend would still loom large in oral tradition, and some flavour of his music might have been heard, or passed on, through first-hand devotees like his brother Felix, Willie Clancy, Martin Rochford, Ted Furey, John Keenan senior and others; but because of one evening in November 1947, on a date that no one seems to know, and when he was apparently not even at his best, he changed the world of uilleann piping forever.

*

Johnny Doran was born into a Travelling family with a long history of piping and was raised in Rathnew, Co. Wicklow. His great-grandfather was John Cash (1832–1909), the most famous Travelling musician of his day. A horse-dealer and tinsmith as well as a performing piper, Cash maintained a home in County Wicklow in tandem with travelling to fairs and events between there and Connemara. He learned his piping from an uncle, James Hanrahan of County Tipperary, and had eight children. He became a man of relative wealth in his time and cuts an imposing figure in his only known portrait.

Francis O'Neill met Cash in 1906 and sourced further recollections from his friend William Rowsome (father of Leo) for *Irish Minstrels And Musicians* (1911):

> John Cash was a man of fine personal appearance, well above medium height, with proportionate muscular development, amiable of disposition and with good conversational powers. Unlike the typical piper and fiddler, he was not loquacious; neither was he an egotist. … The young people always expected a rare treat when 'Cash the Piper' was around, and it is but the simple truth to say they were never disappointed, although their patience was sorely tried occasionally by the piper's protracted delay in getting started. … He had a long and honourable career as an Irish piper. Otherwise he was an industrious man who led a useful and, it must in truth be stated, a blameless life.[256]

One of John's children, James Cash (1853–1890), who died young and without progeny, was said to be an even more brilliant piper than his father, and was a particular influence on the pipers in the Rowsome family. Another of his offspring was Margaret Cash, who married a fellow Traveller, and piper, named John Doran. They in turn had a son named John Doran, who also took up the instrument. This John Doran married Kate McCann of Rathnew and they were to have eight children, among whom was Johnny Doran.

Johnny's father, whilst a piper who like John Cash before him performed at country events, was primarily a labouring man who spent time in England and Dublin, and served (with two brothers) in the British forces during the Great War before settling in Rathnew, where Johnny attended primary school. A John Doran (possibly Johnny's father or even his grandfather), listed as being of the Pipers' Club, Dublin, won the Gaelic League's Oireachtas piping competition in 1904. Similarly, a piper named John Doran (conceivably Johnny or his father) gave a broadcast on 2RN, forerunner of Radio Éireann, in 1934.

Travelling pipers entertaining crowds at fairs were once common in Ireland. Brian Ó Dochartaigh, a retired Garda officer writing in 1969, fondly recalled encountering in his youth (in the 1900s and 1910s) such people, most of whom played flat sets (pre-concert pitch) and some of whom played with a double chanter in order to harmonise with themselves. The most valuable information he gives, though, is on the respect given to itinerant pipers by the mainstream 'settled' community:

> The itinerant pipers always had common ground with their more fortunate brethren, and mixed with and visited them as an accepted practice – and, of course, gave and received additions to their repertories as the case might be.
>
> I never saw an itinerant piper badly dressed, and for the most part they wore the old-fashioned long body coats or frock coats as they were called, black, tall crowned soft hats and invariably a green coloured cravat with some gold adornments, which might be a harp or a shamrock on the knot of the cravat.
>
> These pipers frequented fairs, races and even sports meetings, and always played to crowds; and also frequented towns on market days, and it was a common sight and a welcome one to see them setting up in the market square of a town and using a crutch which they invariably carried, on which to rest a leg so that the chanter of the instrument could be 'popped' or the valve at its end effectively used off the knee. If there was a convenient window sill it would suit as well as the crutch, as the piper could then play in the orthodox position, which is seated of course. …
>
> [A]nother very marked characteristic of these men – they hardly ever solicited money for their art as is the way with ordinary itinerants. … Generally the money came to them [by tacit understanding among the crowd] … They were received with open arms wherever they went, and people drew a wide distinguishing line between them and the ordinary itinerants or street performers. It was well understood that Dinny Delaney of Ballinasloe or the Cashes and Dorans … did not acquire their craft from the inhabitants of canvas tents on the roadsides …

> I often thought what a great loss it was that in those days we did not possess the means we have now of recording music. What a wonderful thing it would be to hear our native music played as it was by our ancient bards, with whom these itinerant pipers must have had direct or semi-direct links.[257]

The only photograph of Johnny Doran's father, sure enough, shows him standing with his pipes in a street in a long dark coat, hat and cravat, with his right foot on a case or suchlike, allowing the chanter to rest on his knee. Johnny Doran would adopt a similar approach, resting his foot on his instrument case but also, to Martin Talty's recollection, using a home-made strap to hold the pipes. In Talty's memory, Johnny always stood up to play at open-air events, whatever the convenience of window ledges, although there is one known exception: a large stone in Ballynacally village near Ennis, Co. Clare, where he often sat to play and which in the 1980s was saved from a council road-widening exercise by public protest; it now rests on a plinth with a plaque honouring the man who once played music there.

Johnny said he was first taught the pipes by a relative, John Cash (presumably a distant cousin), before gaining further knowledge from his father. For their book *Free Spirits* (2011), Fegan and O'Connell tapped into Doran family lore, particularly from his daughters Eileen and Nan, to chart Johnny's path from a child prodigy at age eight to a man who made essentially the whole of his living from the pipes. They state that in the summer of 1918, Johnny accompanied his father to a fair in Carlow town where they performed on the street, walking away with £4/9 shillings and sixpence: 'a substantial amount of money for a day's work, and it would feed the Doran family for at least four weeks'.[258]

They date Johnny's first trip to Clare – the county with which he would become particularly associated – to 1922, and specifically to Kilkishen, a small village in East Clare. Martin Rochford, a young man from the Feakle area, was there and recalled John Doran senior bringing Johnny to the Black Sticks pub, where the 14-year-old played at the request of a local shoemaker and traditional music buff who had the distinction of owning a gramophone.

In 1923, Johnny won the junior section of the Dublin Feis piping competition, with one Edmund Potts coming second.* The following year the positions were reversed: Potts scoring 90 and Doran 87.

---

* Johnny's name was spelt 'Johnnie' in the Feis records. On an engraved stock of a set of pipes belonging to him, now owned by NPU, the name is spelt 'Johney'. It seems likely that the Edmund Potts against whom he competed in 1923–24 was Eddie Potts, son of John Potts (another piping legend from the time of John Cash). Eddie Potts was an uncle of Seán Potts, a tin-whistling member of The Chieftains from 1962 to 1979.

The pub performance that Martin Rochford had seen Johnny give in Kilkishin left an impression – although, as he stated in *Johnny Doran: A Famous Piper*, a 1988 RTÉ radio documentary: 'He didn't appear again till 1937 … [but] he seemed to hang around here a lot in '38."

By 1937 Johnny was married, to Mary Cash (herself a great-grandchild of 'Cash the Piper'), and was pursuing life as a travelling piper with a horse-drawn 'flat cart' caravan and a copy of *Old Moore's Almanac* to chart his course around Ireland in a given year. As Clare man P.J. Curtis put it in his book *Notes From The Heart* (1994):

> With the lengthening of the days and the coming of the hawthorn blossom and the mayfly, Johnny Doran's gaily-coloured horse-drawn caravan could be seen drifting lazily towards a sheep or cattle fair in Ennistymon or Kilrush or a wedding or house-dance in Miltown Malbay or Quilty. … The sight and sound of Johnny Doran playing his pipes on the streets of a village in Clare in the 30s must have been both exotic and exciting to all who witnessed it. He was a small, wiry, good-looking man with dark skin and black hair. According to the fiddler John Kelly, 'He looked for all the world like an Indian.' The few photos of Johnny still extant – swarthy, black-haired, with high cheekbones, intelligent eyes – would seem to confirm John Kelly's description of him. … It is said by some that he did not drink, would never play his pipes past midnight and would often go into the fields after dark to play a tune for the little people. Wherever lies the truth, it was said of Johnny Doran that as both man and musician, you could meet no better.[259]

*

Writing back cover notes to *The Last Of The Travelling Pipers*, Topic Records' posthumous collection of recordings made of Felix Doran (Johnny's younger brother, who had passed on in 1972), Seán Reid began with a caveat:

> This short account of the personal recollections of one man can be no substitute for proper biographies of both Felix Doran and his brother Johnny, which should now be compiled as a matter of urgency. They were the last of a great and illustrious line of travelling pipers, and the end of an era; it is unlikely that we shall ever see their likes again.[260]

---

* Fegan and O'Connell note in *Free Spirits* (2011) that Johnny tended to play in West Clare and his brother Felix in East Clare.

Regrettably, Seán's call went unanswered. Aside from the family lore in *Free Spirits* and scraps of reminiscences here and there, published often long after his death in 1950, the hour-long RTÉ documentary *Johnny Doran: A Famous Piper*, compiled and broadcast in two parts in 1988, must remain the key source of primary information about the short life of Johnny Doran. Many of those who knew him were interviewed, their even-then distant recollections of his performing and his personality often vivid decades on. He is universally recalled as friendly, popular, a family man and a near-abstainer from alcohol, drinking only moderately to be sociable.*

He was around five foot six, swarthy and had prominent white teeth. Martin Talty, of Clare, remembered him as a quiet man who never said a rude word to anyone, drank little, smoked Woodbine cigarettes, had two horses, owned three or four sets of pipes (preferring a quiet flat set if playing in his caravan) and who, beyond music, seemed to have few interests.

Shooting the odd rabbit with an old shotgun, presumably for the pot, is all Martin could recall of any extra-musical activity on Johnny's part. He did, though, recall Johnny's fingers as being extremely long and flat, like Séamus Ennis' fingers, only wider – a natural advantage for any piper. While Martin believed that Johnny never did any horse-dealing (in contrast to his brother Felix, who later moved into scrap-dealing and then haulage), other sources suggest that he did do a little of this, albeit only as a sideline.

> **Martin Talty**: He was a tremendously skilful man with his hands … I distinctly remember him making keys [for his pipes] and things like that and using the iron band in the wagon wheel as an anvil … He'd be tapping it with a hammer, shaping it gently, and he'd turn round and talk to you, wouldn't be looking, and he'd still be tapping …[261]

Margaret Cash recalled Johnny making keys from silver spoons, making reeds from cane and working on Felix's pipes. He seems also to have bought and sold pipes, to an extent, though perhaps as much to help out protégés as for profit.

In Martin Talty's memory, Johnny generally wore grey trousers, sports coat and sandals when he played in public. The best-known formal portrait photo taken of Johnny shows him (with his pipes) wearing white collar and tie, a wide-checked sports coat and, unusually for the time, white shoes or clogs of some

---

* Felix Doran wore the badge of the Pioneer Total Abstinence Association during the 30s, but succumbed to alcoholism in later life.

sort.* Johnny Cleary, a farmer from Claremorris, Co. Mayo, recalled him as 'a grand little fellow, as far as I can remember now. He wasn't too big – and well-dressed. You wouldn't think he was a knight of the road, anyhow. He was a respectable kind of fellow and grand company.'[262]

The only person who tempers, if only slightly, this picture of openness and conviviality is Margaret Cash, a relative of similar age who grew up with Johnny and kept in touch:

> **Margaret Cash**: He was a very nice chap … [His brother] Felix was an all-round man, he'd play for anybody. Johnny was a very funny-going fellow. He didn't mix in with much of his own people, he always kept to himself … He kept in more with the farming types and the piping people, the musicianers … He didn't play much for [you] – you'd have to coax him to play a tune for you. He'd want to like you very much before he'd play for you.[263]

---

* This portrait photo, which can be seen online, in *Free Spirits* and on the cover of Touhy and Ó hAodha's *Postcolonial Artist*, is notable in that Johnny had clearly prepared for it: it represents how he chose to present himself. A second portrait-style photo, seemingly taken for a newspaper, was discovered by Wilbert Garvin and reprinted in *An Píobaire* Vol. 6 No. 2, April 2010. In this one, Johnny, with differently styled hair, wears the same sports coat and tie, but with the addition of a waistcoat. The few other genuine known photographs of Doran are chance snapshots. Essentially, these are: one at St Brigid's Well (seemingly from the early 30s, showing a younger man than the other photos); two taken by John McCaffrey, of Johnny with Pat Cash in Dublin, around Christmas 1941; one on a street flanked by two women (seemingly in Clare, published by *Dál gCais* Vol. 2, 1975); one dated to the early 40s, on a street in Mayo flanked by onlookers; and one seated on a wall, with his pipes, in a group. The St Brigid's Well shot shows a young man tie-less in a loose grey suit. The McCaffrey shots, taken in a non-public performance situation, are the only ones showing Johnny in a cap, which Séamus Ennis recalled Doran wearing even indoors (though clearly not when performing in public), and in more casual clothing. The Clare and Mayo street shots both show Doran with his checked sports jacket, without and with a tie, respectively, and with a cigarette in his mouth in the former. Indeed, his attire and haircut are so similar to the formal portrait in the Mayo shot that one imagines they were taken around the same time. In the Clare shot we can clearly see the strap that Martin Talty recalled. The seated shot shows Johnny with sports coat, grey trousers and a white silk scarf or cravat. The photo of a standing piper taken at The Oul' Lammas Fair in Ballycastle(-o) is commonly attributed as Johnny Doran. It remains enigmatic. The agency from which it appears to be sourced (which acquired it together with the stock of a now-defunct agency) dates it roughly to 1955 and credits it to George Pickow, an American who was never in Ireland prior to 1952, two years after Johnny's death. It is of markedly higher quality than any of the other known Doran shots. Nevertheless, the shape and length of the fingers is very redolent of Doran's in other photographs, while both Wilbert Garvin and Brian Vallely believe the pipes themselves display peculiar aspects (e.g. the end of the chanter) which point to the pipes in other photos of Johnny.

Johnny Doran may not have returned to East Clare until 1937, as Martin Rochford clearly recalled, but he was often in West Clare (the two halves of the county being geographically isolated from each other) from the early 30s onward. Fiddler John Kelly, who would remain close friends with Johnny thereafter, first met him in Kilkee, performing upright, his leg on a box to support the chanter, and was mesmerised by the man's playing. It was an experience shared by many others.

'I'd never heard anything like him,' said Johnny Cleary, of Claremorris. 'He could do anything with the uilleann pipes. And he was a fantastic set dancer.'[264]

'It was love at first sight when I heard him playing the pipes,' said Martin Rochford. 'He got a practice set in Ennis for me. I think it was only £2 – but £2 was a lot of money then.'[265]

'I was so confounded by the music,' was the response of Paddy Philbin, a dancing teacher from County Galway who first encountered Johnny teaching Felix the pipes at his caravan by the roadside. Paddy later danced to Johnny and Felix's music, opposite the Imperial Hotel in Eyre Square, Galway (one of Johnny's regular spots) on a Saturday evening in 1934: 'He was such a great traditional player for Irish dancers. One of the greatest players, [in] rhythm, time and style. His style of playing was second to none.'[266]

Despite purportedly being a good dancer himself, Johnny is believed to have disliked playing for set dances (although he is known to have done so) because of the many notes he had to leave out, sacrificing variation and free-wheeling improvisation for rhythm.

In the RTÉ documentary, Nick Kinsella recalled a race meeting in Lingstown, Co. Wexford, in the early 30s, which offers a glimpse of a confident performer in his natural environment:

> He stood up to play the pipes, which was unusual … He laid one foot on the case of the pipes and … he played the pipes. … He was a young, slight lad at the time and he seemed very much at his ease playing, no trouble in the world. And then later on that year I heard him again at an athletic sports meeting at Kilmore Quay. And of course he had all the music fans around him, because a piper was very rare in this area and everyone wanted to hear him.[267]

If standing pipers from the Travelling community had once been commonplace (at least in the memory of Brian Ó Dochartaigh), they had become a rarity by the 1930s. There may have been one or two others about, but save for his brother Felix and one Tom Rainey, a man who played in Clare and inspired Martin Rochford, no other standing piper from Johnny Doran's time is ever referred to. Possibly Doran's towering brilliance made any other piper of the time an irrelevance, a memory not worth keeping; perhaps likelier, Johnny and Felix Doran were, as Seán Reid believed, more or less the last of a kind.*

Muiris Ó Rócháin, an old friend of Willie Clancy's, was inclined to this view:

> Johnny Doran was probably unique. He came in the 30s and the piping tradition in Clare at the time would have been at a very low ebb ... practically non-existent. Folk memory there would have been of Garrett Barry. Whatever it was, they took to Doran – his personality, the impact he made, his charisma, of course his music. [People were] hearing the pipes for the first time on many occasions. One man, Thomas Power of Quilty, a noted step-dancer and set dancer, would be talking about setting up benefit dances in Quilty, when he came, to hold him there – benefit dances happening in different houses at night.[268]

Willie Clancy and Martin Talty were ecstatic at meeting Doran for the first time on their way to the Miltown Races near Spanish Point in 1936, just six years before the same thing would happen to Michael Falsey.† Fiddler Junior Crehan was also present on that occasion, his own first encounter with Doran:

> I remember to hear [sic] the music and of course I made for it. There, also near Johnny, was Willie Clancy and Martin Talty and Thady Casey and 'Scully' Casey. Anyone interested in traditional music, Johnny drew them towards him. We followed him all day and didn't bother with the races. We were after Johnny all day. We gave him a couple of pennies and went into Miltown then. When the last race would be won they would all go into Miltown, 'twas about a mile from where the course was. Johnny would sit up in The Square ... All the town would be around him and they pitching in two bob or half a crown and maybe a fist of coppers. All around where he'd be would be covered with money. He might move away then to some other quarter, but he would have the crowd all the time.

---

* Felix Doran last visited Clare in 1950. He moved to Manchester in 1952 and built a haulage business, pursuing piping only as a hobby thereafter. He won a Fleadh competition in 1963 in Ireland and was recorded at the traditionally-focused Keele Folk Festival in 1965. The only caveat to himself and Johnny being 'the last of the Travelling pipers' is the enigmatic photograph of an unnamed piper, standing, at a fair in Ballycastle, referred to in the footnote above – assuming it really was taken circa 1955. It seems likelier that it does in fact depict Johnny Doran, and was taken in the 1930s by an unknown professional photographer.

† Clancy and Talty's account of their meeting and later associations with Johnny are found in the chapter on Clancy.

At the horse races again the next year we would go in the town first, and when we'd be going in the Mullagh Road you would hear the sound of the pipes, and it was something lovely; Johnny playing with his left leg up on his pipes case and he playing away. And I used to try and give him … well, a penny or tuppence was great at that time. He had a little bag and he would go around saying, 'Assist the music.'

And if you paid him he was thankful, and if you didn't, it made no difference. But I'd try and manage the sixpence for him always. And when he would have the round of collecting done he'd come back:

'Would you like me to play something now for you?'

He would ask me, I suppose, for giving the most money.

But the first day he came, when he left the racecourse he had £13 in coppers, and 'twas a big load to carry in.* He went in to McDonagh's pub and he had a drink and asked the woman would she change the money for him. So the counting started. And she was delighted to get the change because there was big business lads drinking and she wanted a lot of change. She gave him silver and a few notes for the heap of coppers. But then he got a lot more around the town after that in the evening.[269]

This anecdote, when repeated, is often rounded off with a statement that the average farm labourer at the time could expect to earn £12 in a year.† Whether or not that is a representative figure, Johnny's earning power – or, more accurately, the power of his music and the consequent gratitude of listeners in hearing it – was certainly extraordinary in such straitened times.

P.J. Curtis: My own father saw Johnny play many times at horse and cattle markets in north Clare and used to say it was the most amazing, magical music he had ever heard in his life. He said that Johnny used to make as

---

* In various forms, this has become a well-worn anecdote. Fegan and O'Connor put the figure at £13/8 shillings and misdate the incident to 1946; in Touhy and Ó hAodha's *Postcolonial Artist*, piper Mickey Dunne, whose father knew Doran, attached the windfall (£3/10 shillings this time) to Michael Falsey's 1942 encounter with Doran at the Miltown Races. Dunne's source was an oral account he had received in 2003 from Michael Falsey, but seemingly two anecdotes had become telescoped into one.

† Irish farm labourers were particularly poorly paid among the workforce in the 1930s and 40s, but online searches have not revealed any figure lower than 15 shillings per week for the period. This extrapolates to £39 per year. Of course, farm labouring has a seasonal aspect and, in any case, this research is far from scientific. But I draw attention to it to show how stories, even those that are essentially true, can become a little fuzzy in the telling.

much as 30 shillings a day busking at the fairs at a time when a labourer earned two shillings a week.[270]

One theme common to all recollections of Doran is how scarce money was at the time and how well he did in attracting it. Johnny Cleary in County Mayo recalls Doran visiting a fair there in 1935 or '36 and coming to his home after, playing and receiving a whip-round of six or seven shillings, which was a lot for that time and place. If we take 15 shillings a week as a farm labourer's wages (see footnote above), Johnny certainly made half that in one evening.

Playing for families and neighbours in their homes or at semi-formal gatherings in domestic settings was part of Johnny's pattern. Martin Talty remembered himself and Willie Clancy spending a night in Johnny's caravan once, when other accommodation couldn't be found, and Mary Doran making them bacon and eggs in the morning: 'Things we couldn't have got at home at the time!' They then went to Kilkee, two flutes and pipes between them on the street, with Willie dancing a hornpipe at one point: 'Ah, we had wonderful times, you know. I was *amazed* at all the money that was being thrown in.'[271]

Johnny seems to have been happy, indeed keen, to play with other musicians if the opportunity presented itself. In line with the free and easy busking trio with Willie Clancy and Martin Talty, a similarly memorable happenstance occurred once with Junior Crehan:

> **Junior Crehan**: One day I happened to be in Kilmahil, looking for a couple of heifers to buy. I bought them on the fair green and came over to the village. It wasn't long till I heard the pipes and saw a crowd around Johnny. He was playing to his heart's content and the money was flowing. So, as I chanced to be on the scene, he asked me:
> 'Is there any chance you could get a fiddle?'
> 'God, I don't know,' I said. 'I don't know where there'd be a fiddle got around.'
> So we adjourned to Carey's public house and some of the family went out and got a fiddle, and a very bad fiddle it was. Well, I tuned up with Johnny and we played and played inside the pub. We were sitting on the end of a form and there was silver all along the form on one side. And there was a table near it and the table was full of bottles of stout for me. If I drank them all I wouldn't see home for a fortnight! But Johnny got the silver. Oh, a bag of money! So we played for two or three hours there, and there was such a crowd that they could not come in, the house was so full. They were

back out across the street and they were looking in the windows and trying to hear the music. But when I went out to go home, my two heifers were let out of a yard. To get home I had to walk them about 10 miles. As someone said to me after: 'You paid for the piper!'[272]

It wasn't always a case of playing for money. Fegan and O'Connell quote another story from Michael Falsey (presumably secondhand, as Falsey only saw Doran performing the once) of a man in Quilty who sought out Johnny to play at a party for his daughter who was emigrating:

> At the end of the night the man of the house put some money into Johnny's pocket, and Johnny took it out and gave it back to his host and said, 'No need to do that.'[273]

Johnny's cousin, Frank O'Brien, recalled that the piper often visited their home in Carlow when Frank was a child:

> He always called to us when he came round. And he was a very popular man, popular with our neighbours and generally in Carlow, because he played in Carlow … It was like Christmas when he'd come, because … there was no radio and no television, so any live music was welcome. … [N]o one could play the pipes like he could play them. He was a master of them. I can remember the open fireplace and the lights on and we all sitting round on the floor, anywhere we could sit, to hear him playing. And there'd be plenty of people out on the street. He'd be in for the night when he called there. The bacon and cabbage would be on and the apple tart … we wouldn't let him go to bed until late. We'd keep him playing … But he was very popular anyway, even if he'd never played the pipes.[274]

*

During the war years (1939–45), while Ireland remained neutral, everyone was subject to rationing, which meant registering with a shop in a static location. For Johnny Doran – who had a wife and several children to support (nine in total, though not all of them were born by 1940) – it meant a significant change to his lifestyle and earning potential. Much of the war era he spent based in Dublin, occasionally visiting Leo Rowsome's recently revived Pipers' Club.

Dónal Glennon: We met Johnny in the Pipers' Club in Thomas Street, and at that time the members that come to my mind who were present were Andy Conroy, Mick Conroy, John Kelly … old John Clark might have been there and Matt Kiernan, I'd say … They were always glad when he came. He didn't come every Saturday night, because he might be travelling round the country. But whenever he came in he was more than welcome. We used to do a whip-round to make sure that we gave Johnny a gratuity for his playing. We all enjoyed listening to Johnny.[275]

Leo Rowsome himself must have heard Doran on occasion. Johnny owned a set of concert-pitch Rowsome pipes, which he favoured when playing (they would be the set he recorded with), so the pair must have met when arranging for the construction and transaction. One assumes they would have had a few tunes together on such occasions. Seán Reid, who knew both men, wrote: 'Johnny Doran, one of the greatest pipers of all time, swore by Leo, and his brother Felix Doran put him at the top of the list.'[276]

Near Christmas 1941, one John McCaffrey was passing by a Travellers' site at Green Lanes, Terenure:

> I have a vivid recollection of a fascinating experience I had in this place one Saturday afternoon preceding Christmas. From a distance I heard the sound of bagpipe music and, as I approached the caravans, I was enchanted with the rousing strains of 'Garryowen'.
>
> Naturally, I stopped and listened until the conclusion of the alfresco entertainment. I then chatted with the two pipers and the little boy, who said he hoped to play as well as his father did when he grew up. The men explained that they were practising playing their 'favourite jigs, reels and hornpipes for the Christmas'. Fortunately I had my camera with me on this occasion and they very kindly agreed to allow me to take their photographs.
>
> They told me that they were traditional Irish pipers and that they toured all Ireland. They played the pipes at Killarney, Killorglin, Ballinasloe and other towns where 'things were stirring'. … These two pipers made a lasting impression on me. They were very intelligent men, with gentle and melodious voices. In a casual manner they mentioned that their ancestors had made their living by doing a bit of piping in addition to their trade as horse-dealers.
>
> They said they would be complimented if I sent the snaps if they came out at all. They were not optimistic, because there was no sunshine and the light in the lane was fading. However, if the results were worth looking at I

was to forward the likenesses to 'Pat Cash, care of the General Post Office, Dublin'. As directed, I sent contact copies of my two negatives which were comparatively successful 'though earth and sky looked dreary'. In due course I received a flattering letter of thanks.[277]

The photos, of Johnny with Pat Cash and Pat's son, all holding pipes, are a window on a passing age. It has been said that Johnny had a wireless in his caravan; if so, he would certainly have heard some of Rowsome's many broadcasts for 2RN and its successor, Radio Éireann.* He may conceivably also, as John McSherry conjectures, have heard and absorbed jazz: the pop music of its day. He would very likely have heard the dance band 'swing' jazz of the 1930s – but just possibly, from the early 40s, on European stations or Voice Of America (though surely not on Radio Éireann), he may also have heard the revolutionary small-group sound of what would become known as be-bop.†

---

* 2RN operated between 1926 and 1933, with its smaller sister station in Cork, 6CK, spanning 1927–33. Both stations used low-power transmitters, hence coverage was limited to a zone around those two cities. In 1933 a much more powerful transmitter came into operation at Athlone, roughly in the centre of Ireland, ensuring coverage to most of the Free State, as it was still called at that time. During the 1933–37 period the station became known as Radio Athlone. 'Éire' was adopted as the name of the state in 1937, and consequently 'Radio Éireann' became the commonly used name of the station, although it was not formally constituted as such until 1960.
† During the 1930s, jazz was known generally as 'swing' and was played by large, formally dressed dance-band ensembles, rather than by the small groups of four or five that became the norm in the be-bop era. Dance bands and their featured vocalists – 'crooners' like Al Bowlly in Britain and Bing Crosby in America – were a radio mainstay on the BBC at this time, often broadcasting live from swish London venues. 'Crooning', though, was believed by some to be the beginning of the end of civilisation. Ireland being a deeply conservative place, the powers that be in the country during the 1930s and 40s were of this view. Maurice Gorham's *Forty Years Of Irish Broadcasting* (RTÉ, 1967) contains various references to the furrowed brows of a series of government-appointed Directors Of Broadcasting on the question of swing music and crooners – despite their popularity with advertisers and the general population to whom they (via their sponsored programmes) were selling. In September 1940, new regulations limited sponsored programmes to two hours per day and none at all after 5.30pm (unless advertisers chose to sponsor an orchestral concert), while various things, such as alcohol advertising, were banned. As Gorham puts it: 'Jazz was to be discouraged though not actually banned.' If Johnny Doran was listening to the radio on his travels during the 1930s, he was probably listening to the BBC or Radio Luxembourg. This latter was a commercial station between 1933 and 1939, using an unauthorised wavelength with a powerful transmitter based in Luxembourg, aimed squarely at British and Irish listeners and broadcasting the popular music of the day without any moral qualms. During the war years of 1940–45, batteries for radios became impossible to acquire in Ireland.

Pat Mitchell, on the evidence of the 1947 recordings, certainly sees a similarity between Doran and two trail-blazers of that era's new jazz:

> Listening to Johnny's music, we are swept along – caught up in the rush of excitement generated by the powerful rhythms on chanter and regulators and variation tumbling out after variation. And if he stumbled occasionally, who can blame him? Johnny's music brings to mind the playing of some of the jazz greats such as Dizzy Gillespie or Charlie Parker, people who were literally driven by the music in their heads to push the boundaries of that music and pile variation upon variation, sometimes with scant regard for intonation and in too great a hurry to pick up the odd dropped note. And as with Johnny, who cares? For me, great music is not defined by focusing on precise tuning and the like, rather by the emotion it generates in the listener. All three played tremendous music whose effect was visceral, making the pulse quicken and heightening the emotions.[278]

Breandán Breathnach, who himself saw Johnny performing once, in Galway's Eyre Square, seemed to concur that the piper had the heart of a jazz man:

> It strikes me that Johnny was playing for himself, in response to some inner kind of urge or feeling, and that he went over and over the tune until he got the whole thing out of his system … It's not surprising that it does have an effect on people and that they immediately succumb to the style.[279]

Johnny performed only Irish traditional material – though, as Breathnach observed on another occasion, with so much improvisation involved that presenting it as such was a harmless sleight of hand: 'In Clare he would say, 'I had this version from the County Longford.' But then in Longford he'd say, 'I had this from County Clare.' … But it was really his own performance.'[280]

Despite the constraints of rationing, there are several anecdotes about Johnny which place him at various points around Ireland during the war years. Aside from the Miltown Races of summer 1942, he played at an Ulster final (hurling or Gaelic football) at Clones, near the Monaghan/Fermanagh border, around 1943, according to Johnny Cleary. Cleary also recalls Johnny smuggling tea across the border into Northern Ireland, using a false bottom in his caravan. He apparently did so many times, but was caught once, was fined and paid the fine.

How widely did Johnny travel? In *Free Spirits*, Fegan and O'Connell reproduce a map by P.J. O'Connell dotted with locations believed to have been visited by Doran:

they span most of the counties of Ireland, North and South, but source information is not provided. Other books list a rather smaller selection of counties (none in the North), while in the RTÉ documentary it was confidently stated that Johnny never ventured north of Bundoran, a coastal town in south Donegal. For once, we can turn to Johnny Doran himself for enlightenment as to the places he preferred, at least.

> **Muiris Ó Rócháin (1972)**: On the back of a photograph [the portrait photo] belonging to him and reproduced in a paper after his death, he said: 'I was always welcome everywhere I went. My favourite counties are Kerry, Clare, Mayo, Donegal, Sligo, Tipperary, Kilkenny and Longford. My best counties are Clare and Galway.'[281]

Did Johnny ever play in Northern Ireland? If we set aside the enigmatic photograph of the man at Ballycastle, on the north coast of County Antrim, there is one story that seems to place Johnny Doran at a fair in Ballymena, also in Antrim. Cecil Colville, who became a piper himself, was around 12 at the time. He was interviewed in 2009 by Wilbert Garvin:

> [I]n Ballymena every year they had a fair – the big fair was always the last Tuesday in October in Bryan Street Square. All sorts of cowboys came there – they broke stones on their chests and they lay on beds of nails, ate glass bottles – you name it – they all came there. There was a guy in the other corner and he used to have a dancing doll and an accordion, and the dancing doll danced to the music – he tapped the board and that made her dance. There was always a crowd about the town.
>
> There was this guy who came to Ballymena, who he was I don't know. He had a metal box and there was a wee girl with him. He opened up this box – it was a clear aluminium box – I really couldn't tell you if it was aluminium or not. He got this contraption out o' the box – he had these things he strapped round his belly for a start. Then he set the box up on its end and he got one leg on it. Then he brought out these other bits and started to assemble the instrument. I watched him very intently and then he gave it two or three squashes on the chanter to see they were OK and then he ran his fingers up and down the keys … Then he started to play.
>
> Now he would have played one or two slow airs, you see, and one or two marches. One march that has stuck out in my mind was 'The Mountains Of Pomeroy'. He played that one first, and he used to accompany himself on the regulators. You know nowadays how … their hand falls on the regulator

and it's just a real mix-up of notes – but this boy didn't do that – he vamped them to marching time. I watched him and watched him and watched him. And then the wee girl came and stood down in front of him and he started to play 'The Blackbird', which was a set dance. The way he played that was something special while the wee girl danced. Nowadays they go like the hammers of hell, but that man played music as it should be played – because, you see, he went according to the proper time. I stood and I watched that man for about an hour and a half. He played hornpipes, jigs and reels, and the quality of his music was so good you would have felt like dancing along with the wee girl – that is exactly how his music sounded. He also played a lot of slow airs. It made some impression on me, I'll tell you that. Then he stopped for a smoke. There were crowds round him and they were throwing in half-crowns in those days. This was round about 1945. He was getting half-crowns the like you have never seen. The wee girl was putting them into a bag with a drawstring on it.

I asked him, I says, 'I'm very interested in music myself. I never saw an instrument like that before and I never heard as much beautiful music. What would you call your instrument?' He says, 'You call it the uilleann pipes. Some people call it the union pipes but we call it the uilleann pipes.' I said to him, 'Where do you come from?' 'I come from a long, long bit away. I do the fairs every autumn – I always go round to play at the fairs.' I then said to him, 'There can't be a lot of people who play this instrument.' 'Well, in the south of Ireland you would maybe get half a dozen in every county that would play them.'

The drones were just like a swarm of bees. I noticed that the head of the chanter went directly into the bag – it wasn't like the modern way. Who made his pipes I don't know. After that I asked everybody about uilleann pipes but nobody knew what I was talking about – they hadn't a clue.[282]

It's tempting to believe that this was Doran, even though the detail about vamping in march-time rather than playing with variety on the regulators contrasts with Doran's only recordings; there's also the matter of the player's speed, and no mention of reels. Nevertheless, as Wilbert noted: 'I took Cecil a couple of photographs of Johnny Doran and let him listen to a recording of Johnny playing 'The Blackbird'. Although [it was] a long time ago, Cecil said that Doran looked and sounded just like the piper he met.'[283]

*

After the war, Johnny's travelling lifestyle resumed in earnest. Paddy McDonagh recalled one post-war visit to a fair in County Sligo:

> [P]eople left the cattle on the streets, left everything there and listened to Doran playing for the whole afternoon. In fact, he wasn't able to continue; he got fatigued in the finish.[284]

One remembrance of Johnny Doran, seemingly from the post-war period, was quoted in a book on Irish dialects, in the context of a discussion about speech patterns of people from different regions of Ireland. The interviewee, a Miltown Malbay man of 75 at the time of the interview in 1978, was referred to only as 'C.O'B.'. Amidst the quirks of speech and transcription is another first-hand insight into the drawing power of Johnny Doran in Clare:

> I didn't know of any other piper around here, but I often heard of Garrett Barry … [But] I do remember Johnny Doran comin' around. … There used [to] be big races in Miltown that time. There was the first place I saw 'im, an' I thought he had the finest music I ever heard, an' even think it still; Johnny Doran. … I thought he had grand time and sweet music. … He was a middle-sized man, middle-aged that time. He died – he died soon after. … I was never talkin' to him at all, but I used to follow him around. I even went up to Lehinch Races – they were small races only – I was expectin' he'd be there, an' he was there. And that's the most thing that brought me up, was to hear him playin'. He was very willin' to play.[285]

Interviewed by Tom Munnelly, Junior Crehan recalled that on one day a year, Garland Sunday (the last Sunday in July), Lahinch was the place to be for music and dancing.* People would visit the nearby Holy well of St Brigid (location of one of the few Doran photographs) in Liscannor on the day before, and then have fun the next day in Lahinch, where a performance platform was erected by the shore:

> **Junior Crehan**: I was often at it. I was there one day with Johnny Doran, and we played together out near the promenade [on the platform] … In some of the pubs in Lahinch there would be sessions. There'd be a couple of lads hired to keep playing and draw in a crowd. Doran might be there one year and he wouldn't be there the next, you know. He could be on his

---

* Lahinch is spelt locally as both 'Lahinch' and 'Lehinch'.

travels around. If he was in this district at the time he'd be in Lahinch and Ennistymon and fair days and sports meetings.[286]

A final story from this period, probably from 1946, touches very slightly on a future great name in piping, Liam O'Flynn. Returning to Dublin from the Atlantic coast one day, Johnny made a point of passing through Kill, in Kildare. He had been encouraged to visit a fiddler named Liam O'Flynn (senior):

> **Liam O'Flynn senior**: One day this man came to the door and he said, 'My name is Doran, Johnny Doran. I'm a piper.' And of course I knew him, knew of him, and had heard him playing in places before, but I'd never actually met him. He told me that he'd been in Newbridge and my good friend Sergeant Tom Armstrong, in the Guards' barracks, told him if he was coming this way to call in on me and we could have some tunes together … So Johnny came in and we had a few tunes together, and Johnny was a marvellous piper, one of the best ever … He played tunes I never heard and I was to try and keep up with him, which I wasn't able to do! He had a wonderful style and a great collection of tunes. He played tunes which I'd really never heard before.[287]

Liam Óg (junior) has said that according to his father, one of the tunes Johnny played was a reel called 'The Sligo Maid'. What else was in Johnny's repertoire that we can be sure of?

Martin Rochford recalls meeting Johnny after the latter had played at a wedding in Bodyke, Co. Clare, in June 1938. After a couple of pints at a local pub they went back to Johnny's wagon, where he wrote out a tune for Martin, 'The Swallow's Tail': 'He used to make a grand job of it. … He'd play every way – tight fingering and open fingering. He never played a tune the same, a different touch every time, but still it was the same tune.'[288]

Tommy Hunt recalled that on one occasion in Bundoran Dick O'Byrne, a hard-to-please son of the man who had taught fiddler and recording icon Michael Coleman, requested 'The High Level' hornpipe from Johnny – a performance which relieved O'Byrne of half a crown (two shillings and sixpence).

Reels (a Scottish-derived form) were the most popular tune type within Irish traditional music at the time, and Johnny had many in his repertoire. Those specifically recalled from his performances, in addition to 'The Sligo Maid', are 'My Love Is In America', 'The Flogging Reel', 'The Cup Of Tea', 'The First House In Connaught', 'The Green Groves Of Erin' and 'The Star Of Munster'. The jig 'Coppers & Brass' is recalled, as is the set dance 'The Three Sea Captains', which Martin Rochford remembered as a request from a local music teacher at an all-night session. Martin Talty recalled that Johnny would play some slow airs, including 'The Dear Irish Boy' and 'The Lark In The Clear Air'. We can add the march 'Garryowen', recalled by John McCaffrey, and we might tentatively add the march 'The Mountains Of Pomeroy' and the set dance 'The Blackbird', from Cecil Colville's recollection of the piper at Ballymena. When he was hospitalised in 1948, Johnny is reputed to have played 'The Collier's' and 'The Fermoy Lasses', both reels, with the assistance of his friends.

Of the above 18 titles, Johnny would include five among the 16 tunes he recorded in 1947 (encompassing jigs, reels, hornpipes, set dances and airs): 'The Blackbird', 'Coppers & Brass', 'My Love Is In America', 'The Fermoy Lasses' and 'The High Level'.

*

In the harsh winter months of 1947 leading into 1948, Johnny and his family were based in Dublin, where he was earning some money as a bricklayer's assistant with Andy Conroy, from the Pipers' Club. John Kelly, an old friend from Clare, had moved to Dublin in 1944 and opened a shop in Capel Street. Johnny was a regular visitor and had a particular fondness for Frances Kelly's tea and home-made bread.

Posterity has John Kelly, and the fortuitous availability of Kevin Danaher, to thank for the only recordings of Johnny Doran that were made. Danaher was a Limerick man who had joined the Irish Folklore Commission (IFC) in January 1940, taking leave to join the Irish Defence Forces later that year (becoming a Captain) before returning to the IFC in 1946. His main thrust was to develop its ethnological dimension, but he also became the staff member most involved, in the organisation's early years, in operating a newly acquired (1945) Presto acetate cutting machine. John and Kevin were both interviewed for the 1988 RTÉ documentary:

> **John**: Every night he could, he came … This night it was the month of November, he was very crestfallen looking … 'I'm very bad,' he says to me. He left his pipes down on the floor. 'I've a pain up under my heart,' he says. 'Oh God, that's terrible,' says I. 'Ah, sure, it'll be alright,' he says … The missus came down and I says, 'Do you know what? I think Johnny Doran is going to die. We'd better get him recorded.' I knew Kevin Danaher of the Folklore Commission, and I walked over [the road] to the phone. And on my way over to the phone I had a feeling Danaher would be away down the country, collecting music. [But] it rang on the other side and there was Danaher. I told him I had Johnny Doran in the house and I'd like to get him recorded … 'Okay,' says he, 'bring him over immediately.'

Kevin: It was on a Saturday evening, late Saturday afternoon in Earlsfort Terrace, University College … because at that time the Folklore Commission was working in two or three small rooms at the top there.* And they came up there with this very pleasant small man with a bag under his arm, carrying his pipes. I rigged up the thing and he tuned up his pipes and started to play. And we made a certain number of recordings then. And they were the only recordings as far as I know that were made from Johnny Doran.

John: He recorded about 10 or 12 tunes that night and he got a pound for his labour, which he thought was great money – and that was out of Kevin's pocket.† Money was terribly scarce in those days. He didn't play his best that night, I thought. … The needle was cutting around like a ball of wool, and Johnny was watching that ball as he was playing – and the ball was getting bigger and bigger as the needle was cutting it. It became as big as a football. Johnny threw down the pipes and he made a dive for that ball and he said, 'Oh, I'll bring that up and let my wife see it.'[289]

In fact, Johnny recorded 19 tunes (three of them repeats, so 16 different tunes) in nine sets, thus nine acetate discs. John Kelly joined him, on fiddle, on one set of reels: 'Tarbolton/The Fermoy Lasses'. The 'ball of wool' was swarf, waste material created when the music was cut into the acetate. Johnny seemed to enjoy the recording process:

Kevin: It didn't worry him in the slightest. Indeed, he thought it a bit of a joke, too, that he was playing for an object rather than for people. He used

---

* Breandán Breathnach, in a piece in *An Píobaire* No. 12, 1981 (which included original John Kelly quotations), gave Monday as the evening in question, and also 82 St Stephen's Green (round the corner from Earlsfort Terrace) as the IFC address at the time. *The Dictionary Of Irish Biography* (CUP, 2009) entry on Danaher also states 82 St Stephen's Green as the location. In *Traveller Piper* (NPU, 2009), John Kelly's son gives the day as Wednesday. In both of these sources an arrangement for a second session the following week is referred to – Breathnach stating that this arrangement was obviated by Johnny's accident occurring in between, Kelly junior mistakenly believing that a second session did take place. John Kelly senior clearly states it was November; Johnny's accident happened in January 1948. Why a second session did not take place in the few weeks between these events could be for any number of reasons. No one at the time could have foreseen the catastrophe. Breathnach adds that pipers Andy and Mick Conroy were with Johnny and John Kelly when the recordings were made.

† When Séamus Ennis joined the IFC in 1942, his salary was £3 per week. While Kevin Danaher was the best-paid member of the IFC's staff, he can hardly (given its ramshackle finances) have been earning a significant sum.

to wink at the machine every now and then! The expression on his face led you to believe that this was fun. He was joking with the pipes, you see, and producing all sorts of marvellous results. Doran was a musical genius, there is no doubt about that. And the sad pity is that much, much more recording wasn't done. We had made a tentative arrangement: 'The next time you're round, Johnny, we'll record again.' And he said, 'Oh yes, certainly, certainly.' He was delighted to hear himself playing. And indeed he criticised himself playing. But 'We'll come again,' he said. 'We'll do it again.'[290]

A general election was taking place in Ireland on February 4 1948, called unexpectedly by the incumbent, and increasingly divisive, Taoiseach (Premier), Éamon de Valera, of the party Fianna Fáil. His intention was to curtail the rise of a new socialist party, Clann na Poblachta, led by Seán McBride.* During December or early January, McBride had heard Johnny playing music on the street in Dublin and asked him to play at a campaign meeting in Phoenix Hall. Following the success of this, Johnny was asked to play at the party's final rally, the night before the election, at College Green. It wasn't to be.

On Friday January 30 1948, Johnny was parked at Back Lane opposite Christchurch Cathedral, near to where his parents were living, at Doyle's Cottages on New Street. In 'a sudden gust of wind' the top four-foot section of a wall was blown down on top of Johnny's caravan. As Dublin's *Evening Mail* reported: 'The wooden walls and roof splintered like matchwood and the six occupants were covered in brick, mortar and flying dust.'[291]

---

* Tuohy and Ó hAodha, in *Postcolonial Artist*, posit the idea that Johnny may have shared Seán McBride's hard-line Republican sympathies (rather than, say, his anti-poverty/anti-corruption stance). Their evidence is an anecdote from a Séamus Mac Mathúna interview with Patrick Kelly, a Clare fiddler, who recalled visiting Kilrush one day, with toothache, as a trial of 'Blueshirts' – members of an Irish fascist organisation with origins in the pre-Civil War IRA – involved in a train derailment was taking place in its courthouse. Kelly recalled that it was a fine day and Johnny Doran turned up to play: 'Well, as soon as the court case was over, the square started to fill. They came from nowhere – you never saw such a crowd! Everyone shoving in to see where the music was coming out of, and good he was getting. But the finish of Johnny and my tooth was that I forgot about my tooth, and I came home without ever having it removed.' The story surely says more about the power of Johnny's music than it does about his politics, if indeed he espoused any. He went where the crowds were, and on this particular occasion they were rubber-necking at a courthouse. Given the proximity to the 1916 Rising and 1922 Civil War, many people and organisations in 1930s Ireland had Republican backgrounds of various hues, but my understanding of Clann na Poblachta is that they were opposed to the fascistic version of Republicanism espoused by the 'Blueshirts'. One suspects that Johnny was a non-prescriptive man and a pragmatist.

Of the six occupants, five of his children were unscathed, but Johnny – standing with his foot on a chair, tying a shoelace as the wall fell – suffered back, stomach and head injuries. Transferred to St Kevin's Hospital, he was crippled from the waist down.

> **Martin Talty**: We went up to Dublin – Seán Reid, Willie Clancy and myself. And Leo Rowsome, we met him, and we went into the hospital, St Kevin's ... Johnny, of course, was lying in the bed and couldn't get up. Of course, we had pipes and played a few tunes ... Leo had really gone to town on 'The Collier's' and things like that.* Seán Reid, with the mind he had, was highly imaginative ... He stood in behind the bed and blew the pipes and passed the chanter to Johnny. He stopped it on his chest and he played 'The Collier's'. You should have heard that. My God, the staccato, the way the whole thing rolled out – it was great![292]

Although unable to walk, Johnny recovered enough to resume the travelling lifestyle for a while. Mary Doran, however, was under great pressure. Margaret Cash recalled four daughters remaining at a paid convent school in Dublin from this point, to ease Mary's burden.†

Frank O'Brien recalled meeting him shortly after he was out of hospital, near the Curragh Camp in Kildare: 'He played the pipes lying on his back and he also played a whistle that day. Felix was there, too.'[293]

Margaret Cash also met him, at a horse fair, shortly after the accident and would see him again toward the end:

> [Just] before he died he had changed a lot, aged. But his voice was just as good as ever. And he was all comical ... good-humoured. A short while after that he went to Athy County Hospital [St Vincent's] and I went to see him there.[294]

The team which made the RTÉ *Long Note* documentary in 1988 had the good

---

* Tuohy and Ó hAodha, in *Postcolonial Artist*, don't mention 'The Collier's' but give instead 'The Fermoy Lasses' as a tune Johnny played in his hospital bed, citing Andy Conroy and Willie Clancy as those who helped him. Their source isn't stated.
† While the winter of 1947–48 was clearly a struggle financially, with Johnny working as a bricklayer's assistant and taking whip-rounds from his friends at the Pipers' Club, putting four children into boarding school can't have been cheap. He is reputed to have left £900 when he died in January 1950.

fortune to find Sister Mary Dominic, one of the nursing staff at St Vincent's, who spoke movingly and with clarity about Johnny's last days:

> I met him on the 27th of October 1949, when he was admitted here. He was sent in by the local doctor in Castledermot [Kildare]. He suffered from spinal injuries but also he was very, very weak and very ill and needed hospital care. He was camping in the area at the time and living with his wife. He was so ill that we did not like asking him any questions. But he rallied for a long time … He never wanted to talk about [his accident]. Before he died I learned he was a famous piper from one of his relatives. And I mentioned to Johnny, 'You never let me know that you were a piper.' And he just smiled. But the following Sunday the pipes were brought in by a relative and we asked Johnny to play. We fixed him up comfortably in the bed so he would be able to manage the pipes. And he played a couple of tunes and we were all delighted. The patients that were up gathered around his bedside to hear him, and it was very moving. Because everybody knew that he was a dying man.

Johnny Doran died on January 19 1950.

> **Sister Mary**: He was very weak all that day and hadn't very much to say to anybody. But he joined in the prayers. And I feel he was very dear to God.

*

> **Séamus Ennis**: Listening to Paddy [Keenan]'s piping brings me back to the many pleasant nights I spent listening to Johnny Doran's music in his caravan, then parked somewhere near Templeogue, south of Dublin. Coldly nights, they were, with Mrs Doran making tea for us while winter howled outside. Johnny was a man of the road in a big way … He was a small, dark man, and he seemed to make himself even smaller when he strapped on his pipes and sat in the caravan's corner beside the stove, his cap on at all times, filling our little night with his music.[295]

Séamus Ennis delivered this fond recollection during an RTÉ radio programme he presented on St Patrick's Day 1974, with Paddy Keenan live in session. Later that year Séamus provided, in the notes to Paddy's eponymous Gael Linn album, similar recollections of nights spent in good company with Doran. Presumably these occasions were during the 1942–47 period in which Séamus was a collector for the

IFC. Finbar Furey, in an interview for this book, raised, with some emotion, the question of why Johnny Doran was not recorded more extensively by the IFC and, specifically, at all by Séamus Ennis:

> **Finbar**: They were sent out with microphones into the countryside – and they went past everybody! They went to other people, but they passed the Travelling people – and, you know, those people had the best music, just sitting there.
> [Yes, Doran was eventually recorded by the IFC, but] for 40 minutes, of his entire life! Isn't it amazing that we shouldn't have more? You must imagine that during this time you had Séamus Ennis wandering the roads of Ireland, and Johnny was alive at the time. Felix Doran was alive at the time; so was Seán McAloon. There was wonderful pipers like Willie Clancy alive at the time. All these guys were about. … No matter which way you go, you still come back to Johnny Doran and the Cashes.

The question is a fair one. Johnny Doran was an exceptional musician, a tradition bearer and an originator, all of which must have been obvious to anyone who heard him. Should the IFC have been more proactive in having his genius recorded? Should Séamus Ennis – a man who knew piping, who knew Doran and who must undoubtedly have recognised his brilliance – have done something toward this end personally?

There are a number of points to consider in Séamus' defence, and in defence of the IFC generally. Firstly, Séamus was being dispatched to specific locales (not chosen by himself), essentially to collect material associated with those areas; hence Travellers might by their very nature not be representative of the areas in question.

Secondly, Séamus travelled by bicycle until 1946, when wartime petrol restrictions ended. Ríonach Uí Ógáin points out that Séamus did not have ongoing access to an Ediphone machine (and if he did, he could hardly have carried it long distances by bicycle), but rather was dependent on locally-based collectors such as Seán Ó hEochaidh in Donegal or Liam Mac Coisdealbha in Galway to lend him their machines, generally for a day or part of a day, as was convenient for them. Hence, if he met Johnny by chance on the road, ad-hoc cylinder recording was unlikely.

Thirdly, Séamus was primarily collecting music in written notation form on his field trips, using expensive wax cylinders as a re-useable tool in this process, rather than routinely collecting permanent audio recordings of individual performers. Only very occasionally, such as with a couple of Colm Ó Caodháin items, referenced in his field diaries, did he record a particular performance with a view to it being a permanent record.

Fourthly, it seems clear that Séamus was principally on the hunt, presumably on the instructions of IFC boss James Delargy, for songs and lore. This is reflected both in Ríonach Uí Ógáin's exemplary edition of his IFC field diaries, *Going To The Well For Water: The Séamus Ennis Field Diary 1942–1946* (Cork University Press, 2009), and in the IFC database of his permanent recordings.

Séamus made 29 permanent recordings of tradition bearers for the IFC between 1945 and 1946, and none before that. Of these, 25 were made jointly with Kevin Danaher, presumably on the IFC's recently acquired Presto acetate machine, either at an Oireachtas event in Dublin or at the IFC's Dublin premises; one was made jointly with visiting American collector Alan Lomax; and three were made by Séamus alone on an Ediphone cylinder machine in Connemara, of singers Colm Ó Caodháin and Joe Heaney. Some of the early acetate recordings of Oireachtas performers were made in co-operation with Radio Éireann. Of the joint 1945–46 recordings made with Kevin Danaher, roughly half were songs and lore, the other half music, specifically fiddle pieces from Frank Cassidy, Agnes White, Neilidh Boyle and Johnny Doherty, plus one solitary piece of piping from Paddy Delaney.

Séamus' name is attached to a further 119 permanent recordings for the IFC in 1947. 41 of these were recorded while in the Hebrides; the rest were made in Ireland. Almost half of Séamus' 1947 recordings (51 in total) were made by him alone; the rest of the Irish-based recordings were made jointly with Kevin Danaher; the Hebridean recordings were made jointly with Calum Mac Ghill Eathain. Virtually all of the 1947 recordings, however, were of songs or of lore. The only exceptions to this were two sets of reels and hornpipes by fiddler Denis Murphy and eight items of Highland war piping from Niall Mhic Dhomhnaill and Aonghus Caimbeul in the Hebrides.

The published field diaries make it clear that uilleann pipers were rare in the Irish localities to which Séamus was sent as a collector: often he himself, as a piper, would be a subject of fascination and delight, in demand for evening entertainments, if he happened to have his pipes with him (they would only be with him if he'd had them sent on by post). Séamus made no recordings of the very few pipers he encountered in these localities.*

Fifthly, Johnny Doran was still young in the 1940s. Who could possibly have imagined that he would not live beyond 1950? Hence, recriminations about the IFC

---

* The one piper whom Séamus would meet occasionally on his travels for the IFC was Peait Canavan in Connemara. Inspired to take up piping after seeing Séamus' father playing at a Feis in Carna, Peait acquired his first full set of pipes in 1940 and learned much of his repertoire from books. Nevertheless, Séamus was able to collect transcriptions of nine pieces from him. A devil's advocate might suggest that the question now becomes: 'Why, then, did Séamus not collect any *transcriptions* of music from Johnny Doran?'

only recording him once (in 1947) and Seamus not recording him at all are surely unreasonable.*

> **Ríonach Uí Ógáin**: I do think that all [these] reasons are valid, overlap and we may never know the full answer. ... The IFC's emphasis was on collecting narrative in Irish. That said, collectors recorded and collected from musicians, singers, thatchers and hundreds of others. The IFC also gave particular attention to song in Irish (e.g. [the work of] Ennis, Liam de Noraidh). The resulting collection – now the National Folklore Collection – reflects very much also the individual interests of collectors.

It must be remembered that the IFC was only established in 1935 and was propelled more by vision and the energy of a few individuals than by funds. Anna Bale, archivist of the National Folklore Collection at University College Dublin, offers some perspective:

> **Anna Bale**: I think that the many cultural, political, linguistic and ideological reasons that led to systematic collection of oral tradition in Ireland in 1935 have to be considered in this instance, i.e. that the imminent decline of the Irish language would mean that a rich oral literature would be irretrievably lost – 'Gather The Fragments Lest They Perish', et cetera.
>
> So, from the start, the collecting of lore and songs in Irish was a priority. Apart from the early cylinder recordings, many of which were donations, the first recording of music on acetate disc by the Commission is the fiddle playing of Neillidh Boyle from Donegal in 1945. This is a full five years after the first discs were cut, and all the material on disc up until then was either tales, lore, songs or poetry in Irish.
>
> Nonetheless, there are over 650 recordings of Traveller song, lore and music in the Sound Archive alone, quite apart from any manuscript or photographic material. I think it can be said that the IFC was very much ahead of its time in acknowledging (and collecting) the wealth and variety of lore, language, song and music in the Traveller community. Séamus Ennis' earliest disc recording from a Traveller is in 1946, when he and Kevin Danaher recorded the fiddle music of Johnny Doherty.

---

* It is, nevertheless, just conceivable, given what we know of Séamus' curious tendency toward self-aggrandisement in later life, that he may have harboured some jealousy of Johnny's abilities. But the impression one gets from his field diaries of the generosity of spirit in Séamus' character in the 1940s, coupled with the widely attested mild-mannered, inclusive character of Johnny Doran, makes the idea of envy as a factor in Séamus' not recording Doran unlikely.

Perhaps most pertinent of all when considering Finbar's question is a fully informed understanding of the nature of the IFC, its resources and its priorities at the time. Mícheál Briody's *The Irish Folklore Commission 1935–1970* (2007) makes it painfully clear how desperately the IFC was hobbling from one inadequate government funding round to the next during much of its existence. It was perpetually trying to acquire adequate recording devices – plus, its initial focus was on lore and language rather than music. Even then, when a collector did record something with a view to its being a permanent record, this was within the context of it being a 'sample' of something, rather than part of an exhaustive collection. The IFC was not in the business of making 'albums'. The first commercially viable 12-inch microgroove record was released in 1948, while 'the album' as a concept arguably began with Frank Sinatra's themed collection *In The Wee Small Hours* in 1955.

In August 1947, shortly before Séamus left IFC employ, he accompanied Kevin Danaher on a trip to Kerry to record songs and lore on gramophone discs, 'albeit with somewhat makeshift apparatus'.[296] The following year, the IFC at last had a disc-cutting mobile recording van, even though magnetic tape was now fast becoming the way forward. Danaher would be the driver and recording engineer up to late 1950, when he was moved to other duties:

> **Briody**: Although it mainly concentrated on recording samples of tales and lore, it did collect a good deal of song and instrumental music. Moreover, if the occasion arose, this unit could be sent to collect specifically the repertoires of folk singers and musicians.[297]

By this time, Ennis was working with Radio Éireann's new Outside Broadcasting unit, steering it toward recording traditional musicians whenever possible. By 1951 he would be with the BBC as a full-time collector of folk song and music, visiting Ireland amongst other parts of the Isles. Had Johnny Doran lived, Séamus would surely have sought him out for the BBC project. Similarly, Séamus' eventual successor at Radio Éireann, Ciarán Mac Mathúna – whose *A Job Of Journeywork* was, from 1955 onward, seeking out great traditional performers for broadcasts – would surely also have recorded Doran. Rather than ask why Johnny Doran was not recorded earlier or in greater quantity by the IFC, we should be thankful that he was recorded at all.

However much it may be regretted now that more of the singular magic of Johnny Doran was not captured for posterity, Kevin Danaher of the Irish Folklore Commission, on the basis of one telephone call from a mutual friend, stopped what he was doing one night in November 1947 and recorded a modern day album's worth of music by a man he had apparently never met, in an era before 'the album' truly existed. He made the process enjoyable and honoured the musician with a significant sum of money from his own pocket. He recommended a further session which, regrettably, did not take place within the few active weeks that were left to Doran.

While a case can easily be made (see above) for Johnny Doran as 'the Jimi Hendrix of the pipes', a case can also be made for him as 'the Robert Johnson of the pipes'. An almost exact contemporary of Doran's, Johnson (1911–38) was born in Mississippi and became acclaimed, as his posthumous legend grew, as 'the King of the Delta blues singers', with a guitar style and vocal style that mesmerised contemporaries and became the cornerstone influence of future blues and blues-rock artists. An itinerant musician, Johnson may have borne no comparison with Doran as regards his known personality and behaviour, but there are many other similarities: he recorded a small body of work (29 songs, 13 alternate takes); he defined a tradition, distilling influences up to that point and adding his own particular magic to create something that would become an essential touchstone for future practitioners; there is intrigue about the proper playback speed of his recordings (although in Doran's case this is now resolved); his recordings first circulated widely in the 1960s (Doran's through a widely taped Ciarán Mac Mathúna Radio Éireann broadcast, Johnson's through a 1961 LP release); and he died young, leaving a legend to grow, with the handful of other musicians who knew him giving interviews about him for decades thereafter. One could go on, but the point is made. The one key difference was that Robert Johnson was actively interested in being recorded, having five 78rpm discs released in his lifetime; Johnny Doran was not. It is only posterity which craves more of Doran's music on record; being recorded was only ever a novelty to Doran himself.

Johnny Doran was a travelling entertainer, a man who made people happy and who clearly made himself happy in doing so. That in itself would be a tremendous achievement for anyone. Yet Doran was also an acclaimed artist in his own time, held in awe by other traditional musicians, and has become a figure of still greater awe in the time since. To an extent, as with Johnson (more so in Johnson's case, given the indestructible fascination with stories of devilish deals down at the crossroads) and as with Hendrix, this posthumous reputation is fuelled by captivating mythology and a yearning for the unobtainable.

Like Jimi Hendrix, a black American who found fame as a charismatic virtuoso among white audiences in 1960s pre-multicultural Britain, Johnny Doran was an 'outsider' who effectively beat the system. There was nothing confrontational about him; rather, despite his Traveller lifestyle and ethnicity, he presented himself well in both manners and dress. In doing so, and also through the sheer captivating brilliance of what he did, he laid waste to any prejudices inherent in the time and place within which he operated.

As Touhy and Ó hAodha suggest, with liberal speech marking:

> Far from marginalising him, Johnny Doran's nomadic lifestyle as a travelling musician may actually have been to his advantage both socially and commercially, at least in relation to his music. He is still remembered as a charismatic (and 'mysterious') figure, an artist who was much respected as an individual living the 'free life' of the road. His music and 'image' attracted much attention in an era before 'image' had become the cultural pre-requisite it is today … While it is dangerous to 'over-emphasise' any parallels between his way of life and his musical style, there is nevertheless a strong argument to be made that the 'freedom' in Johnny Doran's playing … was (almost certainly) perceived – in the minds of those who heard him – to be a direct reflection of his lifestyle. It is as if the 'freedom' that was a tenet of his 'nomadic' way of life was being sonically articulated in the free-flowing experimentation and variation of the music which Doran played.[298]

Johnny Doran's 43 minutes of immortality were first released commercially in 1988, by Comhairle Bhéaloideas Éireann on cassette, as *The Bunch Of Keys*. In 2002 they were deftly remastered by Harry Bradshaw and released on CD, with an insightful booklet of notes and photographs, by Na Píobairí Uilleann as *The Master Pipers Vol. 1*. One listen to the medley of 'Colonel Fraser/My Love Is In America/Rakish Paddy' should be enough to convince anyone of the man's extraordinary technical gift and emotional power.

Still, there is always a danger that in venerating the musician we misplace the man. Current piper Peter Laban provided this story to an online Doran appreciation site. While second-hand and vague in attribution, one hopes it is true, for it gives a sense of fun to a human being who is perhaps sometimes in danger of becoming a character of myth in view of the earnest weight of historical significance placed upon him:

> **Peter Laban**: One story I got from an old piper called Rourke … now living in North England. He told me how he got his first set when living in Armagh when he was young. There had been a horse fair and the Travellers were passing through the village. Anyway, he was sitting there, a young piper proud of his new pipes, when in comes these two young Travellers; they sit in for a while listening. After a while one of them said: 'My brother here plays a bit on the pipes – would you let him have a go at your set?'

Well, okay, fine. So the young fellow straps on the pipes and takes playing like mad, all over the regulators, really amazing. He plays a couple of tunes and gives back the pipes, says 'Great set, lad – keep going', and goes. Leaving the young piper completely baffled with disbelief. Anyway, the man who told this story said that years later he was listening to a radio program on Felix Doran and in this program Felix told the story of the trick he and his brother once played on a young piper. The now old piper at last understood what had happened when he was young.[299]

As another current piper, Mickey Dunne, wisely observed, from the standpoint of the 21st century, whatever Johnny Doran's qualities as a musical icon across generations, he had something perhaps greater in his own lifetime to which surely everyone can relate. Pipers can aspire to the way Johnny Doran played music; the rest of us can aspire to the way he lived.

Mickey Dunne: The freedom he had. … No one to tell him what to do – he did his own thing. … And if you see where he parked [near Miltown] – you could see the sea, and the day I was there, like, there was a nice breeze blowing – lovely and warm – and I thought, 'Jesus, that man had it sorted out'![300]

Chapter 13
The Only Patsy Touhey

Séamus Ennis: You couldn't fault Patsy Touhey. He was the greatest I've heard of the men before my father's time.[301]

Finbar Furey: He was a true *entertainer*. If there are great pipers, you have to be entertainers as well. Patsy Touhey told jokes for a living – he was a cabaret artist who played the pipes. Chief O'Neill couldn't do without him, because he would draw everybody in, draw in other pipers.* Patsy Touhey and Johnny Doran were the two greatest exponents of uilleann pipes ever – *ever*. And on the regulators my *whole* inspiration, not for the playing on the regulators but for the *tone* he got from his regulator playing, was Patsy Touhey. It was nothing to do with the reeds, it was how much air he was putting into the regulators. He played in that jumpy style, which Felix Doran [emulated] – like dance music, like Donegal musicians.

Patsy Touhey (1865–1923) was born near Loughrea, Co. Galway, became a star in America and lives on as almost the first recorded uilleann piper – and certainly the first that mattered. He saw recorded sound as an economic and career-building opportunity and, via newspaper adverts from 1901 onward, dealt directly with the public – offering 'Original Phonograph Records of the Irish pipes made to order by the Best Irish Piper in America'. This was in a time almost before a commercial music industry. Save for the bespoke nature of his wax cylinder performances ($1 each, $10 for a dozen), Touhey's approach remains a striking portent of the way most professional musicians, in a virtually post-music-industry landscape, operate today.

*

---

* Francis O'Neill, Chicago police chief and hugely important, as a writer and collector, in the preservation of Irish traditional music in America during the late 19th and early 20th centuries. Finbar: 'Francis O'Neill – a fantastic man. They landed in New York and he got them a room, there were no badges … I found that every time I came back to Ireland after the 70s there was a new tradition, a new badge, a new schism … They broke Ireland up into so many different flags, different styles. And if you look, really, it's all the same style. It's just different accents.'

Patsy Touhey's family emigrated to New York when he was around three, in 1868. Although his father, grandfather and two uncles were all pipers, Patsy had not taken up the instrument by the time his father died in 1875. He subsequently took lessons from one of his father's pupils. In 1886, aged 21, he began to play professionally, touring up and down the East Coast for a year with fellow piper John Egan. In contrast to his respectful and humble offstage character, he embraced professionally his vaudeville stage billing as 'The Only Patsy Touhey'.

A great friend of future Chicago police chief Francis O'Neill, who would often write admiringly of his friend's character and musicianship, Patsy appears to have had a breakthrough moment with his appearance at Mrs Hart's 'Donegal Castle' within the Chicago World's Fair in 1893. Outside the exhibition, the suitably venerable, dour and be-whiskered Turlough McSweeney (shipped in from County Donegal) represented the 'old music' and the 'old country'; inside, a clean-shaven, youthful Patsy Touhey (albeit wearing knee breeches and a deerstalker hat) represented the new world. As Francis O'Neill described it 20 years later: 'the hopes and aspirations of a regenerated nation were pleasingly typified in 'Patsy' Touhey, the spruce young man in corduroy breeches and ribbed stockings, whose expert manipulation of a great set of Taylor pipes made him the centre of attraction within.'[302]

Patsy had embraced the innovations of the Taylor brothers (from Drogheda, by then based in Philadelphia) in pipes construction. Specifically designed to be more effective on the US vaudeville stages, Taylor pipes were louder than previous designs and were, for the first time, in concert pitch. It was the final step in the evolution of the uilleann pipes as we know them today.

Francis O'Neill provides a compelling sketch of Touhey in action at the height of his fame in 1903:

> When Myles Murphy, manager of the 'Irish Village' at the Louisiana Purchase Exposition held at St Louis, Missouri, in 1903, determined to obtain the best talent for his concession, he engaged 'Patsy' Touhey at the latter's own price. And it proved a capital stroke of business for Mr. Murphy at that.
>
> So novel and captivating was his performance of all varieties of music on the Irish pipes on the stage of the Irish Theatre, that the members of the 'International Association of Chiefs of Police', about 200 in number, who attended the play in a body, encored his playing repeatedly, and wanted him to continue his wonderful music indefinitely but four encores were all the stage manager would allow. Neither sentiment nor early associations had much to do with this acclaim, for the majority of those present were of other than Irish ancestry, and of the latter less than half were of Irish birth.

As comedian and piper Touhey has been before the American public all over the United States for years, and while at this writing many hundreds of theatrical people are out of employment, it speaks well for his standing with the public that he is rarely without an engagement.[303]

One of Patsy's greatest hits as a comic performer was a bit of stage business in which he fell off the end of a bench. One could keep the punters roaring indefinitely with such a routine in those days. Four years later, Francis O'Neill posted a number of wax cylinders of Irish musicians as a Christmas present to an associate, a Reverend Richard Henebry in Waterford. The Reverend was effusive in his response:

> The five by Touhey are the superior limit of Irish pipering. One of his, especially, 'the Shaskeen Reel', is so supreme that I am utterly without words to express my opinion of it. … It represents to me human man climbing empyrean heights and, when he had almost succeeded, then tumbling, tumbling down to hell and expressing his sense of eternal failure on the way. The Homeric ballads and the new Brooklyn Bridge are great, but Patsy Touhey's rendering of 'The Shaskeen Reel' is a far bigger human achievement. Why there is no Irish musician alive now in his class.[304]

Ironically, O'Neill himself could disagree with that view. Bernard Delaney, to whom he had given employ in the Chicago Police Department, was, he felt, a better player for dancers, though Touhey was superior on the regulators.* In terms of personality, however, the pair could hardly be further apart:

> **Francis O'Neill**: Delaney, although picked off the streets by me and given a chance which made him wealthy, is disobliging, greedy and most ungrateful. … Touhey has no disagreeable qualities at all, being kindly, obliging and not at all troubled with conceit.[305]

While a tremendous patron of Irish music, owner of a number of Touhey cylinder recordings himself, and a huge fan of Touhey in live performance, Francis O'Neill did not share Reverend Henebry's unbridled enthusiasm for his recorded works:

> I never heard a record of Touhey's to do him anything like justice. The drones being pointed away from the horn are scarcely audible and as his chanter is

---

* Cylinder recordings of Delaney made in 1898 in Chicago survive and do indeed reveal him to have been a very fluent player.

always sharp concert pitch and the regulators toned accordingly, they sound somewhat harsh and jarring when reproduced on the phonograph.[306]

Patsy Touhey was, in general, somewhat brighter in outlook than his friend. By 1911 O'Neill could foresee only false dawns (momentary faddish 'revivals') and inexorable decline for Irish traditional music. His letters blame the Irish in general, particularly those in America, for abandoning their heritage for alternative entertainments and Irish musicians in America for falling out with each other. He was also dubious about the opportunities attainable through commercial recordings:

> If the genuine demand for Irish pipe music existed, it would be gladly supplied, but it doesn't. … Patsy Touhey could not get enough for his time from the record people. His theatrical business is more profitable. They found a cheaper man, McAuliffe, and cheaper work of course. He is now dead.[307]

Eventually, though, Patsy Touhey did throw in his lot with the 'record people'. Accepting that the time of the wax cylinder had passed, he recorded four 78rpm sides for Victor in 1919, although only three sides would be released. While around 58 of his recordings are known to survive, these three sides have an appreciably better sound quality. Even Francis O'Neill, one imagines, must have been impressed.

Touhey died in January 1923, aged only 57 and still at that time a popular presence on the American theatrical scene. He lives on because he embraced technology. There are always more cylinders to be unearthed, but of his known works, 58 are transcribed in Pat Mitchell and Jackie Small's *The Piping Of Patsy Touhey* (NPU, 1986), with excellent biographical material, while 36 are presented on a CD of the same title (NPU, 2005). Save for the pratfalls on benches, most of those involved professionally in Irish music today are following the Touhey model exactly: touring for a living, releasing music direct to consumers (websites replacing newspaper ads, CDs and downloads replacing cylinders) as a sideline. And perhaps all those so engaged today also hope that beyond making them a living in the here and now, their works might ensure them the afterlife of that man born 150 years ago. For Patsy Touhey's music traverses the bridge between archaeology and living influence. It still has the power to connect.

Chapter 14
Uilleann Piping Before 1900

Until the modern era, the uilleann pipes were a relatively obscure instrument, limited almost entirely to Ireland and the Irish diaspora in America. The players, at any given time, of this beguiling but fiendishly complex machine were never numerous. Around 1700 the instrument, in a form more or less recognisable to the modern player, fades into view; somewhere around 1800 it attains the end point in its evolution; and somehow, over the following 150 years or so, it makes it, alive and well (just about), into the modern age of global communications and professional recording artistry.[*]

The instrument's popularity, and consequently its very chances for survival, ebbed and flowed several times over those three centuries. There was a legal framework for the prohibition of Irish music during the Penal Laws era in the 18th century; piping having outlived that, the post-Famine (1845) period in Ireland looked bleak for its survival; but the tradition clung on and even prospered toward the end of the 19th century in America, with pipers visible as entertainers on the vaudeville stage. Indeed, recordings of Irish pipers in America – epitomised by Patsy Touhey, the greatest of all recorded pipers from that time and place – pre-date by several years the earliest recordings of indigenous American jazz and blues. Yet even during this relative boom time for the instrument, Francis O'Neill, Chicago's chief of police and a tireless enthusiast and chronicler of Irish music, to whom we owe much of our knowledge of pre-20th century pipers, was prophesying doom for the instrument within a generation.

Following a brief flurry of interest in the pipes back in Ireland during the 'Gaelic Revival' of the 1890s, things again began to look rather lean, although the Travelling community was sustaining the instrument and its repertoire away from the spotlight of public revivals – its own tradition of piping having a kind of

---

[*] 'End point in its evolution' might be going too far. The instrument in its standard current form was essentially complete by around 1800: chanter, drones, regulators, keys. Nevertheless, the Taylor brothers of Drogheda would standardise its pitch and dimensions in the late 19th century, while others after that, including R.L. O'Mealy, would experiment with adding a contrabass regulator and suchlike. Innovations in the uilleann pipes' design are certainly still possible today.

fountainhead in the figure of John Cash, a celebrated virtuoso from the mid to late 19th century, and reaching an apex in the extraordinary recordings of his great-grandson Johnny Doran in 1948: 43 minutes whose impact within the world of piping might be said to equate to Elvis Presley's influence, eight years later, on the course of popular music.

In addition to Doran, who remains an almost mythical figure, the middle years of the 20th century were dominated by three individuals – longer-lived and more frequently recorded – who bridged the centuries of oral tradition, passing it from a handful of people in one generation to a handful in the next and on into the safety of the modern commercial recording era: Leo Rowsome, Willie Clancy and Séamus Ennis. All three were very different characters and musicians, but the sounds and styles of practically all modern pipers of note, including John McSherry, can be traced back to these few individuals (together with Johnny Doran and, to a lesser extent, Patsy Touhey) – either directly or via others, like Finbar Furey, Paddy Keenan and Liam O'Flynn, whom they influenced and whose own recordings, within the modern popular music arena and within the cult of virtuosity (as integral to Irish traditional music as it is to rock and jazz), have been great in number and globally accessible to the masses.

While there are great sweeping vistas of pure speculation and deserts of ignorance in the long history of Irish traditional music, there are still enough tantalising scraps, going back to the Dark Ages of European history in the first millennium AD, upon which to build plausible conjectures. The same can be said of the pipes themselves, from the primitive mouth-blown instruments of the ancient world in the Middle East to the many-tentacled Irish device, and its various European relatives, of the present. Along the way, the insights and oversights and internecine squabbles of the individuals who undertook early attempts at scholarship and historical enquiry provide not only evidence but a certain amount of fun in themselves. For all the arguments between, and subsequent criticisms of, the early historians, we must be grateful for their interest and their efforts. Something is better than nothing. Any advantage a prospective cultural historian in, say, the 18th or 19th century had in terms of proximity to 'the source' of the tradition he or she was examining must be counterbalanced by the sheer logistical difficulties of those times in communication, in travel, in transcription, in ensuring accuracy of information and in so many other areas.

One might say that Séamus Ennis – a man whose own character and wisdom seemed so delightfully to fulfil all the mystical, magical attributes of 'the piper' in lore – embodied the last hurrah of the old-style historian of the culture (through his professional engagement in field recording and music collecting in the 1940s and 50s) while also providing the template for the modern traditional musician as professional recording artist. As a great eccentric, he was but the latest in a long line.

*

'We cannot find that the Bagpipe was indigenous to the Irish. To the Caledonians, we believe, they must be content to owe it. We got it, as it were, in exchange for the harp.'
— Joseph Walker, 1786[308]

Joseph Walker was a founding member of the Royal Irish Academy, with antiquarian interests in the history of Irish music, art and clothing and in Italian drama. By the time he was putting into print his ideas on bagpipes, toward the end of the 18th century, in a well intentioned, ground-breaking and entertaining (if wildly speculative) work entitled *Historical Memoirs Of The Irish Bards*, the creature then known as the union pipes, which had emerged from the impenetrable mists of history earlier in that century, was coming to the apex of its development. By 1800 the instrument had become, and would remain, the most complex and versatile of all the many varieties of bagpipes around the world, with under-arm bellows, an eight-hole chanter, three drones, three regulators and a number of keys, giving a range of two octaves with options for chordal accompaniment.

'Though the Bagpipe,' Walker continued, 'was the solace of the Scotch Chieftain, and though the Scotch Piper received his musical education from a College of Pipers, yet this instrument never received any considerable improvements from the Scots. It was reserved for the Irish to take it from the mouth and to give it its present complicated form ...'[309]

In attempting to chronicle the history of Irish music, Walker was doing something not quite, but almost, unprecedented.† His efforts would not necessarily be appreciated by all who came later, but they were a marked improvement in credibility on those of his immediate predecessor in the field, General Charles Vallancey, and a vast improvement in tone from the originator of the genre, Giraldus Cambrensis, or Gerald of Wales.

---

* There is a tradition of a piping college operating on Skye in the Early Modern era, with anecdotal evidence of regular traffic between the pipers of Scotland and Ireland. Similar-period suggestions of a school of piping in Ireland are less well attested.
† 'I trust I am offering to my countrymen an acceptable present: the gift has novelty, at least, to recommend it,' Walker wrote, in a preface to his work. 'Though Ireland has long been famed for its poetry and music, these subjects have never yet been treated of historically. I do not pretend to have done completely, what has lain so long undone ... However, I have marked out a path which may facilitate the pursuit of those who shall hereafter follow me.'

Vallancey was an Englishman who began the pseudo-etymological process that resulted in the union pipes of the 18th and 19th centuries becoming, by 1905, the uilleann pipes of the 20th century and beyond. Gerald of Wales would not have recognised either term – nor, indeed, the instrument itself. He was, unsurprisingly, a Welshman, who visited Ireland twice during the 1180s, as a clerk in the service of King Henry II. His *Topographia Hibernica* was published around 1188, in the first of many editions, and in it he may or may not have documented the ancestor of the Irish bagpipes in the form of a mysterious instrument he called a *Chorus*.

'The Irish are a rude people,' wrote Gerald, 'subsisting on the produce of their cattle only, and living themselves like beasts – a people that has not yet departed from the primitive habits of pastoral life ... They neither employ themselves in the manufacture of flax or wool or in any kind of trade or mechanical art; but abandoning themselves to idleness, and immersed in sloth, their greatest delight is to be exempt from toil, their richest possession, the enjoyment of liberty ... This people then, is truly barbarous, being not only barbarous in their dress but suffering their hair and beards to grow enormously in an uncouth manner ... Whatever natural gifts they possess are excellent, in whatever requires industry they are worthless ...'[310]

The 'enormous' hair and beards that so vexed Gerald would reappear the better part of a millennium later, as Irish traditional musicians carved out a viable space in the stadium rock era of the 1970s. Nevertheless, amidst all this opprobrium toward the lifestyle, habits and morality of the inhabitants of Ireland, Gerald made an exception for one activity:

> I find among these people commendable diligence only on musical instruments, on which they are incomparably more skilled than any other nation I have seen. Their style is quick and lively. It is remarkable that, with such rapid finger-work, the musical rhythm is maintained and that, by unfailingly disciplined art, the integrity of the tune is fully preserved throughout the ornate rhythms and the profusely intricate polyphony.[311]

It is tempting to think of piping as being hinted at in this reference to rapid finger-work and polyphony. Gerald's book is notable for listing various native instruments, among them the enigmatic *Chorus*, but notable too for containing no more obvious mention of pipes. Given that the man clearly knew a bagpipe when he saw or heard one (calling a bagpipe a bagpipe in other works on the Scots and Welsh), this seems curious.' But the history of any instrument or musical tradition will be riddled with tantalising glimpses, vague references, things that are lost and, just occasionally, things that are found. And across all of it will be a great deal of speculation. The story of Irish piping does not, in any of these aspects, disappoint.

Topographia Hibernica was to be the first significant work on Ireland, its people and its customs from the perspective of an outsider, albeit one who apparently couldn't abide foreigners. General Vallancey's series of six volumes published between 1770 (the year of his arrival in Ireland) and 1804, as *Collectanea De Rebus Hibernicis*, was the next.† It was a case of quantity over quality. As one biographical resource puts it: 'in the light of modern research his theories and conclusions – a fanciful compound of crude deductions from imperfect knowledge – are shown to be without value.'[312]

Vallancey's successors could hardly do worse, even if the mists of time might be said to have become a great deal foggier after his intervention than they were before it. But he remains, in a way, the man who may be said to have 'invented' the uilleann pipes: seeing a passing mention of 'woollen bagpipes' in an edition of Shakespeare's *The Merchant Of Venice*, he presumed 'woollen' to be an mishearing

---

* Captain Francis O'Neill, in *Irish Minstrels And Musicians* (1913), reported that the bagpipe in Wales had died out around the beginning of the 14th century. The bagpipe as an instrument in regular use in England is referred to in Chaucer's *Canterbury Tales*, the writing of which began in the 1380s. It was, in England, an instrument associated with fairs and entertainment, which eventually developed two drones. (A third drone was only added to the Great Highland Bagpipe in the late 18th century, marking the end of its development.) The English bagpipe was favoured by various kings but apparently never used in a military context, unlike its cousins from Scotland and Ireland – instruments that *were* used within the British military. As O'Neill puts it, writing in 1913: 'The English bagpipe survived with varying degrees of popularity until early in the 18th century, although the Northumbrian pipes – a distinct and much improved variety – remained in favour for a generation or two afterwards; and from recent accounts it is not altogether extinct.'

† Charles Vallancey (1721–1812) came to Ireland with the military in 1770 and immediately set his antiquarian interests to work on the hitherto ignored field of Irish history. In that respect, one has to admire his energy and pioneering interest. Unfortunately, he was no good. Alfred Webb's online *Compendium Of Irish Biography* quotes 19th century Irish music collector George Petrie as saying: 'It is a difficult and rather unpleasant task to follow a writer so rambling in his reasonings and so obscure in his style; his hypotheses are of a visionary nature.' The *Compendium* quotes another source, the *Edinburgh Review*, as saying: 'To expose the continual error of his theory will not cure his inveterate disease. It can only excite hopes of preventing infection by showing that he has reduced that kind of writing to absurdity, and raised a warning monument to all antiquaries and philologians that may succeed him.' The *Quarterly Review* appears to summarise historiography's debts to the man: 'General Vallancey, though a man of learning, wrote more nonsense than any man of his time, and has unfortunately been the occasion of much more than he wrote.'

or Anglicisation of 'uilleann', the Irish word for elbow. W.H. Grattan Flood was peddling the same notion more than a century later. In fact, the very appearance of the word in Shakespeare would seem to be a misprint, 'swollen' making much more sense. Writing a decade or so later, even Joseph Walker had the sense to note that 'a late learned and ingenious commentator on Shakespear,' reads *swol'n* for woollen bagpipe ... This may be the right reading, but we are not certain that it is; it does not, therefore, preclude conjecture.'[313]

He wasn't wrong there: that single leap from a probable misprint of one word to a speculative corruption of an unrelated Irish word has given the whole concept of 'uilleann pipes', as both an instrument and a name, a bogus backdating to the 16th century. A tad unfairly for both Vallancey and Walker, their role in the naming of the uileann pipes is largely forgotten – the phrase being typically described as 'a 20th century Irish Gaelic neologism'[314] or, more bluntly, as an invention of W.H. Grattan Flood in his 1905 work *A History Of Irish Music*.

Despite adding his footnote on the notion that basing anything on Shakespeare's 'woollen' might be a waste of time, Joseph Walker nonetheless allowed himself to state the then-current (1786) position on the nomenclature of the Irish pipes – the word on the street, as it were – in an effort to justify Vallancey's etymology:

> At this day the Pipers call their bellows *bollog na Cuisli*, the bellows of the Cuisli, or veins of the arms on the inside, on the first joint; and as this joint on the outside is denominated Ullan or Uilean (i.e. Elbow), Vallancey concludes that Ullan pipes and Cuisli pipes are one and the same.† In Ullan pipes we have, perhaps, the woollen Bagpipe of Shakespear, to which he attributes an extraordinary effect ...[315]

And what was this extraordinary effect? As the playwright puts it, quite bafflingly, in *The Merchant Of Venice*:

> 'And others, when the bagpipe sings i' th' nose,
> Cannot contain their urine.'[316]

---

* Walker is referring here to *Comments On The Last Edition Of Shakespeare's Plays* (1785) by Dublin scholar John Monck Mason. As Mason's dates are 1726–1809, Walker's 'late' translates as 'recent' – the previous year, in fact, to his own book.
† Denis Brooks, in an essay in *The Pipers' Review* (Vol. 1 No. 2, 1980), explores many names in Irish and Scots Gaelic used during the 18th century for the pipes and their constituent parts. As well as 'Union pipes', he says the instrument, by 1800, was also sometimes referred to as *cuislean* and *cuisle-ciuil*.

After a couple of centuries of clear-headed reflection, Breandán Breathnach, in the very first issue of *An Píobaire* (journal of the then-recently formed Irish piping organisation Na Píobairí Uilleann), after dutifully reprinting some of Walker and Vallencey's views on the matter, was able to caution subscribers that 'Ullan pipes ... would seem to denote an instrument then in existence, but the term is not found independent of Vallancey ... The remarks about the veins and the elbows strike one as fanciful.'[317]

And while he was at it, it was time to take the sanctimonious W.H. Grattan Flood down a peg or two. Breathnach reprinted a 1904 letter from Grattan Flood to a journal, in which the latter's idea that 'Union' was 'an Anglicised corruption of uilleann (Shakespeare's woollen)'[318] was propounded as if it were fact; the letter also stated: 'Everybody knows the old proverb 'more power to your elbow', which had a special significance in the case of the Uileann or Union pipes.'[319]

'The suggestion of Vallancey has become a fact with Grattan Flood,' rued Breathnach. '[But] I had always thought that the expression 'more power to your elbow' referred to drinking ... It may be added that Grattan Flood is even less reliable than either Walker or Vallancey.'[320]

*

Writing in 1971, in his *Folk Music And Dances Of Ireland*, Breandán Breathnach summed up the state of learning at that time on the antiquity of the bagpipes in Ireland. What he wrote remains a valid summary today:

> It seems safe to take it the bagpipe was known in 11th century Ireland ... The earliest mention of it occurs in the 9th century; by the 11th century pipes had spread like wildfire throughout Western Europe.[321]

Sculptural evidence suggests some form of bagpipes as far back as the Hittite Empire in the Near East, circa 1,000 BC. Second century Roman writer Suetonius, the man who set in motion the story that the Emperor Nero (54–68 AD) fiddled (or, to put it more accurately, lyred) while Rome burned, suggests that the same Emperor could also play the bagpipes, mouth-blown but seemingly involving under-arm bellows.' Whatever their role in the ancient world, the things were all over Europe by the second millenium AD. In medieval Ireland, the successor to Nero's lyre was the king of instruments. As Joseph Walker put it: 'The Bagpipe has always been obliged to yield ... amongst the Irish, to the Harp; but it has ever been a favourite instrument of the vulgar.'[322]

---

* As Derek Scott, a leading Popular Culture academic and bagpiping enthusiast, notes: 'I seem to recollect reading that he won every bagpipe competition he entered.'

Walker's book, *Historical Memoirs Of The Irish Bards* (1786), was published just six years before the Irish harp tradition's swansong at the Belfast Festival of Harpers in 1792. Virtually all that is now known of the lifestyle and repertoire of the itinerant harper in Ireland – a noble tradition dating at least back to the era of the 8th century Brehon Laws (which gave a harper the legal value of four cows) – derives from the 'eleventh hour' notation and observations of Edward Bunting at that 1792 event. It had been held specifically to document an all-but-dead tradition, which duly fulfilled its destiny and perished more or less immediately. Largely by chance, the union pipes and their players were poised to move into the recently vacated space once occupied in Irish music and society by harps and harpers.

'Household pipers became the vogue as the harp declined,' wrote Francis O'Neill, in 1913, 'and a capable performer was never at a loss for an engagement at castle, or hall, in the homes of the gentry … In a sense, the wandering piper … was a combination of mail service, news agency and general entertainer.'[323]

Travelling back the better part of a thousand years, we find ancestors of both harp and pipes on Muiredach's High Cross at Monasterboice, dated to the 9th or 10th century. On one side of the decorated edifice is a lyre, on the other are 'triple pipes' (a mouth-blown instrument) – supposed to represent, respectively, 'the blessed' and 'the damned'.[324]

Writing in 2012, Keith Sanger identifies instruments on similar crosses in Scotland as 'a mouth blown triple pipe similar to the Launeddas still played today in Sardinia':

Keith Sanger: The potential change from a Launeddas type of instrument using the mouth as the air reservoir and circular breathing to adding a bag for a reservoir is technical rather than musical. By providing a bigger reservoir it simply allows the instrument to increase in size and therefore volume and there is certainly some evidence in Scotland that the bagpipe may have still been growing in size over the course of the 16th century.

[But] exactly when the 'bagpipe' first appeared in the British Isles is not easy to determine. Some have argued the case for a bagpipe in Ireland by the 11th or early 12th centuries having appeared in Britain and Europe at that time. Actually these claims are based on references using various words translatable as 'pipe/piper' with no indication of a bag. But comparison with later sources suggests that a bagpipe could be covered by these terms. Investigation is showing that of some 300 contemporary references to named Scottish bagpipers pre 1800, none of them actually mention a bag; however the earliest firm reference which does comes from the household accounts of Edward I of England in 1285–86.[325]

Nailing down precisely what is being referred to in pre-18th century sources that appear to be talking about 'pipes' or 'pipers' of some kind is indeed the big difficulty. Drag that back to the first millennium AD and the difficulty becomes even bigger.

In 'Of Music And Musical Instruments In Ancient Erinn', one of his lectures to the Royal Irish Academy in the late 1850s, the pioneering Irish linguist and cultural historian Eugene O'Curry described nine classes of musicians attested to in the Brehon Laws (which he dated to the 5th century):

> The fifth is the *Cuislennach*, who played the *Cuislenna Ciuil*, or musical tubes, whatever they were … The ninth performer on my list is the *Pipaire*, or piper, who is mentioned in the Brehon Laws among the lower class of artists, ranking with the mechanics … *Ergolan* and *Scalfortach* are names for a piper preserved in some of our latter-day glossaries but, as both words imply a loud noise, they must apply to that species of pipes which we know at present as the Highland Pipes of Scotland.[326]

We are left with the impression that, whatever they were in Brehon Ireland, 'pipers' and 'pipe-blowers' were distinct entities. Then again, in his own glossary of terms, O'Curry identified both *Cuisleanna* and *Pipaí* as the same thing: 'bag-pipes'.*

O'Curry and subsequently others have cited a poem on the fair at Carman, from *The Book Of Leinster* (compiled around 1160), as a further indication of some form of bag-blown pipes in Ireland. A couple of tantalisingly opaque lines in it mention:

> *'Pipes, fiddles, shackle men,*
> *Bonemen and tube-players …'*

Early illustrations of bagpipes in Europe, from illuminated manuscripts, woodcuts and the like, are fascinating things, most coming with a variety of caveats about their representational veracity. One famous illustration of a bagpiper (specifically, a German one) is a wood engraving by Albrecht Dürer, dated to 1514. The instrument depicted – two long drones and a long chanter – is similar to those in three illustrations purportedly of Irish pipers from the latter third of the century, the first (dated sometime after 1567) being by a Belgian, Lucas De Heere. It has

---

* Alternative views are, of course, possible. Denis Brooks, in *The Pipers' Review* (Vol. 1 No. 3, June 1980), argues that the presence of both 'cuslennaig' [players of cuisle] and 'pipaí' in the same text, *The Book Of Leinster*, invalidates the notion that the 'cuisle' was a bagpipe of any sort, meaning that it must instead be 'perhaps a primitive reed-pipe of some sort'.

been suggested that, even aside from questions over the player's costume, the substantial instrument depicted 'resembles quite clearly the large Belgian bagpipe of the later 16th century'.³²⁷

It might be presumed that John Derricke's *Image Of Ireland* of 1581,⁎ a work of 12 woodcuts and prose concerned with an English trouncing of Irish rebels in the 1570s – containing representations of the Irish lifestyle of which Giraldus Cambrensis would surely have approved – would be more accurate. Apparently not.

> **Denis Brooks**: It is questionable whether [Derricke] had even been in Ireland … [his] piper closely resembles De Heere's: as it is unlikely that an artist (and [an] English [one] at that) would have been present and close enough to the Irish to render an illustration of a raiding party, it must be concluded that the work was a studio job.³²⁸

Brooks dismisses a third illustration from the period, captioned 'Irish Warpiper', as an obvious copy of Derricke, and of no value.

Whatever such an instrument looked like, the earliest certain knowledge of its being used in a theatre of war by Irish musicians dates to Henry VIII's siege of Boulogne in 1544 (although there are, naturally, vague possible references going still further back). The last documented sighting of Great Irish War Pipes on the field was in Belgium, in the service of George II at the Battle of Fontenoy, in 1745 – almost exactly 200 years after Boulogne.†

Writing within living memory of Fontenoy, the antiquarian Joseph Walker told his readers: 'We cannot find that the Bagpipe was indigenous to the Irish. To the Caledonians, we believe, they must be content to owe it. We got it, as it were, in exchange for the harp.'³²⁹

Written evidence for Scottish war pipes of some sort goes back to 1396 and a skirmish in Perth, although a tradition has been propounded (more out of desire for it to be true than on any reliable evidence) that pipes were present at the Battle of Bannockburn, scene of a still-resonant Scots triumph over England a century

---

⁎ All 12 visual plates of Derricke's work, from its sole surviving copy, can be viewed at: en.wikipedia.org/wiki/The_Image_of_Irelande,_with_a_Discoverie_of_Woodkarne

† Writing in 1971, Breandán Breathnach noted that, through the proliferation of pipe bands, their Associations and their competition culture, 'the war pipes are much more popular than the Uilleann pipes in Ireland'. He did, however, note: 'The traditional manner of playing on the war pipes was lost sometime during the 18th century. The present vogue dates back to the opening years of the present century, when members of [newly founded] pipers' clubs in Cork and Dublin strove to re-awaken an interest in the instrument.' (*Folk Music And Dances Of Ireland*, 1971; revised 1977)

earlier. Nevertheless, while the written evidence for the Great Highland Bagpipes of Scotland certainly predates that for the Great Irish War Pipes, the two instruments were, in all probability, always identical.

The parallel development situation is reflected in anecdotes of pipers travelling between 'colleges of piping' in Skye and in Ireland at the time: however one interprets the concept of a 'college', the frequency of the travelling and the sharing of music and technique between the two nations is not in doubt. All the 16th century illustrations of these instruments depict two drones and a chanter, with a large bag held at the front of the player, although Denis Brooks notes that 'curiously, it seems that the bass drone was known in Ireland by at least 1500, predating its appearance in Scotland'.[330] Thus, we may be forgiven for thinking that the causal relationship between Highland and Irish pipes, at their inception, was not dissimilar to the matter of bovine tuberculosis in the 21st century: of the badgers and the cows, we may never know who was to blame.

> **Francis O'Neill (1913)**: In the more ancient pictures of pipers … the bag rests on the performer's breast and stomach … This style would naturally be called the '*Cuisle* pipes', as the pressure on the bag to expel the air is exerted by the forearms or wrists – hence, *cuisle*, or pulse. A later development of the warpipe was in placing the bag, much diminished in size, under the arm, in which position the necessary pressure is administered by the elbow or *Uilleann* … However, the *Uilleann pipes* of those days were still the warpipes or *Piob Mor*;* and they must not be confounded with the *Uilleann* or Union pipes, which were practically a new instrument, developed in the early years of the 18th century …. [Precisely] when the Piob Mor or warpipe was transformed into the Irish or Union pipes, is largely a matter of conjecture …[331]

As with the origins of any music born of an oral tradition, it is only to be expected that there comes a point where facts disappear into the mists of speculation: the event horizon of certainty. Irish piping is no exception. It is nonetheless surprising to learn that, very largely through the efforts of Francis O'Neill, there is considerably greater source material on the nature and personalities of Irish piping before the

---

* Writing in 1980, Denis Brooks argues that, in Ireland: 'The mouth-blown bagpipe was known most often by the simple piob mala (not piob mor, a distinctly Scottish Gaelic term). The bag of the pipes was mala or bolg; as part of the name for 'bagpipe', mala is found in less frequently used denominations, such as mail-phiob and mala ceoil, and boilg may also have occurred.' (*The Pipers' Review*, Vol. 1 No. 2, 1980)

20th century than on, say, the origins of the blues in America.*

The instrument we know now as the uilleann pipes dovetailed conveniently into prominence as the harp declined. Travelling pipers (often blind) in effect took the place in Irish society and music that had previously belonged to the harpers. It was not a case of supplanting, but rather one of survival of the fittest, given a variety of social and economic factors – the two instruments having co-existed happily for around a century by the time of the valedictory Belfast Festival Of Harpers in 1792. Whether the uilleann pipes, or union pipes as they were known at the time, can be traced back much further than the early years of that century, in any recognisable form, remains a question that will doubtless continue to be asked, attacked and circled around for a long time yet. And the answer will likely continue to remain impenetrable.

*

Moving beyond the world of vague references and scattered, dubious artistic representations, we arrive, by the 1700s, at the point where Irish traditional music, previously an oral tradition, begins at last to be captured in amber, although it may be said that several of the early attempts somewhat damaged the specimen in transit.† Irish tunes appear to have been popular in genteel circles in England during the 1500s, Francis O'Neill finding references in Shakespeare to at least nine identifiable Irish songs. A few traditional tunes from Ireland appeared in published

---

* Blues scholarship can only go back as far as 1900 with any accuracy. Pianist Jelly Roll Morton (1890–1941), a key figure in early jazz, attested in an interview with a folklorist in 1938 that he'd heard a prostitute sing a blues song in New Orleans around 1900, recalling the words and structure. W.C. Handy (1873–1958), often referred to – including by himself – as the 'Father Of The Blues', was an educated African-American musician, schooled in orchestral and brass band music, who took rustic folk forms and made them palatable to mainstream audiences. His description, in his 1941 autobiography, of hearing, at a Mississippi railway station in 1903, a rough-hewn solo musician singing and playing guitar with a knife (used like a bottleneck across the strings), 'playing the weirdest music I had ever heard', is often cited by blues scholars. On the origins of the blues form and traditions prior to 1900, there is general agreement that the ingredients in the cauldron included Scots-Irish music (secular and spiritual, familiar to southern blacks from white neighbours of similar social class in the Appalachian states) and pre-Islamic West African music.

† A regular bugbear for scholars is the tendency for early collectors, including Bunting (despite his own avowals of absolute accuracy) to shoehorn traditional melodies into keys in which they could not possibly have been played, adding notes that could not possibly have been played on the instruments in question and adding counterpoint and bass notes that owe more to the passing fashion for European art music than to any native tradition. Aside from that, it was all fine.

form, in England and Scotland, during the late 1600s. The first all-Irish collections appeared during the first half of the 1700s, beginning in 1724 with John and William Neale's *A Collection Of The Most Celebrated Irish Tunes*, only one copy of which survives.[*]

> **Breandán Breathnach**: With the advance of the century, Irish airs appeared in increasing numbers in English and Scots publications, in the operas of the period, and in local collections published by the Lees[†] and other Dublin music publishers.[332]

Samuel Lee published, circa 1774, *Jackson's Celebrated Irish Tunes*, which included several items sourced from the remarkably prolific 'gentleman piper' of that period, Walker 'Piper' Jackson. Many more tunes by or associated with Jackson, generally with his name in the title – effectively making him the Bo Diddley of diddly-dee[‡] – ended up in other published or manuscript collections over the next few decades.[§]

The first performer on the instrument that became known as the uilleann pipes whose name was recorded was one Laurence Grogan of Johnstown Castle, Co. Wexford; his playing career is dated to the first quarter of the 18th century. Thanks to the testimony of descendants, Grattan Flood goes into some detail on Grogan, another 'gentleman piper' who composed a number of pieces for the instrument, including 'The Girl I Love' and 'Ally Croker' (firmly dated to 1725–26); this latter had evolved into 'Oh The Shamrock!' by the time of *Moore's Irish Melodies* (1859), a widely popular publication for piano.

---

[*] The publishing date is sometimes stated as 1726. The sole copy extant belonged to collector Edward Bunting. The Neales were involved in Dublin musical life and helped to build the venue at which Handel's *Messiah* debuted in 1742.

[†] Manuel, John, Samuel and Edmund Lee (seemingly three generations) published various collections in the late 1700s. There is still debate over whether their famous collection of Turlough O'Carolan harp pieces – published in various editions around 1780, in settings for harpsichord, piano and various baroque melody instruments – was original or a reprint of an earlier (lost) Manuel Lee book – or indeed a 1748 (lost) book published by Dennis Connor in association with O'Carolan's son.

[‡] Rock'n'roll pioneer Ellas McDaniel aka Bo Diddley (1928–2008) specialised in songs with his name in the title. Even the rhythm used in many of his hits is now, appropriately, known as the 'Bo Diddley beat'. Whether 'Piper' Jackson's repertoire contained more variety than Bo's limited, if hugely successful, formula is for others to say.

[§] There are over 100 Irish traditional tunes beginning with 'Jackson's', most of them associated with the Limerick piper (whose forename is sometimes given erroneously as 'Walter' rather than Walker). His tunes can be found in Canon Goodman and Patrick Gunn's manuscripts as well as in Mr O'Farrell's celebrated pipes tutor of c. 1800. Jackson died c. 1798.

The Irish elbow-driven pipes in their first recorded century found favour, for different reasons, with the highest and lowest echelons. Grattan Flood noted that 'during the period of the iniquitous Penal Laws – from 1703 to 1746 – Catholic priests occasionally went about in the guise of pipers, and even bishops are recorded to have passed as performers on the pipes.'[333] This seems curious, given that Irish culture was, on paper at least, as little tolerated as Catholicism. One might think that a priest dressing up as a piper would be no more effective than a turkey disguising itself as a Brussels sprout in December. Nevertheless, the instrument was to prove just as popular with Protestant clergymen as with their Catholic peers.

One Protestant cleric, Reverend Dr Thomas Campbell, an associate of the eminent lexicographer Dr Johnson, wrote, after visiting a gentleman friend in Tipperary in 1775:

> Here we were at meals, even on Sunday, regaled with the bagpipe, which to my uncultivated ear is not an instrument so unpleasant as the lovers of Italian music represent it.[334]

At the other end of the social scale, Joseph Walker quotes from the 1767 *Letters*, published by Samuel Derrick (a Dublin literary man, and yet another acquaintance of the well-connected Dr Johnson), on an encounter Derrick had made among the rural poor:

> He and his fellow traveller, being driven by a shower of rain, into a hut near Killarney, entered into conversation with their hosts, a poor old couple – 'We asked the woman (says he) how she intended to support her family. Some of them, she answered, as they grow up, shall go out to service, and one or two help me, in and about my grounds at home: as for Donough, my eldest boy, who was blinded by the Small-pox, we have got a man to teach him the Bagpipes, with which and begging, there is no fear, under God, but he may get an honest livelihood, and live very comfortably: at any rate, it is better than being a sorry tradesman.[335]

'However, the Bagpipe,' Walker goes on to say, 'in the hands of a good performer, is not unworthy [of] the ears of royalty … I have been informed that George II [who reigned 1727–60] was so much delighted with the performance of an Irish gentleman on the Bagpipes, that he ordered a medal to be struck for him.'[336]

'Apparently, Irish pipers were not infrequent performers in England in 1730,' Grattan Flood declared, 'as, from the London *Evening Post*, under date of June 17th,

1732, there is mention of 'a noted Irish bagpiper' who was concerned in a quarrel in a brandy-shop 'by Mermaid Court, near Charing Cross.'[337]

As the century wore on, the instrument and its practitioners would be increasingly observed, in their country of origin, by literary and musical passers-by. Grattan Flood suggests that George Frideric Handel, on his 1742 trip to Dublin to premiere his *Messiah*, took note of the melodies of a couple of Irish tunes, 'Eileen Aroon' (a song he would reputedly have traded his entire *oeuvre* to have written) and 'The Poor Irish Boy' (a piping tune).

One anonymous correspondent to the *Gentleman's Magazine* in 1751 commented, after a trip to Ireland:

> Every village has a Bagpiper, who every fine evening after working hours, collected all the young men and maids in the village about him, where they dance most cheerfully; and it is really a very pleasing entertainment to see the expressive though awkward attempts of nature to recommend themselves to the opposite sex.[338]

The piper in the 18th century clearly occupied a space that fell uniquely between the rustic art that caught Handel's attention; the functionality – a bearer of news, a guest at weddings, a necessary cog in the wheel of neighbourhood dances – required by rural society at the time; and, as with the tradition of harping that was coming to an end, a kind of employment safety valve against otherwise crippling illness (so many pipers of the 18th and 19th centuries being the victims of blindness through one health issue or another).

Having said that, not all blind pipers were born into poverty:

> **Finbar Furey**: They were blind from syphilis, mostly, or they were blind from birth; there was leprosy, there was everything in this country. It wasn't just travelling people. There's a great painting in the National Museum, 'The Blind Piper' [by Joseph Haverty (1794–1864)] – he wasn't a Traveller, he was a man of the world. My father pointed that out years ago: with a great set of pipes and the way the man is dressed and his legs crossed like that, the man is comfortably off.

It seems fair to say that, in tandem with their roles as heralds at formal events like weddings and funerals and as accompanists at dances, the notion of the piper as both a *bon viveur*, or loveable rogue, and as an individual somehow in league with otherworldly forces (invariably fairies) took hold in the 18th century. The piper's long association, deserved or otherwise, with excessive revelry also begins here.

Writing in his loquaciously whimsical memoir, *Personal Sketches Of His Own Times*, Sir Jonah Barrington (1760–1834) recounts arriving one day at his brother's hunting lodge:

> We had intended to surprise my brother; but had not calculated on the scene I was about to witness. It was about ten in the morning: the room was strewed with empty bottles – some broken – some interspersed with glasses, plates, dishes, knives, spoons, etc, all in glorious confusion. Here and there were heaps of bones, relics of the former day's entertainment, which the dogs, seizing their opportunity, had cleanly picked. Three or four of the bacchanalians lay fast asleep upon chairs; one or two others were on the floor, among whom a piper lay on his back, apparently dead, with a table-cloth spread over him, and surrounded by four or five candles burnt to the sockets; his chanter and bags were laid scientifically across his body, his mouth was quite open, and his nose made ample amends for the silence of his drone … Had I never viewed such a scene before, it would have almost terrified me; but it was nothing more than the ordinary custom which we called 'waking the piper', when he had got too drunk to make any more music.[339]

Boozing and piping coincide in a number of Barrington's anecdotes, such as this one concerning the father of a friend, one John, Earl of Ormonde:

> He was well-read and friendly, a *hard-goer* (bon vivant) as it was called, and an incessant talker. His Lordship occasionally adjourned to a kind of tavern in the city, of which a certain widow Madden was the hostess,* and where one Mr Evans, surnamed 'Hell-cat', together with the best boozers and other gentlemen of Kilkenny, assembled to amuse his Lordships by their jests and warm punch … These boozing matches sometimes proceeded rather too far … [One night] on departing from the tavern, far more full of liquor than wit, some wild young man in company suggested the demolition of the doctor's windows. No sooner said than done. The piper played, the stones flew and [Dr] Duffy's shivered panes bore ample testimony to the strength of the widow's beverage.[340]

In defence of the uilleann piper's reputation, it is worth noting that tomfoolery

---

* Any connection with Madden's, a bar in Belfast frequented by pipers in recent years, must surely be coincidental.

and piping were bedfellows long before the elbow-driven variant of the instrument even existed. Writing around 1584, Dublin-born scholar and alchemist Richard Stanyhurst noted, of the bagpiping scene of his day:

> [I]f anyone were to make a puncture in the bag, even with the point of a needle, the instrument would be spoiled, and the bag would immediately collapse, and this is frequently done by humorous people when they wish to irritate the pipers.[341]

This practice, should it still survive, must be one tradition which pipers today would be happy to see die out.

*

An interest in collecting and preserving Irish music went hand in hand with efforts to document something of its history, which is where the well-meaning gentleman antiquaries Charles Vallancey (1721–1812) and Joseph Walker (1761–1810) came in. More remarkably, however, a trio of elusive pipers in the 18th and 19th centuries managed to make their own invaluable contributions to latter-day listings of the world's rarest books: John Geohegan, Henry Colclough and the enigmatic 'Mr O'Farrell', the sort of figures, like 'Piper' Jackson, for whom knowledge of life dates or other biographical information would only spoil the mystery.

Mr O'Farrell's Collection Of National Irish Music For The Union Pipes was published in London around 1800 (some suggest a year or two earlier, but it was certainly no later than 1804). Patrick Sky, who edited a facsimile edition in 1995, puts it in context:

> O'Farrell's book represents a number of probable firsts: the first significant collection of Irish dance tunes collected and written down by a traditional musician and performer – not a scholar; [the] first tutor for the Union pipes; and finally the first Irish dance music collection by an Irishman, containing the earliest examples of many of the tunes that are in our current repertory.[342]

The union pipes, O'Farrell himself asserted, were 'an instrument now so much improved as renders it able to play any kind of Music, and with the additional accompanyments which belong to it produce a variety of pleasing Harmony which forms as it were a little Band in itself.'[343] O'Farrell was writing his 'treatise' because 'gentlemen often expressing a desire to learn the Pipes have been prevented by not meeting with a proper Book [of] Instructions'.[344]

For all the book's importance in historical terms, it might be conjectured that not too many gentlemen took O'Farrell up on his offer. A century later, it would take several years of earnest enquiries to antiquarian booksellers and a fat wallet before even Francis O'Neill was able to secure a battered but complete copy of the work. Writing in 1972 in an introduction to a new edition of O'Neill's *Irish Folk Music: A Fascinating Hobby* (1910), which had included from day one a facsimile reprint of O'Farrell's treatise, Barry O'Neill was able to say that: 'O'Neill's copy of O'Farrell's tutor had previously been owned by Robert Reid (1774–1837) of North Shields, Northumberland, England, a maker of Uilleann pipes and umbrellas …'[345] Few indeed are the uilleann pipers, then as now, who have not found it useful to diversify.

Even today there are reputedly only a handful of copies of O'Farrell's tutor. To some extent, he bears comparison to Robert Johnson (1911–1938), the influential Delta bluesman whose biography is littered with mysteries and intrigue, not least a mythical Faustian pact at a crossroads at midnight. While there's no suggestion that O'Farrell was doing deals with Beelzebub, he certainly covered his tracks: almost no biographical information is known about him, and the little that is seems built on sand. He may have been called Patrick (the British Library copy of his book is inscribed 'P. O'Farrell'); he may have been born in Clonmel, Co. Tipperary (although no records have ever been found to confirm this); he may have been born in Limerick (Francis O'Neill posits such an idea, given the man's composition 'O'Farrell's Welcome To Limerick').*

Yet, despite rigorous research on the matter, Patrick Sky could only attest to four certain facts about the author. The first two derive from the book itself: O'Farrell's address in London and, from a frontispiece illustration, his participation in a performance of a pantomime at Covent Garden. The third and fourth facts came courtesy of a monumental scholarly work on London stage performers of the era.† O'Farrell, we learn, had performed, with harper John Erhardt Weippert, an air in a ballet called *The True Lover's Knot*, which was incorporated around 1795 into a sonata published by Thomas Costellow. In addition, O'Farrell and Weippert are

---

* 'O'Farrell's Welcome To Limerick' was later used as the air to a bawdy song in Irish, 'An Phís Fhliuch' – the title of which later stuck to the tune itself. Consequently, Liam O'Flynn's early 1970s recording of 'An Phís Fhliuch', which so excited the young John McSherry, can be traced back to the pen of the mysterious Mr O'Farrell nearly 200 years earlier. A continuum indeed.

† *A Biographical Dictionary Of Actors, Actresses, Musicians, Dancers, Managers, And Other Stage Personnel in London, 1660–1800*, by Philip Highfill *et al*, Southern Illinois University Press, 1973–93.

noted as accompanying the ballet *The Black Knight* in June 1803.*

Yet even with these few apparent facts there are complications. No sooner has a fragment of information on O'Farrell been placed on the table than it floats away on a breeze. The frontispiece illustration, purportedly of O'Farrell playing the union pipes in Irish playwright/actor James Byrne's *Oscar And Malvina* in the Theatre Royal, Covent Garden, at the work's debut in August 1791, is suspiciously similar to a contemporary illustration of Dennis Courtney, an Irish piper born in 1760 and well known on English stages. Patrick Sky's enquiries reveal that Courtney, not O'Farrell, accompanied *Oscar And Malvina* at Covent Garden every year between 1791 and 1794, and did so with John Erhardt Weippert on harp.†

Courtney died later in 1794 and, for a performance of the pantomime on March 12 1795, *The London Stage* advertises, along with the ever-present Weippert, 'The UNION PIPES by an Eminent Performer (his 3rd appearance in public)'. It is hard not to hope that such a tantalising reference may indeed be but a thin veil over the presence of the elusive O'Farrell. Writing in 2002, subsequent to Sky's reprint, Seán Donnelly stated: 'There is a hint in a work published in 1795 that [O'Farrell] was already performing by the early 1770s, but against such an early date for him is that he was last heard of playing in Edinburgh in 1832.'[346] (Donnelly was referencing here a piece by Keith Sanger: 'Irish Pipers And Scotland, III,' *Piping Times*, 10/98.)

The one fact in all of this which seems to have passed scholars by – certainly to the extent of specifically pointing it out – is that *The London Stage* announcement of Dennis Courtney playing the union pipes at Covent Garden in August 1791 is the earliest occurrence of the name 'union pipes' in print. It has long been accepted that the name predated the 1801 Act Of Union and, consequently, is not in any way connected to that geo-political context, but the source usually cited is the occurrence of 'union pipes' in a poem of 1796. As for what the name does reflect, it is merely an educated guess, oft repeated, that it reflects the 'union' of chanter, drones and regulators.

O'Farrell's tutor included 69 tunes. He went on to publish another work, *O'Farrell's Pocket Companion For The Irish Or Union pipes* (1810), which contained

---

* A fifth piece of information, gleaned from the tutor itself, is that the work was available for purchase not only at O'Farrell's address but at Mr Gow's music shop at 31 Carnaby Street – future beacon of 'Swinging London' in the 1960s. Mr Gow was John Gow, son of the legendary Scots fiddler Neil Gow. Writing in his 1972 Introduction to Francis O'Neill's *Irish Folk Music: A Fascinating Hobby* (1910), Barry O'Neill attests that O'Farrell also performed in *The Country Girl* at London's Theatre Royal in 1803.

† Séamus Ó Casaide, writing in the journal of Irish pipers, *An Píobaire*, in 1972, notes that Dennis Courtney also performed in a production of *Oscar And Malvina* in Dublin in January 1792.

many more, including the earliest known version of 'The Fox Chase', an epic descriptive piece in several sections, attributed to blind piper Edward Keating Hyland, and to this day a test piece for pipers.

> **W.H. Grattan Flood**: He was an accomplished musician as well as piper, and got lessons in theory and harmony from Sir John Stevenson. When George IV visited Dublin in 1821, he ordered a new set of pipes for Hyland, at a cost of 50 guineas, as a mark of recognition of his performance.[347]

Writing in *An Píobaire* in 1977, in an argument that builds on a 1973 piece by blues writer Eric Thatcher, Pat Mitchell makes a fascinating case for 'The Fox Chase' being a bridge between 18th century Irish piping and 20th century African-American harmonica blues. 'The Fox Chase', while quintessentially a pipe tune, did have a life for a while as a fiddle piece, certainly in Donegal, and likely in the Appalachian states of America, where the fiddle was as popular in the late 19th century among African-Americans as it was with white 'hillbillies' of Scots-Irish descent. Thatcher argued that a fiddle version in the southern states was the link between blind Edward Hyland's epic and the briefer 'Fox Chase' of blind Sonny Terry, on harmonica, in the recording era of the mid-20th century – the harmonica having by then become popular as a cheaper alternative to the fiddle.

Mitchell points to the smoking gun of an eight-note musical phrase shared between the piping tune and a 1965 recording of the similarly-titled harmonica blues by Dr Isaiah Ross – much later than Sonny Terry's first recording of it but indicative, he felt, of an earlier source tradition.

More generally, though, the blues writer Eric Thatcher had sensed something in Irish piping which can be felt instinctively to this day by anyone listening to traditional laments on the instrument:

> The curious phrase-delineations and 'tone-bending' techniques ('tipping', 'cranning', 'pinching', 'shivering', etc), and the general improvisational approach may seem, aurally at least, as close to the blues as anything recorded in Africa. After hearing [Séamus] Ennis play slow themes like 'Were You At The Rock?' and 'The Lament Of The Fox' I can never again be quite sure that 'blue notes' are an African gift to America.[348]

O'Farrell had one more mystery to throw at the scholars of the future. The discovery of the planet Neptune (in 1846) was based entirely on the implication of a hitherto-unknown outer planet provided by the curious orbital deviations of Uranus; similarly,

O'Farrell provided a clue to a yet more venerable published tutor for the pipes. His cover blurb for *Mr O'Farrell's Collection Of National Irish Music For The Union Pipes* had promised 'a Treatise with the most perfect Instructions ever yet Published'. This, of course, implies the existence of at least one predecessor.

Writing in 1972, Séamus Ó Casaide wondered whether the predecessor in question might have been a certain Colclough, who was known to have written a pipes tutor through a passing reference by tune collector Canon Goodman in the 19th century. But, as he noted, 'no copy of Colclough's appears to have survived'.[349] He was to be proved wrong on both counts. Barring its front cover, the manuscript of Colclough's tutor *had* survived, but it would be dated to around 1830. More excitingly, at least two different London-published editions of a hitherto unknown work dated to around 1743–46, by one John Geohegan, would turn up.

Titled *The Compleat Tutor For The Pastoral Or New Bagpipe*, Geohegan's work was the first of its kind (or at least was asserted to be such on its cover) and provides an invaluable marker in the known development of the union pipes.

> **Geohegan**: The Bagpipe, being at this Time brought to such Perfection as now renders it able to perform the same Number of Notes with the Flute or Hautboy,* I thought it might be acceptable to the curious to set forth this small Treatise, and I hope my labour will not be entirely unworthy of their Notice, having taken the same with a View of explaining all the Difficulties in the Musick of this Instrument. I have known some young Gentlemen, who had not only a fine Taste for all sorts of Musick, but also a sane Genius, to have a great Desire to play the Bagpipe, yet have been hindered from what their Inclinations so urged them to, by this Instrument's wanting a Scale or Gamut to learn by, which all other Musical Instruments of any Value have …[350]

Geohegan, like O'Farrell half a century later, was clearly responding to some level of demand. While the musical items in his tutor were generally familiar Scottish and English airs, its chief value to history is that it provides a definite, clearly lit beacon along the hazy path of the union pipes' early development.

The pastoral pipes are generally accepted as the union pipes' immediate forerunner, being an instrument with two (sometimes three) drones and a two-octave chanter, identical to the union pipes chanter save for a 'long foot' – an extension that allowed the instrument to access a low 'C', albeit with compromises in terms of fingering and

---

* Hautboy = Oboe.

tuning. It was an instrument without, in the early 1700s, a keyed regulator – although Patrick Sky, who edited a combined reprint of Colclough and Geohegan's tutors in 2000, notes that some specimens of the pastoral pipes (later in date, overlapping with the emergence of the union pipes proper) have been found with a regulator containing four or five keys. There are also rare examples with two regulators.

While Geohegan describes an instrument with two drones, Wilbert Garvin – having examined an enlargement of the frontispiece of Geohegan's *Compleat Tutor* from the British Museum – noted that there were, in fact, clearly three drones visible.* Union pipe drones would give D in three octaves; from the lengths of the drones on Geohegan's frontispiece, Denis Brooks could conclude:

> What we have here, of course, is typical Northumbrian drone tuning, two drones in octaves and a third sounding a fifth, between. In D, these would be: D, A, D. This instrument is the Northumbrian Long Pipes, a bagpipe which was known of for a long time only because of the existence of Northumbrian Half Long Pipes. Because of the lack of knowledge in the north of England's own folk memory of the Long Pipes, it must be assumed that the Long Pipes never caught on.[351]

Capturing a magical moment in the transition of the pastoral pipes – notwithstanding any momentary diversion via Northumbria – to what became the union pipes, Geohegan notes in his preface that one instrument maker 'I am inform'd has of late invented a way of fixing two Keys to ye Chanter … [though as yet] I have not met with any Pipe of that kind.'[352]

Ross Anderson has sleuthed extensively on the pastoral pipes and their repertoire in recent years, uncovering hitherto neglected or miscategorised manuscripts of pastoral pipe music in archives and throwing a great deal of light on the overlapping histories of the pastoral and union instruments.† He summarises the pastoral pipes as being essentially a baroque oboe with a bellows, 'the fascinating 'missing link' between the [Scottish] Border pipes of 1700 and the Union pipes of 1800'.[353]

While noting various tuning eccentricities characteristic of the instrument, eased by certain fingering manoeuvres and compensations in the chanter design, his analysis demonstrates that speedy transition into the second octave (previously thought doubtful) was possible:

---

* *An Píobaire*, June 1982
† Ross Anderson's fascinating website, including several of his articles and links to pages that feature people playing the pastoral pipes, can be found here: www.cl.cam.ac.uk/~rja14/music/

In its fundamental register, the pastoral chanter plays a nine-note scale of an octave plus a flattened lower seventh. Essentially, it plays the Highland pipe scale, but with an extra octave available by squeezing harder, and many accidentals available by cross-fingering …

So why, then, did the Pastoral pipe fall out of fashion sometime in the first half of the 19th century? A hint may come from Haynes' history of the baroque oboe.* Seventeenth and 18th century woodwind development was driven by the search for more expressive instruments. The move from the shawm to the oboe, with its lipped reed, was one innovation in this line; so was the move from the recorder to the traverse flute, and many of the subsequent more technical evolutions. The Pastoral pipe may simply have gone against this grain. Although it could play the Highland repertoire, it lacked the bottom-hand punch of the Highland chanter with its more conical bore and harder reed. Although it could play the Northumbrian repertoire, it could not do staccato in the way a Northumbrian or Union chanter can.[354]

The long foot joint of the pastoral pipes made staccato playing impossible; by removing the foot joint, a whole new way of playing was rendered possible:

> If playing on the knee became fashionable because of the staccato, the improved dynamics and the greater range of tone colour – in short, as it made the instrument more eloquent – then in time the instruments would be tuned for performance on the knee rather than off, and the foot joint would fall into disuse. Losing the low C was a small price to pay for the increased expressiveness.[355]

The pastoral instrument, with its chanter and fingering notably different from its union pipe cousin, seems not to have effectively died out until the 1830s. The dominance of the union pipes appears to have been assured by the 1770s. For the history of piping, the pastoral and union pipes of the 18th and early 19th centuries may bear comparison with the blurry overlap of Neanderthal and Cro-Magnon Man (once, also, thought to have been strictly sequential) in the progress toward *Homo sapiens*.

Denis Brooks has suggested that once the foot joint associated with the pastoral pipes had been removed, allowing staccato playing by resting the chanter on the player's thigh, another happy consequence was that 'the regulator was easily appended

---

* *The Eloquent Oboe – A History Of The Hautboy 1640–1760*, (OUP, 2001), B Haynes to the pipes'.³⁵⁶ Based on the evidence of surviving pipes, Brooks suggests that 'the foot joint may have been abandoned in Ireland between 1746 and 1770'. Once the foot joint had been removed, fingering that had previously produced C, D, E miraculously now sounded D, D sharp, E: 'This phenomenon remains the most peculiar part of the Irish chanter to this day.' ³⁵⁷

> **Ross Anderson**: The early chanters from [celebrated Dublin pipe maker] James Kenna (from about the 1760s) were like pastoral chanters, with a quiet tone and an E flat pitch, while in time his instruments became louder and the pitch moved down to [the key of] C. The foot joint was forgotten: its remnant today is the tenon cut around the foot of the modern uilleann chanter. But this change took some time …
>
> The new chanters (both long and short) spread through both Ireland and Scotland in the 18th century, with makers in Dublin, Edinburgh, Aberdeen and Newcastle competing and copying each others' ideas. Tunes and musicians also passed back and forth. The new instrument's popularity peaked in Edinburgh in the third quarter of the 18th century, and the Highland Society in London had both Pastoral and Highland pipers playing at its dinners from about 1780–1820. By about 1780 Dublin had become a centre too.³⁵⁸

Edinburgh, Anderson argues, was an Enlightenment boom town during the latter half of the 18th century:

> By the early 1770s its music scene rivalled Salzburg or Vienna.* Folk music prospered as well as classical; dancing moved indoors, people wanted instruments to play it, and bellows pipes competed with fiddles imported from Italy. Dublin was also growing vigorously, and the union pipe became fashionable among its middle classes from about 1780–1830. Competition between makers in Dublin, Edinburgh, Aberdeen and Newcastle seems to have driven innovation. By the 1820s the bellows pipes played by Scots musicians like Robert Millar and Donald MacDonald were Union pipes incorporating the innovations of Dublin makers like the Kennas.³⁵⁹

*

Irish linguist and historian Eugene O'Curry (1794–1862) had a significant influence

---

* Derek Scott makes the point that Albrechtsberger, Dittersdorf, Hoffman, and Wagenseil were all active in Vienna in the 1770s, as were Mozart and Haydn in the next decade, all of which tempers Anderson's comparison – but not his enthusiasm.

on the two great Irish music historians of the late 19th and early 20th centuries, Captain Francis O'Neill and W.H. Grattan Flood, on the matter of the earliest apparent written reference to pipers in Ireland, although large pinches of salt would need to be involved today.

O'Curry had been born and brought up in County Clare, exposed to a living tradition of language and culture. Having worked as a teacher, a manual labourer and a mental hospital warden, he made his first contribution to written history only after being invited, in the 1830s, by Dublin publisher George Smith (who also arranged a job for O'Curry with the Ordinance Survey), to join the Royal Irish Academy. Dublin, at that time, was almost a separate country in itself, culturally and intellectually focused more on Britain and Europe than on the rest of Ireland.

> **Muiris Ó Rócháin**: The Royal Irish Academy, founded in 1795 for the study of polite literature and antiquities, opened the breach of walls of Anglo-Irish Dublin through which the first scientific knowledge of Gaelic culture began. There it was in the hands of men who were but little competent to understand it, but this despicable school did produce one useful result: it awakened the undying opposition of three giant men, [John] O'Donovan, [George] Petrie and [Eugene] O'Curry and gave birth to their immortal work.[360]

Petrie had joined the Academy in 1827 and soon began a collection of historic Irish manuscripts; O'Donovan joined in 1832 and O'Curry in 1835. The trio worked on an epic survey of Irish history and antiquities, as an adjunct to a government land survey, up to 1842, when funding was withdrawn. O'Curry catalogued the Academy's Irish manuscripts in 1842, and – alongside much other work on Irish language and literature – in 1849 catalogued the Irish manuscripts at the British Museum. After scraping a living for years, in 1852 both O'Curry and O'Donovan were employed by the newly created Brehon Law Commission to transcribe the ancient material in question for publication. O'Curry subsequently took a post at the newly created Catholic University in Dublin as Professor of Irish History & Archaeology. From 1857 to 1862 he delivered a series of lectures on the manners and customs of the Ancient Irish, later published in two volumes.

Both Petrie and another collector, Henry Hudson, collected huge quantities of music from Paddy Coneely, a blind piper of Galway who flourished in the second quarter of the 19th century, playing pipes that had once belonged to an even more illustrious forebear: John Crump, 'the Munster piper'.* Drawn by Coneely's

---

* Petrie noted 17 tunes from Coneely, while Hudson noted 138, all of which were published in printed collections during their lifetimes.

reputation, Petrie and his associates travelled to Galway in 1839, didn't find him at home, bumped into him later on a Connemara highway and – despite his protestations that he had a gig that night – bundled him off for some serious anthropology:

> His captors explained to him that the Galway gentlemen could often hear him, while they may not have the opportunity again of doing so. So he had to come. … After keeping the kidnapped piper with them for two weeks, he was brought home safe and sound and financially better off than if he had kept his engagement with the gentlemen of the regatta.[361]

Petrie waxed lyrical about Coneely in *The Irish Penny Journal* the following year, after waxing even more lyrical about the man's legendary predecessor, Mr Crump:

> Musical reader! Do not laugh at the epithet we have applied to the sounds of the bagpipe: the music of Crump … was truly delicious even to the most refined musical ears. … Truth to tell, Paddy Coneely is not to be compared with John Crump who, according to the recollections of him which cling to our memory, was a Paganini in his way – a man never to be rivalled – and who produced effects on his instrument previously unthought of, and which could not be expected. …
>
> Paddy can play not three tunes, but three thousand; in fact, we have often wished his skill more circumscribed, or his memory less retentive, particularly when, instead of firing away with some lively reel, or still more animated Irish jig, he has pestered us … with a set of quadrilles or a galloppe, such as he is called on to play by the ladies and gentlemen at the balls in Galway. But what a monstrosity – to dance quadrilles in Galway! … Fair Galwegians, for assuredly you are fair, put aside this sickly affectation of refinement … Be yourselves, and let your limbs play freely, and your spirits rise into joyousness to the animating strains of the Irish jig, the reel, and the county dance; so it was with your fathers, and so it should be with you. But we are wandering, perhaps, from our subject…
>
> Paddy … is a happy man – a happier man we never saw. He is always singing – in sunny weather, sprightly airs, and in gloomy weather, pathetic ones; but he never looks or is sad … He has … a high opinion of his musical talents, and a strong feeling of decent pride. He will not lower the dignity of his professional character by playing in a tap-room or for the commonality – except on rare occasions, when he will do it gratuitously, and for the sole pleasure of making them happy. …

> Paddy is as temperate as he is a prudent man. ... 'You don't drink hard, Paddy,' we remarked to him. 'No, sir,' he replied; 'I did once, but I found it was destroying my health, and that if I continued to do so, I would soon leave my family after me to beg ...'[362]

Nevertheless, as Francis O'Neill observed 70 years later:

> Popular and patronized [sic] as he was in his prime, poor 'Paddy', like many other celebrities, outlived his fame. ... The famine years proved disastrous to him in many ways. Sadness instead of gaiety universally prevailed, and music had lost its appeal even were our [man] here – then in broken health – capable of furnishing it. Paralysis gradually sapped his strength and he passed away in 1850, relieved of anxiety for the welfare of his two boys, who were cared for by the Christian Brothers.[363]

This fate, sadly, would be familiar even into the early years of the 20th century, with elderly pipers momentarily dragged into the limelight by well-wishers in the Gaelic League, only to wind up in a workhouse a few years later. Perhaps the most notable collector of the 19th century in Ireland was James Goodman, later Canon Goodman in the Church Of Ireland. As Breandán Breathnach observed, Goodman 'really possessed the qualities for treating Irish music properly. He was literate musically, a native speaker of Irish, and an excellent performer on the pipes – Douglas Hyde [founder of the Gaelic League] declared him to be the best piper he had ever heard.'[364]

Though he lived to 1896, Goodman collected only during 1860–66, but did so voraciously, acquiring around 150 tunes from Thomas Kennedy, a blind piper from Dingle. A statue of Goodman, playing his pipes, was erected in his former parish in Skibbereen in 2006.*

*

The names Kenna, Coyne and Egan are the great ones in uilleann pipe making of the late 18th and early-to-mid-19th centuries. Within that sentence is a whole chasm of complexity – explored by Seán Donnelly in mind-boggling depth in the 2002 edition of *The Seán Reid Society Journal*.† Not only were there multiple makers called Kenna and Egan in this period, but pinning down their forenames and chronology

---

* Goodman was reputed to have had his set of Taylor pipes buried with him, although some sources suggest they were passed on to a friend.
† Seán's fascinating piece can be found online, and is recommended: www.seanreidsociety.org/SRSJ2/a%20century%20of%20pipe-making.pdf

is immensely complicated, not helped by erroneous identifications made by the well-meaning Francis O'Neill in his works of the early 20th century.

Nevertheless, O'Neill made a statement in *Irish Folk Music: A Fascinating Hobby* (1910) that stands as an accurate summary to this day:

> [Michael Egan] improved and multiplied the concords or regulators of the Irish pipes, which up to his time were exceedingly limited. In short, he was to the Irish or Union bagpipes what Stradivari was to the violin.[365]

As Seán Donnelly noted, in a compelling essay on the Kennas and Coynes in *The Seán Reid Society Journal* in 2002:

> The now standard account of Kenna and Coyne, the famous Irish pipe-makers, appears in Francis O'Neill, *Irish Minstrels And Musicians* (1913). There had been an 'elder' and a 'younger' Kenna, probably father and son. … Arguably Timothy Kenna [the younger one, misidentified as the elder by O'Neill] was the great pipe-maker of the early 19th century – perhaps one of the most important innovators in the development of the Irish pipes – and he was the maker Michael Egan eclipsed [in the 1840s]. …
>
> Around 1851 or 1852 Michael Egan left for New York from Liverpool, where he had settled in 1845, after brief periods spent in various places in Ireland. One tradition had it that Egan was brought to New York specially to make a set of pipes for Patrick Coughlan, then a promising young piper, who was to leave the United States for Australia on the outbreak of the American Civil War. A less-edifying story was that Egan had to flee Liverpool, having stabbed a client with a reamer. But whatever his immediate motive for emigrating, since 1848 Egan would have seen stupendous numbers of poverty-stricken and fever-ridden Irish pour into Liverpool, the chief port of the Irish Sea and the principal embarkation point for the United States, and possibly he saw the writing on the wall for the practice of his craft in either Ireland or England.[366]

While Egan became the gold standard, O'Neill goes on to mention one or two blind alleys in 19th century pipe making, notably one William Talbot of Roscrea, a blind genius who tuned pianos and repaired pipe organs for fun and also constructed a set of 'Grand Pipes' to his own specification. O'Neill quotes one witness as saying: 'His pipes were indeed a very wonderful instrument, or rather combination of instruments, being so complicated that no one could play upon them but himself.'[367]

He went on to say:

> [T]he sentiment prevails among pipers to this day that it is doubtful if Egan's pipes have ever been equalled, not to say excelled, for mellowness of tone and adaptability as a parlour instrument. The music of lower than concert pitch was sweet and soothing, and on certain temperaments it exercised a peculiar fascination not easily explained.[368]

That being said, O'Neill then went on to declare that 'the instruments now being manufactured by Mr Rowsome, of Dublin, are modelled after the Egan type of Union pipes and are quite as complete and well finished.'

When William Rowsome's pipe making business, established in Dublin in the very early years of the 20th century, passed to his son Leo, the journey of the pipes into precisely the instrument that remains standard today was complete. Rowsome had taken note of recent developments in America, pioneered by William and Charles Taylor, late of Drogheda.

> **Breandán Breathnach (1978)**: Billy Taylor is one of the great names in the history of Irish piping. Not alone was he regarded by many judges as the greatest piper of his time, he also enjoyed the reputation of being a pipe maker of the highest order. The quality of his work may be gauged from the fact that offers of sums in excess of £1,000 fail to induce their fortunate owners to part with their Taylor set. ... He and his step-brother, Charley, emigrated to the States in 1872. They stayed with a friend in New York for about two years and then moved to Philadelphia, where they spent the rest of their lives. ...
>
> As well as being a superb craftsman, [Billy] Taylor possessed inventive genius and he developed an instrument of powerful tone and in concert pitch which suited admirably the requirements of the concert hall and other places of public entertainment in the States, and so well was his work received that soon the Taylor set superseded the old mellow-toned sets, a note or more below concert pitch, which up to then had been in vogue.[369]

Before leaving Drogheda, Billy Taylor had tutored Nicholas Markey in piping. Markey would go on to tutor James Ennis at the Dublin Pipers' Club in the early 1900s; James Ennis, in turn, taught his son Séamus everything he knew. Billy died in 1901, his brother shortly afterward. They had made the last great innovation in uilleann pipe making, but never enjoyed much wealth – their generosity being abused, as Francis O'Neill put it, by a nefarious bar owner and a crowd of hangers-on.

Their innovations in regard to pitch, bore and volume were taken up by the next great makers of the instrument, as Seán Donnelly, in The Seán Reid Dociety Journal, explained:

> William Rowsome appears to have been the first maker in 20th century Ireland to manufacture the modern wide-bore, concert-pitch chanter. The Taylor brothers of Drogheda and Philadelphia are credited with developing this type of chanter in the United States during the 1870s and 80s to suit professional pipers playing in music halls and other spacious venues. It is, however, claimed that the Taylors had made a few of these new-style chanters before leaving Drogheda c. 1870. When Leo Rowsome succeeded his father in 1925, his concert-pitch pipes and chanters became almost the standard type and very much remain so. But while his father did make the older low-pitched flat pipes and chanters, Leo himself appears to have made few of these. In contrast [R.L.] O'Mealy seems to have made few concert-pitch pipes and chanters, preferring to produce flat sets.[370]

By that point, from the 1920s to the 1940s, Leo Rowsome in Dublin and R.L. O'Mealy in Belfast, along with the Crowley brothers in Cork, were just about the last remaining uilleann pipe makers in the world.

*

> The great famine of 1847 almost extinguished the last vestige of the people's customs. That calamitous period, when starvation, disease, death and emigration absorbed the people's minds, and its long aftermath of years of despondency almost obliterated the aspirations, musical and otherwise, of that generation. The succeeding generation was more susceptible to the Anglicizing [sic] methods of England's representatives in Ireland. The 'snobbery' germ entered the hearts of the people and propagated a race of nondescripts who were neither Irish nor English. Everything Irish became repugnant to them, the pipes, the dances, the language, the music itself, everything was discarded but the 'brogue' which, happily, was unshakable, as if stamped on their tongues by Providence as a reminder of their infidelity.[371]

Such was the view, in 1902, of Tom Ennis. Ennis was a piper in Chicago who would later record some of the earliest 78rpm discs of Irish music. As he valiantly declaimed:

> During the long languishment of the pipes in Ireland the sons of Erin in

America did not allow it to fall into entire desuetude. Its popularity in this country never waned. ... The great popularity Irish music has gained in Chicago is not to be attributed to any special efforts of the representative Irish organisations or the Irish press. For some incomprehensible reason it is almost totally ignored by both. ... The success attendant on the Irish music, the Irish piper and the Irish fiddler in Chicago can be safely said to be in no small measure due to the efforts and fostering care of Francis O'Neill, chief of police. ... For some years Mr O'Neill has been engaged in compiling a book of Irish music that in quality and comprehensiveness will be far superior to the famous collections of Bunting and Dr Petrie.[372]

And thus it proved. Francis O'Neill (1848–1936) was born near Bantry in County Cork, emigrated to America as a young man and rose to become Chief Of Police in Chicago between 1901 and 1905. He used his patronage to give jobs on the force to numerous Irish traditional musicians. Chicago became a cultural escape capsule from an economically and culturally collapsed Ireland – a microcosm of its musical heritage:

Within the city limits, a territory comprising about 200 square miles, exiles from all of Ireland's 32 counties can be found. ... Among Irish and Scotch music lovers, every new arrival having musical taste or talent is welcomed ... and there is as much rejoicing on the discovery of a new expert as there is among astronomers on the announcement of a new asteroid or comet.[373]

There were plenty of piping stars in the Captain's orbit: he was very friendly with Patsy Touhey, whom he admired greatly as a person and a player, and Bernard Delaney, whom he despised as a person but rated above even Touhey as a player. O'Neill pursued his passion for Irish music and used his organisational skills, energy and financial resources (many thousands), particularly after retiring, toward accumulating musicological and biographical material on Irish music and its practitioners past and present, with a particular bent toward pipers (being one himself). With his cohorts Sergeant James Early and James O'Neill, originally of Belfast, helping in the transcription of music, Francis published nine books between 1903 and 1922.

Originally there was no intention of compiling more than a private manuscript collection of those rare tunes remembered from boyhood days. ... Drawing the line anywhere was found to be utterly impracticable, so we never knew when or where to stop.[374]

Irish music owes O'Neill a monumental debt for not doing so. He is, in a nutshell, the man whose intervention single-handedly saved Irish music from the bonfire of neglect. One book, *The Dance Music Of Ireland* (1907), became and remains the cornerstone of the Irish traditional repertoire, containing 1,001 tunes. On the prose front, his books *Irish Folk Music: A Fascinating Hobby* (1910) and *Irish Minstrels And Musicians* (1913) assembled a tremendous amount of information and anecdote that would otherwise have been all but lost.

As Breandán Breathnach put it:

> He counted neither time nor money in his crusade to preserve this music. …. O'Neill also designed [his books] to develop confidence and self-respect in musicians by making them aware of the history of their music and the value of the heritage which they had in their possession. He was acutely aware of the contempt in which the music was held. … What a strange spectacle – the Chief of Police in Chicago … striving to preserve and promote, from a distance of 5,000 miles, the old culture of rural Ireland while the people of Ireland were rejecting it as if the Almighty had ordered them to do so.[375]

Over in Ireland, in parallel with O'Neill's years of nurturing, researching and publishing, a revival of interest in Irish culture was under way. The Gaelic League (Conradh Na Gaeilge) was formed in 1893, inspired by one Douglas Hyde and populated by middle-class intellectuals. One result was the founding in 1897 of annual Feis Ceoil events with the joint aims of promoting Irish music and collecting and publishing any hitherto unknown pieces of music. The first Feis, in Dublin, included pipes and harp in the 'Competitions Of Archaeological Interest' category, with £1 for the winner in performance of each category and £3 for the performance of any unpublished air.

The ambition to collect and publish uncollected music became somewhat farcical over the ensuing years, as various collected airs were found to be already known or popped up in a trickle of other collections that kept being published just as the Gaelic League book was about to go to press. Eventually, in 1914, a slim volume appeared, optimistically referred to as 'Volume One'.

Seven pipers were gathered together for the 1897 uncollected airs event: Turlough McSweeney of Donegal; John Flanagan and Thomas Rowsome of Dublin; Denis Delaney of Galway; Robert Thompson of Cork; John Cash of Wicklow; and R.L. O'Mealy of Roscommon (later domiciled in Cork and then in Belfast). McSweeney took first prize in the airs competition, Thompson in the general piping performance competition, with McSweeney and Rowsome taking second and third places. Only O'Mealy, of the seven, was described as a non-professional at the time. Remarkably, eight wax cylinder recordings made at the airs competition – of performances by McSweeney, Thompson, Flanagan and O'Mealy – were preserved from 18 that were recorded. These were surely the earliest recordings of uilleann piping ever made. Breandán Breathnach noted, in a 1986 magazine piece, that 46 cylinders survived from the early years of the Feis events, being donated to the Irish Folklore Commission in 1955 – albeit some having deteriorated past saving. They were duly inherited by UCD's National Folklore Collection.

Breathnach said that 23 cylinders were suitable for having audio extracted. UCD today has a list of 38 Feis Ceoil cylinders in its possession, of which 34 have recently been digitised. Twelve of the cylinders are of piping, of which 10 are among those digitised (the other two are by Martin Reilly and 'Mr Sullivan', presumably Mící 'Cumbá' O'Sullivan). Of these 10, four are of tantalisingly unidentified performers, while the rest feature (according to handwritten notes with the cylinders) Denis Delaney, Thomas Cash (possibly a confusion between Thomas Rowsome and John Cash), George McCarthy, Dan Markey and Martin Reilly.

Breathnach concluded:

> The pipers and fiddlers who attended the Feis Ceoil in its first years were the last in a line of professional performers. Men in their 60s and 70s, they would have acquired their skills and repertoire from musicians born in the previous century. What an immense treasure we should now possess had the sound of their music been systematically recorded for posterity.[376]

In 1898, the centenary of the Belfast Harp Festival of 1798 (at which the last gasp of the Irish harping tradition was celebrated and captured in some sort of amber by Edward Bunting's notes and transcriptions), the Feis Ceoil was held in Belfast.[*] Many of the old stagers appeared again: John Cash, Denis Delaney, Robert Thompson, Turlough McSweeney, John Flanagan. Thompson got first prize in the piping competition this time.

A new competitor that year was Michael 'Mící Cumbá' O'Sullivan of Kerry, born in the 1830s and 'discovered' by John Wayland of the recently founded Cork Pipers' Club. Wayland had had Mící 'imported to Cork, where he was received with due honours; and as he was a sweet, expressive player, I had several of his masterpieces recorded, such as the 'Maidrín Ruadh' and 'Gol na mBan'.'

A wax cylinder recording of O'Sullivan playing 'Gol na mBan' at the end of the

---

* One wonders whether any of the organisers considered that harping died out practically overnight after the 1792 event. Hardly a happy portent.

19th century has long been the most accessible of these early cylinder recordings. Quite when it was recorded seems to be a bit of a hazy question. The 'Mr Sullivan' cylinder in the UCD collection that was too damaged to digitise in 2008 was a recording of 'Women After The Battle', a paraphrase of 'Gol na mBan' in English. Had it been dubbed in the 1980s, from whence the copies online originate? Who knows. Writing in *Ceol* in 1986, Breandán Breathnach stated that the tune was recorded from O'Sullivan at the 1898 Belfast Feis. Writing in *An Píobaire* a year later, he said it was from the 1899 Feis in Dublin, citing a report on the event in *The Gael* (New York) that mentions O'Sullivan playing the piece.

Whatever the chronology, it remains an atmospheric glimpse into a lost world.* Quite how remote this world was from the modern era is illustrated by this anecdote from Francis O'Neill relating to Wayland's activities:

> Obligingly [O'Sullivan] played his best tunes into an Edison phonograph, but a scowl instead of a smile overspread his handsome features when he heard the machine reproduce the tunes. Evidently regarding this as another instance of the devil's handiwork, he aimed several whacks of his cane at the enchanted box before he could be restrained.

As Wayland himself observed: 'My experiences with 'Mickey' would fill a volume; he was such a funny little man with a head full of 'quare' notions, pishogues and the like.'

In a way, the tale of Michael O'Sullivan is totemic of the well-meaning revival fad of the 1890s and early 1900s: haul an eccentric old musician out of the backwoods, push him into competitions on public stages and stick an Ediphone machine under his nose. It was never going to end well.

Francis O'Neill provides a compelling glimpse of the situation:

> From the start, the blind musician was liberally patronized [sic], but, unfortunately, one of his many whims seized him and put an end to his dreams of prosperity. A hallucination that it was fairy butter the landlady put before him changed the whole current of his thoughts and caused him to quit the house [in which he had been set up in Cork] on short notice.
> A very pious man in his way, he had a habit of crossing himself repeatedly when

---

* A good place to hear 'Gol na mBan' (though retitled 'Alasdrum's March') is at Ross Anderson's Music Page: www.cl.cam.ac.uk/~rja14/music/ – where 1898 recordings of Bernard Delaney, the star piper of the USA, can also be accessed, along with much else of interest.

he thought he was in the company of uncongenial spirits. Often would he caution Mr. Wayland, 'Look out for yourself now, Mr. Whalen, you have enemies here.' …

Under the guardianship of the indefatigable Wayland, 'Mickey' journeyed to Dublin and tied with Denis Delaney for second prize at the Feis Ceoil competition in 1899, but not being awarded the first prize, he attributed his ill success to the fairy butter served him at Mrs Moore's establishment, and also to the malign influence of a dead man's breeches he wore.

It appears that certain members of the Cork Pipers' Club had fitted him out for the occasion with a suit from a 'ready made' shop, but nothing could convince 'Mickey' that he had not been draped in a dead man's garments. Rather than run any future risks of being 'overlooked', he decided to hasten back to his friends in Kerry; but before setting out on the journey he carefully parcelled up the bewitched breeches and flung it violently into the little shop where it had been purchased, remarking that it was hard for him to take first prize with the fairy butter stuck to him and a dead man's spirit haunting him, or, in other words, 'with God in his heart and the devil in his breeches'. …

Old, feeble, and friendless, and far from those upon whom he had legal and sentimental claims, Michael Sullivan, talented, eccentric, and a scion of illustrious ancestry, found a final refuge in the Cahirciveen poorhouse, where he died soon after; but, whether numbered among the living or the dead, his memory will remain ever fresh and green with Mr Wayland and the other members of the Cork Pipers' Club …[377]

O'Neill wrote with a veneer of positivity in *Irish Minstrels And Musicians* (1913) about John Wayland's Pipers' Club in Cork and its counterpart in Dublin, founded in 1900 by Mícheál Ó Duibhginn. He marvelled that the latter had managed to corral no less than 17 pipers for the 1912 Oireachtas ('the largest number of the fraternity ever assembled at such a gathering') and included a group photo in his book – albeit cautioning that 'we regret to foresee the day that it may be historical'.[378]

As he bullishly put it, before outlining the various obstacles of poverty and boycotts over which Wayland had triumphed:

> Great movements develop from small beginnings as great oaks from little acorns grow. Who could have foreseen the far-reaching influence which the Cork Pipers' Club – the pioneer of its kind – exercised in the revival of music and dancing in Ireland?[379]

Yet O'Neill's prose works are veiled in melancholy. It was as if, by trumpeting achievements of spirited individuals and movements in Ireland and America, he were willing into existence a genuine flourishing of the music he loved, most especially the subset within it of union piping. But he couldn't quite bring himself to believe it. Partly, he was a man who, by 1905, had seen all five of his children die of various illnesses, and who allowed no music in his home after that; partly, he was an enthusiast but not a fool. He had lived through one revival in Ireland, observing it from afar, and had drawn together for mutual warmth the best of those bearers of tradition who had come to America. Patsy Touhey and Bernard Delaney had even thrived on the popular stage. But the writing appeared, nonetheless, to be on the wall.

> **Breandán Breathnach**: Even while engaged in writing *Irish Minstrels And Musicians* O'Neill had begun to abandon hope for the future of Irish music. He became convinced that nothing of enduring value could be expected from Irish revivals, musical, literary or linguistic, which ever and always flared up and then subsided like bonfire conflagrations.[380]

He was right to be sceptical. The last entry in the minute book of the Dublin Pipers' Club was dated January 15 1914. It revived in November 1921, but was dissolved again at some point during or after the Civil War of 1922. The Cork Pipers' Club had similarly declined toward dissolution during the First World War period.* The Oireachtas Feis Ceoil had begun declining from 1905 onward, to the extent that no events were held between 1924 and 1939. This was more or less parallel to the period in which the Dublin Pipers' Club was inactive, from a fuzzy point around the Civil War to its resurrection by Leo Rowsome in 1936.

It is hardly an exaggeration to say that as the elderly eccentrics of the 19th century passed on, as the Gaelic Revival ran out of steam, and as the early 20th century wars in Europe and Ireland took their toll, the continuum of union piping had dwindled to a slender and precarious thread. Luckily, the man left holding that thread was Leo Rowsome; and Leo Rowsome was no quitter.

---

* The Cork Pipers' Club has been revived in the modern era. Rightly claiming the club to be the oldest piping club in existence, given its founding in 1898 (notwithstanding the evidence suggesting that the club itself didn't open its doors until the following year), its website is largely silent on the 50-odd years during which it was out of action. A few days before this book was typeset, Northern piping supremo Brian Vallely chanced upon a 1907 poster referencing a hitherto undocumented pipers' club in Belfast. The past is full of surprises.

Chapter 15
Piping In Ulster

Writing in 1980, in *Pipers' Review*, Denis Brooks made a statement that retains the power to infuriate Northern pipers 35 years later: 'The union pipes never took hold in Ulster; in a century and a half, to 1900, the new pipes were equally known, more or less, in the other three provinces.'[381]

There are, of course, exceptions to any generality.* While the nine counties in question – Antrim, Armagh, Derry/Londonderry, Donegal, Down, Cavan, Fermanagh, Monaghan and Tyrone – may not, until recently, have been awash with union/uilleann pipers, one might say the same of any of the four provinces of Ireland. There have been piping notables in Ulster from the instrument's earliest days; in recent times it has become an international piping hotbed, with a style of teaching and, some believe, of playing distinct from the Dublin-based Na Píobairí Uilleann stable. There's room for everyone.

William Kennedy

Pipe maker William Kennedy, of Tandragee, Co. Armagh, represents Ulster's first claim to piping notoriety. Born near Banbridge, Co. Down, in 1763, William was blind from the age of four. From the age of 13, typically for a blind child of that time, he learned music – from a Mr Moorehead in Armagh.† Lodging there with a cabinetmaker, he also learned how to use tools. Within a year or so, he began to repair instruments.

William returned to his parents' home in Church Street, Tandragee, where his father built him a workshop, the ruins of which remain, behind the Montagu Arms pub. He specialised in furniture and subsequently clock making. A commission in 1786, for a Mrs Reilly, of Scarva House and Tallyho Castle, led to William discovering

---

* Ulster has tended to be known for its song tradition, while the fiddle style and tradition of Donegal (drawing influences from Scottish fiddle music) is a distinctive sub-genre in Irish instrumental music.
† While there is, curiously, no reference to Kennedy in Francis O'Neill's *Irish Minstrels And Musicians*, O'Neill does mention Mr Moorehead's son, John Moorehead, who is credited with composing the tune 'Speed The Plough'.

the pipes. Mrs Reilly was a piping devotee, and she arranged for the young man to hear a celebrated piper named Downey. William was intrigued:

> He purchased an old and defective set that gave him so much trouble he set about contriving to make a new set instead. In that he succeeded, and after a lot of practice he learned how to play them.[382]

The first Kennedy set was completed in nine months. William married in 1793 and continued making and repairing instruments, clocks, looms and furniture, but most often making pipes. The couple were particularly friendly with Brigadier General and Lady Olivia Sparrow, who settled in Tandragee at Sparrow Castle in 1796. William was involved in Lady Sparrow's founding of a new church in the town, which was completed in 1812. As Lady Sparrow wrote in a memoir:

> After the death of my husband … in 1805 my good friend William Kennedy and his dear wife helped out with many chores as he only lived across the road from my castle a matter of yards away.[383]

Save for a period spanning 1798–99 (when he lived in Mullabrack, tutoring an apprentice in clock making) William remained in Tandragee until his death in 1834. An obituary in the *Newry Telegraph* noted:

> Mr William Kennedy [was] one of the most extraordinary men who have appeared in these latter times. Though totally deprived of sight, he was enabled, through his industry, his perseverance, and his genius, to execute with precision, taste and judgement, various elaborate works of a nature which have heretofore required the utmost exertions of well-trained artists, in full possession of all the senses and faculties with which nature had endowed them. This ingenious man fabricated his own tools, and with ease he constructed time-tellers, bagpipes, flutes, and various other instruments of music. He invented also a particular kind of bagpipe, by means of which he was enabled to regulate the bass at pleasure, so as to render it at all times accordant with the varied modulations of the airs which he chose to perform. It possessed great sweetness, depth, and organic power … Add to this, that he was a kind-hearted, friendly, industrious, moral and religious man; an affectionate husband, a fond parent, and, in all respects, a useful and justly esteemed member of society.[384]

William's accomplishments as a blind person, especially in the 18th century, are extraordinary. Yet aside from mechanical competency, he has also been credited with significant innovations in the evolution of the uilleann pipes.

A Biography Of The Blind by James Wilson, published in 1821, includes an interview with William and – along with scattered magazine pieces that were printed during his lifetime – provides a remarkable richness of information. No other pipe maker of the period is better documented. Francis Joseph Bigger, writing for the *Ulster Journal Of Archaeology* in 1906, built on Wilson's text and described what he believed to be the design innovations that William had made. Among these were: the addition of keys to the chanter, allowing flats and sharps; extending the range of the chanter, enabling a high E; and the addition of extra notes to the regulator.* Some of Bigger's other identifications, though, remain obscure or ambiguous and, given that only a handful of Kennedy sets have come to light, the exact status of his contribution to pipe making remains enigmatic.

Brian Vallely of Armagh Pipers' Club unveiled a plaque to William in Tandragee in March 2015. The club inaugurated a William Kennedy Piping Festival in 1994. They sum him up thus:

> Was Kennedy the first to put keys on a chanter? O'Farrell's *Treatise* [c. 1800] does not mention keys. Kenna, Coyne and Egan pipes [from the 19th century] generally have at least four keys. Did Kennedy invent a high E key? … With all the unanswered questions about Kennedy, we still know more about the man than any of his contemporaries. What comes across clearly in all the writings, which now span almost 200 years, is the esteem in which he was held and the impression he made on all who met him.[385]

Walker 'Piper' Jackson

One more 18th century figure who had a major impact within piping, specifically on its repertoire, was Walker 'Piper' Jackson. For many years little was known of his life, but there seemed to be a good chance that he came from County Monaghan.

---

* Ken McLeod, founder of the Seán Reid Society, adds: 'Although [it was] claimed by F.J. Bigger that Kennedy invented what is now known as the 'regulator' this is untrue and I believe that this may have been either James Kenna of Mullingar or Robert Reid of North Shields. I have owned a set of pipes by James Kenna (father of Timothy) which was made around 1770 or 1780. Regulators were first added to pastoral pipes but we don't know when James Kenna started out, although it is believed to be by 1770.' See the chapter on 'Uilleann Piping Before 1900' for more on pastoral pipes.

Or, at least, *someone* named Jackson who played and composed for the union pipes certainly did.

Samuel Lee of Dublin published, circa 1774, *Jackson's Celebrated Irish Tunes*, including several items sourced from the 'gentleman piper'.* Many more tunes by or associated with Jackson, generally with his name in their titles, appeared in other collections over the next few decades.†

In Grove's *Dictionary Of Music And Musicians*, Jackson is described thus:

> The most noted composer of tunes for the Irish pipes during the 18th century. His melodies (of great excellence) were among the most popular tunes of the day, both in Ireland and in England ... [They] were reprinted over and over again in collections of the period ... Practically nothing is known of his biography ... There is a passing reference to him in O'Keeffe's *Reminiscences* of 1826, by which it appears that he was 'a fine gentleman of great landed property'.[386]

The question of whether this celebrated piper/composer was a man of Ballingarry, Co. Limerick, or of Creeve, Co. Monaghan, has been rumbling along since the time of Bunting's *Ancient Music Of Ireland* (1840). Bunting declared Jackson for Monaghan; Grattan Flood, in his *History Of Irish Music* (1905), opted for Limerick.

In *Irish Minstrels And Musicians* (1913), Francis O'Neill quotes correspondence to himself from a Patrick O'Leary, by then 'a man of prominence' in Australia,[387] who knew the Monaghan Jacksons as a boy and recalled them as a wealthy Ulster linen-manufacturing, mill-owning and racehorse-owning family.

> **Patrick O'Leary (1913)**: Differing materially from the Anglo-Scottish squirearchy of Ulster of their time, or any other time, they were liberal, broad-minded and hospitable. During my boyhood I have heard 50 or 60 tunes, reels and jigs, that were credited to the famous piper ...[388]

O'Leary went on to explain how the reel 'Jacky Latin' was composed by the Monaghan Jackson for one Jack Duffy, who came from Lattan, near Creeve – the true title being

---

* The non-extant Samuel Lee edition is inferred from known editions by John Lee in 1780 and Edmund Lee in 1790.

† There are at least 90 extant Irish traditional tunes attributed to the piper (whose forename is sometimes given erroneously as 'Walter'), many of them with titles beginning 'Jackson's'. His tunes can be found in Canon Goodman's and Patrick Gunn's manuscripts as well as Mr O'Farrell's celebrated tutor of c. 1800. Jackson died c. 1798.

'Jack O'Lattan'. One uncredited sleuth, writing for *Treoir* in 1971, felt it only fair to point out that a tune called 'Jack Lattin' had appeared in *Waylet's Collection Of Country Dances*, published in 1749, and that, in a further layer to the probability onion, there is a place in County Limerick called Lattin.

The *Treoir* writer established that there were indeed wealthy, sporting Jacksons of Creeve and also cited Robin Morton's research on the Ulster song 'Jackson And Jane', about a sporting Hugh Jackson in the linen industry. Might this fellow also be the piping Jackson of the area? Or might he be a son or grandson? Morton quotes an 1801 survey showing a Hugh Jackson to be prominent in linen bleaching in the area, noting that his descendants lived in the area until the 1960s.[389]

Writing in 1976 about the elusive piper, Breandán Breathnach began with a hitherto neglected source, Ferrar's *History Of Limerick*, published in 1787. Would it shed light on the mystery? Seemingly so:

> Walker Jackson is a native of the county of Limerick and a good musician, who has composed a number of excellent pieces of music which are much admired for their harmony and expression. The most favourite of Mr Jackson's compositions are: 'Jackson's Morning Brush; 'The Turret'; 'The Humours Of Castle Jackson'; 'Jackson's Ramble'; 'Roving Blade'; and 'The Cream Of The Jest'.[390]

The first two tunes cited are included in the Lee collection *Jackson's Celebrated Irish Tunes*. Clearly, this is the man we're after. Or at least one of them.

Breathnach goes on to provide further evidence from contemporary documents and local tradition in the Ballingarry area about these Jacksons and their castle, and the interesting fact, drawn from *Limerick Chronicle* adverts of 1785, that Walker Jackson – whose tunes are so associated with conviviality – was president of a society known as Cuideachda Gan Cúram ('Companionship Without Care'). What it is that they did or subscribed to remains a mystery, but one may infer that a good time was had by all.

The Breathnach investigation went on to cite further oral history from Counties Limerick and Monaghan on the two Jacksons – the Monaghan man's racehorses, for example, being named after parts of the pipes – including testimony from one Limerick man who believed they were the same person, with properties and business interests in both places. Breathnach subscribed to the 'two people' theory and noted:

> It would seem from the type of tunes attributed to the two Jacksons, mostly jigs to Walker, mostly reels [a Scottish import into Irish music] to the northern piper, that the latter lived some decades later than the former.[391]

The legend of the Piper/Pipers Jackson lives on, defiant of mundane truths. Ninety extant tunes with upward of 270 titles are attributed to 'Jackson', with a further 12 titles attributed to him in various sources for which a tune cannot be found.

> **Breandán Breathnach**: It is most unlikely that Jackson composed a tenth of the tunes attributed to him. Some were in print before his time, many must have been composed after his time. The reels associated in northern sources with the name are most likely to be related to Jackson of Creeve, who, doubtless like his southern counterpart, is given credit for tunes which are not his at all. Of those tunes which can with certainty be attributed to Walker Jackson his 'Morning Brush', with all due respects to O'Neill, is his best and most popular.[392]

Turlough McSweeney

'No Irish piper of ancient or modern times … has been the subject of so much publicity as McSweeney, 'the Donegal Piper', since brought to light by Mrs Hart and installed at 'Donegal Castle' on the Midway of the World's Columbian Exposition at Chicago in 1893.'[393]

So declared Francis O'Neill, to whom we owe most of our knowledge of this curious man. Born in 1829 and still pursuing his eccentric course in 1913, when *Irish Minstrels And Musicians* was published, McSweeney could purportedly trace his ancestry back to Eremon, first king of Ireland, in 1690 BC. Not quite the last of the line, Turlough had two sons and five daughters (one possibly a piper) but his extraordinary character, and his skill in piping, ensured that the royal line, in somewhat reduced circumstances, went out with a bang.

Turlough McSweeney, as the representative of the 'old music', played outside 'Donegal Castle' at the 1893 Chicago World's Fair mentioned above, while the new age was embodied by Patsy Touhey, the piping king of American vaudeville, playing inside. As O'Neill affirmed: 'No two musicians on the Midway, representing their respective countries, won more attention or elicited more praise than they.'[394]

McSweeney, however, was a difficult man to get along with. Aside from his dour disposition, he fervently believed that his gift of piping had been acquired from the king of the fairies, after a moonlit visit to a knoll in Gweedore. He also jealously guarded a mysterious 'book of instructions'. On the latter point, at least, O'Neill could shed some light:

> As McSweeney enjoyed the hospitality of Sergeant Early from Saturday

evening until Monday morning, during his six months' stay in Chicago, we were afforded ample opportunity to hear him at his best. For an Irish piper, his coldness and reticence were in marked contrast with the manners of most persons of his class. This taciturnity may have been constitutional; yet who knows but it was the visible effect of maintaining the dignity befitting a distinguished piper, conscious of his descent from the chieftains of the once powerful Clan MacSuibhne of Tir-Conaill. Be that as it may, he rarely relaxed his reserve. With his host and benefactor, Sergeant Early, and with Mr Gillan, a great admirer of his music, he was more communicative and almost cordial.

Being in line with the tales of fairy enchantment, his mysterious allusions to a book of 'instructions' all through his career have served to make him an object of peculiar interest to people of his class everywhere. No human eye, except his own, has ever been permitted to profane this treasure by even a glance. As a concession to his benefactors before named, he presented them with a scale of the natural notes on the Irish chanter, which, upon comparison, we find is identical with that to be found in *O'Farrell's National Irish Music* [of which O'Neill knew of two other extant copies] … The 'Donegal Piper', may well regard his treasure as priceless, cherishing, as he undoubtedly does, the hallucination that he possesses the only copy in existence of one of the rarest and most unique works ever printed on a British press.[395]

McSweeney was among the handful of venerable pipers corralled by Gaelic League revivalists into Feis Ceoil competitions. He took second prize to Robert Thompson of Cork at the inaugural Feis in Dublin in 1897. Amazingly, one performance, of his own 'MacSweeney's March' [sic], was recorded on wax cylinder during the 'unpublished airs' part of the competition.*

Francis O'Neill recounted several stories of Turlough's dealings with the little people, including one account of a party held in his honour in Chicago where 'under the mollifying influence of a few tumblers of screeching hot punch, 'the Donegal Piper' relaxed his customary reserve and became almost sociable'.[396] The newly agreeable McSweeney proceeded to scare the living daylights out of fellow piper, and fan, Billy McCormick when he appeared to introduce him to an invisible host of his mystical associates outside the kitchen door – a host for whom he proceeded to play, his performance outstripping that given to his human associates earlier that evening. McCormick made his excuses and left as quickly as propriety would allow.

---

* While the Feis Ceoil cylinders were donated to the IFC in 1955 and later inherited by UCD, Turlough's performance cannot be found or accurately identified.

Turlough travelled around the northern counties of Ireland and also into Scotland, but took no pupils and guarded his piping techniques as he did his 'book of instructions'. He was consequently the last of a kind. In 1944 Séamus Ennis, travelling in Donegal for the Irish Folklore Commission, was intrigued to meet a priest who knew the already legendary character and who had been left his pipes. Ennis was delighted to see them. On that occasion, as far as we know, the instrument – which had reportedly once played on its own for a fairy visitor to McSweeney's home – was silent.

R.L. O'Mealy And Brother Gildas

Asked once about styles of piping, Séamus Ennis declared that there were three: loose or open fingering, such as that used by street musicians who played 'off the knee' to gain volume (e.g. Johnny Doran); the 'normal or Drawing Room style, which tended to be more musical', as favoured by Séamus; and the ultra-close fingering of the North: 'Brother Gildas of Belfast was the closest I've ever heard.'[397]

Brother Gildas (1882–1960), born Patrick O'Shea in Ballinskelligs, Co. Kerry, is generally associated with Belfast, where he taught at the De La Salle School. Friendly with many of the Dublin pipers, including Leo Rowsome, he was eccentric in his approach to performing.

> **Robbie Hughes**: Brother Gildas was a well known collector and a capable piper, but I remember being told by a very old man who had heard him playing that, such was Gildas' fascination and awe for the haunting acoustical qualities of the C natural note on the chanter scale, he often would hold this note for a longer time than could be considered reasonable by either the composer or indeed the audience.[398]

Wilbert Garvin, himself one of the great characters of Northern piping, never met Gildas but heard an addendum to this stretching of the C: that Gildas would make the sign of the cross while holding it. Seán Reid invited Gildas to holiday with the Reid family on a couple of occasions. Mrs Reid (with whom Gildas differed on the right approach to quality cooking) was convinced she could hear Gildas' pipes playing long after he had retired for the night. She maintained that this happened again when Seán inherited Gildas' Egan set in 1960 – Seán eventually finding that life was made easier by passing them on to another piper.*

---

* The full story can be found in *The Seán Reid Society Journal*, Vol. 2, March 2002. The pipes are currently in the possession of Wilbert Garvin.

Gildas, however, was but one exponent of what some call 'the Belfast style', a curious style that seems to have originated, certainly as a geographical descriptor, with prominent piper and pipe maker Richard (R.L.) O'Mealy (1873–1947), who was likewise not native to the city but forever associated with it. The 'Belfast style' may actually have developed much earlier, in Dublin:

> **Terry Moylan**: Unfortunately, there are no recordings of Brother Gildas. Breandán Breathnach knew Gildas, and Gildas was a visitor to John Potts' house. And Breandán learnt from old John Potts and learnt from Gildas, and Breandán had a very slow, deliberate, quite tight style – and Matt Keirnan had the same tight style. And apparently this was the style, Breandán said, that the older pipers around Dublin all shared. It didn't have any of the flowing effect that Leo or Willie or Seamus had. You couldn't dance to it.

In a detailed appreciation of O'Mealy in *The Seán Reid Society Journal* – a tremendous piece of sleuthing and reminiscence, freely available online – Ronan Browne describes O'Mealy as 'central to the continuance of piping in the north-east of Ireland in the early 20th century'.[399]

A man of many surnames, O'Mealy represented the fourth generation of pipers and pipe makers in his family, his father being steward of the Tristernagh Estate in Westmeath.* The first tune Richard learned on pipes was 'St Patrick's Day', learned on that very day from his brother Ned. During the late 1890s, through employment in drapery retail, he moved between Dublin, Boyle and Cork. He took part in competitions during this period, including the inaugural 1897 Feis, winning awards for pipe making in the 1901 and 1902 Oireachtas. He was present at the March 1898 meeting that led to the founding of the Cork Pipers' Club (two years before its Dublin cousin). In 1900, the Dublin club funded Richard and his brother Ned to attend the Leinster Feis. A year or so prior to this, Richard had married Eleanor Williams, and around 1900 they moved to Belfast, where Richard had secured a job as chief floor-walker with Arnott's, a prestigious department store.

---

* Known as 'Melia' locally, the family name was given as 'Mealy' on R.L.'s birth certificate. On a press advert for his services as a pipes repair man in Cork in 1899, the name is still Mealy. He is listed as 'Mealey' in the annual Belfast Street Directories until 1903, when it becomes 'O'Mealey'. The second 'e' is dropped in this source from 1926. Wilbert Garvin: 'Apparently [R.L.] had a couple of sets that he had made but couldn't sell them. Brother Gildas was very friendly with him. He said he was going to Dublin and he would get a stamp made to stamp the pipes. He arrived back and showed the stamp and here it said 'R.L. O'Mealy'. Richard said to Gildas, 'But my name is Mealy'. 'Ah,' says Gildas, 'with the O in front you'll be able to sell the pipes far better.' And so he did!'

Richard would remain in Belfast for the rest of his life. The first 10 years of the new century, seemingly up to a time when Eleanor became seriously ill (finally dying in 1920, after a long illness), were his most prolific as a performer. Onstage, he dressed in a somewhat absurd faux-Bardic costume. This apparently irritated at least one early reviewer, Éamonn Ceannt (1916 revolutionary and piper), who wrote of a double bill with 'Professor [Robert] Thompson' of Cork:

> Thompson was wretched and Mealy spoiled his playing by the ridiculous costume he wore. … [A]sk your grandfathers and grandmothers if they ever beheld a piper in long-tailed green coat, yellow knee-breeches, blue stockings and buckled shoes, not forgetting a patch near the throat which was covered by a loose cloth resembling a handkerchief. Mr Mealy also wore spectacles and beard while performing.[400]

There are several photos of O'Mealy in this get-up, including an image on his own publicity material dated around 1904/05. The very fact that, in this era, a piper *had* publicity material – a compliment slip with 'Bardic dress' photo in one corner and two pages of glowing extracts from press reviews – was extraordinary. O'Mealy was vigorous in self-promotion and unapologetic about his fees. A surviving letter to Lord Castletown, after a now-lost exchange around a potential engagement, reveals 'The Prince Of Irish Pipers' in bullish form:

> My fee is two guineas … I have sacrificed much for the pipes and my ability, as a performer, has cost me a life-long study together with what my fore fathers left on a sure foundation. I have heard that an ordinary piper from Cork is [now] engaged. …
> PS Canon Goodman, Skibbereen, and I used to play together.[401]

Ken McLeod, Ronan Browne, Wilbert Garvin and their associates in the Seán Reid Society managed to find numerous contemporary references to O'Mealy performing around the North, from Strabane on the Donegal border to Glenarm in deepest Antrim, during the first decade of the century. Writing in 1913, Francis O'Neill was able to apply his delightfully circuitous prose to the man:

> Much that would be interesting to the general reader … and rather complimentary than otherwise, is omitted in deference to our subject's wishes. Biography of the living is as much out of place, anyway, as ante-mortem epitaphs, for be it known we are all prone to view ourselves in the delusive

mirror of self-esteem. … A man of education and ability, Mr O'Mealy … was born generations too late for his merits to be appreciated as they deserve. … In his young days Mr O'Mealy had the pleasure of playing at a concert with the renowned Canon Goodman, who in his opinion was the best piper in the province of Munster. … Liberally endowed with the artistic temperament, O'Mealy seems well equipped for his profession. He claims to have worked certain improvements in various parts of the instrument …[402]

Writing privately, however, in a letter of 1912, O'Neill was less circumlocutory: 'Mr O'Mealy of Belfast may be a good piper but he is a supersensitive egotist, unjustifiably sarcastic in referring to possible rivals.'[403]

The 1911 Census listed O'Mealy as 'Musician, Maker of Irish Uilean [sic] Bagpipes, Artist'. Beyond that, until 1924, he disappears from view. An anguished letter of August 1910 from O'Mealy to F.J. Bigger marks perhaps the beginning of Eleanor O'Mealy's terminal illness. Conjecturally, Richard curtailed his performing career to care for his wife, alongside his ongoing day job as a floor-walker.*

He reappeared in public, and in print, as an adjudicator at a piping competition within the Tailteann Games, a revival of an ancient sporting event, in August 1924. James Ennis, father of Séamus, took first prize and earned the O'Mealy remark of being 'a very interesting player'.[404]

The following month, on September 30 1924, Richard gave the first of many broadcasts on the BBC.† Belfast's BBC outpost 2BE had opened only 15 days previously, with studios in Linenhall Street and with initially limited transmitter reach. Northern Ireland as a whole would be able to hear the local BBC from 1936. Richard made two further solo broadcasts for 2BE in this period (in November 1924 and September 1925). He also made at least one very early broadcast in Dublin for 2RN, founded in 1926.

While the years between 1925 and 1934 would seemingly be fallow for airtime, R.L. made at least 32 further BBC appearances (some for the British Forces Service during wartime) between 1934 and 1943.‡ Typically, these 1934–43 appearances

---

* A kind of retail *maître d'*, as portrayed by 'Captain Peacock' in the 1970s sitcom *Are You Being Served?*
† His repertoire on this occasion, in a 20-minute solo programme, was 'Irish Jig' (9/8 time), 'The Copper Lass' (6/8 time), 'Erin Is My Home' (air), 'Billy Byrne Of Ballymanus' (march), 'The Donegall Reel' [sic], 'O'Mealy's Hornpipe'. He also did a spot the same evening on a news and variety programme.
‡ The years between 1925 and 1934 would see no 2BE broadcasts involving uilleann pipes, apart from one solitary programme in 1930 that featured Liam Walsh.

would be on *The Children's Hour* or *Piping, Fiddling And Singing*; only once did he provide music within a drama. During the same period, in 1938, he made his sole appearance on celluloid, in the Richard Hayward film *Devil's Rock*, playing the pipes outside a rural cottage as a character walks into the distance. It is an atmospheric one-minute sequence and anticipates the modus operandi of the McPeake Family by several years in having a singer (Hayward) join the piping halfway through.

Exploring *Radio Times*' listings is helpful for getting a sense of the uilleann pipes' 'visibility' within the catchment area of the BBC in Northern Ireland during O'Mealy's time. Aside from Richard, only five other pipers can be found to have broadcast from Belfast between 1924 and O'Mealy's death in 1947, all of them between 1930 and 1940: one broadcast apiece for County Waterford's Liam Walsh, Dublin's William Andrews and Belfast's Patrick Maxwell (O'Mealy's odd-job man and pupil); two from Belfast's Frank McFadden; and 12 from County Fermanagh's Philip Martin, described in *Radio Times* as 'one of the few well-known exponents of the Uillean [sic] pipes in Ulster'.*

O'Mealy's dominance of the Belfast airwaves was akin to Leo Rowsome's dominance of those from Dublin. The pair certainly knew each other – they each appeared regularly at the Tristernagh Feis, held every June between 1924 and 1946 (barring two years) near O'Mealy's family home in Westmeath. Anecdotally, Leo was said to have practically fallen off his chair when he heard O'Mealy for the first time, though with quite what emotion remains obscure.

> **Ronan Browne**: The annual trip to Tristernagh must have been a huge part of his year and we are told … that when he arrived, great crowds would gather in Templecross; he would hold forth and might talk on any subject; often the night would pass without a note being played, but the next evening he might play all night, hardly stopping; sometimes he would just play the whistle.[405]

From 1931, married to his second wife Letitia, Richard lived at 45 Rugby Avenue in Belfast. He had a pipe making workshop with a treadle lathe in his attic, which boasted an apparatus to ring downstairs for cups of tea, and passers-by in the street below would often be bemused by the sounds emanating from same. A couple of those who knew him claim that Richard kept a hoard of gold coins in his workshop, but routinely pleaded poverty during these later years.

> **Ronan Browne**: In the 1930s, writing to [friends], he laments the amount of

---

* Phil Martin also broadcast on Radio Éireann, as 2RN had become named by the mid-30s, and made one 78rpm record for Regal Zonophone in the same decade, both sides of which can be heard at the remarkable Internet Archive (archive.org). Phil died in the early 1940s.

work available to him, citing Belfast pipers of indifferent ability and Dublin pipers poaching performance opportunities. He goes as far as pleading with them in 1936 to write to the BBC asking to hear more of him on the radio; he states that without the odd engagement from the BBC he wouldn't be able to carry on living at his present address.[406]

Andy Conroy, the Dublin-based piper who was present at Johnny Doran's only recording session, and who was himself described as 'a gentleman, wit, black belt karate master and a *very* tight piper',[407] met Richard in 1942:

> **Andy Conroy**: I worked in Belfast building air raid shelters for the British. I visited his home through Brother Gildas. Brother Gildas was taking lessons from him, although he doesn't agree to that now, that he was taking lessons from him. … [O'Mealy] said that he thought that the Dublin pipers were shivering afraid of him. He mentioned one man – I won't mention his name – there was a … concert or something. And this man, he landed at the concert … and he said he'd left his pipes in the tramcar because when he heard that O'Mealy was there he got scared. A well known man on paper … He would speak of other people with scorn such as … I don't know can I mention names … Well, the pipers of that day that were in Belfast, shall we say?[408]

Richard had made Francis McPeake a set of pipes around 1904, but had fallen out with him long before 1942.

The last broadcasts he made were in 1943. The online *Radio Times* database lists three, the last being in June. Nevertheless, 10 tunes were cut to disc, purportedly during a broadcast on August 28 1943. It would hardly be O'Mealy without a frisson of mystery, though: BBC Archives researcher Kate O'Brien has checked all possible files and there is not a shred of R.L. O'Mealy documentation extant at the BBC Written Archives Centre. More to the point, the 'Programmes As Broadcast' file on the August 28 1943 Forces Service programme *Irish Dance*, the only programme that may conceivably have featured O'Mealy that day, merely confirms that it did not.

Whatever their date or circumstances, these 10 short recordings, which reveal his playing to be redolent of a concertina, such was the tightness of his style, are almost the only ones he ever made.* The BBC recordings were reputedly made discreetly –

---

* According to Breandán Breathnach, two tunes by R.L. were recorded on wax cylinder (along with tunes from the 'wretched' Robert Thompson, John Flanagan and Turlough McSweeney) at the 1897 Dublin Feis. Neither can now be found at UCD's Folklore Collection, although there remain four unidentified piping cylinders in its Feis Ceoil collection.

an amusing example of the corporation wilfully bootlegging one of its own sessions – as R.L. was against recording on principle, believing, according to his nephew, that 'if his public had access to recordings of him, they would be less likely to come out to see him in concert'.[409]

This seems an eccentric view, although R.L. was 70 in 1943 and had grown up in an era long before commercial recordings. Leo Rowsome had been among the vanguard in embracing the medium in the 1920s and 30s. Far from diluting an audience, recordings expanded it. But one gets the impression that R.L. O'Mealy was not a man to take advice, least of all from pipers in Dublin.

> **Ronan Browne**: In those later years … he took pupils – or, more correctly, he built up relationships with the people who bought his pipes and this led to tuition. From his letters alone one could publish a full manual on learning to play the Irish pipes, including the care of the instrument and most importantly the making of reeds for it. … His pupils all felt honoured to learn from the great man; they listened closely and did it his way, always. It is no wonder that so many of his instruments survive in perfect order, many of them still in original cases lined by Letitia along with original embroidered chanter, bag and bellows covers.[410]

Richard was in fairly poor health by the 1940s, possibly due to his workshop environment. After the worst winter on record, he died on March 14 1947. Two of his students, Jim McIntosh and Jack O'Rourke, were among a small gathering at his funeral. He left nearly £1,600 (all to Letitia), which certainly came as a surprise to all those visitors who had gone away thinking the man existed in penury – including Seán Reid, who after one visit had bags of coal sent round.

*

Volume 3 of *The Seán Reid Society Journal* does a great service to knowledge by exploring the ripples outward from R.L. O'Mealy, shining a light on several of his pupils. Perhaps against perceptions then or now, 'the vast majority of the persons R.L. made pipes for and taught to play were of Protestant background'.[411]

> **Ken McLeod**: The religious divide has played a part in the North of Ireland's history going back long before the Union pipes emerged. For example, two of O'Mealy's pupils, Jack O'Rourke and Jim McIntosh, came from backgrounds of the strongest and most opposing kind. Jack from the republican Falls Road and Jim from the loyalist Shankill Road.

They remained friends for life but their friendship was virtually kept secret. After O'Mealy died and Jim McIntosh bought his tools he was living in the Donegal Road area, another strong loyalist district. After a year or two he sold them on to Seán Reid in Ennis. Jack O'Rourke was the go-between who arranged this and I clearly remember Jack telling me that the matter had to be kept quiet. Both Jack and Jim had considerable concerns as to how their neighbours might react to such an alliance. Sad but true. This type of unfortunate attitude might help explain why Jack and Seán McAloon, to name but two [Catholic] Belfast pipers, never even met Billy Hope and knew only of his existence as far as we know. …

[Yet] Highland pipers on the Shankill Road seemed to have known about R.L. and after taking up and playing the Highland instrument saw the 'uilleann' pipes as acceptable because of the religious background of the maker and teacher.[412]

R.L. O'Mealy was from a Church Of Ireland background. His pupil Billy Hope (1880–1959), as Ken McLeod implied, had an Ulster-Scots Presbyterian background, and was a joiner and a teacher of Highland pipe bands. He seems also to have been a friend of Francis Bigger, the 'Celtic Revivalist' who pops up a lot in these tales. On Saturdays during the 1920s, Billy co-opted part of his first wife's drapery shop on the Shankill Road to sell piping-related goods – which, as McLeod notes, 'gives one a clear feeling for the very serious interest in bagpiping which existed there between the wars'. His advertising slogan was 'Don't Hope For The Best, Come To Hope's And Get It.' He taught Highland piping at Campbell College, a prestigious private school in East Belfast, between 1916 and 1959, and taught woodwork at its preparatory school. Somehow, alongside this, tutoring several other pipe bands and looking after a large family, he found time to build a house on King's Road – the scene of photographs taken with Leo Rowsome in the 1950s.

Billy had become interested in uilleann piping early enough for R.L. to make him a set – seemingly a flat set, for he later asked Leo Rowsome for a set in D, in order to be able to play with his friend Davy Mawhinney, (a fiddler) and his pals in the Antrim & Derry Fiddlers' Association.

Another O'Mealy pupil was Miles Delap, son of a Church Of Ireland minister from Strabane, who had a tin whistle and a Highland piping background. He commissioned a set of O'Mealy pipes in the 1930s before moving to England, where he served in the RAF, sinking the first U-boat of WWII.

On the other side of the wearisome Northern Ireland religious divide amongst

R.L.'s pupils was Jack O'Rourke, a house painter from the Falls Road area of Belfast. Jack was a great friend of the Fermanagh piper Seán McAloon, who lived nearby.

> **Ken McLeod**: Jack played on BBC radio, most probably during O'Mealy's lifetime, because I remember one evening when Seán McAloon said to Jack, 'I'll never forget that night you played on the BBC, you had just got the double-bass [sic] regulator from O'Mealy and when you hit it, it sounded like a ship going down the Lough.'[413]

O'Mealy was known for the baritone-bass-contrabass (as opposed to the standard tenor-baritone-bass) alignment of his regulators. There is no obvious record of Jack's BBC appearance – but perhaps, as with fellow O'Mealy pupil Patrick Maxwell (who broadcast in December 1937), O'Mealy may have made the opportunity happen. Maxwell was an odd-job man, with a background in the Craobh Rua Uilleann Pipe Band (which played outside GAA matches and had a clubhouse on Crown Entry off High Street in Belfast), who came twice a week to help R.L. with things, receiving a set of pipes for his trouble.

The most intriguing of O'Mealy's known pupils is 'Miss Johnston': Netta Jane Johnston (1878–1952), a general store proprietor of Carnlough on the County Antrim coast. A multi-instrumentalist, Miss Johnston was for many years organist at St Mary's (Church Of Ireland) parish church in the village. Wilbert Garvin, himself an organist and piper living in deepest Antrim, looked back fondly on his forebear:

> Regarding her organ-playing she apparently had a running argument with the local rector because of her habit of practising the organ at Ardclinis Church between three and four in the middle of the night! She was eventually banned from playing the church organ since no agreement could be arrived at. She played and taught classical violin, being much in demand as a music teacher; she was also competent on the piano, flute and pipe organ. She formed what she appropriately called the 'Carnlough Non-Sectarian Flute Band' which ran for many years in the 1920s and 1930s. With respect to her Uilleann piping, it was very unusual to find a lady piper, particularly in the earlier part of the 20th century in a small village like Carnlough …
>
> Refined, cultured and dignified, she was nevertheless somewhat of an eccentric (I use this term very much in the complimentary sense). She was well known as a 'night owl', being often seen walking around Carnlough in the wee small hours. When approached about the possible dangers associated with such an activity she would demonstrate her method of protection – her

long walking cane was in fact a sword-cane! She would produce this long blade (which she kept sharpened like a razor) from the cane with a flourish and dared anyone to try her on. There is no doubt that she would have used it if and when necessary. Apparently she was also proficient in judo and was purported to have a loaded shotgun under her bed.[414]

On the origins of Miss Johnston's interest in piping, once again Francis Bigger is involved. The first 'Feis Of The Glens' was held in 1904 – and there he was on the organising committee, along with a 26-year-old Miss Johnston:

> **Wilbert Garvin**: [I]t is likely that it was F.J. Bigger who invited R.L. O'Mealy to be the music adjudicator and one of the performers at the evening concert. This is probably where Miss Johnston may have first come across the pipes and R.L. O'Mealy, and been fascinated by both. She also knew that R.L. made pipes since Neil McCurdy from Rathlin Island won the piping competition on war pipes at the Feis … [and] his prize was a set of uilleann pipes by O'Mealy. She travelled regularly to Belfast for lessons with R.L. usually on a Wednesday afternoon when the shop shut early. Being a reasonably accomplished, determined and versatile musician she bought a set from him and progressed quite rapidly. She played the pipes at the Feis in Ballymena in the 1930s. The Ballymena Feis is still held today … I remember that when I first came to the Ballymena area in the late 60s, I entered the Feis so that people would have an opportunity to hear the pipes. Unfortunately the only class that I could enter was the 'miscellaneous instrument class', to the chagrin of the adjudicator, none other than the redoubtable Breandán Breathnach, who of course couldn't resist making a few pertinent remarks![415]

Willie Clarke

Like (perhaps) the mysterious Piper Jackson, William 'Willie' Clarke (1889–1934) came from County Monaghan. A Presbyterian of Scottish descent, Willie became a watchmaker, with premises in Ballybay. He also became one of the earliest uilleann pipers to be commercially recorded, and might have represented a wellspring of piping and pipe making in Monaghan had his life not been cut short.

Willie was inspired to take up both the Highland and uilleann pipes by Pat Ward from nearby Doohamlet – the same Pat Ward who influenced Séamus Ennis' father. Unusually, Willie also owned a set of Lowland pipes.

Harry Bradshaw: Pat Ward ... was one of a small group of pipers who kept interest in the instrument alive when it had almost become extinct at the end of the 19th century. ... [Nevertheless] there was a strong pocket of Uilleann Pipers in the Monaghan area in Willie's youth and when the Feis Ceoil was staged in Belfast in 1898 and 1900, the pipers entered included: Philip Goodman 'who had walked all the way from his native Carrickmacross', Dan Markey from Castleblayney and George McCarthy also from Carrickmacross.

Pat Ward, as Willie's teacher, was one of his greatest influences: other less well-known pipers in the area who had contact with Willie were: William Carolan who came from the townland of Dopeymills ... Mick Keenan, a piper and pipe-maker, who lived in Glassleck in County Cavan ... another keen young exponent on the pipes was Philip Martin who lived quite a distance away in Kilturk near Lisnaskea in County Fermanagh. ... Philip would make the long and arduous trip by bicycle to visit Willie Clarke in Ballybay. Philip's only free day to do this was Sunday but Willie being a firm up-holder of the Sabbath would not take his pipes out of their box or play music on Sundays. Philip Martin was to die a young man having made one impressive piping recording in Dublin in 1937.

A piping visitor from further afield was Brother Gildas who at that time was teaching in Downpatrick, County Down. He regularly visited and stayed as a guest at the Clarke home. These visits were remembered by Willie's son, Reverend Bill Clarke: 'Brother Gildas, a delightful man, used to come and visit us. The evenings would end up in a piping session part of which I would be allowed to listen to and then I would have to go to bed. I remember he spoke with a lovely Southern accent, a most beautiful brogue, and this used to fascinate us children.'

Brother Gildas was a well-known figure in the piping world at that time ... a Kerryman and a native speaker of Irish. The spectacle of a De La Salle Brother staying in a strong Presbyterian house in North Monaghan in the mid-1920s must have raised eyebrows at the time, but Willie Clarke's attitude to such things is remembered by his son: 'He liked the person, he was interested only in the person, he wasn't interested in anything else.'

Another visitor from [far] afield was James Ennis of Finglas 'a Dublin civil servant, a bit taciturn and a gifted piper and fiddler' as Reverend Bill Clarke remembers. 'He was a very frequent visitor to our home. His wife was from Farney in County Monaghan and he and my father used to play together and have some lovely evenings.' Two Belfast pipers Frank

McFadden and Francis McPeake occasionally called at the Clarke home on piping matters as did Leo Rowsome …[416]

Bradshaw concedes that 'Willie Clarke's name … would probably be long forgotten if it were not for his recordings'. These had come about by chance. Willie regularly attended a gathering of pipers at Bellingham in Northumberland in the 20s and at one such, in 1928, a man from Columbia Records recruited three pipers – players of uilleann, Northumbrian and Highland pipes – to come to London and make a three-disc set entitled *The Pipes Of Three Nations*. Willie later created a pipe making workshop in his loft (just as O'Mealy had done in Belfast) but succumbed to TB in 1934. The brief flowering of uilleann piping in County Monaghan was ended.

The McPeake Family

The first Francis 'Frank' McPeake (1885–1971) was born in Belfast to a mother from Belfast and father from Derry/Londonderry. 'Though I'm Belfast born, my heart is in Derry,' he said, 75 years later.[417] His father was a singer and flautist, and by the time he was about 11 Frank had joined his two brothers in the O'Connell Flute Band. Around the beginning of the 20th century, F.J. Bigger introduced Frank to the uilleann pipes. In 1904, he gave Frank an O'Mealy flat set and arranged for blind John O'Reilly, from County Galway, to come to Belfast for some months to give Francis lessons. As the now defunct family website put it: 'One day during a lesson, Francis began to sing *with* the pipes! John O'Reilly couldn't believe this as it was totally unheard of for someone to do this …'[418]

Frank became the best-known player to do this, but he wasn't the first. Aside from R.L. O'Mealy's turn, with pipes and voice, at the end of *Devil's Rock* (1938), Breandán Breathnach noted of Canon Goodman in the 19th century that he 'was wont to sing in unison with the pipes'.[419] Additionally, Séamus Ennis' field diary for May 23 1946, while in Clare, includes this:

> John Tom [Ó Mianáin] came to spend part of the evening here again. I got him to sing unaccompanied his song with the pipes. Well, do not talk! Everyone was smitten by this and we had to sing and play three or four of them before John got a rest. John was very proud of this. I put him in front of the Ediphone and as luck would have it the soundbox failed completely. John was not too pleased.[420]

Séamus played pipes with singers informally on at least two further occasions during this trip, but it would never become part of his own act. Thus, the still singular aspect of singing to one's own piping remains largely the preserve of Frank McPeake and his descendants. In time for the 'British folk revival' of the 1960s, they would form themselves into a multi-generational band, made all the more confusing for outsiders as almost everyone in it appeared to be called Francis.

Francis I (Frank), the first of the line, later described himself as 'a lone piper in the North' during these early years of the century.[421] He won a Belfast Feis in 1906 and an Oireachtas learners' event in 1912, and was invited to attend, with harper John Page, the Pan-Celtic Congress in Brussels in 1911. His Oireachtas adventure received a mention in O'Neill's *Irish Minstrels And Musicians* in 1913:

> The singing of the young man from the north to the accompaniment of his pipe music was a performance highly appreciated. Originally a pupil of R.L. O'Mealy of Belfast, temperamental difficulties came between them, so he placed himself under the tuition of [John] O'Reilly, who spent some months in the Ulster metropolis.[422]

In 1917, Frank's son Francis II was born; in 1942, his grandson Francis III was born. Both would become pipers in due course.[*]

While one or both of the first two Francis McPeakes made local BBC broadcasts of solo piping between 1949 and 1957, the McPeake Trio first appears in BBC documentation from August 1957. The previous year, Francis I and Francis II had performed as a duo at the Royal Albert Hall, invited by BBC folk music collector Peter Kennedy. The trio combined the two Francis McPeakes with James McPeake (b. 1936) on harp. When Frank had found an old minstrel harp, made by McFall of Belfast, abandoned in a Downpatrick convent, his son James had been persuaded to learn it.

The extremely odd combination of pipes and harp had been no accident. Frank had fond memories of playing with a Welsh harpist (probably John Page) and was keen to explore the combination again.

In 1957, the trio accompanied Ewan MacColl, Peggy Seeger and others from the leftist beginnings of the British folk music revival on a memorable trip to the World Youth Festival. As Peggy recalls: 'We went from London to Moscow on the train: three days. And they never stopped – they never stopped playing.'

It was under the patronage of Peter Kennedy, Ewan MacColl and others in Britain that platforms were created upon which first the McPeake trio and then the

---

* The late Peter Kennedy noted on his Folktrax website: 'Francis II became interested in playing the instrument at the end of [WWII] and first played on the radio in 1949.'

double trio could become a touring, recording and broadcasting entity. *The McPeake Family* LP (featuring the original trio) was released in 1961, on US label Prestige, through MacColl's connections. By the next album, for Topic in 1963, they were a double trio. There would be six LPs and two EPs between 1961 and 1967, plus numerous national broadcasts.

It is difficult to view the McPeakes' records as a body of work created by a unit focused on an artistic career or legacy, as such. Given the heavy repetition of material (at least six versions of 'Jug Of Punch' released during the 1960s alone), McPeake records appear to have been ephemeral items, souvenirs for people unlikely to collect them all. Alex Campbell, the godfather of British folk troubadours, operated in this way, too, purportedly recording 100 albums in his career. He certainly didn't have 100 albums' worth of material.

In 1960 Frank felt emboldened to phone Diane Hyde, producer of BBC radio's *Ulster Magazine*, to say that he would not be willing to accept further engagements at present BBC fees. He pointed out to Ms Hyde that 'even Radio Éireann pays more', and suggested that 15 guineas might be more acceptable. Ms Hyde told her superiors she would be sorry to lose the McPeakes, but left it up to them, adding: 'I don't know whether you would consider their uniqueness, together with their [first prize] at Llangollen this year …'*

An executive responded, saying: 'They are not used very often and I should think 15 guineas wouldn't break us, but perhaps [we] could get away with less. It might be worth trying 12.' But it seems Frank had his way. One 1963 contract is notable for having a fee of 12 guineas scored out and the figure of 15 inserted.

The BBC association proved useful when it came to international credibility. In December 1961 Frank wrote to a local producer asking for a reference toward acquiring a visa for a US and Canadian tour sponsored by businessman Paul Endicott. H.S. Denton replied that while the BBC had rarely been asked for such a thing, he was happy to provide it and wished them a pleasant trip.

A second US tour, of five weeks, would take place in February-March 1965, at the height of the 'British Invasion' spearheaded by The Beatles. US trade paper *Variety* described the tour as 'another twist on the invasion of talent from the British Isles'.[423] The trip was co-sponsored by Pete Seeger, godfather of American folk music. Pete had met the McPeakes in Belfast the previous year, making a short film of them playing music at home, with various neighbours looking on – among them the father of flautist Marcas Ó Murchú.

---

* Ms Hyde was referring to the annual Welsh Eisteddfod, which the McPeake trio were to win in their category on the three occasions they entered.

Marcas: The Pete Seeger film of the McPeakes in Belfast – my daddy is there eight seconds into it with a checked jacket on. It's just lovely. You can play music very simply. … What the McPeakes were doing was a full sound, it was like a bowl of stew – it warmed you up, you felt at home. I have a postcard from Francis I to my dad, written when they were touring America in the 60s, and in it he apologises for not having much Irish – the irony being that it's all written in Irish!

These tours would have been rare occasions for Americans, even Irish-Americans, to see uilleann pipes, but the McPeakes' principal platform during their 1960s heyday was in Britain. Intriguingly, their appeal seems to have ebbed more swiftly at home than it did in England.

From April 1963 to January 1965 the group were a regular broadcasting turn in Northern Ireland. After that, things dried up, just as they appeared to be taking off in mainland Britain. In January 1967, Frank wrote to H. Waldo Maguire, controller of BBC Northern Ireland, outlining his family's credentials and availability. Maguire replied congenially that while he was, of course, aware of the McPeakes' achievements, 'fashions change and just at the moment there is no suitable placing for the special skill and entertainment you have to offer.' Three months later, perhaps as a bit of a sop, Frank received a solo booking on *Country Céilí*. It would be the last McPeake booking for BBC NI that decade.

Nevertheless, broadcasts and recordings were only part of any folk artist's activities in this era of an unrepeatably rich harvest of opportunities around the folk clubs, nascent festivals and concert halls of Britain. Most artists on this scene had one or two 'big songs', which could sustain them. Martin Carthy had 'Scarborough Fair'; Jackson Frank had 'Blues Run The Game'; Alex Campbell had 'Been On The Road So Long'; the McPeakes had 'Wild Mountain Thyme' aka 'Will Ye Go, Lassie, Go?'.

Frank had based the composition on 'The Braes Of Balquhither', by early 19th century Scottish poet Robert Tannahill. The first release of the song, by Francis I and Francis II, was on *Folk Song Today*, a various-artists LP on HMV, from a recording made by Peter Kennedy in 1952. There would be several further McPeake recordings of the song and covers by artists around the world, from Judy Collins (1961), The Clancy Brothers (1962) and Joan Baez (1965) onward. The relative dearth of 1960s British artists recording it perhaps reflects an understanding within the 'folk revival' community that this was the McPeakes' signature song, and should be left to them.

Whether the McPeakes were a 'revival' act or a 'source' act was a moot point at the time. In July 1967, Karl Dallas opined: 'The McPeakes … have been singing together with the Irish pipes and harp for so long most people think of them as traditional singers [not 'revival singers'] …'424

Their bookings tended toward the 'traditional' end, barring odd shared bills with the likes of guitar virtuoso Gordon Giltrap. One fascinating line-up, mixing Glasgow comedy with London social comment and various hues of English and Irish tradition, occurred in February 1968 at London's Festival Hall: The Young Tradition, Matt McGinn, Leon Rosselson, Anne Briggs, The McPeake Family and Bob Davenport, with compère Sydney Carter.

Unusually, while the McPeakes were accepted as 'tradition bearers', they seemed to have no problem appealing to Light Entertainment producers. Their sentimental sound was easy on the ear and there was obviously human interest in the extended family aspect.

One interface between the McPeakes and popular culture was when they were booked to play at The Beatles' wrap party for their TV film *Magical Mystery Tour*. John Lennon had reportedly seen them on a TV programme, which must have been *Line Up*, tele-recorded on December 14 1967 (although the broadcast date remains elusive).*

From May 1968 the McPeakes were being represented in Britain by NEMS, founded by the recently deceased Beatles' manager Brian Epstein. A year later, their representation was with Apple Corps, a multi-faceted organisation run by the steadily-imploding Beatles themselves. A series of internal BBC memos from May and June 1969, over the failure of Frank McPeake to appear on *My Kind Of Folk* – a booking supposedly handled by Apple's Alastair Taylor – reveals the chaos at first hand.† By June, the family's representation had reverted to Roger Rushton, their former manager. Not uncommonly, the McPeakes' association with Apple proved that not everything touched by The Beatles turned to gold.

The McPeakes as a creative, touring entity are defined by the 1960s almost exactly. Their first album was released in 1961; their last, *Pleasant And Delightful*, appeared at the end of 1967. Their broadcasting career survived up to 1970; their British touring career up to 1972.‡

There would be a 'comeback' period, beginning with an Ulster Museum concert in December 1977, a UTV documentary and a return to Britain in February 1979,

---

* For more on the McPeakes' broadcasting history, see the Discographies & Sessionographies appendix.

† See the Discographies & Sessionographies appendix for details.

‡ The now defunct McPeake family website declared that the band ceased when Francis I died in 1971, but a version of the group, certainly featuring both Francis II and Francis III, toured British clubs in October-November 1972.

for a concert in Purley with The Boys Of The Lough. While the essence of their act in the 60s had been nostalgia, the reunion added a new layer to it: they were now themselves a kind of nostalgia act for the epochal 1960s. Odd concerts aside, from the late 70s onward the McPeake family would focus on music tuition in Belfast. They had certainly been a 'unique' act, as Diane Hyde had conceded back in 1960, but that novelty aspect – like everything in music – had had its time.

Seán Reid

'We have come a long way in traditional music since the early 30s,' said Seán Reid in 1974. 'Happily we have made progress and most changes have, I suppose, been for the better.'[425]

Though he was too modest to say so, most of those leaps of progress bore his own fingerprints. An educated, organised man, Seán Reid (1907–78) was a fiddler, pianist and piper from the North who had a significant role in the (re)founding of the Dublin Pipers' Club in the 1930s, The Tulla Céilí Band in the 1940s, Comhaltas Ceoltóirí Éireann (CCÉ) in 1951 and Na Píobairí Uilleann (NPU) in 1968. It's entirely appropriate, for such an advocate of organisations, that the Seán Reid Society now exists in his honour, publishing detailed historical knowledge on piping and pipers.

Seán was born in Castlefin, Co. Donegal, moving to Dungannon, Co. Tyrone, as a child. His father and uncle were fiddlers, and as a child he was surrounded by music:

> Music seemed to melt away whatever religious and political differences there were and the belief that music transcends these divisions was planted early in [my] mind and has ever since influenced my attitudes to Irish music and the Irish question.[426]

In 1927 he went to Queen's University Belfast to study civil engineering, and while there joined the Officers' Training Corps:

> At that stage I was unaware of the existence of the uilleann pipes, although I used to pass the house of R.L. O'Mealy [then at 109 Rugby Avenue] on the way from my lodgings to the university. … I picked up a recording by a piper called Tom Ennis who lived in Chicago and died in 1920. The music he played had a haunting and lasting effect on me. … [But] it was the year before I finished Queens that I first heard the uilleann pipes played.[427]

The occasion was the Glens Feis (Feis na nGleann) at Cushendun. Having taken part in athletics, Seán left the track to hear distant music: 'a very sweet music, which at first I took to be played on the fiddle. But this was not so: the musical instrument was the uilleann pipes and the musician was O'Mealy. Unfortunately he was gone before I had time to get to him.'

Later, working in Armagh, he saw one of the earliest sets of pipes made by Leo Rowsome. Moving to Dublin in 1934, he fell in with piper John Potts, who became a mentor. In 1937, having revived the Dublin Pipers' Club with Rowsome, Seán moved to Ennis, Co. Clare, as a county engineer. Almost immediately becoming friendly with Johnny Doran and then Willie Clancy, Seán was to remain intimately involved with the Clare music scene. This involvement led to the founding of a national and still-dominant organisation for the promotion of traditional music:

> Those of us who were attending and promoting Feiseanna came to the conclusion that it was necessary to have a nationwide organisation that would bring musicians together and publicise and propagate their music. The feeling for such a body was as strong among the rural organisers as it was in the Pipers' Club and finally, in 1951, Comhaltas Ceoltóirí Éireann was established. It was born out of the Pipers' Club, and its first constitution, a short, flexible document which lasted for many years, was drafted by Tommy Rowsome.[428]

Seán was happiest when CCÉ was still an organisation of modest size and informal spirit. Its principal outworking was the system of Fleadh competitions. In 1956, the year of the first Ennis Fleadh, CCÉ, at Seán's encouragement, made its first official contact with traditional musicians in Northern Ireland: the Antrim & Derry Country Fiddlers' Association.

> This organisation was not exclusively Protestant; it contained a fair number of Catholics, and it seemed to bear out what I long believed, that music does not naturally recognise political and religious divisions. The many Protestant musicians I met were on the same wavelength music-wise and there were many of us in Comhaltas who believed we should establish strong relations with the Northern musicians. The time seemed to be ripe and, as Francis McPeake senior put it, 'the Protestants were interested, very interested.'[429]

A period of co-operation ensued, with the Fiddlers' Association sending adjudicators and prizes to *fleadhanna* in the South. But events, and knee-jerk reactions to them, eventually got in the way:

> There was, on the Northern side, a widespread fear of the politicians, and when the 1970 Fleadh was cancelled as a gesture of support for the Nationalists in Ulster all co-operation came to an end. I opposed the decision of Comhaltas at the time. I felt the cancellation was a sectarian move not likely to improve relations between North and South. I still have no reason to change my opinion. … At least I am happy to say that a number of us did try to bring all traditional musicians together. We believed in keeping Comhaltas non-political and non-sectarian; it was a pity we did not succeed.[430]

Seán had better fortune in this regard with NPU, founded in 1968 as a more focused, manageable and non-competition-based interest group around piping. One or two Northern musicians would be involved in its founding – not least Brian Vallely, founder in 1966 of Armagh Pipers' Club (see the following chapter) and Wilbert Garvin, a beacon of ecumenism and good humour in life and music.

Wilbert Garvin

One of the most intriguing creations in Tolkien's *The Lord Of The Rings*, an anomaly which the author was happy to leave enigmatic, is Tom Bombadil – a whimsical forest-dweller and nature spirit whose light-hearted, mischievous and rather scatty persona masks great wisdom and age. One thinks of Bombadil when meeting Wilbert Garvin. Wilbert's cheery outlook and carefree way are worn lightly on a career in third-level science, with a number of biology textbooks to his name, not to mention the cracking of the pipe makers' code and the creation of a first-ever manual on the construction of uilleann pipes. Added to this are a lifelong involvement in Presbyterianism – as organist and latterly as historian – and a gift for cartooning. He may not wear a blue feather in his hat, and his good lady may prefer 'Elizabeth' to 'Goldberry', but he really does live in a lonely cottage on the edge of a wood. And, as he'll admit with a bit of chuckle, younger members of NPU are occasionally amazed to find that there is still someone alive and well who hobnobbed with the likes of Rowsome, Ennis and Clancy.

Born in North Belfast in 1938, Wilbert had an early interest in Highland piping through the Boys' Brigade. Aged 13 or 14, he joined the Field Marshal Montgomery Pipe Band, playing the 'Brian Boru pipes' – a variation on Highland pipes with keys allowing notes above and below the standard Highland pipe scale, hence chromatic enough to allow playing within military brass bands. With this fairly exotic musical background (along with church organ playing) and a science degree, Wilbert arrived in Newry in the early 60s for his first job in teaching:

> There wasn't much music in the school – it was non-existent. So I took the bull by the horns and suggested we do a Gilbert & Sullivan opera [*The Pirates Of Penzance*]! I put a lot of wee notices around Newry: 'If anyone would like to help out …' and we got a very good orchestra. People really helped out. One of them was a chap called Eddie Ruddy who played a Boehm flute.
>
> Eddie had said to me they had a wee traditional music group 'and we meet at a back room in the cathedral'. The piano player was sick and could I vamp? I didn't know what he was talking about but I decided to go anyway, and found the vamping was quite straightforward.
>
> Then he said, 'Do you play anything else?'
>
> 'My main instrument is the pipe organ, and I play the Highland pipes'.
>
> And he said, which really opened my mind, 'Do you realise they used to play a bagpipe they called the 'Irish organ'?'
>
> I said, 'Did they? And do you know anybody who plays it?'
>
> 'Well, I'm not sure.'
>
> 'Could you find out if you could get me an Irish organ?'
>
> 'Well, I'll get the word out and see what happens.'
>
> So about a month later he knocked at the flat door and came in and says, 'I've good news for you, Wilbert. I know where there's an Irish organ.' And you can imagine these are all boys connected with Roman Catholics in Newry. 'You've to go to the Orange Hall on Saturday night. They have a wee céilí and there's a chap there, his name's Harold Stewart, and his father played the Irish organ. As far as we know the son still has the pipes.'
>
> So I went up on the Saturday night to meet Harold. Yes, his father's pipes were in the attic and, yes, if I would like to come up I could see them. So I went up the following week to Harold's house in Tandragee and when I went in the living room he had this onion bag, a red net bag, and in it were these bits of fusty leather and bits and pieces. And I could see there were obviously two sets in there. One set was made by Frank McFadden and his father Peter. 'The other set,' he said, 'I'm not sure who made them.' They were actually made by Williamson of Belfast in the early 20th century – the only known set by Williamson, who was friendly with O'Mealy. He brought

out a letter from an antiquarian in London offering him £150 for these pipes. But it was quite obvious that he really wanted them to be played.

He says, 'Do you play any musical instruments?' And I says, 'Yes, well my main instrument's the pipe organ.' 'Oh,' he says, 'that's strange. Is it meant to be? I'm an organist – in Tandragee Presbyterian Church. I wonder could you help me? I learned by ear and I don't read music too well, and there's a soloist coming next Sunday and she's sent me the music and I can't get it right.' So we went into the front room, he set it down on the piano and I rattled through it, I could see where the problems were. I sat him down and went through it until he had it just right and then he says, 'Are you interested in taking up the pipes?' I said, 'I am indeed.' So you can imagine he sold me the pipes for the right price. And then he told me about Frank McFadden, who his father went to in Belfast.

So then I went to Frank – this was 1963. Frank had bronchitis, but he literally cried when he saw the pipes, cos it was the first set he had worked on with his father. And of course he got them together, he put a new bag on, he made a new set of bellows and got the thing going – and I think he only charged me a fiver. So that's how I got started. I was obviously playing tunes that I had played on the Highland pipes and the Brian Boru pipes – marches mostly, and odd things like hornpipes turned into marches. I could hear Frank playing and was amazed at this staccato playing, like O'Mealy's: Belfast style, very tight fingering.

Wilbert's pals in Newry suggested he ought to 'go and meet a wee man in Ennis called Seán Reid', which he did during the next school holiday. Both men being Northerners with Queen's University backgrounds, 'we'd all sorts of things in common and we became close, close friends from that day on':

> The second time I went down to see Seán, he had it all planned out. He said, 'I'm going to teach you in the evening – then when I go to work the next day, you've to practise all day, and then when I come home after tea I'll check up, and then I'll teach you some more.' So we started with the fingering and then he started to teach me the ornaments, and Seán taught me *all* the stuff I needed to know on the uilleann pipes – and we spent the whole week doing that. Just chanter stuff. But that got me on the right track.
>
> Seán took me up [to Miltown Malbay] to meet Willie Clancy. I had the set going okay, but Willie was left-handed. He took it and turned it round. And when he found out I was a Highland piper, well … You don't

take a tape recorder the first time you meet somebody, but I am so sorry I didn't tape that evening, because he took the mickey out of the Highland pipes so much, it was absolutely brilliant. So I formed then a very close relationship with Willie and went down regularly to stay with him. And that was a real good experience. He was a lovely, lovely man. Willie told me a very interesting thing when I was starting the pipes. He says, 'Wilbert, the Irish music is in the airs and the jigs.' And I've concentrated on the airs and the jigs ever since. When they're rattling away in sessions on these reels, I'm sort of cringing!

So in the 60s I would have been up and down to County Clare and travelling around ... 'piping pilgrimages', that's what I called them. Being a biologist, I worked out that if there was any species that was particularly rare, [it] would probably be in a geographically isolated area! So the far west of Ireland: go there and maybe you'll find out ...

In '64 I was on one of my piping pilgrimages, up the west coast along from Galway. I was in Spiddal in a wee restaurant/pub, and I was sitting playing the pipes when these two fellows arrived and were sitting watching me, listening. And then they asked me where I was from and I asked them who they were. And the wee one said, 'I'm Paddy Moloney.' And the other fellow said, 'I'm Seán Potts.' [Paddy] looked just the same as he does now! He was fascinated to find this fellow from Belfast who was playing the pipes and [wondered] how did I find out about them.

It was a lovely day, so I went down to the beach, which was totally deserted. There was a big rock, I got my bathing togs out and went for a swim. I came out again and the seagulls were around and I thought, 'Ah, I must play you a wee tune ...' After a while I sensed something and turned round, and who was standing five paces back from me with the tears streaming down his face but Harold Stewart from Tandragee. Hadn't heard his father's pipes played for years. He was a commercial traveller, which I didn't know. How could you explain something like that? I never got over that.

In due course Wilbert got to meet venerable figures Tommy Reck, Séamus Ennis and Leo Rowsome as well as one or two younger people, like Pat Mitchell, who were also taking up the instrument. The piping world was so small then that practitioners eventually gravitated toward each other. Wilbert was particularly fascinated during one of his Clare trips to encounter one of Seán Reid's uncharacteristically less-than-successful schemes. It would be a scheme that he himself would see through to completion more than 30 years later:

Ennis was down in Ennis, and it was the bold Seán Reid who had got him to put together a tutor for the pipes. He was working on it in the early 60s. I was a real wee magpie. Seán would be away at work and he'd say, 'You can hunt through whatever you want [in the study]' … and here was this folder with these notes by Ennis, beautifully written. So I copied everything down by hand – just in case it was ever lost! And then [later] I found another version he had done in the NPU archives, and that formed the basis for *The Master's Touch* [published in 1998]. Ken McLeod, the originator of the *Seán Reid Society Journal*, and Robbie Hannan and I started talking about Séamus, and that was when we decided to do something. Ken said he would put some money together to support it. There wasn't really enough in his writing to make a whole book, so I thought, 'How can we extend it a bit?' So that's why I did the introduction, the biographical stuff, got a few photographs, and then wrote a bit about the tutor.

With seemingly no other pipers around,* during the 60s in Belfast Wilbert was learning most regularly from Frank McFadden – an exponent of the old 'Belfast style'. In 1964 or '65, Wilbert found himself entered, by a pal in Newry, into an Oireachtas piping contest in Dublin:

We had to do an air, a jig and a reel, I think. … I was on last. Anyway, these other three [entrants], I was listening to them and they were all Rowsome pupils and they were playing with this very open style, like chamber music. I was sitting there thinking, 'I don't play the pipes like this!' Eventually I come up and I played and it was this sort of tight style. It was really funny. I still have the cheque somewhere. I think I won because it was so different!

Wilbert, a distinctive grinning figure in bohemian beard amid the sea of dark suits and conservative haircuts, was one of the 47 pipers assembled at Bettystown in 1968 at the gathering which led to the founding of NPU:

Seán Reid and Séamus Ennis spoke so eloquently when it was set up. But they came to the conclusion that there would be three clear objectives: 1) promoting the playing of the union or uilleann pipes; 2) collecting and preserving the music of these pipes; and 3) promoting the manufacturing

---

* In the early 60s, Wilbert met flautist and future piper Brian Vallely from Armagh: 'When I started playing the pipes, I don't know how Brian found out, but he appeared in Newry at my flat. He played the flute. I sat and played for him most of the evening …'

and servicing of these pipes. I went along to every annual *tionól* and it was great to meet all these other pipers from all over the place …

In 1976, Armagh Pipers' Club had published a piping tutor, *Learn To Play The Uilleann Pipes* – the first since Leo Rowsome's in 1936. Publishing a tutor was one thing; publishing a manual for the instrument's construction was quite another. There were few left alive by this point who knew how such a thing could be done. Frank McFadden died in 1976. If there were ever to be a serious piping revival, it would not take long for the world's stock of McFadden, Rowsome, Kennedy, Crowley, O'Mealy, Egan and Kenna sets to become exhausted. Breandán Breathnach decided the solution lay in Northern Presbyterianism:

Wilbert: I'm a naturally curious individual, and a lot of pipes [at the NPU *tionóls*] were set out on benches for people to look at, and I started measuring them, looking at the differences, and realised very early on that the bores on things like the chanter were more important than anything on the outside. In 1977, at the *tionól*, Breandán approached me. He says, 'Wilbert, could I have a word with you?' I knew it was something very serious coming up.

'What do you want, Breandán?'

'Well,' he says, 'it's the 10th anniversary next year. Up until now we have dealt with the first two objectives of Na Píobairí Uilleann but we have completely ignored the third one. Now, Wilbert, I have watched you over the last few *tionóls* and you're doing a lot of measuring and so on. I've a wee job for you. I want you to write a book on the construction and maintenance of the pipes, to be published for next year's *tionól*.'

'You must be joking, Breandán!'

'No.'

'Why are you asking me?'

'Well, there's not much time left to get this together. I know if you agree to do it that, as a Presbyterian from the North, it will be done.'

So he threw the gauntlet down and I couldn't resist. … The pipe makers were dying off. The information was all going to be lost and that was, I suppose, my motivation in putting something together. I had to start and make them. I'd never done any lathe work before. I just learnt everything from scratch. What else could you do?

The Irish Bagpipes: Their Construction And Maintenance was first published in 1978. It has been republished by Wilbert several times since, his autobiographical illustrations ensuring the book's iconic status.

Wilbert: When I went to Blackstaff [Press, Belfast] first, they had only published poetry. I went to them with the book, and they were surprised I had completed it. They asked how many I thought should be printed and I said, 'Maybe 300' – and they were very impressed by my realistic approach! To date, over 5,000 have been sold. I think people like the cartoons – there aren't that many people who make pipes! One of the best letters I got, which made it worth my while, was a letter from a guy in England who had been badly injured in a car crash and was paralysed from the waist down and he was going to attempt suicide. And he happened to come across my book in a library and he thought, 'Oh, I could sit at a wee lathe and make things ...' And that's what he did. To me, it was worthwhile writing the book for that.

It's a very basic book, but I never decided to change it. It was the first of its kind. I won an Irish book design award for it, because of the cartoons, I think. And the only reason there were cartoons [was because] I wrecked my back and I was in bed for a fortnight and I'd finished the book and I was thinking, 'There's no humour in it ... I can't have something without a bit of craic in it.' So I drew those cartoons lying on my back in bed.

Only in recent years has Wilbert turned his hand to commercial recording, releasing CDs with two distinct performing units: Ceol na gCapall, a duo with Barbara Gray, whose compositions feature on the album *Breath Of Fresh Air* (1997); and Ailsa, with Barbara Gray and Michael Sayers, who have released *Misty Burn* (2003) and *Sam M'Guffin's Kitchen* (2004), setting to music the words of County Antrim vernacular poets.

Wilbert served on the NPU board for many years and has often contributed wonderful material to *An Píobaire* and *The Seán Reid Society Journal*. He remains a happy advocate of the uilleann piping world and its values: 'When I went to Dublin and NPU, the way I was accepted and brought into the fold – I couldn't have asked for better. I found that the Presbyterian minister in Ballyclare played an O'Mealy set, the Reverend MacBeth. There were no barriers then, and I've found that with NPU. I must admit I have enjoyed my years in piping.'

Even now, his curious mind is poking around for solutions to modern piping problems:

> You can't get good ivory now, but I have devised a machine to make artificial ivory that has the grain in it, to make it exactly the same way as the elephant makes its tusks. So I'm working on that at the minute. It might also help to save the elephant.

Belfast In The 1960s

Portadown man Robin Morton, who would go on to found Scots/Irish traditional group The Boys Of The Lough˙ and later Temple Records, was at Queen's University Belfast on two occasions in the 60s, with a year at London's LSE (and immersion in that city's folk revival scene) in between.

> **Robin**: The McPeakes – that was the first uilleann piping I saw, and it made the hairs stand on the back of my head. Phil Coulter got them up to the Glee Club at Queen's, in '63/'64. It was 'me da', middle Francie, young Francie and Kathleen – three pipers and a harp player – and it was amazing.

In Robin's memory, 60s Belfast was a rich tapestry of overlapping scenes: 'an exciting time'. Returning from London in 1964, fired by Ewan MacColl's influence, Robin started both a folk club at Queen's and the Ulster Folk Music Society, which brought over performers including MacColl, Bob Davenport and The Spinners for concerts at a small hall in the city centre. Robin was keen to find traditional singers and record them on reel-to-reel:

> **Robin**: At that time it felt like we were saving Irish traditional music, but I began to realise, as we met more and more musicians, that we weren't saving it – it was there, it was just hidden.
>
> What was happening in England was a song revival – and it was a *revival*. We were thinking it was a revival in Ireland in the early 60s, but really it was a rediscovery. We had a very living tradition – and we started to discover it. 'Go and collect Ulster songs and sing in your own accent!' Ewan would say. One of the first things I did when I got back was get these people together round a tape recorder: [flautist] Cathal O'Connell, [fiddler] Tommy Gunn, [piper] Seán McAloon and [hammered dulcimer player] John Rea. Topic were doing records of songs, not music, at this point, but I sent this tape to Bill Leader, hoping to interest them in an album – but they weren't interested. In fact, they lost the bloody tape as well.

˙ A proto version of The Boys Of The Lough (minus the name), featuring Robin Morton, Tommy Gunn and Cathal McConnell, existed between 1965 and 1968, touring England a few times under Ewan MacColl's patronage. The band proper started in 1972, in Edinburgh, with Robin Morton, Cathal McConnell, Aly Bain and Mike Whellans. Remarkably, Tommy Gunn had a son called Bren Gunn. Wilbert Garvin recalls this causing some problems once when the pair's car was pulled over at an army checkpoint.

Two other Belfast folk clubs are recalled: one near department store Robinson & Cleaver in the early 60s and another – the Pike Folk Club – off Grosvenor Road, later in the decade; while music and song were regularly to be heard at Pat's Bar near the docks. Sessions would also happen at Tommy Gunn's house on Botanic Avenue, involving the likes of Seán McGuire – a fiddle virtuoso and piper who had toured America and performed on *The Ed Sullivan Show* in the 50s:

> **Robin**: Seán was playing in London a lot, because he was a superstar – playing in the Irish clubs, making a *lot* of money. Nobody would pay him money in Ireland – in the North, anyway. Tommy Gunn ran these sessions at his house, and Seán McGuire would come, but Tommy didn't play like Seán – so he wasn't a threat, as it were.

One character often at these sessions was local CCÉ representative Brian O'Donnell, who was involved in a relative wealth of traditional music on the local airwaves (although this rarely included piping – that being said, Seán McAloon was filmed at least once by UTV) in the 60s:

> **Robin**: Everybody knew Brian O'Donnell. He was an important man, though he liked a drink. I saw him at one of the Fleadhs in Clones, getting up in the morning and pouring brandy on his cornflakes! There was a producer at UTV who put out programmes of traditional music, and Brian was employed by him as an advisor. They used to spend their time at 'Studio 3', which was the pub round the corner. If you rang up UTV, they might say, 'I think they're in Studio 3 …' If you were in the know, you'd know where to find them.
>
> Maurice Leech was a local BBC producer doing interesting stuff. The BBC at that time seemed to bring in people like Leech, Sam Hanna Brown, later Paul Muldoon – almost like a way of subsidising the arts. These people were writers who turned out a few dozen programmes a year. They weren't under great pressure. Maurice Leech did a series of radio programmes from Donegal, Fermanagh, Antrim, where he would gather round local musicians and singers plus one or two 'stars'. It was called *Come Listen Here A While*. So that involved music as well as song.
>
> I came back from London with the idea of doing a half-hour 'Radio Ballad' [like those created by Ewan MacColl for national radio] about unemployment in Belfast, which was broadcast locally. Cathal McConnell and Seán Quinn on accordion were involved. I'm still very proud of it. And Maurice Leech produced that.

Via the BBC's own Radio Enterprises label, David Hammond – another producer/auteur who had once been Van Morrison's school teacher – brought out an LP, *Ulster's Flowery Vale*, in 1969. It was a marriage of music and song featuring himself singing alongside Tommy Gunn, Cathal McConnell, Seán McGuire, Seán McAloon and Dubliners banjoist Barney McKenna.

Fermanagh-born piper McAloon (1923–98) lived at 52 St James Road and became a magnet for young pipers throughout the 70s and into the 90s, an era during which he was rarely visible as a performer. He was more visible in the 60s, when he was the most prominent piper in Belfast:

> **Robin**: Seán was a nice man – eccentric, quiet, rather reserved; quite a sensitive man. You'd hardly get any talk out of him, but you'd get great music. … He'd gone to America to work, lived in the Bronx in New York when all the best Irish music was there, but he never went out of his flat! From what I understand, he never played a note while he was there. He was that sensitive, and quite scared in some ways. It was the same when the Troubles started and Seán didn't go out that often.

Cecil Colville, an admirer of R.L. O'Mealy who met McAloon often as a young man interested in piping, gave this recollection to Wilbert Garvin – which, while not date-specific, gives a compelling impression of a trio of somewhat irascible Belfast pipers, all of whom knew each other, in the blurry years before the 70s: pipe maker Frank McFadden, Seán McGuire (1927–2005) and Seán McAloon.

> **Cecil Colville**: Seán McGuire lived nearly next door to Frank. If you went in and got Frank in a bad mood, you knew that McGuire had been in. He said to me, 'I made that so-and-so a set of pipes – a lovely set of pipes – going great – didn't please him. He had to be into them, hoking at them.' Then McGuire says to me, 'Them's not going.' I says, 'What have you done to them? They were perfect when they left here.' He said, 'I started to adjust the reed, and then it cracked. I'm just after throwing them out.' Jack O'Rourke [one of O'Mealy's pupils] used to go down to Seán McAloon's. Jack had a lot of bits and pieces of pipes … from O'Mealy when he died, and he had had them for years. McAloon, he moaned and moaned until he got them off Jack. He had a set of regulators – they were beautiful – a tenor, a baritone and a normal bass. No matter what you gave McAloon, it would need to have been better. I used to call in with Jack after early Mass and he says, 'I haven't long to stop because I'm going up to see McFadden' – there

were a few bits he wanted McFadden to make for him on the lathe. I was up with McFadden this day and McFadden says to me, 'What time is it?' 'It's five minutes to two.' 'McAloon will be coming shortly with his bits and pieces. He is a terrible man. He brings an armful of bits and pieces. Could you do this and could you do that. He even tells you how to do it. Sure, when he's telling me how to do it, could he not do it himself?'[431]

During 1968 or '69, Robin – with Wilbert Garvin as intermediary – brought Willie Clancy to Queen's University for a concert. Seán McAloon was in the audience:

> **Robin**: I did something unforgiveable, in a way, but I was thinking, *'This is wonderful – we've got these two great pipers here …'* I said, 'Here we've Willie Clancy, a legend in his own lifetime from County Clare, and here we've got Seán McAloon, this great piper from Roslea living in Belfast – Seán, maybe you'll play a set and we can compare Willie to [a] great Northern piper?' What a stupid thing to do! And McAloon put his head down and played like I'd never heard him playing. This was *Gunfight At The OK Corral*. McAloon wasn't putting Willie Clancy in his place – he wasn't that kind of man – but he was laying it down. You make things up after 40-odd years, but I'm sure Willie came up to me after and said, 'Christ, McAloon was in great shape!' It was amazing.

In 1970 Robin recorded McAloon in pipes/fiddle and hammered dulcimer duet with Glenarm man John Rea, at a Dublin studio, for *Drops Of Brandy*, an LP released on Mercia Records in Dublin and reissued in 1976 by Topic. Robin explained Seán's discovery of the pipes as a young man in his cover notes:

> He saw a piper called Phil Martin playing at a Feis in Roslea – he had heard him many times on radio – and resolved to go and see him about getting a set of pipes. Martin, who lived at Ballagh in Co. Fermanagh, gave him the address of Crowley the Cork pipe-maker and musician. Seán sent for his practice set by post; they cost him £7.50.
>
> He battled away at them and about a year later he was ready to fit the drones. When he had done this he went to see Phil Martin again in the hope of getting some further hints. Unfortunately he found him on his death bed.[432]

Robin went on to recount that Seán exchanged the Crowley pipes for a Rowsome set, from Leo himself, after a couple of years. He quotes Seán as declaring Leo 'the greatest piper of them all'.

> **Helena Rowsome**: My father was very fond of Seán McAloon – I wrote a piece for *An Píobaire* after his death. Seán was in regular contact with my father, asking him for the notation of tunes he would have heard him playing on radio and at concerts. It was no trouble for Dad to write a tune and pop it in the post. In a letter, Seán complimented him on his playing of 'The Salamanca' and 'The First House In Connaught', commenting 'I think it's the greatest piping that has ever been recorded.'

Belfast In The 1970s

> **Breandán Breathnach (1978)**: William Carleton, the Ulster novelist and antiquarian, writing on these pipes 150 years ago, declared that they were most popular in the primitive provinces of Munster and Connacht; that they were less common in Leinster and could be described as rare in Ulster. Times have changed. There are now over 30 exponents in the province and schools of piping at Armagh and Belfast add yearly to their number.[433]

Seven years later, Robbie Hannan wrote to *An Píobaire* to declare: 'Piping is alive and well in Belfast presently. There are probably 12 pipers, young and old, spread throughout the city.'[434]

In relative terms, especially given that barely 50 pipers could be gathered at Bettystown in 1968, these figures sound impressive. Piping was certainly being clawed back from the brink of extinction during the 70s, not least through the efforts of the NPU and Brian Valley's Armagh Pipers' Club – but underneath the bullish exterior, piping was still not quite out of the woods during the 70s and 80s.

Belfast in the 1970s was grim. When John McSherry was learning the pipes in Belfast in the early 80s, it was a pretty odd thing to be doing. There were not, it seemed to him, many others doing so; plus, most of the musicians he met in pub sessions were roughly a generation older, regardless of what instrument they played. The pub session, as the entity we know today, was itself only a child of the 70s. Anecdotally, urban centres like Belfast seem to have led the way into this now-standard model of traditional music gatherings. Éamonn Curran, now a pipe maker and tutor at Armagh Pipers' Club, was living in rural Monaghan in the 60s:

> **Éamonn**: The social fabric wasn't the same then as now. A lot of what took

place would be in parish halls, places like that. If there was something on in the local hall, people might go out, have a few drinks and then go round to the hall and finish up there for the night. It wasn't so much that it was more formalised [than a pub session], but it was in a more social setting – tea and sandwiches would have been the norm and soft drinks for children, more family-oriented.

So what had been happening in piping and traditional music in general in Belfast during the 70s, in the period just before John McSherry took up the instrument? John (b. 1970) and myself brought together two of his old friends, Marcas Ó Murchú (b. 1961) and Neil Martin (b. 1962), for an evening of reminiscence, to see what could be collectively recalled about this apparent 'dark age' in the city's musical heritage. As with all 'dark ages', it is remarkable how much can be retrieved – although the recollections below (with others from Robin Morton and Barry Kerr added in) are of course impressionistic of those individuals' experience at the time and not a comprehensive record.

There is a kind of standard narrative that paints 1970s Belfast as a place entirely avoided by touring musical artists because of 'The Troubles'. One of the last concerts before darkness descended was Led Zeppelin at the Ulster Hall on March 5 1971, famously the first concert at which they played 'Stairway To Heaven'. And then it all went to hell. Or, at least, that's the standard narrative. The truth is more nuanced. Several international rock and folk artists continued to give concerts in Belfast during the decade (Rory Gallagher, Horslips, Ralph McTell), and from 1977, under Geoff Harden's inspirational leadership, the Sunflower Folk Club was regularly hosting top-division English and Scottish folk artists. Tony McAuley, at BBC NI, brought in several major names in pro Irish traditional music for TV concerts, including Planxty in 1974 and The Bothy Band in 1977. There were publicly accessible trad concerts, too:

Marcas Ó Murchú: I remember seeing a poster at the Athletic Stores in [1972]: 'The Boys Of The Lough and support group Na Bucculí', and that was Dermy Diamond and his mates, and I remember thinking, 'Wow, I know those people' – a poster on a bombed-out Athletic Stores on Queen Street!

Robin Morton: It wasn't anything to do with politics; we just came over to play music. We were getting gigs at the drop of a hat, like, 'Will you come and play the Olympia in Paris?' at three weeks' notice. It wasn't like now! I was a tutor at Edinburgh University, had my students set up: if I don't make my next tutorial, you'll know we have a gig. ... That time I came back and they said, 'Sorry, Robin, one of the staff came round ... we had to tell them you were in Belfast.' It was that gig [that Marcas saw]. I went to tell the Prof and he said, 'Oh, thank God you're back – we thought you'd been shot!' He didn't know I was getting pissed and playing music. But we were getting offered so many gigs that I said to Cathal [McConnell], 'We're going to have to stop this or else we go pro ...' And so we were the first professional Irish music band – The Chieftains weren't professional at that point.* We went straight to the States that summer, played Philadelphia Folk Festival, met a guy who became our agent and the rest is history, really. We filled the Usher Hall twice: 3,500 people. It was amazing, actually, to be a part of it.

Marcas: I had two sisters who sang in Irish, and in May '72 they were performing with The Chieftains in Clonard Hall. I remember the promoter, Jim Aiken, saying it was difficult to persuade anybody to come. But, to be fair, I [still] remember The Chieftains in the Grosvenor Hall, at Clonard Hall, at the Lyric Theatre and at the McMordie Hall in Queens University in the early 70s. There was Na Filí who would come up, they played in Cluain Árd and they were incredible – Neil's uncle, Tomás Ó Canainn [on pipes], was an inspiration to a lot of people. Liam O'Flynn and Paddy Glackin played in the late 70s in St Joseph's Training College. I remember De Danann at the Ulster Museum, and the McPeakes coming back in 1977.

Mícheál Ó Domhnaill was a friend of our family for years, and I remember going with a group of musicians from our school to see The Bothy Band and being totally inspired [Paddy] Keenan nearly bringing the house down. I remember him playing 'Fraher's Jig' and 'The Harvest Home' and 'The Bucks Of Oranmore', which was unbelievable.

Neil Martin: I remember great Bothy Band concerts in the Ulster Hall in Belfast. I remember Keenan doing a gig in 1973, before The Bothy Band, up in the Ulster Museum: [with] Tony MacMahon and Seán Corcoran, an Arts Council funded thing, just the three solo performers. And I remember

---

* The Chieftains' eponymous first LP was released, on Claddagh, in 1964; *Chieftains 2* in 1969, after which they become a regular recording and touring group, though semi-professional. Their first BBC session was on *Country Meets Folk* in August 1970, followed by a session for John Peel (the first of five between 1970 and 1975) in September. *Chieftains 5* in 1974 was their first release, of several, on British label Island, at which point they become fully professional.

the utter magic of Keenan's piping. I'd only been playing pipes a short time myself then.

Marcas: Nowadays in Belfast on a Saturday night, you could have the Cultúrlann with a gig, An Droichead with a gig, the Dirty Onion with a gig, the Sunflower Club with a gig, three or four sessions going on. Whereas in those days, if Planxty were coming, that was it, it was like the Messiah coming up the road! That's why they were packed out. Always boys with long hair, like myself, at those kind of shows, whereas The Chieftains was more of a family audience.

*

Marcas Ó Murchú was born in 1961 and raised in West Belfast, attending St Mary's Grammar School, the University of Ulster, St Mary's University College and Madrid University, all places where he met and shared tunes with musicians. Now a languages teacher, Marcas is a master of the wooden flute, a life-long enthusiast for traditional music and the Irish language, and widely admired as a spare-time Irish music broadcaster (for the BBC and RTÉ). He is a senior tutor at the annual Willie Clancy Summer School in Clare, and has also taught at the Frankie Kennedy Winter School in Donegal and many others in Ireland and elsewhere. His knowledge of traditional music, like the sharpness of his memory, is exceptional.

Marcas' father, who had the distinction of winning an All-Ireland title in Irish singing despite being directed into the wrong Oireachtas competition (one for *native* Irish speakers) in Dublin in 1961, was chairperson of an Irish-language cultural centre in Belfast, the Cluain Árd, on Hawthorn Street, operating since 1936. While there may only have been limited grass-roots traditional music activity in Belfast during the 70s and 80s, Marcas was perfectly placed to observe it.

During that period, he made over 1,000 hours of recordings of local musicians and traditional music broadcasts, later kindly donated to the Irish Traditional Music Archive (ITMA), as well as Irish language and cultural interviews, which he donated to the Linenhall Library – but he's always been less concerned with making commercial recordings himself than with the joy of playing. Nevertheless, he has made two albums: *Ó Bhéal Go Béal* (1997) and *Turas Ceoil* (2007). In 2013 he was awarded Music Laureate Ard-Ollamh by CCÉ. But long before that he was a crucial early mentor to John McSherry.

Neil Martin was born in 1962 and raised in North Belfast, attending St Malachy's College. Learning piano from around age seven, whistle from age nine and pipes from age 11 along with the cello, Neil has carved out a career as a composer, arranger and recording artist with skills in both art music and traditional music. He has written for orchestra, and has recorded both as a solo artist and with his own West Ocean String Quartet. He also often performs as an accompanist (on cello and whistle) to his early piping hero Liam O'Flynn. Around 1987 he produced a now-lost album with John McSherry's family group Tamalin.

Neil: I was aware of the pipes through my uncle Tomás Ó Canainn, who played with Na Filí, and my father had records of Séamus Ennis. My parents had a very broad collection – Nioclás Tóibín, The Beatles, Ry Cooder, Beethoven, Brahms, Mozart, Louis Armstrong & The Hot Five   When I went to St Malachy's, in my first year, there was an Irish teacher there, Phil Stewart, and he had a practice set of pipes, which he couldn't make a fist of – and he said to me, 'Do you want the loan of these for a year?' And I was kind of interested. When I got them, I phoned up my uncle Tomás in Cork and said, 'I've got this set of pipes, there's no reed in the chanter. What'll I do?' He sent me over to 'middle Francie' McPeake in Theodore Street and Francie reeded the chanter. And for a lot of years I would have gone for pipe lessons to middle Francie – Francis II.

Marcas: I remember, as a child, Francis I. My daddy used to go round to Jackie Vernon's, who was an international footballer but also a butcher. His place was on the Springfield Road and Francis I, who died St Patrick's Day 1971 – he used to be sitting there in an armchair, and I was always impressed because on the wall of the house was a picture of two pipers: [one was] Francis II, who died 1985 or '86, and it was painted. I remember as a child of five or six, looking up at this thinking, 'Wow.' The painting was lovely, but the fact that it was traditional musicians in a painting – you never saw that.

When Neil and I were at school it was Emerson Lake & Palmer, The Sweet, Roy Wood & Wizzard – there weren't too many tin whistles around St Malachy's or St Mary's! I was the oddball in our school. My father in the 1950s had bought a Ferrograph reel-to-reel, so he had recorded the Seán Ó Riada programmes [*Our Musical Heritage*, 1962] off the radio, the ones that RTÉ lost. I would record Ciarán Mac Mathúna every Sunday morning [on RTÉ], Tommy Sands [on Downtown Radio] when he started as well.

Neil: When I was starting on pipes, you could have counted on one hand, at best, the number of young people playing pipes – mostly in Belfast. Noel

Fitzpatrick [the shoemaker] had a nephew, John Fitzpatrick, who took a hand to them for a while, but there would have been very, very few.

Aside from Seán McAloon and Noel Fitzpatrick, a handful of other pipers from Belfast and the North are recalled from the 1970s and early 80s. From Belfast, there were: Robbie Hannan, another student of McAloon; Francis McPeake IV; his cousin Francis McIlduff, who has often performed and recorded with John McSherry; Des McCabe; Patrick Davey; and one Ailish (whose surname not even Marcas can recall) from O'Neill Street. Elsewhere in the North, there were the veterans Wilbert Garvin in Kells and Brian Vallely in Armagh, along with Wilbert's friends Ken McLeod from Antrim and Robbie Hughes (who also made pipes) from Down. From Derry/Londonderry there was Finbar McLaughlin, who won an All-Ireland title in 1976, and from Antrim, there was Trevor Stewart, who won it a year or so later and who performed in the trio Shannon, Stewart & Baillie.

There was Michael Horgan, from Newcastle, with whom Marcas played in a group in 1977 called Hewlett (practising in a Newcastle Scout hut). There were Fergus Henderson from Ballymena; Tarlach Connolly (a student of Brian Vallely) who attended Coleraine University during Marcas' time there; Feargal French from Lurgan; Billy McCormick from Carrickfergus, famously given a set of Taylor pipes by a passing nun; and Jack Wade, a policeman from Monaghan who took lessons from McAloon.* Marcas also recalls meeting two Finbar McLaughlin pupils at a session in Buncrana: Brian Stafford, a connoisseur of 'the old music, like the Goodman collection'; and Joe McLaughlin, who played a flat set and favoured Donegal tunes, 'which is hard enough on the pipes'.

If this all begins to sound like a horde of pipers, the impression is illusory. As Marcas says, 'Over a period of 15 to 20 years, you'd meet these people once or twice.' The scattered nature of Northern pipers meant that having someone like Seán McAloon on tap in Belfast was a blessing to young pipers:

> **Neil**: He was such an odd, unique individual. I loved his madness, I loved his enthusiasm for pipes, I loved his forthright way. 'Do you like the flute, Neil?' 'I do, I like the flute.' *'Ah fuckin' hate it!'* And two weeks later you'd have the same conversation. A terrific man! I have many happy memories of bottles of whiskey getting walloped of a Saturday afternoon with him.

---

* Online searches reveal a further handful of names of scattered Northern pipers from those times: Sammy Wade and Willie Simpson in North Antrim; Maurice Bradley in Draperstown; John McCarron, Joe McHugh and Brendan Begley from Derry; and Eamon Dillon from Belfast. No doubt there are a few others.

John: One day my dad brought him a bottle of whiskey: no hesitation, straight into it. I put the pipes on and kept on playing, and it must have been within half an hour he was on the floor, crawling around on his hands and knees, grooving to the music. He was such a great character.

Neil: At one stage Seán only had one glass in the house, and I brought him a half bottle of whiskey on a Saturday afternoon. Seán would take a drink, fire it back, no bother, and he'd give me the glass and the bottle. I'd give him the glass back. And then at a certain point he'd get hungry, go out to the kitchen: soda farls and three quarters of an inch of butter. It would kill you!

Barry Kerr: Seán used to make my reeds when I was a kid [in the early 90s]. Seán was a character. I loved him, a great man. There were certain people he wouldn't have let into his house. He was good to me, though. I'd have brought him down a few boxes of cigarettes and a bottle of *poitín* and he'd have made me a few reeds.

Marcas: When I went up to his house he was playing the fiddle. He was one of the closest you'd ever hear to Michael Coleman. He'd draw the bow and you knew there was something special coming.

Neil: He would rarely have played [pipes] in the house. But I remember him playing really nicely at a thing in the mid-1980s down in Denvir's Hotel in Downpatrick. He was dressed up in hat, shirt and tie – playing in public.

Marcas recalls that by the late 70s there were sessions in Belfast based around three distinct sets of musicians. Firstly, at the Rossa Club on Falls Road on Thursday nights, where people would gather around Dermy Diamond: 'You could have had 15 flute players turn up at a session there, including [future Altan flautist] Frankie Kennedy. One night Maurice Lennon [future fiddler with Stockton's Wing] turned up, and the next time I saw him he was participating in the All-Ireland and he won it.' Secondly, there was a session at Charlie Murray's Bar, also on Falls Road, where Marcas got his first flute from maker Sam Murray. The third session was at O'Donnell's on Whiterock Road.

Marcas: But before [all of those] – I wasn't part of it, though my father was – was the Old House in Albert Street. That would have had people like Joe Heaney coming to it, Nioclás Tóibín, the *sean-nós* singer from

Waterford, Caitlín Maude – because they were performing at the Cluain Árd in Hawthorn Street, and my daddy and those involved in the committee would have been taking them out for a drink, and that's where they would have been performing. I heard it said that there was one particular man was listening to Joe Heaney singing and the tears were running down his eyes. So there was music happening.

Marcas later became friendly with the late Kevin McClafferty, who revealed he had played pipes in the early to mid-60s in Belfast at a regular house session on Derryvolgie Avenue. Brian Vallely was a regular at these and recalls others there including James McMahon, box player Tom Maguire, fiddler Fergus McTaggart, Seán McAloon and sometimes John Rea, plus a couple of others on flute.*

Neil: I used to go to a session in Joy Street on a Saturday afternoon at the house of Alastair Herron, the fiddle maker. Trevor Stewart, Deirdre Shannon, Sam Murray, Nigel and Diane Boullier, Jim McKillop and a guy from down south who played pipes a bit   You were hungry [to meet other traditional musicians]. You'd go to sessions at the Cluain Árd and Joy Street, and Sam Murray there would know other people, so it kind of spread out from that.   You gravitated towards Fleadhs, and there was a little Comhaltas meeting that used to happen in a Scout Hall near my parents' [house] around '76. I would go up there on a Monday night and play tunes. The other people would have been well my senior – in their 60s.

Marcas: I remember a conversation I had with Neil, in 1979, just after he had spent some time with the Belfast Youth Orchestra in America. He was thinking of giving up traditional music, because he was totally taken with the orchestra. I encouraged him to keep the pipes going. For me, Neil at that time was one of the inspiring musicians, the other ones being Frankie Kennedy and Mairéad Ní Mhaonaigh [both later of Altan], who would have come around Christmas to the Cluain Árd.

One of my prayers was that Antrim would win the All-Ireland at hurling, which almost happened in '89. But another was that every child in my area would be playing traditional music. As I grew up, there was nobody,

---

* Several evenings of music from this era in Belfast, spanning 1967, were recorded on reels by future Sunflower Folk Club organiser Geoff Harden at the Pike Folk Club, off Grosvenor Road. Among those recorded were visitors Ted Furey and Joe Heaney and locals Seán McAloon (seven excellent solo piping pieces), Seán McGuire and others.

really, in my age group – the closest was Davy Maguire, who lived about half a mile away. [But] I was at Cluain Árd five or six nights a week playing music … And through that I would have met various musicians like Leslie Bingham. When I was 16 Leslie took me to my first Fleadh, down to Ennis, an All-Ireland.

Tuition in Belfast, which created a new generation of traditional musicians, began from the late 70s with the McPeake family operating out of Clonard Monastery. Other tuition circles later formed around Seán McGuire in Andersonstown and, in the 80s, around Marcas Ó Murchú at a school in Fortwilliam.

Marcas: The whole teaching thing with the McPeakes – that was my prayer answered. You'd see kids on a Saturday night passing our door, on O'Neill Street, going up with pipes. I thought I'd never see this. I remember Francie II saying, 'If you've got any spare time on Saturday nights, come along.' And I did – I would teach up there. When I started playing music, the only published learning we had were the Armagh Pipers' [Club] books, which came out for about a shilling, *Learn To Play The Tin Whistle* and *Whistle And Sing* by Eamonn Jordan from Portadown. I remember them for sale in Matchett's.

Neil: When 'me da' McPeake came up, he had played fife and flute in various bands and you would use the tips of your fingers for such instruments. So when he took up pipes he used the tips, which technically restricts massively what you can do. And indeed I started playing pipes like that. Only after a lot of work with Liam O'Flynn did I change that.

In 1976, aged 14, Neil won a series of junior piping competitions, including an All-Ireland. The week before the All-Ireland event there was a Scoil Éigse tuition week with Liam O'Flynn:

Neil: That was a really focused week. I would have been playing with the tips of my fingers, and O'Flynn said to me, 'Now, I think you're going to be hampered considerably. I would encourage you to change.' So I spent nine, 10 months – it took a huge amount of effort, having played that way for two or three years. But once I got over it, I could see there were things you could do a million times better. He was kind of my deity, my hero, anyway – which of course gave me a huge buzz, aged 14. I would bump into him after that and talk a little. We started working together from 1986. I was playing cello and keyboards initially, and we'd do stuff on two pipes occasionally.

Traditional music pub sessions in Belfast only began in the mid-70s. Before that, the impression is of house sessions – like those attended by Brian Vallely in the 60s and Neil Martin in the early 70s – and slightly more formalised gatherings, such as the Pike Folk Club and Friday nights at the Cluain Árd, where people would take turns to perform. Politics had no impact when it came to musicians playing music together:

> **Neil**: I remember when we'd be approaching army checkpoints and we'd turn down the music on the car cassette player. I remember I was 15 and assumptions being made by civilian searchers [on the gates around Belfast city centre] saying, 'What's that?' 'Uilleann pipes.' 'I suppose you're going up to play Republican tunes in the West now?' You don't really have the answer at 15.

> **Marcas**: I never heard politics discussed at all [in sessions]. It was a breath of fresh air. You'd go out to play music and people would be saying, 'What goes after this tune here?' Or, 'Do you know this version of 'The Chicago Reel'?' Happy days! You didn't care if the boy was Sammy or Séamus. And it's still the same. Seán McAloon played on the [*Drops Of Brandy*] record with John Rea, and I remember sitting in a session with John Rea and a crowd of boys from Ballymena, a Saturday night in Ballycastle, and come twelve o'clock, the Sabbath, all the instruments [went] back in their cases. And I said, 'Well, fair play to you, boys, I enjoyed the two or three hours I had with you. That's your way …' I played on for another two or three hours with a crowd of boys from Donegal or somewhere. Nobody ever said they didn't want to play with me cos I was from West Belfast. They all thought I had something special, and I thought they had something special. All those people I mentioned earlier on, I don't know what church they went to, what jobs they had, what they earned; but I know they were great musicians.

Sheila Friel

After a fallow period of a hundred years or thereabouts, living on the legend of Turlough McSweeney, Donegal has another piper of profile – and, adding a further layer of rarity, that piper is a woman. Female uilleann pipers have been notable by their absence during much of the instrument's history, and yet there has never been any obvious reason for such a situation. Perhaps the cost and availability of the instrument until recent times was a factor, along with general social norms of yore on the respective roles of women and men.

Francis O'Neill, in *Irish Minstrels And Musicians* (1913), profiled Miss May McCarthy of the Cork Pipers' Club, whose virtuosity surpassed that of her teacher, club founder John Smithwick Wayland. May performed in Britain and won a number of regional *Feiseanna*. As O'Neill noted: 'while neither big nor brawny this versatile Irish colleen can handle with ease a full-size instrument … [and has] even successfully competed with men on the Warpipes.'[435]

May McCarthy was still playing pipes in the late 1960s. O'Neill also found space to give a passing mention to a Mrs J.J. Murphy of Limerick, who won second prize to Frank McPeake's first in the 1912 Oireachtas learners' competition, and to doff his cap more loquaciously at Miss Mollie Morrissey, another Wayland protégée. A 1912 photograph of Dublin Pipers' Club members in his book includes one unidentified female piper. Fifteen years on from the founding of the Cork club, O'Neill could applaud its achievements in piping suffrage:

> The Cork Pipers' Club survived many difficulties since its inception in March, 1898, and blazed the way to success which similar organizations [sic] subsequently followed. In precept and example it was an inspiration, and not only that but convention was disregarded, barriers were broken down, and the musical franchise conferred on the fair sex. The latter have since earned distinction in every branch of study whether vocal, instrumental or terpsichorean, and thus proved the wisdom of the innovation.[436]

After this triumphant breakthrough, and notwithstanding the singular Miss Johnston of Carnlough (see above), little is heard of women pipers until Betty Nevin, a pupil of Leo Rowsome's, who began attending Dublin Pipers' Club in the late 1940s, appearing in a famous group photograph of Leo instructing a class which also included a short-trousered Paddy Moloney. There were surely other women pipers during the subsequent 30 or 40 years, but the only one to have attained much notice was Máire Ní Ghráda, who appeared on a 1978 Claddagh LP, *The Piper's Rock*, featuring various young pipers including Davy Spillane, Mick O'Brien and Gabriel McKeon.

Lately, more female pipers are becoming prominent, in the sense of releasing recordings and pursuing semi-professional performing careers. Along with Louise Mulcahy from Cork, Sheila Friel (b. 1990), from Glasgow with a proud Donegal heritage, is one such. With siblings Clare and Anna, she released *The Friel Sisters* in 2013, and in May 2014 Sheila joined the board of NPU: no small commute from Glasgow to Dublin.

> **Sheila**: I began on the flute and tin whistle in Glasgow. I always listened to the pipes from a young age. I guess my first exposure would have been through the likes of The Bothy Band and Planxty. Mum always listened to them, so we were brought up with that. … Marcas [Ó Murchú] would have been a big influence on us. He used come and stay with us up in Donegal [at] our great granny's house, near Ranafast. … There are four Comhaltas [branches] in Glasgow and we came up through that, till I was about 15, when I got the pipes.

Sheila met a fellow Donegal piper, Ciarán McPhilemy, in Buncrana around 2005, and he recommended a pipe maker. Irish music in Sheila's family comes from her mother's side: her grandmother played the fiddle.

> **Sheila**: My granny told me [that] when she was growing up, [the pipes] wasn't really an instrument for a girl – which only made me want to play it more! There was maybe a bit of a stigma. And they're quite physical instruments – my arms are quite muscly. Maybe some of the old sets were [even more] difficult to play.

Sheila is keenly interested in any link between piping and Donegal, including her peers Ciarán McPhilemy from Lifford and Conor Day, originally from Belfast but living in Donegal. She knows of two pipe makers in the county: Martin Crossan and Ray Sloan, with rumours of a third in Letterkenny. Born in the CD era but collecting vinyl of pipers recorded long before it, she also has a keen interest in piping history – and was amazed to find that a colleague in her profession of dentistry was a relative of the late Séamus Ennis. Through him, she has acquired a signed copy of *The Fox Chase* (1978): 'One of my most treasured possesions!'

> **Sheila**: [When] I started getting tuition in Ireland and getting versions of tunes, you're almost encouraged to look back. Maybe I'm just nosy. And if you're going to a lot of commemorative events, like the Breandán Breathnach Weekend, you feel you should 'know'. The Willie Clancy school, too. I was there last year and met someone who didn't know Willie Clancy played music!
>
> Looking through Leo Rowsome's letters with Helena [Rowsome] I was interested to see there were two sets he sent to Donegal, one of them to a person called Friel. I think I know the family. I've made a phone call to see if I can find these pipes. …
>
> I always keep my flute on the table if I'm at a session in a remote area

of Donegal, where there might be more 'hard core' tunes. Some of those Donegal tunes I can play on pipes, but they can sound harsh and they're not particularly suited to pipes. It can be an assault on people's ears. Some of them suit really nicely, though: some of the waltzes and Highlands. The more I put the flute down, the more I'm discovering some of these tunes really do suit the pipes – maybe tweaking one or two of the notes, though.

Sheila is young enough to look up to John McSherry – albeit, at well over six feet tall, not literally:

Sheila: I remember his bellows broke one year [at the Celtic Connections festival in Glasgow], and I don't think I'd met him at this point, but I got a manic phone call from someone at Celtic Connections. I'd been playing for maybe three years by then. *'Can we get a lend of your pipes?'* … I don't think I've learned any tunes from John, but we've partied a lot!

He hates *tionóls*, he told me, but … I laugh when I hear that. For me, *tionóls* were a lifeline! I would frequently pop into NPU [in Dublin] when I was learning the pipes, because I didn't have anyone to teach me in Scotland and I didn't have anyone to maintain my set here either. So I would pop in with my set falling to bits and get someone in Henrietta Street to help me!

I'm a dentist, so when I play music I don't have to worry if it's marketable – if people like it, they like it. I've something else on the go, anyway. [But] I'm hoping to go professional at some point.

*

This doesn't seem like a region bereft of uilleann piping, does it? A bit threadbare at times, perhaps, but hardly any more so than anywhere else in Ireland during the ebb and flow of the instrument's fortunes. At this point, 15 years into the 21st century, it seems fair to say that through the efforts of a handful of individuals, most especially Brian Vallely – who defies the uilleann piping stereotype of the 'awkward loner' in being a supremely committed, sociable and effective organisation man – Ulster has become central to the future well-being of uilleann piping. Even John McSherry is getting organised:

Brian Vallely: In the 60s, piping was 'backs to the wall' – it wasn't even accepted in traditional music circles. Quite often, a piper – when he went into a session, the other musicians would stop playing. The situation now is that the pipes are a worldwide, iconic instrument. It's just mushroomed out. There are probably far more non-Irish people playing pipes and making pipes now than Irish people.

Sheila Friel: Being involved on the board of NPU, there's an incredible amount of work that goes into furthering the instrument. But now it's going from strength to strength. They're more accepted within the session scene and within Irish traditional music.

John McSherry: There's a lot of great pipers in the North today, like Cillian Vallely, Francis McIlduff, Tiarnán Ó Duinnchinn, Darragh Murphy, Paddy O'Hare, Barry Kerr and a lot more young, up-and-coming players like Aaron O'Hagan and Conor Lamb (both from the band Réalta), Conor Mallon, Jamie Murphy, Chris McMullan, Mark Doherty, Matthew McAstocker, Liam McCullagh – the list goes on. And they're all quite different to the Dublin style of playing. A lot of those players have come through the Armagh Pipers' Club. When you talk about the rise of piping in the North, Brian Vallely has to be given due credit.

I've been running classes in Belfast for about five years, teaching in An Droichead [cultural centre in Belfast]. I'd started a Pipers' Club there, but I was never able to give it the impetus it needed. But now, since I started a piping session in the Sunflower Bar [early in 2014], there seem to be pipers popping up from everywhere. A few times we've had eight or 10 pipers there at the one session. And we're all of the same mind: it's time to do something. It's probably not that different from the likes of Leo Rowsome, Seán Reid and Tommy Reck reviving the Dublin Pipers' Club in the 1930s – the enthusiasm is exactly the same.

So we've started up The Northern Pipers' Society, to run tuition and put on concerts, et cetera. We've constituted it as a not-for-profit organisation: myself, Darragh Murphy, Edel Ní Churraoin, Jamie Murphy and Mark Doherty. We're based in the fantastic new Duncairn arts centre, Antrim Road, and have Belfast cultural guru Ray Giffen to thank for that. We're planning to hold concerts, run reed-making classes, tuition, everything that will be helpful to pipers in the North. It'll be complementary to what Brian [Vallely] has been doing in Armagh.

Barry Kerr: Belfast now is mind-blowing. You've the best pipers in Ireland living here, without a doubt. There always has been a piping tradition in Belfast. John of late has been teaching a lot, which I think is fantastic because he has so much to give. For a long time he would have been away a lot on tour, so less able to give time to teaching, but now some young pipers are coming through from John's 'stable' and they're fantastic players. A lot of people would look to John as one of the masters of the tradition, so I've no doubt he's attracting a lot of Northern pipers because of that.

John McSherry: There has always been a strong pipe and reed making presence in the North with the likes of O'Mealy, the McPeakes, McFadden and McAloon which has continued right up to the present day. Today you have people like Robbie Hughes, Martin Preshaw, Martin Gallen, Martin Crossin and Adrian Jefferies, who have been making their mark, I should give special mention to Paddy O'Hare. As far as reed making is concerned, he's one of the best. He's been making reeds since he was a teen and has been keeping so many pipers in constant supply. He has recently published a manual on the subject entitled *A Guide To Reed Making For The Uilleann Pipes*, for which I was delighted to write a foreword. He's also a great piper. There's also Aaron O'Hagan who learnt his reed making skills from Paddy. He's also making great pipes. This young, up and coming pipe maker will be one to watch out for in the future. It's a very healthy situation at present – very good for the Pipers' Society

There are pipers in Belfast who most definitely wouldn't be picking up their instruments that often if it wasn't for the Society. These things renew people's enthusiasm. It seems that even pipers, despite all the evidence to the contrary, are social animals underneath it all!

We're thinking in cross-community terms as well, thinking about putting on Highland piping classes. There's one fellow in the Society from the Field Marshal Montgomery Pipe Band who's learning the uilleann pipes – aspiring to that second octave – and we're hoping a number of his colleagues in the pipe band world will also show an interest. I think the time is right for this to happen.

There's always been an ecumenical basis to uilleann piping, even in the North, although it tilted towards Catholics during the conflict in the 70s and 80s. But that non-sectarian, open-to-all spirit is coming back now, I believe. When people play music together, their politics and their religion don't matter. It's just never come up in any session I've been involved in, and I hope it never will.

Amen to that.

Chapter 16
Brian Vallely & Armagh Pipers' Club

> **Marcas Ó Murchú**: People like Brian and Eithne Vallely are unsung heroes of our native tradition. While Brian is respected as a wonderful artist, and deservedly so, he is also a giant of northern piping and musicianship in the second half of the 20th century.

One day in 2011, an extraordinary number of uilleann pipers gathered on one stage for one remarkable event, in a small town 40 miles west of Belfast and 80 miles northwest of Dublin.* The occasion was the 45th anniversary of Armagh Pipers' Club. The number of pipers involved, all of them members of the club, was also 45: virtually equivalent to the number of pipers that could be assembled back in 1968, from the whole of Ireland and beyond, for the Bettystown gathering from whence sprang Na Píobairí Uilleann (NPU).

That achievement alone – an isolated, independent club with such a concentration of pipers, thriving within a generation of the art's near-extinction – is monumental. More remarkably still, the club was founded and has been sustained through the musical passion, organisational skill and sheer bloody-mindedness of one man, Brian Vallely, and his wife Eithne. Brian has not so much beaten the system as simply tried it, rejected it and created one that is better. An artist by profession, Brian has never taken a penny for what is now, at the time of writing, nearly 50 years of unrelenting effort in building the club up from one student and one tutor (himself) in 1966 to currently around 270 students (not only in piping but in many of the instruments of Irish traditional music) and over 30 tutors, each one paid nearly double the teaching rate available through other institutions.

If the question 'Who is the most important uilleann piper of the past 50 years?' were asked, the natural instinct would be to ponder the handful of internationally known professional pipers of that period – Liam O'Flynn, Paddy Keenan and the rest. But among the cognoscenti of piping, no one would laugh, and many would nod sagely, if the answer advanced were 'Brian Vallely'. The man himself would balk at the notion and change the subject very quickly, but he is the architect, builder and

---

* Armagh is technically a city, but you'd never guess.

caretaker of an engine room in uilleann piping that has chugged away, the outside world often oblivious to its activities, for half a century and produced more pipers – and pipers of skill and solid grounding – than surely any other institution worldwide. Indeed, one might even say that Armagh Pipers' Club has produced more pipers and pipe teachers than almost any other *country* worldwide, with the probable exception of America.

In the context of piping, Brian Vallely's achievement in Armagh is akin to the work of a handful of Irish monasteries in keeping alive and well the flames of literacy and learning for the whole of Europe during the 'Dark Ages'. Eventually, the efforts involved bear fruit and the learning spreads outward. The only difference, perhaps, is that 6th century purveyors of illuminated manuscripts didn't have to deal with cold-callers selling website services, insurance companies arguing about premises refurbishments and half the perambulating population of a small city wanting to stop and say hello every time you walk down the street. Even the quietest of men, after 50 years in a cultural powerhouse, starts to get noticed.

*

In a way, Brian Vallely (b. 1941) owes his Irish traditional music odyssey to Dave Brubeck, the jazz man who took five. It happened in Glasgow in 1961. But even then, he had some knowledge of the Irish tradition and of the pipes, rare as they were at that point in time:

> **Brian**: You could carry the whole of recorded Irish traditional music on LP and EP in one hand in those days. It started in the late 50s with Seán Ó Riada, then [Leo] Rowsome, on Claddagh, and in London I discovered Willie Clancy's recordings with Michael Gorman and Margaret Barry. I did drawings of old Francie McPeake in 1959 when I was at Belfast College Of Art [1959–61]. My father had organised the Feis Mór Ard Mhacha in Armagh and Ted Hart played the pipes at that – that was in the 30s and 40s, after which the Feis faded. So I knew *of* the pipes.
>
> But when I was listening to Seán Ó Riada, I wasn't sure what I was listening to. I played the records in my studio when I was a student and then when I was working as a painter in Edinburgh. I [had] started playing flute when I was a student in Scotland. I was friendly with a group of Italian guys at art college and they were all jazz players, and they took me to a Dave Brubeck concert in Glasgow, which blew my mind completely. I told them I'd always regretted not playing music and they said, 'But why? You like Irish music, why don't you play it?'

> 'I don't have an instrument; I don't know how to.'
> 'Well, what instrument do you like?'
> 'I really like the flute …'

Back in Ireland by the mid-60s, having progressed on the flute, Brian acquired a practice set of pipes from Matt Kiernan in Dublin:

> **Brian**: I hadn't met any other pipers when I got my first practice set, though I could already play stuff on the flute and the whistle. The chanter looked quite similar, so I blew it up and tried a couple of tunes. It sounded roughly in tune, but bit by bit as I found out more, from Matt Kiernan and Frank McFadden [in Belfast] – though none of those guys were teachers … But then I discovered Willie Clancy. Myself and my brother cycled down – three days on bad roads – to Clare. Willie didn't formally teach any more than Séamus Ennis, who [later] came up to Armagh for concerts and stayed in our house for a week or two weeks. Séamus played; you just watched him. [But] one day [Willie] took a chanter and played about 10 airs slowly onto a tape for me in his house. So by trial and error I learned, and when you learn that way, you get an idea of how it should be taught.

Brian admits to having always had an inherent 'organisational drive'. Comhaltas Ceoltóirí Éireann (CCÉ) had been founded in 1951, and its regional and national Fleadhs had become significant events by the early 60s, attracting casual revellers as well as musicians. Totally focused on the music, Brian became enthusiastically involved in the local branch of CCÉ, moving up to the County Board, then the Ulster Council and thence as a delegate to the National Board. As he reflects today, 'I took it that the object was the development of the uilleann pipes and the harp.' He was to be disillusioned.

Brian found not only that CCÉ in the North seemed to have an institutional view of uilleann pipes as almost an 'alien instrument' but also that some, at national level, seemed to be caught up in financial cronyism and self-interest:

> **Brian**: I started the Pipers' Club [in 1966], totally disillusioned by Comhaltas, even though I'd been delighted when it started. But it was already developing at national level into a sort of centralist, scratch-my-back, money-making organisation. It didn't appear to put music first – despite the incredible dedication and hard work to be found in Comhaltas branches throughout the country. That's why I've always said I would never do it for money.

It's quite bizarre, looking back on it now. I really don't know what their thinking was [in the Northern Comhaltas]. If you imagine, all these pipers up here who were Presbyterians and Freemasons and Orangemen, the only Catholic pipers that were around would have been old Francie McPeake and [Seán] McAloon – who I met at the sessions at Derryvolgie Avenue [in Belfast] in the 60s.

When we started [the Pipers' Club], I was the only piper. The plan then was [that] to be a member of the club you had to learn the uilleann pipes. It was difficult to get them – I didn't know where to look. Immediately after we got the first set from Matt Kiernan, we discovered Frank McFadden. Frank deliberately kept a low profile. He spent his entire life in terror of the Inland Revenue – he'd nearly be looking up and down the street before taking two and six for a reed! But he made loads of sets for us. Everybody came to him – Ennis, Paddy Moloney – because he was renowned as a reed maker.

Frank used to say to me, 'So-and-so was just in with me, he's a Grand Master in the Orange Lodge … and somebody else was in, he's a minister in Larne …' He'd say to me, 'I always like them to come in at different times to the likes of you'! He'd say these people were very quiet about their piping, but it turns out there was this whole group of people piping for a hundred years or more, but it didn't fit into the simplistic equation of music with nationalism. But they regarded themselves 100 per cent as Irish musicians. I'd heard of Billy Hope. And then there was Robbie Hughes, who started making pipes [in the 70s], whose father was a minister in the Church Of Ireland down in Fermanagh. …

The Arts Council once said to me, 'You'd need to get more Protestants involved.' And I said to them, 'Look, the problem is that I don't know any *Catholic* pipers. All my piping friends are Protestants. There *are* no Catholic pipers!'

When NPU began in 1968, Brian admits he was 'wild-eyed for it', but after three years as its secretary, he felt that the organisation's priorities weren't quite in tune with his own. Specifically, he believed that more should be done about tuition if the instrument were ever going to prosper; also, he was uncomfortable with a prescriptive aspect as to how the instrument should be taught and played – it seemed as though the people involved were 'deifying' Séamus Ennis and his style of piping without understanding that the man was a total one-off.

Brian and his new wife Eithne focused instead on Armagh Pipers' Club as a long-term labour of love. Brian, rare in being a skilled organisational operator who isn't also a self-aggrandiser or control freak (of the sort that treats an organisation as a vainglorious platform or personal income stream) – is also the even rarer sort of person who can quietly, over the course of decades, get on with creating something for the greater good against all manner of logistical, cultural and financial obstacles.

> **Brian**: I had met Eithne, who was teaching in Monaghan, so I was over in Monaghan a lot in '68. Her father had been very friendly with Ned Curran, and he asked me would I teach his son Éamonn. So Éamonn was my first piping pupil.*

With perfect symmetry, Éamonn Curran went on himself to become a pipe maker and one of the tutors at the club. But back then, seeing the pipes in Brian's hands in mid-60s Monaghan was a revelation:

> **Éamonn**: He was immensely committed to the pipes – that came through everything he did. And it could be argued that piping then was on the verge of extinction. … [Before I met Brian], I would only have seen the pipes on RTÉ – that would have been the closest I had come to them: on a children's programme that Séamus Ennis had.† … Looking back, [the situation] wasn't great. Quite often musicians didn't want to see pipers coming! There would have been traditional musicians and if you'd brought out a set of pipes they'd have asked you what they were. The piping world was on a knife edge at that stage.
>
> It was a great honour to be involved with the club from its inception. In the early days it was very much hand-to-mouth. We were in very poor venues: the venues would change from month to month as places became available.

Finding adequate premises was not the only headache:

> **Éamonn**: It was also a time when it was very difficult to travel in the North due to the Troubles, so there was very little coming and going of music – not as much as there is now. Here in the border areas, travelling late at night generally wasn't a great idea. I'm sure it was the same in Belfast, from a different angle.

---

* Éamonn now teaches at Armagh Pipers' Club in addition to making pipes for club members. His father Ned was a well known traditional flute and fiddle player.
† Probably *Séamus Ennis Sa Cathoir* ('Séamus Ennis In The Chair') in 1963.

Around 1969, having moved to Armagh and married Brian, Eithne Valleley became involved in the club. Primarily a fiddler, she had attended college in Dublin with Helena Rowsome and had given the pipes a go herself while there, being taught for a while by Dan Dowd. As she puts it now: 'I thought I could just pick it up. But I was no good at it!' Nevertheless, her fiddling skills would help Brian's pet project toward diversifying, which has been part of its pragmatic formula for success:

> **Eithne**: The club was a hobby at the start, a bit of fun. But Brian had an evangelistic attitude with pipes – they were dying out, and the only way to avoid that was to get people to play them and people to make them. … I just helped with fiddle classes. It was very tiny at that stage.
>
> **Brian**: [As already mentioned, the original] plan was [that] to be a member of the club you had to learn the uilleann pipes. We then realised it was going to be impractical, so we started just on a concept of teaching traditional music and hoped to recruit people to learn pipes out of that.
>
> **Eithne**: The club started really just as things were absolutely falling apart here. The music depended on the people who were playing – and how many of them were going to stay around? So many of them got to the end of school but didn't go to the universities here, as they do now – they got as far away as possible, and generally stayed there. Armagh was a depressing place then. You didn't think then past what you were doing at that moment – trying to keep a normal life going. … We had pipes, fiddle and flute in the early days, and it just kind of grew slowly. Initially, Brian would have taught all the pipes and all the flute [students], and then eventually some of his pupils were able to move into the teaching – Éamonn Curran, Mark Donnelly …

*

Writing in 1972 to *Treoir*, the monthly journal of CCÉ, Brian sought to inform people of what he was up to, having noticed references to the club in recent issues of the magazine. He dutifully pointed out that the club was not affiliated to CCÉ but that it was convivial with the nearby Portadown CCÉ branch, with which it had collaborated on joint events. The club's membership at that point was 39: 32 children and seven adults. It was running classes on three weeknights as well as Saturdays, and generally undertook two concerts a year in Armagh in addition to odd engagements elsewhere. He explained the simple framework:

All our pupils learn the tin-whistle and attend singing classes in English and Irish. Once they have mastered some tunes and show a musical sense, children are encouraged to try flute (when available), fiddle and pipes. Some now play two or three of these instruments.[437]

That same year, the club published a three-part series of books, *Learn To Play The Tin Whistle*. It was the first time they had sought external funding, which inevitably began a process of professionalising the club's operation.

Eithne: We decided the books would be a useful thing to produce – because there wasn't anything else [equivalent]. They were initially done with an old-fashioned hand-cranked duplicator, but then we had them printed. We shipped piles of them to America and France and so on. We've met loads of people since who say, 'Oh, I started off on your tin whistle book!' I think summer schools were the next project we sought external funding for. Everything had been voluntary up till then – if we put on a concert, we'd pay people from what was taken on the door. Once you get funding, you have to be accountable, though in the early days it wasn't like it is now – you didn't have to produce a receipt for every stamp you bought! But you don't let the bureaucracy stop you.

Multi-instrumentalist and composer Neil Martin (b. 1961) was present at one of the club's 'outside events' around this time:

Neil Martin: Back in the early 1970s, at 10 years of age, I attended an Irish language summer course for young people held in the Servite Priory in Benburb, County Tyrone, under the stewardship of Paul McAvinchey, a key figure in the encouragement of arts and the Irish language. In the evenings, various activities and diversions were arranged, and on one occasion Brian Vallely and others from the Armagh Pipers' Club came and performed. I knew something already of the uilleann pipes through my uncle, Tomás Ó Canainn, and his group Na Filí. But hearing pipes played in Benburb that night further drew me in towards piping. That I can still clearly see that evening in my mind's eye, more than 40 years later, obviously underlines its importance to me. My father subsequently bought for me the books of tunes published by the club, and they were an important and welcome resource for me as a young piper – the landscape for modern collections of tunes was fairly barren back then.

I have admired ever since Brian's selfless and relentless promotion and encouragement of piping, and over those 40 years many fine pipers have emanated from that Armagh stable. I recently collaborated with one such, Conor Mallon – the inaugural recipient of a substantial Arts Council/BBC Bursary.

Four years after the tin whistle tutor, Brian and Eithne published a piping tutor, *Learn To Play The Uilleann Pipes* – the first since Leo Rowsome's in 1936, and one that is still in print. Frank McFadden, a tremendous resource to the Pipers' Club in these early years, died not long after seeing Brian's tutor dedicated to him.

The club's membership reached 100 during the 70s, plateaued for a while before reaching 150, then moved upward to its current level (approaching 300). From 1980 to 1985, Brian organised a residential tuition week during the summer, named the Bunting Residential School, at Benburb Priory, with kids from Belfast coming down from the McPeakes' school at Clonard. Among those at the first one was Marcas Ó Murchú, while those at the second included John McSherry (only playing the tin whistle at the time) and his siblings, whom Brian recalls as among the better behaved of what was a fairly riotous assembly.

John McSherry: I remember meeting Brian for the very first time when I was 10 or 11. He organised a summer school of traditional music in Benburb, which I attended with a group of Belfast kids. I think we got up to a lot of mischief during the week, but despite this we managed to learn quite a bit. Fond memories!

Marcas Ó Murchú: Brian was ahead of most traditional teachers of his era, in that he published books to help his pupils. *Learn To Play The Tin Whistle* Volumes 1 and 2 were influential in the early 70s on people like me … I longed to meet the Valleys in person and share some musical experiences with them. I was not disappointed. … I attended their gathering in Benburb … Music and people were central to them, participation and enjoyment were crucial, it appeared to me. [Brian] shared his skills with one and all with grace and character. When I began teaching music, I am sure that some of the techniques they employed were knitted into my own teaching. The Valleys were very affable and well organised in their delivery of musical classes [at Benburb]. They are still as modest and approachable as when I first met them, something I regard as a sign of great musicians. This is why their school is so successful, no doubt.

From 1994 onward, the club's now numerous events have included the annual William Kennedy Piping Festival – now a major international event in the Irish traditional music calendar. Brian's position remains one of total integrity, total non-sectarianism and total openness to giving a platform to new ideas in presenting traditional music. He's even reticent in talking about this sort of thing, 'waving flags' about it, in case it attracts nutcases, naysayers and bigots from any side. He just wants to carry on promoting the enjoyment of and participation in traditional music – and he has been doing exactly that, ignoring the naysayers, for nearly 50 years:

> **Brian**: No amount of money will bring people together, but actions will. The Piping Festival – that was our first big breakthrough, in 1994. The week after it, when I walked up Scotch Street I doubled the number of people who said, 'Hello Brian.'
>
> I have never taken a penny, [and] nor [has] my wife, for any of the work we do. I have a profession: I'm a full time painter, I make my living that way. Eithne, for most of her life, was a teacher. It's a matter of principle. People might fantasise, 'Brian Vallely must be getting something out of it,' but our records are totally open. If I go somewhere, I pay my own way. Initially we didn't even charge for music classes. But I know that what we have created here in Armagh is totally unique.

In 2006, members of the club past and present – including pipers Cillian Vallely, Jarlath Henderson and Tiarnán Ó Duinnchinn, among many well regarded names in traditional music – created a double disc *40th Anniversary Album*. Even Brian Vallely allowed himself a bit of the fun by appearing on one track, piping with his wife Eithne and son Caoimhín on fiddles. In 2011, for the 45th anniversary, a sumptuous and well illustrated book[*] was produced, which tells the story in full. Onstage, Brian marked the milestone in style:

> **Brian**: I organised this performance by 45 pipers from the club, and asked Dónal O'Connor to score a four-part performance called 'Song Of The Chanter'. Some people in Na Píobairí Uilleann would object to two pipers at the one time! It would have been impossible anywhere else. There's no

---

[*] *45 Years: Armagh Pipers Club* (2012), by Brian and Eithne Vallely, tells the club's story in full, with contributions from many of the musicians associated with it, past and present. The book is available, along with the club's tutorial publications and other products, from: www.crowvalleymusic.com

other club with such a concentration of pipers – even though we've far more fiddlers in the club!

Dónal O'Connor: I'm immensely proud to have been involved in bringing 45 pipers together on one stage, from seven years of age to 70 plus and of varying abilities, creating a glorious sound. It's something that probably has never been achieved before and may well never happen again. The chorus of 45 chanter reeds blowing at once was reminiscent of a cacophony of excited hyenas or a Maasai tribe striking up in vocal unison on the plains of Tanzania.

Financial transparency has remained crucial to Brian:

Brian: We're [now] a charitable organisation; I'm on the board, so I can't benefit from it legally – but I was already [giving my time free of charge] anyhow, long before we had that status. It was my passion, and I just had the feeling that if I started taking money from it, it would become something else. I mean, I like money as much as anyone else … But then again, [with] the amount of work we put in, money literally could not pay us! We have 50 classes every week, we have hundreds of pupils coming through, we have festivals, all these sorts of things – we have to reinvent ourselves every week and produce volumes of documentary evidence for the Arts Council.

The club now boasts a strong committee, its chairman a former Head Of Sound at UTV and BBC Scotland, who handles technical matters that even Brian Vallely, master of much, would otherwise have to outsource. A full-time secretary and social media buff is also employed, not least to handle the hugely time-consuming dealings with various international funding bodies. 'And it is a full-time job,' says Eithne. 'It all helps to keep us going. Mind you, sorting out a hole in the roof and getting central heating in isn't going to come from a funding body!'

One of the current tutors at the club is Barry Kerr (b. 1978), a professional musician, as both a piper and singer-songwriter, and a painter – a calling he shares with Brian:

Barry Kerr: Brian Vallely is a hero of mine. He gives up a serious amount of his time, but it's because he's such a passionate person, whether it's about art or music. I've been honoured, as a painter myself, to have exhibited with him. … What he has done for generations, now, of musicians in the North and indeed throughout Ireland is unbelievable. People come from all over to learn at the Pipers' Club because of the quality of the teachers. [Some of] the students that have grown up there are now teaching there. He draws in the best of [touring] acts to expose the kids to all sorts of styles. He has a great outlook for the music – he's not stuck in the past, he totally embraces forward thinking.

Éamonn Curran, Brian's very first pupil and now himself a teacher at the club, concurs:

> **Éamonn**: Every teacher would have their own take on music, but one thing that comes through very strongly from Brian's influence is getting the basics very right for beginners. A lot of times we'd get pupils coming in who'd maybe have learned a bit of piping skills elsewhere, and quite often the very basic stuff hasn't been covered, which means bad habits, which contribute to sloppy piping, which is out of tune. Unless you can get the finger-work exact, you're not going anywhere as a finished musician.

Largely unconcerned with the professional end of traditional music (notwithstanding his son Cillian's fully professional membership of Lúnasa and sons Niall and Caoimhín's semi-professional membership of Buille), Brian's interest is purely in music itself and the joy of playing it. He holds the view that professional standards exist at the amateur level:

> **Brian**: The level of music with our top pupils, even with some very young ones, is in my view truly frightening in comparison with what would have been accepted years ago. When we started the Pipers' Club, we were looked down on by the middle class of Armagh – they wouldn't send their kids here. It's now become a desirable acquisition. A lot of them are going to the youth orchestras as well as doing traditional music – my sons did the same. It made my sons better musicians and didn't in any way take away from their traditional playing. Musical literacy became a policy of the club over the years. I get fed up with people being proud of being musically illiterate. I didn't learn music [as a kid], but I did teach myself to read it later.

Counting John McSherry's brief cameo as a summer school pupil in 1981, a second generation of the family is now benefiting from its wisdom and camaraderie: John's neice Miadhach Lughain O'Donnell. Having achieved All-Ireland level at flute,

Miadhach Lughain is now in the enviable position of learning the uilleann pipes from both Armagh Pipers' Club and her uncle John.* John is more than happy to share that responsibility:

> **John McSherry**: The Armagh Pipers' Club has done an awful lot for piping in the North. There has been a constant flow of great pipers and other musicians coming through the ranks – from Tiarnán Ó Duinnchinn, Brian Finnegan and Cillian Vallely right up to young Conor Mallon – all down to the hard work and dedication of Brian Vallely, who works tirelessly in the teaching and promotion of the instrument. When you talk about the rise of piping in the North, Brian Vallely has been the main man from day one.

So what does Miadhach Lughain make of the club?

> **Miadhach Lughain O'Donnell**: I'm 15 years old. I started playing pipes at the Armagh Pipers' Club five months ago and I absolutely love it. I just love the sound the pipes make, and it's because of my Uncle Johnny that I want to play them – he's a real inspiration to me. Having the opportunity to go and play in a place where there's lots of enthusiastic people my own age is really class – the place is just hiving with people every Monday night. I think it's amazing that Brian and Eithne have been doing this for 50 years, and even more amazing that they've been doing it voluntarily the whole time! They are so dedicated, and I think we all have a lot to be thankful for because of them. Brian's such a gentle, unassuming and generous character. I have a huge amount of respect for him.

Asked what she is most proud of from her time with the club, Eithne Vallely has no hesitation:

> **Eithne**: I think it's just the fun that youngsters get from being involved in traditional music, and the family relationships – a seven-year-old, a daddy, a granny, and they're all able to enjoy things together. With a lot of sports, for example, kids are only involved with their own age group, so you only mix with those people – you don't learn how to relate to other ages. It's fun to watch it in our monthly group sessions: they're not conscious of people being different ages, they just hear a tune and join in together. It brings a lot

---

* While Armagh Pipers' Club doesn't encourage students to take part in competitions, Brian has always been relaxed if an individual club member wishes to do so.

of shy children out of themselves, and helps ADHD children – we don't set out to do that, it just happens. And they make great friendships, too.

*

Asked to summarise Brian's famously unquenchable reserves of willpower and enthusiasm for the project he created in 1966, Éamonn Curran laughs out loud:

> **Éamonn**: I think anyone who knows Brian is totally amazed and is gobsmacked at the level of input and passion! He truly is an amazing man, in all respects – as an artist, as a piper and as a promoter of traditional music and particularly piping. Brian pulled it back from the brink, certainly in the North. He's a man in a million.

Nearly 50 years on, Brian Vallely is still the voice of common sense, a man who gets things done and creates opportunities. As Eithne says, 'It's what keeps him going.' He wants to enrich people with knowledge of history, give them an interest in traditional music and create something positive with no badge attached to it:

> **Brian**: Traditional music is 'the art of composition' – it's not a museum piece. Piping styles and piping have changed so much in the last 40 years. There's a repertoire of ornamentation that's now a given, but I can honestly tell you it didn't exist before that; it wasn't how people played. Some people did try to standardise uilleann piping, almost like Highland piping, based on [the playing of] Séamus Ennis. But none of them came near Séamus Ennis: Séamus Ennis wasn't up for cataloguing or quantifying, he would play whatever the hell he wanted to.

There are very few people left who not only knew the masters of piping in the mid-20th century – Ennis, Rowsome and Clancy – but are also still active in music at a very significant level. Brian is surely the most prominent of those. He has a rich history of personal experiences and contact with the greats from which to draw as a teacher and facilitator of music – but, as Barry Kerr observed, there's nothing about the fellow that's stuck in the past. He'll happily chat about Ennis and Clancy, Moloney and O'Flynn, over a cup of coffee if you want him to – and any fan of Irish music would be delighted to hear those recollections – but there's no sense of a man wallowing in rose-tinted reverie or name-dropping in an effort to prop up his own credibility through past associations. He's far more interested in keeping the club afloat, sorting out that hole in the roof with the insurance people, organising the next event and making sure that what's happening today and tomorrow with the students coming through the club is as good as it was yesterday. And he is no more stuck in any tired socio-cultural past than he is in a musical past:

> **Brian**: One of the things that probably annoys the trad brigade [about the club] is that for a number of years we've been focusing our attention on the Scottish islands – not the Ulster-Scots thing, [but] real Scottish music. We've been doing these exchange visits for 15 years. And because Skye is full of people speaking Gaelic, from the Presbyterian Church or the Free Church, it disabuses our pupils of the idea that the music is tied to this or that philosophy. … I wouldn't be a great performer, but I like to think I can teach.

And, on that, an awful lot of people would agree.

Appendix 1
Melody Maker Interviews, 1976 & 1978

During the 1960s and 70s, British music weekly *Melody Maker* managed to cover many genres of music in detail, with a more 'musicianly' focus than other music weeklies of the time, having entered the 'rock era' as a long-established magazine with jazz coverage at its core. Eric Winter and Karl Dallas had pioneered its folk music coverage in the 60s, with Colin Irwin becoming a prolific *Melody Maker* staff writer on the subject during the 70s. Many of his pieces not only give a flavour of the times, but also allow penetrating glimpses into the character of the musicians concerned. The presentation of Irish traditional music in the 21st century commercial arena is still built very largely on the templates and foundations of a very few bands in the 1970s. Here, with Colin Irwin's generous agreement, are two of the chief culprits caught in the moment: The Bothy Band, word-of-mouth sensations in 1976; and a reflective Liam O'Flynn, in between Planxtys, in 1978.

Bothy Band: *Melody Maker* Band Breakdown
Colin Irwin
(Originally published 1/5/76)

One of the foremost characteristics of Southern Ireland has always been its abundance of excellent traditional musicians, receiving and seeking no fame or acclaim outside of their immediate environment.

Recently, The Chieftains and Planxty have proved it's possible to achieve much more widespread popularity for Irish folk music without aborting it seriously, and The Bothy Band are in the process of achieving much more than that – attempting to transplant the fire and informal spirit of the spontaneous crack in its entirety to a concert platform.

They came together about 15 months ago when Mícheál Ó Domhnaill, his sister Tríona, Dónal Lunny and Paddy Glackin were invited to play at the 21st birthday celebrations of the Irish record label Gael Linn. Further sessions ensued, RTÉ television producer Tony MacMahon sat in with them on melodeon and slowly the informal sessions developed into something more lasting. Their reputation spread so rapidly that they decided to turn professional, resulting in the departure of MacMahon and Glackin for Tommy Peoples, an old friend of Matt Molloy, who had already been incorporated along with Paddy Keenan.

They obviously owe much to The Chieftains and Planxty for opening the way, and certain parallels can be drawn in their music, though their style has more drive and gut appeal. The Domhnaills and Lunny provide a solid rhythmic base (and occasional vocals), and Keenan, Peoples and Molloy do the rest, weaving pipes, fiddle and flute in arresting and electrifying fashion. Mícheál Ó Domhnaill indicated the atmosphere of music they had in mind by naming them after the old bothy bands – those unplanned sessions enjoyed by migrant Irish workers.

Their rise has been astonishing; the excitement they created in Ireland caused much anticipation in England before they arrived. When they came for the first time at the end of last year [1975] they played to mainly Irish communities, and fulfilled all the promise. When they returned for their first full British tour they'd made great strides. Dónal Lunny formed his own label, Mulligan, to issue their first album in Ireland, which has now just been put out in Britain by Polydor.

Over Easter they were at the Inverness Folk Festival and this summer they are set to appear at the Cambridge, Sidmouth and Durham festivals. The one thing that seems capable of holding them back would appear to be within their own character and lifestyle.

Dónal Lunny
Initially the temptation was to think of the group as Dónal Lunny's band – he was, after all, the one member who had a big reputation outside Irish traditional music circles. Lunny's standing as one of the most imaginative and fertile minds involved in folk was born when he became a founder-member of Planxty, contributing substantially to the spirit that made their first album such a classic.

Lunny left Planxty in 1973 to form a new band, which spent six months rehearsing but never got off the ground. In the time before The Bothy Band came together just over a year ago, Lunny concentrated on production, working on the first Spud album, Tommy Makem's *Ever The Wind* and Christy Moore's *Whatever Tickles Your Fancy*.

'Andy Irvine influenced me a lot. Before Planxty I gigged with him and started playing bouzouki rather than guitar and I began to look at things from a different angle. The reason I left Planxty was to play with someone else – the pull from another direction was stronger. I had certain regrets about it after but I tend to accept the inevitability of a situation.'

He missed playing, however, and was delighted with the promise shown by the early Bothy Band gigs, and when they decided it was time to make an album Lunny formed his own record label, Mulligan, based in Dublin, to do it.

'There are some really excellent singers and players in Ireland who would do very well on an album. We'd like to record some of them. It's worth it to have your own label, there isn't the problem of album deadlines and all that. Keep it simple is my motto, and I have the advantage of bitter experience.'

He says The Bothy Band intend to keep to their policy of playing their own interpretations of traditional music. Their approach to traditional music is a natural development of their own backgrounds – 'It's fine to add influences as long as the essence remains undiluted. We are very happy with the way things are going.'

Mícheál Ó Domhnaill

'I never got into groups like Fairport or Steeleye at all people like Swarbrick, René from Stivell's band, Peter Knight there are boys of seven or eight years in Ireland who could have them for breakfast.'

Forthright views from Mícheál Ó Domhnaill, the guitarist/vocalist who is often considered the mastermind behind The Bothy Band, although he strenuously disputes it. That myth has arisen, he says, because he was in at the very beginning and, working at Gael Linn, was in a position to do much of the organising.

Born in Dublin but brought up in County Meath, and the son of a collector of wax cylinder recordings, he spent 13 years studying classical piano with little exposure to traditional music – the influence of musicians like Jansch and Renbourn was more profound. He joined a group called Skara Brae with his sister Tríona and cut an album with them for Gael Linn ('We were really successful only with the Irish speaking population') and then joined Monroe, who had the distinction of gigging with Planxty for six months in Ireland.

They went to Brittany where they were quite successful, and Mícheál came back to collect songs for the Folklore Commission:

'They were looking for collectors and my brief was Donegal. They had the text but not the melodies. Tom Munnelly in Dublin has collected 6,000 songs but there are countless airs, and I had to try and find them. I suppose I found about 300 or 400, some of them from my aunt.'

Having left Monroe, he missed playing but stayed in touch by doing some radio work with Tony MacMahon and doing freelance work at Gael Linn. He was full of ideas of how to treat traditional music by the time The Bothy Band were born.

'I'd love to be in a rock band. During the two-year period where I was doing nothing but listening to traditional music I found myself completely closed off from everything else. Recently I've been listening to records made in '73 like early Little

Feat albums, which I think are amazing, and all the Clapton and Derek & The Dominos stuff. I also always had a hankering to get an electric traditional music group going because I don't think any band has done it properly yet. There haven't been bands with good traditional music players in them. There hasn't been an ace fiddle player or piper among them, that's why the treatment of the music hasn't really come off.'

Matt Molloy
Molloy, a softly spoken friendly man from County Roscommon, has established himself as one of Ireland's finest traditional musicians – he's a former all-Ireland champion. Now that the controlled drive of his flute playing and his striking blend with Keenan and Peoples has lifted The Bothy Band to a position of some eminence, Molloy is somewhat bewildered that Irish traditional music is so much in demand and it's possible to make a living out of playing it.

'I wouldn't have thought it possible four or five years ago,' he says. 'I've no idea why it is, although The Chieftains have done great work, they are fine musicians – particularly Seán Keane. But if this thing fell in the morning, I'll still be playing traditional music, if I make money at it or not.'

He started playing whistle when he was seven and graduated to flute a couple of years later having been taught by his father (the whole family were traditional musicians). He became an aircraft technician with Aer Lingus, spent the rest of his time playing at informal sessions, appearing at the Fleadhs, and putting on small concerts with other likeminded musicians, which led directly to the Bothy Band.

'We were all quite well-established as traditional musicians and we'd advertise these concerts in the local paper, and the profits from the concert would pay for the crack which would go on all weekend. There was a lot of drinking involved.'

That's how it was at the beginning of the band, and though it's grown rapidly and has become much more than the means to a crack, he says there's still a lot of fun involved. 'I suppose there's a certain amount of discipline once you're in a group but we still have sessions after concerts and wreck ourselves staying up all night.'

Naming Willie Clancy and Séamus Ennis as his most admired and influential musicians ('I've always had a fascination for the pipes'), he makes an additional point about the current popularity of traditional music. 'There are folk-rock bands who don't impress me. They are supposed to be progressing but the sad part about it is they have no traditional background to progress from. They just can't play the bloody stuff.'

Paddy Keenan
It had been a heavy night (and I mean really heavy), and Paddy Keenan appeared

to be suffering the worst – the combination of his strong accent and the obvious discomfort of struggling to coax his brain into working order resulting in a largely incomprehensible mumble in answer to my questions. Certain facts were gleaned, however: he's 26, was brought up on an unrelenting diet of traditional music, coming from a long line of travelling musicians, and learnt to play the pipes from his father while a young boy.

He was 16 when he started playing a full set of pipes and played regularly at informal sessions and concerts with other members of his family. He admits to a period when he became attracted to the rock revolution, and briefly concentrated on guitar when he heard Dylan and Donovan and fancied himself as a singer-songwriter. But he met up with Matt Molloy and became enmeshed in the Dublin folk scene.

It's the wild excitement of Keenan's playing that contributes so much electrifying edge to the Bothy Band – on the two occasions I've seen him he's won standing ovations for astonishing solos. Keenan – tall, swarthy and youthful looking – shrugs aside awed enquiries about his attitude to playing and how he acquired such venom in his piping. He names his greatest influence as the late Johnny Doran, also stating his admiration for the playing of Patsy Touhey and Leo Rowsome. He can't see anything extraordinary about his own playing: attributing his style to the influence of these pipers.

'Rowsome did more than anyone for the pipers,' he says. 'I'm only learning.' He rates Paddy Moloney as 'quite a good player,' adding that the only piper he really listens to now is Séamus Ennis. 'There's a lot of good young pipers coming up in Ireland now though.'

The impression gained is that Keenan is a naturally informal musician who would be just as happy playing in Dublin pubs as he would be travelling around playing in concert halls with the same musicians. Keenan maintains he prefers it this way, though. 'I like playing with a permanent band, I always wanted to play with musicians like Matt.'

Tríona Ní Dhomhnaill
The diminutive Tríona was, like her brother Mícheál, born in Dublin but brought up in Meath, and studied classical music and piano. She got into traditional music through Tony MacMahon, who had the idea of presenting a series of radio programmes involving 10 musicians from different backgrounds.

This was her first experience of playing with traditional musicians, and after a period with Skara Brae, [she] went to Brittany (she recently married a Breton). On returning to Dublin she worked at Gael Linn 'answering the phone and dealing with the public' and not playing herself until The Bothy Band arose. Now she generally concentrates on adding to the rhythms on clavinet, although she also sings a bit with a vast repertoire she learnt from her aunt, Nelli Ní Dhomhnaill, of Donegal. She's recently made a solo album.

'My aunt's style of singing has influenced me an awful lot. I used to listen to The Beatles and Pentangle and people like that but I got out of touch – I was always more interested in things like Romanian and Bulgarian folk songs.

'My aunt is amazing though, she has about 300 songs she could give you in the space of a week and she doesn't jealously guard them or anything like that. Donegal was a big immigration county and the seasonal workers would go off and come back with these songs as presents.'

She's had experience of songwriting and arranging, as well as being involved in radio and television music programmes, but now considers herself irretrievably immersed in traditional music. 'I'd have to start again from scratch to play classical music. There was a lot of advanced stuff I could play, which I couldn't even attempt now.'

Tommy Peoples
As aggressive as is the piping of Keenan, it's matched all the way by the robust fiddling of Tommy Peoples – the two of them blend together in breath-taking fashion when they cut loose. Peoples hails from Donegal, an area of strong fiddle traditions – 'in Donegal you rarely saw another instrument' – and was taught to play by his family as a young boy.

Peoples – a man of burly, rugged physique – moved to Dublin in his mid-teens and had a long succession of jobs 'doing anything and everything, building work mainly', and spending most of his free time playing in the Dublin clubs. His reputation grew as he came into contact with other traditional musicians and he moved to Clare, joining the celebrated Kilfenora Céilí Band and playing on their 1974 album for Transatlantic (TRA 283), and he stayed with the Kilfenoras for about four years.

He returned to Dublin about nine months ago and 'fell in with this lot', being enlisted as the replacement for the departing Paddy Glackin. He'd known most of the band for several years and had played with them informally on various occasions and was a natural choice, despite his horror about being part of a disciplined line-up.

'Discipline always came hard to me,' he says, 'but I enjoy playing with the other people in the band, and everybody has enough material to keep it interesting. I don't find it that hard to rehearse.'

Like Keenan, he's dismissive when you refer to the fire in his playing and ask him who he admires. He pays tribute to The Chieftains' Seán Keane. He and Keane have played together on various occasions, in fact he's played along with most of the traditional musicians of note at some point. He's never been exposed to any great degree to other forms of music – traditional music has always dominated his life and he's happy to keep it that way.

The Enigmatic Piper Supreme
Colin Irwin
(Originally published 25/2/78)

You'll doubtless be amused by the extravagance of the comparison, but being an ex-member of Planxty is the folk world's equivalent to being an ex-Beatle.

Liam Óg O'Flynn snorts audibly, and the overwhelming impression is that he doesn't think a great deal of the suggestion. Planxty never were a band to relish publicity, always largely unimpressed and indifferent to high praise. And Liam O'Flynn (the Óg, which means young, and was used to identify him from his father, is optional) was without doubt the most reticent of them all.

Pipers, it's said, are a race apart. God departs to a special vault and concocts a completely new mould every time he contemplates depositing a piper in Ireland. The great pipers – Clancy, Rowsome, Ennis, etc – are all legends, and the current giants like Paddy Moloney and [Paddy] Keenan (and two characters don't contrast more sharply than those two) are well on the way to joining them.

O'Flynn (probably considered by the vast majority of aficionados to be vastly superior to both) is different again, enigmatic in his introspection.

It came as quite a pleasant shock when Liam, in Britain for his first solo tour, agreed (though one feels with great reluctance) to my request for an interview. Despite immaculate politeness and willing consideration of every question aimed at him during the couple of hours of our encounter, he's a discernibly uncomfortable interviewee. There have, in the history of the world, been more voluble men.

But what an uilleann piper! He was fortunate to benefit from the tuition of three of the greatest pipers Ireland ever produced – Leo Rowsome, Willie Clancy and Séamus Ennis – and his own highly individual fluent and economical style has resulted from an amalgam of all three influences plus other traditional instrumentalists.

He's actually the son of a Kerry fiddler, and though brought up in County Kildare – not an area famous for its traditional music – he was still surrounded by the music as a kid through his parents (his mother comes from Clare) and their friends. He was playing the tin whistle at six, and was 11 when he got his first set of practice pipes.

Leo Rowsome, a good friend of Liam O'Flynn Snr, was his first teacher. He'd go and see Rowsome once a week for a half-hour session (increased to an hour as he became more proficient) and that, he tells you emphatically, was the high point of the week. He was Rowsome's pupil for two years until he went off to boarding school.

Later, he took some guidance from Willie Clancy, one of many traditional musicians encountered on visits to the country, and after him Séamus Ennis, with whom he formed a strong friendship that survives today – they even shared a flat in Dublin at one time.

At no time during this development did he consider there was a possibility of playing the pipes for a living. He was a teacher who regarded the pipes as a spare time passion when Christy Moore invited him to join the sessions of his *Prosperous* album in the spring of 1971.

Immediately after that he took himself off to America on his holidays and wound up staying for six months, eventually returning to Ireland to find an invitation to join the other musicians from the session in a group they were forming.

'I had reservations about joining Planxty ... naturally,' he tells me with a slight grin. 'But it came at the right time for me, having just got back from America, and we said we'd see how it went for three months and I don't think any of us thought it would last very long. So it didn't worry me too much.

'But as we got more involved in each other's music we tried to sort out ways in which to use the instruments together and use them with the music. There were people who said I shouldn't be playing in a group like that, with guitars and things, but we tried to deal with the music in a sensible way ... and I think we managed very well.

'I continued to play informally – it was always very important for us not to lose touch, to keep in contact, and we did.'

They immediately made a bit of a name for themselves supporting Donovan on a concert tour in Ireland, and their single, 'Three Drunken Maidens', received extensive airplay; and they were away, quickly realising they'd become involved in something that was going to be much bigger than any of them had initially envisaged.

O'Flynn characteristically refuses now to glorify the achievements of Planxty. No, he says, he doesn't think the reputation of the band has become inflated – 'the thing has mushroomed so much now it's natural for people to talk about Planxty' – but he won't hear of any suggestions that they brought about a revolution in Irish music, however modestly.

Sure, he's proud of the music Planxty created, but he feels their role was merely incidental in the flood of Irish traditional music that would have occurred anyway.

'Planxty might have accelerated it slightly,' is the most he'll concede. 'The whole thing's mushroomed so much in the last few years – The Chieftains are going to parts of the world that have probably never heard anything remotely connected with Irish music before.

'I think it's a good thing that there are so many people playing the music now. There are people who do it specifically for money and that's undesirable, but I think the music will remain basically the same. When the old folks, the original musicians go, they have a style, a way of playing that younger people don't ever have, because lifestyles are different and in every area lifestyles change.

'I don't see much point in bemoaning the fact. You aren't permanently going to have people like Willie Clancy – they're particular to a particular life and that's got to change.'

I ask him – classic ex-Beatle question this – whether there's any likelihood of Planxty re-forming, just for a one-off tour or concert (there have inevitably been rumours). There's such a long silence that I wonder if he's heard me. Probably not, it seems … 'I don't really have any feelings about whether it should or shouldn't happen.' And that was that.

Would you ever consider joining a formal group of any sort again? This time the pause isn't so excruciating. 'No, I wouldn't want to be involved in a group of that sort again, mainly because a lot of it would have to do with the whole business and the facts of life in a group.

'You have very little control over your own circumstances and you probably spend time working off overheads and so on. I just prefer to be that much more in control.'

He has positively no regrets about the group's split, whatever fame and commercial rewards may have been one more album away – and it's widely believed they were about to hit the treble chance when they decided to split. Material considerations have evidently never been high on the list of priorities with this man.

'We could have been very big internationally, maybe not, I don't know. We just knew it was time to break up, we wanted to go our separate ways and there was no consideration at all of this business of potential that was there. It would have been very much going against the grain to continue for any material rewards that might have been coming.

'I'm not so sure that there were any great mistakes which caused the group to disband. There were things we might have done differently – simple things like if we'd formed our own record label we'd have gained a lot more financially. But the group didn't exist for all that long; through that first year we didn't have time to think about things like that.'

Like the others he had no precise plans for life after Planxty and it's come as quite a delightful surprise to discover that there's now sufficient awareness and interest in the pipes to enable him to do solo tours. And he still gets to play with the others in various combinations either at concerts (recently, for example, he toured Belgium with Paul Brady) or informally with reasonable regularity. The casual arrangement, he observes, is infinitely more preferable than a regular group structure.

And from a time not so long ago when piping seemed like a doomed art, this most complex and intriguing of instruments can scarcely have known such flourishing popularity. Liam is gratified to see it and speaks warmly of young players like Paddy Keenan, though his particular admiration is for a lesser-known piper who rarely plays in public called Tommy Reck.

He's loath to make comparisons between the three masters – Rowsome, Clancy and Ennis – all brilliant pipers with individual styles, and all immense characters.

He talks of Rowsome's open style of playing, the 'wildness and gaiety' of Clancy as a musician and a character, and the 'amazing' Ennis, proud and delighted to play for whoever asks him. 'People keep saying he's over the hill but he always comes back and plays this dazzling stuff.' He refuses to differentiate between the influence they had over him and though it's not voiced, it's evident they all hold honoured places in his affections.

'You can see their personalities strongly in their playing. The more you listened to these fellows the more you realised they themselves were actually in there with the music. I would agree with those who say there is something magic about the pipes.

'They can be so frustrating. It takes so long to learn and they're always prone to tuning difficulties – there are times when you want to give up, when you envy fiddle players. But there's an excitement about it that's special. It's something I can't explain but it's there.'

Appendix 2
Discographies & Sessionographies

The information below has been compiled from an array of sources including: original records; online discographical resources (e.g. 45cat.com, discogs.com, mainlynorfolk.info, folktrax-archive.org); the Irish Traditional Music Archive (ITMA) in Dublin; the BBC Written Archive Centre (WAC) in Caversham; *Radio Times* (BBC Project Genome online); *Melody Maker*; the RTÉ TV archive database; the British Library/National Sound Archive; the BBC Sound Archive database; Ken Garner's *In Session Tonight* (BBC Books, 1993) and *The Peel Sessions* (BBC Books, 2007); artist websites; and sundry other print and online sources.

In some cases I've provided only a Select Discography, in others I've tried to be comprehensive. Inevitably, with any undertaking like this, there will be items missed. Ironically, the shakiest discography is John McSherry's. He has played on recordings by many other artists and never kept a diary, let alone acquiring the records themselves.

Contents

John McSherry Discography
Albums As Band Member/Featured Artist
Soundtracks & Collaborative Projects
Albums As Backing Musician/Guest

Séamus Ennis Discography
Part 1: Recordings Released During Séamus Ennis' Lifetime
Solo Albums & EPs
Shared Albums
Appearances On Various-Artists/Themed Releases
Recordings As An Accompanist
Part 2: Posthumous Releases
Part 3: The Folktrax Releases 1975–2002
Séamus Ennis Albums On Folktrax

BBC Broadcasts Featuring Séamus Ennis On Folktrax Albums
Various-Artists Folktrax Albums Including Séamus Ennis

Finbar & Eddie Furey Discography 1968–76
Albums & Singles 1968-76

Finbar & Eddie Furey BBC Sessionography 1967–75
BBC Radio
BBC TV

Paddy Keenan Select Discography
Solo & Duo Albums
The Blacksmiths
The Bothy Band

The Bothy Band BBC Sessionography
BBC Radio
BBC TV
Miscellaneous BBC Radio Coverage

McPeake Family Discography 1955–75
Albums & EPs
Exclusive McPeake Recordings On Various-Artists Releases

McPeake Family BBC Sessionography 1949–70
BBC Radio
BBC TV
Addendum: Extant RTÉ Radio Recordings

Willie Clancy Discography

Leo Rowsome Selected Discography
Vinyl Releases
Exclusive Recordings On Various-Artists Releases

John McSherry Discography

Albums As Band Member/Featured Artist

Rhythm & Rhyme (Grapevine GRACD227) 1997
Tamalin
Rhythm And Rhyme; Skipping Over The Bogs; In The Morning; Jim Donoghue's/The Tempest/The Fair Wind; Words; Kerreg Beg An Triez; Land Of Love; Crazy Man Michael; Reaping The Rye/Unknown Slip; Gort Na Sailéan; Some Day Soon; Poor Tom; Unknown/ The Reconciliation/The Steeplechase
Note: Tamalin included all John's siblings (Tíona, Joanne and Paul) plus Kevin Dorris.

In The Morning (single) (Grapevine CD6PS217) 1997
Tamalin
Tracks: In The Morning (Radio Edit); Crazy Man Michael; Skipping Over The Bog; In The Morning (Album Version)

Coolfin (Hummingbird/RTÉ CDHBRTE 221) 1998
Dónal Lunny
Spanish Point; The Lowlands Of Holland; Glentown; Mouseskin Shoe And Dancing In Allihies; Moldavian Triptych; Butler's; False Fly; Polkas: Trip To Sado/Dan-Ti Dan-Dan; Slides: Coolfin/Nóra Críona; Kickdancer; Siúl A Rúin; Lucky Lucky Day
Note: The musicians involved in this album toured as Coolfin or Dónal Lunny's Coolfin.

Lúnasa (own label LSA001) 1998
Lúnasa
Eanair; Feabhra; Márta; Aibreán; Bealtaine; Meitheamh; Iúil; Meán Fomhair; Deireadh Fómhair; Mí Na Samhna; Mí Na Nollaig; Jacky Molard's/The Hunter's Purse
Note: Sometimes known as 'Lúnasa Mk 1', the musicians involved in this record were John McSherry, Michael McGoldrick, Seán Smyth, Donogh Hennessy and Trevor Hutchinson. *Lúnasa* was made widely available in 2002 on Compass Records.

Otherworld (Green Linnet GLCD 1200) 2000
Lúnasa
Goodbye Miss Goodavich/Rosie's Reel; The Floating Crowbar/McGlinchey's/The Almost Reel; The Butlers of Glen Avenue/Sliabh Russell/Cathal McConnell's; January Snows/ Laura Lynn Cunningham; The Miller of Drohan; Dr Gilbert/Devils Of Dublin/Black Pat's; Autumn Child/Heaton Chapel; Stolen Apples; Taylor Bar, 4am/Ceol Na Mara; Lafferty's/Crock Of Gold/Lady Birr/Abbey Reel; O'Carolan's Welcome/Rolling In The Barrel

At First Light (Vertical Records VERTCD061) 2001
Michael McGoldrick & John McSherry
Farewell To Connaught; Rolling Waves; Doinna; Ornette's Trip To Belfast; Lucy Campbell's; Lady Lane; Trip To Ireland; The Bloom Of Youth; Lacey's Jig; The Graf Spee; Road To Taynuilt

Tripswitch (Vertical Records VERTCD076) 2006
John McSherry, Dónal O'Connor
Rose In The Gap; Tripswitch; Seán Maguire's; Both Ghé; Spanish 5's; Antón; Commonality Set; Áille's Arabesque
Note: Code on the back of the album allows access to a free *Live EP* download via www.atfirstlight.net with exclusive versions of: Ornette's Trip To Belfast; The Rolling Waves; Commonality.

Six Days In Down (Riverboat Records TUGCD1057) 2010
Bob Brozman, John McSherry & Dónal O'Connor
Hardiman The Fiddler; Brelydian; A Mháire Bruineall; Portaferry Swing; Róise Na bhFonn

(Tuneful Rose); Pota Mór Fataí; The Slide From Grace; Bean An Fhir Ruaidh (The Red Haired Man's Wife); Beer Belly Dancing; The Beauty Spot; Cailleach A Shúsa (The Hag In The Blanket)
Note: Also released in 2013 as a double CD special edition with various-artists compilation *The Rough Guide To Irish Music* (World Music Network RGNET1294CD).

Soma (Compass Records 7 4538 2) 2010
John McSherry
An Bhean Chaointe; Atlantic Drive; The Stone of Destiny; Bádaí Na Scanán; The Wave-Sweeper; The Rambles Of Kitty; The Maid Of Murlough; Aisling Gheal; The Slide From Grace; Áille's Antics
Note: Includes among the backing musicians At First Light's Dónal O'Connor and Francis McIlduff and Tamalin's Paul and Joanne McSherry.

Idir (At First Light AFLCD201101) 2011
At First Light
The Magnificent Six; Ar Thóir An Donn; Aird Uí Chuain (The Quiet Land Of Erin); Máire An Chúil Ór Bhuí; Bethan's Dance; Rolling In Rosemount; Courting Is A Pleasure; El Garrotín; Roy's Hands; The Pipers Of Roguery
Note: The band 'At First Light' consists of three people: John McSherry, Dónal O'Connor and Francis McIlduff. Various others are featured on this record and in ongoing live performances.

The Olllam (Compass Records 7 4584 2) 2012
The Olllam
Prolllogue; The Belll; Three Signs Of A Bad Man; The Devilll For My Hurt; The Follly Of Wisdom; The Tryst After Death; Bridge Of Glllass; Prayer For Tears
Note: As with *At First Light*, The Olllam comprise three members (John McSherry, Tyler Duncan, Michael Shimmin) with additional musicians for live appearances.

Soundtracks & Collaborative Projects

Sult: Spirit Of The Music (Hummingbird HBCD0009) 1996
Collaborative Project
Musicians: John McSherry (uilleann pipes), Dónal Lunny (bouzouki), Nollaig Casey (fiddle), Pat Crowley (keyboards), Steve Cooney (bass, guitar), Noel Bridgeman (drums), Van Morrison (guitar, vocals), Mary Black (backing vocals), Brendan Power (harmonica), Richie Buckley (sax), Keith Donald (sax)
Note: Highlights from a music TV series presented by Dónal Lunny.

Marginal Moon (Ki/oon Records KSC2232) 1998
Soul Flower with the Dónal Lunny Band
Note: Japanese release.

Waking Ned (Decca 460 939 2) 1998
Film Soundtrack (Shaun Davey)
Musicians: John McSherry (pipes, whistle), Nollaig Casey (fiddle), Arty McGlynn (guitar), Liam Ó Maonlaí (whistle, bodhrán, vocals), The Waterboys (vocals), Shaun Davey (keyboards), Rita Connolly (vocals), The Voice Squad (vocals), Colm Ó Maonlaí (vocals), James Nesbitt (vocals)

This Is My Father (Hummingbird HBCD 0019) 1999
Soundtrack
Musicians: Dónal Lunny (bouzouki, guitar, keyboards, mandolin, bodhrán), Sharon Shannon (accordion), Nollaig Casey (violin, viola), John McSherry (pipes, whistle), Kieran Hanrahan (banjo), Vinnie Kilduff (whistle), Séamus Glackin (fiddle), Jimmy McGreevy (accordion)

Duiseacht (Experience Ireland, no catalogue number) 2000
Musicians: RTÉ Concert Orchestra,

Dónal Lunny (bodhrán), Greg Sheehan (percussion), Lloyd Byrne (percussion) Róisín Elsafty (vocals), John McSherry (low whistle, pipes), Nollaig Casey (fiddle)

St Patrick 2000 (Keltia Musique KMCD 105) 2000
Collaborative Project
Musicians: Dónal Lunny (bouzouki, guitar, keyboards, mandolin, bodhrán), Nollaig Casey (violin, viola), John McSherry (low whistle, pipes), Richard Buckley (sax), Karl Ronan (trombone), Stephen McDonnell (trumpet), Máiréad Nesbitt (fiddle)

The Irish Sea Sessions 2011 (Liverpool Philharmonic LPISSCD002) 2012
Collaborative Project
Musicians: Bernard O'Neill (Musical Director), David Munnelly (accordion, piano), Terry Clarke-Coyne (flute, whistle, vocals), John McSherry (pipes, whistle), Méabh O'Hare (fiddle), Jennifer John (vocals), Damian Dempsey (vocals, guitar), Alan Burke (vocals, guitar), Ian Prowse (vocals, guitar), Graham Dunne (vocals, guitar)

Albums As Backing Musician/Guest

Loosely Connected (Greentrax CD TRAX 052) 1992
Niamh Parsons
Musicians: Niamh Parsons (vocals), John McSherry (pipes, whistle), Paul McSherry (guitar), Eddie Friel (piano), Dee Moore (bass), Dave Early (drums, percussion)
Note: Includes the first recording of John's 'Katie Campbell's Rambles'. John performed live as a member of Parsons' band around this time.

Different Worlds (Greentrax CTRAX055) 1992
Paul Herron

Instinctive Behaviour (Munich Records MRCD 167) 1993
Melanie Harrold & Olly Blanchflower

Celtic Connections (SLAM CD 01) 1993
Celtic Connections

Money's Gone (own label) 1996
Strawman

Eleanor Shanley (Grapevine GRACD206) 1995
Eleanor Shanley

Weather In The Heart (I&E CD102) 1995
Carmina

Little Bruises (Columbia 478573 2) 1995
Gary Kemp
Note: John toured as a member of Gary's band in support of this album.

Aoife (Gael Linn CEFCD172) 1996
Aoife Ní Fhearraigh

The Very Best Of Philomena Begley (Ritz RITZ SC 431) 1996
Philomena Begley

Each Little Thing (Grapevine GRACD226) 1997
Sharon Shannon

Wandering Home (Rykodisc HNCD1410) 1997
Maura O'Connell

When Two Lovers Meet (Mongrel Music MMCD001) 1997
Sarah McQuaid
Note: Mostly Irish songs and instrumentals on this debut album from the gifted singer/songwriter/guitarist – and proofreader of this book – who has had to deal with everyone thinking she's an 'Irish trad' artist ever since. Subsequently reissued on other labels.

Atlantic Roar (Chyme Music PTICD 1090) 1997
Paul Bradley

Finisterres (Byg Production SAN4891672) 1997
Dan Ar Braz & L'Heritage Des Celtes
Musicians: Dan Ar Braz (guitar), Dónal Lunny (bouzouki, guitar, bodhrán, claviers, tambourine), Noel Bridgeman (percussion), Nollaig Casey (fiddle), John McSherry (uilleann pipes), Graham Henderson (mandola), Karen Matheson (vocals), Eoghan O'Neill (bass), Elaine Morgan (vocals)

Landmarks (Atlantic 83083-2/SonyBMG 74321560072) US 1997 / UK 1998
Clannad
Note: John toured as an additional member of Clannad in support of this album.

Man Of The House (Outlet PTICD1091) 1998
Ray Gallen
Note: This instrumental album, credited to bódhran player Ray, has become the source of three tracks usually credited 'John McSherry', which have popped up ever since on a raft of cheapo compilations on the labels Outlet, Chyme, Sounds Irish and others.

Restless Spirit (Dara/RTÉ TORTE CD 224) 1998
Tommy Fleming

Idir An Dá Sholas = Between Two Lights (Gael Linn/Hummingbird GLHCD9002) 1999
Maighréad & Tríona Ní Dhomhnaill with Dónal Lunny

Zenith (Live) (Sony International 491811) 1998
Dan Ar Braz & L'Héritage Des Celtes

Note: Dan Ar Braz (Breton electric guitar maestro) plus most of Coolfin, Capercaillie and others.

The Dust Bowl Symphony (Elektra 7559-62418-2) 1999
Nanci Griffith

Blackbirds And Thrushes (Green Linnet GLCD 1197) 1999
Niamh Parsons

Otherworld (Green Linnet GLCD 1200) 1999
Lúnasa
Note: Includes John McSherry on four tracks.

On Song (Curb CURCD 128) 2003
Brian Kennedy

Bye A While (own label, no cat #) 2005
Pádraig Rynne

Home (Warner Atlantic 5051011 0293 2 5) 2005
The Corrs

Má Bhíonn Tú Liom, Bí Liom: New And Traditional Songs From Connemara (Vertical Records VERTCD080) 2006
Róisín Elsafty

Songs From The Heart (EMI) 2011
Celtic Woman

Dream Of You (Rhino 2564678839) 2010
Sharon Corr

Triad (own label RLBCD001) 2013
Sylvain Barou / Dónal Lunny / Pádraig Rynne

The Wayland Man (own label MMC0001CD) 2014
Michael McCague

Séamus Ennis Discography

Pat Mitchell observed, in *The Dance Music Of Séamus Ennis* (NPU, 2007), that 'unfortunately Ennis allowed a number of records to be released on which his playing would suggest that he was definitely not on top form, but there are still riches to be gleaned even from these'. What records Pat had in mind he didn't reveal. Strictly speaking, Séamus Ennis created and released only seven full albums and one EP in what might be termed his recording career, between 1959 and 1982. During that time he also contributed an EP's worth of tracks apiece to two albums shared with other solo musicians. In addition, from 1954 onward – predating his solo releases – an array of otherwise unavailable Séamus Ennis tracks would appear on various-artists studio and live albums.

Posthumously, numerous further otherwise unavailable tracks have continued to appear, scattered around various-artists releases, while a superb and well-annotated collection of hitherto unreleased material, *The Return From Fingal*, appeared in 1997. A 2CD set bringing together the best of Séamus' surviving BBC recordings (music and speech) would be both possible and desirable, representing the most significant corner of his career yet to be documented on record. Similarly, a 2CD/2DVD set of his complete surviving RTÉ TV/film material (with English subtitling where relevant), incorporating the two-hour radio documentary *The Séamus Ennis Story*, would be a wonderful thing. These are both projects which, for a prospective third-party licensor, with willpower and access to arts subsidies, are both achievable and desirable – such was Séamus' uniqueness and import as a cultural figure.

Counterintuitively (for those interested in it), Séamus' piping is best heard in the context of a fuller exposition of his art: within a programme of songs, tunes and spoken word. The best example of this is *Masters Of Irish Music* (Leader, 1969) – which, alas, through the vagaries of catalogue ownership, has never been available in any digital format and may never be. Secondhand vinyl copies should be sought out. The next best example is available on iTunes: *Féidlim Tonn Rí's Castle Or The King Of Ireland's Son* (Claddagh, 1977).

Of the totally-piping records, by far the best is *The Return From Fingal* (RTÉ, 1997), comprising Radio Éireann/RTÉ recordings spanning 1940-80. This was followed by an even more expansive 2CD Willie Clancy release in 2007.

Peter Browne: The reason we did the CDs of Willie and Séamus was because I was in a particular position: first of all as a piper who had learned from both, and there was also a lot of personal family contact with both, so I knew them well; and then, being in RTÉ, I became aware that the material was there, and the opportunity and the will existed to do it in the various different sections of the organisation necessary to bring it to a good conclusion. So you could describe it as self-propelling!

In Séamus' case, the fact that the recordings were so early in his life and so good was a revelation – they were all from within RTÉ. For Willie, it was slightly different in that we selected the best of what was in RTÉ but also trawled as far and wide as we could to produce what would be a comprehensive collection 'under one roof'. But in both cases the quality of the piping is exceptional and iconic and its availability does actually have a 'hearable' bearing on present day players' (not just pipers') styles, repertoire, etc.

One key to fully appreciating Séamus' piping is knowing that when he played song airs (his forte), he had in mind the Irish-language song lyrics when he chose his phrasing. The

Bonny Bunch Of Roses (Tradition, 1959) is an entertaining and varied album, available on CD and important as Séamus' first commercial release and one of the earliest LPs of uilleann piping by anyone. The two Tara albums (*The Pure Drop* and *The Fox Chase*) are available on a double CD under the ghastly title *The Best Of Irish Piping* and with an even ghastlier sleeve design. *Ceol, Scéalta Agus Amhráin* (Gael Linn, 1961) is available on CD, though some complain about harsh mastering. *The Wandering Minstrel* (Topic, 1974) is available to download with booklet from Topic/iTunes. *Forty Years Of Irish Piping,* first released in 1974 (US) and 1976 (UK), also remains available on CD, although its lack of annotation frustrates. Further frustration accompanies the bewildering array of Séamus Ennis material circulated in small quantities under shifting titles between 1975 and 2002 by the Folktrax cassette label run by Peter Kennedy. These are addressed in a separate section below.

Part 1: Recordings Released During Séamus Ennis' Lifetime

Solo Albums & EPs

The Bonny Bunch Of Roses (Tradition TLP 1013) 1959
Prod: Robin Roberts / Edited: Liam Clancy
A Little Bench Of Rushes; The Kerry Recruit; The First House In Connaught/The Copper Plate Reel; The Farmer's Cursed Wife; An Leanbh Sidhe (The Fairy Boy); An Clar Bog-Deil (The Bog Deal Board); The Thrush In The Straw; The Cuckoo's Hornpipe; The Bonny Bunch Of Roses-O; Gol Na Mban 'San Ar (The Women's Lament in Battle); The Wealthy Squire; Hogan's Favourite/The Connaught Man's Rambles/The Lark In The Morning/When The Cock Crows It Is Day; Marrow Bones; Will You Come With Me Over The Mountain

Note: Reissued many times under this and other names, including in 1976 as *Irish Pipe And Tin Whistle Songs* (Olympic Records OL-6129) and *Visit To Ireland Volume Three* (Fat Boy Records FATCD 419/3). Available on CD in at least three other editions: two under the original title (albeit one using the spelling 'Bonnie'), one as *Two Centuries Of Celtic Music* (Legacy 499). In 1960 'The Fairy Boy' appeared on *The Tradition Folk Sampler* (TSP1) LP.

The Ace And Deuce Of Piping EP (Collector Records JEI 6) 1960
The Ace And Deuce Of Piping; The Dark Woman Of The Glen; Paddy O'Rafferty; Sixpenny Money; The Clay Of Kilcreggan
Note: Never available on CD. The Collector label was active in issuing folk music recordings on single and EP between 1959 and 1964, beginning with a trio of Robin Hall & Jimmie Macgregor singles in 1959. The JEI Irish music EP series, of which Séamus' sole release for the label was a part, had eight releases: JEI 1–4 were all by Dominic Behan; JEI 5 and 7 were by Joe Heaney; and JEI 8 was *Shirley Sings Irish*, by English singer Shirley Collins.

Ceol, Scéalta Agus Amhráin (Gael Linn CEF 009) 1961
Rec: Dublin
Song: Na Ceannbháin Bhána; Pipes: The Gold Ring; Song: Bean Dubh An Ghleanna; Pipes: Úirchill An Chreagáin; Song: Johnny Seoighe; Tin Whistle: Pat Ward's Hornpipe; Song: An Binsín Luachra; Pipes: Salamanca/Duke Gordon/Jenny's Welcome To Charlie; Song: Casadh An tSúgáin; Tin Whistle: An Bearach Connachtach; Song: Dónall Óg; Pipes: Cornphíopa Na Sióg
Note: Available on CD as Gael Linn CEFCD 009, 2006. The CD cover is a photo of a rather austere Séamus, taken in his later years. The original LP, now very rare, had a much more playful cover featuring a smiling painting

of Séamus with inset photos of the man as musician, singer and storyteller. Two of the pieces included here with spoken introduction tales in Irish, 'The Gold Ring' and 'The Fairies' Hornpipe' ('Cornphíopa Na Sióg'), would be revisited on his LP for Leader (below), with introductory tales in English.

Séamus Ennis (Masters Of Irish Music Series) (Leader LEA 2003) 1969
Rec: 5 Camden Villas, London / Prod: Bill Leader
A Pinch Of Snuff; The Fairies' Hornpipe; The Gold Ring; The Fairy Straying; The False Hearted Lover; Ditherum Doodah; The Bird's Chorus; The Lark In The Morning; The Lark's March
Note: Never available on CD.

Strains On Wind Once Blown – Vol. 1: The Pure Drop (Tara TARA 1002) 1973
Rec: Dublin
The Pure Drop/The Flax In Bloom; The Fairy Boy; The Groves Hornpipe/Dwyer's Hornpipe; O'Sullivan The Great; When Sick, Is It Tea You Want?/The Humours Of Drinagh; By The River Of Gems/The Rocky Road To Dublin; Ask My Father/Pat Ward's Jig; Valencia Harbour; The Standing Abbey/The Stack Of Barley; The Leitrim Thrush/Miss Johnson; The Return From Fingal; Chase Me, Charlie/The Dingle Regatta; White Connor's Daughter, Nora; Slieve Russell/Sixpenny Money; Stay For Another While/I Have No Money/The Cushogue
Note: On 2CD with *The Fox Chase* (TARA 1009) as *The Best Of Irish Piping* (TARA CD1002/9), 1995.

The Wandering Minstrel (Topic 12TS250) 1974
Rec: Livingstone Studios, Barnet / Prod: Tony Engle
The Wandering Minstrel/Jackson's Morning Brush; The Boys Of Bluehill/Dunphy's Hornpipe; The Glen-Nephin Cuckoo/The Little Fair Cannavans; The Frieze Britches; The Flags of Dublin/The Wind That Shakes The Barley; The Little Stack Of Barley/Cronin's Hornpipe; The New Demesne; The Blackbird; Gillan's Apples/The Walls Of Liscarroll/The Stone In The Field; Molly O'Malone; Kiss The Maid Behind The Barrel; Happy To Meet And Sorry To Part
Note: On two CD editions in 1993: Green Linnet GLCD 3078 and Ossian OSS CD 12. Various tracks have appeared on various-artists compilations on Topic and Globestyle/Ace, including *Gentlemen Pipers* (Globestyle/Ace ORBD 084) in 1994, which used four tracks, while 'The Blackbird' appeared on Topic's epic 7CD survey of the label's past: *Three Score And Ten: A Voice To The People* (Topic TOPIC70) in 2009. *The Wandering Minstrel* has been available since 2009 as a Topic download (TSDL250).

Forty Years Of Irish Piping (Innisfree SIF1000) 1974
Rec: Various dates and locations / Prod: Patrick Sky
The Merry Blacksmith/The Rainy Day/The Silver Spear; First You Must Learn The Grip; The Bucks Of Oranmore; The Bucks Of Oranmore/The Sligo Maid's Lament; The Praties Are Dug And The Frost Is All Over*; The Fox Chase*; If All The Young Maidens Were Blackbirds And Thrushes; The Copperplate Reel; The Silver Spear/The Dublin Reel/Miss Monahan; Salamanca/Duke Gordon; Don Niperi Septo; Donegal Reel; Paudeen O'Rafferty/The Friar's Jig; Speed The Plough/The Merry Blacksmith/The Forge Music; The Lark's March; Sixpenny Money/When The Cock Crows It Is Day*; Piper Of The Embers/Down The Back Lane/Sixpenny Money/Paudeen O'Rafferty; I'll Mend Your Pots And Kettles O; The Broken Pledge; Paddy Killoran's Reel*; Gentle Philip Fahey*

Note: Notable in being the first release on US label Innisfree (later rebranded Green Linnet), founded by Patrick Sky, and the first release on UK label Free Reed (Free Reed FRR 001/002), founded by Neil Wayne. By 1974 it was time for a Séamus Ennis 'best of'. This collection, however, has a dearth of source information. It was 'produced and recorded' by Patrick Sky, a professional recording artist with a developing interest in uilleann piping. The original LP notes conceded that the five tracks marked (*) were collected by George and Jean Ritchie Pickow, presumably during their Irish field trip in 1952. They all differ from the three Séamus recordings on the previous relevant Ritchie collections, *Field Trip* (1954) and *As I Roved Out (Field Trip – Ireland)* (1960) – details below.

The album notes do, however, thank various people, including Liam O'Flynn, Liam Clancy, Tara Records, Breandán Breathnach, the IFC and Séamus himself. (Breathnach recorded Séamus privately many times from the mid-1950s onward – the results being now accessible at the ITMA, Dublin.) The album title seems unlikely: can anything herein date back further than the mid-1940s? *Thirty Years Of Irish Piping* is perhaps more accurate. One or two tracks also play fast.

Patrick Sky: Séamus did not directly participate in the production of the album. He did write a letter of introduction that I would show to friends that [might] have recordings. The main sources of the album were Jean and George Pickow, Liam Clancy and Diane Meek. Other sources were RTÉ, my own recordings of Séamus, and various reel-to-reel and cassette recordings by people that I ran across and was introduced to by Séamus … I should have made a better effort to document the tunes, but looking back, I wasn't very interested in documentation. I could kick myself. As to *Forty Years Of Irish Piping*, the title was more of a guess than fact. Liam Clancy did tell me that some of his reel-to-reels were transferred over from older wire recordings, probably sometime in the early 40s.

Forty Years Of Irish Piping was the first album on the Innisfree record label, later becoming Green Linnet, founded by myself and Lisa Null. I produced all of the early records, such as Tim Lyons' *Easter Snow*, Tommy Reck's *The Stone In The Field*, Joe Ryan and Eddie Clarke's *Sailing Into Walpole's Marsh*, et cetera. In general I should have done a better job on *Forty Years Of Irish Piping* and other recordings.

I knew that some of the tracks were fast, but recording equipment at that time did not have the ability to speed up or slow down. Someone today could re-edit the record and correct the pitch with no problem.

Féidlim Tonn Rí's Castle Or The King Of Ireland's Son (Claddagh CC 19) 1977
Rec: Dublin
A long folk tale including the following pieces of music on pipes and whistle: The Rocky Road To Dublin; The Eagle's Whistle; The Rambling Pitchfork; The Stone In The Field; The Fisherman's Hornpipe; The Walls Of Liscarroll; The Boys Of The Lough; Banish Misfortune; Easter Snow; The Dublin Reel
Note: Never released on CD, but currently available for download via iTunes. 'Easter Snow' was later used on the 1984 label compilation *Claddagh's Choice* (Claddagh CC 40).

The Fox Chase (Tara TARA 1009) 1978
Rec: Dublin
Music At The Gate/The Pigeon On The Gate; The Blooming Meadows/Kitty's Rambles; Ned Of The Hill; Smash The Windows/The Dark Girl In Blue; The Derry Hornpipe/The

Cuckoo's Nest; The Trip We Took O'er The Mountain; The Merry Sisters/Music In The Forge/Castle Kelly; Johnny Cope; The Rainy Day/A Fair Wind; The Fox Chase; The Braes Of Busby/Colonel Frazer
Note: On 2CD with *The Pure Drop* (TARA 1002) as *The Best Of Irish Piping* (TARA CD1002/9), 1995.

Shared Albums

Seoda Ceoil 2 (Gael Linn CEF 022) 1968
Séamus Ennis, Seán Keane, Seosamh Ó hÉanaí [Joe Heaney], J.J. Gannon
Rec: Dublin
Séamus Ennis tracks: O'Calllaghan's Hornpipe; The Flags Of Dublin/Hand Me Down The Tackle; Fr. Jack Walshe; Colonel Frazer/The Braes Of Bushy; O'Keefe's Plough/The Merry Blacksmith/The Music Of The Forge
Note: Séamus' tracks are all piping tunes. Available as a 2CD with *Seoda Ceoil 1* as Gael Linn CEFCD 203.

The Drones And The Chanters: Irish Pipering (Claddagh CC 11) 1971
Rec: Dublin
Séamus Ennis tracks: Jenny's Welcome To Charlie; The Wounded Hussar; Pat Ward's; The Trip We Took Over The Mountain; Bean Dubh An Ghleanna; The Bucks Of Oranmore
Note: Shared with Leo Rowsome, Willie Clancy, Paddy Moloney, Peadar Broe, Tommy Reck and Dan Dowd, with notes by Séamus' old Radio Éireann colleague Seán Mac Réamoinn. It was the first in a proposed series of albums featuring piping from around the world. Released on CD in 2000 and on CD/download in 2011.

Appearances On Various-Artists / Themed Releases

Field Trip (Collector Limited Editions CLE 1201) 1954
Rec: Ireland
Séamus Ennis tracks: Bog Down In The Valley; Uncle Frog Went Out To Ride
Note: Recorded by Kentucky singer Jean Ritchie. On this record she shares space with singers she recorded while on a field trip through Ireland, Scotland and England in 1952-53 with George Pickow. The photo of Séamus on the cover of *The Bonny Bunch Of Roses* was taken by Pickow during this trip. On *Field Trip*, Jean often pairs her own Appalachian versions of songs with those sung by the likes of Séamus, Jeannie Robertson and Sarah Makem. On CD as *Jean Ritchie – Field Trip* (Greenhays GREEH-CD0726), 2001.

The Columbia World Library Of Folk And Primitive Music Vol. 2: Ireland (Columbia SL-204 / KL-204) 1955
Rec: Ireland
Séamus Ennis tracks: The Banks Of The Roses; The Rocks Of Bawn; The Copperplate Reel [Steven Folan/Séamus Ennis]; Whiskey In The Jar; The Woman Of The House; Molly Bawn; Were You At The Rock?; Mrs. McGrath; The Bucks Of Oranmore
Note: Recorded by Alan Lomax and Séamus Ennis (1951) and Brian George (1947) in Ireland. This was one of 18 volumes of a projected 44 compiled by Alan Lomax for Columbia Records' Masterworks between 1955 and 1964. Reissued on Columbia vinyl as ML 4941 and AKL 4941. Available on CD as Rounder CD1742, 1998.

As I Roved Out (Field Trip – Ireland) (Folkways FW 8872) 1960
Rec: Ireland
Séamus Ennis track: The Sound Of The Drum

Note: Another selection from Jean Ritchie's 1952 Irish field recording trip. Séamus here sings a brief (0:47) song collected from Colm Ó Caodháin of Glinsk: a version of 'Soldier, Soldier', one of the few Colm sang in English. Other singers featured include Sarah Makem, Elizabeth Cronin and Frank McPeake. A companion volume, *Field Trip – England* (FW 8871), was also released in 1960. Both are available from Folkways as CD or download.

A Jug Of Punch: Broadside Ballads Old And New (HMV CLP 1327) 1960
Rec: Cecil Sharp House, London / Prod: Peter Kennedy
Séamus Ennis tracks: Brian O'Linn; Football Crazy
Note: Other artists included Steve Benbow, Jimmie Macgregor, Shirley Collins and Frank McPeake. Uniquely, Séamus recorded here with others backing him: Jimmie Macgregor plays mandolin on both tracks; Vic Pitt plays bass on 'Football Crazy'. Séamus contributes tin whistle to Shirley Collins' 'Higher Germanie' and 'The Horse Named Bill' and Jimmie Macgregor's 'Grat For Gruel'. There were two other volumes in the series, all recorded at Cecil Sharp House with a similar cast: *A Pinch Of Salt* (on which Séamus also appears) and *Rocket Along*.

A Pinch Of Salt: British Sea Songs Old And New (HMV CLP 1362) 1960
Rec: Cecil Sharp House, London / Prod: Peter Kennedy
Séamus Ennis tracks: The Mary Anne McHugh; Fine Girl You Are (The Holy Ground)
Note: The second LP from the Cecil Sharp House sessions (see above). Séamus sings unaccompanied on the first track; on the second, he is backed by Perry Friedmann (banjo) and Vic Pitt (bass). Séamus contributes tin whistle to Shirley Collins' 'Long Years Ago'.

The Folk Songs Of Britain Volume I: Songs Of Courtship (Caedmon Records TC1142) 1961
Séamus Ennis tracks: The Brown Thorn; As I Roved Out
Note: Séamus contributes a pipe tune and song to this themed collection featuring traditional singers including Elizabeth Cronin, Paddy Tunney, Bob and Ron Copper, Frank McPeake and Jimmy McBeath. This was the first in a 10-volume series collected and edited by Peter Kennedy and Alan Lomax, assisted by Shirley Collins – with additional help from Séamus Ennis on this and other volumes. The series came out on Caedmon (US) in 1961 and on Topic (UK) in 1968-70.

The Folk Songs Of Britain Volume II: Songs Of Seduction (Caedmon Records TC1143) 1961
Séamus Ennis tracks: Dublin City; Behind The Bush In The Garden
Note: A song and pipe tune, respectively. Reissued in 1968 on Topic 12T158. Both of Séamus' tracks appear on an extended version of the album, with further tracks added by Peter Kennedy, released on CD in 2000 as *Folk Songs Of England, Ireland, Scotland & Wales: Songs Of Seduction* (Rounder 11661-1778-2).

The Folk Songs Of Britain Volume III: Jack Of All Trades (Caedmon Records TC1144) 1961
Séamus Ennis track: I'll Mend Your Pots And Kettles
Note: Séamus' short piping tune ends this 25-track collection. Frank McPeake also contributes a track, singing with pipes. Reissued in 1968 as Topic 12T159.

The Folk Songs Of Britain Volume IV: The Child Ballads 1 – 'The English And Scottish Popular Ballads' Numbers 2–95 (Caedmon Records TC1145) 1961
Séamus Ennis track: Captain Wedderburn's Courtship
Note: Reissued in 1968 on Topic 12T160. As with Volume II in the series, Rounder released a version on CD in 2000 with additional tracks from Peter Kennedy – making the original title even more unwieldy: *The Folk Songs Of England, Ireland, Scotland & Wales: Classic Ballads Of Britain And Ireland Volume 1: Storytelling Ballads, As Included In Francis James Child's English & Scottish Popular Ballads #2-106*. Unfortunately, Kennedy dropped Séamus' song, replacing it with an alternative version, 'Captain Woodburn', by Thomas Moran of County Leitrim. However, the missing Ennis recording reappears on Topic's 2012 3CD themed compilation *The Voice Of The People Volume 23: Good People, Take Warning* (Topic TSCD673T). The track is here titled 'Captain Wedderburn' and is the only Ennis performance on the set, which features numerous British and Irish artists recorded between the 1940s and 1960s, mostly from the Peter Kennedy archive. Séamus' performance on the 1961 LP was a Kennedy edit of 3'16", but the version on *Good People, Take Warning* is 4'10", the complete version.

Traditional Music At Newport 1964 Part 2 (Vanguard VRS 9183 / VSD 79183) 1965
Rec: Newport Folk Festival, America
Séamus Ennis tracks: Did The Rum-Do-Daddy; Piper On The Hearth; What'll Ye Do; Father's Maid
Note: Recorded at Newport, July 23-26, on Séamus' only US trip, and issued in mono and stereo versions. Séamus shares the vinyl with Mississippi John Hurt, Jean Ritchie and others. Records had been released of performances from the Newport Folk Festival since 1959, but the 1964 event would be the most heavily documented. In addition to two volumes of traditional music, there were two volumes of *The Blues At Newport 1964* and three volumes of *Evening Concerts*. All of these bar Part 2 of the blues set and Part 2 of the traditional music set (with Séamus) were also issued in Britain on Fontana. Released on CD in 1991 in Japan as *Traditional Music At Newport 1964 Part 1 And 2* (King/Vanguard KICP 2116/7).

Irish Music In London Pubs (Folkways FW03575 / FG 3575) 1965
Rec: Camden, London
Séamus Ennis tracks: Rakish Paddy (performed by Michael Gorman, Séamus Ennis and Tommy McGuire in the middle of a medley with Margaret Barry); Casadh An t-Súgáin (The Twisting Of The Hay-Rope)
Note: Recorded in mono, seemingly in 1958, at the King's Arms and the Bedford Arms by Ralph Rinzler and Barry Murphy, using equipment borrowed from Ewan MacColl. Séamus was a rare performer on the London Irish music scene. His performance here is either fortuitously captured or deliberately given (because someone was recording it). Reissued on Transatlantic's budget imprint (XTRA 1090) in 1969 under the original title but as a Margaret Barry & Michael Gorman album. Released on CD and download by Smithsonian Folkways in 2012.

Voices Of Radio 1926–1976 (EMI/RTÉ 50) 1976
Séamus Ennis track: Threshing Dance At Ballinamona, County Tipperary (1949)
Note: An LP of great orators and events from the Radio Éireann archive. Séamus' report from 1949, from his days as an Outside Broadcast Officer, follows Taoiseach Éamon De Valera's 'Reply To Churchill' from 1945. Others featured include Seán O'Casey, Brendan Behan and Patrick Kavanagh.

Our Musical Heritage (RTÉ/Funduireacht An Riadaigh FR 001/002/003) 1981
Séamus Ennis tracks: Bean Dubh A'Ghleanna; The Frieze Breeches
Note: A 3LP box set, credited to Seán Ó Riada but essentially a various-artists set, with booklet by Tomás Ó Canainn. The LPs featured music used in Seán Ó Riada's ground-breaking 1962 RTÉ radio series *Our Musical Heritage*; in many cases, performances recorded especially for the series at that time. Séamus' tracks may fall into that category. The first LP features *sean-nós* singing; the second features pipes and fiddle; the third features the flute, whistle, accordion and concertina. The other pipers featured are Johnny Doran and Tommy Reck.

Recordings As An Accompanist

So Early In The Morning: Irish Children's Traditional Songs, Rhymes And Games (Tradition TLP 1034) 1960 LP
Peg & Bobby Clancy and the Clancy Grandchildren
Rec: Ireland
Note: Séamus plays tin whistle with Bobby Clancy (guitar, harmonica) and Diane Hamilton (harp) on songs collected by Diane. Various tracks subsequently appeared on other Clancy Brothers & Tommy Makem albums, including *At Home With …* (Tradition/Everest TR 2060) in 1967 (released in the UK as Emerald Gem 1006 in 1968) and *Irish Folk Airs* (Tradition/Everest 2083), also in 1967. Available in original form on two CD editions: Tradition/Rykodisc TCD1053 (1997); Essential Media Group 942-31197-0 (2009).

The Green Crow Caws (EMI Tuatha EMA 793) 1980
Seán O'Casey
Rec: Ireland
Séamus Ennis tracks: A Rare Time For Death In Ireland; All Around Me Hat
Note: An LP tribute to playwright Seán O'Casey, arranged and associate-produced by singer/multi-instrumentalist Paul Brady. John Kavanagh is the featured singer throughout. Séamus contributes pipes to the above two tracks. The album was reissued on CD in 1993, jointly credited to Seán O'Casey and Paul Brady (See For Miles SEECD 376).

Part 2: Posthumous Releases

Master Of The Uilleann Pipes (Skylark SK 1001) 1985
Séamus Ennis
Rec: Dublin, mid-70s / Prod: Patrick Sky
Séamus Ennis introducing tunes to Patrick Sky: Callahan's Hornpipe; The Gold Ring; Jenny's Welcome To Charlie; The Monk's Jig; The Pinch Of Snuff; The Fairy Boy; The River James; The Swamp; The Lark's March; The Smoke House; The Longford Collector; The Lark's March; Munster Buttermilk; Lament For The Fox; The Fox Hunter; The Blackbird; The Humours Of Drinagh; Phillip Martin's Jig; Páidín O'Rafferty; Chief O'Neill's; The Kid On The Mountain; The Derry Hornpipe; The Bucks of Oranmore
Note: A 60-minute US cassette, released by Séamus' piping protégé Pat Sky. All but the last three tracks are recorded in a relaxed setting in good fidelity, with Séamus taking requests from Pat and one or two friends. The final three tracks are recorded at a Dublin folk club with a noisy but enthused audience. Séamus' performance of 'The Bucks Of Oranmore' is taken at manic speed but with remarkable control, the audience erupting at its conclusion. Deserving of remastering and re-release.

The Séamus Ennis Story (RTÉ MC 115) 1988
Documentary
Note: A double-cassette release in Ireland of a four-part tribute to Séamus produced by Peter Browne and broadcast on RTÉ in spring 1988. It features many of Séamus' friends reminiscing, along with music and interviews from Séamus himself, some of the music from (still) otherwise unreleased RTÉ recordings: a terrific insight into the man, now almost impossible to find.

Roaratorio (Mode 28/29) 1992
John Cage
Note: A double CD including the 60-minute 1979 recording of *Roaratorio: An Irish Circus On Finnegan's Wake For Speaker, Irish Musicians And 62-Track Tape* originally broadcast on 22/10/79 on German radio station WDR3. Musicians throughout are Paddy Glackin, Matt Molloy, Séamus Ennis, Peadar and Mel Mercier and Joe Heaney, subsumed into the avant-garde collage of sound.

The Lark In The Clear Air: Mo Cheol Thú: Ciarán Mac Mathúna Introduces Irish Music, Song And Poetry From His Popular Sunday Morning RTÉ Radio 1 Programme (RTÉ MC125) 1995
Various Artists
Note: This RTÉ cassette release includes one piping tune from Séamus, although it's unclear whether or not this is an otherwise unavailable performance.

Denis Murphy – Music From Sliabh Luachra (RTÉ CD 183) 1995
Denis Murphy
Séamus Ennis track: The Woman Of The House (with Denis and Julia Clifford on fiddles)
Note: The notes to this album on the legendary fiddler from the Sliabh Luachra (Cork/Kerry) tradition state that it was compiled from recordings made between 1948 and 1969 by Séamus Ennis, Ciarán Mac Mathúna and Aindreas Ó Gallchóir. (Séamus also made several 1947 acetate recordings of Denis for the IFC, seemingly not used herein.) Denis Murphy and Julia Clifford had already been featured on a 1977 album, with fiddler Pádraig O'Keeffe, called *Kerry Fiddles: Music From Sliabh Luachra Vol. 1* (Topic 12T309) – the content of which had been entirely recorded, for the BBC, by Séamus Ennis at Charlie Horan's Bar, Castleisland, Co. Kerry, on 9/9/52. The Topic album included no performances from Séamus himself. On this RTÉ release, Séamus' trio recording with Denis and Julia is attributed to an undated session for Raidió Na Gaeltachta (RTÉ's Irish-language service). Bafflingly, Raidió Na Gaeltachta was only founded in 1972, without the 1948-69 span stated in the notes.

Ceol Na hÉireann: The Traditional Music Of Ireland From The Sound Archives Of RTÉ (RTÉ CEOCD 001) 1996
Various Artists
Séamus Ennis track: Reels: The Silver Spear/ The Dublin Reel
Note: Includes apparently otherwise unreleased performances by Planxty, The Bothy Band, The Chieftains, Seán Ó Riada and others. Séamus' track was the blistering 1959 performance from a concert in Clare subsequently included on *The Return From Fingal* (RTÉ 199CD).

The Return From Fingal (RTÉ 199CD) 1997
Séamus Ennis
Rec: Ireland, 1940-80
Bonny Kate/The Milliner's Daughter/The Flannel Jacket (1940); The Pipe On The Hob/An Buachaillín Buí/East Of Glendart (1940); An Droighnean Donn/The Garden Of Daisies (1940); The Bantry Hornpipe/

The Pleasures Of Hope (1940); Smash The Windows/The Drops Of Brandy/The Tenpenny Piece/A Fig For A Kiss (1940); The Mountain Lark/The Sligo Maid's Lament/The Flax In Bloom (1940); The Tailor's Twist/Kelly's Hornpipe (1940); The Ace And Deuce Of Piping (1940); The Fair-Haired Girl/The Bucks Of Oranmore (1940); Ballymanus Fair/The Standing Abbey (1940); The Gold Ring/Úirchill An Chreagain (1948); The Salamanca/Hand Me Down The Tackle (1948); The Return From Fingal (1948); An Droimeann Donn Dilis (1949); An Cruiscin Lan; Eamon A' Chnoic; Seán Ó Duibhir An Ghleanna; Tatter Jack Walsh (1950); The Butcher's March/When The Cock Crows It Is Day/Sixpenny Money (1959); The Silver Spear/The Dublin Reel (1959); Ballymanus Fair (1971); Lady Carbury (The Mason's Apron) (1975); The Frieze Breeches (1975); The Morning Thrush (1980); The Dusty Miller (1978); Easter Snow (1978)

Note: The best of Séamus' surviving Radio Éireann and RTÉ recordings, with a well annotated booklet from producer Peter Browne. This is the most essential of all Séamus' instrumental releases.

Song Of A Road (Topic TSCD802) 1999
Various Artists
Rec: London / Prod: Ewan MacColl, Peggy Seeger, Charles Parker
Séamus Ennis track: Hot Asphalt
Note: Originally broadcast in 1959, this was the second of Parker, MacColl and Seeger's eight BBC 'Radio Ballads', this one on motorway building. See 'Séamus Ennis At The BBC' chapter.

Past Masters Of Irish Dance Music (Topic Records TSCD604) 2000
Various Artists
Séamus Ennis track: Reels: The Cavan Brigade/When The Cock Crows It Is Day/Sixpenny Money

Note: A compilation of Irish music spanning 1927-49, restored from British, Irish and American 78rpm discs plus a few 2RN and BBC recordings. Séamus' track is from his BBC Library session at Broadcasting House, London, 22/9/49.

Sing Christmas And The Turn Of The Year: The Live Christmas Day 1957 Broadcast On BBC Radio (Rounder 11661-1850-2) 2000
Various Artists
Séamus Ennis track: The Dublin Reel
Note: Dragged from Peter Kennedy's bottom drawer. As well as his featured track, Séamus had been booked to play tin whistle, pipes and sing in chorus, so he is no doubt part of the melee throughout. See 'Séamus Ennis At The BBC' chapter.

Tuning The Radio: Early Traditional Music Recordings From The RTÉ Libraries And Archives (RTÉ285CD) 2010
Various Artists
Séamus Ennis track: The First House In Connaught/Miss Monaghan
Note: Featuring a 1940s photo of Séamus with his Radio Éireann Outside Broadcast colleagues on the cover, this includes the above performance recorded on 7/11/40, when Séamus was just 21 and which is otherwise unavailable, not being among the 1940 tracks on RTÉ's 1997 Ennis CD *The Return From Fingal*. This release also includes a unique Leo Rowsome performance.

King's Head Folk Club: Traditional Performers At This London Folk Club 1968-1970 (Musical Traditions MTCD356-7) 2012
Various Artists
Séamus Ennis tracks: Kitty From Ballinamore; Fairies' Hornpipe; Pinch Of Snuff; False Bride
Note: These tracks were recorded at Séamus'

King's Head club performance on 16/7/69, the night before he recorded *Masters Of Irish Music*. Run by Rod and Danny Stradling between 1968 and 1970, and booking exclusively traditional performers, the club was modelled on Bob Davenport's 1964-66 club at the Fox in Islington. Many of the King's Head performers were recorded on reel-to-reel, hence this expertly annotated souvenir in 2012 on Rod's own label. From his notes: 'Séamus was a great hero of anyone interested in traditional music; singer, astonishing piper and a wonderful storyteller. That night there were more people in the club room than you would believe possible!' Photos from this King's Head gig adorn the covers of both *Masters Of Irish Music* (1969) and *The Wandering Minstrel* (1974). Available from www.mustrad.org.uk

Part 3: The Folktrax Releases 1975–2002

Séamus' rarest albums are the four 'released' in surely very limited form on cassette by his former BBC colleague Peter Kennedy. Kennedy remains controversial for his views and practices around intellectual property in traditional music. Setting aside arguments on his right to exploit material actually recorded by himself from traditional musicians, often while employed for the BBC under its not-for-profit field recording scheme in the 1950s, his subsequent cassette label Folktrax also marketed his off-air copies of BBC broadcasts and, in Séamus' case, an album's worth of master-quality material recorded for the BBC Permanent Library with its provenance disguised. Séamus was presumably at least aware of *Music At The Gate* in 1975; his three other full albums on Folktrax appeared in the year of his death. There are several other themed albums from Folktrax that also include possibly exclusive Séamus Ennis tracks, along with at least three albums sourced from BBC broadcasts that certainly do – all of which are detailed below. The ITMA in Dublin holds digitised copies of most of this material. The Kennedy archive is now owned jointly by the British Library and Topic Records, who have to date used some of it within their ongoing *Voice Of The People* series of themed multi-disc sets.

Séamus Ennis Albums On Folktrax

Music At The Gate (Folktrax 079) 1975
My Father And Mother Were Irish; The Banks Of The Roses; Molly Bawn; The Praties Are Dug; The New Demesne; The Bonny Boy Is Young But He's Growing; The Whistling Thief; The Trip Over The Mountain; Brian O'Linn; Captain Wedderburn's Courtship; The Mountain Dew; Uncle Rat Went Out To Ride; The Boyne Hunt; Sho-Hee Sho-Sho; Music At The Gate; The Old Orange Flute; Calm Avonree; Cucanandy Nandy/The Old Woman Tossed Up In A Blanket; Lord Gregory; The Brown Thorn; Football Crazy; The Herring Song
Note: Purportedly recorded by Peter Kennedy in London, 22/3/58 – which is probably true. It includes: 15 songs in English with one, a fairy lullaby, in Gaelic; two dandling songs; five tunes on pipes; some mouth-music, tin whistle and fiddle playing. While seven song titles overlap with material recorded by Séamus during his September 1949 BBC sessions, the timings are all markedly different. This set would appear to be a genuine Peter Kennedy recording. This recording of 'Captain Wedderburn's Courtship' is almost certainly the one Kennedy edited for use on *The Folk Songs Of Britain Volume IV: The Child Ballads 1 – 'The English And Scottish Popular Ballads' Numbers 2-95* (Caedmon Records TC1145) in 1961, which was later restored to full length in 2012 on Topic's *The Voice Of The People*

Volume 23: Good People, Take Warning (Topic TSCD673T). It seems possible that 'The Brown Thorn' here was also the one used by Kennedy on another LP in the Caedmon series, *The Folk Songs Of Britain Volume I: Songs Of Courtship* (Caedmon Records TC1142) in 1961.

John Airy: Séamus Ennis Stories & Pipe Tunes aka ***The Fairy Piper*** (Folktrax 302) 1982
John Airy And St Peter; The Three Daughters; Henry Bohannon And The Fairy Piper; The Lark's March; The Bachelor And The Fairy Wedding + The Pinch Of Snuff; The Fairy Hornpipe; The Little Fairy Ring + Golden Jig; The Fairy Feast + The Fairy Straying; I'll Mend Your Pots And Kettles; The Frieze Breeches
Note: Seven stories (the title one 20 minutes long) and seven pipe tunes, purportedly recorded by Alan Lomax, George Pickow and Peter Kennedy in 1952. *John Airy* seems to have been the original title, although online sources suggest the latter title was also used at some point. It would appear, based on a sampling of parts of this album at the ITMA, that – barring the long title track – most or all of the tracks, their titles altered, are lifted from the 1969 Leader LP *Masters Of Irish Music*.

Rocking The Cradle (Folktrax 169) 1982
The Limerick Rake; Will You Marry Me?; Soldier, Soldier; Green Grass It Grows Bonny; The Rare Bog, A Rattling Bog (The Tree Down In The Valley); The Summer Is Come; Uncle Frog; Dance To Your Daddy-O; Molly Malone; If All The Young Maidens; The Woman Of The Fairy Mound; The Stolen Pig; Mrs McGrath; Too Much Butter; The Lost Puppy; As I Walked Through Dublin City; I'll Go To Kannore; Lullaby; The Old Man Rocking The Cradle
Note: Mostly children's songs, some in English and some in Gaelic, purportedly recorded by Peter Kennedy in London, 1958. 'Dublin City' is likely the version Kennedy used on *The Folk Songs Of Britain Volume II: Songs Of Seduction* (Caedmon Records TC1143) in 1961. It also seems probable that at least three performances come from the Jean Ritchie/George Pickow recordings of 1952: 'The Rare Bog …' aka 'Bog Down In The Valley' and 'Uncle Frog', which had appeared in 1954 on *Field Trip*, and 'Soldier, Soldier' aka 'The Sound Of The Drum', which had appeared in 1960 on *As I Roved Out (Field Trip – Ireland)*. And, yes: it's hard to make sense of the Folktrax catalogue number and release date.

The Morning Brush aka ***The Mountain Of Women*** aka ***The Pied Piper Of Dublin*** (Folktrax 374) 1982
The Mountain Of The Women; The Lament Of The Fox; The Morning Brush/The Dublin Reel; Chief O'Neill's/The Boys Of Bluehill; Jockey To The Fair; Tatter Jack Welch/Paddy O'Rafferty; The Groves; The Connaught Heifer/The Braes Of Busby; The Dark Lady Of The Glen; The Leitrim Lilt; Kelly's/Ballymanus Fair; Were You At The Rock?; Twisting The Hayrope; Cavan Brigade/When The Cock Crows/Sixpenny Money; Rainy Day/Merry Blacksmith's/Miss Lane's Fancy
Note: Purportedly recorded by Peter Kennedy in London, 22/3/58, this in fact constitutes almost all of Séamus' two piping sessions for the BBC Permanent Library on 22/9/49 and 7/2/58. The only items missing are 'Tuning-Up/Dublin Reel' and 'Tipperary Wedding' from the 1949 session. *The Morning Brush* appears to have been the original title of this release – a miscrediting of 'The Morning Thrush' (composed by Séamus' father), Kennedy possibly assuming it was 'Jackson's Morning Brush'. Séamus is on superb form throughout, especially on 'Were You At The Rock?' and 'Twisting The Hayrope'.

BBC Broadcasts Featuring Séamus Ennis On Folktrax Albums

Wassail Wassail (Folktrax 253) 2002
Séamus Ennis tracks: The Merry Blacksmith/ Mrs McLeod's (pipes), with Peter Kennedy (fiddle); Untitled Jig (whistle); The Mountain Dew (song); Jennie Jenkins (song), with Brian George; Kelly's/Off To California (pipes), with Peter Kennedy (melodeon)
Note: This release comprises two episodes from the BBC series *As I Roved Out*, the first (from 27/12/53) being a Christmas session in a Sussex pub with Séamus, Bob and Ron Copper, Isla Cameron and others.

The Gaelic West – The West of Ireland & The Western Isles (Folktrax 275) 2002
Séamus Ennis tracks: Soldier, Soldier; Were You At The Rock?/The Bucks Of Oranmore
Note: A 1951 BBC programme presented by Séamus, which includes the above performances (see 'Séamus Ennis At The BBC' chapter).

Alan Lomax Presents Sing Christmas 1957 (Folktrax 950) 2002
Note: The same BBC broadcast that Kennedy supplied to Rounder for their 2000 CD *Sing Christmas And The Turn Of The Year: The Live Christmas Day 1957 Broadcast On BBC Radio*.

Various-Artists Folktrax Albums Including Séamus Ennis

As I Roved Out: Songs Of Courtship (Folktrax 60013) Undated, probably 1975

A-Going To The Fair: Songs Of Diversion (Folktrax 60027) 1975

The Seeds Of Love: A Study Of English Folksong (Folktrax 60136) 1979
Blow The Winds-i-o: Ballads Of Storm & Shipwreck (Folktrax 60512) 1979

The White Cockade: Ballads Of Soldiers And Sweethearts (Folktrax 60518) 1979

Finbar & Eddie Furey Discography 1968–76

Albums & Singles 1968–76

I Know Where I'm Going (Waverley ZLP 2104) 1968
Paddie Bell with Finbar & Eddie Furey
Rec: Edinburgh, late 1967/early 1968
Personnel: Paddie Bell – vocal, guitar (P); Tom Smith – guitar (T); Finbar – pipes (F); Eddie – guitar, bodhrán (E)
I Know Where I'm Going (P, F, E); The Lark In The Morning (F, E); Come By The Hills (P, T); Star Of The Munster (F, E); The Lark In The Clear Air (P); Pretty Saro (F, E); If I Were A Blackbird (P, T); Three Lovely Lassies From Bannion (P, T); The Sligo Maid (F, E); The Verdant Braes Of Screen (P,F,E); Down By The Sally Gardens (P, T); The Spanish Lady (F, E); My Lagan Love (P); Róisín Dhu (F, E)
Note: Released in an alternative sleeve on Capitol (USA) in 1968 and in another alternative sleeve on EMI (Ireland) in 1974, credited to 'Eddie & Finbar Furey with Paddie Bell'. On CD with Paddie's previous LP: *Paddie Herself/I Know Where I'm Going* (Alauda Records, 2001). The original sleeve misspells Finbar as 'Finbah'.

Finbar & Eddie Furey (Transatlantic TRA168) 1968
Prod: Bill Leader / Rec: London, 1968 / Rel: August 1968
The Spanish Cloak; Come By The Hills;

Sliabh Na mBan (The Mountain Of The Women); Dainty Davy; Tattered Jack Welch; The Flowers In The Valley; Pigeon On The Gate; Graham's Flat; Leezy Lindsay; Piper In The Meadow Straying; The Curragh Of Kildare; Eamonn An Chnuic (Ned Of The Hills); This Town Is Not Your Own; Rocking The Baby

Traditional Irish Pipe Music (Transatlantic XTRA1077) 1969
Finbar Furey
Prod: Bill Leader / Rec: Livingstone Studios, Barnet, c. February–March 1969 / Rel: July 1969
Rakish Paddy; The Hag With The Money; Castle Terrace; Madame Bonaparte*; The Young Girl Milking Her Cow; Fin's Favourite; Peter Byrne's Fancy; O'Rourke's Reel; Roy's Hands*; Planxty Davy; The Bonny Bunch Of Roses; Eddie's Fancy; The Silver Spear
Note: A 24-minute solo LP, but with Eddie backing on (*). Reissued in Germany in an alternative sleeve in 1974 (Transatlantic: TRANS 201029) and in the US in 1972, in another alternative sleeve, as *The Irish Pipes Of Finbar Furey* (Nonesuch H72048).

The Lonesome Boatman (Transatlantic TRA191) 1969
Finbar & Eddie Furey
Prod: Bill Leader / Rec: Livingstone Studios, Barnet, c. February–March 1969 / Rel: July 1969
Bill Hart's Favourite; Dance Around The Spinning Wheel; Let Me Go To The Mountains; McShane; Colonel Fraser; The Lonesome Boatman; Carron Lough Bay; The Prickly Bush; Bogy's Bonny Belle; The Fox Chase
Note: In 1979, The Fureys & Davey Arthur released a re-recording of 'The Lonesome Boatman' as a single A-side in Ireland (Banshee Records SHE 003).

The Bold Fenian Men (Columbia CS 9805 USA / CBS 63635 UK) 1969
The Clancy Brothers & Tommy Makem
Prod: Teo Macero / Rec: London, late 1968 / Rel: 1969
Bold Tenant Farmer; Seeds Of Love; Navvy Boots; The Banks Of The Roses; Early Morning Rain; Fare Thee Well Enniskillen; All For My Grog; Come By The Hills; (Down By The Glen) The Bold Fenian Men; Frog In The Well; The Old Triangle
Note: Finbar & Eddie are uncredited backing musicians.

The Clancy Brothers Christmas (Columbia USA) 1969
The Clancy Brothers
Prod: Teo Macero / Rec: London, August 1969 / Rel: late 1969 (USA only)
Jingle Bells (Buala Bas); Sing We The Virgin Mary; The Holly Tree; Angels We Have Heard; When Joseph Was An Old Man; Christmas In Carrick; Silent Night; Lovely Far Off City; Christ Child Lullaby; Curoo, Curoo; The Wren Song
Note: Finbar & Eddie are uncredited.

Flowers In The Valley (CBS UK / Columbia US) UK 1969 / US 1970
The Clancy Brothers
Prod: Teo Macero / Rec: London, August 1969 / Rel: late 1969
Beer, Beer, Beer; Dirty Old Town; Flowers In The Valley; Easy And Slow; Banks Of Sicily; Sullivan's Son; Jennifer Gentle; The Upside Down Blackbird; Water Is Alright In Tay; Bill Brown; Cruiskeen Lawn
Note: Finbar & Eddie are uncredited.

Beer, Beer, Beer / Jennifer Gentle (Columbia 4-45014) 1969
The Clancy Brothers
Rel: 15/10/69
Note: A single from *Flowers In The Valley*. The B-side is credited 'E. Furey, F. Furey' but is

solely an Eddie Furey composition. In 1979 The Fureys & Davey Arthur released a re-recording of 'Beer! Beer! Beer!' as a single in Ireland (Banshee Records SHE 004).

The Dawning Of The Day (Dawn DNLS 3037) 1972
Finbar & Eddie Furey
Prod: Barry Murray / Rec: 1972 / Rel: May 1972
Drops Of Brandy; My Lagan Love; Farewell To Tarwathy; Locks And Bolts; William Hollander; Crowley's Reel; Jennifer Gentle; Barney Hare; Her Father Didn't Like Me Anyway; Reynardine; The French Drink Wine; Blackbird; The Dawning Of The Day; Coppers And Brass; Tie The Bonnet; Sally Sits Weeping
Note: Brian Brocklehurst plays bass throughout.

Her Father Didn't Like Me Anyway / Reynardine (Dawn DNS 1025) 1972
Finbar & Eddie Furey
Rel: 19/5/72
Note: A single from *The Dawning Of The Day*. A re-recording by The Fureys & Davey Arthur was released as a single by Polydor Ireland in 1977.

Four Green Fields (Plane S12 F200) 1972
Eddie & Finbar Furey
Prod: Conny Plank / Rec: Windrose Studio, Hamburg, February 1972
Enniskillin Dragoon; Lark In The Morning; October Song*; Rocky Road Reel; Four Green Fields; Lonesome Boatman; Night Visiting Song; The Ould Bush; Highland Paddle; Terror Time; Roy's Hands*
Note: A German release with Wolfgang Florey (cello) on (*). Also released in France on Arfolk. Released on CD in 1993 and in 2003.

A Dream In My Hand (Intercord Xenophon 26 429-1) 1974
Eddie & Finbar Furey
Prod: Carsten Linde/Eddie & Finbar Furey / Rec: Windrose Studio, Hamburg, January 1974
Lark On The Strand/Bunch Of Keys; Cock Of The North; Pipe On The Hob; Dónal Óg; Road To Derrytown; Pollution*; Peggy And The Soldier; Seán The Ceo; Glen In Ahadoe; Life Is Just That Way; John Blunt; Plains Of Waterloo
Note: A Germany-only release. Jörg Suckow plays bass and cello on (*).

Irish Folk Festival: Live 1974 (Intercord Xenophon INT 181.000) 1974
Various
Prod: Carsten Linde / Rec: Stadthalle, Karlsruhe, 4/5/74
Finbar & Eddie Furey: Cock Of The North; Uilleann Pipes Introduction/Anac Cuan; The Town I Love So Well
Eddie Furey: The Whole World Turning Paddie
The Furey Family (Ted, George, Paul, Eddie, Finbar): The Cry Of The Workers/Tie The Bonnet/Rakish Paddie
The Furey Brothers: I Know Where I'm Going
All Musicians (finale): The Fox Hunter's Reel & Jigging In Germany; Sally Gardens; The Dingle Regatta
Note: A Germany-only double LP from a multi-artist tour. Other artists featured are: Ted Furey & George Furey; Bobby Clancy; The Buskers; Miko Russell.

I Live Not Where I Love (Intercord Xenophon INT 161.010) 1975
Eddie & Finbar Furey
Prod: Carsten Linde/Finbar & Eddie Furey / Rec: Conny Plank's studio, Neunkirchen, May 1975
I Live Not Where I Love; The Wind That

Shakes The Barley; Lord Lovell; Hush Hush; The Road To Ballyer; St. Patrick's Day; Crossmaglen; Matt Highland; Miss McDonald's/Tarbolton; Whiskey In Me Tay; Tribute To Leo Rowsome; Wounded Knee
Note: A Germany-only release. Reissued on CD by Claddagh in 2008. While only Finbar and Eddie are credited, the back cover also states: 'Special thanks to our brothers George & Paul and to Davey Arthur for the help in making this record.'

The Farewell Album (Intercord Xenophon INT 181.010) 1976
Eddie & Finbar Furey
Prod: Carsten Linde/Eddie & Finbar Furey / Rec: Conny Plank's studio, Neunkirchen and Folk Club Witten, June 1976
STUDIO DISC: Pretty Saro; Carsten's Jig; The Grimsby Lads; Graham's Flat; The Grave Of Wolfe Tone; Spalpin Aroon/Kiss The Maid Behind The Barrel; She Came To Me; Boat Me Over; Ted Furey's Fancy/The Skylark; Leaving Belfast Town; Ban Dubh Aglana; William Hollander; She's Touched You
LIVE DISC: The Bold Tenant Farmer; Lord Gregory; Fin's Favourite/Sixpenny Money; I Live Not Where I Love; The Dowie Dens Of Yarrow; From Clare To Here; The West Wind; Still He Sings; Princess Royal; Farewell To Tarwathie; Ned Of The Hill; The Lancashire Lads
Note: A Germany-only double LP. Hannes Wader is credited with 'vocal, guitar', presumably on the studio disc. As with the previous LP, the back cover states: 'Special thanks to our brothers George & Paul and to Davey Arthur for the help in making this record.' The live disc is clearly a recording featuring the line-up that would become, via Tam Linn, The Fureys & Davey Arthur.

Finbar & Eddie Furey BBC Sessionography 1967–75

BBC Radio

(?) *Night Ride*, BBC Radio 1
Rec: 27/8/69 / Tx: 10/9/69
Note: The BBC contract lists this as 'John Peel Programme', with the producer as Pete Ritzema; the title of Peel's 1969 Wednesday night show was *Night Ride*. Ken Garner's two rigorous books on BBC radio sessions have missed this one – although they include all the other Finbar & Eddie broadcasts for Peel, most (though not all) of which have surviving contracts. Garner's research method was 'Programmes As Broadcast' files rather than contract files, although no set of extant BBC paperwork is 100 per cent accurate. Suggestively, one session that was certainly broadcast on 10/9/69, by the little-known Andy Fernbach, was recorded on 27/8/69 by Pete Ritzema, at Maida Vale studios, London. Conceivably, both the Fureys and Fernbach could have been recorded, a three-hour session each, on the same day. The Furey contract requires '25 minutes approximately' of music. Finbar & Eddie were certainly in England at the time – recording with the Clancy Brothers and performing at least once, on 22/8/69 in Bradford. It's possible that this session might have been cancelled for reasons unknown – although when that was the case the contract was usually stamped 'cancelled'.

Country Meets Folk, BBC Radio 1 and 2
Rec/Tx: 6/12/69 from the Playhouse Theatre, London / Prod: Bill Bebb
Note: Wally Whyton introduces the Fureys plus The Johnny Young Four, surprise guests and Brian Brocklehurst on bass.

Country Meets Folk, BBC Radio 1 and 2
Rec: 14/11/70 at the Playhouse Theatre, London / Tx: 21/11/70 / Prod: Colin Chandler
Note: Wally Whyton introduces the brothers plus The Spinners, The Hillsiders and a surprise guest, with Brian Brocklehurst on bass.

Folk On Friday, BBC Radio 2
Rec: 17/11/70 at the Playhouse Theatre, London / Tx: 27/11/70 / Prod: Frances Line
Note: Jim Lloyd introduces the Fureys and Mike Harding.

Country Meets Folk, BBC Radio 2
Rec: 13/2/71 at the Playhouse Theatre, London / Tx: 14/2/71; repeated 20/2/71 / Prod: Bill Bebb
Note: Wally Whyton introduces The High Level Ranters and Mr Fox, plus Brian Brocklehurst on bass with the Fureys. Their fee on this occasion was £18.

Twelve Noon, BBC Radio 4
Rec/Tx: 5/5/71 from Edinburgh.

Country Meets Folk, BBC Radio 2
Rec/Tx: 29/1/72 from the Playhouse Theatre, London / Prod: Bill Bebb
Note: This was rearranged from an original booking for the edition broadcast on 18/12/71 – presumably the chaps had a clash of engagements. Wally Whyton introduces the show, also featuring The Southern Ramblers, The Yetties and Alan Taylor, with Brian Brocklehurst on bass.

Folk On Sunday, BBC Radio 2
Rec: 13/6/72 / Tx: 30/7/72 / Prod: Frances Line
Note: The contract asks for five numbers, three of them 'bright', not more than 15 minutes in duration. Presented by Jim Lloyd.

Curiously, the BBC WAC artist file on Finbar & Eddie Furey ends at this point. However, Ken Garner, working from different files (see above), documents four further sessions, all for John Peel, listed below along with the track titles as they were scribbled down (sometimes inaccurately) by the engineer on the day.

Top Gear, BBC Radio 1
Rec: 12/6/72 / Tx: 27/6/72 / Prod: Bob Conduct
Tracks: The Bonnet/Crowley's; Reynardine; Spanish Cloak/Dingle Regatta; Pretty Sara; Farewell To Tarwathy

Top Gear, BBC Radio 1
Rec: 7/11/72 / Tx: 9/1/73 / Prod: Bob Conduct
Tracks: Jennifer Gentle; Bobly And Spike's Reel; Life Is Just That Way; Tattered Jack Walsh

Folk On 2, BBC Radio 2
Rec: ? / Tx: 20/11/72 / Prod: Frances Line
Note: Jim Lloyd introduces a Christmas Céilí with The Ranchers, Finbar & Eddie Furey and Barry Skinner.

Top Gear, BBC Radio 1
Rec: 5/11/74 / Tx: 14/5/74
Tracks: Peggy And The Soldier; John Peel's Favourite Pipe Jig; Lament For Anacuion/Ace And Deuce Of Pipery; Sailor Come Home From The Sea; Crowley's Reel

Top Gear, BBC Radio 1
Rec: 25/2/75 / Tx: 3/3/75
Tracks: Tam Linn's Opener; Gypsey Davey; Ask Me Father; Heart's Lament
Note: Recorded at Maida Vale, producer unknown, as 'Tam Linn' (forerunner to The Fureys & Davey Arthur) with Finbar, Eddie, Paul and Davey Arthur.

BBC TV

Degrees Of Folk, BBC1
Rec: 12/12/67 / Tx: 10/6/68
Note: Hosted by The Corries and filmed at a different UK university each week. This debut episode was live at Napier College, Edinburgh, and also featured one Bernadette, and The Manhattan Brothers. Finbar & Eddie's fee was £35.

Corrie Folk, BBC1
Rec: 19/2/69 / Tx: 1969
Note: Filmed live at Hamilton College of Education in Scotland, with rehearsals the previous day.

Se Ur Beatha, BBC Scotland
Rec: 12/7/70 / Tx: 1970?
Note: The producer, John McPherson, asked for two instrumentals: one pipes/guitar, one whistle/bodhrán, requesting 'Pigeon On The Gate' and 'Tattered Jack Welch'.

Roy Castle Beats Time, BBC1
Rec: ? / Tx: 16/5/75
Note: As *Radio Times* put it, 'Roy meets music-makers from Scotland, Ireland and Wales.' Guests were Finbar Furey, The Alexander Brothers, The Pontarddulais Male Voice Choir and The Ted Kavanagh Irish Dancers.

Paddy Keenan Select Discography

Paddy Keenan has a slender discography. Aside from a few recordings as a sideman (including the Gael Linn solo albums from Tríona Ní Dhomhnaill and Maighréad Ní Dhomhnaill in 1974 and 1976 respectively), his oeuvre consists of five albums more or less under his own name, two albums with The Blacksmiths (which he'd rather forget about) and four albums as a member of The Bothy Band.

The Bothy Band LPs were originally released in Ireland on Mulligan and in the UK on Polydor. The fate of these albums since then is a sorry tale. One posthumous BBC concert set was released in 1998.

During the course of working on this book, it was a pleasure to initiate, with Dónal Lunny's authority, a deeper trawl of extant BBC recordings, with a view to a band-approved album drawn from these sources. Hopefully such a disc will be released, on Hux Records, in 2015.

Solo & Duo Albums

Paddy Keenan (Gael Linn CEFC045) 1975
Paddy Keenan
The Steam Packet/McLeod's Reel; Drops Of Brandy; The Lark In The Strand; The Humours Of Ballyconnell/Toss The Feathers; Dunphy's Hornpipe/The High Level; Tarbolton/The Longford Collector; Barbara Allen; Coppers And Brass/The Rambling Pitchfork; The Ace And Deuce Of Piping; The Blackbird; The Job Of Journeywork; Farewell To Erin/The Youngest Daughter; Paddy Keenan's Jig; The Swallow's Tail; The Wild Irishman/The Sailor's Bonnet; Colonel Frazer/My Love Is In Amerikay
Note: With John Keenan, Thomas Keenan and Paddy Glackin.

Doublin' (Tara TARA2007) 1978
Paddy Keenan & Paddy Glackin
Reels: The Mountain Road/The Congress Reel; Hornpipes: The Plains Of Boyle/Cronin's Hornpipe; Reel: Castlekelly; Reel:

The Bunch Of Keys; Jigs: Tripping Up The Stairs/Fraher's Jig; Reel: Jenny's Welcome To Charlie; Reels: The Boyne Hunt/Toss The Feathers; Reels: The Dublin Reel/The Woman of The House; Jigs: The Sporting Pitchfork/The Rambling Pitchfork; Reels: Last Night's Fun/The Salamanca; Jigs: My Darling Asleep/Garrett Barry's Jig; Slow Air: Róisín Dubh; Reels: The Old Bush/The Bucks Of Oranmore
Note: With Dónal Lunny and Noel Kenny.

Poirt An Phíobaire (Gael Linn CEF099) 1983
Paddy Keenan & Arty McGlynn
Condon's Frolics/The Eavesdropper; The Factory Girl; Man Of The House; The Maid Behind The Bar/O'Rourke's/Eilish Brogan; The Monaghan Twig/Collier's; The Ballintore Jig; Marig Ar Pollanton/Cahir's Kitchen; O'Neill's March; Jezaique; The Green Gates/George White's Favourite; Cape Clear

Ná Keen Affair (Hot Conya HCR01) 1997
Paddy Keenan
Jenny's Wedding/Craig's Pipes; The Cuckoo's Nest; The Flagstones Of Memories/Anderson's/Molly Bawn; Killdevil Air; The Corner House/Paddy Taylor's/Reevey's; Herb Reid's/She Said She Couldn't Dance/Shooting The Bull; Dinny O'Brien's/The Garden Of Daisies; Andy McGann's/The Old Copperplate; Johnny's Tune, For The Avalon; Scotch Mary/The Earl's Chair/Pigeon On The Gate; Out On The Ocean; Bonny Kate/Rakish Paddy/The Ivy Leaf
Note: With Arty McGlynn, Tommy Peoples, Séamus Creagh, Niall Vallely, Tommy O'Sullivan and others.

The Long Grazing Acre (Hot Conya HCR03) 2002
Paddy Keenan & Tommy O'Sullivan
Jigs: The Lost And Found/The Hag At The Churn/The Wind Off The Lake; Tunes:

Eímhín's/Cahír's Kitchen; Song: The Maids of Culmore; Reels: O'Rourke's/The Spike Island Lassies/Lord McDonald; Tune: Jutland; Jigs: Brother John/The Pavee Jig; Song: Stranger To Himself; Jigs: Sliabh Russell/The Blarney Pilgrim/The Clare Jig; Tune: Mary Bravender; Reels: Antara/The Twirly Haired Girl/The Mountain Road; Song: Killing The Blues; Jigs: Kitty O'Neil's/The Kerry Jig
Note: With James Blennerhassett, Stephen Housden, Greg Sheehan, Tríona Ní Dhomhnaill and others.

The Blacksmiths

Merrily Kissed The Quaker (EMI/Aran ISLE3010ARAN) 1974
Arthur McBride; Denis Murphy; O'Keeffe's; The Skillet Pot; Tabhair Dom Do Lámh; Go To Sea Once More; The Foxhunter's; Cooley's Reel; Merrily Kissed The Quaker; The Jolly Beggarman; The Rakes Of Mallow; Grafton Street; Nancy Whiskey; The Bucks Of Oranmore; Planxty Irwin; The Blacksmith; Duelling Bodhráns; Whiskey In The Jar
Note: Also issued as Bellaphon BI15167 (1975).

The Blacksmiths 2 (EMI/Talisman STAL1048) 1976
The Circle; Amazing Grace; Morrison's Jig; Farewell To Erin; The Whistling Gypsy; A Job Of Journeywork; Theme From Deliverance; Reel On The Flute; The Lively Reel; Rag Time Annie; The Lark In The Morning; The Blacksmith; Bill Harte's Jig; Scottish Jig; Arthur McBride; Cooley's Reel; Amazing Grace

The Bothy Band

The Bothy Band (aka 1975) (Mulligan LUN 02) 1975
The Kesh Jig/Give Us A Drink Of Water/The Flower Of The Flock/Famous Ballymote; The

Green Groves Of Erin/The Flowers Of Red Hill; Do You Love An Apple; Julia Delaney; Patsy Geary's/Coleman's Cross; Is Trua Nach Bhfuil Mé In Éirinn; The Navvy On The Line/The Rainy Day; The Tar Road To Sligo/Paddy Clancy's; Martin Wynne's/The Longford Tinker; Pretty Peg/Craig's Pipes; Hector The Hero/The Laird Of Drumblaire; The Traveller/The Humours Of Lissadel; The Butterfly; The Salamanca/The Banshee/The Sailor's Bonnet

Old Hag You Have Killed Me (Mulligan LUN 007) 1976
Music In The Glen; Fionnghuala; The Laurel Tree; Farewell To Erin; Maid Of Coolmore; The Kid On The Mountain; Cunla; Untitled Reel; Sixteen Come Next Sunday; The Ballintore Fancy; Calum Sgaire; Old Hag You Have Killed Me; Tiocfaidh An Samhradh (Summer Will Come); Michael Gorman's

Out Of The Wind Into The Sun (Mulligan LUN 013) 1977
The Morning Star/The Fisherman's Lilt/ The Drunken Landlady; The Maids Of Mitchelstown; The Leitrim Fancy/Round The World For Sport/Rip The Calico/ Untitled Reel/ The Enchanted Lady/The Holy Land; The Streets Of Derry; The Pipe On The Hob/The Hag At The Churn; The Sailor Boy; The Blackbird; The Strayaway Child; The Factory Girl; The Priest/Mary Willie's/This Is My Love, Do You Like Her?

After Hours (Mulligan LUN 030) 1979
The Kesh Jig/Give Us A Drink Of Water/ Famous Ballymote; The Butterfly; Casadh An tSúgáin; Farewell To Erin; The Heathery Hills Of Yarrow; The Death Of Queen Jane; The Pipe On The Hob/The Hag At The Churn; The Priest/Mary Willie's/This Is My Love, Do You Like Her?; How Can I Live At The Top Of A Mountain; Rosie Finn's Favourite/Over The Water To Charlie/The Kid On The Mountain; The Green Groves Of Erin/The Flowers Of Red Hill

Ceol Na hÉireann: The Traditional Music Of Ireland From The Sound Archives Of RTÉ (RTÉ CEOCD 001) 1993
Various Artists
Bothy Band track: Reels: The Navvy On The Line/The Rainy Day
Note: Includes otherwise unreleased RTÉ performances by Planxty, Séamus Ennis, The Chieftains, Seán Ó Riada and many others.

Live In Concert (Strange Fruit SFRCD 063) 1996
Note: Two of the band's BBC radio concerts, from 15/7/76 and 24/7/78 (see BBC sessionography below).

The Bothy Band BBC Sessionography

BBC Radio

Unknown Title (Radio Ulster)
Tx: 5/9/75
Jackson's Jig/Paddy Clancy's Jig; Reels: Salamanca/Banshee/Sailor's Bonnet; The Death Of Queen Jane; The Kesh Jig/Give Us A Drink Of Water/The Flower Of The Flock/ The Ballymote Reel; When I Was A Fair Maid; The Butterfly; The Green Groves Of Erin/The Flowers Of Redhill
Note: Known from a master copy in a private collection.

John Peel Show (Radio 1)
Rec: 9/3/76, Maida Vale / Tx: 26/3/76 / Prod: Jeff Griffin
The Maid Of Coolmore; When I Was A Fair Maid; Fionnghuala; The Morrison Selection (Old Hag You Have Killed Me/Danny Delaney's/Morrison's); Music Of The Glen/ The Humours Of Scariff/Poll An Madadh Uisce
Note: All tracks survive at source. Four of the

five were rebroadcast with a new contract on *The Alan Freeman Show* (one per week) on April 10, April 17, April 24 and May 1 1976. The missing track was 'Fionnghuala'.

In Concert (Radio 1)
Rec: 15/7/76, Paris Theatre / Tx: 11/9/76 / Prod: Pete Dauncey
Martin Wynne's/The Longford Tinker; Two Jigs/The Kid On The Mountain; Patsy Geary's/Coleman Cross; Sixteen Come Next Sunday; Michael Gorman's/The Road To Lisdoonvarna/Joe Cooley's; Lucy Campbell/The Laurel Tree; Fionnghuala; Farewell To Erin; The Kesh Jig/Give Us A Drink Of Water/The Flower Of The Flock/Famous Ballymote
Note: The concert survives at source and appeared, with some spoken intro edits, on *Live In Concert* (Strange Fruit, 1996).

Both Sides Now (Radio 2)
Tx: 29/7/76 / Prod: Bill Bebb
Note: Wally Whyton presents a 60-minute show featuring guests The Bothy Band and The Teesside Fettlers. Produced by Bill Bebb.

Folkweave (Radio 2)
Rec: 2/8/76 / Tx: 12/5/77 / Prod: Peter Pilbeam
Note: This was a 55-minute broadcast, recorded at the Sidmouth Folk Festival, featuring The Bothy Band, Jackie Daly & Séamus Creagh, Packie Byrne & Bonnie Shaljean. While this doesn't survive in the Sound Archive, 30-minute edits of *Folkweave*'s 1977 series were cut to transcription disc for rebroadcast on the BBC World Service and are extant in that form. That may be the case with some of the 1976 *Folkweave* series.

John Peel Show (Radio 1)
Rec: 19/10/76, Maida Vale / Tx: 24/11/76 / Prod: Jeff Griffin
Billy Banker/The Shores Of Loughrea/The Laurel Tree; Bonny Kate/Jenny's Chickens; Michael Gorman's/The Frieze Britches/All The Way To Galway/Fairhead Mary; Sixteen Come Next Sunday; The Hare In The Heather; Garret Barry's/Coppers And Brass [piping solo].
Note: All of the tracks survive at source.

Both Sides Now (Radio 2/Radio 1)
Rec: 21/10/76 / Tx: 23/10/76 / Prod: Bill Bebb
Note: A one-hour programme presented by Wally Whyton, with Brian Golbey, Harvey Andrews and The Bothy Band, and Brian Brocklehurst as 'house bass player'.

John Peel Show (Radio 1)
Rec: 14/3/78, Maida Vale / Tx: 21/3/78 / Prod: Malcolm Brown
O'Neill's March; The Strayaway Child; The Maids Of Mitchelstown; Lord Franklin
Note: There's a curiosity with this session: piecing together evidence from both the BBC WAC and the BBC Sound Archive database, it appears that all four tracks were featured (with a separate contract for their use) on *The Alan Freeman Show* on April 1, April 8, June 3 and July 22 1978 (one track per show). The same four tracks were also broadcast at some point on *The Friday Rock Show*, presented from its inception (which was on 17/11/78) by Tommy Vance (though no separate contract for this exists). This session does not survive at source, but does in off-air form from the Peel broadcast.

Folk 78 (Radio 2)
Rec: 18/6/78, Broadcasting House, London / Tx: 5/9/78 / Prod: Ray Harvey
Note: The Bothy Band in concert for 28 minutes, one of a series of Broadcasting House folk concerts broadcast between July and September 1978. No copy is known to survive.

John Peel Show (Radio 1)
Rec: 20/11/78, Maida Vale / Tx: 28/11/78 / Prod: Tony Wilson
The Hunter's Purse/The Sailor On The Rock; The Death Of Queen Jane; Jigs; Mulqueeny's (Hornpipe)/Farrell O'Gara/Drag Her Round The Road; Crazy Dreams
Note: This was a session by the touring 'Mulligan Roadshow' quartet of three Bothy Band members (Kevin Burke, Matt Molloy, Mícheál Ó Domhnaill) and guitarist/vocalist Paul Brady. It would appear that each man fronted one of the five tracks recorded. The Roadshow quartet were also recorded for *Folkweave* and *Folk 79* while on tour during November 1978 (see below).

Folk 79 (Radio 2)
Rec: 24/7/78, National Club, Kilburn / Tx: 1/5/79; repeated on 28/8/79 / Prod: Ray Harvey
The Tar Road To Sligo/Paddy Clancy's; The Maids Of Mitchelstown; I Wish My Love Was A Red Red Rose; Piping Solo: Garret Barry's/The Bucks Of Oranmore; The Morning Star/The Fisherman's Lilt/The Drunken Landlady; Do You Love An Apple?; A Jig And Five Reels: The Leitrim Fancy/Around The World For Sport/Rip The Calico/Martin Wynne's/Enchanted Lady/The Holy Land
Note: This broadcast appeared on *Live In Concert* (Strange Fruit, 1996) and was a series of four 29-minute concert broadcasts. The other broadcasts featured Ewan MacColl & Peggy Seeger and two instalments of Paul Brady. While the contract suggests that all three shows were recorded at the Purcell Room, *Radio Times* bills The Bothy Band performance as having been recorded at the National Club, Kilburn. *Melody Maker* reported on 10/3/79 that the recording for the whole *Folk 79* series would take place (as had the whole of the previous year's *Folk 78* series) at Broadcasting House, giving details for the artists appearing. The concerts would take place at 5.30pm with tickets available by application to the BBC Ticket Unit. The Bothy Band were also booked to play a (presumably late-night) concert at the Venue, London, on the same night as the advertised Broadcasting House recording (18/3/79). However, the extant broadcast is introduced as being from the summer of 1978 at the National Club. One might speculate that either *Melody Maker* got it wrong or there was a problem with putting on the 18/3/79 concert. But, if so, how come the BBC had an unbroadcast concert from the National up their sleeve? Despite being managed by National Club owner Kevin Flynn at the time, The Bothy Band did not play the National on their March 1979 final UK tour.

Folk 79 (Radio 2)
Rec: 11/78 / Tx: 30/1/79 / Prod: Ray Harvey
Note: Thirty minutes of the Mulligan Roadshow quartet (Burke, Ó Domhnaill and Molloy with Paul Brady).

Folkweave (Radio 2)
Rec: 11/78, Wythenshawe Forum / Tx: 17/5/79 / Prod: Peter Pilbeam
Note: Advertised in *Radio Times* as 'Kevin Burke & Mícheál Ó Domhnaill' in a concert segment within this 50-minute show, this was in fact recorded during the Mulligan Roadshow tour. The material was either repeated, or further tracks aired, on the edition broadcast on 21/6/79.

Folkweave (Radio 2)
Rec: 11/78, Wythenshawe Forum / Tx: 24/5/79 / Prod: Peter Pilbeam
Note: Advertised in *Radio Times* as 'Matt Molloy' in a concert segment within this 50-minute show, this was in fact recorded during the Mulligan Roadshow tour. (Paul Brady's performance from Wythenshawe was broadcast in *Folkweave* on 7/6/79.)

BBC TV

Twndish: 1 (BBC Wales)
Tx: 21/1/77
Note: First episode of a Welsh-language pop music programme. Dewi Pws Morris introduces a montage of highlights from the forthcoming series, seemingly featuring The Bothy Band. The highlights programme survives at source.

Gig In The Round (BBC Northern Ireland)
Rec: ? / Tx: 11/3/77 / Prod: Tony McAuley
Note: A 30-minute concert in BBC NI's Belfast studios, split with Paul Brady & Andy Irvine. The show survives at source.

The Val Doonican Music Show
Rec: ? / Tx: 27/5/78 / Prod: Yvonne Littlewood
Note: The Bothy Band perform a three-minute piece, 'Tar Road To Sligo/Paddy Clancy's', on Season Two of this long running Light Entertainment show (1976-85). US crooner Andy Williams was also a guest on this episode. The show survives at source.

Arena: Bring Me Back A Song (BBC2)
Rec: May 1977 to early 1978 / Tx: 27/2/80; repeated 3/3/80
Note: The *Radio Times* blurb for this 45-minute episode of the long-running arts series reads: 'As the Sense Of Ireland festival of arts comes to London, *Arena* presents some of the finest Irish musicians of today. In tonight's programme The Bothy Band and Planxty … play and sing with their families and friends on location in Dublin and on the west coast of Ireland.' By that time The Bothy Band were defunct, although Planxty had recently reformed. A version of this film was screened at the Dublin Folk Festival in August 1978, at which stage it was within the BBC's *Omnibus* strand. For whatever reason, it was never broadcast under this banner. *Omnibus* had 16 BBC1 slots between July and December 1978 within which to broadcast the film, but didn't; it had a further 16 slots during 1979; and, most bafflingly, it was also on air across the first quarter of 1980, when a 38½ minute edit of the film was finally broadcast within the *Arena* strand on BBC2. Possibly the Bothy Band sabbatical during the latter half of 1978 had meant that a broadcast was held back. The widely publicised Planxty reunion and the 'A Sense Of Ireland' events in London in February 1980 (referenced in Alan Yentob's intro on the broadcast version) provided a new peg upon which to hang it. Why it went out on BBC2's *Arena* rather than BBC1's *Omnibus*, for which it had been commissioned, is a mystery. The programme survives at source.

Twndish: Steeleye Span (BBC Wales)
Rec: ? / Tx: 14/8/78
Note: Iestyn Garlick introduces traditional music from Steeleye Span, Ossian and The Bothy Band. The programme survives at source.

Miscellaneous BBC Radio Coverage

Radio Times details this handful of further programmes with Bothy Band content, almost certainly all being record- and discussion-based rather than featuring exclusive recordings.

Sounds Interesting (Radio 2)
Tx: 13/6/76
Note: Derek Jewell reviews and plays newly released music from Jethro Tull, Harris Chalkitis, Kim Carnes and The Bothy Band.

Sounds Interesting (Radio 3)
Tx: 28/11/76
Note: Derek Jewell reviews and plays newly released music from Stanley Clarke, The Bothy Band and Led Zeppelin.

Late Night Folk (Radio 3)
Tx: 25/9/77 / Prod: Tony McAuley
Note: Although apparently featuring no exclusive Bothy Band recordings (there is no contract), this was a one-off 25-minute programme dedicated in full to the band.

Tony McAuley had previously produced their *Gig In The Round* TV concert for BBC NI. Perhaps this Radio 3 show used audio from that TV recording – but if so, it's strange that no separate contract was drawn up. No copy of this Radio 3 show is known to survive.

McPeake Family Discography 1955–75

The McPeake Family offered a very particular kind of music, using the uilleann pipes less as a solo instrument than as a texture within easily accessible balladry with a certain nostalgic or nationalistic flavour. They were essentially a vocal group, although a few instrumental items were usually included. Their folk club performances were doubtless the first opportunity many in Britain had to experience the pipes in person and as such, while of limited musical interest, they retain historical importance. In a sense, they filled the gap in Britain between Séamus Ennis' period of prolific BBC radio broadcasting (including piping) in the 1950s and the rise of Finbar & Eddie Furey as a hugely popular British folk club act, featuring piping in a more visceral, virtuosic context, from 1967 onward.

Albums & EPs

The McPeake Family Of Belfast (Prestige PREST-INT 13018) 1961
Jug Of Punch; The Verdant Braes Of Skreen; Slieve Gallon Brae; Durd Fainne; Little Red Fox; A Maid Going To Comber; Will You Go Lassie Go; Weavers And Doffers Song; Ireland Boys Hurrah; Bucket Of Mountain Dew; The Road To Balynure; The Banks Of The O.B.D.; Susie Maquire; Maggie Pickens; On Carrick Down; Erin The Tear; Monaghan Fair; My Singing Bird

Note: A US-only release, likely secured through Ewan MacColl, who had several previous releases on this New York jazz label – which would launch a dedicated folk imprint, Folklore, in 1963. Transatlantic reissued this album in the UK in 1966 (XTRA 5012). The release date is sometimes cited as 1959 or 1960, but the 1961 date comes from a vinyl first pressing. The Family were a trio on this release, which included 'Will Ye Go, Lassie, Go' aka 'Wild Mountain Thyme' – for neither the first nor the last time.

The McPeake Family (Topic 12T87) 1963
McLeod's Reel; A Bucket Of The Mountain Dew; Eileen Aroon; An Durd Fainne; My Singing Bird; The Lament Of Aughrim; Carraig Dun; The Derry Hornpipe; The Old Piper; Slieve Gallon Brae; Ireland, Boys, Hurrah; Cock Robin; An Coolin; The Verdant Braes Of Skreen
Note: The Family were a double trio on this album recorded by Bill Leader in between gigs on an early folk club tour: Francis I, II and III (all on vocals, pipes), James McPeake (vocals, harp), Kathleen McPeake (vocals, harp) and Tommy McCrudden (vocals). Available on CD as *Wild Mountain Thyme* (Topic TSCD583), 2009.

Wild Mountain Thyme EP (Topic TOP92) 1963
Juanita; Jug Of Punch; Will Ye Go Lassie, Go; I Know My Love
Note: Four non-album songs, including the

third release for their best-known number, recorded by Bill Leader during the above LP sessions. No fewer than six of the Prestige LP items were repeated for Topic – a recycling pattern of a limited repertoire that would continue. Available on CD as *Wild Mountain Thyme* (Topic TSCD583), 2009.

Irish Folk (Fontana Special SFL 13068) September 1964
Brennan On The Moor; Alabama; Ballynure Ballad; The Winding Banks Of Erne; Belfast Street Songs; Out In The Open; The Next Market Day; Dumb, Dumb, Dumb; Banks Of The Roses; Maggie Pickens; On The Banks Of The O.B.D.; Lament For Owen Roe; Jute Mill Song; Ducks Of Magherlin
Note: A six-piece here. That's the simple bit. This album comes in two variants: the 14-track stereo release (above) with a brightly coloured photo of the group standing by a vintage fireplace; and the 16-track mono release (Fontana TL5214) – entitled *Irish Folk!* (in italics and with an exclamation mark added, as if it were a threat) – with the group pictured by a river. The two added tracks are 'Buncrana Train' and 'Corrie Doon'. But the confusion doesn't end there. In 1965 the album was repackaged, with an alternative sleeve (its third variant in two years) as *Introducing The McPeake Family* (Fontana MGF 27536/SRF 67536). This time the album was presented in both mono and stereo versions as a 16-tracker, meaning 'Buncrana Train' and 'Corrie Doon' made their debut in stereo.

Ducks Of Magherlin EP (Fontana TE 17440) 1964
Belfast Street Songs; The Winding Banks Of Erne; The Ducks Of Magherlin; Buncrana Train; The Next Market Day
Note: None of these EP tracks are exclusive – unless one had bought only the stereo version of the accompanying *Irish Folk* LP, in which case 'Buncrana Train' would be rolling up to the station for the first time.

At Home With The McPeakes (Fontana TL 5258/STL 5258) November 1965
Jugs Of Punch; Roisin Dhu; The Stuttering Lovers; The Bonnie Bunch Of Roses O; Molly Baan; Finnigan's Wake; The Famine Song; The Anti-Recruiting Song; The Cotton Mill Song; Top Of The Cork Road; Bonnie Boy; My Own Native Land; I Wish, I Wish; The Blackbird; Love Will Never, Never Conquer Me; Henry Joy
Note: Still a six-piece. Released in both mono and stereo pressings.

'Sé Do Bheatha, A Bhaile/Welcome Home (DTS Records LFX3) 1966
Marches: The Fairy Revels/The Green Flag; General Munro; Susan McGuire; The Verdant Braes Of Skreen;
Reels: George White's Fancy/The Queen's Wedding; The Bonny Bunch Of Roses O; Seó h-In Seó; The Jug Of Punch; Roisin Dhu; Kneel To The Tomb; Jigs: Out Of The Ocean/Kittys Bonnet; An Coulin; Oro Sé Do Bheat A Bhaile
Note: A very obscure label, DTS was a contraction of Davies Transcription Service – under which name seemingly at least eight EPs appeared during 1961–63, of which three are discoverable online (The Sheaf River Jazz Band and verité of Sheffield trams and the Flying Scotsman). As DTS, they released two EPs and three known LPs in the traditional music sphere (the other LPs being by English singers Cyril Tawney and Harry Cox); one online source suggests five LPs in total. Even more intriguingly, an album was released in 1969 on the similarly obscure label Evolution (Evolution Z1002), again as *Welcome Home* or *'Sé Do Bheatha, A Bhaile*, depending on whether one takes the title from the discs

(English) or cover (Irish) – but with a different track listing, one that matches the track listing of the 1972 Windmill release *Irish To Be Sure* (see below). Evolution would appear to have released at least six LPs and at least three singles during 1969–70, all by psychedelic rock bands – except for those by the McPeakes.

Pleasant And Delightful (Fontana TL 5433/STL5433) November 1967
Rennnafeirste; She Moved Through The Fair; Take The Flag Down; Lowlands Of Holland; Pleasant And Delightful; Bold Fenian Men; Boulavogue; My Lagan Love; Ploughboy; Terry's Fancy; The Constitutional Movement; Don't Stick Knives In Babbies' Heads; Sean South Of Garryowen; Irish Peasant Girl; My Love Is An Arbutus; Will You Buy Me A Banana; The Wind That Shakes The Barley; Rifles, The 'Skins And The Fusiliers
Note: More confusion. This also appeared in 1967 with the same cover photo but different title and graphics as *The Delightful McPeakes* (Philips 6856 017). Fontana was a UK subsidiary of Philips, a Dutch company. Who knows why there were apparently two UK releases for this record. The cover photo itself, of the six members standing outside an old cottage, was from the same session from whence came the cover shot for the stereo version of *Irish Folk*.

Jug Of Punch/Courting In The Kitchen (Banshee Records 3103) 1960s?
Note: There is no date on this single and no indication of how many members were involved, but the label typography, style and information ('Recorded in Ireland') suggests it is a 1960s release, and on an Irish-based label. This Banshee Records is not the one operated by the Fureys from the late 1970s.

Irish To Be Sure (Windmill WMD 151) 1972
Ducks Of Magheralin; Roisin Dhu; General Munro; Alabama; Out Of The Ocean; Kitty's Bonnet; The Constutional Movement; Belfast Brigade; George White's Fancy; The Queen's Wedding; Kneel To The Tomb; An Raibh Tu A A'Carraig; Brennan On The Moor
Note: Another discographical mystery: is this a unique album or a compilation/retitling of previous recordings? The brief back cover notes state: 'Father, son and grandson, all blessed with the gift of playing the pipes and harp, combine here with sister Kathleen and cousin Frank …' suggesting that this is a five-piece version of the group. But it also suggests the blurb writer has only got a vague grasp of who's in the group, what each one plays and what their names are. If Francis I (d. 1971) is here, the LP had been recorded a year or more prior to release – which makes sense in view of the fact that the tracklisting is identical to that on the above-mentioned 1969 Evolution release. The Windmill label was UK-based and specialised in cheapo easy-listening releases: its other albums of 1972–73 were mostly all 'sounds like' tribute albums to Bert Kaempfert, Engelbert Humperdinck, Andy Williams, Glenn Miller et al. For the McPeakes, the end of the road collided firmly with the middle of the road.

The Jug Of Punch (Folktrax 60071) 1975
The Jug Of Punch; Maidrín Rua; My Singing Bird; The Fairy Revels/The Green Flag; Bonny Bunch Of Roses, O [Frank solo]; Miss McCloud's/Swallow's Tail; An Doro Fáinne; The Blackbird (song, air and hornpipe); Erin, The Tear; Lament For Aughrim; The Mountain Dew; The Verdant Braes Of Screen; Ireland, Boys, Hooray; The Coulin; Siubhán Ní Dhuibhir (Susan Maguire); Blackthorn Stick/Saddle The Pony; Carrick Donn; Sé Fáth Mo Bhuartha (The Cause Of

My Sorrow); The Road To Ballynure; Juanita; Seothín Seó; The Wild Mountain Thyme
Note: A 60-minute cassette release from Peter Kennedy's label. Purportedly recorded by Kennedy in London on 15/1/61. The Family featured are Francis I, Francis II and James, with some duo and solo items. 'The False Young Man' is almost certainly the recording heard on *The Folk Songs of Britain Volume I*, released in 1961 and compiled by Kennedy.

The Rights Of Man: Francis McPeake – The Singing Piper (Folktrax FTX 176) 1975
Francis I tracks: The Rights Of Man; The Grave Of Wolfe Tone; Monaghan Fair; The Constitutional Movement; My Lagan Love; The Jug Of Punch; The Next Market Day; The Wild Mountain Thyme; The Old Piper; The Coolin; General Munro; Seothin Seo
Francis I & II tracks: The Dawning Of The Day; Annie Laurie; Slieve Gallon Braes; The Verdent Braes Of Skreen
Francis II tracks: She Moved Through The Fair; My Singing Bird
Note: Recorded by Peter Kennedy on 7/7/52. Francis I talks about his life and music, and sings with and without pipes. On some tracks he is joined by Francis II.

Exclusive McPeake Recordings On Various-Artists Releases

Folk Song Today: Songs And Ballads Of England And Scotland (HMV DLP 1143) 1955
Various Artists
Includes: Will You Go, Lassie Go? – Frank McPeake and son
Note: A 10-inch LP of songs collected by Peter Kennedy. This was the first appearance on record of the McPeakes' signature song, performed here by Francis I and II. The record also includes Shirley Collins, Harry Cox, Rory & Alex McEwen, Bob & Ron Copper, John Macdonald, Jeannie Robertson, Davie Stewart, Fred Lawson and Bob Roberts.

As I Roved Out (Field Trip – Ireland) (Folkways FW 8872) 1960
Includes: Monochan Fair [sic] – Frank McPeake
Note: Recordings made by Jean Ritchie in 1952. Frank McPeake sings one song with brief piping intro. Other singers featured include Sarah Makem, Elizabeth Cronin and Séamus Ennis. A companion volume, *Field Trip – England* (FW 8871), was also released in 1960. Both are available from Folkways as CD or download.

A Jug Of Punch: Broadside Ballads Old And New (HMV CLP 1327 / EMI XLP 5003) 1960
Various Artists
Includes: Monaghan Fair/Irish Reel; Jug Of Punch – Frank McPeake
Note: This was the first of three themed HMV albums recorded at Cecil Sharp House, London, by Peter Kennedy. The others were *A Pinch Of Salt* and *Rocket Along*. All featured more or less the same cast of people, often collaborating on each other's recordings, although Frank appears only on *A Jug Of Punch* and performs only the above two solo items. Others on this record include Séamus Ennis, Steve Benbow, Shirley Collins, Bob & Ron Copper and Jimmie Macgregor.

The Folk Songs Of Britain Volume I: Songs Of Courtship (Caedmon TC1142) 1961
Various Artists
Includes: Our Wedding Day – Francis McPeake; The False Young Man – Frank and Francis McPeake
Note: The first in a series of 10-inch LPs, collected and edited by Peter Kennedy and Alan Lomax. The series was originally released in 1961 on New York's Caedmon Records,

with UK releases in 1968–70 on Topic (this volume being Topic 12T157). The songs were collected from traditional singers all over the British Isles by the editors mainly in England, by Hamish Henderson in Scotland, and by Séamus Ennis and Seán O'Boyle in Ireland. Others on this volume include Bob & Ron Copper, Jeannie Robertson, Paddy Tunney and Séamus Ennis himself.

The Folk Songs Of Britain Volume III: Jack Of All Trades (Caedmon TC1144) 1961
Various Artists
Includes: The Ould Piper – Frank McPeake
Note: Another in the series, this one including Davie Stewart, Bob & Ron Copper and Séamus Ennis again. It also, amazingly, features someone other than a McPeake – one Edward Quinn of County Tyrone – singing 'The Jug Of Punch'. Reissued in 1968 as Topic 12T159.

Folksound Of Britain (EMI/HMV CLP 1910) 1965
Various Artists
Includes: The Verdant Braes of Skreen – The McPeake Family
Note: This was a live LP recorded at a concert presented by the English Folk Dance & Song Society at the Royal Festival Hall, London, on June 4 1965. It was produced by Roy Guest, recorded by Seán Davies and edited by Peter Kennedy. Other artists include Jack Elliot, Louis Killen, The Watersons, Bob & John Copper, Cyril Tawney and Bob Davenport.

Song Of A Road (Topic TSCD802) 1999
Various Artists
Note: Originally broadcast in 1959, this was the second of Charles Parker, Ewan MacColl and Peggy Seeger's series of eight BBC 'Radio Ballads'. MacColl brought Francis McPeake in (see BBC Sessionography below) as both a singer and instrumentalist (pipes) on the project.

Sing Christmas And The Turn Of The Year: The Live Christmas Day 1957 Broadcast On BBC Radio (Rounder 11661-1850-2) 2000
Various Artists
Includes: The Jug Of Punch – The McPeake Trio (performed in a shared sequence with The Ravenhill Temperance Flute Band)
Note: See BBC Sessionography below.

McPeake Family BBC Sessionography 1949–70

In 1949, Francis McPeake's Belfast address is listed in WAC documents as 15 Connedagh Drive; by late 1951 it is 5 Farmview Street; by January 1967 it is 30 Theodore Street. Francis is always engaged to perform in a solo capacity between 1949 and 1957. While Francis (either I or II) continues to perform solo on some céilí-based broadcasts up to 1965, from August 1957 onward the engagements are generally for 'The McPeake Trio', which becomes a quartet or quintet on occasions during the 1960s. In comparison, all of the group's LP and EP releases of the 1960s (bar their first) are as a sextet. The contracts for the 1949–54 broadcasts do not specify whether they are recording (Rec) or broadcast (Tx) dates, although these were almost certainly all live broadcasts during this period.

BBC Radio

Piping And Fiddling (Northern Ireland Home Service)
22/11/49
Francis to play '4 minutes of traditional dances'.

Piping, Fiddling And Singing (Northern Ireland Home Service)
17/4/50
Francis to play '5–6 minutes of traditional music'.

Piping, Fiddling And Singing (Northern Ireland Home Service)
16/1/51
Francis to play '5–6 minutes of traditional music'.

Piping (Scottish Home Service)
15/6/51
Francis (recorded in Belfast) to play '5 minutes of jigs and reels'.

Piping (Scottish Home Service)
14/12/51
Francis (recorded in Belfast) to play '5 minutes of traditional tunes'.

Songs That Have Stayed (Northern Ireland Home Service)
4/9/52
Francis to play 'traditional Irish airs which will be supplied'.

Piping Round Up (Scottish Home Service)
5/6/53
Content to be decided.

Country Dancing (Home Service)
Tx: 22/12/53
No contract extant; known from *Radio Times*. A 30-minute show presenting traditional music from around the British Isles. Frances McPeake plays pipes with The Jackie Hearst Trio. Northumbrian piper Jack Armstrong also appears (with his Barnstormers), as do Scots accordionist Jimmy Shand and others.

Accent On Melody (Northern Ireland Home Service)
1/12/54
Francis to play 'a medley of jigs and a medley of reels, approximately 2 minutes each'.

Country Dancing (Home Service)
Tx: 9/3/55 / Prod: Jack McGeagh
No contract extant; known from *Radio Times*. A 30-minute country céilí from Lurgan, with St Peter's Céilidhe Band [sic], Francis McPeake (pipes) and Marie Cunningham (accordion).

Accent On Melody (Northern Ireland Home Service)
Tx: 16/1/56
Francis to play '3 minutes approx. of Irish dances'.

Traditional Irish Dances (Northern Ireland Home Service)
Tx: 17/5/56
Francis to play 'attractive Irish dances to last approx. 4/4½ minutes'.

Accent On Melody (Northern Ireland Home Service)
Tx: 14/1/57
Francis to play a 'medley of jigs or reels to last 3 minutes approximately'. WAC documents, though incomplete, suggest that this broadcast may have been cut to disc by the BBC Transcription Service.

Country Dancing (Home Service)
Tx: 6/3/57 / Prod: Sam Denton
No contract extant; known from *Radio Times*. 15 minutes from a céilí at Newry, with The Jackie Hearst Trio, Liam O'Connor (songs) and Francis McPeake (pipes).

Country Céilí (Home Service)
Tx: 22/5/57 / Prod: Sam Denton
No contract extant; known from *Radio Times*. From Clady, with Bridie Gallagher, The Fred Hanna Band, Francis McPeake on pipes and Kenny Thompson on accordion.

Country Dancing (Home Service)
Tx: 7/8/57/ Prod: Sam Denton
No contract extant; known from *Radio Times*. A 15-minute show from a céilí in Glenavy, with St Peter's Céilí Band, Teresa Clifford (songs) and The McPeake Trio.

Country Dancing (Home Service)
Tx: 13/11/57/ Prod: Sam Denton
No contract extant; known from *Radio Times*. A 15-minute show from a céilí in Gilford, with St Peter's Céilí Band, Teresa Clifford (songs) and The McPeake Trio.

Sing Christmas And The Turn of The Year (Home Service)
Rec: live broadcast (in Birmingham) / Tx: 25/12/57
This was song collector Alan Lomax's last BBC project: a wildly ambitious Christmas morning regional round-up programme, following the Queen's Speech. While there is no extant McPeake Trio contract for this broadcast, they did appear, performing 'Jug Of Punch'. Peter Kennedy later released the broadcast on his own Folktrax label and subsequently on CD via Rounder in 2000. (See 'Séamus Ennis At The BBC' chapter.)

Come Into The Parlour (Light Programme)
Tx: 28/12/57; edited repeat (30 minutes) 4/1/58
No contract extant; known from *Radio Times*. A 45-minute show with the Light Orchestra conducted by David Curry, Henry Hinds (bass vocalist) and The McPeake Trio.

Country Dancing (Home Service)
Tx: 16/4/58 / Prod: Sam Denton
No contract extant; known from *Radio Times*. A 15-minute show from a céilí in Crossgar, with The Jackie Hearst Quartet, Annie Gray (songs) and The McPeake Trio.

Country Dancing (Home service)
Tx: 13/8/58 / Prod: Sam Denton
No contract extant; known from *Radio Times*. A 20-minute show from a céilí in Tullyallen, with The Vincent Lowe Céilí Band, Teresa Clifford and Frank McElroy (songs) and Francis McPeake (pipes).

Country Dancing (Home Service)
Tx: 18/2/59 / Prod: Sam Denton
No contract extant; known from *Radio Times*. A 30-minute show from a céilí in Portadown, with The McCusker Brothers Céilí Band, David Hammond (songs with guitar) and The McPeake Trio.

Country Dancing (Home Service)
Tx: 15/4/59 / Prod: Sam Denton
No contract extant; known from *Radio Times*. A 20-minute show from a céilí in Ballycastle, with Charlie Kelly's Céilí Band, Una O'Callaghan and William Stevenson (songs) and Francis McPeake (pipes).

Children's Hour (Home Service)
Tx: 10/5/59
Incongruously, a 50-minute show, this episode themed around Irish music and stories, including The McPeake Trio.

Traditional Music (Northern Ireland Home Service)
Rec: 27/5/59 / Tx: 11/6/59
Francis to play 'traditional music lasting 13½ minutes'.

Song Of A Road (Midland Programme)
Rec: 2-3/10/59 / Tx: 5/11/59
Note: For a £10 'special' fee plus travelling expenses 'to be notified', Francis is 'to sing and play the uilleann pipes'. Rehearsals for the programme were from 30/9/59 to 1/10/59 at BBC Maida Vale and Portland Place studios, London. This was the second of the 'Radio Ballads' (1958–64) created by Birmingham producer Charles Parker with Ewan MacColl and Peggy Seeger. Francis sang 'Come All You Gallant Drivers' and was also among nine instrumentalists on the broadcast. (See also 'Séamus Ennis At The BBC' chapter.)

3/8/60 *Memo to superiors from Diane Hyde, producer of* Ulster Magazine *(NI Home Service):* Ms Hyde wants to use the McPeakes (at this point a trio), but there is an issue: 'Mr McPeake telephoned to say that they would be free but would not be willing to accept a further engagement from the BBC at their present fee. He added: "Even Radio Éireann pays more than the BBC", and he thought 15 guineas would be a reasonable fee … I would be sorry to lose the McPeakes but I must leave it to you and the NI Programming Executive to decide what they are worth. I don't know whether you would consider their uniqueness, together with their [first prize] at Llangollen this year …'

On 15/8/60 E.W. Boucher replies: 'I think it is [acceptable] to increase the McPeake Trio's fee. They are not used very often and I should think 15 guineas wouldn't break us, but perhaps Programming Executive could get away with less. It might be worth trying 12.'

Country Dancing (Home Service)
Tx: 29/3/61 / Prod: Sam Denton
No contract extant; known from *Radio Times*. A 30-minute show from a céilí in Dungannon, with The McCusker Brothers Céilí Band, Teresa Clifford and Robert McKeown (songs) and Francis McPeake (pipes).

Country Dancing (Home Service)
Tx: 25/10/61 / Prod: Sam Denton
No contract extant; known from *Radio Times*. A 30-minute show from a céilí in Keady, with The McCusker Brothers Céilí Band, Annie Gray (folk singer), John Hughes (songs with guitar) and Francis McPeake (pipes).

Come Into The Parlour (Light Programme)
Tx: 23/3/62 / Prod: Sam Denton
No contract extant; known from *Radio Times*.

A 30-minute show with the Light Orchestra conducted by David Curry, John Hughes (songs with guitar) and The McPeake Trio.

Country Dancing (Home Service)
Tx: 23/5/62 / Prod: Sam Denton
No contract extant; known from *Radio Times*. A 20-minute show from a céilí in Coleraine, with Charles Kelly's Céilí Band, Sheila Gillespie and Robert McKeown (songs) and Francis McPeake (pipes).

Calling The Tune (London Home Service)
Tx: 28/1/63
Two Francis McPeake solo performances are played ('Blackthorn Stick' and 'Saddle The Pony'), from a source not specified – possibly a Transcription Service disc. Francis McPeake is posted a retrospective fee for this broadcast by Maureen Moore (NI Home Service).

On With The Dance (Light Programme)
Tx: 25/4/63
Fee: 15 guineas (12 guineas is entered on the contract but scored out), plus repeat fees
A 30-minute show with David Curry conducting the Light Orchestra and The McPeake Family. The McPeakes, it seems, have won their battle for 15 guinea fees. Two sets of tunes for this programme are required, of 3 minutes' duration each – recorded at BBC Belfast studios. The tunes/sets are listed thus: Out On The Ocean/Kitty Bonnet [sic]; Derry Hornpipe/Harvest Home; Holland Is A Fine Place/Little Red Box; The Blackbird.

Country Dancing (Home Service)
Tx: 30/10/63 / Prod: Sam Denton
No contract extant; known from *Radio Times*. A 30-minute show from a céilí in Londonderry, with Charlie Kelly's Céilí Band, Marion Walker and James Shaw (songs) and Francis McPeake (pipes).

Come Into The Parlour (Light Programme)
Tx: 25/2/64
No contract extant; known from *Radio Times*. A 30-minute show featuring the Light Orchestra conducted by David Curry and The McPeake Trio.

Country Dancing (Home Service)
Tx: 25/3/64 / Prod: Sam Denton
No contract extant; known from *Radio Times*. A 30-minute show from a céilí in Beragh, with The Malachy Doris Céilí Trio, Elizabeth Keith and Eric Hinds (songs) and Francis McPeake (pipes).

Ulster Magazine (General Overseas Service)
Rec: 27/1/65
An interview with either Francis McPeake or the trio.

Country Céili (Home Service)
Tx: 25/3/65 / Prod: Sam Denton
No contract extant; known from *Radio Times*. A 30-minute show from a céilí in Ballerin, with The McCusker Brothers Céilí Band, Teresa Clifford and Frank McElroy (songs) and Francis McPeake (pipes).

Folk-Song Cellar (Home Service)
Tx: ?/8/66 / Prod: Maude Hamill
Note: *Folk-Song Cellar* was a 45-minute live music programme that ran for seven weekly episodes between 13/8/66 and 24/8/66, hosted by Robin Hall and Jimmie Macgregor and produced in collaboration with the English Folk Dance & Song Society (EFDSS). See below.

1/9/66 *Memo from E.W. Boucher (BBC Belfast) to a colleague in London:* It seems the McPeakes were broadcast on *Folk-Song Cellar* [a Home Service programme, also cut to transcription disc for overseas broadcast] shortly before this memo, their performance having been recorded at Cecil Sharpe House, home of the EFDSS, in London. Boucher's text is a rebuke under the guise of a missive offering his availability for 'advice' should producers from London want to book Northern Ireland artists. The reply, from someone connected with *Folk-Song Cellar*, explains that the artists involved in the series were booked by the EFDSS, not the BBC. Boucher replies saying that, nonetheless, 'regions appreciate and find helpful the normal courtesy of information regarding the use of their local artists'. One wonders whether producers at BBC Merseyside expected to be similarly informed every time some other region booked The Beatles, Cilla Black or any of the dozens of other 'local artists' from their patch. Boucher's memo, while absurd, indicates the sheer novelty of a Northern Ireland act in the 1960s being booked for broadcast by other BBC regions.

Folk Concert From Lancaster (North Of England Home Service)
Rec/Tx: 4/5/67
Fee: £24
Presumably the McPeakes are recorded in concert (the contract reveals no details). Eleven days later, presumably still on tour in Britain, they are featured on record on *A Cellar Full Of Folk* (Light Programme).

Country Meets Folk (Radio 1)
Rec/Tx: 13/7/67, probably Playhouse Theatre, London / Prod: Ian Grant
Fee: £25
The McPeakes are named as a trio in this contract: Francis, Francis and Kathleen. The show was presented by Wally Whyton; other guests are The Mustangs and Gordon Giltrap, plus Brian Brocklehurst as house double bassist.

My Kind Of Folk (Radio 1)
Rec/Tx: 17/7/68, Studio 2, Broadcasting House, London / Prod: Frances Line
Fee: £25

The McPeakes are again listed as a trio. A 30-minute show presented by Cyril Tawney. Other guests are Johnny Handle and The High Level Ranters.

Shamrock Time (Radio 2)
Rec: 21/8/68 / Tx: 6/9/68 / Prod: Alan Tongue
Fee: £31/10
The McPeake Family (four members this time) are to record 'probably 5 or 6 pieces' at the BBC Belfast studio. Introduced by Brendan O'Dowda, with other guests being Eileen Donaghy and an unnamed orchestra conducted by Terence Lovett.

Country Meets Folk (Radio 1)
Rec/Tx: 31/8/68, Playhouse Theatre, London / Prod: Ian Grant
Fee: £25
The McPeakes are listed as a trio. Other live guests are Noel Murphy and The Lorne Gibson trio, plus Brian Brocklehurst on bass. Introduced by Wally Whyton.

Country Meets Folk (Radio 1/Radio 2)
Rec/Tx: 1/3/69, Playhouse Theatre, London / Prod: Ian Grant
Fee: £25
The McPeakes are listed as a trio. Other live guests are Stefan Grossman and The Western Union, plus Brian Brocklehurst on bass. Introduced by Wally Whyton.

6/5/69 *Memo from MJ Quinault to Patrick Newman (Light Entertainment Booking Manager):* Quinault explains that around 10/4/69 he was asked to book Francis McPeake I as a guest of The Spinners on *My Kind Of Folk* (Radio 2), to be recorded 16/4/69 and broadcast 23/4/69.

On 14/5/68 Roger Rushton (McPeakes' manager) had written to BBC Contracts informing them that NEMS (the late Brian Epstein's agency/management organisation) were now the McPeakes' sole representatives. Quinault rang NEMS, to be informed that they no longer handled the McPeakes; the agency advised him to call Alastair Taylor at The Beatles' Apple organisation.

Quinault had 'several conversations' with Taylor on April 10 and 11. Finally, he asked Taylor to name a fee and supply a letter of authority from the McPeakes to ensure that Apple were now their representatives:

'Mr Taylor said he was going on leave the following day, but he would make sure that Francis McPeake got the message … On the 16th April 1969 I had a phone call from the Producer [Frances Line] to say that Francis McPeake had not appeared in the studio. When she rang him at home he said he had heard nothing about this other than a casual message from The Spinners … I rang Apple and spoke to several people there none of whom knew anything about the booking at all.'

Alastair Taylor's secretary assured Quinault he would call to sort the whole thing out when he had returned from leave. On May 5, having heard nothing since, Quinault rang Apple again, to be told that Taylor had left their employ 'and they do not know his whereabouts. Apparently it was known he was leaving before he went on leave … I seem to have difficulty in finding someone in authority to whom I can put my complaint …'

7/5/69 *Letter from Patrick Newman to 'The McPeake Family' at 30 Theodore Street, Belfast:* Newman explains that their BBC contact card had listed Apple Management Ltd (replacing NEMS) but that a recent attempt at applying this booking mechanism 'produced a totally unsatisfactory state of affairs'. Newman says that the BBC are happy to contact the McPeakes in future, but if they prefer to remain represented by Apple 'it would be nice if we could be convinced of their ability to handle matters in a satisfactory manner'. Newman copies the letter to BBC Northern Ireland and Apple Corps Ltd. He suggests that if Francis would prefer to reply by phone he is welcome to reverse the charges.

15/5/69 *Memo from Maureen Moore (BBC NI Programme Executive) to Patrick Newman:* Moore thanks Newman for copying her into the letter above and explains that BBC NI has for years simply booked the family directly. She mentions that Francis McPeake had phoned her after April 16 to say that he hadn't heard about the *My Kind Of Folk* engagement. She gives Newman a note of caution: 'If he does 'phone you and reverse the charges, I wish you luck as I must warn you that he is a bit long winded – to put it mildly!'

23/6/69 *Letter to the BBC from Roger Rushton:* The McPeakes' former manager, Roger Rushton, notifies the BBC that representation for the family is now via himself.

Folk On Friday (Radio 2)
Rec: 14/3/70, Playhouse Theatre, London / Tx: 24/4/70 / Prod: Frances Line
Fee: £30
A 60-minute show introduced by Jim Lloyd, also featuring Barry Skinner.

Folk On Friday (Radio 2)
Tx: 15/5/70 / Prod: Frances Line
There is no surviving contract for this, but the McPeakes are listed in *Radio Times* as 'studio guests', with Tony Rose, on this 60-minute show introduced by Jim Lloyd.

Country Meets Folk (Radio 2)
Rec: 17/10/70, Playhouse Theatre, London / Tx: 18/10/70; repeated 17/10/70 and 24/10/70 / Prod: Colin Chandler
Fee: £30
A 60-minute show introduced by Wally Whyton, featuring The McPeakes, Phil Brady & The Ranchers and Robin & Barry Dransfield.

BBC TV

Tonight (BBC TV)
Rec: 26/3/64, Lime Grove Studios, London
Fee: £52/10 (£10/10 per member) + rehearsal fee: £10/10 + repeat fee: £26/5
Rehearsals for this TV show were held the day before tele-recording, both sessions at Lime Grove Studios, London. The McPeakes are a quintet here: Francis I, II and III, James and Thomas. They perform two songs, one of which will be broadcast (date unspecified).

Line Up (BBC2 TV)
Rec: 14/12/67
Fee: £52/10
Broadcast date is TBA when the contract is signed. The fee suggests that the McPeakes were a quintet here. Famously, John Lennon saw the group on this programme, which led to their booking for The Beatles' *Magical Mystery Tour* filming wrap party. Pre-eminent Beatles scholar Mark Lewisohn has searched 'Programmes As Broadcast' files at the WAC but has found no trace of the McPeakes appearing in any episode of the show – and yet it definitely happened. *Radio Times* is also silent on the matter.

? Folk (BBC2 TV)
A *Melody Maker* 24/8/68 news item mentions that the McPeakes would 'probably' be guests on this forthcoming BBC2 colour programme. There is no BBC written record of this happening. It's possible that bookings for this show were taking place during the McPeakes' chaotic representation by Apple Corps (see above). Perhaps an offer to appear fell down the back of an Apple Corps sofa. The group did, however, appear on regional ITV station ABC's *Eamonn Andrews Show* on Friday 9/8/68.

Addendum: Extant RTÉ Radio Recordings

There are two vintage McPeakes-related RTÉ recordings, both available to be heard at the ITMA, Dublin. The first is listed as an RTÉ studio recording made at Phoenix Hall, Dublin, 12/5/59, of 'The McPeake Family' singing in English with Francis McPeake Jnr and James McPeake specified as uilleann pipers. Twelve tracks are performed. The second is a concert recording from Ennis, Clare, 6/8/62, involving 'The McPeake Family' along with fiddler Paddy Canney, piper Peadar O'Loughlin, singer Robbie McMahon and The Kilfenora Céilí Band. Fifteen tracks are performed.

Willie Clancy Discography

Irish Jigs, Reels & Hornpipes (Folkways FW6819) 1956
Michael Gorman & Willy Clancy [sic]
Promenade Step; Side Step; Ask Me Father/Carry Me Down To Carlow; The Mug Of Brown Ale; The Fair-Haired Boy; The Mountain Road; Fermony [sic] Lasses; The Flogging Reel; Humours Of Lissadel/Doctor Gilbert; Hornpipe [untitled]; Chief O'Neill's Favourite; Rodney's Glory; Little Red Lark
Note: A 10-inch US-only LP. Although the front cover stated 'Recorded In Ireland', it was actually recorded by Ewan MacColl at his home in Croydon, in 1955. Currently available from Smithsonian Folkways as a download.

Diarmuid Ó Flatharta – 'An Seánduine' / Willie Clancy – 'Na Connerys' (Gael Linn CE 12) 1960

Seán 'ac Dhonncha – 'Tá Na Páipéir Dhá Saighneáil' / Willie Clancy – 'The Old Bush/The Ravelled Hank Of Yarn' (Gael Linn CE 14) 1960

Seosamh Ó hÉanaí [Joe Heaney] – 'Sadhbh Ní Bhruinneallaigh & Is Measa Liom Bródach' / Willie Clancy – 'The Plains Of Boyle/The Leitrim Fancy' (Gael Linn CE 18) 1960
Note: Irish label Gael Linn released a series of 20 (CE1-CE20) now-rare 78rpm discs between 1957 and 1961, with each disc split between two different traditional solo performers (including pipers Tommy Reck on two sides as well as the above three discs involving Willie Clancy). Twenty-one of the 43 tracks across these 78s – including one, 'Na Connerys', of Willie's three – were compiled on the 1978 LP *Na Ceirníní 78 1957–1960* (Gael Linn CEF 075). All 43 tracks were compiled on the 2004 2CD *Seoltaí Séidte (Setting Sail): Ceolta Éireann 1957–1961 – Forty-Three Historic Recordings* (Gael Linn CEFCD184).

Irish Pipe & Fiddle Tunes EP (Topic TOP89) 1963
Margaret Barry, Willie Clancy, Michael Gorman
Willie Clancy tracks: Hardiman The Fiddler; Chief O'Neill's Favourite [with Michael Gorman]; The Chanter's Song; The Mountain Road [with Michael Gorman]
Note: All of the tracks involving Willie were recorded by Ewan MacColl at his Croydon home in 1955. The sole track by Margaret Barry (with Gorman) was recorded by Bill Leader in 1957. These were all leftovers from other projects. 'The Chanter's Song' was later included on the LP *From Erin's Green Shore: Songs, Pipes & Fiddle Tunes In The Irish Tradition* (Topic TPS168), in 1966. 'Chief O'Neill's Favourite' and 'The Mountain Road' were included on the Michael Gorman

double-CD anthology *The Sligo Champion* (Topic TSCD 525 D) in 2001.

The Minstrel From Clare (Topic 12T175) 1967
Willie Clancy
Langstern Pony; The Templehouse/Over The Moor To Maggie; Bruachna Carraige Báine (The Brink Of The White Rock); Erin's Lovely Lea; The Killavel Fancy/The Dogs Among The Bushes; The Family Ointment; The Dear Irish Boy; Caoineadh An Spailpín (The Spalpeen's Lament)/The Cuckoo's Nest; The Pipe On The Hob; The Gander; The Legacy Jig; The Flogging Reel; The Song Of The Riddles (Captain Wedderburn's Courtship); Spailpín A Rúin (Spalpeen, My Love)
Note: Willie's first solo LP, recorded in a pub in Carraroe, Galway, by Bill Leader. Six tracks appeared in 1995 on the various-artists CD *Farewell To Lissycasey: The Traditional Music Of County Clare* (Ossian OSSCD 79). 'The Song Of The Riddles' was included on the 1998 CD *The Voice Of The People Volume 1* (Topic TSCD651); 'Erin's Lovely Lea' was included on the 1998 CD *The Voice Of The People Volume 4* (Topic TSCD654). The album has been available in full on Green Linnet CD (GLCD 3091) from 1994 and as a Topic download (TSDL175) from 2009.

Seoda Ceoil 1 (Gael Linn CEF18) 1968
Seán Ó Ceallaigh [John Kelly], Willie Clancy, Seán Ó Conaire [Seán Conroy]
Willie Clancy tracks: Old Hag, You Have Killed Me/Old Tipperary; The Boy In The Gap/Seán Reid's Fancy; The Bold Trainer O; Little Garden Fling; Jim Ward's/Strop The Razor; The Jolly Banger/The Ravelled Hank Of Yarn; The Humours Of Derrykrosane/Hardiman The Fiddler; Fraher's Jig
Note: Translating as 'Musical Treasures', this is a shared LP, with the three artists each performing solo. Available from 2013 on CD with Vol. 2 (not featuring Willie) as *Seoda Ceoil 1 & 2* (Gael Linn CEFCD203).

The Breeze From Erin: Irish Folk Music On Wind Instruments (Topic 12T184) 1969
Various Artists
Willie Clancy tracks: An Phis Fhliuch (The Choice Wife); The Morning Dew/The Woman Of The House; Táimse Im Chodlatha.
Note: Other artists are Festy Conlan (whistle), Eddie Corcoran (whistle), Tim Lyons (accordion), Tony MacMahon (accordion) and Séamus Tansey (flute, whistle), with Reg Hall accompanying some on piano. Tracks were recorded during Bill Leader's field trip to Clare in 1967 (these include all of Willie's) and at Reg Hall's home in Croydon. 'The Choice Wife' was included on the 7CD set *Three Score And Ten: A Voice To The People* (Topic TOPIC70) in 2009.

Tutor For The Feadóg Stáin [Tin Whistle]: Foilsithe Ag Comhaltas Ceoltóirí Éireann (CCE, no cat. no.) 1971
Performers: Mícheál Ó hAlmhain (speech); Willie Clancy, Mary Bergin, Micho Russell, Deirdre Collis (whistles)
Note: A 60-minute cassette release of a tin whistle tutor with English language instruction and examples of tunes.

The Drones And The Chanters: Irish Pipering (Claddagh CC11) 1971
Various Artists
Willie Clancy tracks: Bímís Ag Ól/Let Us Drink!; Loch Na gCaor; The Lady's Pantalettes; Kitty Got A Clinking Coming From The Fair
Note: An LP shared with Séamus Ennis, Peadar Broe, Leo Rowsome, Paddy Moloney, Dan Dowd and Tommy Reck. Released on CD in 2000 and on CD/download in 2011.

The West Wind (Folktrax FTX 173) 1975
Willie Clancy & Bobby Casey
Solo piping tracks: Rowsome's Slip Jig; The Harvest Home; The Sweep's Hornpipe; Give Us A Drink Of Water; The Dear Irish Boy; Rakish Paddy; Connacht

Heifers; Varsoviana; The Foxhunter's; Polka Mazurka; Banish Misfortune; Old Hag You Have Killed Me; Top It Off; [plus four Untitled Jigs, three Untitled Slow Airs and one Untitled Reel]
Solo whistle tracks: The Flogging Reel; The Bright Lady; The Red Haired Man's Wife; Jumping Charlie; Thompson Catty
Pipes & fiddle duets: The Bush/Chicago Reel; Ask My Father; The West Wind/Seán Reid's Fancy; Munster Buttermilk
Note: A 60-minute cassette on Peter Kennedy's label. In addition to the above Willie Clancy content were five solo fiddle pieces from Bobby Casey. The tracks were purportedly 'recorded by Séamus Ennis & Peter Kennedy in London in 1956' and 'edited by Peter Kennedy'. There seems no reason to doubt this (unlike the stated provenance of some Folktrax releases): both Clancy and Casey were in London during that period, as was Ennis.

The Pipering Of Willie Clancy: Volume 1
(Claddagh CC32) 1980
Willie Clancy
The West Wind/Seán Reid's Fancy; The Rocks Of Bawn; The Old Bush; Will You Come Down To Limerick?; The Bold Trainer O; The Rolling Wave; An Ghaoth Aniar-Aneas (The South-West Wind); Garret Barry's Mazurka; Jenny Picking Cockles/My Love Is In America; The Bright Lady; The Lady's Pantalettes/The Crooked Road To Dublin/ The Ravelled Hank Of Yarn; Purty Molly Brannigan/The Green Fields Of America; Kitty Got A Clinking Coming From The Fair; The Bonny Bunch Of Roses/An Binnsín Luachra (The Little Bench Of Rushes); Down The Back Lane; Páidín Ó Raifeartaigh (Little Pat Rafferty); Clancy's Jig; Jenny, Tie The Bonnet; Corney Is Coming
Note: Performances recorded for Radio Éireann/RTÉ, 1958-73 – though no specific track dates are given.

The Pipering Of Willie Clancy: Volume 2
(Claddagh CC39) 1983
Willie Clancy
Seán Ó Duibhir A' Ghleanna; Caisleán Dhun Guaire (Dungaire Castle); McKenna's/ Colonel Rodger's Favourite/The Happy Days Of Yore; Casadh An tSúgain; Harvest Home; I Buried My Wife And Danced On Top Of Her; 'Chailligh, Do Mhairis Mé (Old Hag You Have Killed Me); The Flower On The Moor; Bímís Ag Ól 's Ag Pógadh Na mBan (Let Us Be Drinking And Kissing The Women); The Milliner's Daughter; The Trip O'er The Mountain; The Connaught Heifers; The Steampacket; The Gold Ring; Kitty Gone A Milking; Banish Misfortune/The Shady Groves Of Peamount; An Buachaill Caol Dubh (The Dark Slender Boy); An Phis Fhliuch (The Choice Wife); Rakish Paddy; Fraher's Jig; Garret Barry's; Dark Is The Colour Of My True Love's Hair; Jenny's Welcome To Charlie
Note: More undated performances recorded for Radio Éireann/RTÉ, 1958-73.

A Clare Session With Willy Clancy [sic] And Friends (Skylark SK1003) 1985
Willie Clancy (pipes), Peadar O'Loughlin (fiddle, flute), Jimmy Ward (banjo), Martin Talty (flute, pipes)
Jenny Picking Cockles; Jenny's Wedding; The Crooked Road To Dublin; The Bunch Of Green Rushes; The Steam Packet; Rakish Paddy; The Skylark; Roaring Mary; The Morning Dew; The Fiddler Leahy's; The Fiddler Cooley's; The Ships Are Sailing; The Queen Of The Fair; Paddy Fahy's; The Reel Of Mullinavat; Tomeen O'Dea's; The Friar's Britches; The Pipe On The Hob; The High Reel; The Boy In The Gap; Paddy Taylor's; The Green Groves Of Erin; Miss Galvin's Reel; The Wild Irishman; Toss The Feathers; Kitty's Rambles
Note: A 60-minute US release on Patrick Sky's cassette label.

Leo Rowsome
Selected Discography

Leo Rowsome recorded at least 36 78rpm shellac discs for a variety of labels between 1925 and 1948. A detailed listing can be found online (www.tedmcgraw.com/iweb%20published%20to%20computer/iWebSite2/LeoDiscog2.html). Leo was only modestly represented on vinyl during his lifetime. Two posthumous LPs collecting some of his 78s were released on Topic in the 1970s; the contents of these have since been edited onto one CD. Further digital-era releases could be created from non-commercial recordings and the handful of extant RTÉ recordings.

Vinyl Releases

Irish Popular Dances: Reels, Jigs, Hornpipes
(Folkways FW 6818) 1951
Various
Note: A 10-inch US-only LP – Leo's first appearance on vinyl, three years after his last shellac (78rpm) release. Leo's tracks: 'Jackson's Morning Brush/The Clare Jig' (probably from HMV IM 525, 1937); 'Boil The Breakfast Early/The Heather Breeze' (probably from HMV BD 1314, 1937). Other artists, all performances of similar vintage, include Michael Coleman, The Flanagan Brothers, The Hyde Brothers and Liam Walsh.

The King Of The Pipers (Claddagh CC1) 1966
Leo Rowsome
The King Of The Pipers; O'Carolan's Concerto/Planxty Davis; The Coolin; Pipe On The Hob/The Bride's Favourite; The Fox Chase; The Dark Slender Boy; Jenny's Wedding/Lord MacDonald; Planxty Browne; The Battle Of Aughrim; The Kerry Jig/The Ballintore Fancy; The Old Man Rocking The Cradle; Molloy's Favourite/My Sweetheart Jane; Madame Bonaparte; The Death Of Staker Wallace; Will You Come Down To Limerick/Hardiman The Fiddler; The Derry Hornpipe
Note: Reissued on CD in 1996 as Claddagh CC1CD. 'The Kerry Jig/The Ballintore Fancy' also appears on the various-artists 1984 LP *Claddagh's Choice* (CC40) and its subsequent CD reissue.

Piper's Choice EP (Claddagh CCE1) 1966
Leo Rowsome
The Stoney Steps/Dillon's Fancy; Casadh An tSúgáin; My Darling Asleep/Tommy Whelan's; The Bright Lady; The Ashplant/Jenny Tie The Bonnet/Drowsy Maggie
Note: Bafflingly, this EP was not added to the CD reissue of *The King Of The Pipers*. Helena Rowsome: 'There was a glitch in the recording and it was not reproduced. Pity, as it is the only recording to my knowledge on which he played the double chanter.' In general, the Irish record industry and specifically labels associated with traditional music have ignored the concept of added value, in both content and annotation, in the CD remastering era.

Classics Of Irish Piping Vol. 1 (Topic 12T259) 1975
Leo Rowsome
Kiss The Maid Behind The Barrel/Touch Me If You Dare; Top Of The Cork Road/The Irish Washerwoman; Boulavogue/The Old Bog Road; The Boys Of Wexford/Kelly The Boy From Killane; Boil The Breakfast Early/The Heather Breeze; Savourneen Deelish/Clare's Dragoons; The Blackbird; St. Patrick's Day; Rights Of Man/Wexford/Dunphy's Hornpipe; The Broom/Star Of Munster/The Milliner's Daughter; Day Dreams/The Low Backed Car; Kitty's Rambles/Donnybrook Fair/The Butcher's March; The Plains Of Boyle/Bantry Bay Hornpipe; The Collier's Reel/The Maid of Tramore

Note: A selection from Leo's 1926-44 78rpm releases for the London, HMV and Columbia labels, sourced from the collections of Tony Engle, Reg Hall and EMI. *Classics Of Irish Piping* (Topic TSCD471), released in 1998, is a CD compiling 12 tracks apiece from the LPs *Vol. 1* and *Vol. 3*: 24 of the 30 vinyl tracks.

Classics Of Irish Piping Vol. 3 (Topic 12T322) 1977
Leo Rowsome
Gillian's Apples/The Maid Of Tramore; The Independent Hornpipe/The Star Hornpipe; The Fairie's Revels/I Won't Be A Nun; Higgin's Hornpipe/The Queen Of May; The Frieze Breeches; Tomorrow Morning/The Cloone Hornpipe; The Bunch Of Keys/Buckley's Fancy; The Sweep's Hornpipe/The Friendly Visit; The Cook In The Kitchen/Rakes Of Kildare; Jockey To The Fair; My Darling Asleep/Tongues Of Fire; Brian O'Lynn/The Newly Married Couple; A Nation Once Again/The Bold Fenian Men/Fainne Geal An Lac; Shandon Bells/Haste To The Wedding; Snowy Breasted Pearl; Rocky Road To Dublin
Note: A further selection from Leo's 78rpm releases (1925-48) for the Rex, Imperial and Winner labels, sourced from Reg Hall's collection. Vol. 2 in this series, incidentally, compiled vintage recordings by William Andrews and Liam Walsh. Partly reissued on *Classics Of Irish Piping* (Topic TSCD471) (see above).

Exclusive Recordings On Various-Artists Releases

The Drones And The Chanters: Irish Pipering (Claddagh CC 11) 1971
Leo Rowsome tracks: My Darling Asleep/ Whelan's Jig; The Castle Of Dromore; The Dear Irish Boy

Note: Seemingly exclusive recordings – although possibly the second track was lifted from the same label's *Piper's Choice* EP – on an album shared with Séamus Ennis, Willie Clancy, Paddy Moloney, Peadar Broe, Tommy Reck and Dan Dowd. Released on CD in 2000 and on CD/ download in 2011.

The Irish Phonograph Vol. 1 (RTÉ/EMI GAE 1003) 1986
Various Artists
Note: Vintage 78rpm recordings by Leo along with Neil O'Boyle, The Tulla Céilí Band, Seán Maguire and others.

Traditional Irish Recordings From 1917 To c. 1950 Vol. 3: Piping Rarities (Oldtime Records OTR103) 2009
Various Artists
Note: Leo Rowsome tracks: Dark Woman Of The Glen; Jackson's Morning Brush/ The Clare Jig. The former is presumably from HMV IM 1016 (1944) and the latter from HMV525 (1937) – the same as had previously been resurrected on the 1951 Folkways LP. Neither of these was on the *Classics Of Irish Piping* compilations.

Tuning the Radio – Early Traditional Recordings From RTÉ Radio (RTÉ 285CD) 2010
Various Artists
Note: Leo Rowsome track: The Sligo Maid/ Miss McLeod's, recorded on 16/2/49 as a music insert for a programme called *Music Stand*. As most of Leo's many Radio Éireann broadcasts were live, this is probably a very rare survival (being a pre-recorded insert). The album comprises unreleased recordings made during the 1940s and 50s by Radio Éireann's Mobile Recording Unit.

Appendix 3
John McSherry Tune Transcriptions

Introduction by John McSherry

From one perspective, I've been part of the popular music industry – Led Zeppelin, The Beatles, Elvis Presley, Frank Sinatra, all the way back to the first blues records in the 1920s. From another, I've been part of a much longer, more organic continuum of uilleann piping and traditional Irish music going all the way back to the 1700s. Curiously enough, Patsy Touhey, one of the very earliest and greatest recorded Irish pipers, and a man felt by some to be 'outside the tradition', was selling cylinder recordings by mail order as early as 1901. He felt that he didn't need record labels, that he could do it himself. And he could. Over a century later and music in the commercial arena has more or less arrived back at that model: individual artists doing it themselves. There will always be a demand for music but there may not always be a demand for a 'music business' as we've known it in the 20th century. Traditional musicians will survive regardless, as they always have.

Nevertheless, musical history in the recording era tends to be measured in recordings and, for me, the first recording of any significance in my own story is *Loosely Connected*, the Niamh Parsons album from 1992 which included my own 'Katie Campbell's Rambles'. The next significant releases were the sole Tamalin album *Rhythm & Rhyme* (1997), the first Lúnasa album, *Lúnasa Live* (1998), and the eponymous *Coolfin* (1998). Of these, only the Tamalin album contained any self-written material. My compositional muse would only start flourishing in the following decade. Nevertheless, for a traditional musician, one can measure one's history in tunes – compositions or interpretations. Musicians have often expressed interest in my style of playing, even of standard piping tunes like 'Colonel Frazer' and 'Miss Monaghan's', so what we've done in this appendix of 25 transcriptions is to present both compositions and traditional tunes from my repertoire. Ultimately, any worth I have as a musician and artist hangs solely on the quality of the work. If I've done anything worth preserving, disseminating and carrying on, a fair part of it will be here.

John Riddell, one of my piping students, has done a tremendous job in transcribing with great accuracy a mix of compositions and traditional tunes from my own performances on record and in person. I've gone through these transcriptions, in draft form, in detail with him and can affirm that the versions printed here really do represent my playing. 'Katie Campbell's Rambles' is here, along with traditional material from the three important 1997–98 albums mentioned above and both compositions and trad tunes from five of the six albums that constitute my key works on record spanning 2001–12. While the format of this book is, we know, not ideal for sheet music presentation, the tunes are printed here as a permanent record (books, after all, hang around for decades) and it's anticipated that anyone wishing to use them for learning or performing will scan/photograph and then print the pages required for convenience. At some stage in the future, myself and John Riddell hope to publish a book of all my compositions. Until then, I hope you enjoy the tunes I've selected!

Background To Tune Transcriptions by John Riddell
It was listening John McSherry's recordings that first drew me to the uilleann pipes and, over time, convinced me that this was an instrument I wanted to learn to play, to whatever standard I could achieve. I soon came to understand that traditional music in general, and arguably pipe music in particular, owes much of its character and appeal to the use of a range of techniques – not just those sometimes referred to as ornaments or embellishments but other methods by which the tonal quality or character of the notes produced may be altered (see the guide to the technique symbols used in the transcriptions). These techniques are used in all tunes and on a large proportion of the notes. A quick glance at the transcriptions on the previous pages, where symbols indicating technique are shown above the notes to which they apply, gives an idea of this. In some tunes you will see that almost every note is adorned with a symbol indicating that it is affected in some way by the application of a specific technique.

These techniques can be thought of as an extension of the player's creative options beyond the bare notes of the tune, which would lack interest on their own but which are brought to life by use of ornamentation and technique. The choice of which techniques to use, and where in a tune to use them, follows no fixed rules, but is a choice made by the player and indeed can define a player's style. John's playing shows a judicious choice of technique, adding just the right character to notes, complementing and emphasising the intrinsic rhythm and shaping the phrasing but always blending seamlessly into the tune – never intruding or disrupting the flow of the music. This is what for me makes him one of the stand-out pipers of his generation. It's what motivated me to study and analyse his playing style and to use this as guidance and inspiration for my own learning.

Learning to play the pipes means much more than just being able to play the naked tune – it is essential to understand the effect that the different techniques create, master the mechanics (including the motor skills) required to execute them fluently, and develop a sense of how and when to use them in a way that is sympathetic and complementary to the tune. Needless to say this is a daunting task for the beginner and the impetus for these transcriptions was born of my own frustrations as I attempted to negotiate this process. I would frequently hear things in recorded performances that I could not understand and could not easily recognise, even with recourse to the piping tutors currently available and the plethora of information on the worldwide web. Distinguishing between the different forms of ornamentation was, to begin with, almost impossible and the techniques underlying some sounds remained a complete mystery. The idea of the transcriptions is to facilitate the learning process to some degree. Music notation is one way of attempting to facilitate the learning and dissemination of tunes. However, in this case music notation alone is not enough. The challenge was to come up with a scheme that could also convey the use of the all-important techniques without which the transcriptions would have limited meaning.

The reason for developing a special notation or set of symbols for this is because the techniques used in traditional music are fundamentally different from the ornamentation used in classical music. In traditional music embellishments such as cuts, taps, rolls and crans involve a sequence of finger movements that open and close different holes. However, the purpose of these is not to produce a sequence of notes of audible pitch, but rather to produce an interruption or disturbance of the otherwise continuous tone of the main note to which the technique is applied. Although some techniques such as cuts and rolls might in some way be represented in a similar manner to the grace notes (small notes) used in classical music to represent certain types of ornamentation (for example mordents or appoggiaturas) to do so can actually be misleading. In addition, because ornamentation appears so frequently in traditional music, they would soon clutter the manuscript and make the music difficult to read. For this reason, a system has been developed where each technique is represented by its own distinct symbol and these are set above the staff with the positioning indicating the timing of the technique in relation to the notes of the tune. The scheme I have devised is an adaptation and development of an idea I came across in a comprehensive guide to traditional flute and whistle playing by Grey Larson. His book, *The Essential Guide To Irish Flute And Tin Whistle*, is an excellent resource and highly recommended read. It is impossible to convey in musical notation all of the nuances of pipe and whistle playing technique – in the end these come from the individual performers – but we hope the transcriptions capture the essential techniques and provide a useful road map to their deployment in the tunes. The transcriptions in most cases remain faithful to the recorded versions on John McSherry's albums. In the few cases where the transcriptions depart from these they reflect John's current preferred configuration of the tune. A larger collection of tune transcriptions and a tutor for the uilleann pipes and low whistle inspired by this project are now in preparation.

How these transcriptions are used is a matter of choice and will depend on the reader's level of familiarity with pipe and whistle playing and access to alternative forms of guidance. With the increasing popularity of the pipes throughout the world, they may be especially valuable to those for whom the opportunity to mix with accomplished players is limited. However, even those lucky enough to be able to learn first-hand by the aural tradition should find them a useful resource. Some characteristic techniques such as tight triplets and popping will be easily recognised, but the difference between different types of rolls and crans is more subtle especially when executed at speed. One effective way of using the transcriptions is therefore to listen along to the recordings with the sheet music in front of you. It will then be possible, while following the music, to identify the techniques used at any point in the tune. Even non-piping musicians may find this an interesting exercise! If played slowly at first, some more experienced pipers might even find it possible to play from the transcriptions in the manner of sight reading. However they are used we hope they will increase the accessibility and enjoyment of the music.

John Riddell, May 2015

1. Katie Campbell's Rambles
This is the first tune I ever wrote which I dedicated to my niece, Katie. From *Loosely Connected*, 1992.

2. The Tempest
I changed a few of the notes of this reel to give it a different feel from the normal version. From *Rhythm & Rhyme*, 1997.

3. Colonel Frazer
This is one of the great piping reels. I got it from the playing of Paddy Keenan but it has a much longer history as a recorded piece, going back to recordings made by Johnny Doran in 1947 and Patsy Touhey at the very dawn of the 20th century. From *Lúnasa Live*, 1996.

4. Miss Monaghan's
This is a lovely trad reel. I changed the end of the tune to give it a more dynamic turn-around. From *Coolfin*, 1998.

5. Lady Lane
I wrote this jig while living in Lady Lane, a quaint row of cottages in Dublin, with my baby girl Áille. From *At First Light*, 2001.

6. Tripswitch
A tune written by myself and Dónal O'Connor while recording in Homestead Studios, Randalstown. Mudd, the engineer, had gone to the pub for the night and we were left to our own devices. I didn't have a light for my cigarette so I used the toaster, which turned out not to be one of my better ideas – in fact, it turned out everything. The fuses all tripped and we finished the tune in the dark. Still, it gave us an idea for a title … From *Tripswitch*, 2006.

7. Áille's Arabesque
An elegant wee tune I wrote for my daughter Áille who was a very keen dancer at the time. From *Soma*, 2010.

8. The Maid Of Murlough
Murlough beach, Newcastle, Co.Down is a favourite retreat of my girlfriend Trisha. She has been such a shining light in my life and this was just a small thank-you. From *Soma*, 2010.

9. The Pipers Of Roguery
I wrote this for all the roguish pipers out there. From *Idir*, 2011.

10. Lord Mayo
An ancient Irish march I got from an early Chieftains album. From *Lúnasa Live*, 1996.

11. Maids Of Mount Cisco
A very popular old reel. From *Lúnasa Live*, 1996.

12. The Rambles Of Kitty
A very popular piping jig I got from the playing of Liam O'Fynn. From *Soma*, 2010.

13. The Rose In The Gap
A great march got from Dónal O'Connor's dad, Gerry, who in turn got it from the Donnellan Collection of Oriel Songs and Dances. From *Tripswitch*, 2006.

14. The Slide From Grace
I wrote this tune while thinking on all those people who had it all but let it slip away. From *Soma*, 2010.

15. The Wave-Sweeper
The third part of this tricky wee waltz changes to a 4/4 time signature. I named it after the sea-borne chariot of the Celtic mythological deity Manannán Mac Lir. From *Soma*, 2010.

16. An Bhean Chaointe (The Keening Woman)
In Ireland 'keening women' were noted for their skill in lamenting the dead and so were invited to wakes to mourn the departed. From *Soma*, 2010.

17. Down The Back Lane
This piping jig was a favourite of the great Willie Clancy. From *Soma*, 2010.

18. Farewell To Connaught
A fine reel I got from the whistle playing of Micho Russell. From *At First Light*, 2001.

19. The Follly Of Wisdom
Yes, the three l's are intentional. A polka with a West Coast vibe. From *The Olllam*, 2012.

20. McSherry's Waltz
A waltz myself and my sister Tíona wrote for our parents, Denis and Olive. A wee thank-you for all they've done for us. From *Soma*, 2010.

21. Rolling In Rosemount
A slide myself and Dónal wrote in about 10 minutes while rolling cigarettes in his home studio in Rosemount Gardens. From *Idir*, 2011.

22. The Gulf Of Mexico
A tune I got from my brother Paul's old band Grianan. I think it's an old American folk song. From *Soma*, 2010.

23. The Maid At The Spinning Wheel
A very popular old piping jig, great for cranning. From *Idir*, 2011.

24. The Limestone Rock
A very popular trad reel. From *At First Light*, 2001.

25. Áille's Antics
Another tune I wrote for my daughter Áille. The title says it all. From *Soma*, 2010.

Key to Technique Symbols

This is a guide to the symbols used in the tune transcriptions to represent techniques applied to the notes above which they are placed. The symbols are shown on the left as they appear in the music notation and a brief description of the technique is given on the right.

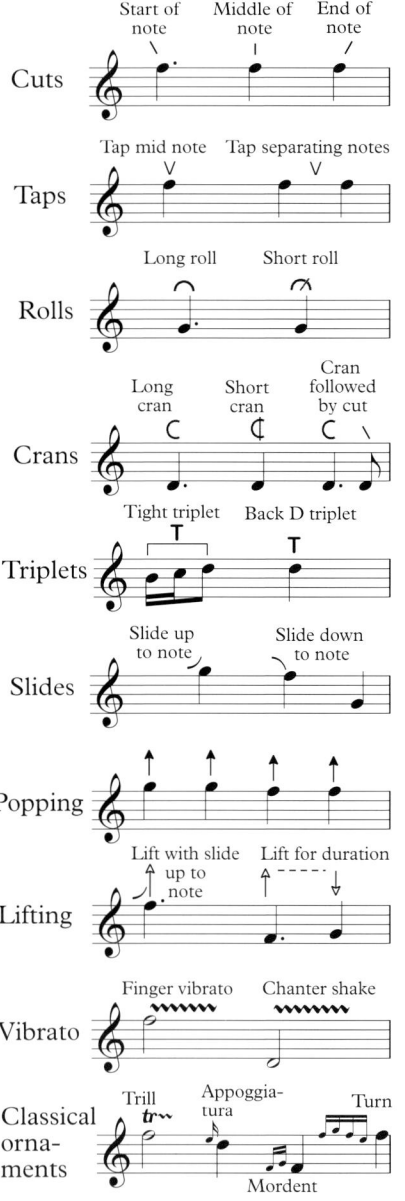

Cuts are produced by a brief lifting and replacing of a finger producing a momentary interruption to the note being played. Cuts are most commonly used at the start of a note and may be used to separate successive notes of the same pitch. They may also be used in the middle, or at the end of a note, especially in slower tunes.

Taps are a brief tapping of a finger over the hole beneath the lowest covered hole, producing a momentary interruption to the note being played. Taps can be used in the middle of a note or to separate two notes.

Rolls are a combination of a cut followed by a tap. Long rolls start with the main note followed by a cut part way into the note, followed by a tap. They are most often used on a note of dotted crotchet value. Short rolls are similar but start with a cut. They are often executed very quickly and are most often used on a crotchet.

Crans are most often used on low D (on which rolls cannot be performed) but may also be used on other notes such as low E. Like rolls they can be played in long and short forms. It is quite common to combine a cran with a cut on the following note resulting in a more complex ornamentation.

Tight triplets are a grouping of three notes, the first two being shorter in value than the third. They can involve groups of varing pitch, usually in ascending or descending order and are played in a short and detached (staccato) style. Tight triplets can also be played on back D by sliding the thumb across the hole.

Slides are executed at the beginning of a note by approaching the note to be played from the note immediately above or below. The pitch is gradually altered by progressive opening or closing of the appropriate holes.

Popping is a tonal effect which can be applied to notes in the upper register by a rapid lifting of the chanter from the knee and immediate replacement. It may be used on occasional notes in a tune or several notes in succession.

Lifting of the chanter from the knee can be used on certain notes mainly in the lower octave to alter their tonal quality. Lifting is often combined with a slide at the beginning of a note the co-ordination of the two giving greater emphasis. Some phrases can be played with the chanter off the knee throughout.

Vibrato may be added to notes, particularly longer notes, by rapid fluttering of a finger over a hole. Applying vibrato to the hole two down from the last hole covered is often effective. For low D the chanter can be shaken to achieve a similar effect.

Classical ornaments are represented by the standard symbols used in classical music notation or by the use of grace notes (notes of reduced size) written on the staff.

Katie Campbell's Rambles

Composed by John McSherry (IMRO/MCPS)
Transcribed by John Riddell

The Tempest

Traditional arranged by John McSherry (IMRO/MCPS)
Transcribed by John Riddell

Colonel Frazer

Traditional arranged by John McSherry (IMRO/MCPS)
Transcribed by John Riddell

Miss Monaghan's

Traditional arranged by John McSherry (IMRO/MCPS)
Transcribed by John Riddell

Lady Lane

Composed by John McSherry (IMRO/MCPS)
Transcribed by John Riddell

Aille's Arabesque

Composed by John McSherry (IMRO/MCPS)
Transcribed by John Riddell

The Maid Of Murlough

Composed by John McSherry (IMRO/MCPS)
Transcribed by John Riddell

The Pipers of Roguery

Composed by John McSherry (IMRO/MCPS)
Transcribed by John Riddell

Lord Mayo

Traditional arranged by John McSherry (IMRO/MCPS)
Transcribed by John Riddell

Maids of Mount Cisco

Traditional arranged by John McSherry (IMRO/MCPS)
Transcribed by John Riddell

The Rambles of Kitty

Traditional arranged by John McSherry (IMRO/MCPS)
Transcribed by John Riddell

The Rose In The Gap

Traditional arranged by John McSherry (IMRO/MCPS)
Transcribed by John Riddell

The Slide From Grace

Composed by John McSherry (IMRO/MCPS)
Transcribed by John Riddell

The Wave Sweeper

Composed by John McSherry (IMRO/MCPS)
Transcribed by John Riddell

An Bhean Chaointe

Composed by John McSherry (IMRO/MCPS)
Transcribed by John Riddell

Down The Back Lane

Traditional arranged by John McSherry (IMRO/MCPS)
Transcribed by John Riddell

Farewell To Connaught

Traditional arranged by John McSherry (IMRO/MCPS)
Transcribed by John Riddell

The Folly of Wisdom

Composed by John McSherry (IMRO/MCPS)
Transcribed by John Riddell

McSherry's Waltz

Composed by John McSherry and Tiona McSherry (IMRO/MCPS)
Transcribed by John Riddell

Rolling In Rosemount

Composed by John McSherry and Dónal O'Connor (IMRO/MCPS)
Transcribed by John Riddell

The Gulf Of Mexico

Traditional arranged by John McSherry (IMRO/MCPS)
Transcribed by John Riddell

The Maid At The Spinning Wheel

Traditional arranged by John McSherry (IMRO/MCPS)
Transcribed by John Riddell

The Limestone Rock

Traditional arranged by John McSherry (IMRO/MCPS)
Transcribed by John Riddell

Aille's Antics

Composed by John McSherry (IMRO/MCPS)
Transcribed by John Riddell

Endnotes

1. *A Touchstone For The Tradition* (Brandon, 2001), Tony Kearns & Barry Taylor
2. 'The quiet man of the pipes', *Folk News*, 8/78
3. Second paragraph from an onstage interview with Finbar by Tony Clayton-Lea at IMRO HQ, Dublin, 30/1/14
4. Partly from an onstage interview with Finbar by Tony Clayton-Lea at IMRO HQ, Dublin, 30/1/14
5. From an onstage interview with Finbar by Tony Clayton-Lea at IMRO HQ, Dublin, 30/1/14
6. Karl Dallas, notes to the LP reissue *1968* by Sweeney's Men (Transatlantic, 1976)
7. From an onstage interview with Finbar by Tony Clayton-Lea at IMRO HQ, Dublin, 30/1/14
8. Second paragraph from an onstage interview with Finbar by Tony Clayton-Lea at IMRO HQ, Dublin, 30/1/14
9. 'Corrie-ing Favour', Andrew Means, *Melody Maker*, 19/12/70
10. *Singing From The Floor: A History Of British Folk Clubs* (Faber & Faber, 2014), J.P. Bean
11. Davey Johnstone, reply to an online question, 15/12/13
12. *Singing From The Floor: A History Of British Folk Clubs* (Faber & Faber, 2014), J.P. Bean
13. From an onstage interview with Finbar by Tony Clayton-Lea at IMRO HQ, Dublin, 30/1/14
14. Nat Joseph, notes to *The Johnstons* (Transatlantic, 1968)
15. Tony Wilson, *Melody Maker*, 24/8/68
16. *Singing From The Floor: A History Of British Folk Clubs* (Faber & Faber, 2014), J.P. Bean
17. *Melody Maker*, 29/3/69
18. *Melody Maker*, 19/7/69
19. *Free Spirit* (2002), RTÉ TV, Dir: Liam McGrath
20. 'Clancys – The Oldest Folk Group Left', Tony Wilson, *Melody Maker*, 15/6/68
21. 'Another Chapter Closes, Makem Leaves Clancys', Tony Wilson, *Melody Maker*, 26/4/69
22. 'A New, Fat Sound From The Clancys', Tony Wilson, *Melody Maker*, 13/9/69
23. 'A New, Fat Sound From The Clancys', Tony Wilson, *Melody Maker*, 13/9/69
24. *Melody Maker*, uncredited, 21/2/70
25. From an onstage interview with Finbar by Tony Clayton-Lea at IMRO HQ, Dublin, 30/1/14
26. 'Bringing Irish Music To The People', Jeremy Gilbert, *Melody Maker*, 13/12/69
27. 'Bringing Irish Music To The People', Jeremy Gilbert, *Melody Maker*, 13/12/69
28. 'Bringing Irish Music To The People', Jeremy Gilbert, *Melody Maker*, 13/12/69
29. *Free Spirit* (2002), RTÉ TV
30. *Melody Maker*, 19/2/72
31. Partly from an onstage interview with Finbar by Tony Clayton-Lea at IMRO HQ, Dublin, 30/1/14
32. Ulrich Olshausen, notes to *A Dream In My Hand* (Intercord, 1974)
33. 'Furey-ous forces behind Tam Linn', Colin Irwin, *Melody Maker*, 4/10/75
34. 'Furey-ous forces behind Tam Linn', Colin Irwin, *Melody Maker*, 4/10/75
35. 'Furey-ous forces behind Tam Linn', Colin Irwin, *Melody Maker*, 4/10/75
36. *Free Spirit* (2002)
37. *Free Spirit* (2002)
38. *The Humours Of Planxty* (Hodder Headline Ireland, 2006), Leagues O'Toole
39. 'Start Following The Leader', Jeremy Gilbert, *Melody Maker*, 7/2/70
40. *The Humours Of Planxty* (Hodder Headline Ireland, 2006), Leagues O'Toole

41 *The Humours Of Planxty* (Hodder Headline Ireland, 2006), Leagues O'Toole
42 *The Humours Of Planxty* (Hodder Headline Ireland, 2006), Leagues O'Toole
43 *The Humours Of Planxty* (Hodder Headline Ireland, 2006), Leagues O'Toole
44 'Moore the merrier', Andrew Means, *Melody Maker*, 11/3/72
45 *No Disco* Planxty documentary, RTÉ, 2002
46 *The Humours Of Planxty* (Hodder Headline Ireland, 2006), Leagues O'Toole
47 'The Celtic Sound: Planxty', Karl Dallas, *Melody Maker*, 11/8/73
48 *The Humours Of Planxty* (Hodder Headline Ireland, 2006), Leagues O'Toole
49 'The Celtic Sound: Planxty', Karl Dallas, *Melody Maker*, 11/8/73
50 'The Easter Resurrection', Colin Irwin, *Melody Maker*, 17/3/79
51 'The Celtic Sound: Planxty', Karl Dallas, *Melody Maker*, 11/8/73
52 'The Easter Resurrection', Colin Irwin, *Melody Maker*, 17/3/79
53 *The Humours Of Planxty* (Hodder Headline Ireland, 2006), Leagues O'Toole
54 *No Disco* Planxty documentary, RTÉ, 2002
55 'The quiet man of the pipes,' Tomás Mac Ruairí, *Folk News*, 8/78
56 'The Easter Resurrection', Colin Irwin, *Melody Maker*, 17/3/79
57 'The Enigmatic Piper Supreme', Colin Irwin, *Melody Maker*, 25/2/78
58 'The Easter Resurrection', Colin Irwin, *Melody Maker*, 17/3/79
59 *The Humours Of Planxty* (Hodder Headline Ireland, 2006), Leagues O'Toole
60 *No Disco* Planxty documentary, RTÉ, 2002
61 *The Humours Of Planxty* (Hodder Headline Ireland, 2006), Leagues O'Toole
62 *Free Spirits: Irish Travellers and Irish Traditional Music* (MPO Productions, 2011), Tommy Fegan and Oliver O'Connell
63 *Traditional Music In Ireland* (Routledge & Kegan Paul, 1978), Tomás Ó Canainn
64 Notes to *Paddy Keenan* (Gael Linn, 1974), Séamus Ennis
65 'The Bothy Band: Guinness Brigade in Nescafé experiment', Fred Dellar, *NME*, 10/4/76
66 *The Humours Of Planxty* (Hodder Headline Ireland, 2006), Leagues O'Toole
67 Notes to *The Best Of The Bothy Band* (Mulligan, 1980), Colin Irwin; later reprinted, incongruously, as notes to the Mulligan CD issue of the first album, *The Bothy Band*
68 'The Bothy Band: Guinness Brigade in Nescafé experiment', Fred Dellar, *NME*, 10/4/76
69 'The Bothy Band: Guinness Brigade in Nescafé experiment', Fred Dellar, *NME*, 10/4/76
70 'The Bothy Band: Guinness Brigade in Nescafé experiment', Fred Dellar, *NME*, 10/4/76
71 Notes to *The Best Of The Bothy Band* (Mulligan, 1980), Colin Irwin
72 'Kevin the great', Colin Irwin, *Melody Maker*, 13/5/78
73 *Melody Maker*, 4/12/76
74 *Melody Maker*, 22/2/77
75 *Melody Maker*, 25/6/77
76 Mary Hardy, *Folk News*, 9/77
77 'Tripping the light fantastic', Colin Irwin, *Melody Maker*, 18/2/78
78 'Tripping the light fantastic', Colin Irwin, *Melody Maker*, 18/2/78
79 'Kevin the great', Colin Irwin, *Melody Maker*, 13/5/78
80 'Kevin the great', Colin Irwin, *Melody Maker*, 13/5/78
81 Colin Irwin, *Melody Maker*, 8/78
82 'A great weekend of music and ecstasy', Tomás Mac Ruairí, *Folk News*, No. 16, 1978
83 *An Bothy Boy – in omós do Mhícheál Ó Domhnaill* (2011), TG4

84 *The Humours Of Planxty* (Hodder Headline Ireland, 2006), Leagues O'Toole
85 'Moore The Merrier', Colin Irwin, *Melody Maker*, 19/8/78
86 'Mulligan Stew', Colin Irwin, *Melody Maker*, 2/12/78
87 'Molloy to quit Bothy Band?', *Melody Maker*, 19/8/78
88 *Melody Maker*, 9/9/78
89 'Matt joins reformed Planxty', *Folk News*, No. 17, 1978
90 *The Humours Of Planxty* (Hodder Headline Ireland, 2006), Leagues O'Toole
91 'Bothies to tour UK', *Melody Maker*, 11/11/78
92 'Mulligan Stew', Colin Irwin, *Melody Maker*, 2/12/78
93 'Mulligan Stew', Colin Irwin, *Melody Maker*, 2/12/78
94 *Melody Maker*, 1/9/79
95 'Beatific Ballisodare', Colin Irwin, *Melody Maker*, 25/8/79
96 'Séamus Ennis Tour', *Melody Maker*, 6/8/77
97 Seán Reid, 23/11/75; from Topic LP notes to Leo Rowsome's *Classics Of Irish Piping*.
98 *The Humours Of Planxty* (Hodder Headline, 2006), Leagues O'Toole
99 *The Séamus Ennis Story* (RTÉ, 1988), Prod: Peter Browne
100 *The Séamus Ennis Story* (RTÉ, 1988), Prod: Peter Browne
101 *The Séamus Ennis Story* (RTÉ, 1988), Prod: Peter Browne – original source uncredited
102 'Willie Clancy: The Man And His Music', Muiris Ó Rócháin and Harry Hughes, *Dál gCais*, Vol. 1 1972
103 'Willie Clancy And The Student Piper', uncredited, *An Píobaire*, 4/73
104 'Calling On The Piper', Seán Laffey, *Irish Music*, 7/98
105 'Willie Clancy: The Man And His Music', Muiris Ó Rócháin and Harry Hughes, *Dál gCais*, Vol. 1 1972
106 Peter Browne, notes to *The Return From Fingal* (RTÉ, 1997)
107 *The Humours Of Planxty* (Hodder Headline, 2006), Leagues O'Toole
108 *Irish Minstrels And Musicians* (1913), Francis O'Neill
109 *Irish Minstrels And Musicians* (1913), Francis O'Neill
110 Notes to *Classics Of Irish Piping* (Topic, 1993), Seán Reid (adapted from 1975 LP notes)
111 Undated radio interview with Rowsome, youtube.com/watch?v=6thedX3R1TE
112 *Irish Minstrels And Musicians* (1913), Francis O'Neill
113 *Irish Minstrels And Musicians* (1913), Francis O'Neill
114 Notes to *Classics Of Irish Piping* (Topic, 1993), Seán Reid (adapted from 1975 LP notes)
115 Essay on Leo Rowsome, Seán Reid, 23/11/75, pipers.ie/about/patrons/leo-rowsome/
116 Undated radio interview with Rowsome, youtube.com/watch?v=6thedX3R1TE
117 Essay on Leo Rowsome, Seán Reid, 23/11/75, pipers.ie/about/patrons/leo-rowsome/
118 Essay on Leo Rowsome, Seán Reid, 23/11/75, pipers.ie/about/patrons/leo-rowsome/
119 Publicity flyer for 'A Grand Ceilidhe', Birmingham 2/9/46, BBC Written Records, Caversham
120 *The Humours Of Planxty* (Hodder Headline, 2006), Leagues O'Toole
121 Notes to *Classics Of Irish Piping* (Topic, 1993), Seán Reid (adapted from 1975 LP notes)
122 *The Chieftains: The Authorised Biography* (Random House, 1998), John Glatt
123 *Melody Maker*, 28/6/69
124 Leo Rowsome addressing the Bettystown meeting of pipers, May 1968, youtube.com/watch?v=668s_qg-a7I

125 'Seán Reid: A Self Portrait', Muiris Ó Rócháin and Harry Hughes, *Dál gCais*, Vol. 2, 1974
126 'Death Of Well-Known Irish Musician', *Treoir*, Samhain/Nollaig, 1970
127 Undated radio interview with Rowsome, youtube.com/watch?v=6thedX3R1TE
128 'Seán Reid: A Self Portrait', Muiris Ó Rócháin and Harry Hughes, *Dál gCais*, Vol. 2, 1974
129 *The Humours Of Planxty* (Hodder Headline, 2006), Leagues O'Toole
130 Introduction to *Ceol An Phíobaire: Music Of The Pipers* (NPU, 2012), Terry Moylan
131 'Séamus Ennis – A Tribute', Ciarán Mac Mathúna, *Irish Times*, c. 6-9/10/82, sourced from *An Píobaire*, 10/82
132 'Séamus Ennis – A Tribute', Ciarán Mac Mathúna, *Irish Times*, c. 6-9/10/82, sourced from *An Píobaire*, 10/82
133 *Going To The Well For Water: The Séamus Ennis Field Diary 1942-1946* (Cork University Press, 2009), Ed: Ríonach Uí Ógáin.
134 'U2's Leading Edge', John Hutchinson, *Musician*, 9/86
135 Notes to *Masters Of Irish Music* (Leader, 1969), attributed to Mary Josephine Ennis
136 *Irish Minstrels And Musicians* (1910), Francis O'Neill
137 'As I Roved Out', Mícheál Ó hAlmhain, *Treoir*, 5/3/73
138 'As I Roved Out', Mícheál Ó hAlmhain, *Treoir*, 5/1/73
139 *Miles And Miles Of Music*, RTÉ, 1975
140 'The Feis Ceoil And Piping', (*Ceol VIII*, 1986)
141 'As I Roved Out', Mícheál Ó hAlmhain, *Treoir*, 5/1/73
142 *The Master's Touch: A Tutor For The Uilleann Pipes* (NPU, 1998), Séamus Ennis, Ed: Wilbert Garvin and Robbie Hannon
143 *The Dance Music Of Séamus Ennis* (NPU, 2007), Ed: Pat Mitchell
144 'As I Roved Out', Mícheál Ó hAlmhain, *Treoir*, 5/1/73
145 'As I Roved Out', Mícheál Ó hAlmhain, *Treoir*, 5/1/73
146 Notes to *Masters Of Irish Music* (Leader, 1969), attributed to Mary Josephine Ennis
147 *The Dance Music Of Séamus Ennis* (NPU, 2007), Ed: Pat Mitchell
148 'As I Roved Out', Mícheál Ó hAlmhain, *Treoir*, 5/3/73
149 *The Séamus Ennis Story* (RTÉ, 1988), Prod: Peter Browne
150 *Miles And Miles Of Music*, RTÉ, 1975
151 *Going To The Well For Water: The Séamus Ennis Field Diary 1942-1946* (Cork University Press, 2009), Ed: Ríonach Uí Ógáin (Ríonach is paraphrasing James Delargy from a 1971 radio interview)
152 Unpublished part of an interview by Mícheál Ó hAlmhain, 16/12/72, ITMA, Dublin
153 *Going To The Well For Water: The Séamus Ennis Field Diary 1942-1946* (Cork University Press, 2009), Ed: Ríonach Uí Ógáin
154 *Miles And Miles Of Music*, RTÉ, 1975
155 Seán Ó hEochaidh, 1/44, quoted in *Going To The Well For Water: The Séamus Ennis Field Diary 1942-1946* (Cork University Press, 2009), Ed: Ríonach Uí Ógáin
156 *Going To The Well For Water: The Séamus Ennis Field Diary 1942-1946* (Cork University Press, 2009), Ed: Ríonach Uí Ógáin
157 Séamus Ennis, notes to *Paddy Keenan* (Gael Linn, 1975)
158 *Going To The Well For Water: The Séamus Ennis Field Diary 1942-1946* (Cork University Press, 2009), Ed: Ríonach Uí Ógáin
159 *Dictionary Of Irish Biography* (Cambridge University Press, 2009), Ed: James McGuire and James Quinn

160 *A Life In The Wild* (Gill & McMillan, 2004), Éamon de Buitléar
161 *The Irish Folklore Commission 1935-1970: History, Ideology, Methodology* (Finnish Literature Society, 2007), Mícheál Briody
162 Unpublished part of an interview by Mícheál Ó hAlmhain, 16/12/72, ITMA, Dublin
163 *Forty Years Of Irish Broadcasting* (Radio Telefís Éireann, 1967), Maurice Gorham
164 Uncredited interview, quoted in *The Dance Music Of Séamus Ennis* (NPU, 2007), Ed: Pat Mitchell
165 Uncredited interview, quoted in *The Dance Music Of Séamus Ennis* (NPU, 2007), Ed: Pat Mitchell
166 Peter Browne, notes to *The Return From Fingal* CD (RTÉ, 1997)
167 Robin Roberts, notes to *The Bonny Bunch Of Roses* (Tradition, 1959)
168 *The Man Who Recorded The World* (Heinemann, 2010), John Szwed
169 *The Man Who Recorded The World* (Heinemann, 2010), John Szwed
170 Unpublished part of an interview by Mícheál Ó hAlmhain, 16/12/72, ITMA, Dublin
171 *Forty Years Of Irish Broadcasting* (Radio Telefís Éireann, 1967), Maurice Gorham
172 Unpublished part of an interview by Mícheál Ó hAlmhain, 16/12/72, ITMA, Dublin
173 Séamus Ennis files, BBC Written Records, Caversham
174 Unpublished part of an interview by Mícheál Ó hAlmhain, 16/12/72, ITMA, Dublin
175 *The Dance Music Of Séamus Ennis* (NPU, 2007), Ed: Pat Mitchell
176 Unpublished part of an interview by Mícheál Ó hAlmhain, 16/12/72, ITMA, Dublin
177 Unpublished part of an interview by Mícheál Ó hAlmhain, 16/12/72, ITMA, Dublin
178 Unpublished part of an interview by Mícheál Ó hAlmhain, 16/12/72, ITMA, Dublin
179 *The Séamus Ennis Story* (RTÉ, 1988), Prod: Peter Browne
180 *The Séamus Ennis Story* (RTÉ, 1988), Prod: Peter Browne
181 *Melody Maker*, 24/6/69
182 Rod Stradling, notes to *Traditional Performers At The King's Head Folk Club 1968-1970* (Musical Traditions, 2012)
183 Notes to *Masters Of Irish Music* (Leader, 1969), attributed to Mary Josephine Ennis
184 'Séamus Ennis Improving', *Treoir*, May/June 1970
185 *The Séamus Ennis Story* (RTÉ, 1988), Prod: Peter Browne
186 Letter from Harold Rogers, 6/12/54 (BBC Written Archives)
187 Seán Mac Réamoinn, *The Séamus Ennis Story* (RTÉ, 1988), Prod: Peter Browne
188 *The Master's Touch: A Tutor For The Uilleann Pipes* (NPU, 1998), Séamus Ennis, Ed: Wilbert Garvin and Robbie Hannon
189 Recalled by Christopher Ennis in *Ina Rothaí Óg Ag Bailiú Ceoil: Ó Bhéal Go Béal* (TG4, 2010)
190 *The Humours Of Planxty* (Hodder Headline, 2007), Leagues O'Toole
191 *The Séamus Ennis Story* (RTÉ, 1988), Prod: Peter Browne
192 'As I Roved Out', Mícheál Ó hAlmhain, *Treoir*, 1973
193 Liam O'Flynn, *Ina Rothaí Óg Ag Bailiú Ceoil: Ó Bhéal Go Béal* (TG4, 2010)
194 'As I Roved Out', Mícheál Ó hAlmhain, *Treoir*, 1973
195 *A Life In The Wild* (Gill & McMillan, 2004), Éamon de Buitléar
196 *The Humours Of Planxty* (Hodder Headline, 2007), Leagues O'Toole
197 *The Séamus Ennis Story* (RTÉ, 1988), Prod: Peter Browne

198 Unpublished part of an interview by Mícheál Ó hAlmhain, 16/12/72, ITMA, Dublin
199 Souvenir programme for the Dublin Folk Festival, July 1977
200 *Folk News*, 10/77
201 *Folk News*, 1/78
202 Unpublished part of an interview by Mícheál Ó Almhain, 16/12/72, ITMA, Dublin
203 Unpublished part of an interview by Mícheál Ó Almhain, 16/12/72, ITMA, Dublin
204 *Journeyman: The Autobiography* (Sidgwick & Jackson, 1990), Ewan MacColl
205 Memorial Address, Seán Reid, 4/7/77, reproduced in *An Píobaire*, Autumn 1977
206 Willie Clancy interview with Breandán Ó Cíobháin, RTÉ, 11/72
207 Junior Crehan interview, Tom Munnelly, *Béaloideas: The Journal Of The Folkore Of Ireland Society*, Vol. 66, 1998
208 'Willie Clancy: The Man And His Music', Muiris Ó Rócháin and Harry Hughes, *Dál gCais* Vol. 1, 1972
209 'Willie Clancy: The Man And His Music', Muiris Ó Rócháin and Harry Hughes, *Dál gCais* Vol. 1, 1972
210 'Garrett Barry', *An Píobaire*, Series 2 Vol. 7, 1980 (a late 1950s interview with Jack Donoghue by Séamus Mac Mathúna)
211 'Garret Barry', *An Píobaire*, 1/92 (Michael Cunningham interviewed by Eugene Lambe, 1961)
212 'Willie Clancy: The Man And His Music', Muiris Ó Rócháin and Harry Hughes, *Dál gCais* Vol. 1, 1972
213 *A Touchstone For The Tradition* (Brandon, 2001), Tony Kearns and Barry Taylor
214 Willie Clancy interview with Breandán Ó Cíobháin, RTÉ, 11/72
215 'Willie Clancy: The Man And His Music', Muiris Ó Rócháin and Harry Hughes, *Dál gCais* Vol. 1, 1972
216 'Seán Reid: A Self Portrait', Muiris Ó Rócháin and Harry Hughes, *Dal gCais*, Vol. 2, 1974
217 *A Touchstone For The Tradition* (Brandon, 2001), Tony Kearns and Barry Taylor
218 'Willie Clancy – A Beloved Genius', Martin Talty with Muiris Ó Rócháin, *Treoir*, 5/2/73
219 'Junior Crehan Of Bonavilla' (Part One), Tom Munnelly, *Béaloideas*, No. 66 (1998)
220 'Seán Reid: A Self Portrait', Muiris Ó Rócháin and Harry Hughes, *Dal gCais*, Vol. 2, 1974
221 Memorial Address, Seán Reid, 4/7/77, sourced from *An Píobaire*, Autumn 1977
222 'Willie Clancy: The Man And His Music', Muiris Ó Rócháin and Harry Hughes, *Dál gCais* Vol. 1, 1972
223 'Willie Clancy: The Man And His Music', Muiris Ó Rócháin and Harry Hughes, *Dál gCais* Vol. 1, 1972
224 Willie Clancy interview with Breandán Ó Cíobháin, RTÉ, 11/72
225 'Junior Crehan Of Bonavilla' (Part One), Tom Munnelly, *Béaloideas*, No. 66 (1998)
226 Pat Mitchell, introduction to the 1993 edition of *The Dance Music Of Willie Clancy* (Ossian)
227 Memorial Address, Seán Reid, 4/7/77, sourced from *An Píobaire*, Autumn 1977
228 *The Dance Music Of Willie Clancy* (1976; rev. Ossian, 1993), Pat Mitchell
229 Pat Mitchell, tune notes in *The Gold Ring* (RTÉ, 2009)
230 Pat Mitchell, tune notes in *The Gold Ring* (RTÉ, 2009)
231 From a Seán Reid memoir extract first printed in *Dál gCais*, early 1978, sourced from 'Echoes Of East Clare', Gearóid Ó hAllmhúráin, *Treoir*, (?)/1980
232 'Willie Clancy: The Man And His Music', Muiris Ó Rócháin and Harry Hughes, *Dál gCais* Vol. 1, 1972

233 'Willie Clancy: The Man And His Music', Muiris Ó Rócháin and Harry Hughes, *Dál gCais* Vol. 1, 1972
234 Letter from Willie Clancy to Leo Rowsome, 27/2/48, courtesy of Helena Rowsome
235 'A Piper By Destination', Séamus Mac Mathúna, *Treoir*, 5/1/73
236 Roger Sherlock, interviewed in *Cérbh É – Willie Clancy* (TG4, 2009), Dir: Philip King
237 *A Touchstone For The Tradition* (Brandon, 2001), Tony Kearns and Barry Taylor
238 'A Piper By Destination', Séamus Mac Mathúna, *Treoir*, 5/1/73
239 'The Tulla Céilidh Band: The Heart Of The Tradition', Barry Taylor, 1997 (revised 2009), clarelibrary.ie/eolas/coclare/music/tulla_ceilidhdh_band/heart_of_the_tradition2.htm
240 'A Last Farewell', uncredited, *Treoir*, 5/2/73
241 *The Seamus Ennis Story* (RTÉ, 1988), Prod: Peter Browne
242 *Melody Maker*, 30/9/67
243 'A Piper By Destination', Séamus Mac Mathúna, *Treoir*, 5/1/73
244 'Willie Clancy: The Man And His Music', Muiris Ó Rócháin and Harry Hughes, *Dál gCais* Vol. 1, 1972
245 'Willie Clancy On Traditional Music', John Vesey and Tom Standheven, 7/62, first published online at: standingstones.com/wclancy.html , accessed: 7/1/15
246 'Willie Clancy: The Man And His Music', Muiris Ó Rócháin and Harry Hughes, *Dál gCais* Vol. 1, 1972
247 'Willie Clancy: The Man And His Music', Muiris Ó Rócháin and Harry Hughes, *Dál gCais* Vol. 1, 1972
248 'Calling On The Piper', Seán Laffey, *Irish Music*, 7/98
249 'A Last Farewell', uncredited, *Treoir*, 5/2/73
250 Pat Mitchell, introduction to the 1993 edition of *The Dance Music Of Willie Clancy* (Ossian)
251 *Cérbh É – Willie Clancy* (TG4, 2009), Dir: Philip King
252 Reported in 'A Last Farewell', uncredited, *Treoir*, 5/2/73
253 Memorial Address, Seán Reid, 4/7/77, sourced from *An Píobaire*, Autumn 1977
254 'Willie Clancy: The Man And His Music', Muiris Ó Rócháin and Harry Hughes, *Dál gCais* Vol. 1, 1972
255 'Memories Of The Dorans In Clare', Michael Falsey, *An Píobaire*, ii No. 22, 9/84
256 *Irish Minstrels And Musicians* (1911), Francis O'Neill
257 'Pipers Of The Past', Brian Ó Dochartaigh, *Treoir*, Márta 1969
258 *Free Spirits: Irish Travellers And Irish Traditional Music* (MPR, 2011), Tommy Fegan and Oliver O'Connell
259 *Notes From The Heart: A Celebration Of Traditional Irish Music* (Torc, 1994), P.J. Curtis
260 Seán Reid, notes to *The Last Of The Travelling Pipers* (Topic, 1976) by Felix Doran
261 *The Long Note – Johnny Doran: A Famous Piper*, RTÉ, 1988
262 *The Long Note – Johnny Doran: A Famous Piper*, RTÉ, 1988
263 *The Long Note – Johnny Doran: A Famous Piper*, RTÉ, 1988
264 *The Long Note – Johnny Doran: A Famous Piper*, RTÉ, 1988
265 *The Long Note – Johnny Doran: A Famous Piper*, RTÉ, 1988
266 *The Long Note – Johnny Doran: A Famous Piper*, RTÉ, 1988
267 *The Long Note – Johnny Doran: A Famous Piper*, RTÉ, 1988
268 *Traveller Piper: A Celebration Of The Piping Tradition Of Johnny And Felix Doran* (NPU, 2009)

269 'Junior Crehan Of Bonavilla' (part one), Tom Munnelly, *Béaloideas*, No. 66 (1998)
270 *Postcolonial Artist: Johnny Doran And Irish Traveller Tradition* (Cambridge Scholars Publishing, 2008), David Touhy and Mícheál Ó hAodha
271 *The Long Note – Johnny Doran: A Famous Piper*, RTÉ, 1988
272 'Junior Crehan of Bonavilla' (part one), Tom Munnelly, *Béaloideas*, No. 66 (1998)
273 *Free Spirits: Irish Travellers And Irish Traditional Music* (MPR, 2011), Tommy Fegan and Oliver O'Connell
274 *The Long Note – Johnny Doran: A Famous Piper*, RTÉ, 1988
275 *The Long Note – Johnny Doran: A Famous Piper*, RTÉ, 1988
276 Essay on Leo Rowsome, Seán Reid, 23/11/75, pipers.ie/about/patrons/leo-rowsome/
277 'A Snap Of The Piper', John McCaffrey, *Irish Press*, 12/6/61. Reprinted: *Treoir*, M'Fomhair/D'Fomhair 1969; and *An Píobaire* Vol. 6 No. 2, 4/10
278 Pat Mitchell, notes to *Johnny Doran: The Master Pipers Vol. 1* (NPU, 1988)
279 Quoted in the notes to *Johnny Doran: The Master Pipers Vol. 1* (NPU, 1988)
280 *The Long Note – Johnny Doran: A Famous Piper*, RTÉ, 1988
281 'Johnnie Doran', Muiris Ó Rócháin, *Dál gCais* Vol. 1, 1972
282 Cecil Colville Interview, Wilbert Garvin, *The Seán Reid Society Journal*, Vol. 3, 2009
283 Cecil Colville Interview, Wilbert Garvin, *The Seán Reid Society Journal*, Vol. 3, 2009
284 *The Long Note – Johnny Doran: A Famous Piper*, RTÉ, 1988
285 *The Grammar Of Irish English: Language In Hibernian Style* (Routledge, 1999), Markku Filppula

286 'Junior Crehan Of Bonavilla' (part two), Tom Munnelly, *Béaloideas*, No. 67 (1999)
287 *The Long Note – Johnny Doran: A Famous Piper*, RTÉ, 1988
288 *The Long Note – Johnny Doran: A Famous Piper*, RTÉ, 1988
289 *The Long Note – Johnny Doran: A Famous Piper*, RTÉ, 1988
290 *The Long Note – Johnny Doran: A Famous Piper*, RTÉ, 1988
291 *The Evening Mail*, 30/1/48
292 *The Long Note – Johnny Doran: A Famous Piper*, RTÉ, 1988
293 *The Long Note – Johnny Doran: A Famous Piper*, RTÉ, 1988
294 *The Long Note – Johnny Doran: A Famous Piper*, RTÉ, 1988
295 Séamus Ennis, RTÉ radio, 17/3/74, youtube.com/watch?v=PILzpd36mSw
296 *The Irish Folklore Commission 1935–1970: History, Ideology, Methodology* (Finnish Literature Society, 2007), Mícheál Briody
297 *The Irish Folklore Commission 1935–1970: History, Ideology, Methodology* (Finnish Literature Society, 2007), Mícheál Briody
298 *Postcolonial Artist: Johnny Doran And Irish Traveller Tradition* (Cambridge Scholars Publishing, 2008), David Touhy and Mícheál Ó hAodha
299 Peter Laban, steampacket.ownit.nu/jdoran.html Accessed: 18/2/15
300 *Postcolonial Artist: Johnny Doran And Irish Traveller Tradition* (Cambridge Scholars Publishing, 2008), David Touhy and Mícheál Ó hAodha
301 'As I Roved Out', Mícheál Ó hAlmhain, *Treoir*, 5/3/73
302 *Irish Minstrels And Musicians* (1913), Francis O'Neill
303 *Irish Minstrels And Musicians* (1913), Francis O'Neill
304 Reverend Heneby to Francis O'Neill, early 1900s, *An Píobaire*, April 1974

305 Combined from letters by Francis O'Neill, 15/11/11 and 28/12/11, *An Píobaire*, April 1974
306 Letter from Francis O'Neill, 28/12/11, *An Píobaire*, April 1974
307 Letter from Francis O'Neill, 28/12/11, *An Píobaire*, April 1974
308 *Historical Memoirs Of The Irish Bards* (1786), Joseph Cooper Walker
309 *Historical Memoirs Of The Irish Bards* (1786), Joseph Cooper Walker
310 *Topographia Hibernica* (c. 1188), Giraldus Cambrensis
311 *Topographia Hibernica* (c. 1188), Giraldus Cambrensis
312 *A Compendium Of Irish Biography*, Alfred Webb, en.wikisource.org/wiki/A_Compendium_of_Irish_Biography/Vallancey,_Charles Accessed: 23/9/13
313 *Historical Memoirs Of The Irish Bards* (1786), Joseph Cooper Walker
314 Denis Brooks, *The Pipers' Review*, Vol. 1 No. 2, 1980
315 *Historical Memoirs Of The Irish Bards* (1786), Joseph Cooper Walker
316 *The Merchant Of Venice*, Act 4, Scene 1 (c. 1596-98), William Shakespeare
317 Unattributed, *An Píobaire*, Issue 1, 1969
318 W.H. Grattan Flood, letter to *Freeman's Journal*, July 1904
319 W.H. Grattan Flood, letter to *Freeman's Journal*, July 1904
320 Breandán Breathnach, *An Píobaire*, No. 1, 1969
321 *Folk Music And Dances Of Ireland* (Mercier Press, 1971; revised 1977), Breandán Breathnach
322 *Historical Memoirs Of The Irish Bards* (1786), Joseph Cooper Walker
323 *Irish Minstrels And Musicians* (1913), Francis O'Neill
324 *A Pocket History Of Irish Music*
325 'Lost Chords', Keith Sanger. Published online with references, 29/2/12: wirestrungharp.com/music/lost_chords.html
326 Collected in *On The Manners And Customs Of The Ancient Irish: A Series Of Lectures* (1873), Eugene O'Curry
327 Denis Brooks, *The Pipers' Review*, Vol. 1 No. 3, June 1980
328 Denis Brooks, *The Pipers' Review*, Vol. 1 No. 3, June 1980
329 *Historical Memoirs Of The Irish Bards* (1786), Joseph Cooper Walker
330 Denis Brooks, *The Pipers' Review*, Vol. 1 No. 3, June 1980
331 *Irish Minstrels And Musicians* (1913), Francis O'Neill
332 *Folk Music And Dances Of Ireland* (Mercier Press, 1971; revised 1977), Breandán Breathnach
333 *A History Of Irish Music* (1905), W.H. Grattan Flood
334 *A Philosophical Survey Of The South Of Ireland* (1778), Thomas Campbell. Quoted from *Irish Minstrels And Musicians* (1913), Francis O'Neill
335 *Letters written from Leverpoole, Chester, Corke, &c.* (1767), Samuel Derrick. Quoted in *Historical Memoirs Of The Irish Bards* (1786), Joseph Cooper Walker
336 *Historical Memoirs Of The Irish Bards* (1786), Joseph Cooper Walker
337 *A History Of Irish Music* (1905), W.H. Grattan Flood
338 Anonymous, *Gentleman's Magazine*, Vol. 21, 1971. Sourced from *Historical Memoirs Of The Irish Bards* (1786), Joseph Cooper Walker. Francis O'Neill repeats the quotation in *Irish Folk Music: A Fascinating Hobby* (1910).
339 *Personal Sketches Of His Own Times* (1830), Sir Jonah Barrington
340 *Personal Sketches Of His Own Times* (1830), Sir Jonah Barrington
341 Richard Stanyhurst, c. 1584, quoted in *Irish Minstrels And Musicians* (1913; Mercier Press, 1987), Francis O'Neill
342 Patrick Sky, Introduction, 1995, to the 1995 Grassblade Music edition of

O'Farrell's Collection Of National Irish Music For The Union Pipes (c. 1800), Mr O'Farrell

343 *O'Farrell's Collection Of National Irish Music For The Union Pipes* (c. 1800), Mr O'Farrell

344 *O'Farrell's Collection Of National Irish Music For The Union Pipes* (c. 1800), Mr O'Farrell

345 Barry O'Neill, 1972, Introduction to the 1973 Norwood Editions reprint of *Irish Folk Music: A Fascinating Hobby* (1910), Francis O'Neill

346 'A Century Of Pipemaking, 1770-1870: New Light On The Kennas And The Coynes,' Seán Donnelly, *The Seán Reid Society Journal*, Vol. 2, 3/02

347 *A History Of Irish Music* (1905), W.H. Grattan Flood

348 Eric Thatcher, *Jazz & Blues*, 5/73, quoted in 'The Fox Chase', Pat Mitchell, *An Píobaire*, Bealtaine 1977

349 Séamus O'Casaide, *An Píobaire*, E 1972

350 *The Compleat Tutor For The Pastoral Or New Bagpipe* (c. 1745), John Geohegan

351 'The Early Pipes', Denis Brooks, *The Pipers' Review*, 12/85

352 *The Compleat Tutor For The Pastoral Or New Bagpipe* (c. 1745), John Geohegan

353 'The Pastoral Repertoire, Rediscovered', Ross Anderson. Published online: cl.cam.ac.uk/~rja14/music/pastoral.pdf

354 'The Pastoral Repertoire, Rediscovered', Ross Anderson. Published online: cl.cam.ac.uk/~rja14/music/pastoral.pdf

355 'The Pastoral Repertoire, Rediscovered', Ross Anderson. Published online: cl.cam.ac.uk/~rja14/music/pastoral.pdf

356 'The Early Pipes', Denis Brooks, *The Pipers' Review*, 12/85

357 'The Early Pipes', Denis Brooks, *The Pipers' Review*, 12/85

358 'The Sutherland Manuscript', Ross Anderson. Accessed online: cl.cam.ac.uk/~rja14/Papers/Sutherland-Manuscript.pdf

359 'The Sutherland Manuscript', Ross Anderson. Accessed online: cl.cam.ac.uk/~rja14/Papers/Sutherland-Manuscript.pdf

360 'Eugene O'Curry: The Neglected Scholar', Muiris Ó Róchain, *Treoir* Vol. 5 No. 3, 1973

361 *Irish Minstrels And Musicians* (1913), Francis O'Neill

362 'Paddy Coneely, The Galway Piper', *The Irish Penny Journal*, 3/10/1840

363 *Irish Minstrels And Musicians* (1913), Francis O'Neill

364 *Folk Music And Dances Of Ireland* (Mercier Press, 1971; revised 1977), Breandán Breathnach

365 *Irish Folk Music: A Fascinating Hobby* (1910), Francis O'Neill

366 'A Century Of Pipemaking, 1770-1870: New Light On The Kennas And The Coynes,' Seán Donnelly, *The Seán Reid Society Journal*, Vol. 2, 3/02

367 *Irish Folk Music: A Fascinating Hobby* (1910), Francis O'Neill

368 *Irish Folk Music: A Fascinating Hobby* (1910), Francis O'Neill

369 'Pipers And Piping In Louth,' Breandán Breathnach, *County Louth Archaeological & Historical Journal* XIX 2, 1978

370 'A Century Of Pipemaking, 1770–1870: New Light On The Kennas And The Coynes,' Seán Donnelly, *The Seán Reid Society Journal*, Vol. 2, 3/02

371 'Irish Pipes And Pipers', Thomas Ennis, *The Gael*, February 1902

372 'Irish Pipes And Pipers', Thomas Ennis, *The Gael*, February 1902

373 *Irish Folk Music: A Fascinating Hobby* (1910), Francis O'Neill

374 *Irish Folk Music: A Fascinating Hobby* (1910), Francis O'Neill

375 'Francis O'Neill: Collector Of Irish Music', Breandán Breathnach, *Dál gCais* III, 1977

376 'The Feis Ceoil And Piping', Breandán Breathnach, *Ceol* VIII (1986)
377 *Irish Minstrels And Musicians* (1913), Francis O'Neill
378 *Irish Minstrels And Musicians* (1913), Francis O'Neill
379 *Irish Minstrels And Musicians* (1913), Francis O'Neill
380 'Francis O'Neill: Collector Of Irish Music', Breandán Breathnach, *Dál gCais* III, 1977
381 Untitled article, Denis Brooks, *The Pipers' Review*, June 1980
382 *A Historic Tribute To Mr William Kennedy* (Tandragee History, Heritage & Discovery Group, 2014)
383 *A Historic Tribute To Mr William Kennedy* (Tandragee History, Heritage & Discovery Group, 2014)
384 *Newry Telegraph*, 11/11/1834, armaghpipers.com/workshop/williamKennedy.html
385 Writer unattributed, armaghpipers.com/workshop/williamKennedy.html
386 *Grove Dictionary Of Music And Musicians*, 5th Edition, Ed: Eric Blom – cited in 'Walter Jackson – The Piper', [uncredited], *Treoir*, Bealtaine 1971
387 *Irish Minstrels And Musicians* (1913), Francis O'Neill
388 Patrick O'Leary, writing to Francis O'Neill. Quoted in 'Walter Jackson – The Piper', [uncredited], *Treoir*, Bealtaine 1971
389 'Walter Jackson – The Piper', *Irish Folk Music Studies* 2, 1976, Breandán Breathnach
390 *History Of Limerick, Ecclesiastical, Civil And Military From The Earliest Records To The Year 1787* (1787), J. Ferrar
391 'Walter Jackson – The Piper', *Irish Folk Music Studies* 2, 1976, Breandán Breathnach
392 'Walter Jackson – The Piper', *Irish Folk Music Studies* 2, 1976, Breandán Breathnach
393 *Irish Minstrels And Musicians* (1913), Francis O'Neill
394 *Irish Minstrels And Musicians* (1913), Francis O'Neill
395 *Irish Minstrels And Musicians* (1913), Francis O'Neill
396 *Irish Minstrels And Musicians* (1913), Francis O'Neill
397 'As I Roved Out', Mícheál Ó hAlmhain, *Treoir*, 5/3/73
398 'A Note On Irish Union Pipes', Robbie Hughes, *Lecale Review*, 2005
399 'The Life And Times Of Richard Lewis O'Mealy', Ronan Browne, *The Seán Reid Society Journal*, Vol. 3, 2009
400 Eamonn Ceannt, *An Píobaire* III, 1901–02
401 'The Life And Times Of Richard Lewis O'Mealy', Ronan Browne, *The Seán Reid Society Journal*, Vol. 3, 2009
402 *Irish Minstrels And Musicians* (1913), Francis O'Neill
403 Letter from Francis O'Neill, 9/3/12, *An Píobaire*, May 1974
404 *Irish Independent*, 5/8/24
405 'The Life And Times Of Richard Lewis O'Mealy', Ronan Browne, *The Seán Reid Society Journal*, Vol. 3, 2009
406 'The Life And Times Of Richard Lewis O'Mealy', Ronan Browne, *The Seán Reid Society Journal*, Vol. 3, 2009
407 Andy Conroy Biography, Ronan Browne, *The Seán Reid Society Journal*, Vol. 3, 2009
408 Andy Conroy Interview, Dave Hegarty, *The Seán Reid Society Journal*, Vol. 3, 2009
409 'Piping Style And Notes On The Tunes', Ronan Browne, *The Seán Reid Society Journal*, Vol. 3, 2009
410 'The Life And Times Of Richard Lewis O'Mealy', Ronan Browne, *The Seán Reid Society Journal*, Vol. 3, 2009
411 'William Hope (1880-1959)', Ken McLeod, *The Seán Reid Society Journal*, Vol. 3, 2009

412 'William Hope (1880–1959)', Ken McLeod, *The Seán Reid Society Journal*, Vol. 3, 2009
413 'Jack O'Rourke (1916–1981)', Ken McLeod, *The Seán Reid Society Journal*, Vol. 3, 2009
414 'Netta Jane Nicholl (Miss) Johnston (1878-1952)', Wilbert Garvin, *The Seán Reid Society Journal*, Vol. 3, 2009
415 'Netta Jane Nicholl (Miss) Johnston (1878-1952)', Wilbert Garvin, *The Seán Reid Society Journal*, Vol. 3, 2009
416 'William Clarke: The Ballybay Piper', Harry Bradshaw, *Musical Traditions*, No. 9, Autumn 1991
417 Quoted in A.L. Lloyd's song notes to the Topic LP *The McPeake Family* (1963)
418 mcpeakemusic.com/heritage.php?eraone
419 *Folk Music And Dances Of Ireland* (Mercier Press, 1971; revised 1977), Breandán Breathnach
420 *Going To The Well For Water: The Séamus Ennis Field Diary 1942-1946* (Cork University Press, 2009), Ed: Ríonach Uí Ógáin
421 Quoted in Sam Hanna Bell's notes to the Topic LP *The McPeake Family* (1963)
422 *Irish Minstrels And Musicians* (1913), Francis O'Neill
423 *Variety*, 13/1/65
424 *Melody Maker*, 17/6/67
425 'Seán Reid: A Self Portrait', Muiris Ó Rócháin, *Dál gCais* Vol. 2, 1974
426 'Seán Reid: A Self Portrait', Muiris Ó Rócháin, *Dál gCais* Vol. 2, 1974
427 'Seán Reid: A Self Portrait', Muiris Ó Rócháin, *Dál gCais* Vol. 2, 1974
428 'Seán Reid: A Self Portrait', Muiris Ó Rócháin, *Dál gCais* Vol. 2, 1974
429 'Seán Reid: A Self Portrait', Muiris Ó Rócháin, *Dál gCais* Vol. 2, 1974
430 'Seán Reid: A Self Portrait', Muiris Ó Rócháin, *Dál gCais* Vol. 2, 1974
431 'Interview With Cecil Colville', Wilbert Garvin, *The Seán Reid Society Journal*, Vol. 3, 2009
432 Robin Morton, notes to *Drops Of Brandy* (Topic, 1976)
433 *The Irish Bagpipes* (Blackstaff Press, 1978), Wilbert Garvin
434 Untitled piece, Robbie Hannon, The *Pipers' Review*, 12/85 in English (translated from the Irish original in *An Píobaire*, 5/85)
435 *Irish Minstrels And Musicians* (1913), Francis O'Neill
436 *Irish Minstrels And Musicians* (1913), Francis O'Neill
437 'Armagh Pipers' Club', Brian Vallely, *Treoir*, 5/2/72

Acknowledgements

This book is a combination of information distilled from published sources, unpublished sources and new interviews by the author. One is always standing on the shoulders of giants – in this case those giants include Francis O'Neill, Breandán Breathnach, Pat Mitchell, Colin Irwin and Wilbert Garvin. Another giant, who offered his metaphorical shoulders as a platform upon which the book could exist, is Nigel Osbourne, wizard behind the curtain at Jawbone Press. This book would not have been possible without him. There were some serious bumps in the road but he stayed the course. And now an ongoing series of huge lunches are owed. Thank you, Nigel.

Author interviews in person/by phone: Jenny Barton, Kevin Burke, Martin Carthy, Éamonn Curran, Bob Davenport, Robin Dransfield, Eddie Furey, Finbar Furey, Wilbert Garvin, Paddy Glackin, Reg Hall, Andy Irvine, Paddy Keenan, Barry Kerr, Bill Leader, Dónal Lunny, John McSherry, Tíona McSherry, Neil Martin, Robin Morton, Terry Moylan, Tríona Ní Dhomhnaill, Miadhach Lughain O'Donnell, Marcas Ó Murchú, Al Ross, Peggy Seeger, Brian Vallely, Eithne Vallely.

Author interviews by email/correspondence quoted: Anna Bale, Peter Browne, Dave Burland, Davey Johnstone, Ken McLeod, Ralph McTell, Matt Molloy, Ríonach uí Ógáin, Ciarán Rowsome, Helena Rowsome, Kevin Rowsome, Patrick Sky. Author interviews from the 1990s: Martin Carthy, John Cook, Shaun Davey, Nathan Joseph, Paddy Keenan, Bill Leader, Liam O'Flynn.

Huge thanks to all the interviewees above for giving me their time. I am also extremely grateful to the staff of the Irish Traditional Music Archive (ITMA), Dublin, particularly Elaina Solon and Treasa Harkin, each a great help on my several visits in person and by email. It's a terrific place – go and visit. My thanks also to the staff of the BBC Written Archive Centre, Caversham, particularly Kate O'Brien and Samantha Blake who were always happy to go extra miles down increasingly arcane avenues. BBC copyright material reproduced courtesy of the British Broadcasting Corporation. All rights reserved. Thanks also to the staff of the National Sound Archive and the British Library, and to David Suff at Topic Records. Hannah Lawrence was enormously helpful as a research assistant, doing Herculean amounts of work on my behalf, with great precision, on a couple of occasions in Caversham. Kal Dhillon at BBC4 was a terrific help, as always, as was 'Irish' Jim Lockhart, prowling the corridors of RTÉ with a cheery smile and a can-do attitude. Ken Garner was always available to exchange views on the oddities of BBC session recordings, and the piping milieu provided a few goodies there.

For image provision and permissions I'm grateful to: Treasa Harkin at ITMA; Terry Moylan at Na Píobairí Uilleann; Kieran Hoare at the James Hardiman Library, NUI Galway; Pearl Quinn at the RTÉ Stills Library; Valerie Wilmer; Andy Irvine; Dónal Lunny; Ken McLeod; Lieve Boussauw; Colin Goldie; Wilbert Garvin; Barry Kerr; Shiela Friel; and Paul Eliasberg at Armagh Pipers' Club.

John Riddell provided the tune transcriptions. Colin Irwin very kindly gave permission to reproduce his two 1970s *Melody Maker* pieces. I'm also grateful to Ciarán Rowsome for taking the time to write his own memoir of Leo Rowsome for inclusion herein.

The creation and publication of this book has been generously assisted by the National Lottery Project Funding scheme administered by the Arts Council of Northern Ireland. John and I are grateful for the opportunity provided, and for the administrative expertise and good humour of Craig Corsar at ACNI throughout the process.

Several people provided great encouragement along the way: Tíona McSherry/O'Donnell, who started the whole thing; Conor Shields, kingpin of community arts in Belfast, nay, the North, who kept the forces of darkness at bay; Cormac O'Kane, wizard of sound and beacon of positivity; Brian O'Reilly, the Huxmeister; fellow chroniclers of music past Mark Lewisohn, Peter Doggett and Mick Houghton; Adele Magee and Cardiff Lou from Wookalily (Mr Lou, Dee McCaskie, makes uilleann pipes: no room in the main text, but here's a mention); Carol-Anne Lennie in Luton; Colin and Anita Davies in Wimbledon; 'Late-Night' Tony Furnell in bed; Trevor 'Legsyboy' Leedon in a variety of locations.

Wilbert Garvin, Ken McLeod and Brian Vallely each read (different) sections of the book and provided both useful feedback and encouragement. Professor Derek Scott, kingpin of the academic popular music community, did likewise. Clare Kieran helped with Irish language matters. I'm most grateful to all. Naturally, any errors that remain – and in a book of this scope there are bound to be some – are mine.

Tom Seabrook typeset and indexed the book, with as much drollery and precision as ever. Sarah McQuaid proof-read and copy-edited the text and did so with an exceptional level of scrutiny, in both Irish and English. We had hours of fun talking about hyphens, commas and apostrophes. I recommend her proofing skills, and her music: www.sarahmcquaid.com I've no idea about Tom Seabrook's music, but I can certainly recommend his textual services.

Time and space prohibit a full bibliography but all works cited are given in the Endnotes. The book was written within a very few months, spanning 2014–15, in order to comply with funding parameters. It was hugely challenging but deadlines do focus the mind. A couple of potential chapters were sacrificed, again through time and space concerns: one on Bill Leader; one on Northumbrian, Border and Lowland piping. Thank you to Roger Trevitt and Colin Ross who gave (unused) interviews toward those potential chapters.

All of my books, the present volume included, would have been impossible without Heather's moral support, bonhomie, tolerance of artistic temperament and potential buffer-zoning against pecuniary anxiety. This volume and my previous books on John McLaughlin and Bert Jansch were all subsidised by one-off tranches of money: house sale equity; redundancy payment; Lottery funding. Writing books of this nature feels a bit like stealing time from your life in order to create something that you hope has lasting worth, something that celebrates and documents people who did great things. The financial returns involved in no way justify the time. It's a case of balancing the greater good (one hopes) against what else one might be doing. Luckily or otherwise, I'm no good at anything else.

It was interesting to come across (in *An Píobaire*, July 1974) a 1913 letter from Francis O'Neill to a purchaser of his then recently published (and self-subsidised) *Irish Minstrels And Musicians*. It seems nobody could really justify the writing of books on music even then. But the world, I believe, would be a poorer place without such works. 'Flattering reviews in the press, and appreciative comments in other ways, are all that could be desired but orders are disappointingly few,' he wrote. 'Should I be fortunate enough to be reimbursed for even half my outlay, not considering years of application and persistent effort I would feel satisfied.'

I'm already satisfied that *The Wheels Of The World* is a useful thing to have done. I'm grateful that John and Tíona nudged me into it; I would never have thought of it as a subject otherwise, nor thought myself able to tackle it. It was a learning curve, full of interesting stuff, plus I got to meet some terrific people I may not otherwise have encountered. And any ongoing series of grateful lunches with Nigel Osborne which may eventuate can, after all, hardly be anything other than a pleasure.

This current edition is strictly limited to 2000 print copies. John and I hope, if demand seems viable, to find a way to publish a second edition in due course. Going into business with a piper: what could possibly go wrong?

John would like to thank:

Colin for taking this project on, for his enthusiasm, skill, creative thinking, dedication and sheer hard graft; all my family and friends and all the pipers in the world, past and present, who have made and continue to make this life such an interesting and magical (if a little crazy) journey. I recommend Aaron O'Hagan's pipe making: www.aaronohagan.com

Index

A Job Of Journeywork (Radio Éireann/RTÉ), 109, 360, 401
Altan, 25, 54, 487–8
Anderson, Ross, 430, 432, 442
Andrews, William (aka Liam), 24, 191, 215, 222, 456
Armagh Pipers' Club, 10, 15, 168, 319, 447, 470, 475, 481, 494, 496–7, 499–500, 502, 507
Armstrong, Jack, 275
Armstrong, Louis, 485
Ash Grove, The, 247–9
As I Roved Out (BBC Northern Ireland), 9, 27, 241
As I Roved Out (BBC Home Servive), 235–6, 245, 255, 273–4, 280–3, 288, 291, 296, 325, 339, 356, 360
At First Light (band), 12, 44–5, 47, 50, 52–3, 305
At First Light (album), 38, 44–5

Baez, Joan, 246, 466
Bagpuss (BBC TV), 223
Bale, Anna, 400
Barry, Garrett, 7, 56, 147, 153, 163, 174, 345–7, 349–51, 353, 361, 369, 374, 382, 391
Barry, Margaret, 78, 108, 236, 253, 300, 359, 497
Barton, Jenny, 215, 219, 240–2, 244, 246, 249–250, 261, 265, 357
Beatles, The, 7, 18, 30, 40, 69, 79, 99, 112–3, 118, 128, 130, 161, 465, 467, 485, 515
Bedford Arms, The, 356–7
Behan, Brendan, 128, 295
Behan, Dominic, 107, 240, 324–5, 328, 330
Bell, Paddie, 77, 82, 99
Benbow, Steve, 242–3, 389
Bennett, Alan, 333
Berry, Chuck, 144

Black Eagles, The, 69
Blacksmiths, The, 133
blues, the, 5, 7, 13, 32, 69, 130, 144, 239, 246–7, 282, 303, 345, 395, 402, 409, 420, 426, 428, 466
Bombadil, Tom, 470
Border pipes, 430
Bothy Band, The, 9–10, 21, 26, 32, 35, 41, 57, 61–2, 69, 114, 116, 125, 133, 135–9, 142–155, 157, 189, 258, 263, 482–3, 492, 510–16
Boys Of The Lough, The, 144, 468, 477, 482
Boys Of Ballisodare, The (Festival), 144
Brady, Paul, 42, 81, 115, 142, 144, 146–7, 150, 519
Bradshaw, Harry, 118, 403, 462–3
Brambell, Wilfred, 324
Bream, Julian, 272
Breathnach, Breandán, 136, 167, 222–3, 313, 361, 388, 394, 415, 421, 435, 437, 440, 441–2, 444, 449, 450, 453, 457, 461, 463, 475, 481, 492
Brennan, Máire, 38–9
Brian Boru pipes, 470, 472
Briggs, Anne, 63, 467
Broe, Peadar, 223
Brogan, John, 223
Browne, Peter, 128, 133, 140, 145, 161, 229, 232, 353
Browne, Ronan, 11, 128, 453–4, 456, 458
Browne, Ronnie, 74, 79
Brozman, Bob, 45
Brubeck, Dave, 497
Bruford, Bill, 51
Bunting, Edward, 416, 420–1, 439, 441, 448, 503
Burke, Ciarán, 68
Burke, Kevin, 61, 139, 140–1, 146, 148, 150, 152, 157, 159, 258, 311
Burke, Pat, 347
Burland, Dave, 101

Burns, Robbie, 74
Bush, Kate, 121
Byrne, Tony, 14, 44, 47
Byrnes, Martin, 78, 236, 240, 252, 258, 356, 359
Byrds, The, 141

Cambridge Folk Festival, 80, 114–15, 311
Campbell, Alex, 100, 465–6
Cannavan, Pat (aka Peait), 342
Carroll, John, 347–8
Carthy, Martin, 64, 76–8, 85, 88, 100, 103, 113, 144, 241, 265, 466
Casey, Bobby, 78, 236–7, 351, 354, 356, 358
Casey, Nollaig, 38–40
Cash, John 'Cash the Piper', 7, 317, 373, 375, 377–8, 410, 440–1
Cash, Margaret, 375, 379–80, 396
Cash, Pat, 316, 380, 387
Celtic Connections, 50, 122, 493
Ceoltóirí Chualann, 152
Chaucer, Geoffrey, 413
Chas McDevitt Skiffle Group, 251
Chieftains, The, 10, 13, 18, 29, 38, 68, 114, 124–5, 137, 142–3, 146, 152, 176, 219, 259, 341, 377, 451, 483, 484, 510–11, 513, 516–17
Claddagh Records, 66, 68, 121, 128, 137, 161, 177, 215, 263, 483, 491, 497
Clancy, Bobby, 89, 101, 341
Clancy, Liam, 89–91, 94
Clancy, Willie, 5, 344–350, 352, 358–9, 361–6, 368–70, 373, 374, 382, 384, 396, 398, 410, 469, 472, 480, 484, 492, 497–8, 513, 516–18
Clancy Brothers, The (aka 'the Clancys'), 18, 88, 90–5, 97–8, 103, 142, 253, 466
Clancy Brothers & Tommy Makem, The, 68, 85
Clannad, 24, 33, 39–40, 101–2, 104, 142–4, 148, 220
Clapton, Eric, 117, 513
Clarke, Willie, 461-3
Clay, Cassius, 56–7

Cleary, Frank, 347, 365, 380–1, 384, 388
Cluain Árd, The, 23, 483–4, 488–90
Colclough, Henry, 175, 425, 429–30
Coleman, Michael, 16, 392, 487
Coleman, Ornette, 12
Collins, Shirley, 243
Colville, Cecil, 389, 393, 479
Comhaltas Ceoltóirí Éireann (CCÉ), 9, 12, 15, 71, 142, 167, 177, 181–2, 360, 468–9, 498
Coneely, Paddy, 433–4
Connolly, Billy, 77, 79
Connors, John, 126, 128–9, 372
Conroy, Andy, 165, 386, 393–4, 396, 457
Conroy, Mick, 386, 394
Cooder, Ry, 141, 485
Cook, John, 60, 110, 117–18, 121
Coolfin (band), 12, 37–9, 40, 42, 46–7, 151, 308
Coolfin (album), 38–9, 42
Cooney, Steve, 14, 28, 36–7, 121, 157
Copper, Bob, 234, 237
Cork Pipers' Club, 441, 443–4, 453, 491
Corries, The, 74, 76–7, 79, 84
Cosma, Vladimir, 116
Cotten, Elizabeth, 251
Coulter, Phil, 60, 114, 477
Country Meets Folk (BBC), 93, 95, 483
Courtney, Dennis, 427
Coyne, Maurice, 169, 223, 351, 435-6, 447
Crehan, Junior, 164, 346, 348–9, 351, 361, 382, 384, 391
Cronin, Elizabeth, 227–8, 233, 269–70, 343
Crowley, Tadhg, 129, 175
Crowley brothers (pipe makers), 129, 438
Crump, John, 433–4
Curran, Eamonn, 481, 500–1, 506, 508, 319
Curtin, Hugh, 346, 349, 351
Cutler, Ivor, 333

Dallas, Karl, 68, 113–14, 150, 264, 466, 510

Danaher, Kevin, 228, 352–3, 393–4, 399–405
Davenport, Bob, 238, 243, 356, 467, 477
Davey, Shaun, 40, 62, 114, 116, 118–121, 178, 210
Davis, Miles, 89
Déanta, 28
De Brún, Garech, 128–130, 177
de Buítléar, Éamon, 229, 260, 342
De Danann, 69, 143, 147–8, 220, 264, 336, 483
Degrees Of Folk (BBC TV), 84
Delaney, Bernard, 407, 439, 442, 444
Delaney, Denis ('Dinny'), 222, 440–1, 443
Delap, Miles, 459
Delargy, James, 225, 239, 268, 330, 339
Demons, The, 68–9, 100
Derricke, John, 418
Dervish, 54, 61
De Valera, Éamon, 395
Diddley, Bo, 421
Dillon, Francis, 239, 243, 274, 277, 285, 292–3, 304, 325, 327, 329–33
Doherty, Johnny, 357, 399–400
Doherty, Mickey, 233, 357
Donnelly, Dezi, 34
Donnelly, Mark, 501
Donovan, 144, 514, 517
Doran, Johnny, 7, 10, 12–14, 24, 39, 56–8, 66, 72–3, 80, 125, 127–8, 133, 138, 153, 163, 165, 174, 179, 198, 219, 228, 316, 349, 350–3, 358, 372–82, 385–7, 389–395, 397–405, 410, 452, 457, 469
Doran, Felix, 59, 65, 66, 72, 88, 163, 174, 181, 215, 349, 351, 358, 365, 378, 379, 382, 386, 398, 404, 405
Dorris, Kevin ('Dod'), 30, 35
Doyle, John, 122, 395
Dowd, Dan, 24, 75, 501
Dowling, Mick, 59
Dransfield, Robin, 75, 364–5
Drew, Ronnie, 68, 341
Dublin Pipers' Club, 59, 172–3, 221, 341, 437, 444, 468–9, 491, 494
Dubliners, The, 63, 85, 100–1, 341, 362

Duncan, Tyler, 11, 49
Dunn, Clive, 294
Dunne, Mickey, 383, 404
Dunne, 'The Pecker', 63

Early, Dave, 35–6
Early, Sergeant James, 439
Earth Celebration Band, 38–9, 42, 308
Edge, The, 220
Edwards, Alf, 289, 334
Egan (pipe makers), 447, 452, 475
Elliott, Jack (of Birtley), 108, 252
Elliott, Ramblin' Jack, 241
Embankment, The, 69–70
Eno, Brian, 220
Eire Apparent, 149
Emerson, Lake & Palmer
English Folk Dance & Song Society (EFDSS), 357
Ennis, Catherine, 238, 245, 256, 344
Ennis, Christopher, 238, 344
Ennis, James, 174, 215, 221–5, 437, 455, 462
Ennis, Séamus, 7–10, 14, 17, 21, 14, 56–8, 60, 91, 108, 111, 114, 117, 133–4, 144, 149, 160, 163–4, 166–9, 179–80, 185, 189, 215, 217–322, 324, 230–1, 234–7, 241, 245–7, 251–2, 255–60, 262, 265–7, 270, 275–6, 279–81, 285, 288, 290–3, 297–9, 301, 313–15, 321–2, 329–30, 332, 334, 336–44, 352–6, 360–2, 368, 370, 379–80, 394, 397–400, 405, 410, 428, 452, 461, 463, 473–4, 485, 492, 498–500, 508, 513–14, 516–17
Ennis, Tom, 172, 438, 468
Estes, Sleepy John, 246
Everly Brothers, 121

Fabri, Marco, 27
Fahey, John, 248
fairies, 6, 226, 284, 326, 423, 450
Fairport Convention, 86, 95–6, 144
Falsey, Michael, 373, 382–3, 385
Feis Ceoil competitions, 221, 451
Feliciano, Jose, 247–8

Field Marshall Montgomery Pipe Band, The, 470, 495
Finbar & Eddie Furey (duo), 10, 13, 57, 64, 77, 85, 97, 99, 101, 102, 189, 309
Fingal Trio, The, 222–3
Fintan Lalor Pipe Band, The, 66
Fisher, Archie, 76, 80, 108
Fisher, Ray, 95, 136
Fitzpatrick, Ciarán, 22
Fitzgerald, Jack, 60, 110–11, 117
Fitzpatrick, Noel, 19–20, 485–6
Flanagan, John, 440–1, 457
Flood, W.H. Grattan, 414–15, 428, 433
Flynn, Kevin, 116, 143–4, 147–8, 150, 152
Fotheringay, 95
Frank, Jackson, 466
Friel, Sheila, 11, 164, 182, 319, 490–2, 494
Fureys & Davey Arthur, The, 60, 64, 101, 104–5
Furey, Eddie, 10, 13, 57, 64, 77, 81, 84–5, 90, 93, 97–9, 101–2, 126,109, 309
Furey, Finbar, 6–7, 9–11, 13, 21, 27, 29, 39, 51, 56–9, 62–3, 65–6, 79, 87, 89, 91, 97 108, 126, 138, 219, 246, 254, 362, 398, 405, 410, 423
Furey, George, 102, 131, 247, 315
Furey, Paul, 131
Furey, Ted, 65, 71–2, 95, 101, 125, 246, 251, 352, 375, 488
Fury, Billy, 63

Gabriel, Peter, 42
Gael Linn Records, 133–4, 137, 154, 240, 244, 254, 262, 359, 361, 397, 510, 512, 514
Gaelic League, 66, 162, 173, 221, 352, 376, 435, 440, 451
Gallagher, Rory, 482
Galway, James, 146
Garryowen Ceilidhe Band, The, 201
Garvin, Wilbert, 15, 182, 223, 245, 313, 318, 368, 380, 389, 430, 452–4, 460–1, 470, 477, 479, 480, 486
Gaughan, Dick, 80
Geohegan, John, 425, 429–30

George, Brian, 230, 232–5, 237, 267, 270, 275, 280, 288, 322, 339
Gerald of Wales (Giraldus Cambrensis), 411–12
Gilbert & Sullivan, 471
Gillespie, Dizzy, 388
Giltrap, Gordon, 467
Glackin, Paddy, 117–20, 132–5, 148, 153, 166, 238, 244, 252, 255–6, 258–60, 262, 264–6, 310–11, 336, 483, 510–11, 515
Gorman, Michael, 78, 108, 236, 253, 356, 358–9, 497
Goodman, Canon (James), 421, 429, 435, 448, 454–5, 463
Goodman, Philip, 462
Graham, Davy, 328
Graham, Seán Óg, 45, 53–4, 320
Green, Peter, 7
Grehan Sisters, The, 362
Griffith, Nanci, 11, 40
Grogan, Laurence, 421
Gunn, Tommy, 477–9
Guthrie, Arlo, 140–1, 152

Halley, Diane, 76
Hamilton, Linley, 11
Hall, Reg, 83, 180, 229, 230, 234, 236–7, 240, 242, 252–4, 356–8, 362–4
Hall, Robin, 241
Hanafin, Billy, 56
Handel, G.F., 421, 423
Harcourt (Hotel), The, 37, 41
Harding, Mike, 108, 113
Harper, Roy, 84, 144, 220
Hart, Tony, 294
Hayes, Martin, 124, 139, 348
Hayes, P.J., 348
Hayward, Richard, 456
Heaney, Joe, 72, 91, 215, 236, 240, 246, 258, 399, 487–8
Hehir, Tom, 347
Henderson, Hamish, 233, 282, 298, 325, 357
Henderson, Jarlath, 504

Hendrix, Jimi, 7, 9, 79–80, 83, 101, 138, 374, 402
Hennessy, Donogh, 37
Higgins, Jimmy, 36–7
High Level Ranters, The, 85, 91, 95, 136
Highland Bagpipes, 419
Hope, Billy, 459, 499
Horslips, 112, 137, 222, 482
House, Son, 345
Howerd, Frankie, 188, 206
Howlin' Wolf, 7
Hudson, Henry, 433
Hughes, Robbie, 182, 452, 486, 495, 499
Hughes, Spike, 281, 285, 339
Humblebums, The, 80
Hurt, Mississippi John, 246, 345–6, 402
Hyland, Edward Keating, 428

Idir, 45
Imlach, Hamish, 79
In Town Tonight (BBC), 176, 205, 208–9, 213–14
Irish Folklore Commission, The (IFC), 91, 134, 225–6, 229, 268, 301, 339, 352, 393, 401, 441, 452
Irish Warpipes (Great Irish Warpipes)
Irvine, Andy, 14, 60, 107, 109, 111, 116, 121, 144, 148, 150, 166, 169, 220, 245, 251, 259, 310, 366, 511
Irwin, Colin, 102, 116–17, 136–7, 139, 143–4, 146, 151, 153, 510, 516
Ives, Burl, 296

Jackson, Walker 'Piper', 421, 447
James, Skip, 246, 345
Jansch, Bert, 80, 146
jazz, 11–13, 25, 50–1, 87, 92, 123, 144, 187, 240, 278, 281–2, 301, 357, 367, 372, 387–8, 409–10, 420, 497, 510
Jefferson, Blind Lemon, 7
Jenkins, Jean, 253
John Peel Show, The, 150, 189
Johnson, Robert, 7, 9, 402, 426
Johnson, Dr (Samuel), 422
Johnston, Netta Jane ('Miss Johnston'), 460

Johnstone, Davey, 79
Johnstons, The, 81
Joseph, Nathan ('Nat'), 80
Joyce, James, 324, 328
Joyce, Patrick Weston, 240, 332, 337

Keane, Seán, 343, 365, 513, 516
Keenan, John (senior), 58, 67, 125–7, 129, 131–2, 134, 156, 315, 375
Keenan, Johnny, 73, 75, 126, 131, 133, 247
Keenan, Paddy, 7, 9–13, 35, 39, 41, 51, 55–9, 61–3, 117, 123–5, 128, 131, 133–6, 138–9, 142, 146–7, 153, 155, 157–9, 163, 165, 179, 227, 262, 264, 308, 311, 315, 372, 397, 410, 483, 496, 511, 513, 516, 519
Kelly, Alan, 36
Kelly, Des, 111–12
Kelly, John, 378, 381, 386, 393–4
Kelly, Tom, 22–4
Kenna (pipe makers), 432, 435–6, 447, 475, 479
Kerr, Barry, 12, 28–9, 319, 487, 494, 505, 508
Kiernan, Matt, 132, 386, 498–9
Kilfenora Céilí Band, The, 361, 515
Killing Joke, 121
Killora, 28, 140
Kemp, Gary, 33, 40
Kennedy, Frankie, 25, 484, 487–8
Kennedy, Peter, 234–5, 239, 243, 263, 273, 280–1, 283–4, 286, 288, 291, 296, 298–9, 301, 321–2, 325, 336–40, 356–7, 464, 466
Kennedy, Thomas, 435
Kennedy, William, 15, 305, 445–7, 504
Kilduff, Vinnie, 32, 36
Killen, Louis, 331
Kodo Drummers, The, 38, 42

Laban, Peter, 403
Laichtín Naofa Céilí Band, The, 361
Lá Lugh, 44, 54

LAPD, 121–2, 310
Larner, Sam, 215
Late Late Show, The (RTÉ), 114, 259, 341
Lead Belly, 296
Leader, Bill, 60, 80–3, 85, 107–8, 111, 161, 252–4, 357–8, 362–4, 366, 477
Led Zeppelin, 25, 45, 121, 482
Lewis, C.S., 167
Linde, Carsten, 96, 101
Line Up (BBC TV), 189, 467
Lloyd, A.L. (Bert), 282, 289, 322, 331
Loose Connections (aka Niamh Parsons' Loose Connections), 32, 36
Lomax, Alan, 232–3, 236–7, 243 246, 272, 274, 280, 282, 296, 298–9, 301, 339, 357, 399
Long Note, The (RTÉ), 135, 396
Lorient (Festival Interceltique de Lorient), 27–8, 34, 50, 320
Lowland pipes, 74, 461
Lynott, Phil, 69
Lúnasa, 11, 36–9, 42–4, 46, 49, 54, 69, 372, 506
Lunny, Dónal, 12, 32–3, 38–43, 46, 60–2, 107, 110–11, 114–15, 119, 121, 134–5, 138–40, 142, 146, 148, 150, 152, 218, 308, 310–11, 510–11
Lunny, Manus, 44

Mac Aonghusa, Prionias, 91, 215, 221, 343
Mac Mathúna, Ciarán, 39, 109, 167, 217–18, 235, 342–3, 353, 355–6, 359–60, 365, 370, 395, 401–2, 485
Mac Mathúna, Séamus, 167, 356, 359, 365, 370, 395
Mac Reámoinn, Seán, 231, 245, 255–6, 341, 344, 355
Macero, Teo, 89–90
MacColl, Ewan, 8, 78, 81, 236-7, 239, 243, 250, 273, 280, 282, 292, 301, 303, 331, 339, 358–9, 464, 477–8
MacMahon, Tony, 255, 264, 311, 341, 483, 510–12, 514, 132–5
MacNeice, Louis, 278, 292, 327
Mahavishnu Orchestra, 138

Maguire, Davy, 22, 489
Makem, Sarah, 281
Makem, Tommy, 68, 85, 88–90, 100, 511
Mallon, Conor, 11, 494, 503, 507
Mantovani, 204
Margaret Barry & Michael Gorman (duo), 78, 108, 236, 359
Markey, Dan, 441, 462
Markey, Nicholas, 172, 221, 437
Martin, Bill, 114
Martin, Neil, 31, 113, 305, 482–4, 490, 502
Martin, Phil, 456, 480
Maxwell, Patrick, 191, 456, 460
McAloon, Seán, 20, 22, 48, 57, 66, 318, 398, 459–60, 477–81, 486, 488, 490, 495, 499
McBride, Seán, 395
McCarthy, May, 491
McCormick, Billy, 24–5, 451, 486
McCullough, Rab, 32
McElholm, Eamon, 34, 43
McFadden, Frank, 191, 456, 471–2, 474–5, 479, 498–9, 503
Macgregor, Jimmie, 243, 331
McGlynn, Arty, 155
McGoldrick, Michael, 11–12, 34, 37, 43–6, 51, 122, 308, 372
McGuire, Seán, 83, 478–9, 488–9
McIlduff, Francis, 29, 39, 45–7, 50, 305, 486, 494
McKenna, Barney, 245, 247, 479
McKeon, Gabriel, 13, 143–4, 491
McLaughlin, Finbar, 486
McLaughlin, John, 12, 138, 304
McManus, Tony, 44
McNulty, Pat, 59, 88, 167
McPeake Family, The, 13, 19, 30, 318, 456, 463, 465, 467–8, 489
McPeake, Frank (Francis I), 30, 464, 466–7, 485
McPhilemy, Ciarán, 492
McSherry, Joanne, 306
McSherry, John, 9–15, 18–55, 56–7, 66, 125, 138, 159, 224, 305–8, 310–11, 320, 372, 387, 410, 426, 481, 485–6, 488, 493, 494–5, 503, 506–7

McSherry, Paul, 47
McSherry, Tíona, 306–7, 310
McSherrys, The, 25–6, 28, 307
McSweeney, Turlough
McTell, Ralph, 80, 144, 482
Miller, Jonathan, 333
Mitchell, Pat, 221–4, 235, 347, 352–3, 369, 388, 408, 428, 473
Molloy, Matt, 35–6, 61, 73, 116, 133–5, 142, 145–6, 150–2, 311, 511, 513–14
Moloney brothers, the, 351–2
Moloney, Paddy, 10–11, 13, 29, 128, 160, 176, 219, 370, 473, 491, 499. 514, 516
Monkhouse, Bob, 207
Moore, Calum, 66
Moore, Dee, 32
Moore, Christy, 26, 60–1, 107, 111, 117, 140, 147–50, 257, 310, 511, 517
Morecambe & Wise, 187
Morrison, Van, 14, 36, 479
Morton, Robin, 482, 449, 477, 482
Mouse, Mickey, 204
Movement, The, 68
Moving Hearts, 10, 26, 46, 61–2, 117, 151, 154, 220
Moylan, Terry, 163, 165–6, 172, 179, 180–1, 222, 453
Mr Fox, 95
Mulcahy, Louise, 491
Mungo Jerry, 97
Munnelly, Tom, 391, 512
Murphy, Denis, 228, 269–70, 339
Murray, Barry, 97, 103
Murray, Sam, 22, 487–8
My Kind Of Folk (BBC), 467

Na Fílí, 335, 342, 483, 485, 502
Na Píobairí Uilleann (NPU), 9, 88, 143, 165–7, 178, 181, 251, 370, 403, 415, 445, 468, 475, 496, 504
Nevin, Betty, 491
Ní Dhomhnaill Maighréad, 42
Ní Dhomhnaill, Tríona, 61, 132–4, 137, 141–3, 146, 151, 153, 157–8, 311, 510, 512, 514

Ní Ghráda, Máire, 491
Ní Mhaonaigh, Mairéad, 488
Nomos, 54
Northern Pipers' Society, The, 53, 494
Northumberland Pipers' Society, 94
Northumbrian pipes, 16, 75, 136, 241, 413

O'Boyle, Seán, 249, 288, 325
Ó Caodháin, Colm (aka Colm Keane), 270, 281, 338
Ó Canainn, Tómas, 126, 158, 335, 342, 483, 485, 502
O'Carolan, Turlough, 421
Ochs, Phil, 247
O'Connell, Blackie, 63, 69, 131, 373, 377–8, 385, 388, 463, 477
O'Connell, Cathal, 477
O'Connor, Dónal, 44, 46, 48, 50–1, 53, 54, 504–5
O'Connor, Sinéad, 42, 121
O'Curry, Eugene, 417, 432–3
Ó Domhnaill, Mícheál, 24, 61, 128, 132–4, 146, 150–2, 155, 311, 483, 510–12
O'Donnell, Al, 24, 61, 133–4, 146, 150–2, 155, 311, 483, 510–12
O'Donnell, Miadhach Lughain, 311, 506–7
O'Donoghue's (Pub), 68, 72, 163, 177, 219, 246, 253, 336, 365
O'Donoghue, Paddy (piper), 77, 353–4
O'Donoghue, Paddy (publican), 72
O'Donovan, John, 433
Ó Duinnchinn, Tiarnán, 494, 504, 507
O'Farrel, 'Mr', 175, 421
O'Flynn, Liam, 7, 9–11, 13, 15–6, 18–19, 21, 35, 40–1, 51, 56–60, 62, 107–8, 111–14, 119–22, 136, 144–5, 147–8, 150, 152, 160, 163–4, 168–9, 176, 178, 180, 221, 223, 256–8, 261, 264–5, 310, 316, 343–4, 368–70, 392, 410, 426, 483, 485, 489, 496, 510, 516–7
O'Flynn, Liam (senior)
O'Hagan, Aaron, 494–5
O'Hara, Mary, 328
O'Hare, Brendan, 25, 27, 41

O'Hare, Paddy, 494–5
Ó hEochaidh, Seán, 227, 398
Ó Lochlainn, Colm, 225, 233, 268
Oldfield, Mike, 121
Olllam, The, 49–53, 320
O'Mealy, Richard Lewis (R.L.), 191
Ó Muchú, Marcas, 12, 23–4, 41, 465–6, 482–490, 492, 496, 503
O'Neill, (Captain) Francis, 162, 167, 170–1, 221, 225, 317, 346, 353, 373, 405–9, 413, 416, 419–20, 426–7, 433, 435–7, 439, 442, 445, 448, 450–1, 454, 491
O'Neill, Terry ('Cruncher')
Ó Riada, Seán, 152, 210, 244, 260, 341, 369–70, 485, 497
Ó Róchain, Muiris, 370, 382, 389, 433
O'Rourke, Jack, 458–60, 479
Orwell, George, 217
O'Shea, Brother Gildas (aka 'Brother Gildas'), 175, 452–3, 457, 462
O'Sullivan, Micí 'Cumbá', 56, 222, 317, 352, 441
O'Sullivan, Jerry, 11
O'Sullivan, Tommy, 156
Overton, Bernard, 87, 112

Parker, Charlie (musician), 388
Parker, Charles (BBC producer), 239, 250, 277, 288, 297, 301, 303, 331
Parsons, Niamh, 28, 32
Parton, Dolly, 125
Pastoral pipes, 429–31, 447
Pat's Bar (Belfast), 23, 478
Patton, Charley, 7
Pavees, The, 131, 133, 247, 315
Paxton, Tom, 148, 247
Peel, John, 60, 90, 98, 102, 113, 136, 146–7, 150, 152, 189, 483
Pentangle, 80, 134, 144, 146, 515
Peoples, Tommy, 61, 133, 135–7, 139, 146, 155–6, 511, 515
Petrie, George, 361, 413, 433
Pickow, George, 380
Plank, Conny, 99

Planxty, 9–10, 18–19, 26–7, 32, 41, 46, 54, 57, 60–2, 111–19, 121–2, 125, 134, 137, 148–50, 152, 160, 168, 220, 245, 247, 259, 264, 310, 336, 410, 368, 482, 484, 492, 510–12, 516, 517–18
Potter, A.J., 178
Potts, John, 174, 377, 453, 469
Potts, Edmund, 377
Potts, Seán, 377, 473
Potts, Tommy, 350
Power. Jimmy, 243, 362
Presley, Elvis, 11, 410
Prosperous, 60, 107–8, 110–11, 113, 517

'Radio Ballads', 239, 280, 331
Rafferty, Gerry, 64, 77, 80, 97
Rea, John, 477, 480, 488, 490
Reader, Eddi, 42
Reck, Tommy, 24, 173, 223, 350, 355, 473, 494, 519
RedBox Studios, 47, 50
Redmond, Mark
Reid, Robert, 426, 447
Reid, Seán, 15, 162, 170–4, 176, 178–9, 345, 348, 350, 352–4, 370, 378, 382, 386, 396, 435–6, 438, 447, 452–4, 458–9, 468, 472–4, 476, 494
Reilly, Martin, 441
Rhythm & Rhyme, 36, 43
Rigler, Eric, 11
Ritchie, Jean, 282, 296, 315
Riverdance, 14, 117, 124
Robertson, Jeannie, 215, 240
Rochford, Martin, 375, 377–8, 381, 392–3
Rock Family Trees, 45
Rogers, Harold, 239, 255, 279–80, 283–4, 287–8, 291, 296, 304, 321, 325, 332, 339
Rolling Stones, The, 69, 354
Ross, Al, 247–9
Ross, Dr Isaiah, 428
Rotterdam Bar, The, 36
Rowsome, Ciarán, 182
Rowsome, Helena, 162, 165, 179,182, 313, 481, 501

Rowsome, Kevin, 12, 181–2, 182, 211
Rowsome, Leo, 6, 8, 10, 12–14, 17, 24, 56–7, 59, 68, 70, 87, 101, 127–8, 130, 132, 160–3, 166, 168, 170, 172–3, 175–7, 179–81, 183, 186–190, 196, 200, 203–4, 206, 210–13, 219, 222, 240, 245, 251–2, 306, 313, 350–2, 355, 358, 361, 385–6, 396, 410, 438, 444, 452, 456, 458–9, 463, 469, 473, 475, 491, 492, 494, 497, 503, 514, 516–17
Rowsome, Leon, 175
Rowsome, Thomas, 440–1
Rowsome, Tom, 170, 182
Rowsome, William, 171, 216, 375, 437–8
Russell, Ken, 328

Sainte-Marie, Buffy, 247
Sands, Tommy, 26, 485
Sayers, Peig, 228, 231, 245, 268
Seachtar, 133–5, 311
Seán Reid Society, The, 435–7, 452–4, 458, 468, 474, 476
Seán Smyth Band, The, 36
Seeger, Peggy, 78, 237, 296, 331, 464
Seeger, Pete, 246, 465–6
Seery, Seán, 59, 355
Shakespeare, William, 120, 413–15, 420
Shannon, Sharon, 33, 37–8
Shaw, Donald, 43–4
Sherlock, Roger, 356
Shirley & Dolly Collins, 263
Simon, Paul, 157
Simpson, Martin, 79
Singers' Club, The, 78
Six Days In Down, 45
Skara Brae, 134, 152, 512, 514
Slattery's (bar/folk clubs, Dublin), 111–12, 131, 133, 135, 245, 247, 251, 258, 261, 315
Sky, Patrick, 111, 263, 425–7, 430
Small, Millie (aka 'Millie'), 77, 152
Smith, John Wayland, 441, 443
Smyth, Seán, 36–7
Spillane, Davy, 10–11, 13, 33, 51, 60, 62–3, 491

Spinal Tap, 45
Spinners, The, 477
Sproule, Dáithí, 152
Steeleye Span, 149
Stewart, Belle, 88, 215
Stewart, Calum, 11
Stewart, Dave, 80
Stewart, Rod, 33
Stewart, Trevor, 486
Stockton's Wing, 34, 117, 220, 487
Stradling, Rod, 253–4
Sult, 42
Sunflower Bar, The, 53, 320, 494
Sunflower Folk Club, The, 482, 488
Sutherland, Isabel, 243
Swarbrick, Dave, 76, 85–6, 144, 512
Sweeney's Men, 63, 81, 107, 112, 115, 366, 368

Talty, Martin, 132, 344, 349, 354, 361, 377, 379–80, 382, 384, 393, 396
Tam Linn, 102–3
Tamalin, 12, 25, 28, 31, 36–7, 40, 42–3, 46, 485
Tawney, Cyril, 243, 331, 336
Taylor, Billy, 25, 221, 437
Taylor brothers (pipe makers), 17, 222, 352, 406, 409, 438, 438
Terry, Sonny, 428
Terry-Thomas, 188, 206
The Brendan Voyage, 62, 118–9
'The Fox Chase' (tune), 82, 85, 166, 178, 370, 428
Them (aka Van Morrison's Them), 14
Thompson, Robert, 440–1, 451, 454, 457
Tolkien, J.R.R., 470
Tom Kelly's (Bar), 22–4
Top Of The Pops (BBC TV), 104
Topic Records, 338, 357, 378
Toss The Feathers (aka 'The Tossers'), 34
Touhey, Patsy, 13–14, 16, 24, 57–8, 172, 174, 221, 317, 405–10, 439, 444, 450, 514
Traditional Irish Pipe Music (Finbar Furey LP), 81, 85, 99

Transatlantic Records, 21, 76, 80–2, 84–6, 90, 97, 107–9, 252, 362, 366, 515
Tripswitch, 45–6
Tulla Céilí Band, The, 348, 353–4, 360–1, 468
Tunney, Paddy, 362

uí Ógáin, Ríonach, 218, 228–9, 353, 398, 400
Usher's Island, 122

Val Doonican Music Show, The (BBC TV), 147
Vallancey, General Charles, 411–15, 425
Vallely, Brian, 10, 15, 168, 250–1, 318–19, 380, 444, 447, 470, 474, 481, 486, 488, 490, 493–4, 496–7, 502, 504–5, 507–8
Vallely, Cillian, 11, 494, 504, 507
Vallely, Eithne, 318, 496, 501, 504, 507
Variety Bandbox (BBC), 176, 187, 205–7, 209–10, 213

Walker, Joseph, 411, 414–15, 418, 422, 425
Wallace, Mudd, 31, 46
Ward, Pat, 221, 342, 461–2
Waters, Muddy, 7
Watersons, The, 113, 144
Watson, Doc, 247
Whelan, Bill, 117–8
Whicker, Alan, 289
Whyton, Wally, 335
William Kennedy Piping Festival, The, 15, 305, 447, 504
Williams, Dave, 48, 129, 156, 308
Williams, John, 328
Williamson, Roy, 74, 77, 79, 86
Willie Clancy Week, 26, 264
Wilson, Keppel & Betty, 187
Winter, Eric, 78, 510
Wishbone Ash, 11, 265–6
Woods Band, the, 144
Woods, Terry, 366

SPECIAL NEW IRISH
EDISON BELL Winner RECORDS

BY IRELAND'S RENOWNED PIPER

2|6 Double-Sided   2|6 Double-Sided

[Photo, Crane & Co., Enniscorthy.

LEO. ROWSOME

1st Prize Winner at the Feis Ceoil, Dublin, 1921, 1922, 1924, 1925.
1st Prize Winner all Ireland, at Cavan and Bray, 1922.
1st Prize Winner at Fr. Matthew Feis, Dublin, 1925.
Also Oireacthas Prize Winner, etc.

4259 { THE COULIN
       THE COPPER PLATE REEL

4260 { SNOWY BREASTED PEARL
       ROCKY ROAD TO DUBLIN (Slip Jig)

4261 { BLACKBIRD (Set Dance)
       JIG MEDLEY

4262 { GOD SAVE IRELAND and
          [THE SOLDIER'S SONG
       JOB OF JOURNEYWORK (Set Dance)

TO BE HAD OF IRELAND'S BEST RECORD DEALERS.